Microsoft® Excel 2000 Power Programming with VBA

Microsoft® Excel 2000 Power Programming with VBA

John Walkenbach

IDG Books Worldwide, Inc.
An International Data Group Company

Foster City, CA ✦ Chicago, IL ✦ Indianapolis, IN ✦ New York, NY

Microsoft® Excel 2000 Power Programming with VBA
Published by
IDG Books Worldwide, Inc.
An International Data Group Company
919 E. Hillsdale Blvd., Suite 400
Foster City, CA 94404
www.idgbooks.com (IDG Books Worldwide Web site)

ISBN: 0-7645-3263-4

Printed in the United States of America

10 9 8 7 6 5 4 3 2

1O/SX/QU/ZZ/FC

Distributed in the United States by IDG Books Worldwide, Inc.

Distributed by CDG Books Canada Inc. for Canada; by Transworld Publishers Limited in the United Kingdom; by IDG Norge Books for Norway; by IDG Sweden Books for Sweden; by IDGBA Ltd. for Australia; by IDGBA (NZ) Ltd. for New Zealand; by TransQuest Publishers Pte Ltd. for Singapore, Malaysia, Thailand, Indonesia, and Hong Kong; by Gotop Information Inc. for Taiwan; by ICG Muse, Inc. for Japan; by Norma Comunicaciones S.A. for Colombia; by Intersoft for South Africa; by Le Monde en Tique for France; by International Thomson Publishing for Germany, Austria and Switzerland; by Distribuidora Cuspide for Argentina; by Livraria Cultura for Brazil; by Ediciones ZETA S.C.R. Ltda. for Peru; by WS Computer Publishing Corporation, Inc., for the Philippines; by Contemporanea de Ediciones for Venezuela; by Express Computer Distributors for the Caribbean and West Indies; by Micronesia Media Distributor, Inc. for Micronesia; by Grupo Editorial Norma S.A. for Guatemala; by Chips Computadoras S.A. de C.V. for Mexico; by Editorial Norma de Panama S.A. for Panama; by American Bookshops for Finland. Authorized Sales Agent: Anthony Rudkin Associates for the Middle East and North Africa.

For general information on IDG Books Worldwide's books in the U.S., please call our Consumer Customer Service department at 800-762-2974. For reseller information, including discounts and premium sales, please call our Reseller Customer Service department at 800-434-3422.

For information on where to purchase IDG Books Worldwide's books outside the U.S., please contact our International Sales department at 317-596-5530 or fax 317-596-5692.

For consumer information on foreign language translations, please contact our Customer Service department at 800-434-3422, fax 317-596-5692, or e-mail rights@idgbooks.com.

For information on licensing foreign or domestic rights, please phone +1-650-655-3109.

For sales inquiries and special prices for bulk quantities, please contact our Sales department at 650-655-3200 or write to the address at left.

For information on using IDG Books Worldwide's books in the classroom or for ordering examination copies, please contact our Educational Sales department at 800-434-2086 or fax 317-596-5499.

For press review copies, author interviews, or other publicity information, please contact our Public Relations department at 650-655-3000 or fax 650-655-3299.

For authorization to photocopy items for corporate, personal, or educational use, please contact Copyright Clearance Center, 222 Rosewood Drive, Danvers, MA 01923, or fax 978-750-4470.

Library of Congress Cataloging-in-Publication Data

Walkenbach, John.

Microsoft Excel 2000 power programming with VBA / John Walkenbach.

p. cm.

Includes index.

ISBN 0-7654-3263-4 (alk. paper)

1. Microsoft Excel for Windows. 2. Microsoft Visual Basic for Windows. 3. Electronic spreadsheets. 4. Computer software–Development. I. Title.

HF5548.4.M523W3459 1999

005.369–dc21 99-18447

CIP

ABOUT IDG BOOKS WORLDWIDE

Welcome to the world of IDG Books Worldwide.

IDG Books Worldwide, Inc., is a subsidiary of International Data Group, the world's largest publisher of computer-related information and the leading global provider of information services on information technology. IDG was founded more than 30 years ago by Patrick J. McGovern and now employs more than 9,000 people worldwide. IDG publishes more than 290 computer publications in over 75 countries. More than 90 million people read one or more IDG publications each month.

Launched in 1990, IDG Books Worldwide is today the #1 publisher of best-selling computer books in the United States. We are proud to have received eight awards from the Computer Press Association in recognition of editorial excellence and three from Computer Currents' First Annual Readers' Choice Awards. Our best-selling *...For Dummies®* series has more than 50 million copies in print with translations in 31 languages. IDG Books Worldwide, through a joint venture with IDG's Hi-Tech Beijing, became the first U.S. publisher to publish a computer book in the People's Republic of China. In record time, IDG Books Worldwide has become the first choice for millions of readers around the world who want to learn how to better manage their businesses.

Our mission is simple: Every one of our books is designed to bring extra value and skill-building instructions to the reader. Our books are written by experts who understand and care about our readers. The knowledge base of our editorial staff comes from years of experience in publishing, education, and journalism — experience we use to produce books to carry us into the new millennium. In short, we care about books, so we attract the best people. We devote special attention to details such as audience, interior design, use of icons, and illustrations. And because we use an efficient process of authoring, editing, and desktop publishing our books electronically, we can spend more time ensuring superior content and less time on the technicalities of making books.

You can count on our commitment to deliver high-quality books at competitive prices on topics you want to read about. At IDG Books Worldwide, we continue in the IDG tradition of delivering quality for more than 30 years. You'll find no better book on a subject than one from IDG Books Worldwide.

John Kilcullen
Chairman and CEO
IDG Books Worldwide, Inc.

Steven Berkowitz
President and Publisher
IDG Books Worldwide, Inc.

Eighth Annual Computer Press Awards 1992

Ninth Annual Computer Press Awards 1993

X
WINNER

Tenth Annual Computer Press Awards 1994

Eleventh Annual Computer Press Awards 1995

IDG is the world's leading IT media, research and exposition company. Founded in 1964, IDG had 1997 revenues of $2.05 billion and has more than 9,000 employees worldwide. IDG offers the widest range of media options that reach IT buyers in 75 countries representing 95% of worldwide IT spending. IDG's diverse product and services portfolio spans six key areas including print publishing, online publishing, expositions and conferences, market research, education and training, and global marketing services. More than 90 million people read one or more of IDG's 290 magazines and newspapers, including IDG's leading global brands — Computerworld, PC World, Network World, Macworld and the Channel World family of publications. IDG Books Worldwide is one of the fastest-growing computer book publishers in the world, with more than 700 titles in 36 languages. The "...For Dummies®" series alone has more than 50 million copies in print. IDG offers online users the largest network of technology-specific Web sites around the world through IDG.net (http://www.idg.net), which comprises more than 225 targeted Web sites in 55 countries worldwide. International Data Corporation (IDC) is the world's largest provider of information technology data, analysis and consulting, with research centers in over 41 countries and more than 400 research analysts worldwide. IDG World Expo is a leading producer of more than 168 globally branded conferences and expositions in 35 countries including E3 (Electronic Entertainment Expo), Macworld Expo, ComNet, Windows World Expo, ICE (Internet Commerce Expo), Agenda, DEMO, and Spotlight. IDG's training subsidiary, ExecuTrain, is the world's largest computer training company, with more than 230 locations worldwide and 785 training courses. IDG Marketing Services helps industry-leading IT companies build international brand recognition by developing global integrated marketing programs via IDG's print, online and exposition products worldwide. Further information about the company can be found at www.idg.com.

1/24/99

Credits

Acquisitions Editor
Greg Croy

Development Editors
Matthew E. Lusher
Scott M. Fulton III

Technical Editor
Scott M. Fulton III

Copy Editors
Amy Eoff
Amanda Kaufmann
Nicole LeClerc
Vicky Nuttall

Production
Foster City Production Department

Proofreading and Indexing
York Production Services

About the Author

John Walkenbach is a leading authority on spreadsheet software and is principal of JWalk and Associates Inc., a Southern California–based consulting firm that specializes in spreadsheet application development. John is the author of more than two dozen spreadsheet books and has written close to 300 articles and reviews for a variety of publications, including *PC World, InfoWorld, Windows,* and *PC/Computing*. Currently, he's a contributing editor for *PC World* and writes the magazine's monthly "Spreadsheet Tips" column. He also maintains The Spreadsheet Page, a popular Internet Web site (`www.j-walk.com/ss`), and is the developer of Power Utility Pak, an award-winning add-in for Microsoft Excel. John graduated from the University of Missouri and earned a master's and a Ph.D. from the University of Montana.

John's other interests include guitar, MIDI music, novels, digital photography, and puttering around in the garden.

For all the family back in St. Louis: Dad, Pat, Ken, Kim, and Steve

Preface

Welcome to *Microsoft Excel 2000 Power Programming with VBA*. If your job involves developing spreadsheets that others will use — or if you simply want to get the most out of Excel — you've come to the right place. By reading this book, you can expand your spreadsheet horizons and get even more power from Excel.

Experience tells me that many spreadsheet users spend much of their time creating spreadsheets that other people use. Increasingly, spreadsheets designed with products such as Excel, 1-2-3, and Quattro Pro are suitable for tasks that once required custom programs written in traditional programming languages. Thanks to their macro and customization features, these products now can serve as development platforms for many types of applications. In this book, I cover every aspect of application development using Excel.

Why I Wrote This Book

Over the past 15 years, I've written scores of spreadsheet reviews for the leading trade magazines. During this time, I've seen spreadsheets evolve from simple accounting worksheets to incredibly powerful applications. Microsoft Excel goes well beyond what most people consider the realm of spreadsheet software. I am particularly impressed with Excel's capabilities in the area of application development, especially development using the Visual Basic for Applications (VBA) macro language.

Quite a few advanced Excel books are available, but this book is still the only one that deals with application development from a larger perspective. VBA is just one component (albeit a fairly large component) of application development. Excel is an extremely deep software product: It has many interesting features that lurk in the background, unbeknownst to the typical user. And you can use some of the well-known features in novel ways.

Millions of people throughout the world use Excel. I monitor spreadsheet-related newsgroups on the Internet, and it's very clear to me that people need (and want) help in the areas that this book covers. My guess is that only five percent of Excel users really understand what the product is capable of. In this book, I attempt to nudge you into that elite company. Are you up to it?

What You Need to Know

This is not a book for beginning Excel users. If you have no experience with Excel, I recommend that you read either of the following books:

- *Excel 2000 for Windows For Dummies,* by Greg Harvey, is written for users who want to know just enough to get by—and want to be entertained in the process.
- *Excel 2000 Bible* (by yours truly) provides comprehensive coverage of all the features of Excel. It is meant for users of all levels.

To get the most out of this book, you should be an experienced Excel for Windows user. I didn't spend much time writing basic how-to information. In fact, I assume that you know the following:

- How to create workbooks, insert sheets, save files, and so on
- How to navigate through a workbook
- How to use the menus and shortcut menus
- How to manage Excel's toolbars
- How to enter formulas
- How to use Excel's worksheet functions
- How to name cells and ranges
- How to use basic Windows features, such as file management techniques and the clipboard

If you don't know how to perform the preceding tasks, you may find some of this material over your head, so consider yourself forewarned.

If you're an experienced spreadsheet user who hasn't used Excel 2000, Chapter 2 presents a short overview of what this product offers.

What You Need to Have

To make the best use of this book, you need the following items:

- A copy of Excel 2000 for Windows (also known as Excel 9) or a copy of Excel 97 for Windows (also known as Excel 8)
- A copy of Windows 95, Windows 98, or Windows NT

Any system that can run Windows will suffice, but you'll be much better off with a fast Pentium-based machine with plenty of memory. (I recommend at least 32MB of RAM, preferably 64MB or more.) Excel is a large program, and using it on a slower system or a system with minimal memory can be extremely frustrating.

When you use multisheet workbooks, you often want to view different sheets in separate windows. Therefore, I recommend using a high-resolution video driver (800 × 600 is okay, 1024 × 768 is excellent, and 1600 × 1024 is sheer heaven). A standard VGA resolution will do in a pinch, but it just doesn't let you see enough on-screen.

Conventions in This Book

Take a minute to skim this section and learn some of the typographic conventions used throughout this book.

Keyboard conventions

You need to use the keyboard to enter data. In addition, you can work with menus and dialog boxes directly from the keyboard — a method you may find easier if your hands are already positioned over the keys.

Input

Input that you type from the keyboard appears in boldface — for example, enter **=SUM(B2: B50)** into cell B51.

More lengthy input usually appears on a separate line in a monospace font. For example, I may instruct you to enter the following formula:

```
=VLOOKUP(STOCKNUMBER,PRICELIST,2)
```

VBA code

This book contains many small snippets of VBA code, as well as complete procedure listings. Each listing appears in a monospace font; each line of code occupies a separate line. (I copied these listings directly from the VBA module and pasted them into my word processor.) To make the code easier to read, I often use one or more tabs to create indentations. Indentation is optional, but it does help to delineate statements that go together.

If a line of code doesn't fit on a single line in this book, I use the standard VBA line continuation sequence: at the end of a line, a space followed by an underscore character indicates that the line of code extends to the next line. For example, the following two lines are a single line of code:

```
If Right(ActiveCell, 1) = "!" Then ActiveCell _
  = Left(ActiveCell, Len(ActiveCell) - 1)
```

You can enter this code either on two lines, exactly as shown, or on a single line without the underscore character.

Key names

Names of keys on the keyboard appear in normal type. When you should press two keys simultaneously, the keys are connected with a plus sign: "Press Alt+F11 to activate the Visual Basic Editor." Here's a list of the key names I refer to throughout the book:

Alt	Backspace	Num Lock	Pause
Caps Lock	Ctrl	PgDn	PgUp
Del	Down arrow	Print Screen	Right arrow
End	Home	Scroll Lock	Shift
Insert	Left arrow	Tab	Up arrow

Functions, filenames, and named ranges

Excel's worksheet functions appear in uppercase monospace font, like so: "Enter a `SUM` formula in cell C20." Macro and procedure names appear in monospace font: "Execute the `GetTotals` procedure." I often use mixed upper- and lowercase to make these names easier to read.

Mouse conventions

If you're reading this book, you're well versed in mouse usage. The mouse terminology I use is all standard fare: pointing, clicking, right-clicking, dragging, and so on.

What the Icons Mean

Throughout the book, I've used icons in the left margin to call your attention to points that are particularly important.

I use this icon to indicate that the material discussed is new to Excel 2000. If you're developing an application that will be used for Excel 97 and Excel 2000, pay particular attention to these icons.

I use Note icons to tell you that something is important—perhaps a concept that may help you master the task at hand or something fundamental for understanding subsequent material.

Tip icons indicate a more efficient way of doing something or a technique that may not be obvious.

These icons indicate that an example file is on the companion CD-ROM (see "About the Companion CD-ROM" later in the preface). This CD holds many of the examples that I cover in the book as well as a trial copy of my popular Power Utility Pak software.

I use Caution icons when the operation that I'm describing can cause problems if you're not careful.

I use the Cross-Reference icon to refer you to other chapters that have more to say on a subject.

How This Book Is Organized

There are hundreds of ways to organize this material, but I settled on a scheme that divides the book into seven main parts. In addition, I've included a few appendixes that provide supplemental information.

Part I: Some Essential Background

In this part, I set the stage for the rest of the book. Chapter 1 presents a brief history of spreadsheets so that you can see how Excel fits into the big picture. In Chapter 2, I offer a conceptual overview of Excel 2000—quite useful for experienced spreadsheet users who are switching to Excel. In Chapter 3, I cover formula essentials, including some clever techniques that may be new to you. Chapter 4 covers the ins and outs of the various files used and generated by Excel.

Part II: Excel Application Development

This part consists of just two chapters. In Chapter 5, I broadly discuss the concept of a spreadsheet application. Chapter 6 goes into more detail and covers the steps typically involved in a spreadsheet application development project.

Part III: Understanding Visual Basic for Applications

Chapters 7 through 11 make up Part III, and these chapters include everything you need to know to learn VBA. In this part, I introduce you to VBA, provide programming fundamentals, and detail how to develop VBA subroutines and functions. Chapter 11 contains tons of useful VBA examples.

Part IV: Working with UserForms

The three chapters in Part IV deal with custom dialog boxes. I introduce the concept in Chapter 12 and provide lots of useful examples in Chapter 13. Chapter 14 continues the saga and demonstrates additional techniques that will definitely add a professional quality to your work.

Part V: Advanced Programming Techniques

Part V covers additional techniques that are often considered advanced. The first three chapters discuss how to develop utilities and how to use VBA to work with pivot tables and charts. Chapter 18 covers event handling, which enables you to execute procedures automatically when certain events occur. Chapter 19 discusses various techniques that you can use to interact with other applications (such as Word). Chapter 20 concludes Part V with an in-depth discussion of creating add-ins.

Part VI: Developing Applications

The chapters in Part VI deal with important elements of creating user-oriented applications. Chapters 21 and 22 provide information on creating custom toolbars and menus. Chapter 23 presents several different ways to provide online help for your application. In Chapter 24, I present some basic information about developing user-oriented applications, and I describe such an application in detail.

Part VII: Other Topics

The five chapters in Part VII cover additional topics that you may find helpful. Chapter 25 presents information regarding compatibility. In Chapter 26, I discuss various ways to use VBA to work with files. In Chapter 27, I explain how to use VBA to manipulate Visual Basic components such as UserForms and modules. Chapter 28 covers the topic of class modules. I finish the part with a useful chapter that answers many common questions about Excel programming.

Appendixes

Five appendixes round out the book. Appendix A contains useful information about Excel resources online. Appendix B is a reference guide to all of VBA's keywords (statements and functions). I explain VBA error codes in Appendix C, and Appendix D is a handy ANSI code reference chart. The final appendix describes the files available on the companion CD-ROM.

About the Companion CD-ROM

The inside back cover of this book contains a CD-ROM that holds many useful examples that I discuss in the text. When I write about computer-related material, I emphasize learning by example. I know that I learn more from a well-thought-out example than from reading a dozen pages in a book. I assume that this is true for many other people. Consequently, I spent more time developing the examples on the CD-ROM than I did writing chapters.

The files on the companion CD-ROM are not compressed, so you can access them directly from the CD.

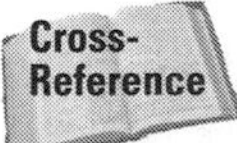

See Appendix E for a description of each file on the CD-ROM.

All CD-ROM files are read-only. Therefore, if you open a file from the CD-ROM and make any changes to it, you need to save it to your hard drive. In addition, if you copy a file from the CD-ROM to your hard drive, the file retains its read-only attribute. To change this attribute after copying a file, right-click the filename or icon, and select Properties from the shortcut menu. In the Properties dialog box, click the General tab, and remove the check mark from the Read-only check box.

About the Power Utility Pak Offer

Toward the back of the book, you'll find a coupon that you can redeem for a free copy of my popular Power Utility Pak software — an award-winning collection of useful Excel utilities and many new worksheet functions. I developed this package exclusively with VBA.

I think you'll find this product useful in your day-to-day work with Excel, and I urge you to take advantage of this free offer. You can also purchase the complete XLS/VBA source files for a nominal fee. Studying the code is an excellent way to pick up some useful programming techniques.

You can take Power Utility Pak for a test drive by installing the shareware version from the companion CD-ROM.

How to Use This Book

You can use this book any way you please. If you choose to read it cover to cover, be my guest. But because I'm dealing with intermediate-to-advanced subject matter, the chapter order is often immaterial. I suspect that most readers will skip around, picking up useful tidbits here and there. If you're faced with a challenging task, you might try the index first to see whether the book specifically addresses your problem.

Reach Out

The publisher and I want your feedback. After you have had a chance to use this book, please take a moment to visit the IDG Books Worldwide Web site to register your book and give us your comments. (See the "my2cents.idgbooks.com" page at the back of this book for more details.) Please be honest in your evaluation. If you thought a particular chapter didn't tell you enough, let me know. Of course, I would prefer to receive comments like "This is the best book I've ever read" or "Thanks to this book, I was promoted and now make $85,000 a year."

Feel free to send me specific questions regarding the material in this book. I'll do my best to help you out and answer your questions, but I can't guarantee a reply. The best way to reach me is by e-mail:

```
author@j-walk.com
```

I also invite you to visit my World Wide Web site, which contains lots of Excel-related material. The URL is

```
http://www.j-walk.com/ss/
```

Acknowledgments

First of all, thanks to everyone around the world who purchased the previous editions of this book. The daily positive feedback from readers continues to astound and encourage me.

Many of the ideas for the topics in this book came from postings to the Excel Internet newsgroups and mailing lists. Thanks to all who frequent these services; your problems and questions were the inspiration for many of the examples I present in this book. I owe special thanks to the following people, who contribute to my daily dose of Excel information: Colin Banfield, Alan Beban, Rob Bovey, Dave Boylan, Stephen Bullen, Shane Devonshire, Jonathan Falk, John Green, David Hager, Myrna Larson, Dave Lewinski, Laurent Longre, Ture Magnusson, Bill Manville, Colin McNair, David McRitchie, Dick Moffat, Brian Murphy, Thomas Ogilvy, Chip Pearson, Jim Rech, David Ringston, Larry P. Shreve, Rick Teale, Tim Tow — and many others whom I haven't mentioned.

This book would not be in your hands if it weren't for the talented people at IDG Books Worldwide, including Matt Lusher, my development editor. Special thanks to Scott M. Fulton, my technical editor. He made countless contributions to this book and set me straight on more than a few issues. Thanks also to the copy editors who made this book more readable. They corrected many of my grammatical mistakes; fixed spelling errors; eliminated, removed, and deleted lots of extra redundancy; and helped me write better than I did.

I'm also indebted to Michie, who kept me happy and amused while I was working on this book.

Finally, thanks to Katlyn, my wonderful daughter and the joy of my life.

Contents at a Glance

Contents

Chapter 13: UserForm Examples 369

Chapter 14: Advanced UserForm Techniques 395

Part VI: Developing Applications 591

PART

I

Some Essential Background

The four chapters in this section provide some useful background information about Excel 2000 and spreadsheets in general. In Chapter 1, you get a brief history of spreadsheets, with insights about why Excel is the superior product for developers. Chapter 2 provides a quick-and-dirty overview of using Excel, complete with lots of tips and helpful suggestions. In Chapter 3, I present some of the formula tricks I've accumulated over the years. Chapter 4 provides many details about the files used and generated by Excel — important information for developers.

✦ ✦ ✦ ✦

In This Part

✦ ✦ ✦ ✦

Excel 2000: Where It Came From

In This Chapter

A history of spreadsheets — where they came from, who makes them, and what differentiates them

A discussion of Excel's evolution

An analysis of why Excel is the best spreadsheet available for developers

To fully appreciate the application development features available in Excel 2000, it's important to understand where this product came from and how it fits into the overall scheme of things. If you've worked with personal computers over the past decade, this information may be old hat. If you're a trivia buff, this chapter is a gold mine. Study this chapter, and you'll be a hit at the next computer geek party you attend.

A Brief History of Spreadsheets

Spreadsheets are a huge business, but most of us tend to take this software for granted. In fact, it may be hard to fathom, but there really was a time when spreadsheets were not available. Back then, people relied instead on clumsy mainframes or calculators and spent hours doing what now takes minutes.

It all started with VisiCalc

The world's first electronic spreadsheet, VisiCalc, was conjured up by Dan Bricklin and Bob Frankston back in 1978, when personal computers were unheard of in the office environment. VisiCalc was written for the Apple II computer, an interesting little machine that is something of a toy by today's standards. But in its day, the Apple II kept me mesmerized for days at a time. VisiCalc essentially laid the foundation for future spreadsheets, and its row-and-column-based layout and formula syntax are still found in modern spreadsheet products. VisiCalc caught on quickly, and many forward-looking companies purchased the Apple II for the sole purpose of developing their budgets with VisiCalc. Consequently, VisiCalc is often credited for much of the Apple II's initial success.

In the meantime, another class of personal computers was evolving; these PCs ran the CP/M operating system. A company called Sorcim developed SuperCalc, a spreadsheet that also attracted a legion of followers.

When the IBM PC arrived on the scene in 1981, legitimizing personal computers, VisiCorp wasted no time porting VisiCalc to this new hardware environment. Sorcim soon followed with a PC version of SuperCalc.

By today's standards, both VisiCalc and SuperCalc were extremely crude. For example, text entered into a cell could not extend beyond the cell — a lengthy title had to be entered into multiple cells. Nevertheless, the capability to automate the budgeting tedium was enough to lure thousands of accountants from paper ledger sheets to floppy disks.

Lotus 1-2-3

Envious of VisiCalc's success, a small group of computer freaks at a startup company in Cambridge, Massachusetts, refined the spreadsheet concept. Headed by Mitch Kapor and Jonathan Sachs, the company designed a new product and launched the software industry's first full-fledged marketing blitz. I remember seeing a large display ad for 1-2-3 in the *Wall Street Journal* — the first time that I'd ever seen software advertised in a general interest publication. Released in January 1983, Lotus Development Corporation's 1-2-3 was an instant success. Despite its $495 price tag (yes, people really paid that much for software), it quickly outsold VisiCalc, rocketing to the top of the sales charts, where it remained for many years — it was, perhaps, the most popular application ever.

Lotus 1-2-3 not only improved on all the basics embodied in VisiCalc and SuperCalc, but also was the first program to take advantage of the new and unique features found in the powerful 16-bit IBM PC AT. For example, 1-2-3 bypassed the slower DOS calls and wrote text directly to display memory, giving it a snappy and responsive feel that was unusual for the time. The online help system was a breakthrough, and the ingenious "moving bar" menu style set the standard for many years. One feature that really set 1-2-3 apart, though, was its macro capability, a powerful tool that enabled spreadsheet users to record their keystrokes to automate many procedures. When such a macro was "played," the original keystrokes were sent to the application — a far cry from today's macro capability but definitely a step in the right direction.

1-2-3 was not the first *integrated* package, but it was the first successful one. It combined (1) a powerful electronic spreadsheet with (2) elementary graphics and (3) some limited but handy database features. Easy as 1, 2, 3 — get it?

Lotus followed up the original 1-2-3 Release 1 with Release 1A in April 1983. This product enjoyed tremendous success and put Lotus in the enviable position of virtually owning the spreadsheet market. In September 1985, Release 1A was replaced by Release 2, a major upgrade that was superseded by the bug-fixed Release 2.01 the following July. Release 2 introduced *add-ins*, special-purpose programs that can be attached to give an application new features and extend the application's useful life. Release 2 also had improved memory management, more @functions, four times as many rows as its predecessor, and added support for a math coprocessor. It also enhanced the macro language, whose popularity exceeded the developers' wildest dreams.

Not surprisingly, the success of 1-2-3 spawned many *clones*—work-alike products that usually offered a few additional features and sold at a much lower price. Among the more notable were Paperback Software's VP Planner series and Mosaic Software's Twin. Lotus eventually took legal action against Paperback Software for copyright infringement (for copying the "look and feel" of 1-2-3); the successful suit essentially put Paperback out of business.

In the summer of 1989, Lotus shipped DOS and OS/2 versions of the long-delayed 1-2-3 Release 3. This product literally added a dimension to the familiar row-and-column-based spreadsheet; it extended the paradigm by adding multiple spreadsheet pages. The idea wasn't really new, however; a relatively obscure product called Boeing Calc originated the 3D spreadsheet concept, and SuperCalc 5 and CubeCalc also incorporated it.

1-2-3 Release 3 offered features that users wanted, features that ultimately became standard fare: multilayered worksheets, the capability to work with multiple files simultaneously, file linking, improved graphics, and direct access to external database files. But it still lacked an important feature that users were begging for: a way to produce high-quality output.

Release 3 began life with a reduced market potential because it required an 80286-based PC and a minimum of 1MB of RAM—fairly hefty requirements in 1989. But Lotus had an ace up its corporate sleeve. Concurrent with the shipping of Release 3, the company surprised nearly everyone by announcing an upgrade of Release 2.01 (the product materialized a few months later as 1-2-3 Release 2.2). Release 3 was *not* a replacement for Release 2, as most analysts had expected. Rather, Lotus made the brilliant move of splitting the spreadsheet market into two segments: those with high-end hardware and those with more mundane equipment.

1-2-3 Release 2.2 wasn't a panacea for spreadsheet buffs, but it was a significant improvement. The most important Release 2.2 feature was Allways, an add-in that gave users the ability to churn out attractive reports, complete with multiple typefaces, borders, and shading. In addition, users could view the results on-screen in a WYSIWYG (What You See Is What You Get) manner. Allways didn't, however, let you issue any worksheet commands while you viewed and formatted your work in WYSIWYG mode. Despite this rather severe limitation, most 1-2-3 users were overjoyed with this new capability, for they could finally produce near-typeset-quality output.

In May 1990, Microsoft released Windows 3.0. As you probably know, this software changed the way people used personal computers. Apparently, the decision makers at Lotus weren't convinced that Windows was a significant product, and the company was slow getting out of the gate with its first Windows spreadsheet, 1-2-3 for Windows, which wasn't introduced until late 1991. Worse, this product was, in short, a dud. It didn't really capitalize on the Windows environment and disappointed many users. Consequently, Excel, which had already established itself as the premier Windows spreadsheet, became the overwhelming Windows spreadsheet market leader. Lotus came back with 1-2-3 Release 4 for Windows in June 1993—a vast improvement over the original. Release 5 for Windows appeared in mid-1994.

In mid-1994, Lotus unveiled 1-2-3 Release 4.0 for DOS. Many analysts (including myself) expected a product more compatible with the Windows product. But we were wrong; DOS Release 4.0 is simply an upgraded version of Release 3.4. Because of the widespread acceptance of Windows, this should be the last DOS version of 1-2-3 to see the light of day.

Over the years, spreadsheets became less important to Lotus (its flagship product turns out to be Notes). In mid-1995, IBM purchased Lotus Development Corporation. Two more versions of 1-2-3 became available, but it seems to be a case of too little, too late. Excel clearly dominates the spreadsheet market.

The most recent versions of 1-2-3 feature LotusScript, a scripting language similar to VBA (see Figure 1-1). Spreadsheet developers haven't exactly embraced this language with open arms. In retrospect, Lotus probably should have licensed VBA from Microsoft.

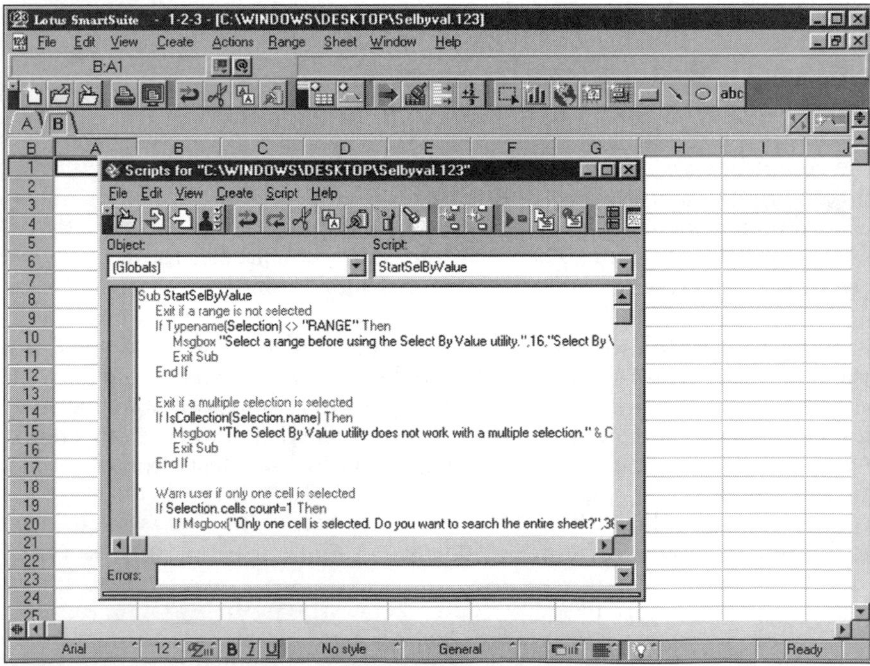

Figure 1-1: Currently, Lotus 1-2-3 includes LotusScript, a VBA-like scripting language.

Quattro Pro

The other significant player in the spreadsheet world is (or, I should say, *was*) Borland International. In 1994, Novell purchased both WordPerfect International and Borland's entire spreadsheet business. In 1996, WordPerfect and Quattro Pro were both purchased by Corel Corporation.

Borland started out in spreadsheets in 1987 with a product called Quattro. Essentially a clone of 1-2-3, Quattro offered a few additional features and an arguably better menu system. And it was also much cheaper. Importantly, users could opt for a 1-2-3-like menu system that let them use familiar commands and also ensured compatibility with 1-2-3 macros.

In the fall of 1989, Borland began shipping Quattro Pro, a more powerful product that built upon the original Quattro and trumped 1-2-3 in just about every area. For example, the first Quattro Pro let you work with multiple worksheets in movable and resizable windows — although it did *not* have a graphical user interface (GUI). More trivia: Quattro Pro was based on an obscure product called Surpass, which Borland acquired.

Released in late 1990, Quattro Pro Version 2.0 added 3D graphs and a link to Borland's Paradox database. A mere six months later — much to the chagrin of Quattro Pro book authors — Version 3.0 appeared, featuring an optional graphical user interface and a slide show feature. In the spring of 1992, Version 4 appeared, having customizable SpeedBars and an innovative analytical graphics feature. Version 5, which came out in 1994, had only one significant new feature: worksheet notebooks (that is, 3D worksheets).

Like Lotus, Borland was slow to jump on the Windows bandwagon. When Quattro Pro for Windows finally shipped in the fall of 1992, however, it provided some tough competition for the other two Windows spreadsheets, Excel 4.0 and 1-2-3 Release 1.1 for Windows. Importantly, Quattro Pro for Windows had an innovative feature, known as the UI Builder, that let developers and advanced users easily create custom user interfaces.

Also worth noting is a lawsuit between Lotus and Borland. Lotus won the suit, forcing Borland to remove the 1-2-3 macro compatibility and 1-2-3 menu option from Quattro Pro. This ruling was eventually overturned in late 1994, however, and Quattro Pro can now include 1-2-3 compatibility features (as if anyone really cares). Both sides spent millions of dollars on this lengthy legal fight, and when the dust cleared, no real winner emerged.

Borland followed up the original Quattro Pro for Windows with Version 5, which was upgraded to Version 6 after Novell took over Borland's spreadsheet business (see Figure 1-2). As I write this, the current version of Quattro Pro is Version 8.

For a while, Quattro Pro seemed the ultimate solution for spreadsheet developers. But then Excel 5 arrived.

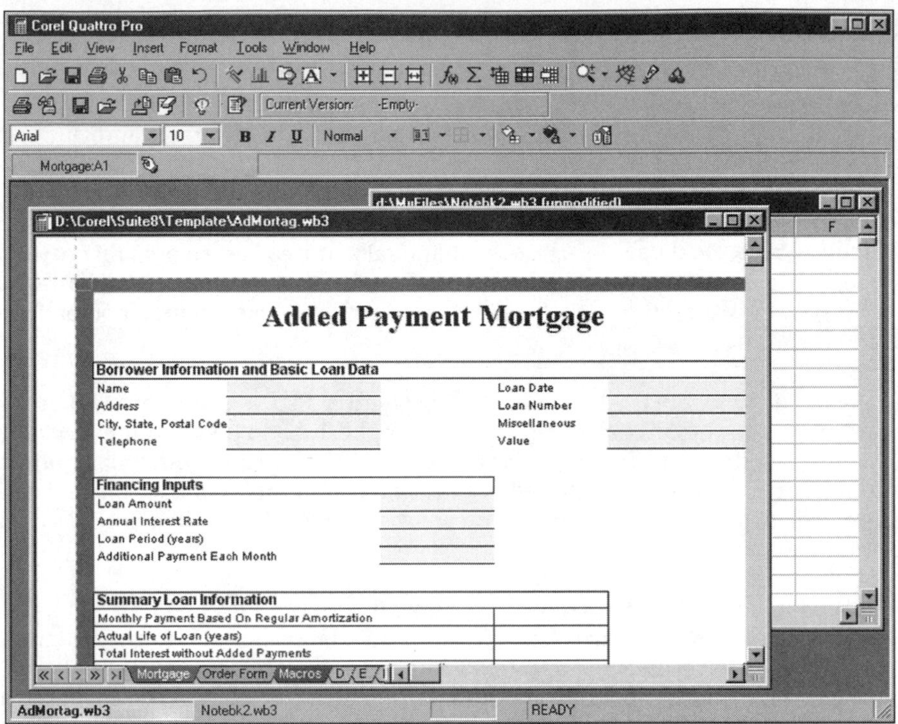

Figure 1-2: Corel's Quattro Pro.

Microsoft Excel

And now on to the good stuff.

Most people don't realize that Microsoft's experience with spreadsheets extends back to the early '80s. Over the years, Microsoft's spreadsheet offerings have come a long way, from the barely adequate MultiPlan to the state-of-the-art Excel 2000.

In 1982, Microsoft released its first spreadsheet, MultiPlan. Designed for computers running the CP/M operating system, the product was subsequently ported to several other platforms, including Apple II, Apple III, XENIX, and MS-DOS.

MultiPlan essentially ignored existing software user-interface standards. Difficult to learn and use, it never earned much of a following in the United States. Not surprisingly, Lotus 1-2-3 pretty much left MultiPlan in the dust.

Excel sort of evolved from MultiPlan, first surfacing in 1985 on the Macintosh. Like all Mac applications, Excel was a graphics-based program (unlike the character-based MultiPlan). In November 1987, Microsoft released the first version of Excel for Windows (labeled Excel 2.0 to correspond with the Macintosh version). Because Windows was not in widespread use at the time, this version included a run-time version of Windows — a special version that had just enough features to run Excel and nothing else. Less than a year later, Microsoft released Excel Version 2.1. In July 1990, Microsoft released a minor upgrade (2.1d) that was compatible with Windows 3.0. Although these 2.*x* versions were quite rudimentary by current standards (see Figure 1-3) and didn't have the attractive, sculpted look of later versions, they attracted a small but loyal group of supporters and provided an excellent foundation for future development. The macro language (XLM) consisted of functions that were evaluated in sequence. It was quite powerful, but very difficult to learn and use.

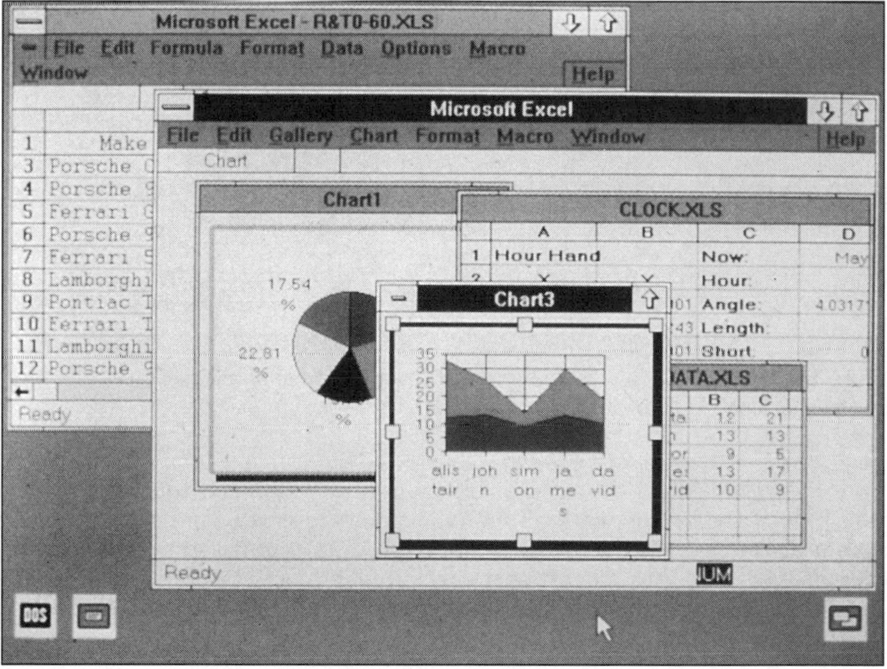

Figure 1-3: The original Excel 2.1 for Windows. This product has come a long way, no? (Photo courtesy of Microsoft)

Meanwhile, Microsoft developed a version of Excel (numbered 2.20) for OS/2 Presentation Manager, released in September 1989 and upgraded to Version 2.21 about ten months later. OS/2 never quite caught on, despite continued efforts by IBM.

In December 1990, Microsoft released Excel 3 for Windows, a significant improvement in both appearance and features (see Figure 1-4). The upgrade included a toolbar, drawing capabilities, a powerful optimization feature (Solver), add-in support, Object Linking and Embedding (OLE) support, 3D charts, macro buttons, simplified file consolidation, workgroup editing, and wordwrap text in a cell. Excel 3 also had the capability to work with external databases (via the Q+E program). The OS/2 version upgrade appeared five months later.

Microsoft Excel - REVENUE.XL3

File Edit Formula Format Data Options Macro Window Help

Normal

F36

Pro Forma Income Statement - Five-year Projection

Revenues (in thousands)	1991	1992	1993	1994	1995
Canada	184,845	203,330	223,663	246,029	270,632
Mexico	49,292	49,785	50,283	50,786	51,294
United States	1,232,300	1,355,530	1,219,977	1,341,975	1,476,173
North America	1,466,437	1,608,645	1,493,923	1,638,790	1,798,099
France	184,845	194,087	203,791	213,981	224,680
Germany	308,075	369,690	373,387	410,726	414,833
Other European	61,615	92,423	184,846	258,784	362,298
United Kingdom	61,615	67,777	74,555	82,011	90,212
Europe	616,150	723,977		965,502	1,092,023
Australia	48,392	53,231		64,409	70,850
Japan	439,931	879,862		2,287,641	2,973,933
Korea	43,993	65,990		148,478	222,717
Taiwan	65,990	82,488	103,110	128,888	161,110
Far East	598,306	1,081,571	2,020,373	2,629,416	3,428,610
Total Revenue	2,680,893	3,414,193	4,350,875	5,233,708	6,318,732
Cost of Goods Sold	1,340,447	1,474,492	1,621,941	1,784,135	1,962,549

Great increase from 1991

Figure 1-4: Excel 3 was a vast improvement over the original release. (Photo courtesy of Microsoft)

Version 4, released in the spring of 1992, not only was easier to use, but also had more power and sophistication for advanced users (see Figure 1-5). Excel 4 took top honors in virtually every spreadsheet product comparison published in the trade magazines. In the meantime, the relationship between Microsoft and IBM became increasingly strained; Excel 4 was never released for OS/2, and Microsoft has stopped making versions of Excel for OS/2.

Excel 5 hit the streets in early 1994 and immediately earned rave reviews. Like its predecessor, it finished at the top of every spreadsheet comparison published in the leading trade magazines. Despite stiff competition from 1-2-3 Release 5 for Windows and Quattro Pro for Windows 5—both were fine products that could handle just about any spreadsheet task thrown their way—Excel 5 continued to rule the roost.

Excel 95—also known as Excel 7—was released concurrently with Microsoft Windows 95. (Microsoft skipped over Version 6 to make the version numbers consistent across its Office products.) On the surface, Excel 95 didn't appear to be much different from Excel 5. Much of the core code was rewritten, however, and speed improvements were apparent in many areas. Importantly, Excel 95 used the same file format as Excel 5—which is the first time an Excel upgrade didn't use a new file format. This compatibility wasn't perfect, however, because Excel 95 included a few enhancements in the VBA language. Consequently, it was possible to develop an application using Excel 95 that would load (but not run properly) in Excel 5.

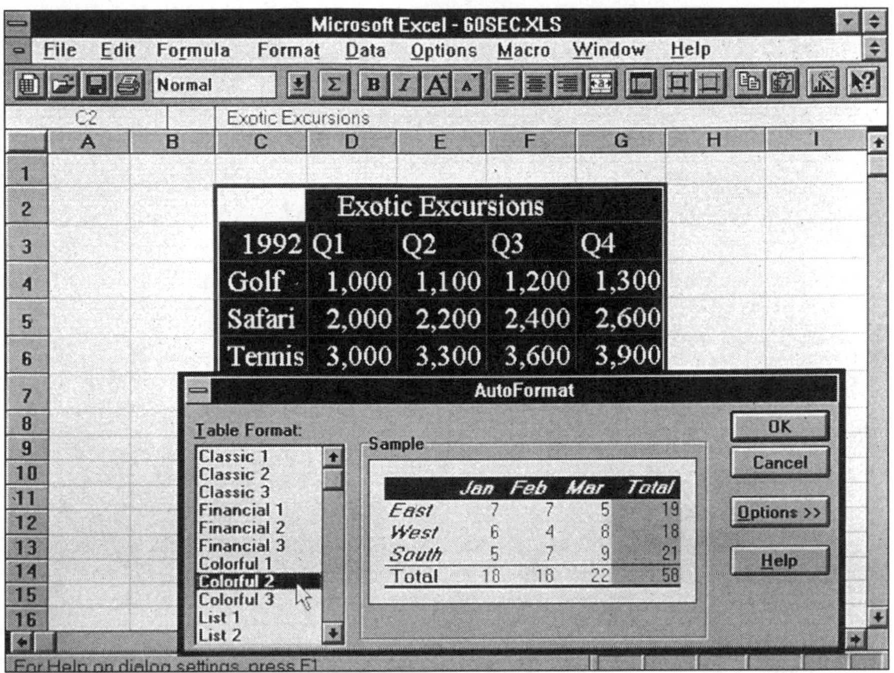

Figure 1-5: Excel 4 was another significant step forward, although still far from Excel 5. (Photo courtesy of Microsoft)

In early 1997, Microsoft released Office 97, which included Excel 97. Excel 97 is also known as Excel 8. This version included dozens of general enhancements plus a completely new interface for developing VBA-based applications. In addition, the product offered a new way of developing custom dialog boxes (called UserForms rather than dialog sheets). Microsoft tried to make Excel 97 compatible with previous versions, but the compatibility is far from perfect. Many applications developed using Excel 5 or Excel 95 require some tweaking before they will work with Excel 97 or Excel 2000.

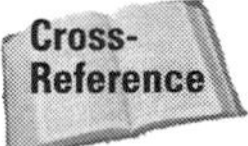

I discuss compatibility issues in Chapter 25.

Excel 2000 was released in early 1999 and is also sold as part of Office 2000. The enhancements in Excel 2000 deal primarily with Internet capabilities, although a few significant changes are apparent in the area of programming.

By any standard, Excel 2000 is an impressive product, and it should remain on top simply because it continues to provide the perfect blend of power and ease of use.

Spreadsheets Today

As I've watched the various spreadsheet products come and go over the years, I've seen some dramatic changes and some astounding shifts in the market. With each version of each product, the designers show a willingness to "borrow" their competitors' successful features. As a result, the three major spreadsheets are now, by and large, virtually identical from the standpoint of the typical user. Excel has, however, continued to chip away at the market share and now commands a huge share of the spreadsheet market.

How do you decide which product to use? Consider these factors:

✦ *Corporate policy*. Of course, most users end up using a particular spreadsheet because of corporate policy. Most companies choose a spreadsheet and stick with it. So, most end users are stuck with a spreadsheet.

✦ *Inertia*. Users tend to stick with a product, upgrading when possible — even if a better product is available. The phrase *if it ain't broke, don't fix it* comes to mind.

✦ *Familiarity*. In the past, 1-2-3 users often found Excel difficult to adapt to — and vice versa. Although the user interfaces of the latest versions are strikingly similar, each product has its own distinct look and feel. Users tend to use products that just "feel" right.

✦ *Standout features*. A standout feature or two can catch a user's fancy. Although today's spreadsheets possess similar features, not all implement these features equally well. For example, all three of the leading spreadsheets offer scenario management, but 1-2-3 far surpasses its competition in this area.

✦ *Recommendations*. Unless they're intimately involved with the spreadsheet industry, most people really don't have the foggiest idea where to start when evaluating spreadsheet products. Consequently, most rely heavily on recommendations from friends, associates, and the media.

✦ *Compatibility*. This is a broad term that covers an application's file formats and menu structures as well as how it works with other software and operating environments (hardware and software).

✦ *Manufacturer stability*. Nobody wants to buy a spreadsheet from a company that may go out of business in six months. That means no support and no upgrades — a dead-end purchase.

✦ *Programmability*. All spreadsheets have some sort of macro capability. But as you'll see, Excel is clearly the winner in this area. VBA is a significant step forward that makes competing macro features pale in comparison.

✦ *Peer support*. A primary source for spreadsheet help is the Internet. Web sites, newsgroups, and online "knowledge bases" provide answers to just about any spreadsheet question that may arise. The amount of material available for the popular spreadsheets varies quite a bit.

✦ *Cost*. Unlike with most products, *price* is not usually a major issue.

Given these factors, it's no wonder Excel remains the leading Windows spreadsheet. It was first on the scene, and I doubt that many original Excel users have switched. It has several standout features (pivot tables, data filtering, and add-ins, to name a few). It almost always comes out on top in head-to-head reviews. Its file format makes it quite compatible with other spreadsheets, and it's also extremely compatible with other Microsoft applications. For application development, Excel is without peer. In addition, many individuals and corporations alike choose Excel because it and Windows come from the same company, Microsoft, which happens to be the world's most successful software company and isn't going to disappear any time in the near future. If you're looking for spreadsheet information on the Internet, about 90 percent of the material deals with Excel. Finally, when you buy Excel as part of the Microsoft Office package, it's dirt cheap.

Why Excel Is Great for Developers

It's a safe bet that spreadsheet-based application development will become increasingly important over the next few years. Excel 2000, a highly programmable product, is easily the best choice for developing spreadsheet-based applications because it supports the VBA language (which is now in widespread use) and offers an easy way to create custom dialog boxes. For developers, Excel's key features include the following:

✦ *File structure*. The multisheet orientation makes it easy to organize elements of an application and store it in a single file. For example, a single workbook file can hold any number of worksheets and chart sheets. UserForms and VBA modules are stored with a workbook but are invisible to the end user.

✦ *Visual Basic for Applications*. This macro language lets you create structured programs directly in Excel. Excel isn't the only spreadsheet to include a structured scripting language (1-2-3 offers LotusScript, for example), but it's certainly the best implementation.

✦ *Easy access to UserForm controls*. Excel makes it very easy to add controls such as buttons, list boxes, and option buttons to a worksheet. Implementing these controls often requires little or no macro programming.

✦ *Custom dialog boxes*. You can easily create professional-looking dialog boxes. Excel 2000's UserForm feature (introduced in Excel 97) is a vast improvement over the old dialog sheets.

✦ *Customizable menus*. You can change menu elements, add to existing menus, or create entirely new menus. Other products enable you to do this as well, but Excel makes it extremely easy.

✦ *Customizable shortcut menus*. Excel is the only spreadsheet that lets you customize the right-click, context-sensitive shortcut menus.

✦ *Customizable toolbars*. It's easy to create new toolbars as another user interface option. Again, other spreadsheets let you do this as well, but Excel outmuscles them all.

- *Microsoft Query*. You can access important data directly from the spreadsheet environment. Data sources include standard database file formats, text files, and Web pages.
- *Data Access Objects and ActiveX Data Objects*. These features make it easy to work with external databases using VBA.
- *Extensive protection options*. Your applications can be kept confidential and protected from changes. Again, pretty standard fare, but Excel has some advantages.
- *Ability to create "compiled" add-ins*. With a single command, you can create XLA add-in files that attach seamlessly. Recent versions of 1-2-3 also include this feature.
- *Custom worksheet functions*. Using VBA, you can create custom worksheet functions to simplify formulas and calculations. Recent versions of 1-2-3 include a similar feature, but the implementation has some serious limitations.

Excel's Role in Microsoft's Strategy

Currently, most copies of Excel are sold as part of Microsoft Office — a *suite* of products that includes a variety of other programs (the exact programs you get depend on which version of Office you buy).

These days, the big topic is *interapplication operability*, or the use of two or more applications at a time. Obviously, it helps if the two or more programs can communicate well with each other. Microsoft is at the forefront of this trend. All the Office products have extremely similar user interfaces, and all support VBA.

Therefore, after you hone your VBA skills in Excel, you'll be able to put them to good use in other applications — you just need to learn the object mode for the other applications.

Summary

In this chapter, I sketched the evolution of spreadsheets. I provided an overview of the various versions of the major spreadsheet product lines, and I explained why Excel is so successful and is an excellent choice for application development. I hope that you gained a new appreciation of Excel while preparing for your next spreadsheet trivia contest.

In the next chapter, I provide a quick-and-dirty overview of Excel for newcomers. *Pssst,* I also reveal some of the program's secrets.

✦ ✦ ✦

Excel in a Nutshell

✦ ✦ ✦ ✦

In This Chapter

An introduction to Excel's "object orientation"

A conceptual overview of Excel 2000, including a description of its major features

Some tips and techniques that even advanced users may find helpful

✦ ✦ ✦ ✦

In this chapter, I provide a broad overview of the major components of Excel 2000. This chapter will prove especially useful for readers who have experience with another spreadsheet and are moving up to Excel. Veteran 1-2-3 users, for example, usually need help thinking in Excel's terms. But even experienced Excel users still may learn a thing or two by skimming through this chapter.

Thinking in Terms of Objects

When you are developing applications with Excel (especially when you are dabbling with VBA), it's helpful to think in terms of *objects*, or Excel elements that you can manipulate manually or via a macro. Some Excel objects include the following:

- The Excel application itself
- An Excel workbook
- A worksheet in a workbook
- A range in a worksheet
- A ListBox control on a UserForm (a custom dialog box)
- A chart sheet
- A chart on a chart sheet
- A chart series on a chart

Notice that something of an *object hierarchy* exists here: The Excel object contains workbook objects, which contain worksheet objects, which contain range objects. This hierarchy is called Excel's *object model*. Excel has more than 100 objects that you can control directly or by using VBA.

Other Office 2000 products have their own object models, and Office itself even has an object model.

Actually, controlling objects is fundamental to developing applications. Throughout this book, you learn how to automate tasks by controlling Excel's objects—and you do so using VBA. This concept becomes clearer in subsequent chapters.

Workbooks

One of the most common Excel objects is a *workbook*. Everything you do in Excel takes place in a workbook, which is stored in a file with an .xls extension.

Excel 97 and Excel 2000 use the same file format. Previous versions of Excel cannot open files from these two versions—although you can save your work in an earlier file format. In addition, Excel 2000 enables you to use HTML as a native file format. In other words, you can save a workbook as an HTML file and then reopen the HTML file with no loss of information.

An Excel workbook can hold any number of sheets (limited only by memory). There are four types of sheets:

- ✦ Worksheets
- ✦ Chart sheets
- ✦ XLM macro sheets (obsolete, but still supported)
- ✦ Dialog sheets (obsolete, but still supported)

Where Are the VBA Module Sheets?

In Excel 5 and Excel 95, a VBA module appeared in a workbook as a separate sheet. A VBA module, as you may know, holds VBA code. In Excel 97 and Excel 2000, VBA modules are still stored with a workbook, but they no longer show up as separate sheets. Rather, you work with VBA modules in the Visual Basic Editor (VB Editor). To view or edit a VBA module, activate the VB Editor by pressing Alt+F11. Subsequent chapters discuss VBA modules in depth.

You can open as many workbooks as you like (each in its own window), but at any given time, only one workbook is the *active workbook*. Similarly, only one sheet in a workbook is the *active sheet*. To activate a sheet, click its sheet tab, which is located at the bottom of the screen. To change a sheet's name, double-click the tab and enter the new text. Right-clicking a tab brings up a shortcut menu.

You can also hide the window that contains a workbook by using the Window ➪ Hide command. A hidden workbook window remains open, but it is not visible.

Worksheets

The most common type of sheet is a worksheet, which is what people normally think of when they think of a spreadsheet. Every Excel worksheet has 256 columns and 65,536 rows (four times as many rows as previous versions of Excel). And, to answer a common question, the number of rows and columns cannot be changed. You can hide unneeded rows and columns to keep them out of view, but you cannot increase the number of rows or columns.

Note Versions prior to Excel 97 had only 16,384 rows.

How Big Is a Worksheet?

It's interesting to stop and think how big a worksheet really is. Do the arithmetic (256 × 65,536), and you'll see that a worksheet has 16,777,216 cells. Remember, this is in just one worksheet. A single workbook can hold more than one worksheet.

If you're using the standard VGA video mode with the default row heights and column widths, you can see 9 columns and 18 rows (or 162 cells) at a time. This works out to less than 0.001 percent of the entire worksheet. Put another way, a single worksheet contains nearly 104,000 VGA screens of information.

If you started entering a single digit into each cell at a relatively rapid clip of one cell per second, it would take you about 194 days, nonstop, to fill up a worksheet. To print the results of your efforts would require more than 36,000 sheets of paper—a stack about six feet tall.

Filling an entire workbook with values is not recommended. Such a file would be huge and extremely slow to work with because Windows would be continually paging information to disk. As you may have surmised, Excel does not allocate memory for each cell; only cells that are actually used take up memory.

The real value of using multiple worksheets in a workbook is not access to more cells. Rather, multiple worksheets enable you to organize your work better. Back in the old days, when a file comprised a single worksheet, developers wasted a lot of time trying to organize the worksheet to hold their information efficiently. Now you can store information on any number of worksheets and still access it instantly. The workbook tabs make it very easy to activate a particular worksheet.

As you know, a worksheet cell can hold a value (including a date), a formula, a Boolean value (True or False), or text. Every worksheet also has an invisible draw layer, which lets you insert graphic objects, such as charts, maps, drawing objects, UserForm controls, pictures, and embedded objects.

You have complete control over the column widths and row heights — in fact, you can even hide rows and columns (as well as entire worksheets). Text in a cell can be displayed vertically (or at an angle) and even wrap around to occupy multiple lines.

Chart sheets

A chart sheet normally holds a single chart. Many users ignore chart sheets, preferring to store charts on the worksheet's draw layer. Using chart sheets is optional, but they make it a bit easier to print a chart on a page by itself, and they are especially useful for presentations.

XLM macro sheets

An XLM macro sheet (also known as an MS Excel 4 macro sheet) is essentially a worksheet, but it has some different defaults. More specifically, an XLM macro sheet displays formulas rather than the results of formulas. In addition, the default column width is larger than in a normal worksheet.

As the name suggests, an XLM macro sheet is designed to hold XLM macros. As you may know, the XLM macro system is a holdover from previous versions of Excel (Version 4.0 and earlier). Excel 2000 continues, however, to support XLM macros for compatibility reasons — although it no longer provides the option of recording an XLM macro. This book does not cover the XLM macro system; instead, it focuses on the more powerful VBA macro system.

Excel 5/95 dialog sheets

In Excel 5 and Excel 95, you created a custom dialog box by inserting a special dialog sheet. Excel 97 and Excel 2000 still support these dialog sheets, but they provide a much better alternative: UserForms. You work with UserForms in the Visual Basic Editor.

When you open a workbook that contains an Excel 5/95 dialog sheet, the dialog sheet appears as a sheet in the workbook.

If, for compatibility purposes, you need to insert an Excel 5/95 dialog sheet, you won't find the command to do so on the Insert menu. The only way to add an Excel 5/95 dialog sheet is to right-click any sheet tab and select Insert from the shortcut menu. Then, in the Insert dialog box, click the MS Excel 5.0 Dialog icon. Be aware that I do not discuss Excel 5/95 dialog sheets in this book (refer to my *Excel For Windows 95 Power Programming With VBA*).

Excel's User Interface

The *user interface* (UI) is the means by which an end user communicates with a computer program. A UI includes elements such as menus, dialog boxes, keystroke combinations, and so on. For the most part, Excel uses the standard Windows UI to accept commands, but it deviates from the standard Windows UI in at least one area — Excel's menus are not "standard" Windows menus.

Menus

The menus in Excel 2000 (and Excel 97) are actually toolbars in disguise. The icons that accompany some menu items are a dead giveaway. As such, they are not affected by systemwide changes. For example, if you use Windows Control Panel to change the font used for menus, this change is not apparent in Excel (or any of the Microsoft Office applications, for that matter).

Excel's menu system is relatively straightforward. Two different menu bars exist (one when a worksheet is active; the other when a chart sheet is active). Consistent with Windows conventions, inappropriate menu commands are dimmed and commands that open a dialog box are followed by an ellipsis. Where appropriate, the menus list any available shortcut key combinations (for example, the Edit menu lists Ctrl+Z as the shortcut key for Edit ⇨ Undo).

Several menu items are *cascading menus* — they lead to submenus that have additional commands (Edit ⇨ Fill is a cascading menu, for example). Cascading menus are indicated by a small arrow.

Beginning with Excel 97, the entire menu system can be customized by the end user or developer. To do so, choose the View ⇨ Toolbars ⇨ Customize command. It's important to understand that menu changes made by using this technique are "permanent." In other words, the menu changes remain in effect even if you close Excel and restart it. This is *very* different from the Menu Editor found in Excel 5 and Excel 95 — and no longer available in Excel 2000.

Excel also features context-sensitive shortcut menus, which appear when the user right-clicks after selecting one or more objects. Importantly, the end user or developer can customize any of the shortcut menus — a feature unique to Excel.

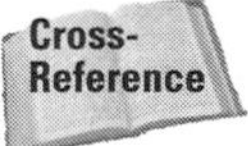

Refer to Chapter 22 for more information about customizing menus.

Dialog boxes

Most of the menu commands in Excel display a dialog box. These dialog boxes are quite consistent in terms of how they operate, except for some subtle differences found in the dialog boxes produced by the Analysis ToolPak add-in (which was written by a third party).

Some of Excel's dialog boxes use a notebook tab metaphor, which makes a single dialog box function as several different dialog boxes. The Options dialog box (choose Tools ➪ Options) is an example of a tabbed dialog box (see Figure 2-1).

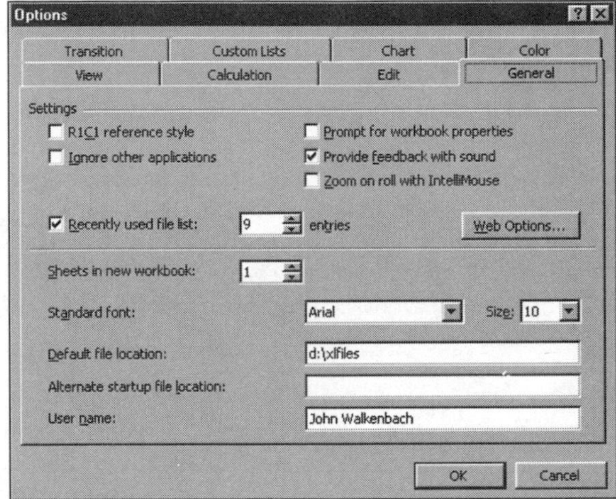

Figure 2-1: Tabbed dialog boxes make many options accessible without overwhelming the user.

The UserForm feature (which debuted in Excel 97) is a significant advancement because it enables the developer to create more robust dialog boxes — including tabbed dialog boxes (using the MultiPage control).

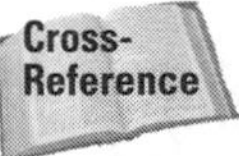

Refer to Part IV for information about creating and working with UserForms.

Toolbars

Excel 2000 ships with 43 predefined toolbars (including the two toolbars that function as menus), and you can create as many new toolbars as you like. Use the View➪Toolbars➪Customize command to customize toolbars or create new ones. You can distribute customized toolbars by attaching them to workbooks.

You can *dock* toolbars (position them along any edge of the screen) or make them *float*. By default, Excel displays the Standard and Formatting toolbars directly below the menu bar.

The toolbar buttons can be displayed in either of two sizes — although the large size buttons are simply too large in my opinion. A crude but effective toolbar button editor is built into Excel (see Figure 2-2). Excel provides a huge assortment of toolbar button images, however, so you probably won't need to use the button editor.

I discuss toolbars in detail in Chapter 21.

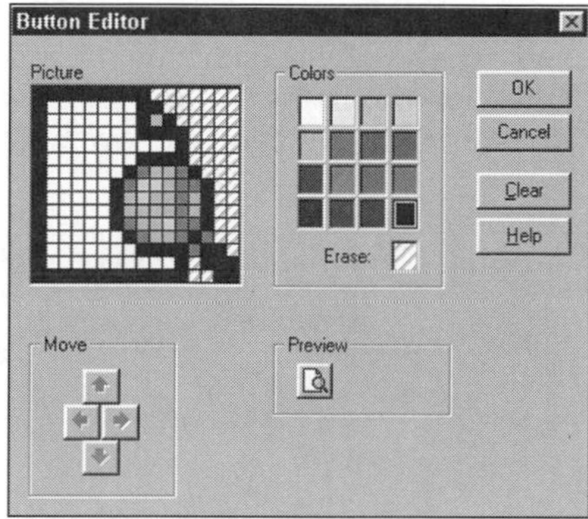

Figure 2-2: Excel's toolbar button editor is nothing to write home about, but it does the job.

Drag-and-drop

Excel's drag-and-drop UI feature enables you to freely drag objects that reside on the draw layer to change their position. Pressing Ctrl while dragging duplicates the selected objects.

Excel also allows drag-and-drop actions on cells and ranges: You can easily drag a cell or range to a different position. And pressing Ctrl while dragging copies the selected range.

Drag-and-drop is optional; you can disable it in the Edit tab of the Options dialog box.

You can also drag a range to the Windows desktop, creating a "scrap" object. You can then drag this object to another workbook (or to another application) and insert it as an OLE object.

Excel 2000, like the other Office 2000 applications, supports a new "Office Clipboard" that enables you to copy as many as 12 items and then selectively paste them.

Keyboard shortcuts

Excel has many keyboard shortcuts. For example, you can press Ctrl+C to copy a selection. If you're a newcomer to Excel—or you just want to improve your efficiency—I urge you to check out the online help (access the *Keyboard Shortcuts* index and go from there). The help file has tables that summarize useful keyboard commands and shortcuts.

Customizing the Display

Excel offers a great deal of flexibility regarding what is displayed onscreen (status bar, formula bar, toolbars, and so on). For example, by choosing View ➪ Full Screen, you can get rid of everything except the menu bar, thereby maximizing the amount of information visible. In addition, by using the View tab in the Options dialog box, you can customize what is displayed in a worksheet window (you can even hide scroll bars and grid lines).

In fact, Excel makes it possible to develop an application that doesn't even look like a spreadsheet.

Data Entry

Data entry in Excel is quite straightforward. Excel interprets each cell entry as one of the following:

- ✦ A value (including date and time)
- ✦ Text
- ✦ A formula
- ✦ A Boolean value (True or False)

Formulas always begin with an equal sign (=). Excel is accommodating to habitual 1-2-3 users, however, and accepts an ampersand (&), a plus sign (+), or a minus sign (–) as the first character in a formula. It automatically adjusts the entry after you press Enter.

Data Entry Tips

The following data entry tips are especially useful for those who are moving up to Excel from another spreadsheet.

- ✦ If you select a range of cells before entering data, you can press Enter to end a cell entry and move to the next cell in the selected range. Similarly, use Shift+Enter to move up, Tab to move to the right, and Shift+Tab to move to the left.
- ✦ To enter data without pressing the arrow keys, enable the Move Selection after Enter option in the Edit tab of the Options dialog box (which you access from the Tools➪Options command). You can also choose the direction that you want to go.

- To enter the same data into each cell of a range, select the range, enter the information into the active cell, and then press Ctrl+Enter.
- To copy the contents of the active cell to all other cells in a selected range, press F2 and then Ctrl+Enter.
- To fill a range with increments of a single value, press Ctrl while you drag the fill handle at the corner of the selection.
- To create a custom AutoFill list, use the Custom Lists tab of the Options dialog box.
- To copy a cell without incrementing, drag the fill handle at the corner of the selection. Or press Ctrl+D to copy down or Ctrl+R to copy to the right.
- You can enter tabs and carriage returns in a cell to make the text easier to read. To enter a tab, press Ctrl+Alt+Tab. To enter a carriage return, press Alt+Enter. Carriage returns cause a cell's contents to wrap within the cell.
- To enter a fraction, press 0, a space, and then the fraction (using a slash). Excel formats the cell using the Fraction number format.
- To automatically format a cell with the Currency format, type a dollar sign before the value. To enter a value in Percent format, type a percent sign after the value. You can also include commas to separate thousands (for example, 123,434).
- Press Ctrl+; to insert the current date and Ctrl+Shift+; to enter the current time into a cell.
- To set up a cell or range so it only accepts entries of a certain type (or within a certain value range), use the Data ⇨ Validation command.

Selecting Objects

Generally, selecting objects conforms to standard Windows practices. You can select a range of cells by clicking and dragging. Clicking an object that has been placed on the draw layer selects the object. To select multiple objects or noncontiguous cells, press Ctrl while you select the objects or cells. To select a large range, click a cell at any corner of the range, scroll to the opposite corner of the range, and press Shift while you click the opposite corner cell.

In versions prior to Excel 97, clicking an embedded chart selected the chart. In Excel 97 and Excel 2000, clicking a chart selects a specific object within the chart. To select the chart object itself, press Ctrl while you click the chart.

Formatting

Excel provides two types of formatting: numeric formatting and "stylistic" formatting.

Numeric formatting

Numeric formatting refers to how a value appears in the cell. In addition to choosing from an extensive list of predefined formats, you can create your own formats (see Figure 2-3) — the procedure is thoroughly explained in the online help system.

Excel applies some numeric formatting automatically, based on the entry. For example, if you precede a value with a dollar sign, Excel applies Currency number formatting.

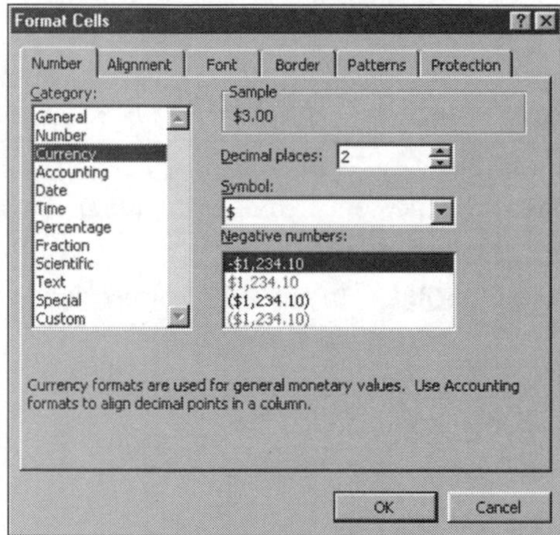

Figure 2-3: Excel's numeric formatting options are very flexible.

Stylistic formatting

Stylistic formatting refers to the formatting that you apply to make your work look good. Many toolbar buttons offer direct access to common formatting options, regardless of whether you're working with cells, drawn objects, or charts. For example, you can use the Fill Color toolbar button to change the background color of a cell, change the fill color of a drawn text box, or change the color of a bar in a chart. But you'll want to access the Format dialog box for the full range of formatting options.

The easiest way to get to the correct dialog box and format an object is to select the object, right-click, and then choose Format *xxx* (where *xxx* is the selected object) from the shortcut menu. This action leads to a tabbed dialog box that holds all the formatting options for the selected object.

Formulas

Formulas are what make a spreadsheet a spreadsheet. Excel has some important formula-related features that are worth knowing. They enable you to write array formulas, use an intersection operator, include links, and create megaformulas (my term for a lengthy and incomprehensible — but efficient — formula).

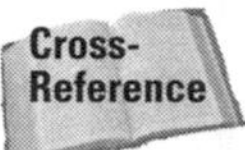

Chapter 3 covers formulas and presents lots of tricks and tips.

Names

All spreadsheets let you use names for cells and ranges, but Excel handles names in some unique ways.

A *name* is an identifier that enables you to refer to a cell, range, value, formula, or graphic object. Formulas that use names are much easier to read than formulas using cell references, and it's much easier to create formulas that use named references.

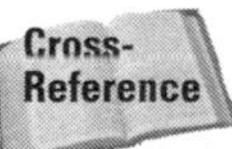

I discuss names in Chapter 3.

Functions

Worksheet functions enable you to perform calculations or operations that would otherwise be impossible. Excel provides a huge number of built-in functions, and you can access even more functions (many of them quite esoteric) by attaching the Analysis ToolPak add-in.

The easiest way to locate the function you need is to use the Paste Function dialog box, shown in Figure 2-4. Access this dialog box by clicking the Paste Function button on the Standard toolbar (or by selecting Insert⇨Function or pressing Shift+F3). If you're not familiar with this feature, I encourage you to check it out. It's very handy.

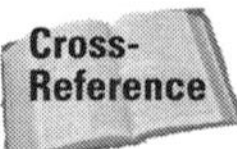

Excel also lets you create your own worksheet functions using VBA. For details about this powerful feature, see Chapter 10.

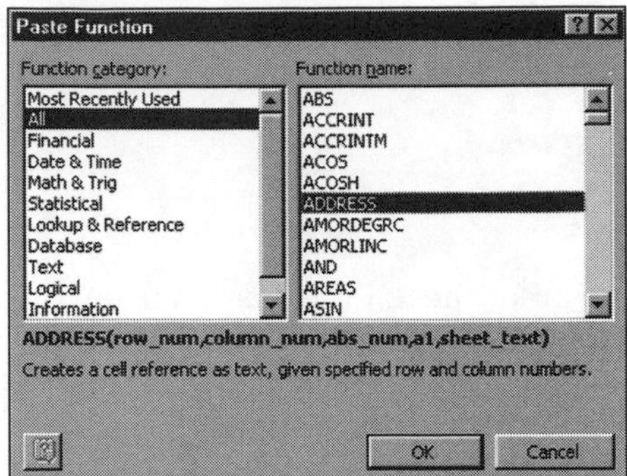

Figure 2-4: The Paste Function dialog box is the best way to insert a function into a formula.

Shapes

As I mentioned earlier in this chapter, each worksheet has an invisible draw layer, which holds charts, maps, pictures, UserForm controls, and shapes.

Excel enables you to easily draw a wide variety of geometric shapes directly on your worksheet, thanks to buttons on the Drawing toolbar. In addition, you should be aware that you can group objects into a single object, which is easier to size or position.

Several drawing objects are worthy of additional discussion:

✦ You can insert AutoShapes from the Drawing toolbar. You can choose from a huge assortment of shapes. Once a shape is placed on your worksheet, you can modify the shape by selecting it and dragging its handles. In addition, you can apply drop shadows, text, or 3D effects to the shape.

✦ The *text box* provides a way to display text that's independent of row and column boundaries — a good way to label rows in a table (see Figure 2-5). Although you can display text vertically in a cell, doing so changes the row height.

✦ For some reason, the designers of Excel make the *linked picture object* rather difficult to generate. Copy a range and then select the Edit➪Paste Picture Link command (which appears on the Edit menu only when you press Shift). The Paste Picture Link command was originally designed to accommodate users who wanted to print a noncontiguous selection of ranges. Users could "take pictures" of the ranges and then paste the pictures together in a single area, which could then be printed.

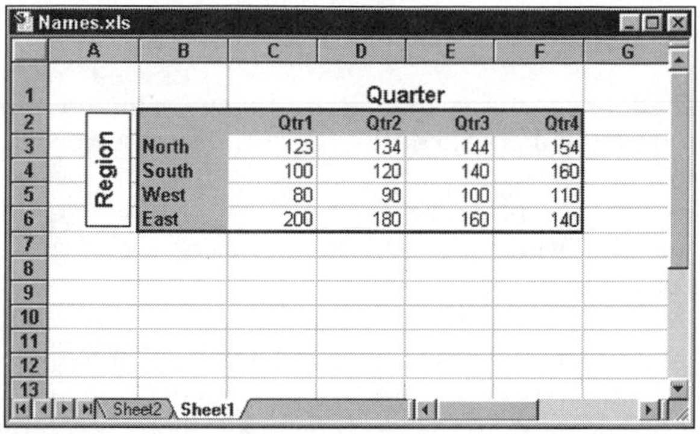

Names.xls

		Quarter			
		Qtr1	Qtr2	Qtr3	Qtr4
Region	North	123	134	144	154
	South	100	120	140	160
	West	80	90	100	110
	East	200	180	160	140

Figure 2-5: The text box drawing object is useful for displaying text vertically.

✦ Finally, many of the UserForm controls (those used in custom dialog boxes) can be placed directly on a worksheet. Doing so can greatly enhance the usability of some worksheets and eliminate the need to create custom dialog boxes. Figure 2-6 shows a worksheet with some dialog box controls added to the draw layer.

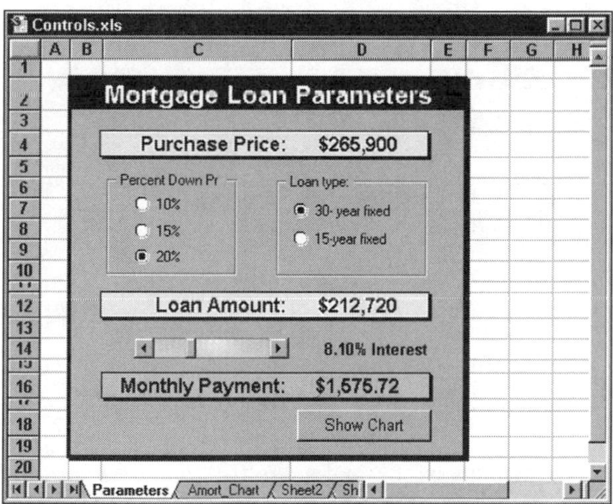

Figure 2-6: Excel lets you add many of the UserForm controls directly to a worksheet.

Charts

Excel, of course, has excellent charting capabilities. As I mentioned earlier in this chapter, you can store charts on a chart sheet or float them on a worksheet.

Excel 2000 supports pivot charts. A pivot chart is linked to a pivot table, and you can view various graphical summaries of your data using the same techniques used in a pivot table.

Excel offers extensive chart customization options. If a chart is free-floating, just click a chart element to select it (or double-click it to display its formatting dialog box). Right-clicking a chart element displays a shortcut menu.

The easiest way to create a chart is to select the data to be charted and then use the Chart Wizard (you can choose the corresponding button on the Standard toolbar). The Chart Wizard walks you through the steps to create a chart that meets your needs.

Excel uses a SERIES function to specify data for the chart (one SERIES formula for each data series). When you select a series in a chart, the SERIES function is displayed in the formula bar (see Figure 2-7). You can modify the SERIES function manually if you like. Often, this is the most efficient way to change the data range used in a chart.

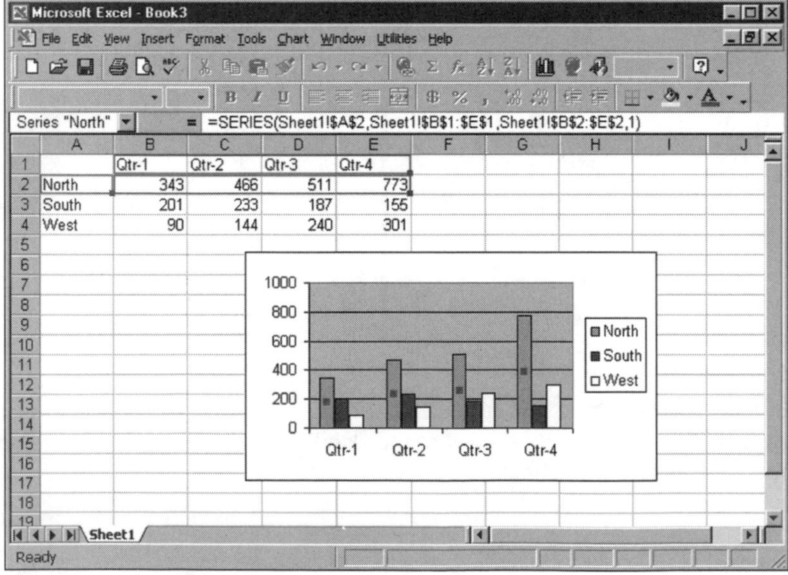

Figure 2-7: Data for a chart series is specified in a SERIES function.

Macros

All the major spreadsheet products have a macro language. Excel has two: XLM and VBA. The original XLM macro language is obsolete and has been replaced with VBA. Excel 2000 still can execute any XLM macro you may run across, but you cannot record such macros. You'll want to use VBA to develop new macros.

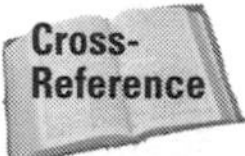

Part III of this book is devoted to the VBA language.

Database Access

Over the years, most spreadsheets have enabled users to work with simple flat database tables (even the original version of 1-2-3 contained this feature). Excel has some slick tools.

Using databases from a spreadsheet falls into two categories:

✦ *Worksheet databases*. The entire database is stored in a worksheet, limiting the size of the database. In Excel, a worksheet database can have no more than 65,535 records (the top row holds the field names) and 256 fields.

✦ *External databases*. The data is stored in one or more disk files and accessed as needed.

Worksheet databases

Generally, when the cell pointer is located within a database, Excel recognizes it and displays the field names whenever possible. For example, if you move the cell pointer within a worksheet database and choose the Data ➪ Sort command, Excel lets you select the sort keys by choosing field names from a drop-down list.

Particularly useful is Excel's AutoFilter feature, which enables you to display only the records that you want to see. When AutoFilter mode is on, you can filter the data by selecting values from pull-down lists (which appear in place of the field names when you choose the Data ➪ Filter ➪ AutoFilter command). Rows that don't qualify are temporarily hidden. See Figure 2-8 for an example.

If you prefer to use the traditional spreadsheet database techniques that involve criteria ranges, choose the Data ➪ Filter ➪ Advanced Filter command.

SalesDatabase.xls

	A	B	C	D	E	F	G
1		Date	SalesPerson	Loc	Product	Num	Price
6	5	7-Oct	Roberts	VIC		907	12.5
8	7	8-Oct	Roberts	VIC		770	12.5
9	8	10-Oct	Smith	NT		223	12.5
19	18	27-Oct	Kee	TAS		706	12.5
24	23	5-Nov	Pradesh	NT		181	12.5
28	27	12-Nov	Smith	NT	Apples	742	12.5
31	30	18-Nov	Roberts	NSW	Apples	27	12.5
36	35	25-Nov	Kee	NSW	Apples	274	12.5
42	41	8-Dec	Roberts	VIC	Apples	390	12.5
43	42	9-Dec	Kee	SA	Apples	32	12.5
45	44	11-Dec	Roberts	QLD	Apples	574	12.5
46	45	15-Dec	Kee	WA	Apples	295	12.5
50	49	17-Dec	Pradesh	SA	Apples	335	12.5
55	54	30-Dec	Smith	VIC	Apples	899	12.5
56	55	1-Jan	Roberts	VIC	Apples	1	12.5
60	59	7-Jan	Roberts	VIC	Apples	292	12.5
70	69	19-Jan	Roberts	TAS	Apples	188	12.5
74	73	27-Jan	Kee	SA	Apples	681	12.5
80	79	5-Feb	Roberts	NT	Apples	922	12.5

(All)
(Top 10...)
(Custom...)
Apples
Mangoes
Oranges
Pears

Sheet1

Figure 2-8: Excel's AutoFilter enables you to view database records that meet only your criteria.

External databases

To work with external database tables, use the Data ➪ Get External Data command, which executes Microsoft Query and enables you to choose your databases and define queries. The results of a query can be directed back to your worksheet.

With Excel 97 and Excel 2000, you can also create Web queries to bring in data stored in a corporate intranet or on the Internet.

Excel also lets you work with data objects independent of Excel through both Data Access Objects and ActiveX Data Objects. Both systems make it easy to access external databases from VBA.

Analysis Tools

Excel is certainly no slouch when it comes to analysis. After all, that's what most people use a spreadsheet for. Most analysis tasks can be handled with formulas, but Excel offers many other options.

Outlines

A worksheet outline is often an excellent way to work with hierarchical data such as budgets. You can collapse or expand an outline to display various levels of detail.

Automatic subtotals

Excel can automatically insert (or remove) subtotal formulas in a table set up as a database. It also creates an outline from the data so that you can view only the subtotals or any level of detail you desire. Figure 2-9 shows some automatic subtotals and the accompanying outline.

outline.XLS

	A	B	C	D	E	I	M	Q
1	**State**	**Jan**	**Feb**	**Mar**	***Q1 Total***	***Q2 Total***	***Q3 Total***	***Q4 Total***
2	California	1,118.00	1,960.00	1,252.00	4,330	4,507	4,722	5,554
3	Washington	1,247.00	1,238.00	1,028.00	3,513	4,703	5,139	4,721
4	Oregon	1,460.00	1,954.00	1,726.00	5,140	4,369	3,786	4,239
5	Nevada	1,345.00	1,375.00	1,075.00	3,795	4,663	4,667	4,624
6	**West Total**	**5,170.00**	**6,527.00**	**5,081.00**	**16,778**	**18,242**	**18,314**	**19,138**
7	New York	1,429.00	1,316.00	1,993.00	4,738	4,763	3,915	4,289
8	New Jersey	1,735.00	1,406.00	1,224.00	4,365	4,316	4,051	4,526
9	Massachusetts	1,099.00	1,233.00	1,110.00	3,442	4,155	4,882	5,376
10	Florida	1,705.00	1,792.00	1,225.00	4,722	4,630	5,062	4,734
11	**East Total**	**5,968.00**	**5,747.00**	**5,552.00**	**17,267**	**17,864**	**17,910**	**18,925**
12	Kentucky	1,109.00	1,078.00	1,155.00	3,342	4,626	4,306	4,526
13	Oklahoma	1,309.00	1,045.00	1,641.00	3,995	5,364	4,338	4,449
14	Missouri	1,511.00	1,744.00	1,414.00	4,669	4,556	4,203	4,279
15	Illinois	1,539.00	1,493.00	1,211.00	4,243	3,623	4,889	4,330
16	Kansas	1,973.00	1,560.00	1,243.00	4,776	4,007	4,322	4,299
17	**Central Total**	**7,441.00**	**6,920.00**	**6,664.00**	**17,683**	**17,550**	**17,752**	**17,357**
18	**Grand Total**	**18,579.00**	**19,194.00**	**17,297.00**	**51,728**	**53,656**	**53,976**	**55,420**
19								

Sheet1

Figure 2-9: Excel can automatically insert subtotal formulas and create outlines.

Scenario management

If you're seeking the ultimate in scenario-management features, 1-2-3's Version Manager is probably your best bet. Excel's scenario manager is quite weak in comparison, but it can handle simple scenario-management tasks, and it's definitely easier than trying to keep track of different scenarios manually.

Analysis ToolPak

The Analysis ToolPak add-in provides 19 special-purpose analysis tools (primarily statistical in nature) and many specialized worksheet functions. These tools make Excel suitable for small- to medium-scale statistical analysis.

Pivot tables

One of Excel's most powerful tools is its *pivot tables*. This special type of object can be manipulated entirely by VBA. Data for a pivot table comes from a worksheet database or an external database and is stored in a special cache, which enables Excel to recalculate rapidly after a pivot table is altered. Figure 2-10 shows a pivot table.

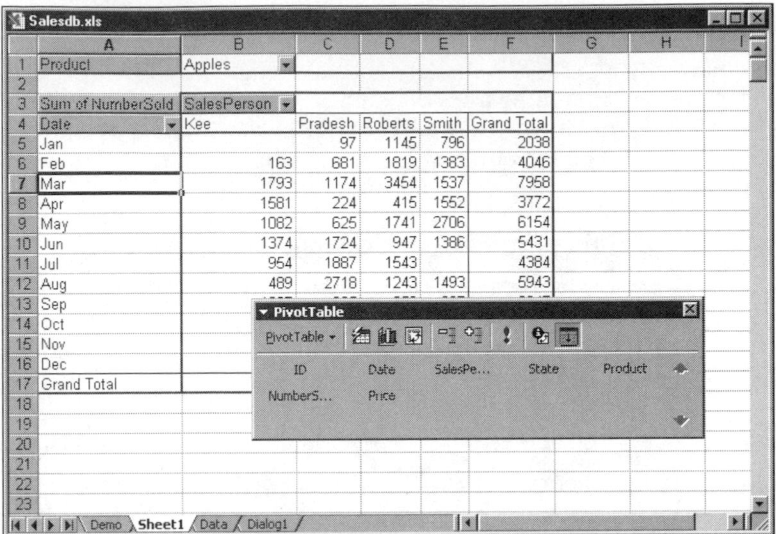

Figure 2-10: Excel's Pivot Table feature has many applications.

Auditing

Excel also has some useful auditing capabilities that help you identify errors or track the logic in an unfamiliar spreadsheet. To access these features, select Tools ⇨ Auditing.

Solver

For specialized linear and nonlinear problems, Excel's Solver add-in calculates solutions to what-if scenarios based on adjustable cells, constraint cells, and, optionally, cells that must be maximized or minimized. Excel's Solver is very similar to the feature found in 1-2-3 for Windows and Quattro Pro for Windows. (This similarity is not surprising when you know that a single company, Frontline Systems, was largely responsible for the feature in all three products.)

Add-Ins

An *add-in* is a program that's attached to Excel to give it additional functionality. To attach an add-in, use the Tools⇨Add-Ins command.

Table 2-1 presents a list of the add-ins that are included with Excel 2000. Depending on how you installed Excel, you may not have immediate access to all of these add-ins. If you attempt to attach an add-in that's not installed, you'll be asked whether you want to install it.

Table 2-1
Add-ins Included with Excel 2000

Add-In	*Description*
Access Links	Lets you use Microsoft Access forms and reports with Excel worksheets (Access must be installed on your system). Adds three new commands: Data ➪ MS Access Form, Data ➪ MS Access Report, and Data ➪ Convert to MS Access.
Analysis ToolPak	Contains statistical and engineering tools plus new worksheet functions. Adds a new command: Tools ➪ Data Analysis.
AutoSave	Automatically saves your workbook at a time interval that you specify. Adds a new command: Tools ➪ AutoSave.
Conditional Sum Wizard	Helps you create formulas that add values in a column only if another value in the row contains a specific value. Adds a new command: Tools ➪ Wizard ➪ Conditional Sum.
Lookup Wizard	Helps you create a formula that returns the value at the intersection of a row and column. Adds a new command: Tools ➪ Wizard ➪ Lookup.
ODBC	Uses Open Database Connectivity functions to connect to external data sources using installed ODBC drivers.
Report Manager	Prints reports that consist of a set sequence of views and scenarios. Adds a new command: View ➪ Report Manager.
Solver	Helps you use a variety of numeric methods for equation solving and optimization. Adds a new command: Tools ➪ Solver.
Template Utilities	Provides utilities used by the Spreadsheet Solutions templates. This is loaded automatically when you use one of these templates.
Template Wizard	Helps you create custom templates. Adds a new command: Data ➪ Template Wizard.
Update Add-in Links	Updates links to MS Excel 4.0 add-ins to directly access the new built-in functionality. Use this only if you open a workbook saved in Excel 4.0 format that uses an older add-in. Adds a new command: Tools ➪ Update Add-In Links.

In addition to these add-ins, there are many third-party add-ins that you can purchase or download from online services. You can use the coupon in the back of the book to acquire a free copy of the Power Utility Pak add-in. And, as I detail in Chapter 20, it's *very* easy to create your own add-ins.

Compatibility

An Excel workbook file is generally specific to the version of Excel that created it. Excel can read workbook files generated by previous versions of Excel, but earlier versions cannot read files produced by later versions unless they were saved in formats compatible with earlier versions.

Excel can import a variety of files generated by other spreadsheet and database products (see Chapter 4 for details).

If you're an experienced 1-2-3 for DOS user, Excel provides detailed online help that's designed to get you to think in terms of Excel. Check out the Help ⇨ Lotus 1-2-3 Help command for more information.

Another aspect of compatibility is compatibility with previous versions of Excel. Developers should be aware of a number of issues. I discuss these in Chapter 25.

Summary

In this chapter, I provided a conceptual overview of Excel 2000 for newcomers to the fold.

Chapter 3 continues the saga with a discussion of formulas.

✦ ✦ ✦

Formula Tricks and Techniques

In This Chapter

An overview of Excel formulas

Differentiating between absolute and relative references in formulas

Understanding and using names

Introducing array formulas

Counting and summing cells

Working with dates and times

Creating "megaformulas"

Virtually every successful spreadsheet application uses formulas. In fact, constructing formulas can certainly be construed as a type of "programming." This chapter provides an overview of Excel's formula-related features and describes some techniques that may be new to you.

About Formulas

Formulas, of course, are what make a spreadsheet a spreadsheet. If it weren't for formulas, your worksheet would just be a static document — something that could be produced by a word processor with great support for tables.

When it comes to formulas, Excel can't be beat. It has a huge assortment of built-in functions, has excellent support for names, and even supports array formulas — a special type of formula that can perform magic.

A formula entered into a cell can consist of any of the following elements:

- Operators such as + (for addition) and * (for multiplication)
- Cell references (including named cells and ranges)
- Values or strings
- Worksheet functions (such as `SUM` or `AVERAGE`)

A formula can consist of up to 1,024 characters. After you enter a formula into a cell, the cell displays the result of the formula. The formula itself appears in the formula bar when the cell is activated, however.

Calculating Formulas

You've probably noticed that the formulas in your worksheet get calculated immediately. If you change any cells that a formula uses, the formula displays a new result with no effort on your part. This is what happens when Excel's Calculation mode is set to Automatic. In this mode (which is the default mode), Excel uses the following rules when calculating your worksheet:

- When you make a change — enter or edit data or formulas, for example — Excel immediately calculates those formulas that depend on the new or edited data.
- If it's in the middle of a lengthy calculation, Excel temporarily suspends calculation when you need to perform other worksheet tasks; it resumes when you're finished.
- Formulas are evaluated in a natural sequence. In other words, if a formula in cell D12 depends on the result of a formula in cell D11, cell D11 is calculated before D12.

Sometimes, however, you may want to control when Excel calculates formulas. For example, if you create a worksheet with thousands of complex formulas, you'll find that operations can slow to a snail's pace while Excel does its thing. In such a case, you should set Excel's calculation mode to Manual. You can do this in the Calculation panel of the Options dialog box.

When you're working in Manual calculation mode, Excel displays *Calculate* in the status bar when you have any uncalculated formulas. You can use the following shortcut keys to recalculate the formulas:

- *F9* calculates the formulas in all open workbooks.
- *Shift+F9* calculates only the formulas in the active worksheet. Other worksheets in the same workbook won't be calculated.
- *Ctrl+Shift+F9* forces a recalculation of everything. This is an undocumented key sequence. Use it if Excel (for some reason) doesn't seem to be calculating correctly.

Excel's Calculation mode isn't specific to a particular worksheet. When you change Excel's Calculation mode, it affects all open workbooks, not just the active workbook.

Cell and Range References

Most formulas reference one or more cells. This reference can be made by using the cell's or range's address or name (if it has one). Cell references come in four styles:

✦ *Relative*. The reference is fully relative. When the formula is copied, the cell reference adjusts to its new location. Example: A1.

✦ *Absolute*. The reference is fully absolute. When the formula is copied, the cell reference does not change. Example: $A$1.

✦ *Row Absolute*. The reference is partially absolute. When the formula is copied, the column part adjusts, but the row part does not change. Example: A$1.

✦ *Column Absolute*. The reference is partially absolute. When the formula is copied, the row part adjusts, but the column part does not change. Example: $A1.

By default, all cell and range references are relative. To change a reference, you must manually add the dollar signs.

Why use references that aren't relative?

If you think about it, you'll realize that the only reason you would ever need to change a reference is if you plan to copy the formula. Figure 3-1 demonstrates why this is so. The formula in cell C4 is

```
=C$3*$B4
```

This formula calculates the area for various widths (listed in column B) and lengths (listed in row 3). After the formula is entered, it can then be copied down to C8 and across to F8. Because the formula uses absolute references to row 3 and column B and relative references for other rows and columns, each copied formula produces the correct result. If the formula used only relative references, copying the formula would cause all the references to adjust — and produce the wrong results.

Book1

	A	B	C	D	E	F	G
1							
2				Length			
3			12	14	16	18	
4	Width	3	36	42	48	54	
5		4	48	56	64	72	
6		5	60	70	80	90	
7		6	72	84	96	108	
8		7	84	98	112	126	
9							
10							
11							

Sheet1

Figure 3-1: An example of using nonrelative references in a formula.

About R1C1 notation

Normally, Excel uses what's known as A1 notation. Each cell address consists of a column letter and a row number. However, Excel also supports R1C1 notation. In this system, cell A1 is referred to as cell R1C1, cell A2 is R1C2, and so on.

To change to R1C1 notation, select Tools ➪ Options, click the General tab, and place a check mark next to R1C1 reference style. After you do so, you'll notice that the column letters all change to numbers. All the cell and range references in your formulas are also adjusted.

Table 3-1 presents some examples of formulas using standard notation and R1C1 notation. The formula is assumed to be in cell B1 (also known as R1C2).

Table 3-1
Simple Formulas in Two Notations Compared

Standard	*R1C1*
=A1+1	=RC[-1]+1
=$A$1+1	=R1C1+1
=$A1+1	=RC1+1
=A$1+1	=R1C[-1]+1
=SUM(A1:A10)	=SUM(RC[-1]:R[9]C[-1])
=SUM($A$1:$A$10)	=SUM(R1C1:R10C1)

If you find R1C1 notation confusing, you're not alone. R1C1 notation isn't too bad when you're dealing with absolute references. But when relative references are involved, the brackets can drive you nuts.

The numbers in brackets refer to the relative position of the references. For example, R[-5]C[-3] specifies the cell that's five rows above and three columns to the left. On the other hand, R[5]C[3] references the cell that's five rows below and three columns to the right. If the brackets are omitted, the notation specifies the same row or column. For example, R[5]C refers to the cell five rows below in the same column.

Although you probably won't use R1C1 notation as your standard system, it *does* have at least one good use. Using R1C1 notation makes it very easy to spot an erroneous formula. When you copy a formula, every copied formula is exactly the same in R1C1 notation. This is true regardless of the types of cell references you use (relative, absolute, or mixed). Therefore, you can switch to R1C1 notation and check your copied formulas. If one looks different from its surrounding formulas, there's a good chance that it may be incorrect.

Referencing other sheets or workbooks

References to cells and ranges need not be in the same sheet as the formula. To refer to a cell in a different worksheet, precede the cell reference with the sheet name followed by an exclamation point. Here's an example of a formula that uses a cell reference in a different worksheet:

```
=Sheet2!A1+1
```

You can also create link formulas that refer to a cell in a different workbook. To do so, precede the cell reference with the workbook name (in square brackets), the worksheet name, and an exclamation point. Here's an example:

```
=[Budget.xls]Sheet1!A1+1
```

If the workbook name in the reference includes one or more spaces, you must enclose it (and the sheet name) in single quotation marks. For example,

```
='[Budget For 1999]Sheet1'!A1+A1
If the linked workbook is closed, you must add the complete
path to the workbook reference. Here's an
example:='C:\MSOffice\Excel\[Budget For 1999]Sheet1'!A1+A1
```

Although you can enter link formulas directly, you also can create the reference by using normal pointing methods. To do so, the source file must be open. When you do so, Excel creates absolute cell references (if you plan to copy the formula to other cells, make the references relative).

Working with links can be tricky. For example, if you use the File ⇨ Save As command to make a backup copy of the source worksheet, you automatically change the link formulas to refer to the new file (not usually what you want to do). Another way to mess up your links is to rename the source workbook when the dependent workbook is not open.

Using Links to Recover Data in a Corrupt File

If you are unable to load a corrupted Excel workbook, you can write a link formula to recover all or part of the data (but not the formulas). You can do so because the source file in a link formula does not need to be open. If your corrupt file is named Badfile.xls, for example, open a blank workbook and enter the following formula into cell A1 of Sheet1 to attempt to recover the data from Sheet1 of the corrupt workbook file:

```
=[Badfile.xls]Sheet1!A1
```

In your new workbook, copy this formula down and to the right to recover as much information as you can. A better approach, however, is to maintain a backup of your important files.

Using Names

One of the most useful features in Excel is its ability to provide meaningful names for various items. For example, you can name cells, ranges, rows, columns, charts, and other objects. An advantage unique to Excel is that you can name values or formulas that don't even appear in cells in your worksheet (see the "Naming constants" section later in this chapter).

Naming cells and ranges

You create names for cells or ranges by using the Insert ➪ Name ➪ Define command (or by pressing Ctrl+F3). An even faster way to create names is to use the Name Box (the drop-down list at the left side of the formula bar). You can choose the Insert ➪ Name ➪ Create command to create names automatically for cells or ranges based on row or column titles on your worksheet. In Figure 3-2, for example, B2:E2 is named *North*, B3:E3 is named *South*, and so on. Vertically, B2:B5 is named *Qtr1*, C2:C5 is named *Qtr2*, and so on.

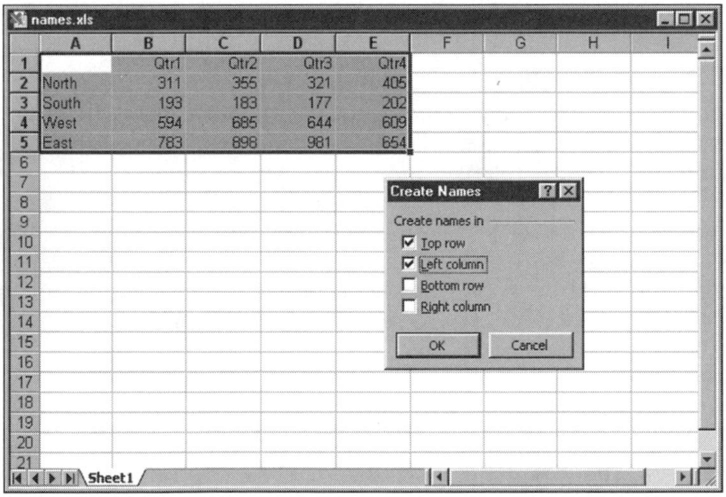

	A	B	C	D	E
1		Qtr1	Qtr2	Qtr3	Qtr4
2	North	311	355	321	405
3	South	193	183	177	202
4	West	594	685	644	609
5	East	783	898	981	654

Create Names
Create names in
☑ Top row
☑ Left column
☐ Bottom row
☐ Right column
OK Cancel

Figure 3-2: Excel makes it easy to create names that use descriptive text in your worksheet.

Using names is especially important if you write VBA code that uses cell or range references. The reason? VBA does not automatically update its references if you move a cell or range that's referred to in a VBA statement. For example, if your VBA code uses a reference to Range("C4"), the code will be invalid if the user inserts a new row above or a new column to the left of the range. Using a reference such as Range("InterestRate") avoids these potential problems.

Excel 2000 includes a new feature that automatically adjusts formulas when you insert a new row or column. For example, assume you have the following formula in cell A5:

```
=SUM(A1:A4)
```

If you then insert a new row directly above row 5, the formula is changed (automatically) to

```
=SUM(A1:A5)
```

In most cases, this is exactly what you want. If you use a named range for the `SUM` argument, no adjustments are made when you insert the new row.

Applying names to existing references

When you create a new name for a cell or a range, Excel doesn't automatically use the name in place of existing references in your formulas. For example, assume that you have the following formula in cell F10:

```
=A1-A2
```

If you define a name *Income* for A1 and *Expenses* for A2, Excel won't automatically change your formula to =Income–Expenses. It's fairly easy to replace cell or range references with their corresponding names, however. Start by selecting the range that you want to modify. Then, choose the Insert ➪ Name ➪ Apply command. In the Apply Names dialog box, select the names that you want to apply and then click OK. Excel replaces the range references with the names in the selected cells.

Unfortunately, there is no way to "unapply" names. In other words, if a formula uses a name, you can't convert the name to an actual cell or range reference. Even worse, if you delete a name that is used in a formula, the formula does not revert to the cell or range address — it simply returns a #NAME? error.

My Power Utility Pak includes a utility that scans all formulas in a selection and automatically replaces names with their references.

Intersecting names

Excel has a special operator, called the *intersection operator*, that comes into play when you're dealing with ranges. This operator is a space character. Using names with the intersection operator makes it very easy to create meaningful formulas. For this example, refer once again to Figure 3-2. If you enter the following formula into a cell

```
=Qtr2 South
```

the result is 183—the intersection of the *Qtr2* range and the *South* range. To get the total for the West region, you can use this formula:

```
=SUM(West)
```

Naming columns and rows

With Excel, you also can name complete rows and columns. In the preceding example, the name *Qtr1* is assigned to the range B2:B5. Alternatively, *Qtr1* could be assigned to all of column B, *Qtr2* to column C, and so on. You also can do the same horizontally so that *North* refers to row 2, *South* to row 3, and so on.

The intersection operator works exactly as before, but now you can add more regions or quarters without having to change the existing names.

When naming columns and rows, make sure that you don't store any extraneous information in named rows or columns. For example, remember that if you insert a value in cell B7, it is included in the *Qtr1* range.

"Natural Language" References

Beginning with Excel 97, you can write "natural language" formulas that use row and column headers. It's not necessary to actually define these names—Excel figures them out automatically. You connect these pseudo names by using the intersection operator (that is, a space character). For example, you might create a formula like this:

```
=January Sales
```

Excel would display the value at the intersection of the column header (Sales) and the row header (January).

While this type of thing may be convenient, I suggest that you avoid this feature like the plague. Using these pseudo names is unreliable and difficult to document, and you cannot use these names in your VBA code.

Scoping names

A named cell or range normally has a workbook-level *scope*—in other words, you can use the name in any worksheet in the workbook. Names that have worksheet-level scope can be used only in the worksheet where they are defined; in fact, a worksheet-level name is not visible in the Name Box in a worksheet where it is not defined. You also cannot find a worksheet-level name in the Define Name dialog box from any sheet where it is not defined.

To create a worksheet-level name, define the name by preceding it with the worksheet name followed by an exclamation point. For example, the name *Sheet1!Sales* is valid only on Sheet1.

Naming constants

Virtually every experienced Excel user knows how to create cell and range names (although not all Excel users actually do so). But most Excel users do not know that you can use names to refer to values that don't appear in your worksheet (that is, *constants*).

Suppose that many formulas in your worksheet need to use an interest rate. Most people would plug the interest rate into a cell and give it a name, such as *RATE*, so that they could use the name in their formulas. The other alternative is to call up the Define Name dialog box and enter the interest rate directly into the Refers to box (see Figure 3-3). Then you can use the name in your formulas just as if the value is stored in a cell. If the interest rate changes, just change the definition for *RATE*, and Excel updates all the cells that contain this name.

Figure 3-3: Excel lets you name constants that don't appear in worksheet cells.

By the way, this technique also works for text. If you define the name IDG to stand for *International Data Group*, when you enter **=IDG** into a cell, the cell displays the full name.

Naming formulas

Besides naming cells, ranges, and constants, you also can enter a formula directly into the Refers to box in the Define Name dialog box to create a named formula. The formula that you enter uses cell references relative to the active cell — the cell that receives the formula. If you use the mouse to indicate related cells in the act of building a formula, however, the references will be absolute.

Figure 3-4 shows a formula entered directly in the Refers to box in the Define Name dialog box. In this case, the active cell is C1, so the formula refers to the two cells to its left (notice that the cell references are relative). After this name is defined, entering **=POWER** into a cell raises the value two cells to the left to the power represented by the cell directly to the left.

Figure 3-4: You can name a formula that doesn't appear in any worksheet cell.

If you use this formula throughout a worksheet, you'll find that it's much easier to enter **=POWER** than to create the formula from scratch. In addition, if you need to modify the formula, you can just change the definition in the Name Box rather than edit each occurrence of the formula.

Naming objects

In addition to providing names for cells and ranges, you can give more meaningful names to objects such as charts and shapes. This can make it easier to refer to such objects — especially when you refer to them in your VBA code.

Contrary to what you might think, the Insert ⇨ Name ⇨ Define command doesn't enable you to name objects (it only works for cells and ranges). The only way to change the name of a nonrange is to use the Name box. Just select the item, type the new name in the Name box, and press Enter.

If you simply click elsewhere in your workbook after typing the name in the Name box, the name won't stick. You *must* press Enter.

Formula Errors

It's not uncommon to enter a formula and receive an error in return. Formulas may return an error value if a cell that they refer to has an error value. This is known as the ripple effect — a single error value can make its way to lots of other cells that contain formulas that depend on the cell. Table 3-2 lists the types of error values that may appear in a cell that has a formula.

Table 3-2
Excel Error Values

Error Value	*Explanation*
#DIV/0!	The formula is trying to divide by zero (an operation that's not allowed on this planet). This error also occurs when the formula attempts to divide by a cell that is empty.
#N/A	The formula is referring (directly or indirectly) to a cell that uses the NA worksheet function to signal the fact that data is not available.
#NAME?	The formula uses a name that Excel doesn't recognize. This can happen if you delete a name that's used in the formula or if you have unmatched quotes when using text.
#NULL!	The formula uses an intersection of two ranges that don't intersect (this concept is described later in the chapter).
#NUM!	There is a problem with a value; for example, you specified a negative number where a positive number is expected.
#REF!	The formula refers to a cell that isn't valid. This can happen if the cell has been deleted from the worksheet.
#VALUE!	The formula includes an argument or operand of the wrong type. An *operand* is a value or cell reference that a formula uses to calculate a result.

Array Formulas

An *array* is simply a collection of cells or values that is operated on as a group. An *array formula* is a special type of formula that works with arrays. An array formula can produce a single result, or it can produce multiple results — with each result displayed in a separate cell (because Excel can fit only one value in a cell).

For example, when you multiply a 1 × 5 array by another 1 × 5 array, the result is a third 1 × 5 array. In other words, the result of this kind of operation occupies five cells; each element in the first array is multiplied by each corresponding element in the second array to create five new values, each getting its own cell. The array formula below multiplies the values in A1:A5 by the corresponding values in B1:B5. This array formula is entered into five cells simultaneously.

```
=A1:A5*B1:B5
```

To remind you that a formula is an array formula, Excel surrounds it with brackets ({ }). Don't enter the brackets yourself.

An array formula example

Excel's array formulas enable you to perform individual operations on each cell in a range in much the same way that a program language's looping feature enables you to work with elements of an array. If you've never used array formulas before, this section will get your feet wet with a hands-on example.

Figure 3-5 shows a worksheet with text in A1:A10. The goal of this exercise is to create a *single formula* that returns the sum of the total number of characters in the range. Without the single formula requirement, you would write a formula using the `LEN` function, copy it down the column, and then use the `SUM` function to add up the results of the intermediate formulas.

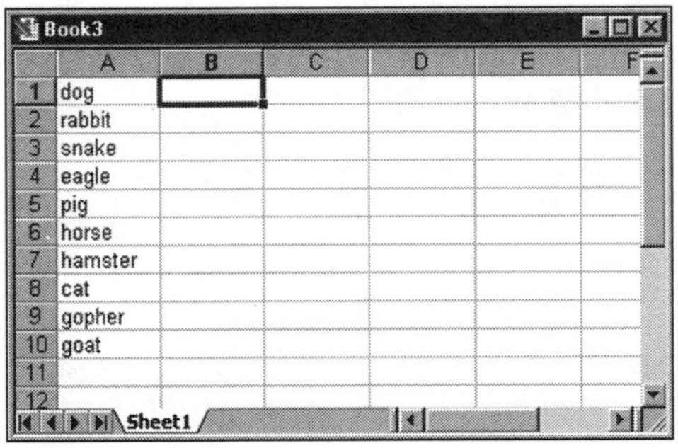

Figure 3-5: You can create an array formula that returns the total number of characters contained in range A1:A10.

To demonstrate how an array formula can occupy more than one cell, create the worksheet shown in Figure 3-5, and then try this:

1. Select the range B1:B10.
2. Type the following formula:

   ```
   =LEN(A1:A10)
   ```

3. Press Ctrl+Shift+Enter.

The preceding steps enter a single array formula into ten cells. Enter a `SUM` formula that adds the values in B1:B10, and you'll see that the total number of characters in A1:A10 is 47.

Here's the key point: It's not necessary to actually *display* those ten array elements. Rather, Excel can store the array in memory. Knowing this, you can type the following single formula in any blank cell (make sure you enter it using Ctrl+Shift+Enter):

```
=SUM(LEN(A1:A10))
```

This formula is displayed surrounded by brackets:

```
{=SUM(LEN(A1:A10))}
```

This formula essentially creates a ten-element array (in memory) that consists of the length of each string in A1:A10. The `SUM` function uses this array as its argument, and the formula returns 53.

An array formula calendar

Figure 3-6 shows a worksheet set up to display a calendar for any month. Believe it or not, the calendar is created with a single array formula that occupies 42 cells.

Calendar Arrays.xls

Month Year

September 1999

Sun	Mon	Tue	Wed	Thu	Fri	Sat
			1	2	3	4
5	6	7	8	9	10	11
12	13	14	15	16	17	18
19	20	21	22	23	24	25
26	27	28	29	30		

Notes Calendar

Figure 3-6: One array formula is all it takes to make a calendar for any month in any year.

The companion CD-ROM contains a workbook with the calendar example as well as several additional array formula examples.

Array formula pros and cons

The advantages of using array formulas rather than single-cell formulas include the following:

- They use less memory.
- They can make your work much more efficient.
- They can eliminate the need for intermediate formulas.
- They can enable you to do things that would be difficult or impossible otherwise.

A few disadvantages of using array formulas are the following:

- Some can slow your spreadsheet recalculation time to a crawl.
- They can make your worksheet more difficult for others to understand.
- You must remember to enter an array formula with a special key sequence (Ctrl+Shift+Enter).

Counting and Summing Techniques

I spend quite a bit of time reading the Excel newsgroups on the Internet. Many of the questions posed in these groups deal with counting or summing various types of cells. In an attempt to answer most of these questions, I present a number of formula examples that deal with counting various things on a worksheet. You can probably adapt these formulas to your own needs.

Using the COUNTIF or SUMIF function

Excel's `SUM`, `COUNT`, `COUNTA`, and `COUNTBLANK` functions are very straightforward, so I'll skip them and get straight to the more useful `COUNTIF` and `SUMIF` functions. `COUNTIF` takes two arguments: the range that holds the data to be counted and the criteria used to determine whether the cell is included in the count. `SUMIF` takes three arguments: the range to be evaluated, the criteria used to determine whether the cell is included in the count, and the range that holds the data to be summed.

Table 3-3 demonstrates a variety of uses for the `COUNTIF` function. The formulas assume that you have a range named *data* (you'll need to substitute the actual range address in these formulas). Also, be aware that the second argument for the `COUNTIF` function can be a reference to a cell that contains the search criteria.

Table 3-3
Examples of Common Uses for the COUNTIF Function

Formula	*Return Value*
=COUNTIF(data,12)	The number of cells that contain the value 12
=COUNTIF(data,1)+COUNTIF(data,12)	The number of cells that contain 1 or 12
=COUNTIF(data,"<0")	The number of cells that contain a negative number
=COUNTIF(data,"<>0")	The number of nonzero values
=COUNTIF(data,">=1")-COUNTIF(data,">10")	The number of cells that contain a value between 1 and 10
=COUNTIF(data,"yes")	The number of cells that contain the word *yes* (not case-sensitive)
=COUNTIF(data,"*")	The number of cells that contain any text
=COUNTIF(data,"*s*")	The number of cells that contain the letter *s* (not case-sensitive)
=COUNTIF(data,"???")	The number of three-letter words

Using array formulas to count and sum

If none of the standard counting techniques fits the bill, you may be able to construct an array formula (see "Array Formulas" earlier in this chapter). Don't forget: When you enter an array formula, press Ctrl+Shift+Enter.

To count the number of numerical values (skipping text and blanks), use this formula:

```
=SUM(IF(ISNUMBER(data),1,0))
```

To count the number of cells that contain an error value, use this formula:

```
=SUM(IF(ISERR(data),1,0))
```

To count the number of unique numeric values (skipping text, blanks not allowed), use this formula:

```
=SUM(IF(FREQUENCY(data,data)>0,1,0))
```

Table 3-4 shows a number of array formula examples based on the worksheet shown in Figure 3-7.

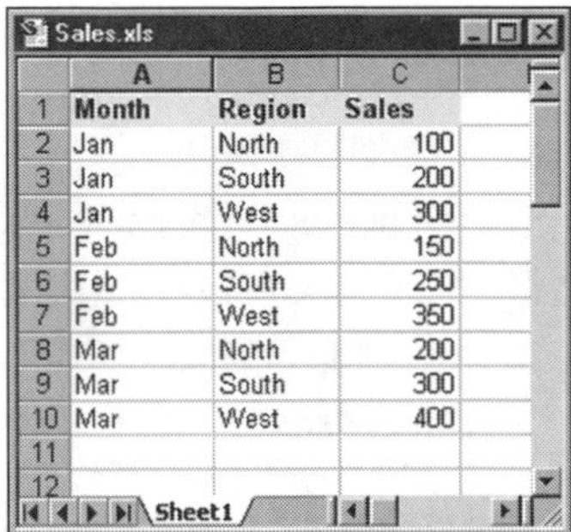

Sales.xls

	A	B	C
1	Month	Region	Sales
2	Jan	North	100
3	Jan	South	200
4	Jan	West	300
5	Feb	North	150
6	Feb	South	250
7	Feb	West	350
8	Mar	North	200
9	Mar	South	300
10	Mar	West	400
11			
12			

Sheet1

Figure 3-7: This simple database demonstrates some useful array formulas for counting and summing.

Table 3-4
Complex Array Formulas Using the SUM Function

Array Formula	*Returns*
`=SUM((A2:A10="Jan")*(B2:B10="North")*C2:C10)`	Sum of Sales where Month="Jan" AND Region="North"
`=SUM((A2:A10="Jan")*(B2:B10<>"North")*C2:C10)`	Sum of Sales where Month="Jan" AND Region<>"North"
`=SUM((A2:A10="Jan")*(B2:B10="North"))`	Count of Sales where Month="Jan" AND Region="North"
`=SUM((A2:A10="Jan")*(C2:C10>=200)*(C2:C10))`	Sum of Sales where Month="Jan" and Sales>= 200
`=SUM((C2:C10>=300)*(C2:C10<=400)*(C2:C10))`	Sum of Sales between 300 and 400
`=SUM((C2:C10>=300)*(C2:C10<=400))`	Count of Sales between 300 and 400

Other counting tools

The COUNTIF function is useful when you have a single counting criterion. For more complex comparisons, you can use the DCOUNT function. To use the DCOUNT function, you must set your data up as a database (with field names in the first row), and you also need to create a separate criteria range to specify the counting criteria. The criteria range can also handle logical OR operations by using additional rows. Consult the online help for details.

Excel's SUBTOTAL function can be very useful when you need to get a count of rows that have been filtered using the AutoFilter feature. The first argument for the subtotal figure determines the type of subtotaling. An argument of 3 represents the COUNTA function, and it returns the number of visible cells in a range.

For the ultimate in counting, consider using a pivot table. If you're not familiar with pivot tables, you're missing out on one of the most powerful tools around.

Working with Dates and Times

Excel uses a serial number system to store dates. The earliest date that Excel can understand is January 1, 1900. This date has a serial number of 1. January 2, 1900, has a serial number of 2, and so on.

Most of the time, you don't have to be concerned with Excel's serial number date system. You simply enter a date in a familiar date format, and Excel takes care of the details behind the scenes. For example, if you need to enter June 1, 1999, you can simply enter the date by typing **June 1, 1999** (or use any of a number of different date formats). Excel interprets your entry and stores the value 36312, which is the serial number for that date.

When working with times, you simply enter the time into a cell in a recognized format. Excel's system for representing dates as individual values is extended to include decimals that represent portions or fractions of days. In other words, Excel perceives all time using the same system whether that time is a particular day, a certain hour, or a specific second. For example, the date serial number for June 1, 1999, is 36312. Noon (halfway through the day) is represented internally as 36312.5. Again, you normally don't have to be concerned with these fractional serial numbers.

Since dates and times are stored as serial numbers, it stands to reason that you can add and subtract dates and times. For example, you can enter a formula to calculate the number of days between two dates.

When performing calculations with time, things get a bit trickier. When you enter a time without an associated date, the date is assumed to be January 0, 1900. This is not a problem — unless your calculation produces a negative time value. When this happens, Excel displays an error (a series of pound signs). The solution? Switch to the 1904 date system. Select Tools⇨Options, click the Calculation tab, and place a check mark next to the 1904 date system check box.

When you add time values, you'll find that you can't display more than 24 hours. For each 24-hour period, Excel simply adds another day to the total. The solution is to change the number formatting to use brackets around the hour part of the format. The following number format, for example, displays more than 24 hours:

```
[hh]:mm
```

Creating Megaformulas

Often, spreadsheets require intermediate formulas to produce a desired result. In other words, a formula may depend on other formulas, which in turn depend on other formulas. After you get all these formulas working correctly, it's often possible to eliminate the intermediate formulas and use what I refer to as a single *megaformula* instead. The advantages? You use fewer cells (less clutter), and recalculation may be faster. Besides, people in the know will be impressed with your formula-building abilities. The disadvantages? The formula may be impossible to decipher or modify.

Here's an example: Imagine a worksheet with a column of people's names. And suppose that you've been asked to remove all the middle names and middle initials from the names — but not all the names have a middle name or initial. Editing the cells manually would take hours, so you opt for a formula-based solution. Although this is not a difficult task, it normally involves several intermediate formulas.

Figure 3-8 shows the results of the more conventional solution, which requires six intermediate formulas shown in Table 3-5. The names are in column A; the end result goes in column H. Columns B through G hold the intermediate formulas.

megaformula - inter.xls

	A	B	C	D	E	F	G	H
1	John Q. Public	John Q. Public	5	8	8	John	Public	John Public
2	Bob Smith	Bob Smith	4	#VALUE!	4	Bob	Smith	Bob Smith
3	Jill Marie Jackson	Jill Marie Jackson	5	11	11	Jill	Jackson	Jill Jackson
4	Amy Young	Amy Young	4	#VALUE!	4	Amy	Young	Amy Young
5	R.J. Smith	R.J. Smith	5	#VALUE!	5	R.J.	Smith	R.J. Smith
6	R. Jay Smith	R. Jay Smith	3	7	7	R.	Smith	R. Smith
7								
8								
9								
10								

Sheet1

Figure 3-8: Removing the middle names and initials requires six intermediate formulas.

Table 3-5
Intermediate Formulas Written in the First Row of Sheet1 in Figure 3-8

Cell	*Intermediate Formula*	*What It Does*
B1	`=TRIM(A1)`	Removes excess spaces
C1	`=FIND(" ",B1,1)`	Locates the first space
D1	`=FIND(" ",B1,C1+1)`	Locates the second space
E1	`=IF(ISERROR(D1),C1,D1)`	Uses the first space if no second space exists
F1	`=LEFT(B1,C1)`	Extracts the first name
G1	`=RIGHT(B1,LEN(B1)-E1)`	Extracts the last name
H1	`=F1&G1`	Concatenates the two names

You can eliminate all the intermediate formulas by creating a megaformula. You do so by creating all the intermediate formulas and then going back into the final result formula and replacing each cell reference with a copy of the formula in the cell referred to (without the equal sign). Fortunately, you can use the clipboard to copy and paste. Keep repeating this process until cell H1 contains nothing but references to cell A1. You end up with the following megaformula in one cell:

```
=LEFT(TRIM(A1),FIND
(" ",TRIM(A1),1))&RIGHT(TRIM(A1),LEN(TRIM(A1))-
IF(ISERROR(FIND(" ",TRIM(A1),FIND(" ",TRIM(A1),1)+1)),
FIND(" ",TRIM(A1),1),FIND(" ",TRIM(A1),FIND
(" ",TRIM(A1),1)+1)))
```

When you're satisfied that the megaformula is working, you can delete the columns that hold the intermediate formulas because they are no longer used.

The megaformula performs exactly the same tasks as all the intermediate formulas — although it's virtually impossible for anyone to figure out, even the author. If you decide to use megaformulas, make sure that the intermediate formulas are performing correctly before you start building a megaformula. Even better, keep a single copy of the intermediate formulas somewhere in case you discover an error or need to make a change.

The only limitation to the megaformula technique is that Excel formulas can contain no more than 1,024 characters. Another way to approach this problem is to create a custom worksheet function in VBA. Then you could replace the megaformula with a simple formula, such as

```
=NOMIDDLE(A1)
```

In fact, I wrote such a function to compare it with intermediate formulas and megaformulas.

Because a megaformula is so complex, you may think that using one would slow down recalculation. Actually, that's not the case. As a test, I created a worksheet that used a megaformula 65,536 times. Then I created another worksheet that used six intermediate formulas. I compared the results with the VBA function I wrote. Statistics regarding the two methodologies were recorded and are shown in Table 3-6.

Table 3-6
Intermediate Formulas versus Megaformula

Method	*Recalculation Time (Seconds)*	*File Size*
Intermediate formulas	7	23.2MB
Megaformula	5	8.2MB
VBA function	66	800MB

As you can see, using the megaformula resulted in significantly faster recalculations as well as a *much* smaller workbook. The VBA function was much slower — in fact, it wasn't even in the same ballpark. This is fairly typical of VBA functions; they are always slower than built-in Excel functions.

The three files used in this time test are available on the companion CD-ROM.

Summary

In this chapter, I examined the many forms that Excel formulas may take and showed how they coalesce to form often intricate mechanisms — which may include the occasional "megaformula."

In the next chapter, I explain how Excel maintains and organizes its many types and formats of files.

✦ ✦ ✦

C H A P T E R

Understanding Excel's Files

✦ ✦ ✦ ✦

In This Chapter

A description of the various ways to start Excel

A discussion of the files used and produced by Excel — including the new HTML file format

Details about how Excel uses the Windows Registry

✦ ✦ ✦ ✦

If you plan to do any advanced work with Excel, it's critical that you become familiar with the various ways to start Excel and with what happens when the application is launched. It's also a good idea to have a good understanding of the various files used and generated by Excel. These topics are covered in this chapter.

Starting Excel

Excel can be started various ways (depending on how it's installed). All methods ultimately execute the Excel.exe executable file.

When Excel starts, it reads its settings from the Windows Registry and opens any add-ins that are installed (that is, those that are checked in the Add-Ins dialog box). It then displays an empty workbook; the number of sheets in the workbook is determined by a user-defined setting that is stored in the Windows Registry. You can change this number by editing the Sheets in the New Workbook setting located in the General tab of the Options dialog box (select Tools➪Options).

If your XlStart folder contains any workbooks, they are opened automatically — and a blank workbook does not appear. If your XlStart folder includes a workspace file, multiple workbooks are opened in a customized workspace. You also can define an alternate startup directory to hold other worksheet or workspace files you want opened automatically. You can set up this alternate startup directory by specifying a path in the Alternate Startup File Location setting located in the General tab of the Options dialog box.

If you want to change the default formats (or content) of blank workbooks that you create, create a default workbook and save it as a template with the name Book.xlt in your XlStart folder. For details on creating and using template files, refer to the online help.

Excel recognizes several command line switches. These are listed in Table 4-1.

Table 4-1
Excel Command Line Switches

Switch	***What It Does***
/automation	Forces Excel to start without loading add-ins and templates or processing files in the XlStart directory or the alternate startup file location. Use this switch to perform a "clean-boot" of Excel.
/e	Forces Excel to start in "embedded" mode. Use this switch when you want to start Excel without creating a new workbook.
/embedded	Same as /e.
/i	Forces Excel to start with a maximized window.
/m	Forces Excel to create a new workbook that contains a single Microsoft Excel 4.0 macro sheet (obsolete).
/o	Causes Excel to reregister itself in the Windows Registry.
/p *directory*	Sets the active path to a directory other than the default directory.
/r *filename*	Forces Excel to open the specified file in read-only mode.
/s	Forces Excel to start in "safe" mode, and does not load any files in the XlStart or alternate startup file directories.
/regserver	Forces Excel to reregister itself in the Windows Registry and then quit.
/unregserver	Forces Excel to unregister itself in the Windows Registry and then quit.

One way to specify any of these switches is to edit the properties of the shortcut that starts Excel. For example, if you want to start Excel without displaying a blank workbook, use the /e switch (as shown in Figure 4-1).

You can run multiple instances of Excel on a single system. Each instance is treated as a separate task.

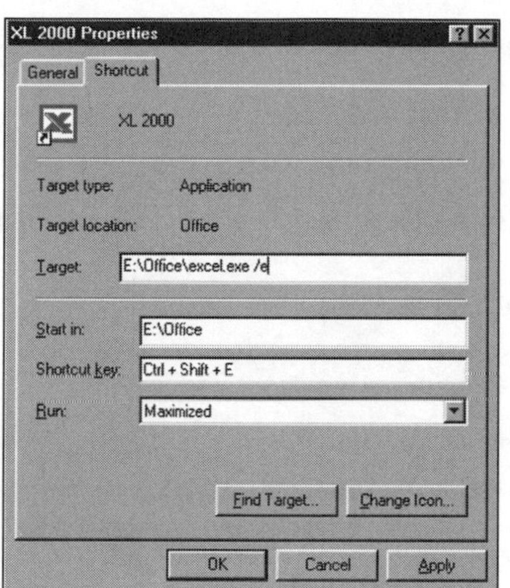

Figure 4-1: Customizing Excel's startup by editing the command line.

Excel's File Extensions

As Excel goes about its business, it uses many files in addition to the Excel.exe executable. These other files are loaded into memory as needed. Table 4-2 presents a summary of the file types that Excel may write to your hard disk during installation.

Table 4-2
File Types Installed by Excel

File Type	*Description*
CHM	A compiled HTML help file.
DLL	A Dynamic Link Library file. DLLs are used by Windows applications to store program code.
EXE	An executable file. Excel.exe is the executable file that runs Excel.
OLB	An object type library file.
TXT	A plain ASCII text file, readable from any text editor (such as WinPad). These files often contain late-breaking information not found in the manuals.
XLA	An Excel add-in file. Several are supplied with Excel, and you can also create your own add-ins.
XLB	An Excel toolbar configuration file. The current toolbar configuration is stored in the Windows directory in a file named Excel9.xlb (the filename is different in a network environment).

Continued

Table 4-2 (continued)

File Type	*Description*
XLC	An Excel 4 chart file (obsolete beginning with Excel 5).
XLL	An Excel link library file. For example, the Analysis ToolPak add-in uses this type of file.
XLM	An Excel 4 macro file (obsolete beginning with Excel 5).
XLS	An Excel workbook file. Unfortunately, there is no way to tell from the extension which version of Excel produced the file.
XLT	An Excel template file.
XLW	A workspace file that contains information about the windows and positions in a workspace. This extension was also used for Excel 4 workbook files (obsolete beginning with Excel 5 because all files are workbooks).

Previous versions of Excel used standard Windows Help files (.hlp). Excel 2000 uses a new type of online help system: HTML Help. This system uses "compiled" HTML files with a .chm extension.

Spreadsheet File Formats Supported

Although Excel's default file format is an XLS workbook file, it can also open and save a wide variety of files generated by several other applications.

An important consideration is whether a particular file type can survive a "round trip." In other words, do you lose any information if you save a file in a particular format and then reopen it in the same application? As you might expect, using Excel's native file format (XLS files) ensures that you'll lose absolutely nothing — as long as you use the latest version of XLS.

Excel 2000 can also use HTML as its native file format. This is actually quite an amazing feat, and I explore this topic in some detail later in this chapter (see "Excel and HTML").

If you save and retrieve a file using a format other than the current XLS format or HTML, you run the risk of losing some type of information – typically formatting and macros, but sometimes formulas and charts.

In the sections that follow, I discuss the various types of files you can and cannot use with Excel.

Lotus 1-2-3 spreadsheet files

Lotus spreadsheets come in several flavors:

- *WKS files* are single-sheet files used by 1-2-3 Release 1.*x* for DOS. Excel can read and write these files.

Excel can also open Microsoft Works files, which also have a .wks extension.

- *WK1 files* are single-sheet files used by 1-2-3 Release 2.*x* for DOS. The formatting for these files is stored in .all files (produced by the Allways add-in) or .fm1 files (produced by the WYSIWYG add-in). Excel can read and write all these files. When you save a file in the WK1 format, you can choose which (if any) type of formatting file to generate.
- *WK3 files* are generated by 1-2-3 Release 3.*x* for DOS, 1-2-3 Release 4.*x* for DOS, and 1-2-3 Release 1.*x* for Windows. These files may contain more than one sheet. The formatting for these files is stored in .fm3 files (produced by the WYSIWYG add-in). Excel can read and write .wk3 files with or without the accompanying .fm3 file.
- *WK4 files* are generated by 1-2-3 Release 4.*x* for Windows and 1-2-3 Release 5.*x* for Windows (Lotus finally got its act together and eliminated the separate formatting file). These files may contain more than one sheet. Excel can neither read nor write these files. If you need to read a .wk4 file into Excel, your only option is to use 1-2-3 Release 4 for Windows (or later) and save the file in WK3 format, which Excel can read.
- *123 files* are generated by 1-2-3 97 and 1-2-3 Millenium Edition. These files may contain more than one sheet. Excel can neither read nor write these files. If you need to read a 123 file into Excel, your only option is to use 1-2-3 and save the file in WK3 format, which Excel can read.

Quattro Pro spreadsheet files

Quattro Pro files also exist in several versions:

- *WQ1 files* are the single-sheet files generated by Quattro Pro for DOS Versions 1, 2, 3, and 4. Excel can read and write these files.
- *WQ2 files* are generated by Quattro Pro for DOS Version 5. Excel can neither read nor write this file format.
- *WB1 files* are generated by Quattro Pro for Windows Versions 1 and 5 (there are no Versions 2 through 4). Excel can read, but not write, this file format.
- *WB2 files* are generated by Quattro Pro for Windows Version 6. Excel can neither read nor write this file format.
- *WB3 files* are generated by Quattro Pro for Windows Versions 7 and 8. Excel can neither read nor write this file format.

You can download a Quattro Pro file converter from Microsoft's Web site. This converter enables you to import Quattro Pro's WB3 files. The URL for download is

```
http://officeupdate.microsoft.com/downloadDetails/
quatt97.htm
```

Database file formats

DBF files are single-table database files generated by dBASE and several other database programs. Excel can read and write DBF files up to and including dBASE 4.

Excel cannot read or write any other database file formats directly. You can, however, use Microsoft Query to access many other database file formats and then copy or link the data into an Excel worksheet. You can run Microsoft Query directly from Excel by using the Data➪Get External Data➪New Database Query command.

Text file formats

Text files simply contain data with no formatting. There are several relatively standard text file formats, but there are no standard file extensions.

- ✦ Each line in *tab-delimited files* consists of fields separated by tabs. Excel can read these files, converting each line to a row and each field to a column. Excel also can write these files, using .txt as the default extension.
- ✦ Each line in *comma-separated files* consists of fields separated by commas. Sometimes text appears in quotes. Excel can read these files, converting each line to a row and each field to a column. Excel also can write these files, using .csv as the default extension.
- ✦ Each line in *space-delimited files* consists of fields separated by spaces. Excel can read these files, converting each line to a row and each field to a column. Excel also can write these files, using .prn as the default extension.

When you attempt to load a text file into Excel, the Text Import Wizard may kick in to help you specify how you want the file retrieved.

To bypass the Text Import Wizard, press Shift when you click OK in the Open dialog box.

You can also perform queries using text files. Use the Data➪Get External Data➪Import Text File command.

Other file formats

- ✦ DIF (Data Interchange Format) file format was used by VisiCalc. I haven't seen a DIF file in ages. Excel can read and write these files.

✦ SYLK (SYmbolic LinK) file format was used by MultiPlan. SYLK files, too, are quite rare these days. Excel can read and write these files.

Files Written by Excel

Excel can write several types of files, which I discuss in this section.

XLS files

The XLS workbook files produced by Excel 2000 use the same file format as Excel 97. These files cannot be opened by any version of Excel prior to Excel 97. You can, however, save a workbook using any of the older Excel file formats. You may lose some information that is specific to the later file format.

An Excel workbook or add-in file can have any extension you like. In other words, these files need not be stored using an .xls or .xla extension.

Which Version Created That XLS File?

Unfortunately, there is no direct way to determine which version of Excel created a particular XLS file. If you have an earlier version of Excel and attempt to open an XLS file that was created in a later version, you'll probably get an error message or a screenful of garbage characters. But if you can open the file successfully, you can use a simple VBA statement to determine the Excel version of the file.

Open the workbook, and make sure it's the active workbook. Press Alt+F11 to activate the Visual Basic Editor, and then press Ctrl+G to activate the Immediate window. Type the following statement, and press Enter:

```
Print ActiveWorkbook.FileFormat
```

The Immediate window displays a value that corresponds to the version of the active workbook. This value is one of those shown in the following table:

Value	*Excel Version*
16	Excel 2
29	Excel 3
33	Excel 4
39	Excel 5/95
-4143	Excel 97/2000

Workspace files

A *workspace file* is a special file that contains information about an Excel workspace. For example, if you have a project that uses two workbooks and you like to have the workbook windows arranged in a particular way, you can save an XLW file (use the File➪Save Workspace command) to save this window configuration. Then, whenever you open the XLW file, Excel restores the desired workspace.

It's important to understand that a workspace file does *not* include the workbooks — only the configuration information that makes those workbooks visible in your Excel workspace. So if you need to distribute a workspace to someone else, make sure that you include the workbook files as well as the XLW file. In addition, the File➪Save Workspace command does not save the workbooks themselves.

Template files

You can save any workbook as a template file (.xlt extension). Doing so is useful if you tend to create similar files on a regular basis. For example, you may need to generate a monthly sales report. You can save some time by creating a template that holds the necessary formulas and charts for your report. When you start new files based on the template, you need only plug in the values.

To create a new workbook that's based on an existing template, use the File➪New command, and select the template from the New dialog box.

Clicking the New toolbar button or pressing Ctrl+N does not enable you to select a template. Rather, a default workbook is created.

You can also create a template named Sheet.xlt, which is used as the basis for new worksheets that you add to a workbook. Note that it is not possible to create a template for chart sheets because Excel handles chart templates differently.

Following is a list of locations where templates are stored.

- ✦ *Your XlStart folder.* This is where you store autotemplates named Book.xlt and Sheet.xlt. You can also put workbook templates in this folder.
- ✦ *Your Templates folder.* Workbook templates stored here appear in the New dialog box.
- ✦ *A folder located inside of your Templates folder.* If you create a new folder within the Templates folder, its name appears as a tab in the New dialog box. Clicking the tab displays the templates stored in that folder. Figure 4-2 shows how the New dialog box looks when there's a new folder (named "John's Templates") in the Templates folder.

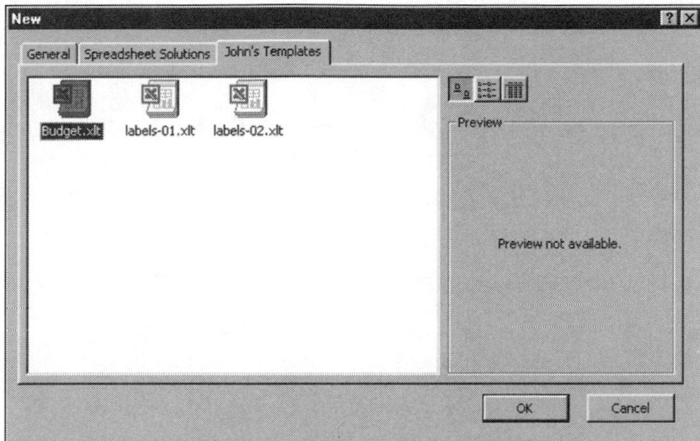

Figure 4-2: Tabs compartmentalize the template files inside the Templates folder.

Toolbar files

Excel stores toolbar and menu bar configurations in an XLB file. When you exit Excel, the current toolbar configuration is saved in a file named Excel.xlb, located in your Application Data\Microsoft\Excel directory. This file contains information regarding the position and visibility of all custom toolbars and custom menu bars, plus modification that you've made to built-in toolbars or menu bars. The file is normally named Excel9.xlb, but it will have a different name if you're on a network.

Add-in files

An *add-in* is essentially a workbook file with a few important differences:

✦ The workbook's `IsAddin` property is True—which means that it can be loaded using the Tools➪Add-Ins command.

✦ The workbook is hidden and cannot be unhidden by the user. Consequently, an add-in is never the active workbook from the perspective of any everyday workbook.

✦ The workbook is not part of the `Workbooks` collection.

Many add-ins provide new features or functions to Excel. You can access these new features as if they were built into the product. For a list of the add-ins included with Excel 2000, refer to Chapter 2.

You can create your own add-ins from XLS workbook files. In fact, creating add-ins is the preferred method of distributing some types of Excel applications. Add-ins have an .xla extension by default, but you can use any extension you like.

Excel add-ins can also be written in the C language and compiled. This type of add-in has an .xll extension. I do not cover this type of add-in.

Chapter 20 covers the topic of add-ins in detail.

Excel and HTML

HTML is the language of the World Wide Web. When you browse the Web, the documents that are retrieved and displayed by your browser are usually in HTML format. An HTML file consists of text information plus special tags that describe how the text is to be formatted. The browser interprets the tags, applies formatting, and displays the information.

Excel 97 included an add-in that converted an Excel range (including charts) to an HTML file. This feature worked fine in most cases, but Excel 2000 takes this concept to a new level.

New Feature

Excel 2000 can use HTML as a native file format. In other words, you can save a workbook in HTML format and then reopen the HTML file, and it will look exactly as it did before you first saved it. All the Excel-specific information (such as macros, charts, pivot tables, and worksheet settings) remains intact. If you're as familiar with HTML as I am, you'll appreciate what a feat this is. HTML is a relatively simple file format. The fact that an Excel workbook can survive the "round trip" is just short of amazing. It seems that Microsoft is attempting to position Excel (actually, all the Office 2000 apps) as an HTML editor.

So how does it work?

The best way to understand how Excel can use HTML as a native file format is to perform some simple experiments. Start with a new workbook, and make sure it has only one worksheet. Enter a few values and a formula, do some simple formatting, and then save the workbook in HTML format. Use the File ➪ Save As Web Page command, and make sure you select the Entire Workbook option. Figure 4-3 shows a very simple workbook consisting of two values and a formula, with the formula cell formatted bold. This is a good candidate for learning about the HTML files saved by Excel.

The remainder of the material in this section assumes that you're familiar with HTML.

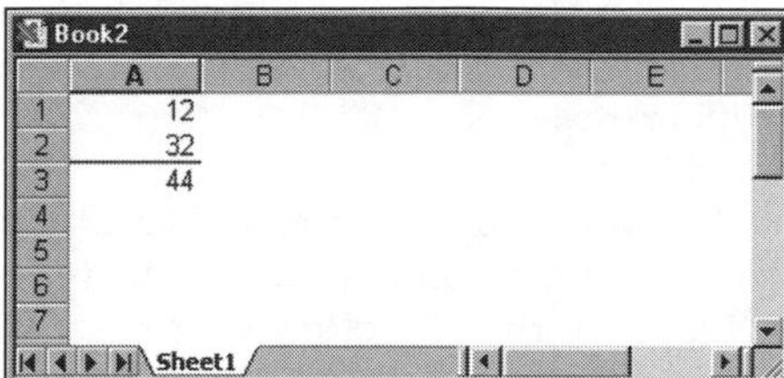

Figure 4-3: Try saving a simple workbook like this in HTML format.

Next, open the HTML file in your browser. It will, or course, look pretty much like the original workbook. Use the browser's View ➪ Source command to view the HTML code. You might be surprised by what you see. Even HTML gurus might be overwhelmed by the complexity of this "simple" Web document.

Following are a few observations about the HTML file.

- The entire Excel workbook can be represented by a single HTML file. In other words, all the information needed to create an exact replica of the original workbook is contained in the HTML file. This isn't always the case, however. Keep reading to find out when a simple HTML file no longer suffices.
- Most of the document is contained within the `<head>` and `</head>` tags.
- A large portion consists of style definitions. This is the information between the `<style>` and `</style>` tags — which is embedded between the `<head>` and `</head>` tags.
- The actual text that's displayed in the browser is contained in a table (between the `<table>` and `</table>` tags).
- The formula is preserved by using a proprietary argument for the `<td>` tag. The proprietary argument is ignored by browsers, but Excel uses this information when the file is reopened.

The HTML file produced for the simple workbook is nearly 4,000 bytes in size — which is quite large considering the simplicity of the displayed page. The extra information, of course, is what Excel uses to create a workbook when the HTML file is reopened.

Adding some complexity

The example workbook used in the preceding section is about as simple as it gets. Now, let's add a small bit of complexity to the workbook and see what happens to the HTML file.

Select A1:A3 and press F11 to create a new chart sheet. Save the file again, and reload it in your browser. You'll find that it closely resembles the Excel workbook—even down to the sheet tabs and navigation arrows!

The HTML file has more than doubled in size. More importantly, the directory in which you saved the file has a new subdirectory that contains additional files (six extra files using my simple workbook). The files in this directory are necessary to display a replica of the workbook in a browser and to recreate the workbook when the HTML file is reopened in Excel.

If you examine the HTML file, you'll see that it's much more complicated than the original one and contains quite a bit of JavaScript code (JavaScript is a scripting language supported by Internet Explorer and Netscape Navigator). At this point, the HTML file has gotten beyond the grasp of your average HTML author. And that's not even taking into account the other files dumped into the subdirectory. The files are

- ✦ Three HTML files (one for each sheet, plus a file that displays the tab strip).
- ✦ A GIF file (the chart).
- ✦ A CSS file (a cascading style sheet that holds formatting and display information).
- ✦ An XML file. This is an "eXtensible Markup Language" file. XML is well beyond the scope of this book. (Hey, I told you this stuff was getting complicated!)

You might want to open some other Excel workbooks and save them as HTML files. You'll soon discover another type of file that's created in the subdirectory, an MSO (for Microsoft Office) file. This is a binary file that holds the information necessary to recreate Excel-specific features such as macros, pivot tables, conditional formatting, and so on.

As you may have surmised by now, saving an Excel workbook in HTML format introduces lots of potential problems. For example, if you need to transfer your file to another location, it's imperative that you include all the supporting files as well. If any of the supporting files is damaged, Excel cannot recreate the workbook. And opening and saving HTML files is much slower than opening and saving normal XLS files. To make a long story short, don't save your workbooks in HTML format unless you have a very good reason to do so.

What about interactivity?

If you're still with me at this point, it's time to introduce yet another level of complexity. Excel 2000 can save HTML files that include spreadsheet interactivity. In other words, when the HTML file is displayed in a browser, the user can actually interact with the document as a spreadsheet—enter data, change formulas, adjust cell formatting, see "live" charts, and even drag data around in pivot tables. This feature, which is called *publishing* (as opposed to *saving*), is limited in that you can only save one sheet (not an entire workbook).

To get a feel for how this works, activate a sheet that contains formulas. Use the File ➪ Save As Web Page command. In the Save As dialog box, choose the Selection: Sheet option, and place a check mark next to Add interactivity. Click the Publish button. You'll get another dialog box (Publish as Web Page). Accept the defaults, and click Publish.

When you open the HTML file in your browser, you'll find that it displays a spreadsheet-like object that is, in fact, interactive. Figure 4-4 shows an example.

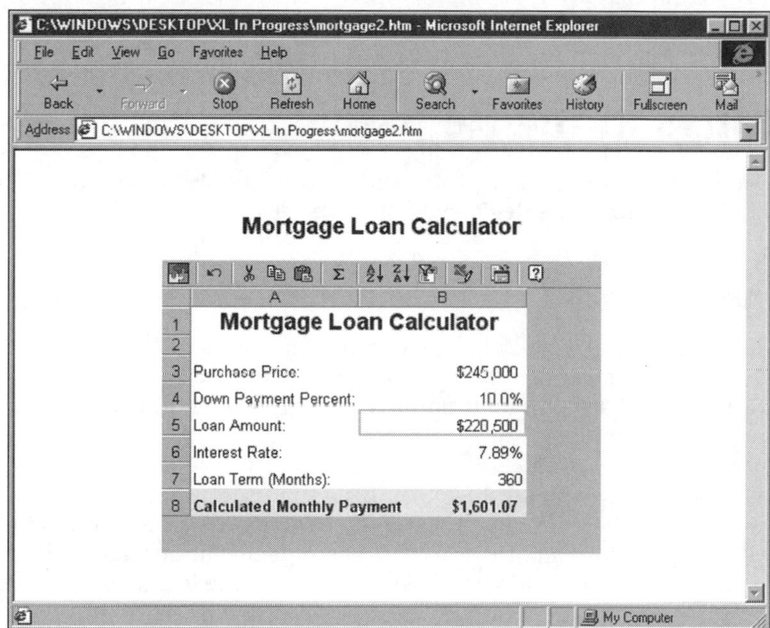

Figure 4-4: An example of an interactive Excel worksheet displayed in a browser.

You might expect that the HTML file generated for an interactive worksheet would be much more complex than the example in the previous section. You'd be wrong. Such a worksheet occupies a single HTML file. Since only one sheet is involved when you publish, there's no need to get involved with the tab strip stuff. The complexity is handled by an ActiveX control. Because of this, the end user must have Office 2000 installed (or have a license for the ActiveX control) to view an interactive Excel file in his or her browser.

This section was intended to provide a brief overview of the HTML feature in Excel 2000. This topic is definitely fodder for a complete book—one that I don't choose to write, thank you.

What about the Script Editor?

You'll find that this book ignores a complete aspect of Excel 2000: the Microsoft Script Editor, which you access by pressing Alt+Shift+F11. The Script Editor is used to edit the JavaScript (or VBScript) code in an HTML document. I consider this topic to be beyond the scope of this book and useful to only a very small number of readers. Consequently, I focus on the real meat of Excel: non-Web-based application development using VBA.

Excel Settings in the Registry

In this section, I provide some background information about the Windows Registry and discuss how Excel uses the Registry to store its settings.

About the Registry

Windows 3.1 used a Registration Database to store information about file association and OLE registration. The Windows 95 (or later) Registry extends this concept by storing configuration information for all types of applications as well as computer-specific information.

The Registry is essentially a hierarchical database that can be accessed by application software. This information is stored in two data files: System.dat (for system-specific information) and User.dat (for user-specific information). Both of these files are located in the Windows folder. In addition, the Registry may use a file named Policy.pol—a file that contains system policies that override the information in the other files.

You can use the Registry Editor program (Regedit.exe, in the Windows folder) to browse the Registry—and even edit its contents if you know what you're doing. Before beginning your explorations, take a minute to read the sidebar titled "Before You Edit the Registry . . ." Figure 4-5 shows what the Registry Editor looks like.

As I mentioned, the Registry is hierarchical. It consists of keys and values. Table 4-3 lists the top-level root keys of the Registry along with a brief description of the type of information stored there.

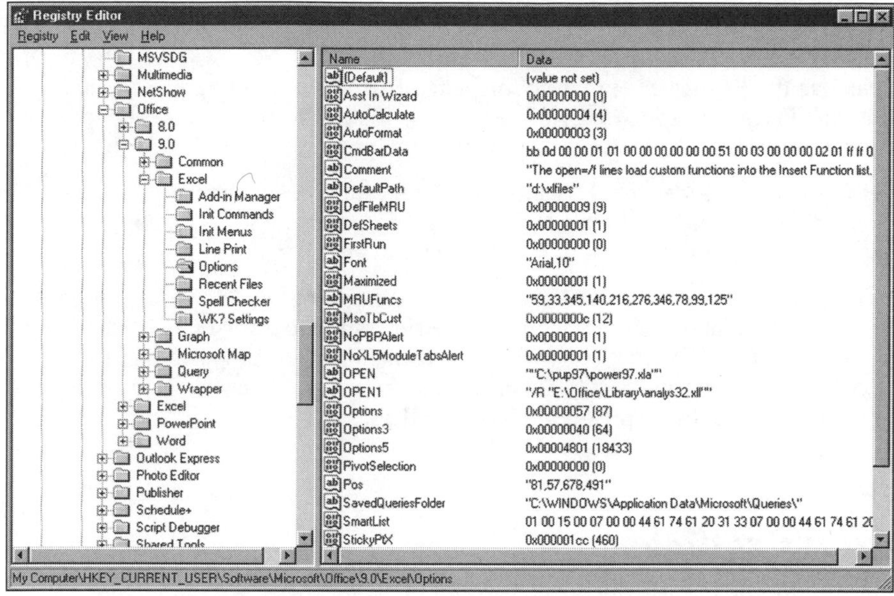

Figure 4-5: The Registry Editor lets you browse and make changes to the Registry.

Table 4-3
Top-Level Keys in the Windows Registry

Key	*Description*
HKEY_CLASSES_ROOT	Information on OLE, shortcut, and other interface features
HKEY_CURRENT_USER	Data from the current user's User.dat file (a duplicate of data found in HKEY_USERS)
HKEY_LOCAL_MACHINE	System-specific information from the System.dat file
HKEY_USERS	Information about all users on the system
HKEY_CURRENT_CONFIG	Hardware information
HKEY_DYN_DATA	Information on installed devices

Before You Edit the Registry . . .

You can use the Regedit.exe program to change anything in the Registry—including information that is critical to your system's operation. In other words, if you change the wrong piece of information, Windows may no longer work properly.

Therefore, it's a good idea to take some simple precautions. First, make sure that you have a startup diskette (you can do this by using the Add/Remove Programs app in the Control Panel). You can use this diskette to start Windows in an emergency.

Second, get into the habit of using the Registry⇨Export Registry File command in Regedit. This command enables you to save an ASCII version of the Registry or just a specific branch of the Registry. If you find that you messed up something, you can always import the ASCII file to restore the Registry to its previous condition (use the Registry⇨Import Registry File command). Refer to the help file for Regedit for details.

Excel's settings

Information used by Excel 2000 is stored in

```
HKEY_CURRENT_USER\Software\Microsoft\Office\9.0\Excel
```

In this section of the Registry, you'll find a number of keys that contain specific values that determine how Excel operates.

The Registry settings are updated automatically by Excel when Excel closes.

It's important to understand that Excel reads the Windows Registry only once—when it starts up. In addition, Excel updates the Registry settings only when Excel closes normally. If Excel crashes your system (unfortunately, not an uncommon occurrence), the Registry information is not updated. For example, if you change one of Excel's settings, such as the visibility of the status bar, this setting is not written to the Registry until Excel closes by normal means.

Table 4-4 lists the registry sections that are relevant to Excel. You may not find all these sections in your Registry database.

Although you can change most of the settings via Excel's Options dialog box, several other useful settings cannot be changed directly from Excel (but you can use the Registry Editor to make changes).

One more warning is in order. Prior to making any changes to the Registry, refer to the sidebar "Before You Edit the Registry . . ."

Table 4-4
Excel Configuration Information in the Registry

Section	*Description*
Add-in Manager	Lists add-ins that appear in the list box when you choose the Tools⇨Add-Ins command. Add-ins that are included with Excel do not appear in this list. If you have an add-in entry in this list box that you no longer use, you can remove it by using the Registry Editor.
Converters	Lists additional (external) file converters that are not built into Excel.
AutoSave	Holds the AutoSave option that you set.
Delete Commands	Enables you to specify which menu commands you don't want to appear.
Init Commands	Holds information about custom commands.
Init Menus	Holds information about custom menus.
Line Print	Holds settings used in 1-2-3 macro printing. Excel updates this section whenever it executes a 1-2-3 macro that has /wgdu (Worksheet Global Default Update) in it.
Options	A catch-all section; holds a wide variety of settings, including the paths to files that are opened automatically when Excel starts (such as add-ins).
Recent File List	Stores the names of the last files saved (up to nine files).
Spell Checker	Stores information about your spelling checker options.
WK? Settings	Contains settings for opening and saving 1-2-3 files (for example, whether to create an FMT or FM3 format file).

Summary

In this chapter, I discussed the files used and created by Excel. I described Excel installation, various ways to load files automatically, Excel's file extensions, and file formats supported by Excel (including the new HTML format). I also discussed some of Excel's settings in the Windows Registry. Information in this chapter that's particularly relevant to application development and programming appears in more detail in other chapters.

This chapter concludes Part I. Part II provides information about developing user-oriented applications with Excel.

✦ ✦ ✦

PART

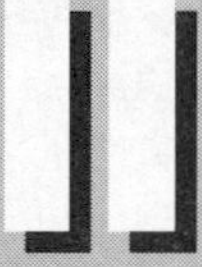

Excel Application Development

This part contains only two chapters, but they are important for readers who want to become effective Excel power programmers. In Chapter 5, I present my views on exactly what constitutes a spreadsheet application. Chapter 6 discusses the general steps involved in creating a spreadsheet application with Excel.

✦ ✦ ✦ ✦

In This Part

✦ ✦ ✦ ✦

What Is a Spreadsheet Application?

✦ ✦ ✦ ✦

In This Chapter

A working definition of a spreadsheet application

The difference between a spreadsheet user and a spreadsheet developer

A system for classifying spreadsheet users to help you conceptualize who the audience is for your applications

A discussion of why people use spreadsheets

A taxonomy of the basic types of spreadsheets

✦ ✦ ✦ ✦

In this chapter, I attempt to clarify how people use spreadsheets in the real world — a topic that's germane to this entire book because it can help you determine how much effort you should devote to a particular development project. By the time you finish this chapter, you should have a pretty good idea of what I mean by a "spreadsheet application." And after you've made it through the rest of the book, you'll be well on your way to developing your own spreadsheet applications with Excel. But first, let's get down to the basics.

You've probably been working with spreadsheets for several years, but chances are good that your primary focus has been on simply generating spreadsheets to get the job done. You probably never gave much thought to more global issues like those discussed in this chapter: the different types of spreadsheet users, how to classify various types of spreadsheets, and even basic questions such as why people use spreadsheets. If the title of this book attracted your attention, it's important for you to understand these issues so that you can become an effective "power programmer." I'll first discuss the concept of a *spreadsheet application*. This is, after all, the desired result of your power-programming efforts.

Spreadsheet Applications

Programming, as it relates to spreadsheet use, is essentially the process of building applications that use a spreadsheet rather than a traditional programming language such as C, Pascal, or BASIC. In both cases, however, these applications will be used by other people — not the developer of the application.

For purposes of this book, **a spreadsheet application is a spreadsheet file (or group of related files) that is designed so that someone other than the developer can perform useful work without extensive training.** According to this definition, most of the spreadsheet files you've developed probably wouldn't qualify as spreadsheet applications. You may have dozens or hundreds of spreadsheet files on your hard drive, but it's a safe bet that most of them aren't really designed for others to use.

A good spreadsheet application has the following characteristics:

- It enables the end user to perform a task that he or she probably would not be able to do otherwise.
- It provides the appropriate solution to the problem. (A spreadsheet environment isn't always the optimal approach.)
- It accomplishes what it is supposed to do. This may be an obvious prerequisite, but it's not at all uncommon for applications to fail this test.
- It produces accurate results and is free of bugs.
- It uses appropriate and efficient methods and algorithms to accomplish its job.
- It traps errors before the user is forced to deal with them. Note that errors and bugs are not the same. Attempting to divide by zero is an error. Failure to identify that error before it occurs is a bug.
- It does not allow the user to delete or modify important components accidentally (or intentionally).
- Its user interface is clear and consistent, so the user always knows how to proceed.
- Its formulas, macros, and user interface elements are well documented, allowing for subsequent changes, if necessary.
- It is designed so that it can be modified in simple ways without making major changes. A basic fact of life is that a user's needs change over time.
- It has an easily accessible help system that provides useful information on at least the major procedures.
- It is designed so that it is portable and runs on any system that has the proper software (in this case, a copy of Excel).

It should come as no surprise that it is possible to create spreadsheet applications for many different usage levels, ranging from simple fill-in-the-blank templates to extremely complex applications that use custom menus and dialog boxes and that may not even look like spreadsheets.

The Developer and the End User

I've already used the terms *developer* and *end user*, terms you'll see frequently throughout this book. Because you've gotten this far, I think I can safely assume that you're either a spreadsheet application developer or a potential developer.

My definitions regarding developers and end users are simple. The person who creates the spreadsheet application is the *developer*. For joint projects, there are multiple developers (a development team). The person who uses the results of the developer's spreadsheet programming efforts is the *end user* (which I often shorten to simply *user*). In many cases, there will be multiple end users, and often the developer is one of the users.

Who are developers? What do they do?

I've spent a good 14 years trading methodologies and basically hanging out with the motley crew of folks who call themselves spreadsheet developers. I divide them into two primary groups:

- *Insiders* are developers who are intimately involved with the users and thoroughly understand their needs. In many cases, these developers are also users of the application. Often, they developed the application in response to a particular problem.
- *Outsiders* are developers who are hired to produce a solution to a problem. In most cases, developers in this category are familiar with the business in general, but not with the specifics of the application they are developing. In other cases, these developers are employed by the company that requests the application (but they normally work in a different department).

Some developers devote full time to development efforts. These developers may be either insiders or outsiders. A fair number of consultants (outsiders) make a decent living developing spreadsheet applications on a freelance basis.

Other spreadsheet developers don't work full time at the task and may not even realize they are developing spreadsheet applications. These developers are often office computer gurus who seem to know everything about computers and software. These folks often create spreadsheet applications as a way to make their lives easier — the time spent developing a well-designed application for others can often save hours of training time and can greatly reduce the time spent answering others' questions.

Spreadsheet developers are typically involved in the following activities, often performing most or all of each task on their own:

✦ Determining the needs of the user
✦ Planning an application that meets these needs
✦ Determining the most appropriate user interface
✦ Creating the spreadsheet, formulas, macros, and user interface
✦ Testing the application under all reasonable sets of conditions
✦ Making the application relatively "bulletproof" (often based on results from the testing)
✦ Making the application aesthetically appealing and intuitive
✦ Documenting the development effort
✦ Distributing the application to users
✦ Updating the application if and when it's necessary

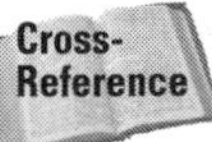

I discuss these activities in more detail in Chapter 6.

Developers must have a thorough understanding of their development environment — in this case, Excel. And there's certainly a lot to know when it comes to Excel. By any standard, Excel is easy to use, but defining what's easy to use depends on the user. Developing nontrivial spreadsheet applications with Excel requires an in-depth knowledge of formulas, functions, macros, custom dialog boxes, custom toolbars, menu modifications, and add-ins. Most Excel users, of course, don't meet these qualifications and have no intention of learning these details — which brings me to the next topic: classifying spreadsheet users.

Classifying spreadsheet users

Over the years, I've found that it's often useful to classify people who use spreadsheets — including both developers and end users — along two dimensions: their *degree of experience* with spreadsheets and their *interest in learning* about spreadsheets.

Each of these two dimensions has three levels. Combining them results in nine combinations, which are shown in Table 5-1. In reality, only seven segments are worth thinking about because both moderately experienced and very experienced spreadsheet users generally have at least *some* interest in spreadsheets (that's what motivated them to get their experience). Users who have a lot of spreadsheet experience and a low level of interest would make very bad developers.

Table 5-1
Classification of Spreadsheet Users by Experience and Interest

	No Interest	*Moderately Interested*	*Very Interested*
Little Experience	User	User	User/Potential Developer
Moderately Experienced	N/A	User	Developer
Very Experienced	N/A	User	Developer

It should be clear that spreadsheet developers must have a great deal of *experience* with spreadsheets, as well as a high *interest* in spreadsheets. Those with little spreadsheet experience — but with a great deal of interest — are potential developers. All they need is more experience. If you're reading this book, you probably fall into one of the boxes in the last column of the table.

The audience for spreadsheet applications

The remaining segments in the preceding table comprise spreadsheet end users — whom you can think of as the consumers of spreadsheet applications. When you develop a spreadsheet application for others to use, you need to know which of these groups of people will actually be using your application.

Users with little experience and no interest are a large percentage of all spreadsheet users — probably the largest segment of all. These are the people who need to use a spreadsheet for their jobs but who view the spreadsheet simply as a means to an end. Typically, they know very little about computers and software, and they usually have no interest in learning anything more than what's required to get their work done. They might even feel a bit intimidated by computers. Often, these users don't even know which version of their spreadsheet they use, and they are largely unfamiliar with what it can do. Obviously, applications developed for this group must be user-friendly — that is, straightforward, unintimidating, easy to use, and as bulletproof as possible.

From the developer's point of view, a more interesting group of users are those who have little or moderate spreadsheet experience but who are interested in learning more. These users understand the concept of formulas, use built-in worksheet functions, and generally have a good idea of what the product is capable of doing. These users generally appreciate the work you put into an application and are often impressed by your efforts. Even better, they'll often make excellent suggestions for improving your applications. Applications developed for this group should also be user-friendly (easy to use and bulletproof), but they can also be more complex and customizable than applications designed for the less experienced and less interested groups.

Why people use spreadsheets

If I asked you why people use spreadsheets, you would probably have to think about it before coming up with an answer. This question is rarely asked, but asking it and arriving at a meaningful answer can have a major impact on your development efforts. The real and not-at-all-surprising answer is that it depends on the user.

Several years ago, I conducted an informal (and not very scientific) survey of spreadsheet users at the company where I was working. Most of the employees were using Excel, but there were also a few staunch 1-2-3 for DOS holdouts in the group. The survey consisted of one question, "*Why do you use a spreadsheet?*" along with a series of check boxes. The survey respondents could choose as many reasons as they liked. After I received the completed survey, I classified each user, based on my knowledge of him or her, into one of two categories: Inexperienced or Moderately/Very Experienced. The results are shown in Table 5-2.

Table 5-2
"Why Do You Use a Spreadsheet?"

Reason *Experienced*	*Inexperienced*	*Moderately or Very*
It makes my work look better.	76%	82%
It helps prevent calculation errors.	76%	82%
I know how to use it.	68%	55%
It's the only way I know to perform a particular task.	72%	36%
Making nice columns is easier with a spreadsheet than with a word processor.	60%	18%
It saves time.	20%	91%
It reduces the amount of work I have to do.	12%	100%
It can handle lots of different tasks.	12%	82%
It was on my workstation when I came here.	36%	18%
It's fun.	12%	73%
It's the most appropriate tool for a particular task.	8%	73%
It's all set up for me.	28%	27%
It makes good graphs.	12%	64%
Everybody else does.	32%	0%
I like the macros.	0%	9%

I certainly don't claim that this survey represents the views of all spreadsheet users, and it's likely that the results would be different if I did the survey today. But I find it interesting, and maybe you will, too. I discuss my interpretations of this data in the following sections.

Inexperienced users

More than three-quarters of the inexperienced users claim to use a spreadsheet because it makes their work look better and helps prevent calculation errors. Other reasons often cited by these users are that it's the only way they know to perform a particular task, they know how to use it, and making nice columns is easier with a spreadsheet than with a word processor.

Only 12 percent claim that it reduces the amount of work they have to do or that it can handle a lot of different tasks. This low percentage suggests that many inexperienced users are missing the point of spreadsheets or that they perceive using a spreadsheet as being work, and they don't understand the spreadsheet's capabilities.

This group often uses spreadsheet software because it's there. In many cases, these users did not choose to have the software—it just happened to be installed on their workstations. Or the person who had the job before they took over used a spreadsheet, and it became a part of the job they inherited. When the time comes to produce the monthly sales report, these users fire up the spreadsheet and repeat the same procedures they've followed for the past 12 months.

My experience with these users tells me that most of them learn only enough to perform basic operations, and they typically ignore about 90 percent of a product's features. My survey supports this perception. Most of these users did not use the charting feature, and none used a spreadsheet because of its macro capability. Only 8 percent said they use a spreadsheet because it's the most appropriate tool.

As a side note, users in this group frequently use software inappropriately. For example, I've seen people attempt to summarize information from massive databases by importing huge files into a worksheet. Others write letters and memos using Lotus 1-2-3. Still others enter tables of numbers into a word processor and compute sums by using a hand calculator. Go figure.

Moderately experienced and very experienced users

The more experienced survey respondents clearly have a better appreciation for the potential uses of spreadsheet software, and generally, they checked off more reasons for using spreadsheets. The reasons most frequently cited by experienced users are usually those that are *not* checked by the inexperienced users, such as reduced workload, time savings, most appropriate tool for a task, and so on. Interestingly, these users also frequently cited the top two reasons that the inexperienced users gave for using a spreadsheet: better-looking work and fewer calculation errors.

Conclusions

This informal survey may shed some light on why people use spreadsheets. The bottom line is that people use spreadsheets

- Because spreadsheets make them (and their work) look good
- Because the results are more accurate
- Because spreadsheets save time and eliminate manual effort

As a developer, you can translate these reasons into goals for the applications you develop. Your application will be successful if it helps the user look good and generates attractive output, produces more accurate results, and saves time and effort.

Solving Problems with a Spreadsheet

I've covered the basic concept of a spreadsheet application, discussed the end users and developers of such applications, and even attempted to figure out why people use spreadsheets at all. Now it's time to take a look at the types of tasks that are appropriate for spreadsheet applications.

You may already have a pretty good idea of the types of tasks for which you can use a spreadsheet. Traditionally, spreadsheet software has been used for numerical applications that are largely *interactive* in nature. Corporate budgets are an excellent example of this. After the model has been set up (that is, after formulas have been developed), working with a budget is simply a matter of plugging in amounts and observing the bottom-line totals. Often, budgeters simply need to allocate fixed resources among various activities and present the results in a reasonably attractive (or at least legible) format. A spreadsheet, of course, is ideal for this.

Budget-type problems, however, probably account for only a small percentage of your spreadsheet-development time. If you're like me, you've learned that uses for spreadsheet software (particularly in recent years) can often extend well beyond the types of tasks for which spreadsheets were originally designed.

Here are just a few examples of nontraditional ways that a spreadsheet such as Excel can be used:

- *As a presentation device.* For example, with minimal effort you can create an attractive, interactive on-screen slide show using only Excel.
- *As a data-entry tool.* For repetitive data-entry tasks, a spreadsheet is often the most efficient route to take. The data can then be exported to a variety of formats for use in other programs.

- *As a forms generator.* For creating attractive forms, many find it easier to use Excel's formatting capabilities than to learn a desktop publishing package such as PageMaker.
- *As a text processor.* The text functions found in all spreadsheets enable you to manipulate text in ways that are impossible using a word processor.
- *As a platform for simple games.* Clearly, Excel was not designed with this in mind. However, I've downloaded (and written) some interesting strategy games using the tools found in Excel and other spreadsheets.

You can probably think of many more examples for this list.

Ironically, the versatility of spreadsheets is a double-edged sword. On one hand, it's tempting to try to use a spreadsheet for every problem that crops up. On the other hand, you'll often be spinning your wheels by trying to use a spreadsheet for a problem that's better suited for a different solution.

Basic Spreadsheet Types

In this section, I classify spreadsheets into several basic types to provide a better perspective on how spreadsheet applications fit into the overall scheme of things. This is all quite arbitrary, of course, and is based solely on my own experience. Moreover, there is quite a bit of overlap between the categories, but they cover most of the spreadsheets I've seen and developed.

My names for these categories are as follows:

- Quick-and-dirty
- For-your-eyes-only
- Single-user applications
- Spaghetti applications
- Utility applications
- Single-block budgets
- What-if models
- Data storage and access
- Database front ends
- Turnkey applications

I discuss each of these categories in the following sections.

Quick-and-dirty spreadsheets

This is probably the most common type of spreadsheet. Most of the spreadsheets in this category are fairly small and are developed to quickly solve a problem or answer a question. Here's an example: You're about to buy a new car, and you want to figure out your monthly payment for various loan amounts. Or perhaps you need to generate a chart that shows your company's sales by month, so you quickly enter 12 values and whip out a chart, which you paste into your word processor.

In both of the preceding cases, you can probably input the entire model in a few minutes, and you certainly won't take the time to document your work. You probably won't even think of developing any macros or custom dialog boxes. In fact, you may not even deem these simple spreadsheets worthy of saving to disk. Obviously, spreadsheets in this category are not applications.

For-your-eyes-only spreadsheets

As the name implies, no one except you — the creator — will ever see or use the spreadsheets that fall into this category. An example of this type might be a file in which you keep information relevant to your income taxes. You open the file whenever a check comes in the mail, you incur an expense that can be justified as business, you buy tax-deductible Girl Scout cookies, and so on. Another example is a spreadsheet that you use to keep track of your employees' time records (sick leave, vacation, and so on).

Spreadsheets in this category differ from quick-and-dirty spreadsheets in that you use them more than once, so you save these spreadsheets to files. But again, they're not worth spending a great deal of time on. You may apply some simple formatting, but that's about it. This type of spreadsheet also lacks any type of error detection because you understand how the formulas are set up; you know enough to avoid inputting data that will produce erroneous results. If an error does crop up, you immediately know what caused it.

Spreadsheets in this category don't qualify as applications, although they sometimes increase in sophistication over time. For example, I have an Excel workbook that I use to track my income by source. This workbook was simple when I first set it up, but I tend to add accouterments to it nearly every time I use it — more summary formulas, better formatting, and even a chart that displays income by month. My latest modification was to add a best-fit line to the chart to project income based on past trends. I'll probably continue to add more to this file, and it may eventually qualify for the single-user application category.

Single-user applications

This is a spreadsheet application that only the developer uses, but its complexity extends beyond the spreadsheets in the for-your-eyes-only category. For example, I developed a workbook to keep track of registered users for my shareware applications. It started out as a simple worksheet database (for my eyes only), but then I realized that I could also use it to generate mailing labels and invoices. One day I spent an hour or so writing macros and then realized that I had converted this application from a for-your-eyes-only application to a single-user application.

No one else will ever use this spreadsheet, but it's a slick little application that's very easy to use. In this particular case, the time I spent modifying the spreadsheet from a for-your-eyes-only spreadsheet to a single-user application was definitely time well spent because it has already saved me several hours of work. The application now has buttons that execute macros, and it has greatly reduced the amount of effort required to deal with the mechanics of tracking my customers and mailing products.

Creating single-user applications for yourself is an excellent way to get practice with Excel's developer's tools. For example, you can learn to create custom dialog boxes, modify menus, create a custom toolbar, write VBA macros, and so on. You'll find that working on a meaningful project (even if it's meaningful only to you) is the best way to learn advanced features in Excel — or any other software, for that matter.

Spaghetti applications

An all-too-common type of spreadsheet is what I call a *spaghetti application*. The term stems from the fact that the parts of the application are difficult to follow, much like a plate of spaghetti. Most of these spreadsheets begin life as a reasonably focused single-user application. But over time they are passed along to others who make their own modifications. As requirements change and employees come and go, new parts are added and others are ignored. Before too long, the original purpose of the workbook may have been forgotten. The result is a file that is used frequently, but no one really understands exactly how it all works.

Everyone who's involved with it knows that the spaghetti application should be completely reworked. But because nobody really understands it, the situation tends to worsen over time. Spreadsheet consultants make a lot of money untangling such applications. I've found that, in most cases, the most efficient solution is to redefine the user needs and build a new application from scratch.

Utility applications

No one is ever completely satisfied with his spreadsheet product. Great as it is, I still find quite a bit lacking in Excel. This brings me to the next category of spreadsheets: *utility applications*. Utilities are special tools designed to perform a single recurring task. For example, if you often import text into Excel, you may want some additional text-handling commands, such as the ability to convert selected text to uppercase (without using formulas). The solution? Develop a text-handling utility that does exactly what you want.

The Power Utility Pak is a collection of utility applications for Excel. I developed these utilities to extend Excel's functionality. These utilities work just like normal Excel commands. You can find the shareware version of the Power Utility Pak on the companion CD-ROM, and you can get a free copy of the full version by using the coupon located at the back of the book. And if you're interested, the complete VBA source code is also available.

Utility applications are very general in nature. Most macros are designed to perform a specific operation on a specific type of data found in a specific type of workbook. A good utility application essentially works like a command normally found in Excel. In other words, the utility needs to recognize the context in which a command is executed and take appropriate action. This usually requires quite a bit of error-handling code so that the utility can handle any situation that comes up.

Utility applications always use macros and may or may not use custom dialog boxes. Fortunately, Excel makes it relatively easy to create such utilities, and they can be converted to add-ins and attached to Excel's user interface so that they appear to be part of Excel.

The topic of creating utilities is so important that I devote an entire chapter to it. Chapter 15 discusses how to create custom Excel utilities using VBA.

Single-block budgets

By a *single-block budget*, I mean a spreadsheet — not necessarily a budget model — that essentially consists of one block of cells. The top row might contain names that correspond to time (months, quarters, or years), and the left column usually contains categories of some type. Typically, the bottom row and right column contain formulas that add the numbers together. There may or may not be formulas that compute subtotals within the block.

This is a very common type of spreadsheet. In fact, VisiCalc (the world's first spreadsheet) was developed with this type of model in mind. In most cases, simple single-block budget models are not good candidates for applications, because they are simple to begin with, but there *are* exceptions. For example, you might consider converting such a spreadsheet into an application if the model is an unwieldy 3D spreadsheet, needs to include consolidations from other files, or will be used by departmental managers who may not understand spreadsheets.

What-if models

Many consider the what-if model category to be the epitome of spreadsheets at their best. The ability to instantly recalculate thousands of formulas makes spreadsheet software the ideal tool for financial modeling and other models that depend on the values of several variables. If you think about it, just about any spreadsheet that contains formulas is a what-if model (which are often distributed as templates). Changing the value of a cell used in a formula is akin to asking "what if . . . ?" My view of this category, however, is a bit more sophisticated. It includes spreadsheets designed exclusively for systematically analyzing the effects of various inputs.

What-if models are often good candidates for user-oriented applications— especially if the model will be used for a lengthy period of time. Creating a good user interface on an application can make it very easy for anyone to use, including computer-illiterates. As an example, you might create an interface that lets the user provide names for various sets of assumptions and then lets you instantly view the results of a selected scenario and create a perfectly formatted summary chart with the click of a button.

Data storage and access spreadsheets

It's not surprising that spreadsheets are often used for keeping lists or modest database manipulations. Most people find that it's much easier to view and manipulate data in a spreadsheet than it is using normal database software. Beginning with Excel 97, each worksheet consists of 65,536 rows, a size increase that greatly extends the potential for database work.

Spreadsheets in this category are often candidates for applications, especially if end users need to perform moderately sophisticated operations. However, Excel's built-in data form dialog box and its auto-filtering commands make working with databases so easy that even beginning users can master simple database operations quickly.

Database front ends

Increasingly, spreadsheet products are used to access external databases. Spreadsheet users can access data stored in external files, even if they come in a variety of formats, using tools that Excel provides. When you create an application that does this, it's sometimes referred to as an *executive information system*, or *EIS*. This sort of system combines data from several sources and summarizes it for users.

Accessing external databases from a spreadsheet often strikes fear in the hearts of beginning users. Creating an executive information system is therefore an ideal sort of Excel application because its chief goal is usually ease of use.

Turnkey applications

The final category of spreadsheet types is the most complex. By *turnkey,* I mean ready to go, with little or no preparation by the end user. For example, the user loads the file and is presented with a user interface that makes user choices perfectly clear. Turnkey applications may not even look as if they are being powered by a spreadsheet, and often, the user interacts completely with dialog boxes rather than cells.

Actually, many of the categories just described can be converted into turnkey applications. The critical common elements, as I'll discuss throughout the remainder of the book, are good planning, error handling, and user-interface design.

Summary

In this chapter, I introduced the concept of a spreadsheet application. I then discussed the distinction between a developer and an end user, and I presented a two-way classification system that describes spreadsheet users. Finally, I classified spreadsheets into several categories, some of which qualify as material for application developers.

Chapter 6 continues this last discussion and goes into more detail about how spreadsheet developers typically go about their business.

✦ ✦ ✦

Essentials of Spreadsheet Application Development

✦ ✦ ✦ ✦

In This Chapter

A discussion of the basic steps involved in spreadsheet application development

Determining end-user needs and planning applications to meet those needs

Guidelines for developing and testing your applications

Documenting your development efforts and writing user documentation

✦ ✦ ✦ ✦

My goal in this chapter is to provide you with some *general* guidelines that you may find useful. There is no simple, surefire recipe for developing an effective spreadsheet application. Everyone has his or her own style for creating such applications, and in my experience, I haven't discovered one "best way" that works for everyone. In addition, every project that you undertake will be different and will therefore require its own approach. Finally, the demands and general attitudes of the people you'll be working with (or for) also play a role in how the development process will proceed.

As I mentioned in the preceding chapter, spreadsheet developers typically perform the following activities:

- ✦ Determine the needs of the user
- ✦ Plan an application that meets these needs
- ✦ Determine the most appropriate user interface
- ✦ Create the spreadsheet, formulas, macros, and user interface
- ✦ Test and debug the application
- ✦ Attempt to make the application bulletproof
- ✦ Make the application aesthetically appealing and intuitive
- ✦ Document the development effort

- ✦ Develop user documentation and online help
- ✦ Distribute the application to the user
- ✦ Update the application when it's necessary

Not all of these steps are required for each application, and the order in which these activities are performed may vary from project to project. Each of these activities is described in the pages that follow; and in most cases, the technical details are covered in subsequent chapters.

Determining User Needs

When you undertake a spreadsheet application development project, one of your first steps is to identify exactly what the end users require. Failure to thoroughly assess the end users' needs early on often results in additional work later when you have to adjust the application so that it does what it was supposed to do in the first place.

In some cases, you'll be intimately familiar with the end users and may even be an end user yourself. In other cases (for example, a consultant developing a project for a new client), you may know little or nothing about the users or their situation.

Following are some guidelines that may help to make this phase easier:

- ✦ Don't presume that you know what the user needs. Second-guessing at this stage almost always causes problems later on.
- ✦ If possible, talk directly to the end users of the application, not just their supervisor or manager.
- ✦ Learn what, if anything, is currently being done to meet the user's needs. You may be able to save some work by simply adapting an existing application. At the very least, looking at current solutions will familiarize you with the operation.
- ✦ Identify the resources available at the user's site. For example, try to determine whether there are any hardware or software limitations that you must work around.
- ✦ If possible, determine the specific hardware systems that will be used. If your application will be used on slower systems, you need to take that into account.
- ✦ Understand the skill levels of the end users. This information will help you design the application appropriately.
- ✦ Determine how long the application will be used. Knowing this may influence the amount of effort you put into the project.

How do you determine the needs of the user? If you've been asked to develop a spreadsheet application, it's a good idea to meet with the end user and ask very specific questions. Better yet, get everything in writing, create flow diagrams, pay attention to minor details, and do anything else to ensure that the product you deliver is the product that is needed.

One final note: Don't be surprised if the project specifications change before you complete the application. This is quite common, and you'll be in a better position if you *expect* changes rather than if you are surprised by them. Just make sure that your contract (if you have one) addresses the issue of changing specifications.

Planning an Application That Meets User Needs

Once you've determined the end users' needs, it's very tempting to jump right in and start fiddling around in Excel—take it from one who suffers from this problem. But try to restrain yourself. Builders don't construct a house without a set of blueprints, and you shouldn't develop a spreadsheet application without some type of plan. The formality of your plan depends on the scope of the project and your general style of working, but you should at least spend *some* time thinking about what you're going to do and coming up with a plan of action.

Before rolling up your sleeves and settling down at your keyboard, you'll benefit by taking some time to consider the various ways that you can approach the problem. Here is where a thorough knowledge of Excel pays off. Avoiding blind alleys before you stumble into them is always a good idea.

If you ask a dozen Excel gurus to design an application based on very precise specifications, chances are you'll get a dozen different implementations of the project that all meet those specifications. And of those solutions, some will definitely be better than others because Excel often provides several different ways to accomplish a task. If you know Excel inside out, you'll have a pretty good idea of the potential methods at your disposal, and you can choose the one most appropriate for the project at hand. Often, a bit of creative thinking yields an unusual approach that's vastly superior to other methods.

So at the beginning of this planning period, you'll be considering some general options, such as those that follow:

- ✦ *File structure.* Think about whether you want to use one workbook with multiple sheets, several single-sheet workbooks, or a template file.
- ✦ *Data structure.* You should always consider how your data will be structured. This includes the use of external database files versus storing everything in worksheets.

✦ *Formulas versus VBA.* Should you use formulas or write VBA procedures to perform calculations? Both have advantages and disadvantages.

✦ *Add-in or XLS file.* In most cases, you probably want your final product to be an XLA add-in, but in some cases, an XLS file is preferable.

✦ *Version of Excel.* Do you want your Excel application to work with Excel 2000 only? With Excel 2000 or Excel 97? What about Excel 95 and Excel 5? Will it also be run on a Macintosh? These are very important considerations because each new version of Excel adds features that aren't available in previous versions.

✦ *How to handle errors.* Error handling is a major issue with applications. You need to determine how your application will detect and deal with errors. For example, if your application applies formatting to the active worksheet, you need to be able to handle a case in which a chart sheet is active.

✦ *Use of special features.* If your application needs to summarize a lot of data, you may want to consider using Excel's pivot table feature. Or, you might want to use Excel's data validation feature as a check for valid data entry.

✦ *Performance issues.* The time to start thinking about increasing the speed and efficiency of your application is at the development stage, not when the application is completed and users are complaining.

✦ *Level of security.* As you may know, Excel provides several protection options to restrict access to particular elements of a workbook. For example, you can lock cells so that formulas cannot be changed, and you can assign a password to prevent unauthorized users from viewing or accessing specific files. Determining up front exactly what you need to protect — and what level of protection is necessary — will make your job easier.

You'll probably have to deal with many other project-specific considerations in this phase. The important thing is that you consider all options and don't settle on the first solution that comes to mind.

Another design consideration is remembering to plan for change. You'll do yourself a favor if you make your application as generic as possible. For example, don't write a procedure that works with only a specific range of cells. Rather, write a procedure that accepts any range as an argument. When the inevitable changes are requested, such a design makes it easier for you to carry out the revisions. Also, you may find that the work you do for one project is similar to the work you do for another. Keeping reusability in mind when you are planning a project is always a good idea.

One thing that I've learned from experience is to avoid letting the end user completely guide your approach to a problem. For example, suppose that you meet with a manager who tells you the department needs an application that writes text files, which will be imported into another application. Don't confuse the user's need with the solution. The user's real need is to share data. Using an intermediate text file to do it is one possible solution to the need. There may be other ways to approach the problem — such as direct transfer of information by using DDE or OLE. In other words, don't let the users define their problem by stating it in terms of a solution approach. Determining the best approach is *your* job.

Learning While You Develop

Now a few words about reality: Excel is a moving target. Excel's upgrade cycle is approximately 18 months, which means that you have one and one-half years to get up to speed with its current innovations before you have even more innovations to contend with.

Excel 5, which introduced VBA, represented a major paradigm shift for Excel developers. Thousands of people up until that point earned their living developing Excel applications that were largely based on the XLM macro language in Excel 2, 3, and 4. Beginning with Excel 5, dozens of new tools became available and developers – for the most part – eagerly embraced them.

When Excel 97 became available, developers faced yet another shift. This new version introduced a new file format, the Visual Basic editor, and UserForms as a replacement for dialog sheets.

VBA is not difficult to learn, but it definitely takes time to become comfortable with it and even more time to master it. The VBA language is still evolving. Consequently, it's not uncommon to be in the process of learning VBA while you're developing applications with it. In fact, I think it's impossible to learn VBA without developing applications. If you're like me, you'll find it much easier to learn VBA if you have a project that requires it. Learning VBA just for the sake of learning VBA usually doesn't work.

Determining the Most Appropriate User Interface

When you develop spreadsheets that others will use, you need to pay special attention to the user interface. By *user interface,* I mean the method by which the user interacts with the application — clicking buttons, using menus, pressing keys, accessing toolbars, and so on.

Again, it's important that you keep the end user in mind. It's likely that you have much more computer experience than the end users, and an interface that's intuitive to you may not be as intuitive to everyone else.

One way to approach the user interface issue is to rely on Excel's built-in features: its menus, toolbars, scroll bars, and so on. In other words, you can simply set up the workbook and then let the user work with it however he or she wants. This may be the perfect solution if the application will be used only by those who know Excel well. More often, however, you'll find that the audience for your application consists of relatively inexperienced (and often disinterested) users. This makes your job more difficult, and you'll need to pay particular attention to the user interface that drives your application.

Excel provides several features that are relevant to user-interface design:

- ✦ Custom dialog boxes (UserForms)
- ✦ ActiveX controls (such as a ListBox or a CommandButton) placed directly on a worksheet
- ✦ Custom menus
- ✦ Custom toolbars
- ✦ Custom shortcut keys

I discuss these features briefly in the following sections and cover them more thoroughly in later chapters.

Creating custom dialog boxes

Anyone who has used Excel for any length of time is undoubtedly familiar with dialog boxes. Consequently, custom dialog boxes play a major role in the user interfaces you design for your applications.

Excel 97 introduced a completely new way to create custom dialog boxes by using UserForms. However, Excel 97 still supports Excel 5/95 dialog sheets. This book focuses exclusively on UserForms.

Figure 6-1 shows a custom dialog box that I developed for an application.

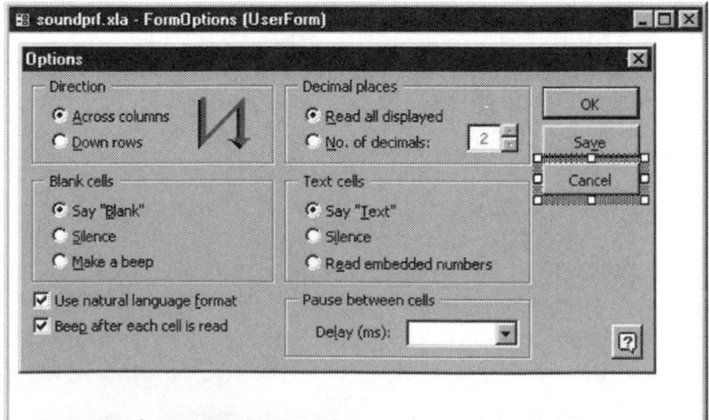

Figure 6-1: Custom dialog boxes are important to an application's user interface.

You can use a custom dialog box to solicit user input, get a user's options or preferences, and direct the flow of your entire application. Custom dialog boxes are stored in UserForms (one dialog box per UserForm). You create and edit custom dialog boxes in the Visual Basic Editor (VB Editor), which you access by pressing Alt+F11. The elements that make up a dialog box — buttons, drop-down lists, check boxes, and so on — are called controls — more specifically, ActiveX controls. Excel provides a standard assortment of ActiveX controls, and you can also incorporate third-party controls.

After adding a control to a dialog box, you can link it to a worksheet cell so that it doesn't require any macros (except a simple macro to display the dialog box). Linking a control to a cell is easy, but it's not always the best way to get user input from a dialog box. Most of the time, you'll want to develop VBA macros that work with your custom dialog boxes.

I cover UserForms in detail in Part IV.

Using ActiveX controls on a worksheet

Excel also lets you add the UserForm ActiveX controls to a worksheet's draw layer. Figure 6-2 shows a simple worksheet model with a UserForm inserted directly on the worksheet.

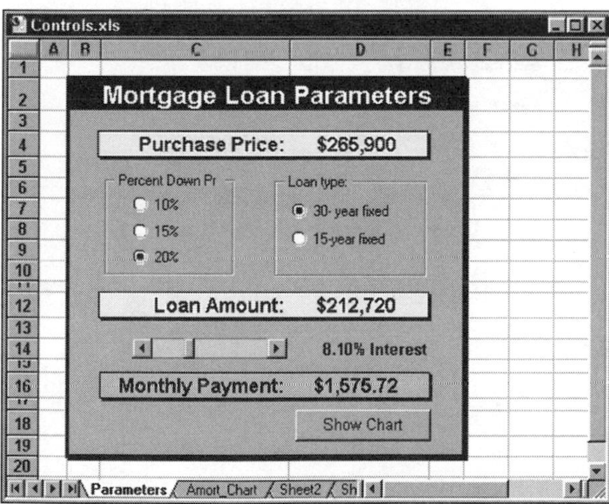

Figure 6-2: Directly adding dialog box controls may make a worksheet easier to use.

Perhaps the most common control is a CommandButton. By themselves, buttons don't do anything, so you have to attach a macro to each button.

Using dialog box controls directly in a worksheet often eliminates the need for custom dialog boxes. You can often greatly simplify the operation of a spreadsheet by adding a few ActiveX controls to a worksheet. This lets the user make choices by operating familiar controls rather than making entries into cells.

The ActiveX controls are found on the Control Toolbox toolbar. You can also use Excel 5/95 compatible controls on a worksheet. These controls, which are not ActiveX controls, are available on the Forms toolbar. (These controls are not discussed in this book.)

Customizing menus

Another way to control the user interface in spreadsheet applications is to modify Excel's menus or to create your own menu system. Instead of creating buttons that execute macros, you can add one or more new menus or menu items to execute macros that you've already created. An advantage to custom menus is that the menu bar is always visible, whereas a button placed on a worksheet can easily scroll out of view.

Beginning with Excel 97, Microsoft has implemented an entirely different way of dealing with menus. As you'll see in Chapter 22, a menu bar is actually a toolbar in disguise. Figure 6-3 shows an example of a new menu – something that might be used in a specialized custom application. Each menu item triggers a macro.

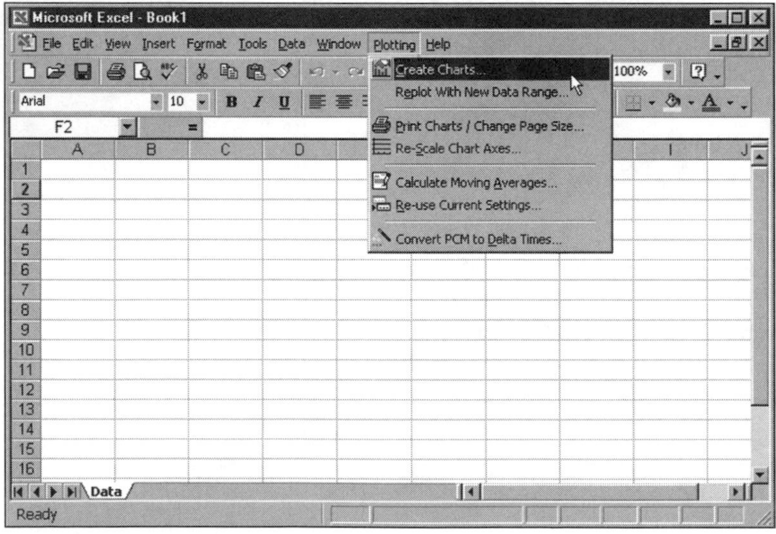

Figure 6-3: This workbook adds a new menu.

There are two ways to customize Excel's menus. You may use VBA code to make the menu modifications, or you can edit the menu directly, using the View ➪ Toolbars ➪ Customize command.

As I explain in Chapter 22, the best approach is usually to use VBA commands to modify the menus. You have complete control over the menus and can even perform such operations as disabling the menu item or adding a checkmark to the item.

Menu modifications that you make using the View ➪ Toolbars ➪ Customize command (see Figure 6-4) are "permanent." In other words, if you make a menu change (such as the removal of a menu item), that change will remain in effect even if you restart Excel.

The Menu Editor (which debuted in Excel 5) was removed, beginning with Excel 97. Menus that were created using the Menu Editor will continue to function when the workbook is loaded into Excel 97 or Excel 2000.

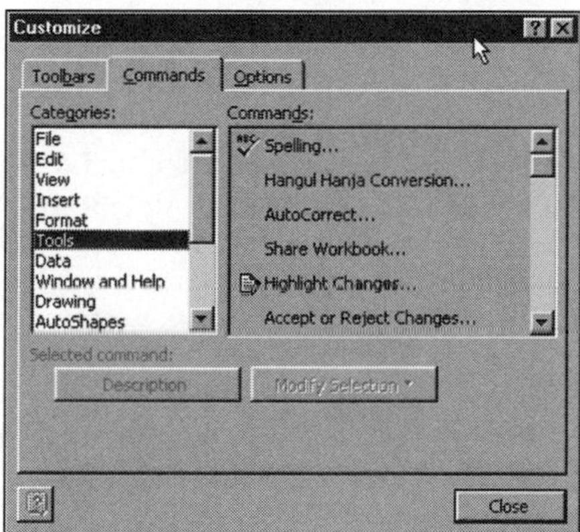

Figure 6-4: The Customize dialog box is where you make changes to Excel's menu system.

You'll find that you can customize every menu that Excel displays — even the shortcut menus that appear when you right-click an object. Figure 6-5 shows a customized shortcut menu that appears when you right-click a cell or range. Notice that this shortcut menu has several new commands that aren't normally available.

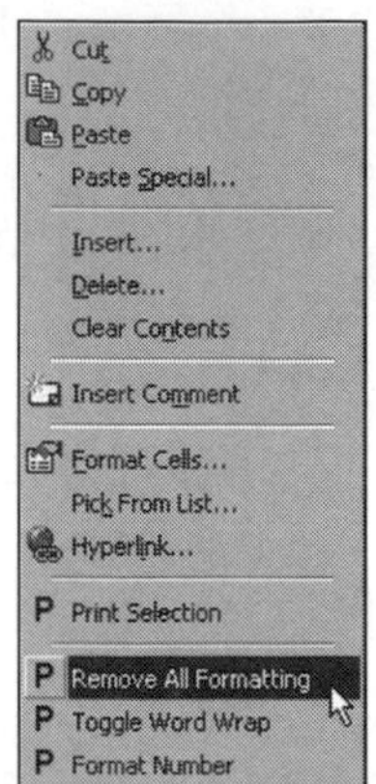

Figure 6-5: An example of a customized shortcut menu.

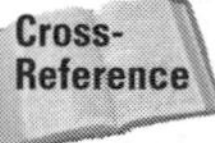

I cover custom menus in detail in Chapter 22.

Customizing toolbars

Toolbars are very common in Windows applications, and Excel offers a huge assortment of built-in toolbars. Generally, toolbar buttons serve as shortcuts for commonly used menu commands to give users a quicker way to issue commands. Because a mouse is required to click a toolbar button, a toolbar button generally isn't the *only* way to execute a particular operation. Excel's toolbars, for example, make it possible to do most of the common spreadsheet operations without even using the menus.

You can create a custom toolbar that contains only the tools you want users to be able to access. In fact, if you attach macros to these tools, a custom toolbar becomes the equivalent of a group of buttons placed on a worksheet. The advantage to using the toolbar in this way is that it is always visible and can be repositioned anywhere on the screen. Buttons inserted on a worksheet are fixed in place and can be scrolled off the screen.

Beginning with Excel 97, you can also add menus to a toolbar.

You can set up your application so that the toolbar appears whenever your application is loaded. You do this by *attaching* a toolbar to a workbook using the Attach button in the Toolbars tab of the Customize dialog box (see Figure 6-6). This lets you store individual toolbars with a workbook application so that you can distribute them to users of your application.

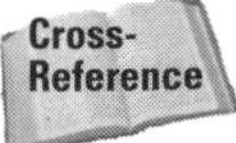

I discuss the topic of toolbars in detail in Chapter 21.

Figure 6-6: You can attach a custom toolbar to a worksheet with the Attach Toolbars dialog box.

Creating shortcut keys

The final user-interface option at your disposal is custom shortcut keys. Excel lets you assign a Ctrl key (or Shift+Ctrl key) combination to a macro. When the user presses the key combination, the macro executes. Obviously, you have to make it clear to the user which keys are active and what they do. However, if speed is essential, pressing a key combination is usually faster than issuing menu commands, using a toolbar, or working with a dialog box.

You need to be careful, however, not to assign a key combination that's already in use for something else. For example, Ctrl+S is a built-in shortcut key used to save the current workbook. If you assign this key combination to a macro, you lose the ability to save the file with Ctrl+S. In other words, a key combination you assign to a macro takes precedence over the built-in shortcut keys. Shortcut keys are case-sensitive, so you can use a combination such as Ctrl+Shift+S.

Executing the development effort

After you've identified user needs, determined the approach you'll take to meet those needs, and decided on the components you'll use for the user interface, it's time to get down to the nitty-gritty and start creating the application. This step, of course, comprises a great deal of the total time you spend on a particular project.

How you go about developing the application depends on your own personal style and the nature of the application. Except for simple fill-in-the-blanks template workbooks, your application will probably use macros. Developing the macros is the tough part. It's easy to create macros in Excel, but it's difficult to create *good* macros. Part III of this book is devoted to VBA, the language you'll use to write your macros.

Concerning Yourself with the End User

In this segment, I discuss the important development issues that surface as your application becomes more and more workable, and the time to package and distribute your work grows nearer.

Testing it out

How many times have you used a commercial software application, only to have it bomb out on you at a crucial moment? Most likely, the problem was caused by insufficient testing that didn't catch all the bugs. All nontrivial software has bugs; but in the best software, the bugs are simply more obscure. As you'll see, you sometimes have to work around the bugs in Excel to get your application to perform properly.

After you create your application, you need to test it. This is one of the most crucial steps; it's not uncommon to spend as much time testing and debugging an application as you did creating the application in the first place. Actually, you should be doing a great deal of testing during the development phase. After all, while you're writing a VBA routine or creating formulas in a worksheet, you'll want to make sure that the application is working the way it's supposed to work.

Bugs? In Excel?

You might think that a product like Excel—which is used by millions of people throughout the world—would be relatively free of bugs. Think again, pal. Excel is such a complex piece of software that it is only natural to expect some problems with it. And Excel *does* have some problems.

Getting a product like Excel out the door is not easy, even for a company like Microsoft with seemingly unlimited resources. Releasing a software product involves compromises and trade-offs. It's commonly known that most major software vendors release their products with full knowledge that they contain bugs. Most of the bugs are considered insignificant enough to ignore. Software companies could postpone their releases by a few months and fix most of them, but software, like everything else, is ruled by economics. The benefits of delaying a product often do not exceed the costs involved. Although Excel definitely has its share of bugs, my guess is that the majority of Excel users never encounter one.

In this book, I point out the problems with Excel that I know about. You'll surely discover some more on your own. Some problems occur only under a specific configuration involving hardware and/or software. These are the worst of all bugs because they aren't easily reproducible.

So what's a developer to do? It's called a *workaround.* If something that you try to do doesn't work—and all indications say that it *should* work—it's time to move on to Plan B. Frustrating? Sure. A waste of your time? Absolutely. It's all part of being a developer.

Like standard compiled applications, spreadsheet applications that you develop are prone to bugs. A *bug* is usually defined as 1) something that does happen but shouldn't while a program (or application) is running, or 2) something that doesn't happen when it should happen. Both species of bugs are equally nasty, and you should plan on devoting a good portion of your development time to testing the application under all reasonable conditions and fixing any problems you find. In some cases, unfortunately, the problems aren't entirely your fault. Excel, too, has its problems (see the "Bugs? In Excel?" sidebar).

I probably don't need to tell you to thoroughly test any spreadsheet development you develop for others. And depending on its eventual audience, you might want to make your application *bulletproof*. In other words, try to anticipate all the errors and screw-ups that could possibly occur, and make efforts to avoid them — or at least handle them gracefully. This not only helps the end user, but also makes it easier on you and your reputation.

Although you cannot conceivably test for all possibilities, your macros should be able to handle common types of errors. For example, what if the user enters a text string instead of a value? What if the user tries to run your macro when a workbook isn't open? What if he or she cancels a dialog box without making any selections? What happens if the user presses Ctrl+F6 and jumps to the next window? As you gain experience, issues like this become very familiar, and you'll account for them without even thinking.

What about Beta Testing?

Software manufacturers typically have a rigorous testing cycle for new products. After extensive internal testing, the prerelease product is usually sent to a group of interested users for *beta testing.* This phase often uncovers additional problems that are usually corrected before the product's final release.

If you're developing an Excel application that more than a few people will use, you may want to consider a beta test. This enables your application to be used in its intended setting on different hardware (usually) and by the intended users.

The beta period should begin after you've completed all of your own testing, and you feel the application is ready to distribute. You'll need to identify a group of users to help you. The process works best if you distribute everything that will ultimately be included in your application – user documentation, installation program, online help, and so on. You can evaluate the beta test in a number of ways, including face-to-face discussions, questionnaires, and phone calls.

You will almost always become aware of problems you need to correct or improvements you need to make before you undertake a widespread distribution of the application. Of course, a beta testing phase takes additional time, and not all projects can afford that luxury.

Making the application bulletproof

If you think about it, it's fairly easy to destroy a spreadsheet. Erasing one critical formula or value often causes errors throughout the entire worksheet — and perhaps other dependent worksheets. Even worse, if the damaged workbook is saved, it replaces the good copy on disk. Unless a backup procedure is in place, the user of your application could be in trouble — and *you'll* probably be blamed for it.

Obviously, it's easy to see why you need to add some protection when users — especially novices — will be using your worksheets. Excel provides several techniques for protecting worksheets and parts of worksheets:

- ✦ You can lock specific cells (using the Protection tab in the Format Cells dialog box) so that they cannot be changed. This takes effect only when the document is protected with the Tools ⇨ Protection ⇨ Protect Sheet command.
- ✦ You can protect an entire workbook — the structure of the workbook, the window position and size, or both. Use the Tools ⇨ Protection ⇨ Protect Workbook command for this purpose.
- ✦ You can hide the formulas in specific cells (using the Protection tab in the Format Cells dialog box) so that others can't see them. Again, this takes effect only when the document is protected with Tools ⇨ Protection ⇨ Protect Sheet command.
- ✦ You can lock objects on the worksheet (using the Protection tab in the Format Object dialog box). This takes effect only when the document is protected with the Tools ⇨ Protection ⇨ Protect Sheet command.
- ✦ You can hide rows (Format ⇨ Row ⇨ Hide), columns (Format ⇨ Column ⇨ Hide), sheets (Format ⇨ Sheet ⇨ Hide), and documents (Window ⇨ Hide). This helps prevent the worksheet from looking cluttered and also provides some protection against prying eyes.
- ✦ You can designate Excel workbooks as read-only to ensure that they cannot be overwritten with any changes. You do this by choosing the Options button in the Save As dialog box.
- ✦ You can assign a password to prevent unauthorized users from opening your file (using the Options button in the Save As dialog box).
- ✦ You can use a password-protected add-in, which doesn't allow the user to change *anything* on its worksheets.

How Secure Are Excel's Passwords?

As far as I know, Microsoft has never advertised Excel as a secure program. And for a good reason: It's actually quite easy to thwart Excel's password system. Several commercial programs are available that can break passwords. Bottom line? Don't think of password protection as foolproof. Sure, it will be effective for the casual user. But if someone *really* wants to break your password, she can.

Making the application aesthetically appealing and intuitive

If you've used many different software packages, you've undoubtedly seen examples of poorly designed user interfaces, difficult-to-use programs, and just plain ugly screens. If you're developing spreadsheets for other people, you should pay particular attention to how the application looks.

The way a computer program looks can make all the difference in the world to users, and the same is true with the applications you develop with Excel. Beauty, however, is in the eye of the beholder. If your skills lean more in the analytical direction, consider enlisting the assistance of someone with a more aesthetic sensibility to provide help with design.

The users of your applications will appreciate a good-looking user interface, and your applications will have a much more polished and professional look if you devote some additional time to design and aesthetic considerations. An application that looks good demonstrates that its developer cared enough about the product to invest some extra time and effort. Take the following suggestions into account:

- Strive for consistency: When designing dialog boxes, for example, try to emulate Excel's dialog box look and feel whenever possible. Be consistent with formatting, fonts, text size, and colors.
- A common mistake that developers make is trying to cram too much information into a single screen or dialog box. A good rule of thumb is to present only one or two chunks of information at a time.
- If you use an input screen to solicit information from the user, consider breaking it up into several, less-crowded screens. If you use a complex dialog box, you might want to break it up by using a MultiPage control (which lets you create a familiar "tabbed" dialog box).
- Use color sparingly, because it's very easy to overdo it and make the screen look gaudy. If your application will be used on laptops, make sure that you use color combinations that also look good (and are legible) in monochrome.
- Pay attention to numeric formats, type faces and sizes, and borders.
- Do whatever you can to make individual parts of the worksheet appear to stay together.

Evaluating aesthetic qualities is very subjective. When in doubt, strive for simplicity and clarity.

Documenting the development effort

Putting a spreadsheet application together is one thing. Making it understandable for other people is another. As with traditional programming, it's important that you thoroughly document your work. Such documentation helps you if you need to go back to it (and you will), and it helps anyone else you may pass it on to.

You may want to consider a couple of things when you document your project. For example, if you were hired to develop an Excel application, you may not want to share all your hard-earned secrets by thoroughly documenting everything. If this is the case, you should maintain two versions: one thoroughly documented and the other partially documented.

How do you document a workbook application? You can either store the information in a worksheet or use another file. You can even use a paper document if you prefer. Perhaps the easiest way is to use a separate worksheet to store your comments and key information for the project. For VBA code, use comments liberally (text preceded with an apostrophe is ignored). An elegant piece of VBA code may seem perfectly obvious to you today — but come back to it in a few months, and your reasoning may be completely obscured.

With regard to user documentation, you basically have two choices: paper-based documentation or electronic (online) documentation. Online help is standard fare in Windows applications. Fortunately, your Excel applications can also provide online help — even context-sensitive help. Developing online help takes quite a bit of additional effort, but for a large project, it may be worth it.

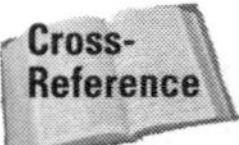

In Chapter 23, I discuss several alternatives for providing online help for your applications.

Distributing the application to the user

You've completed your project, and you're ready to release it to the end users. How do you go about doing this? You can choose from many ways to distribute your application, and the method you choose depends on many factors.

You could just hand over a disk, scribble a few instructions, and be on your way. Or, you may want to install the application yourself — but this is not always feasible. Another option is to develop an official setup program that performs the task automatically. You can write such a program in a traditional programming language, purchase a generic setup program, or write your own in VBA.

Note

The Developers Edition of Office 2000 includes a Setup Wizard that helps you prepare your applications for distribution.

New Feature

Excel 2000 uses Microsoft Authenticode technology to enable developers to digitally "sign" their applications. This process is designed to help end users identify the author of an application, ensure that the project has not been altered, and help prevent the spread of macro viruses or other potentially destructive code. To digitally sign a project, you must first apply for a digital certificate from a formal certificate authority (or you can self-sign your project by creating your own digital certificate). Refer to the online help or Microsoft's Web site for additional information.

Another point to consider is support for your application. In other words, who gets the phone call if the user encounters a problem? If you aren't prepared to handle routine questions, you'll need to identify someone who is. In some cases you'll want to arrange it so that only highly technical or bug-related issues escalate to the developer.

Updating the application when necessary

After you distribute your application, you're finished with it, right? You can sit back, enjoy yourself, and try to forget about the problems you encountered (and solved) during the course of developing your application. In rare cases, yes, you may be finished. More often, however, the users of your application will not be completely satisfied. Sure, your application adheres to all of the *original* specifications, but things change. Seeing an application working frequently causes the user to think of other things that the application could be doing. We're talking *updates*.

When you need to update or revise your application, you'll appreciate that you designed it well in the first place and you fully documented your efforts. If not, well . . . we learn from our experiences.

Why Is There No Run-Time Version of Excel?

When you distribute your application, you need to be sure that each end user has a licensed copy of the appropriate version of Excel. It's illegal to distribute a copy of Excel along with your application. Why, you might ask, doesn't Microsoft provide a run-time version of Excel? A run-time version is an executable program that can load files but not create them. With a run-time version, the end user wouldn't need a copy of Excel to run your application (this is common with database programs).

I've never seen a clear or convincing reason why Microsoft does not have a run-time version of Excel, and no other spreadsheet manufacturer offers a run-time version of its product either. The most likely reason is that spreadsheet vendors fear that doing so would reduce sales of the software. Or, it could be that developing a run-time version would require a tremendous amount of programming that would just never pay off.

Actually, there *is* a spreadsheet product that can generate executable files. Visual Baler, from TechTools Software (`http://www.techtools.com/`), is a unique product that enables you to create spreadsheet applications and distribute them, royalty-free, to any number of users. The end users need no additional software to run it. Unfortunately, Baler seems to have been designed more for users of 1-2-3 and Quattro Pro (it bears little resemblance to Excel).

On a related note . . . Microsoft does offer an Excel file *viewer*. This product lets you view Excel files if you don't own a copy of Excel. Even better, it's free. You can get a copy from Microsoft's Web site (`http://officeupdate.microsoft.com`).

Other Development Issues

You need to keep several other issues in mind when developing an application—especially if you don't know exactly who will be using the application. If you're developing an application that will have widespread use (a shareware application, for example), you have no way of knowing how the application will be used, what type of system it will run on, or what other software will be running concurrently.

The user's installed version of Excel

With every new release of Excel, the issue of compatibility rears its head. As I write this, Excel 2000 is just about ready to be released, yet many large corporations seem to be stuck in a time warp and still use Excel 5 and Windows 3.*x*.

Unfortunately, there is no guarantee that an application developed for Excel 5 will work perfectly with later versions of Excel. If you need your application to work with Excel 5, Excel 95, Excel 97, and Excel 2000, you're going to have to work with the lowest common denominator (Excel 5)—and then test it thoroughly with all other versions.

Things get even more complicated when you consider Excel's "sub-versions." Microsoft distributes service releases (SRs) to correct problems. For example, users might have the original Excel 97, Excel 97 with SR-1, or Excel 97 with SR-2. And some might even have Excel 97 with the *original* SR-1—which was released and then withdrawn by Microsoft because it caused more problems than it fixed!

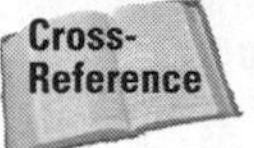

I discuss compatibility issues in Chapter 25.

Language issues

Consider yourself very fortunate if all of your end users have the English language version of Excel. Non-English versions of Excel aren't always 100 percent compatible, so that would mean additional testing on your part.

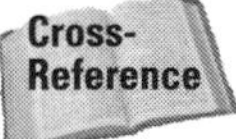

I briefly discuss language issues in Chapter 25.

System speed

You're probably a fairly advanced computer user and tend to keep your hardware reasonably up-to-date. In other words, you have a fairly powerful system—better than the average user. In some cases, you'll know exactly what hardware the end users of your applications are using. If so, it's vitally important that you test your application on that system. A procedure that executes almost instantaneously on your system may take several seconds on another system. In the world of computers, several seconds may be unacceptable.

As you gain more experience with VBA, you'll discover that there are ways to get the job done, and there are ways to get the job done *fast*. It's a good idea to get into the habit of coding for speed. Other chapters in this book will certainly help you out in this area.

Video modes

As you may know, most Windows users use one of three standard video modes: 640 × 480 (i.e., standard VGA mode), 800 × 600, and 1024 × 768. If you develop an application in anything but VGA mode, the application may look terrible when it runs on a VGA system.

I certainly don't recommend developing your apps in VGA mode! You should, however, test them in that mode if there's a likelihood that they will be used in that mode.

This can be a big problem if your application relies on specific information being displayed on a single screen. For example, if you develop an input screen using 800 × 600 mode, users with a standard VGA display may not be able to see all of the input screen without scrolling. Also, it's important to realize that a restored (that is, not maximized or minimized) workbook is displayed at its previous window size and position. In the extreme case, it's possible that a window saved using a high resolution display may be completely off the screen when opened on a system running in VGA mode.

Although advanced users tend to use higher resolutions in Windows, using VGA is unavoidable in some cases. Some laptop systems, for example, support only VGA for their built-in display. There's no way to automatically scale things so that they look the same regardless of the display resolution. Unless you're certain of the video resolution that the users of your application will be using, it's important that you test your application using the lowest common denominator — VGA mode.

As this book will show you (see Chapter 11), it's possible to determine the user's video resolution by using Windows API calls from VBA. In some cases, you may want to programmatically adjust things depending on the user's video resolution.

Folder structure

Another issue you need to think about is the structure of the user's hard drive — how the folders are arranged and named. For example, you can't assume that Excel is installed in a folder named C:\Program Files\Microsoft Office\Office. And you can't even assume that it's installed on drive C. Similarly, you can't assume that Windows is installed in a directory named Windows. Although these are the default installation locations, many systems won't adhere to these conventions. Fortunately, it's possible to use VBA to determine file storage locations.

Summary

In this chapter, I outlined the basic process for developing a spreadsheet application. Much of the information in this chapter is discussed in more detail later on in the book.

This chapter concludes Part II. Part III discusses the ins and outs of Visual Basic for Applications (VBA) — Excel's power programming language and a key element in application development. Chapter 7 begins with a general introduction to VBA.

✦ ✦ ✦

P A R T

Understanding Visual Basic for Applications

This part is the heart of the book. It begins with an introductory overview of VBA and continues through key topics that get you started developing professional applications. You'll learn about VBA procedures (Sub procedures and Function procedures) and get up to speed with essential programming concepts. In addition, you'll find many practical examples that you can adapt for your own use.

✦ ✦ ✦ ✦

In This Part

✦ ✦ ✦ ✦

Introducing Visual Basic for Applications

In This Chapter

An introduction to VBA — the programming language built into Excel 2000

How VBA differs from traditional spreadsheet macro languages, and from the Visual Basic language

How to use the Visual Basic Editor (VBE)

How to work in the code windows in the VBE and customize the VBE environment

The macro recorder in more detail

An overview of objects, collections, properties, and methods

A case study of the `Comment` object

Specific examples of working with `Range` objects

How to access a lot of information about Excel objects, properties, and methods

Programming Excel essentially boils down to manipulating objects — which you do by writing instructions in a language that Excel can understand. This chapter introduces you to that language and to the objects that make up Excel.

Some BASIC Background

Many hard-core programmers scoff at the idea of programming in BASIC. The name itself (an acronym for **B**eginner's **A**ll-purpose **S**ymbolic **I**nstruction **C**ode) suggests that it's not a professional language. In fact, BASIC was first developed in the early 1960s as a way to teach programming techniques to college students. BASIC caught on quickly and is available in hundreds of dialects for many types of computers.

BASIC has evolved and improved over the years. For example, BASIC was originally an *interpreted* language. Each line was interpreted before it was executed, causing slow performance. Most modern dialects of BASIC allow the code to be compiled, resulting in much faster execution and improved program portability.

BASIC gained quite a bit of respectability in 1991 when Microsoft released Visual Basic for Windows (which is currently in Version 6.0). This product made it easy for the masses to develop stand-alone applications for Windows. Visual Basic has very little in common with early versions of BASIC, but BASIC is the foundation on which VBA was built.

About VBA

Excel 5 was the first application on the market to feature Visual Basic for Applications. VBA is best thought of as Microsoft's common application scripting language, and it's now included with all Office 2000 applications — and even applications from other vendors. Therefore, if you master VBA using Excel, you'll be able to jump right in and write macros for other Microsoft (and non-Microsoft) products. Even better, you'll be able to create complete solutions that use features across various applications.

Object models

The secret to using VBA with other applications lies in understanding the *object model* for each application. VBA, after all, simply manipulates objects, and each product (Excel, Word, Access, PowerPoint, and so forth) has its own unique object model. You can program an application using the objects that the application *exposes*.

Excel's object model, for example, exposes several very powerful data analysis objects, such as worksheets, charts, pivot tables, scenarios, and numerous mathematical, financial, engineering, and general business functions. With VBA, you can work with these objects and develop automated procedures. As you work with VBA in Excel, you'll gradually build an understanding of the object model. Warning: it will be very confusing at first. Eventually, however, the pieces will come together and all of a sudden you'll realize that you've mastered it!

VBA versus XLM

Before Version 5, Excel used a powerful macro language called XLM. Excel 2000 still executes XLM macros, but the ability to record macros in XLM was removed beginning with Excel 97. As a developer, you should be aware of XLM (in case you ever encounter macros written in that system), but you should use VBA for your development work.

Figures 7-1 and 7-2 show a simple procedure coded in both XLM and VBA. This macro works on the selected cells. It changes the cell background color and the text color, and it makes the text bold. You probably agree that the VBA code is much easier to read. More important, however, the VBA code is also easier to modify when the need arises.

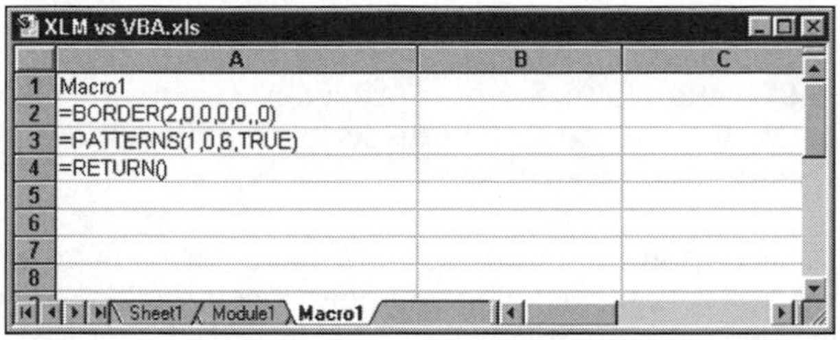

XLM vs VBA.xls

	A	B	C
1	Macro1		
2	=BORDER(2,0,0,0,0,,0)		
3	=PATTERNS(1,0,6,TRUE)		
4	=RETURN()		
5			
6			
7			
8			

Sheet1 / Module1 / Macro1

Figure 7-1: A simple macro coded in Excel's XLM language.

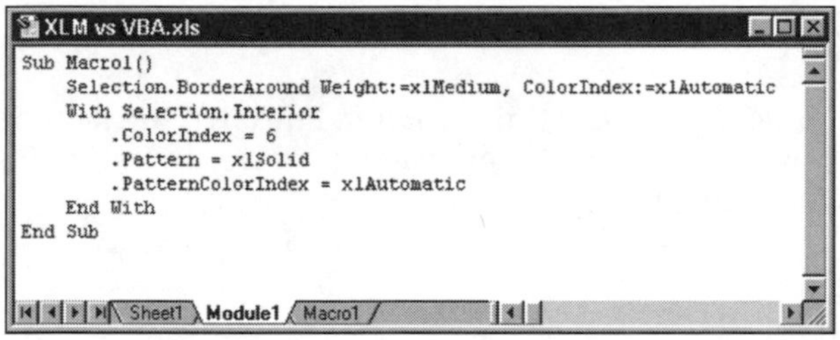

XLM vs VBA.xls

```
Sub Macro1()
    Selection.BorderAround Weight:=xlMedium, ColorIndex:=xlAutomatic
    With Selection.Interior
        .ColorIndex = 6
        .Pattern = xlSolid
        .PatternColorIndex = xlAutomatic
    End With
End Sub
```

Sheet1 / Module1 / Macro1

Figure 7-2: A simple macro coded in Excel's VBA language.

VBA versus Lotus macros

Lotus 1-2-3 (the DOS version) was the first spreadsheet to incorporate macro capability. Although this feature was great in its day, it's quite crude by today's standards. The original 1-2-3 for DOS macros were based on simple keystroke recording, and then playing back those keystrokes to execute the macro. For example, a 1-2-3 for DOS macro that names a range might look like this:

```
/RNC~
```

This represents the following 1-2-3 command sequence:

```
/Range Name Create (Enter)
```

The keystroke-oriented macro language in 1-2-3 was eventually replaced by a command-oriented language. The most recent versions of 1-2-3 include a scripting language similar to VBA (see the next section).

VBA versus LotusScript

Later editions such as 1-2-3 97 feature LotusScript, a procedural language that has much in common with VBA. My experience with LotusScript is limited, but from what I've seen, VBA offers many advantages.

In light of the fact that VBA has become a "standard" and users have a huge code base to draw on, one wonders why Lotus developed a new (incompatible) language rather than simply licensing VBA from Microsoft.

The Basics of VBA

Before I get into the meat of things, I suggest that you read through the material in this section to get a broad overview of where I'm heading. These are the topics that I cover in the remainder of this chapter.

VBA in a nutshell

Following is a quick-and-dirty summary of what VBA is all about:

✦ You perform actions in VBA by executing VBA code.

✦ You write (or record) VBA code, which is stored in a VBA module.

VBA modules are stored in an Excel workbook, but you view or edit a module in the VB Editor.

✦ A VBA module consists of procedures.

A procedure is basically computer code that performs some action on or with objects. Here's an example of a simple a procedure called `Test`:

```
Sub Test()
    Sum = 1 + 1
    MsgBox "The answer is " & Sum
End Sub
```

✦ A VBA module can also have Function procedures.

A Function procedure returns a single value. A function can be called from another VBA procedure or used in a worksheet formula. Here's an example of a function named `AddTwo`:

```
Function AddTwo(arg1, arg2)
    AddTwo = arg1 + arg2
End Function
```

✦ VBA manipulates objects contained in its host application (in this case, Excel 2000).

Excel provides you with more than 100 classes of objects to manipulate. Examples of objects include a workbook, a worksheet, a range on a worksheet, a chart, and a drawn rectangle. Many, many more objects are at your disposal, and you can manipulate them using VBA code.

✦ Object classes are arranged in a hierarchy.

Objects can act as containers for other objects. For example, Excel is an object called `Application`, and it contains other objects, such as `Workbook` and `CommandBar` objects. The `Workbook` object can contain other objects, such as `Worksheet` objects and `Chart` objects. A `Worksheet` object can contain objects such as `Range` objects, `PivotTable` objects, and so on. The arrangement of these objects is referred to as Excel's *object model.*

✦ Like objects form a *collection.*

For example, the `Worksheets` collection consists of all the worksheets in a particular workbook. The `CommandBars` collection consists of all `CommandBar` objects. Collections are objects in themselves.

✦ When you refer to a contained or member object, you specify its position in the object hierarchy using a period as a separator between the container and the member.

For example, you can refer to a workbook named Book1.xls as

```
Application.Workbooks("Book1.xls")
```

This refers to the Book1.xls workbook in the `Workbooks` collection. The `Workbooks` collection is contained in the Excel `Application` object. Extending this to another level, you can refer to Sheet1 in Book1 as

```
Application.Workbooks("Book1.xls").Worksheets("Sheet1")
```

You can take it to still another level and refer to a specific cell as follows:

```
Application.Workbooks("Book1.xls").Worksheets("Sheet1").Range
("A1")
```

✦ If you omit a specific reference to an object, Excel uses the *active* objects.

If Book1 is the active workbook, the preceding reference can be simplified as

```
Worksheets("Sheet1").Range("A1")
```

If you know that Sheet1 is the active sheet, you can simplify the reference even more:

```
Range("A1")
```

✦ Objects have *properties.*

A property can be thought of as a *setting* for an object. For example, a `Range` object has properties such as `Value` and `Name`. A `Chart` object has properties such as `HasTitle` and `Type`. You can use VBA to determine object properties and also to change them.

✦ You refer to properties by combining the object with the property, separated by a period.

For example, you can refer to the value in cell A1 on Sheet1 as

```
Worksheets("Sheet1").Range("A1").Value
```

✦ You can assign values to VBA variables.

To assign the value in cell A1 on Sheet1 to a variable called *Interest*, use the following VBA statement.

```
Interest = Worksheets("Sheet1").Range("A1").Value
```

✦ Objects have *methods*.

A method is an action that is performed with the object. For example, one of the methods for a `Range` object is `ClearContents`. This method clears the contents of the range.

✦ You specify methods by combining the object with the method, separated by a period.

For example, to clear the contents of cell A1 on the active worksheet, use

```
Range("A1").ClearContents
```

✦ VBA also includes all the constructs of modern programming languages, including arrays, looping, and so on.

Believe it or not, the preceding section pretty much describes VBA. Now it's just a matter of learning the details, which is what I cover in the rest of this chapter.

An Analogy

If you like analogies, here's one for you. It may help you understand the relationships between objects, properties, and methods in VBA. In this analogy, I compare Excel with a fast-food restaurant chain.

The basic unit of Excel is a `Workbook` object. In a fast-food chain, the basic unit is an individual restaurant. With Excel, you can add workbooks and close workbooks, and all the open workbooks are known as `Workbooks` (a collection of `Workbook` objects). Similarly, the management of a fast-food chain can add restaurants and close restaurants—and all the restaurants in the chain can be viewed as a collection of `Restaurant` objects.

An Excel workbook is an object, but it also contains other objects such as worksheets, charts, VBA modules, and so on. Furthermore, each object in a workbook can contain its own objects. For example, a `Worksheet` object can contain `Range` objects, `PivotTable` objects, `Shape` objects, and so on.

Continuing with the analogy, a fast-food restaurant (like a workbook) contains objects such as the `Kitchen`, `DiningArea`, and `ParkingLot`. Furthermore, management can add or remove objects from the `Restaurant` object. For example, management may add a `DriveupWindow` object. Each of these objects can contain other objects. For example, the `Kitchen` object has a `Stove` object, `VentilationFan` object, a `Chef` object, `Sink` object, and so on.

So far, so good—this analogy seems to work. Let's see if I can take it further.

Excel's objects have properties. For example, a `Range` object has properties such as `Value` and `Name`, and a `Shape` object has properties such as `Width`, `Height`, and so on. Not surprisingly, objects in a fast-food restaurant also have properties. The `Stove` object, for example, has properties such as `Temperature` and `NumberofBurners`. The `VentilationFan` has its own set of properties (`TurnedOn`, `RPM`, and so forth).

Besides properties, Excel's objects also have methods, which perform an operation on an object. For example, the `ClearContents` method erases the contents of a `Range` object. An object in a fast-food restaurant also has methods. You can easily envision a `ChangeThermostat` method for a `Stove` object or a `SwitchOn` method for a `VentilationFan` object.

With Excel, methods sometimes change an object's properties. The `ClearContents` method for a `Range` object changes the `Range`'s `Value` property. Similarly, the `ChangeThermostat` method on a `Stove` object affects its `Temperature` property.

With VBA, you can write procedures to manipulate Excel's objects. In a fast-food restaurant, the management can give orders to manipulate the objects in the restaurants ("Turn the stove on and switch the ventilation fan to high."). Now is it clear?

Introducing the Visual Basic Editor

In Excel 5 and Excel 95, a VBA module appeared as a separate sheet in a workbook. Beginning with Excel 97, VBA modules no longer show up as sheets in a workbook. Rather, you use the Visual Basic Editor (VBE) to view and work with VBA modules.

VBA modules are still stored with workbook files; they just aren't visible unless you activate the VBE.

The VBE is a separate application that works seamlessly with Excel. By *seamlessly,* I mean that Excel takes care of the details of opening the VBE when you need it. You can't run the VBE separately; Excel 2000 must be running in order for the VBE to run.

Activating the VBE

When you're working in Excel 2000, you can use any of the following techniques to switch to the VBE:

✦ Press Alt+F11.

✦ Select Tools➪Macro➪Visual Basic Editor.

✦ Click the Visual Basic Editor button, which is located on the Visual Basic toolbar.

Don't confuse the Visual Basic Editor with the Microsoft Script Editor. These are two entirely different animals. The Script Editor is used to edit HTML scripts written in VBScript or JavaScript. The Script Editor is not covered in this book.

Figure 7-3 shows the VBE. Chances are, your VBE window won't look exactly like the window shown in the figure. This window is highly customizable — you can hide windows, change their sizes, "dock" them, rearrange them, and so on.

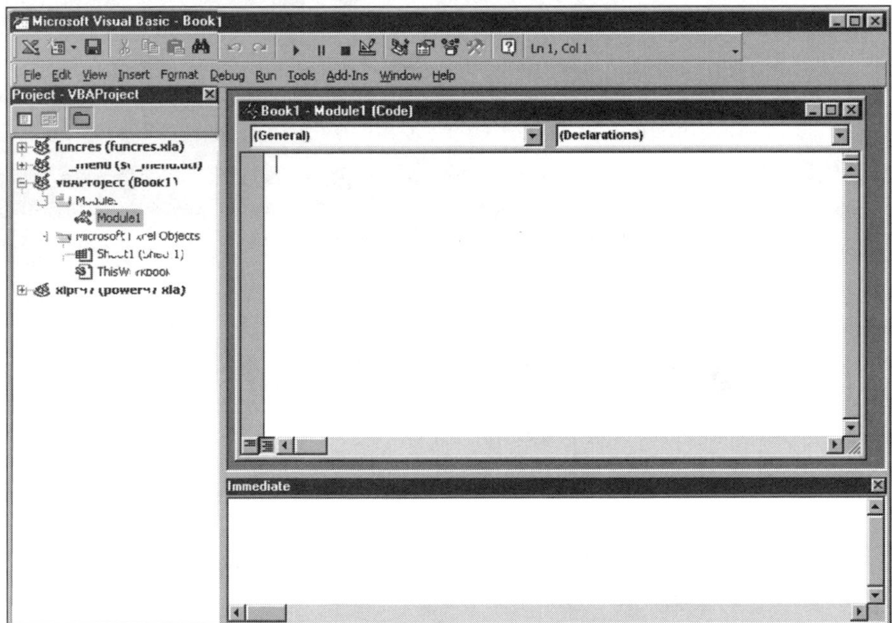

Figure 7-3: The Visual Basic Editor window.

The VBE windows

The VBE consists of a number of parts. I briefly describe some of the key components in the sections that follow.

Menu bar

The VBE menu bar, of course, works like every other menu bar you've encountered. It contains commands that you use to work with the various components in the VB Editor. Many of the menu commands have shortcut keys associated with them. For example, the View ➪ Immediate Window command has a shortcut key of Ctrl+G.

The VBE also features shortcut menus. As you'll discover, right-clicking virtually anything in a VBE window displays a shortcut menu of common commands.

Toolbars

The Standard toolbar, which is directly under the menu bar by default, is one of six VBE toolbars available. VBE toolbars work just like those in Excel: You can customize toolbars, move them around, display other toolbars, and so forth. Use the View ➪ Toolbars ➪ Customize command to work with VBE toolbars.

Project Explorer window

The Project Explorer window displays a tree diagram that consists of every workbook that is currently open in Excel (including add-ins and hidden workbooks). Each workbook is known as a *project*. I discuss the Project Explorer window in more detail in the next section ("Working with the Project Explorer").

If the Project Explorer window is not visible, press Ctrl+R. To hide the Project Explorer window, click the Close button in its title bar (or right-click anywhere in the Project Explorer window, and select Hide from the shortcut menu).

Code window

A code window (sometimes known as a module window) contains VBA code. Every item in a project has an associated code window. To view a code window for an object, double-click the object in the Project Explorer window. For example, to view the code window for the `Sheet1` object, double-click Sheet1 in the Project Explorer window. Unless you've added some VBA code, the code window will be empty.

I discuss code windows later on in this chapter (see "Working with Code Windows").

Immediate window

The Immediate window is most useful for executing VBA statements directly, testing statements, and debugging your code. This window may or may not be visible. If the Immediate window isn't visible, press Ctrl+G. To close the Immediate window, click the Close button in its title bar (or, right-click anywhere in the Immediate window and select Hide from the shortcut menu).

Working with the Project Explorer

When you're working in the VBE, each Excel workbook and add-in that's currently open is considered a project. You can think of a project as a collection of objects arranged as an outline. You can "expand" a project by clicking the plus sign (+) at the left of the project's name in the Project Explorer window. You "contract" a project by clicking the minus sign (–) to the left of a project's name. Figure 7-4 shows a Project Explorer window with three projects listed (one add-in and two workbooks).

If you try to expand a project that's protected with a password, you'll be prompted to enter the password.

Figure 7-4: A Project Explorer window with three projects listed

If you have many workbooks and add-ins loaded, the Project Explorer window may be a bit overwhelming. Unfortunately, it's not possible to hide projects in the Project Explorer window. However, you'll probably want to keep the project outlines contracted if you're not working with them.

Every project expands to show at least one "node" called Microsoft Excel Objects. This node expands to show an item for each worksheet and chart sheet in the workbook (each sheet is considered an object) and another object called `ThisWorkbook` (which represents the `ActiveWorkbook` object). If the project has any VBA modules, the project listing also shows a Modules node, and the modules are listed there. A project may also contain a node called `Forms`, which contains UserForm objects (also known as custom dialog boxes).

Adding a new VBA module

To add a new VBA module to a project, select the project's name in the Project Explorer window, and choose Insert ➪ Module. Or you can right-click the project's name, and choose Insert ➪ Module from the shortcut menu.

When you record a macro, Excel automatically inserts a VBA module to hold the recorded code.

Removing a VBA module

If you need to remove a VBA module from a project, select the module's name in the Project Explorer window and choose File ➪ Remove *xxx*, (where *xxx* is the name of the module). Or you can right-click the module's name, and choose Remove *xxx* from the shortcut menu. You'll be asked whether you want to export the module before removing it. See the next section for details.

Exporting and importing objects

Every object in a project can be saved to a separate file. Saving an individual object in a project is known as *exporting*. And it stands to reason that you can also *import* objects into a project. Exporting and importing objects might be useful if you want to use a particular object (such as a VBA module or a UserForm) in a different project.

To export an object, select it in the Project Explorer window, and choose File➪Export File (or press Ctrl+E). You'll get a dialog box that asks for a filename. Note that the object remains in the project (only a copy of it is exported). If you export a UserForm object, any code associated with the UserForm is also exported.

To import a file into a project, select the project's name in the Explorer window, and choose File ➪ Import File. You'll get a dialog box that asks for a file. You can import only a file that has been exported using the File ➪ Export File command.

If you would like to copy a module or UserForm object to another project, it's not really necessary to export and then import the object. Make sure both projects are open. Then simply activate the Project Explorer, press Ctrl, and drag the object from one project to the other.

Working with Code Windows

As you become proficient with VBA, you'll be spending *lots* of time working in code windows. Each object in a project has an associated code window. To summarize, these objects can be

✦ The workbook itself (ThisWorkbook in the Project window)

✦ A worksheet or chart sheet in a workbook (for example, Sheet1 or Chart1 in the Project window)

✦ A VBA module

✦ A class module (a special type of module that lets you create new object classes)

✦ A UserForm

Minimizing and maximizing windows

At any given time, VB Editor may have lots of code windows. Figure 7-5 shows an example of what I mean.

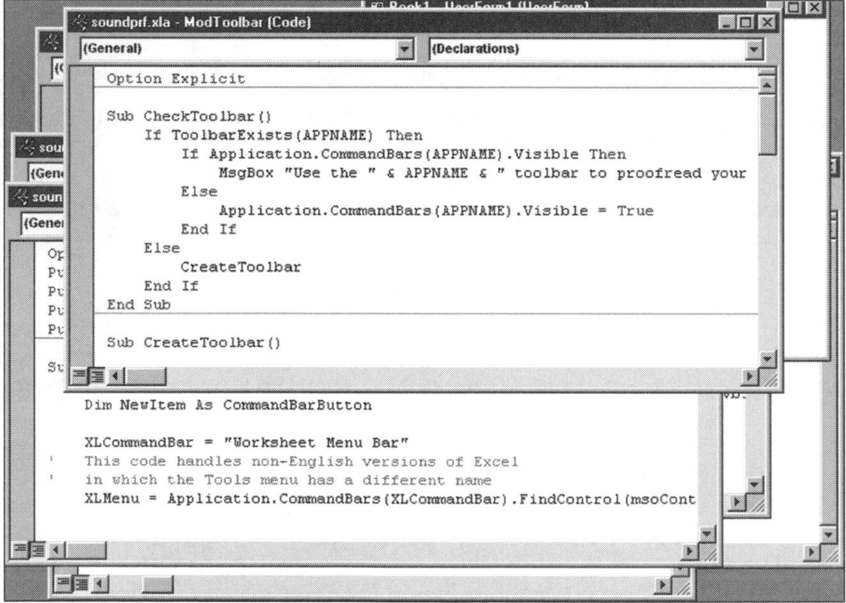

Figure 7-5: Code window overload.

Code windows are much like worksheet windows in Excel. You can minimize them, maximize them, hide them, rearrange them, and so forth. Most people find it much easier to maximize the code window that they're working on. Doing so enables you to see more code and keeps you from getting distracted. To maximize a code window, click the maximize button in the window's title bar, or just double-click the title bar. To restore a code window, making it nonmaximized, click the restore button in the window's title bar.

Sometimes, you may want to have two or more code windows visible. For example, you might want to compare the code in two modules or copy code from one module to another.

Minimizing a code window gets it out of the way. You can also click the Close button in a code window's title bar to close the window completely. To open it again, just double-click the appropriate object in the Project Explorer window.

The VBE doesn't let you close a workbook. You must reactivate Excel and close it from there. You can, however, use the Immediate window to close a workbook or add-in. Just activate the Immediate window, type a VBA statement like the one below, and press Enter.

```
Workbooks("myaddin.xla").Close
```

As you'll see, this statement executes the `Close` method of the `Workbook` object, which closes a workbook.

Storing VBA code

In general, a code window can hold four types of code:

✦ *Sub procedures.* A *procedure* is a set of instructions that performs some action.

✦ *Function procedures.* A *function* is a set of instructions that returns a single value or an array (similar in concept to a worksheet function such as `SUM`).

✦ *Property procedures.* These are special procedures used in class modules.

✦ *Declarations.* A *declaration* is information about a variable that you provide to VBA. For example, you can declare the data type for variables you plan to use.

A single VBA module can store any number of Sub procedures, Function procedures, and declarations. How you organize a VBA module is completely up to you. Some people prefer to keep all their VBA code for an application in a single VBA module; others like to split up the code into several different modules.

Although you have lots of flexibility regarding where to store your VBA code, there are some restrictions. Event-handler procedures must be located in the code window for the object that responds to the event. For example, if you write a procedure that executes when the workbook is opened, that procedure must be located in the code window for the `ThisWorkbook` object, and the procedure must have a special name. This concept will become clearer when I discuss events (Chapter 18) and UserForms (Part IV).

Entering VBA code

Before you can do anything meaningful, you must have some VBA code in a code window. For now, I'll focus on one type of code window: a VBA module.

You can add code to a VBA module in three ways:

- ✦ Enter the code the old fashioned way — type it from your keyboard.
- ✦ Use Excel's macro recorder feature to record your actions and convert them into VBA code.
- ✦ Copy the code from another module and paste it into the module you are working in.

Pause for a Terminology Break

Throughout this book, I use the terms *routine*, *procedure*, and *macro*. Programming people typically use the word *procedure* to describe an automated task. Technically, a procedure can be a Sub procedure or a Function procedure, both of which are sometimes called *routines*. I use all these terms pretty much interchangeably. There is, however, an important difference between Sub procedures and Function procedures. This distinction will become apparent in Chapters 9 and 10.

Entering code manually

Sometimes, the most direct route is the best. Entering code directly involves . . . well, entering the code directly. In other words, you type the code using your keyboard. You can use the Tab key to indent the lines that logically belong together — for example, the conditional statements between an `If` and an `End If` statement. This isn't really necessary, but it makes the code easier to read, so it's a good habit to acquire.

Entering and editing text in a VBA module works just as you would expect. You can select text, copy it or cut it, and then paste it to another location.

A single instruction in VBA can be as long as you need it to be. For readability's sake, however, you might want to break a lengthy instruction into two or more lines. To do so, end the line with a space followed by an underscore character; then, press Enter, and continue the instruction on the following line. The code below, for example, is a single statement split over four lines.

```
MsgBox "Can't find " & UCase(SHORTCUTMENUFILE) _
  & vbCrLf & vbCrLf & "The file should be located in  _
  " & ThisWorkbook.Path & vbCrLf & vbCrLf & _
  "You may need to reinstall BudgetMan", vbCritical, APPNAME
```

Notice that I indented the last three lines of this statement. Doing so is optional, but it helps clarify the fact that these four lines are, in fact, a single statement.

Like Excel, the VBE has multiple levels of Undo and Redo. Therefore, if you find that you deleted an instruction that you shouldn't have, you can click the Undo button (or press Ctrl+Z) repeatedly until the instruction comes back. After undoing, you can press F4 to redo changes that were previously undone. This feature can be a lifesaver, so I recommend that you play around with it until you understand how it works.

Try this: Insert a VBA module into a project, and then enter the following statements into the code window of the module:

```
Sub SayHello()
    Msg = "Is your name " & Application.UserName & "?"
    Ans = MsgBox(Msg, vbYesNo)
    If Ans = vbNo Then
        MsgBox "Oh, never mind."
    Else
        MsgBox "I must be clairvoyant!"
    End If
End Sub
```

Figure 7-6 shows how this looks in a VBA module.

As you enter the code, you might notice that the VBE makes some adjustments to the text you enter. For example, if you omit the space before or after an equal sign (=), the VB Editor inserts the space for you. In addition, the color of some of the text is changed. This is all perfectly normal, and you'll appreciate it later.

To execute the SayHello procedure, make sure that the cursor is located anywhere within the text you typed. Then, do any of the following:

- ✦ Press F5.
- ✦ Select Run➪Run Sub/UserForm.
- ✦ Click the Run Sub/UserForm button on the Standard toolbar.

If you entered the code correctly, the procedure will execute, and you can respond to a simple dialog box (see Figure 7-7). Notice that Excel is activated when the macro executes. At this point, it's not important that you understand how the code works; that becomes clear later in this chapter and in subsequent chapters.

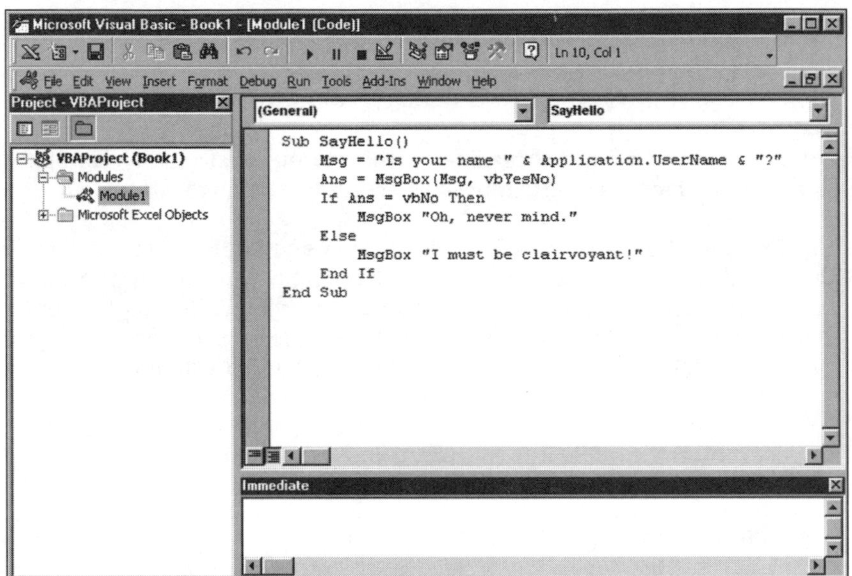

Figure 7-6: Your first VBA procedure.

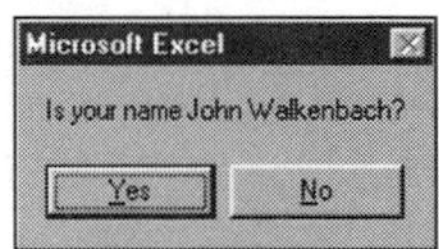

Figure 7-7: The result of running the procedure in Figure 7-6.

Most of the time, you'll be executing your macros from Excel. Often, however, it's more efficient to test your macro by running it directly from the VB Editor.

What you did was write a VBA procedure (also known as a *macro*). When you issued the command to execute the macro, the VB Editor quickly compiled the code and executed it. In other words, each instruction was evaluated, and Excel simply did what it was told to do. You can execute this macro any number of times, although it tends to lose its appeal after a while.

For the record, this simple procedure uses the following concepts (all of which are covered later):

- Declaring a procedure (the first line)
- Assigning a value to variables (`Msg` and `Ans`)
- Concatenating strings (using the `&` operator)
- Using a built-in VBA function (`MsgBox`)
- Using built-in VBA constants (`vbYesNo` and `vbNo`)
- Using an `If-Then-Else` construct
- Ending a procedure (the last line)

Not bad for a first effort, eh?

Using the macro recorder

Another way to get code into a VBA module is to record your actions using Excel's macro recorder.

No matter how hard you try, there is absolutely no way to record the `SayHello` procedure shown previously. As you'll see, recording macros is very useful, but it has its limitations. In fact, when you record a macro you almost always need to make some adjustments or enter some code manually.

The next example shows how to record a macro that simply changes the page setup to Landscape orientation. If you want to try this, start with a blank workbook, and follow these steps:

1. Activate a worksheet in the workbook (any worksheet will do).
2. Select the Tools ➪ Macro ➪ Record New Macro command.

   Excel displays its Record Macro dialog box.
3. Click OK to accept the defaults.

   Excel automatically inserts a new VBA module into the project. From this point on, Excel converts your actions into VBA code. While recording, Excel displays the word *Recording* in the status bar and also displays a miniature floating toolbar that contains two toolbar buttons (Stop Recording and Relative Reference).
4. Select the File ➪ Page Setup command.

   Excel displays its Page Setup dialog box.
5. Select the Landscape option, and click OK to close the dialog box.

6. Click the Stop Recording button on the miniature toolbar (or select Tools ➪ Macro ➪ Stop Recording).

   Excel stops recording your actions.

To take a look at the macro, activate the VB Editor (Alt+F11 is the easiest way), and locate the project in the Project Explorer window. Click the Modules node to expand it. Then click the Module1 item to display the code window (if the project already had a Module1, the new macro will be in Module2). The code generated by this single command is shown in Listing 7-1.

Listing 7-1: Macro for changing page setup to landscape orientation

```
Sub Macro1()
    With ActiveSheet.PageSetup
        .PrintTitleRows = ""
        .PrintTitleColumns = ""
    End With
    ActiveSheet.PageSetup.PrintArea = ""
    With ActiveSheet.PageSetup
        .LeftHeader = ""
        .CenterHeader = "&A"
        .RightHeader = ""
        .LeftFooter = ""
        .CenterFooter = "Page &P"
        .RightFooter = ""
        .LeftMargin = Application.InchesToPoints(0.75)
        .RightMargin = Application.InchesToPoints(0.75)
        .TopMargin = Application.InchesToPoints(1)
        .BottomMargin = Application.InchesToPoints(1)
        .HeaderMargin = Application.InchesToPoints(0.5)
        .FooterMargin = Application.InchesToPoints(0.5)
        .PrintHeadings = False
        .PrintGridlines = True
        .PrintNotes = False
        .CenterHorizontally = False
        .CenterVertically = False
        .Orientation = xlLandscape
        .Draft = False
        .PaperSize = xlPaperLetter
        .FirstPageNumber = xlAutomatic
        .Order = xlDownThenOver
        .BlackAndWhite = False
        .Zoom = 100
    End With
End Sub
```

You may be surprised by the amount of code generated by this single command (I know I was the first time I tried something like this). Although you changed only one simple setting in the Page Setup dialog box, Excel generated code that reproduced *all* the settings in the dialog box.

This brings up an important concept. Often, the code produced when you record a macro is overkill. If you want your macro only to switch to landscape mode, you can simplify this macro considerably by deleting the extraneous code. This makes the macro easier to read, and the macro also runs faster because it doesn't do things that are not necessary. In fact, this macro can be simplified to

```
Sub Macro1()
    With ActiveSheet.PageSetup
        .Orientation = xlLandscape
    End With
End Sub
```

I deleted all the code except for the line that sets the `Orientation` property. Actually, this macro can be simplified even more because the `With-End With` construct isn't needed to change only one property:

```
Sub Macro1()
    ActiveSheet.PageSetup.Orientation = xlLandscape
End Sub
```

In this example, the macro changes the `Orientation` property of the `PageSetup` object on the active sheet. By the way, `xlLandscape` is a built-in constant that's provided to make things easier for you. Variable `xlLandscape` has a value of 2, and `xlPortrait` has a value of 1. Most would agree that it's easier to remember the name of the constant than the arbitrary numbers. You can use the online help to learn the relevant constants for a particular command.

You could have entered this procedure directly into a VBA module. To do so, you would have to know which objects, properties, and methods to use. Obviously, it's much faster to record the macro, and this example has a built-in bonus: You also learned that the `PageSetup` object has an `Orientation` property.

A point I make clear throughout this book is that recording your actions is perhaps the *best* way to learn VBA. When in doubt, try recording. Although the result may not be exactly what you want, chances are that it will steer you in the right direction. You can use the online help to check out the objects, properties, and methods that appear in the recorded code.

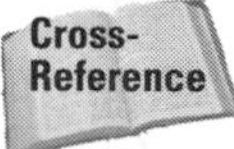

I discuss the macro recorder in more detail later in this chapter.

Copying VBA code

So far, I've covered entering code directly and recording your actions to generate VBA code. The final way to get code into a VBA module is to copy it from another module. For example, you may have written a procedure for one project that would also be useful in your current project. Rather than reenter the code, you can simply open the workbook, activate the module, and use the normal Clipboard copy-and-paste procedures to copy it into your current VBA module. After you've finished pasting, you can modify the code as necessary.

As I noted previously in this chapter, you can also import an entire module that has been exported to a file.

Customizing the VBE Environment

If you're serious about becoming an Excel programmer, you'll be spending a lot of time with the VB Editor window on your screen. To help you make things as comfortable as possible, the VB Editor provides quite a few customization options.

When the VB Editor is active, choose Tools ➪ Options. You'll see a dialog box with four tabs: Editor, Editor Format, General, and Docking. I discuss some of the most useful options on these tabs in the sections that follow.

Using the Editor tab

Figure 7-8 shows the options you access by clicking the Editor tab of the Options dialog box.

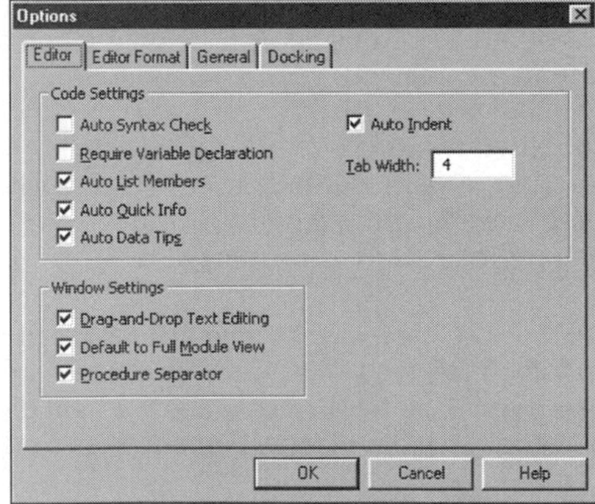

Figure 7-8: The Editor tab of the Options dialog box.

Auto Syntax Check option

The Auto Syntax Check setting determines whether the VB Editor pops up a dialog box if it discovers a syntax error while you're entering your VBA code. The dialog box tells you roughly what the problem is. If you don't choose this setting, the VB Editor flags syntax errors by displaying them in a different color from the rest of the code, and you don't have to deal with any dialog boxes popping up on your screen.

I usually keep this setting turned off because I find the dialog boxes annoying and I can usually figure out what's wrong with an instruction. But if you're new to VBA, you might find this assistance helpful.

Require Variable Declaration option

If the Require Variable Declaration option is set, VB Editor inserts the following statement at the beginning of each new VBA module you insert:

```
Option Explicit
```

If this statement appears in your module, you must explicitly define each variable that you use. This is an excellent habit to get into. If you don't declare your variables, they will all be of the variant data type, which is flexible but not efficient in terms of storage or speed. I'll discuss this in more depth later.

Changing the Require Variable Declaration option affects only new modules, not existing modules.

Auto List Members option

If the Auto List Members option is set, the VB Editor provides some help when you're entering your VBA code by displaying a list of member items for an object. These items include methods and properties for the object you typed.

This option is very helpful, and I always keep it turned on. Figure 7-9 shows an example of Auto List Members (which will make a lot more sense when you actually start writing VBA code).

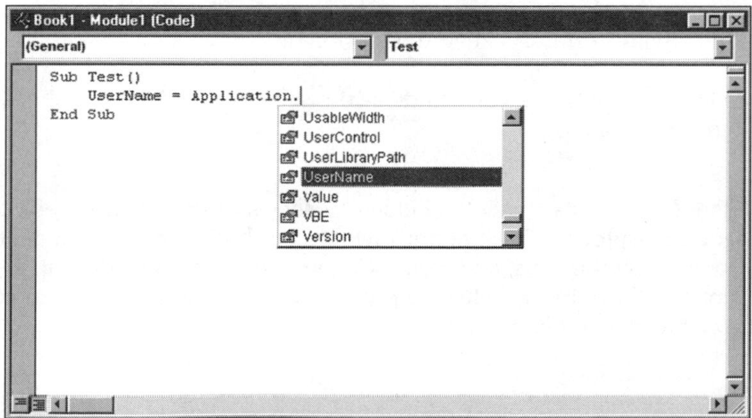

Figure 7-9: An example of Auto List Members

Auto Quick Info option

If the Auto Quick Info option is set, the VB Editor displays information about functions and their arguments as you type. This can be very helpful, and I always leave this setting on. Figure 7-10 shows this feature in action.

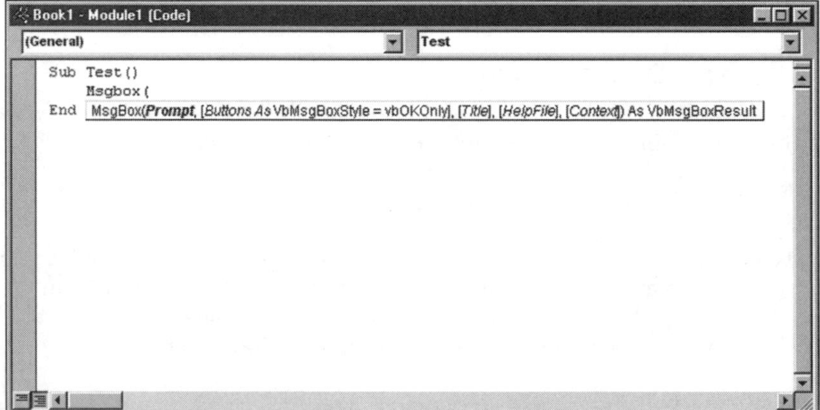

Figure 7-10: An example of Auto Quick Info offering help about the MsgBox function.

Auto Data Tips option

If the Auto Data Tips option is set, the VB Editor displays the value of the variable over which your cursor is placed when you're debugging code. When you enter the wonderful world of debugging, you'll definitely appreciate this option.

Auto Indent option

The Auto Indent setting determines whether the VB Editor automatically indents each new line of code by the same amount as the previous line. I'm a big fan of using indentations in my code, so I keep this option on.

Tip

Use the Tab key, not the space bar, to indent your code. You can also use Shift+Tab to "unindent" a line of code.

Tip

The VB Editor's Edit toolbar (which is hidden by default) contains two useful buttons: Indent and Outdent. These buttons let you quickly indent or "unindent" a block of code. Select the code, and then click one of these buttons to change the indenting of the block. These buttons are very useful, so you may want to copy them to your Standard toolbar.

Drag-and-Drop Text Editing option

When enabled, the Drag-and-Drop Text Editing option lets you copy and move text by dragging and dropping. I keep this option turned on, but I almost always use keyboard shortcuts for copying and pasting.

Default to Full Module View option

The Default to Full Module View option sets the default state for new modules (it doesn't affect existing modules). If set, procedures in the code window appear as a single scrollable window. When this option is turned off, you can see only one procedure at a time. I keep this setting turned on.

Procedure Separator option

When the Procedure Separator option is turned on, it displays separator bars at the end of each procedure in a code window. I like the visual cues of knowing where my procedures end, so I keep this option turned on.

Using the Editor Format tab

Figure 7-11 shows the Editor Format tab of the Options dialog box.

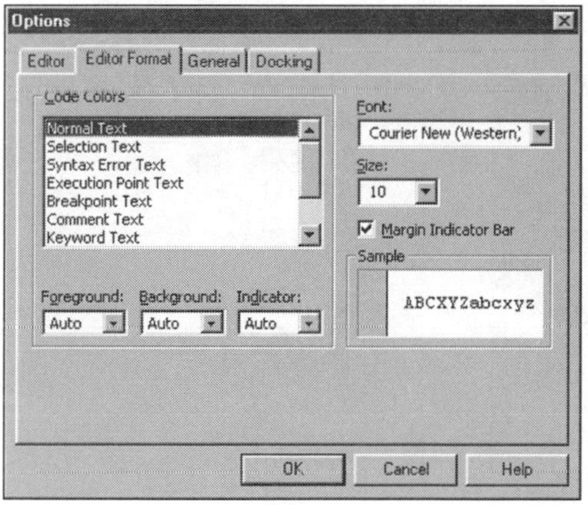

Figure 7-11: The Editor Format tab of the Options dialog box.

Code Colors option

The Code Colors option lets you set the text color (foreground and background) and indicator color displayed for various elements of VBA code. This is largely a matter of individual preference. Personally, I find the default colors to be just fine. But for a change of scenery, I occasionally play around with these settings.

Font option

The Font option lets you select the font that's used in your VBA modules. For best results, stick with a fixed-width font such as Courier New. In a fixed-width font, all characters are exactly the same width. This makes your code much more readable because the characters are nicely aligned vertically and you can easily distinguish multiple spaces.

Size setting

The Size setting specifies the size of the font in the VBA modules. This setting is a matter of personal preference determined by your video display resolution and your eyesight. The default size of 10 points works for me.

Margin Indicator Bar option

This option controls the display of the vertical margin indicator bar in your modules. You should keep this turned on; otherwise, you won't be able to see the helpful graphical indicators when you're debugging your code.

Using the General tab

Figure 7-12 shows the options available under the General tab in the Options dialog box. In almost every case, the default settings are just fine.

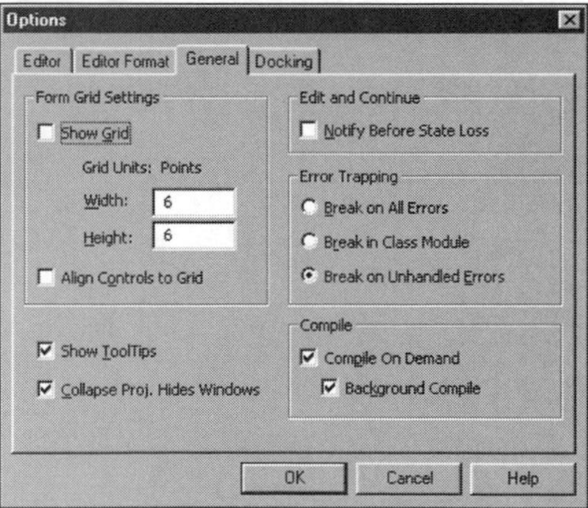

Figure 7-12: The General tab of the Options dialog box.

The Error Trapping setting determines what happens when an error is encountered. If you write any error-handling code, make sure that the Break on Unhandled Errors option is set. If the Break on All Errors option is set, error-handling code is ignored (which is hardly ever what you want). I discuss error-handling techniques in Chapter 9.

Using the Docking tab

Figure 7-13 shows the Docking tab of the Options dialog box. These options determine how the various windows in the VBE behave. When a window is docked, it is fixed in place along one of the edges of the VBE window. This makes it much easier to identify and locate a particular window. If you turn off all docking, you'll have a big mess of windows that is very confusing. Generally, you'll find that the default settings work fine.

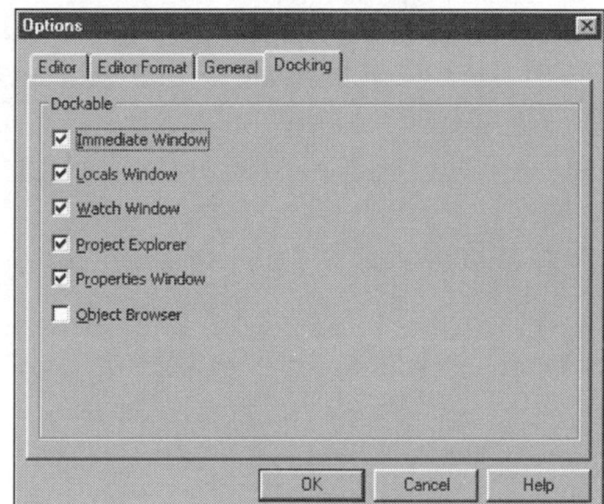

Figure 7-13: The Docking tab of the Options dialog box.

The Macro Recorder

Earlier in this chapter, I discussed the macro recorder, a tool that converts your Excel actions into VBA code. This section covers the macro recorder in more detail.

Excel's Visual Basic toolbar has several useful buttons for you. On this toolbar, you'll find the Run Macro, Record Macro, Stop Macro, and Visual Basic Editor buttons useful.

The macro recorder is an *extremely* useful tool, but it's important to remember the following points:

- ✦ The macro recorder is appropriate only for simple macros or for recording a small part of a more complex macro.
- ✦ The macro recorder cannot generate code that performs looping (that is, repeating statements), assigns variables, executes statements conditionally, displays dialog boxes, and so on.
- ✦ The code that is generated depends on certain settings that you specify.
- ✦ You'll often want to clean up the recorded code to remove extraneous commands.

What is recorded

As you know, Excel's macro recorder translates your mouse and keyboard actions into VBA code. I could probably write several pages describing how this is done, but the best way to show you is by example. Follow these steps:

1. Start with a blank workbook.
2. Make sure Excel's window is not maximized.
3. Press Alt+F11 to activate the VB Editor window, and make sure *this* window is not maximized.
4. Arrange Excel's window and the VBE window so both are visible. (For best results, minimize any other applications that are running.)
5. Activate Excel, Choose Tools ➪ Macro ➪ Record New Macro, and click OK to start the macro recorder.

   Excel inserts a new module (named Module1) and starts recording on that sheet.
6. Activate the VB Editor window.
7. In the Project Explorer window, double-click Module1 to display that module in the code window.

Your screen should look like the example in Figure 7-14.

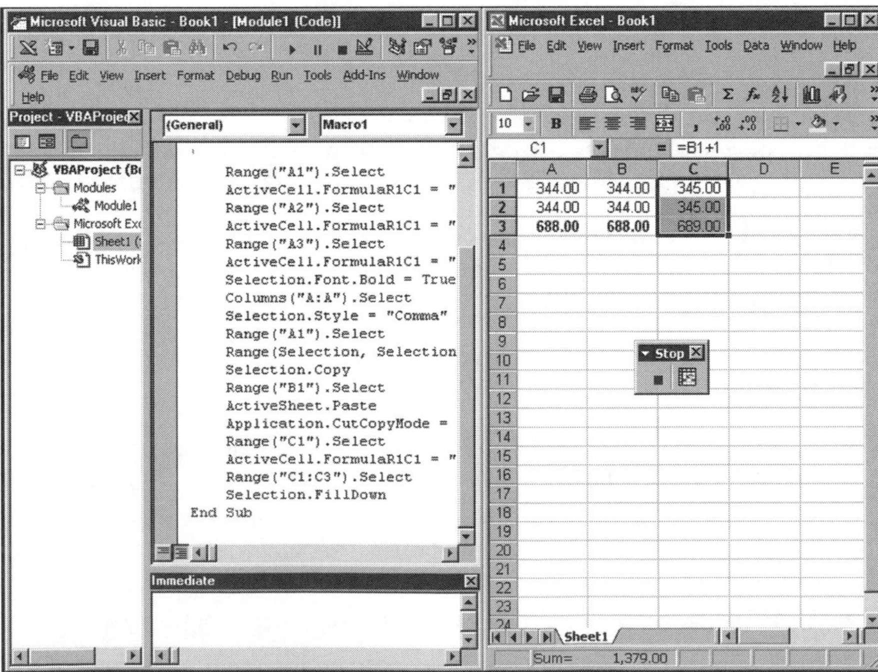

Figure 7-14: A convenient window arrangement for watching the macro recorder do its thing.

Now, move around in the worksheet, and select various Excel commands. Watch as the code is generated in the window that displays the VBA module. Select cells, enter data, format cells, use the menus and toolbars, create a chart, manipulate graphic objects, and so on. I guarantee that you'll be enlightened as you watch the code being spit out before your very eyes.

Relative or absolute?

When recording your actions, Excel normally records absolute references to cells. For example, perform these steps, and examine the code:

1. Activate a worksheet, and start the macro recorder.
2. Activate cell B1.
3. Enter **Jan** into cell B1.
4. Move to cell C1, and enter **Feb**.
5. Continue this process until you've entered the first six months of the year in B1:G1.
6. Click cell B1 to activate it again.
7. Stop the macro recorder.

Excel generates the following code:

```
Sub Macro1()
    Range("B1").Select
    ActiveCell.FormulaR1C1 = "Jan"
    Range("C1").Select
    ActiveCell.FormulaR1C1 = "Feb"
    Range("D1").Select
    ActiveCell.FormulaR1C1 = "Mar"
    Range("E1").Select
    ActiveCell.FormulaR1C1 = "Apr"
    Range("F1").Select
    ActiveCell.FormulaR1C1 = "May"
    Range("G1").Select
    ActiveCell.FormulaR1C1 = "Jun"
    Range("B1").Select
End Sub
```

To execute this macro, choose the Tools ➪ Macro ➪ Macros command (or press Alt+F8), select Macro1 (or whatever the macro is named), and click the Run button.

When executed, the macro re-creates the actions you performed when you recorded it. These same actions occur regardless of which cell is active when you execute the macro. Recording a macro using absolute references always produces the exact same results.

In some cases, however, you'll want your recorded macro to work with cell locations in a *relative* manner. For example, you'd probably want such a macro to start entering the month names in the active cell. In such a case, you'll want to use relative recording to record the macro.

The Stop Recording toolbar, which consists of only two buttons, is displayed when you are recording a macro. You can change the manner in which Excel records your actions by clicking the Relative Reference button on the Stop Recording toolbar. This button is a toggle. When the button appears in a pressed state, the recording mode is relative. When the button appears normally, you are recording in absolute mode. You can change the recording method at any time, even in the middle of recording.

To see how this works, erase the cells in B1:D1, and then perform the following steps:

1. Activate cell B1.
2. Choose Tools ⇨ Macro ⇨ Record New Macro.
3. Name this macro Relative.
4. Click OK to begin recording.
5. Click the Relative Reference button (on the Stop Recording toolbar) to change the recording mode to relative.

   When you click this button, it appears pressed.
6. Enter the first six month names in B1:G1, as in the previous example.
7. Select cell B1.
8. Stop the macro recorder.

With the recording mode set to relative, the code that Excel generates is quite different:

```
Sub Macro2()
    ActiveCell.FormulaR1C1 = "Jan"
    ActiveCell.Offset(0, 1).Range("A1").Select
    ActiveCell.FormulaR1C1 = "Feb"
    ActiveCell.Offset(0, 1).Range("A1").Select
    ActiveCell.FormulaR1C1 = "Mar"
    ActiveCell.Offset(0, 1).Range("A1").Select
    ActiveCell.FormulaR1C1 = "Apr"
    ActiveCell.Offset(0, 1).Range("A1").Select
    ActiveCell.FormulaR1C1 = "May"
    ActiveCell.Offset(0, 1).Range("A1").Select
    ActiveCell.FormulaR1C1 = "Jun"
    ActiveCell.Offset(0, -5).Range("A1").Select
End Sub
```

You can execute this macro by activating a worksheet and then choosing the Tools ➪ Macro command. Select the macro's name, and click the Run button.

You'll also notice that I varied the procedure slightly in this example: I activated the beginning cell *before* I started recording. This is an important step when you record macros that use the active cell as a base.

Although it may look strange, this macro is actually quite simple. The first statement simply enters *Jan* into the active cell. (It uses the active cell because it's not preceded by a statement that selects a cell.) The next statement uses the `Offset` method to move the selection one cell to the right. The next statement inserts more text, and so on. Finally, the original cell is selected by calculating a relative offset rather than an absolute cell. Unlike the preceding macro, this one always starts entering text in the active cell.

Note You'll notice that this macro generates code that references cell A1—which may seem strange because cell A1 was not even involved in the macro. This is simply a by-product of the way the macro recorder works. (I discuss the `Offset` method later in this chapter.) At this point, all you need to know is that the macro works as it should.

By the way, the code generated by Excel is much more complex than it need be, and it's not the most efficient way to code the operation. The macro that follows, which I entered manually, is a simpler and faster way to perform the same operation. This example demonstrates that VBA doesn't have to select a cell before it puts information into it—an important concept that can also speed things up considerably.

```
Sub Macro3()
    ActiveCell.Offset(0, 0) = "Jan"
    ActiveCell.Offset(0, 1) = "Feb"
    ActiveCell.Offset(0, 2) = "Mar"
    ActiveCell.Offset(0, 3) = "Apr"
    ActiveCell.Offset(0, 4) = "May"
    ActiveCell.Offset(0, 5) = "Jun"
End Sub
```

In fact, this macro can be made even more efficient by using the `With-End With` construct:

```
Sub Macro4()
    With ActiveCell
        .Offset(0, 0) = "Jan"
        .Offset(0, 1) = "Feb"
        .Offset(0, 2) = "Mar"
        .Offset(0, 3) = "Apr"
        .Offset(0, 4) = "May"
        .Offset(0, 5) = "Jun"
    End With
End Sub
```

The point here is that the recorder has two distinct modes, and you need to be aware of which mode you're recording in. Otherwise, the result will not be what you expected.

Recording options

When you record your actions to create VBA code, you have several options. Recall that the Tools ➪ Macro ➪ Record New Macro command displays the Record Macro dialog box before recording begins. This dialog box gives you quite a bit of control over your macro. The following paragraphs describe your options.

Macro name

You can enter a name for the procedure that you are recording. By default, Excel uses the names Macro1, Macro2, and so on for each macro you record. I usually just accept the default name and change the name of the procedure later. You, however, may prefer to name the macro up front — the choice is yours.

Shortcut key

The Shortcut key option lets you execute the macro by pressing a shortcut key combination. For example, if you enter **w** (lowercase), you can execute the macro by pressing Ctrl+W. If you enter **W** (uppercase), the macro comes alive when you press Ctrl+Shift+W.

You can add or change a shortcut key at any time, so you don't need to set this option while recording a macro.

Store macro in

The Store macro in option tells Excel where to store the macro that it records. By default, Excel puts the recorded macro in a module in the active workbook. If you prefer, you can record it in a new workbook (Excel opens a blank workbook) or in your Personal Macro Workbook.

Description

By default, Excel inserts five lines of comments (three of them blank) that list the macro name, the user's name, and the date. You can put anything you like here, or nothing at all. As far as I'm concerned, typing anything in is a waste of time because I always end up deleting this in the module.

In versions of Excel prior to Excel 97, the Record Macro dialog box provided an option that let you assign the macro to a new menu item on the Tools menu. For some reason, this option was removed from Excel 97 and later versions. If you want to be able to execute a macro from a menu, you need to set this up yourself. See Chapter 22 for more information.

The Personal Macro Workbook

If you create some VBA macros that you find particularly useful, you may want to store these routines on your Personal Macro Workbook. This is a workbook (Personal.xls) that is stored in your XlStart directory. Whenever you start Excel, this workbook is loaded. It's a hidden workbook, so it's out of your way. When you record a macro, one of your options is to record it to your Personal Macro Workbook. The Personal.xls file doesn't exist until you record a macro to it.

Cleaning up recorded macros

Earlier in this section, you saw how recording your actions while you issued a single command (the File ⇨ Page Setup command) can produce an enormous amount of VBA code. In many cases, the recorded code includes extraneous commands that you can delete.

It's also important to understand that the macro recorder doesn't always generate the most efficient code. If you examine the generated code, you'll see that Excel generally records what is selected (that is, an object) and then uses the `Selection` object in subsequent statements. For example, here's what is recorded if you select a range of cells and then use the buttons on the Formatting toolbar to change the numeric formatting and apply bold and italic:

```
Range("A1:C5").Select
Selection.NumberFormat = "#,##0.00"
Selection.Font.Bold = True
Selection.Font.Italic = True
```

If you use the Formatting dialog box to record this macro, you'll find that Excel records quite a bit of extraneous code. Recording toolbar button clicks often produces more efficient code.

The preceding example is just *one* way to perform these actions. You can also use the more efficient `With-End With` construct, as follows:

```
Range("A1:C5").Select
With Selection
    .NumberFormat = "#,##0.00"
    .Font.Bold = True
    .Font.Italic = True
End With
```

Or you can avoid the `Select` method altogether and write the code even more efficiently, like this:

```
With Range("A1:C5")
    .NumberFormat = "#,##0.00"
```

```
    .Font.Bold = True
    .Font.Italic = True
End With
```

If speed is essential in your application, you'll always want to examine any recorded VBA code closely to make sure that it's as efficient as possible.

You will, of course, need to understand VBA thoroughly before you start cleaning up your recorded macros. But for now, just be aware that recorded VBA code isn't always the best, most efficient code.

About the Code Examples

Throughout this book, I present many small snippets of VBA code to make a point or to provide an example. Often, this code may consist of just a single statement. In some cases, the example consists of only an *expression,* which isn't a valid instruction by itself.

For example, the following is an expression:

```
Range("A1").Value
```

To test an expression, you must evaluate it. The `MsgBox` function is a handy tool for this:

```
MsgBox Range("A1").Value
```

To try out these examples, you need to put the statement within a procedure in a VBA module, like this:

```
Sub Test()
' statement goes here
End Sub
```

Then put the cursor anywhere within the procedure, and press F5 to execute it. Make sure that the code is being executed within the proper context. For example, if a statement refers to Sheet1, make sure that the active workbook actually has a sheet named Sheet1.

If the code is just a single statement, you can use the VB Editor's Immediate window. The Immediate window is very useful for executing a statement "immediately"—without having to create a procedure. If the Immediate window is not displayed, press Ctrl+G in the VB Editor.

Just type the VBA statement, and press Enter. To evaluate an expression in the Immediate window, precede the expression with a question mark (?). The question mark is a shortcut for `Print`. For example, you can type the following into the Immediate window:

```
? Range("A1").Value
```

The result of this expression is displayed in the next line of the Immediate window.

About Objects and Collections

If you've worked through the first part of this chapter, you have an overview of VBA, and you know the basics of working with VBA modules in the VBE. You've also seen some VBA code and were exposed to concepts such as objects and properties. This section gives you some additional details about objects and collections of objects.

As you work with VBA, you must understand the concept of objects and Excel's object model. It helps to think of objects in terms of a *hierarchy.* At the top of this model is the `Application` object — in this case, Excel itself. But if you're programming in VBA using Microsoft Word, the `Application` object is Word.

The object hierarchy

The `Application` object contains other objects. For example, Excel 2000 (the `Application` object we're interested in) contains 47 objects (many of which are collections). Here are a few examples of objects contained in the `Application` object:

`Workbooks` (a collection of all `Workbook` objects)

`Windows` (a collection of all `Window` objects)

`AddIns` (a collection of all `AddIn` objects)

`AutoCorrect`

Each of these objects can contain other objects. For example, the `Workbooks` collection consists of all open `Workbook` objects, and a `Workbook` object contains other objects, a few of which are listed below:

`Worksheets` (a collection of `Worksheet` objects)

`Charts` (a collection of `Chart` objects)

`Names` (a collection of `Name` objects)

Each of these objects, in turn, can contain other objects. The `Worksheets` collection consists of all `Worksheet` objects in a `Workbook`. A `Worksheet` object contains many other objects, which include the following:

`ChartObjects` (a collection of `ChartObject` objects)

`Range`

`PageSetup`

`PivotTables` (a collection of `PivotTable` objects)

If this seems confusing, trust me, it *will* make sense, and you'll eventually realize that this whole object hierarchy thing is quite logical and well structured. By the way, the complete Excel object model is diagrammed in the online help system.

About collections

Another key concept in VBA programming is *collections.* A collection is a group of objects of the same class (and a collection is itself an object). As I noted above, `Workbooks` is a collection of all `Workbook` objects currently open. `Worksheets` is a collection of all `Worksheet` objects contained in a particular `Workbook` object. You can work with an entire collection of objects or with an individual object in a collection. To reference a single object from a collection, you put the object's name or index number in parentheses after the name of the collection, like this:

```
Worksheets("Sheet1")
```

If Sheet1 is the first worksheet in the collection, you may also use the following reference:

```
Worksheets(1)
```

You refer to the second worksheet in a `Workbook` as `Worksheets(2)`, and so on.

There is also a collection called `Sheets`, which is made up of all sheets in a workbook, whether they're worksheets or chart sheets. If Sheet1 is the first sheet in the workbook, you can reference it as follows:

```
Sheets(1)
```

Object referral

When you refer to an object using VBA, you often must qualify the object by connecting object names with a period (also known as a "dot operator"). What if you had two workbooks open and they both had a worksheet named Sheet1? The solution is to qualify the reference by adding the object's *container,* like this:

```
Workbooks("Book1").Worksheets("Sheet1")
```

To refer to a specific range (such as cell A1) on a worksheet named Sheet1 in a workbook named Book1, you can use the following expression:

```
Workbooks("Book1").Worksheets("Sheet1").Range("A1")
```

The fully qualified reference for the preceding example also includes the `Application` object, as follows:

```
Application.Workbooks("Book1").Worksheets("Sheet1"). _
 Range("A1")
```

Most of the time, however, you can omit the Application object in your references (it is assumed). If the Book1 object is the active workbook, you can even omit that object reference and use this:

```
Worksheets("Sheet1").Range("A1")
```

And — I think you know where I'm going with this — if Sheet1 is the active worksheet, you can use an even simpler expression:

```
Range("A1")
```

Contrary to what you might expect, Excel does not have an object that refers to an individual cell that is called "Cell." A single cell is simply a Range object that happens to consist of just one element.

Simply referring to objects (as in these examples) doesn't do anything. To perform anything meaningful, you must read or modify an object's properties or specify a method to be used with an object.

Properties and Methods

It's easy to be overwhelmed with properties and methods; there are literally thousands available. In this section I describe how to access properties and methods of objects.

Object properties

Every object has properties. For example, a Range object has a property called Value. You can write VBA code to display the Value property or write VBA code to set the Value property to a specific value. Here's a procedure that uses VBA's MsgBox function to pop up a box that displays the value in cell A1 on Sheet1 of the active workbook:

```
Sub ShowValue()
    Answer = Worksheets("Sheet1").Range("A1").Value
    MsgBox Answer
End Sub
```

MsgBox is a useful keyword that you'll often use to display results while your VBA code is executing. I use it extensively throughout this book.

The code in the preceding example displays the current setting of the `Value` property of a specific cell: cell A1 on a worksheet named Sheet1 in the active workbook. Note that if the active workbook does not have a sheet named Sheet1, the macro will generate an error.

Now, what if you want to change the `Value` property? The following procedure changes the value displayed in cell A1 by changing the cell's `Value` property:

```
Sub ChangeValue()
    Worksheets("Sheet1").Range("A1").Value = 123
End Sub
```

After executing this routine, cell A1 on Sheet1 has the value 123. You might want to enter these procedures into a module and experiment with them.

Every object has a default property. For a `Range` object, the default property is the `Value` property. Therefore, you can omit the `.Value` part from the preceding code, and it will have the same effect. It's usually considered good programming practice, however, to include the property, even if it's the default property.

Object methods

In addition to properties, objects also have methods. A *method* is an action that you perform with an object. Here's a simple example that uses the `Clear` method on a `Range` object. After you execute this procedure, A1:C3 on Sheet1 will be empty.

```
Sub ZapRange()
    Worksheets("Sheet1").Range("A1:C3").Clear
End Sub
```

Most methods also take arguments to define the action further. Arguments for a method are placed in parentheses. Here's an example that copies cell A1 to cell B1 by using the `Copy` method of the `Range` object. In this example, the `Copy` method has one argument (the destination of the copy). Notice that I used the line continuation character sequence (a space followed by an underscore) in this example. You can omit the line continuation sequence and type the statement on a single line.

```
Sub CopyOne()
    Worksheets("Sheet1").Range("A1").Copy _
       Worksheets("Sheet1").Range("B1")
End Sub
```

Specifying Arguments for Methods and Properties

An issue that often leads to confusion among VBA programmers concerns arguments for methods and properties. Some methods use arguments to further clarify the action to be taken, and some properties use arguments to further specify the property value. In some cases, one or more of the arguments are optional.

If a method uses arguments, place the arguments after the name of the method, separated by commas. If the method uses optional arguments, you can insert blank *placeholders* for the optional arguments. Consider the `Protect` method for a `Workbook` object. Check the online help, and you'll find that the `Protect` method takes three arguments: password, structure, windows. These arguments correspond to the options in the Protect Workbook dialog box.

If you want to protect a workbook named MyBook.xls, for example, you might use a statement like this:

```
Workbooks("MyBook.xls").Protect "xyzzy", True, True
```

If you don't want to assign a password, you can use a statement like this:

```
Workbooks("MyBook.xls").Protect , True, True
```

Notice that the first argument is omitted and that I specified the placeholder with a comma.

Another approach, which makes your code more readable, is to use named arguments. Here's an example of how you use named arguments for the preceding example:

```
Workbooks("MyBook.xls").Protect Structure:=True, Windows:=True
```

Using named arguments is a good idea, especially for methods that have lots of optional arguments and also when you need to use only a few of them.

For properties that use arguments, you must place the arguments in parentheses. For example, the `Address` property of a `Range` object takes five arguments, all of which are optional. The following statement is not valid because the parentheses are omitted:

```
MsgBox Range("A1").Address False   ' invalid
```

The proper syntax for such a statement requires parentheses, as follows:

```
MsgBox Range("A1").Address(False)
```

The statement could also be written using a named argument:

```
MsgBox Range("A1").Address(rowAbsolute:=False)
```

These nuances will become clearer as you gain more experience with VBA.

The Comment Object: A Case Study

To help you better understand the properties and methods available for an object, I focus on a particular object: the `Comment` object. You create a `Comment` object when you use Excel's Insert ➪ Comment command to enter a cell comment. In the sections that follow, you'll get a feel for working with objects. If you're a bit overwhelmed by the material in this section, don't fret. These concepts will become much clearer over time.

Online help for the Comment object

One way to learn about a particular object is to look it up in the online help system. Figure 7-15 shows the main help screen for the `Comment` object.

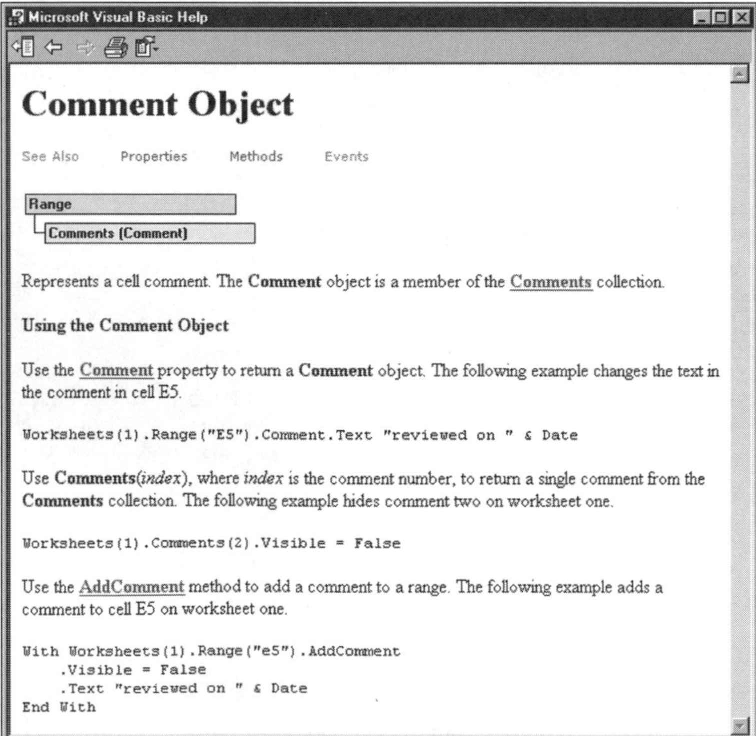

Figure 7-15: The main help screen for the Comment object.

Notice that the underlined words are "jumps" that display additional information. For example, you can click Properties to get a list of all properties for the `Comment` object. Or, click Method to get a list of the object's methods.

Using the Online Help System

The easiest way to get specific help about a particular object, property, or method is to type the word in a code window and press F1. If there is any ambiguity about the word you typed, you'll get a dialog box like the one shown in the accompanying figure.

Unfortunately, the items listed in the dialog box are not always clear, so it may require some trial and error to locate the correct help topic. The dialog box in the figure appears when you type **Comment** and then press F1. In this case, although `Comment` is an object, it may behave like a property. Clicking the first item displays the help topic for the `Comment` object; clicking the second item displays the help topic for the "`Comment` property."

Properties of a Comment object

The `Comment` object has six properties. Table 7-1 contains a list of these properties, along with a brief description of each. If a property is *read-only,* your VBA code can read the property but cannot change it.

Table 7-1
Properties of a Comment Object

Property	*Read-Only*	*Description*
`Application`	Yes	Returns the name of the application that created the comment (that is, Excel).
`Author`	Yes	Returns the name of the person who created the comment.
`Creator`	Yes	Returns a number that specifies the application that created the object. Not used in Excel for Windows (relevant only for Excel for Macintosh).
`Parent`	Yes	Returns the `Parent` object for the comment (it is always a `Range` object).
`Shape`	Yes	Returns a `Shape` object that represents the shape attached to the comment.
`Visible`	No	Is True if the comment is visible.

Methods of a Comment object

Table 7-2 shows the methods that you can use with a `Comment` object. Again, these methods perform common operations that you may have performed manually with a comment at some point — but you probably never thought of these operations as methods.

Table 7-2
Methods of a Comment Object

Method	*Description*
`Delete`	Deletes a comment.
`Next`	Returns a `Comment` object that represents the next comment.
`Previous`	Returns a `Comment` object that represents the previous comment.
`Text`	Sets the text in a comment (takes three arguments).

You may be surprised to see that `Text` is a method rather than a property. This leads to an important point: The distinction between properties and methods isn't always clear-cut, and the object model isn't perfectly consistent. In fact, it's not really important that you distinguish between properties and methods. As long as you get the syntax correct, it doesn't matter if a word in your code is a property or a method.

The Comments collection

Recall that a collection is a group of like objects. Every worksheet has a `Comments` collection, which consists of all `Comment` objects on the worksheet. If the worksheet has no comments, this collection is empty.

For example, the following code refers to the first comment on Sheet1 of the active workbook:

```
Worksheets("Sheet1").Comments(1)
```

The following statement displays the text contained in the first comment on Sheet1:

```
MsgBox Worksheets("Sheet1").Comments(1).Text
```

Unlike most objects, a `Comment` object does not have a `Name` property. Therefore, to refer to a specific comment, you must use an index number or use the `Comment` property of a `Range` object to return a specific comment (keep reading, and this will make sense).

The `Comments` collection is also an object and has its own set of properties and methods. For example, the following example shows the total number of comments:

```
MsgBox ActiveSheet.Comments.Count
```

The Comments collection here has a Count property that stores the number of objects in the active worksheet. The next example shows which cell has the first comment:

```
MsgBox ActiveSheet.Comments(1).Parent.Address
```

Here, Comments(1) returns the first Comment object in the Comments collection. The Parent property of the Comment object returns its container, which is a Range object. The message box displays the Address property of the Range. The net effect is that the statement displays the address of the cell that contains the first comment.

You can also loop through all the comments on a sheet by using the For Each-Next construct (this is explained in Chapter 8). Here's an example that displays a separate message box for each comment on the active worksheet:

```
For Each cmt in ActiveSheet.Comments
    MsgBox cmt.Text
Next cmt
```

About the Comment property

In this section I've been discussing the Comment object. If you dig through the online help, you'll find that a Range object has a property named Comment. This property returns an object: a Comment object. For example, the statement below refers to the Comment object in cell A1:

```
Range("A1").Comment
```

If this were the first comment on the sheet, you could refer to the same Comment object as follows:

```
Comments(1)
```

To display the comment in cell A1 in a message box, use a statement like this:

```
MsgBox Range("A1").Comment.Text
```

The fact that a property can return an object is a very important concept—a difficult one to grasp, perhaps, but critical to mastering VBA.

Objects within a Comment object

Working with properties is confusing at first because some properties actually return objects. Suppose that you want to determine the background color of a particular comment on Sheet1. If you look through the list of properties for a Comment object, you won't find anything that relates to color. Rather, you must do this:

1. Use the Comment object's Shape property to return the Shape object that's contained in the comment.
2. Use the Shape object's Fill property to return a FillFormat object.
3. Use the FillFormat object's ForeColor property to return a ColorFormat object.
4. Use the ColorFormat object's RGB property to set the color.

Put another way, getting at the interior color for a Comment object involves accessing other objects contained in the Comment object. Here's a look at the object hierarchy that's involved.

Application (Excel)
  Workbook object
    Worksheet object
      Comment object
        Shape object
          FillFormat object
            ColorFormat object

I'll be the first to admit it: This can get very confusing! But, as an example of the "elegance" of VBA, code to change the color of a comment can be written with a single statement:

```
Worksheets("Sheet1").Comments(1).Shape.Fill.ForeColor.RGB _
  = RGB(0, 255, 0)
```

This type of referencing is certainly not intuitive and can be difficult to get used to. Fortunately, recording your actions in Excel almost always yields some insights regarding the hierarchy of the objects involved. And, if you work with this long enough, it all makes perfect sense. Trust me.

Adding a new Comment object

You may have noticed that the list of methods for the Comment object doesn't include a method to add a new comment. The reason for this is that the AddComment method belongs to the Range object. The following statement adds a comment (an empty comment) to cell A1 on the active worksheet:

```
Range("A1").AddComment
```

If you consult the online help, you'll discover that the AddComment method takes an argument that represents the text for the comment. Therefore, you can add a comment and then add text to the comment with a single statement, like this:

```
Range("A1").AddComment "Formula developed by JW."
```

The AddComment method generates an error if the cell already contains a comment.

If you'd like to see these Comment object properties and methods in action, check out the example workbook on the companion CD-ROM. This workbook contains several examples that manipulate Comment objects with VBA code. You probably won't understand all the code, but you will get a feel for how you can use VBA to manipulate an object.

Some useful Application properties

As you know, when you're working with Excel, only one workbook at a time can be active. And if the sheet is a worksheet, one cell is the active cell (even if a multicell range is selected).

VBA knows this and lets you refer to these active objects in a simplified manner. This is often useful because you won't always know the exact workbook, worksheet, or range that you want to operate on. VBA handles this by providing properties of the Application object. For example, the Application object has an ActiveCell property that returns a reference to the active cell. The following instruction assigns the value 1 to the active cell:

```
ActiveCell.Value = 1
```

Notice that I omitted the reference to the Application object in the preceding example because it is assumed. It's important to understand that this instruction will fail if the active sheet is not a worksheet. For example, if VBA executes this statement when a chart sheet is active, the procedure halts and you'll receive an error message.

If a range is selected in a worksheet, the active cell will be one of the corner cells of the range (which corner is determined by how the range was selected). In other words, the active cell is always a single cell.

The Application object also has a Selection property that returns a reference to whatever is selected, which could be a single cell (the active cell), a range of cells, or an object such as ChartObject, TextBox, or Shape.

Table 7-3 lists the other Application properties that are useful when working with cells and ranges.

Table 7-3
Some Useful Properties of the Application Object

Property	*Object Returned*
`ActiveCell`	The active cell.
`ActiveSheet`	The active sheet (worksheet or chart).
`ActiveWindow`	The active window.
`ActiveWorkbook`	The active workbook.
`RangeSelection`	The selected cells on the worksheet in the specified window, even when a graphic object is selected.
`Selection`	The object selected (it could be a `Range`, `Shape`, `ChartObject`, and so on).
`ThisWorkbook`	The workbook that contains the procedure being executed.

The advantage of using these properties to return an object is that you don't need to know which cell, worksheet, or workbook is active or to provide a specific reference to it. For example, the following instruction clears the contents of the active cell, even though the address of the active cell is not known:

```
ActiveCell.ClearContents
```

The example that follows displays a message that tells you the name of the active sheet:

```
MsgBox ActiveSheet.Name
```

If you want to know the name of the active workbook, use a statement like this:

```
MsgBox ActiveWorkbook.Name
```

If a range on a worksheet is selected, you can fill the entire range with a value by executing a single statement. In the following example, the `Selection` property of the `Application` object returns a `Range` object that corresponds to the selected cells. The instruction simply modifies the `Value` property of this `Range` object, and the result is a range filled with a single value:

```
Selection.Value = 12
```

Note that if something other than a range is selected (such as a `ChartObject` or a `Shape`), the preceding statement will generate an error because `ChartObjects` and `Shape` objects do not have a `Value` property.

The statement below, however, enters a value of 12 into the Range object that was selected before a non-Range object was selected. If you look up the RangeSelection property in the online help, you'll find that this property applies to a Window object only.

```
ActiveWindow.RangeSelection.Value = 12
```

Working with Range Objects

Much of the work you will do in VBA involves cells and ranges in worksheets. After all, that's what spreadsheets are designed to do. The earlier discussion on relative versus absolute macro recording exposed you to working with cells in VBA, but you need to know a lot more.

A Range object is contained in a Worksheet object and consists of a single cell or range of cells on a single worksheet. In the sections that follow, I discuss three ways of referring to Range objects in your VBA code:

✦ The Range property of a Worksheet or Range class object

✦ The Cells property of a Worksheet object

✦ The Offset property of a Range object

The Range property

The Range property returns a Range object. If you consult the online help for the Range property, you'll learn that this property has two syntaxes:

```
object.Range(cell1)
object.Range(cell1, cell2)
```

The Range property applies to two types of objects: a Worksheet object or a Range object. Here, cell1 and cell2 refer to placeholders for terms that Excel will recognize as identifying the range (in the first instance) and *delineating* the range (in the second instance). Following are a few examples of using the Range method.

You've already seen examples like the following one earlier in the chapter. The instruction that follows simply enters a value into the specified cell. In this case, it puts a 1 into cell A1 on Sheet1 of the active workbook.

```
Worksheets("Sheet1").Range("A1").Value = 1
```

The Range property also recognizes defined names in workbooks. Therefore, if a cell is named "Input," you can use the following statement to enter a value into that named cell:

```
Worksheets("Sheet1").Range("Input").Value = 1
```

The example that follows enters the same value into a range of 20 cells on the active sheet. If the active sheet is not a worksheet, this causes an error message.

```
ActiveSheet.Range("A1:B10").Value = 2
```

The next example produces exactly the same result as the preceding example.

```
Range("A1", "B10") = 2
```

The sheet reference is omitted, however, so the active sheet is assumed. The value property is also omitted, so the default property (which is `Value`, for a `Range` object) is assumed. This example also uses the second syntax of the `Range` property. With this syntax, the first argument is the cell at the top left of the range and the second argument is the cell at the lower right of the range.

The following example uses Excel's range intersection operator (a space) to return the intersection of two ranges. In this case, the intersection is a single cell, C6. Therefore, this statement enters 3 into cell C6:

```
Range("C1:C10 A6:E6") = 3
```

And finally, the next example enters the value 4 into five cells, that is, a noncontiguous range. The comma serves as the union operator.

```
Range("A1,A3,A5,A7,A9") = 4
```

So far, all the examples have used the `Range` property on a `Worksheet` object. As I mentioned, you can also use the `Range` property on a `Range` object. This can be rather confusing, but bear with me.

Following is an example of using the `Range` property on a `Range` object (in this case, the `Range` object is the active cell). This example treats the `Range` object as if it were the upper-left cell in the worksheet and then enters a value of 5 into the cell that *would be* B2. In other words, the reference returned is relative to the upper-left corner of the `Range` object. Therefore, the statement that follows enters a value of 5 into the cell directly to the right and one row below the active cell:

```
ActiveCell.Range("B2") = 5
```

I *said* this is confusing. Fortunately, there is a much clearer way to access a cell relative to a range, called the `Offset` property. I'll discuss this property after the next section.

The Cells property

Another way to reference a range is to use the `Cells` property. Like the `Range` property, you can use the `Cells` property on `Worksheet` objects and `Range` objects. Check the online help, and you'll see that the `Cells` property has three syntaxes:

```
object.Cells(rowIndex, columnIndex)
object.Cells(rowIndex)
object.Cells
```

I'll give you some examples that demonstrate how to use the `Cells` property. The first example enters the value 9 into cell 1 on Sheet1. In this case, I'm using the first syntax, which accepts the index number of the row (from 1 to 65536) and the index number of the column (from 1 to 256):

```
Worksheets("Sheet1").Cells(1, 1) = 9
```

Here's an example that enters the value 7 into cell D3 (that is, row 3, column 4) in the active worksheet:

```
ActiveSheet.Cells(3, 4) = 7
```

You can also use the `Cells` property on a `Range` object. When you do so, the `Range` object returned by the `Cells` property is relative to the upper-left cell of the referenced `Range`. Confusing? Probably. An example might help clear this up. The following instruction enters the value 5 into the active cell. Remember, in this case, the active cell is treated as if it were cell A1 in the worksheet:

```
ActiveCell.Cells(1, 1) = 5
```

The real advantage of this type of cell referencing will be apparent when I discuss variables and looping (see Chapter 8). In most cases, you will not use actual values for the arguments. Rather, you'll use variables.

To enter a value of 5 into the cell directly below the active cell, you can use the following instruction:

```
ActiveCell.Cells(2, 1) = 5
```

Think of the preceding example as though it said this: "Start with the active cell and consider this cell to be cell A1. Return the cell in the second row and the first column."

The second syntax of the `Cells` method uses a single argument that can range from 1 to 16,777,216. This number is equal to the number of cells in a worksheet (65,536 rows × 256 columns). The cells are numbered starting from A1 and continuing right and then down to the next row. The 256th cell is IV1; the 257th is A2.

The next example enters the value 2 into cell H3 (which is the 520th cell in the worksheet) of the active worksheet:

```
ActiveSheet.Cells(520) = 2
```

To display the value in the last cell in a worksheet (IV65536), use this statement:

```
MsgBox ActiveSheet.Cells(16777216)
```

This syntax can also be used with a Range object. In this case, the cell returned is relative to the Range object referenced. For example, if the Range object is A1:D10 (40 cells), the Cells property can have an argument from 1 to 40 and return one of the cells in the Range object. In the following example, a value of 2000 is entered into cell A2 because A2 is the fifth cell (counting from the top and to the right, then down) in the referenced range:

```
Range("A1:D10").Cells(5) = 2000
```

In the preceding example, the argument for the Cells property is not limited to values between 1 and 40. If the argument exceeds the number of cells in the range, the counting continues as if the range were larger than it actually is. Therefore, the statement above could change the value in a cell that's outside of the range A1:D10.

The third syntax for the Cells property simply returns all cells on the referenced worksheet. Unlike the other two syntaxes, in this one, the return data is not a single cell. This example uses the ClearContents method on the range returned by using the Cells property on the active worksheet. The result is that the contents of every cell on the worksheet are cleared:

```
ActiveSheet.Cells.ClearContents
```

The Offset property

The Offset property (like the Range and Cells properties) also returns a Range object. But unlike the other two methods I discussed, the Offset property applies only to a Range object and no other class. Its syntax is as follows:

```
object.Offset(rowOffset, columnOffset)
```

The Offset property takes two arguments that correspond to the relative position from the upper-left cell of the specified Range object. The arguments can be positive (down or right), negative (up or left), or zero. The example that follows enters a value of 12 into the cell directly below the active cell:

```
ActiveCell.Offset(1,0).Value = 12
```

The next example enters a value of 15 into the cell directly above the active cell:

```
ActiveCell.Offset(-1,0).Value = 15
```

By the way, if the active cell is in row 1, the Offset property in the preceding example generates an error because it cannot return a Range object that doesn't exist.

The Offset property is quite useful, especially when you use variables within looping procedures. I discuss these topics in the next chapter.

When you record a macro using the relative reference mode, Excel uses the Offset property to reference cells relative to the starting position (that is, the active cell when macro recording begins). For example, I used the macro recorder to generate the following code. I started with the cell pointer in cell B1, entered values into B1:B3, and then returned to B1.

```
Sub Macro1()
    ActiveCell.FormulaR1C1 = "1"
    ActiveCell.Offset(1, 0).Range("A1").Select
    ActiveCell.FormulaR1C1 = "2"
    ActiveCell.Offset(1, 0).Range("A1").Select
    ActiveCell.FormulaR1C1 = "3"
    ActiveCell.Offset(-2, 0).Range("A1").Select
End Sub
```

You'll notice that the generated code references cell A1, which may seem a bit odd, because that cell was not even involved in the macro. This is a quirk in the macro recording procedure that makes the code more complex than necessary. You can delete all references to Range("A1"), and the macro still works perfectly:

```
Sub Modified Macro1()
    ActiveCell.FormulaR1C1 = "1"
    ActiveCell.Offset(1, 0).Select
    ActiveCell.FormulaR1C1 = "2"
    ActiveCell.Offset(1, 0).Select
    ActiveCell.FormulaR1C1 = "3"
    ActiveCell.Offset(-2, 0).Select
End Sub
```

In fact, here's a much more efficient version of the macro (which I wrote myself) that doesn't do any selecting:

```
Sub Macro1()
    ActiveCell = 1
    ActiveCell.Offset(1, 0) = 2
    ActiveCell.Offset(2, 0) = 3
End Sub
```

Things to Know about Objects

The preceding sections introduced you to objects (including collections), properties, and methods. But I've barely scratched the surface.

Esoteric but essential concepts to remember

In this section, I'll add some more concepts that are essential for would-be VBA gurus. These concepts become clearer as you work with VBA and read subsequent chapters:

- Objects have unique properties and methods.

  Each object has its own set of properties and methods. Some objects, however, share some properties (for example, `Name`) and some methods (such as `Delete`).

- You can manipulate objects without selecting them.

  This may be contrary to how you normally think about manipulating objects in Excel, especially if you've programmed XLM macros. Fact is, it's usually more efficient to perform actions on objects without selecting them first. When you record a macro, Excel generally selects the object first. This is not necessary and may actually make your macro run slower.

- It's important that you understand the concept of collections.

  Most of the time, you'll refer to an object indirectly by referring to the collection that it's in. For example, to access a `Workbook` object named Myfile, reference the `Workbooks` collection as follows:

  ```
  Workbooks("Myfile.xls")
  ```

  This reference returns an object, which is the workbook with which you are concerned.

- Properties can return a reference to another object. For example, in the following statement, the `Font` property returns a `Font` object contained in a `Range` object:

  ```
  Range("A1").Font.Bold = True
  ```

- There can be many different ways to refer to the same object.

  Assume that you have a workbook named `Sales` and that it's the only workbook open. Then assume that this workbook has one worksheet, named Summary. You can refer to the sheet in any of the following ways:

  ```
  Workbooks("Sales.xls").Worksheets("Summary")
  Workbooks(1).Worksheets(1)
  Workbooks(1).Sheets(1)
  ```

```
Application.ActiveWorkbook.ActiveSheet
ActiveWorkbook.ActiveSheet
ActiveSheet
```

The way you choose is usually determined by how much you know about the workspace. For example, if more than one workbook is open, the second or third way is not reliable. If you want to work with the active sheet (whatever it may be), any of the last three ways would work. To be absolutely sure that you're referring to a specific sheet on a specific workbook, the first way is your best choice.

Learn more about objects and properties

If this is your first exposure to VBA, you're probably a bit overwhelmed by objects, properties, and methods. I don't blame you. If you try to access a property that an object doesn't have, you'll get a run-time error, and your VBA code will grind to a screeching halt until you correct the problem.

Fortunately, there are several good ways to learn about objects, properties, and methods.

Read the rest of the book

Don't forget, the name of this chapter is "Introducing Visual Basic for Applications." The remainder of this book covers lots of additional details and provides many useful and informative examples.

Record your actions

Without question, the absolute best way to become familiar with VBA is simply to turn on the macro recorder and record some actions you make in Excel. This is a quick way to learn the relevant objects, properties, and methods for a task. It's even better if the VBA module in which the code is being recorded is visible while you're recording.

Use the online help system

The main source of detailed information about Excel's objects, methods, and procedures is in the online help system.

Figure 7-16 shows the help topic for the `Value` property. This particular property applies to a number of different objects, and the help topic contains hyperlinks labeled See Also, Example, and Applies To. If you click See Also, you get a list of related topics. If you click Example, another window opens with one or more examples (you can copy the example text and paste it into a VBA module to try it out). Clicking Applies To displays a window that lists all objects that use this property.

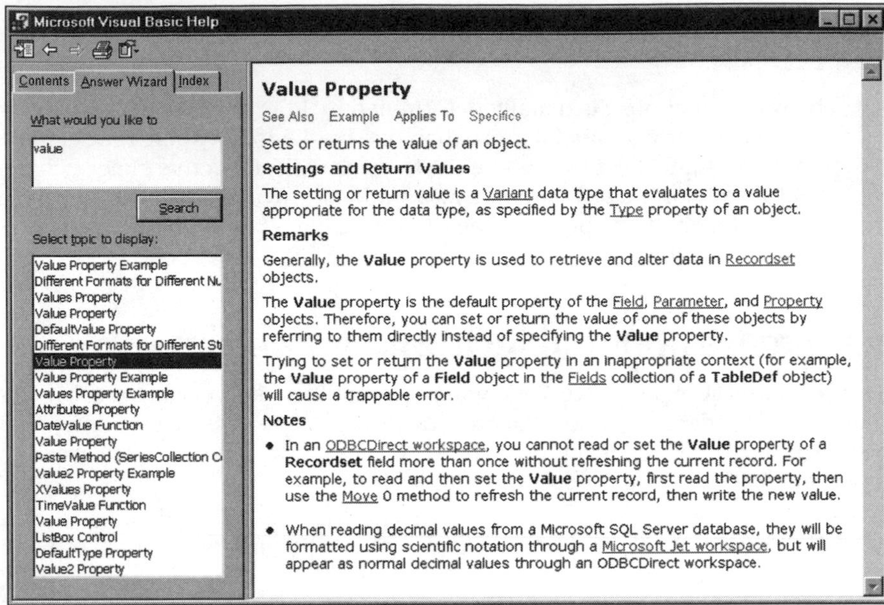

Figure 7-16: A typical VBA help screen.

Use the Object Browser

The Object Browser is a handy tool that lists every property and method for every object available. When the VBE is active, you can bring up the Object Browser in any of the following three ways:

✦ Press F2.

✦ Choose the View ⇨ Object Browser command from the menu.

✦ Click the Object Browser tool on the Standard toolbar.

The Object Browser is shown in Figure 7-17.

The drop-down list in the upper-left corner of the Object Browser includes a list of all object libraries that you have access to:

✦ Excel itself

✦ MSForms (used to create custom dialog boxes)

✦ Office (objects common to all Microsoft Office applications)

✦ Stdole (OLE automation objects)

✦ VBA

✦ Each open workbook (each workbook is considered an object library because it contains objects)

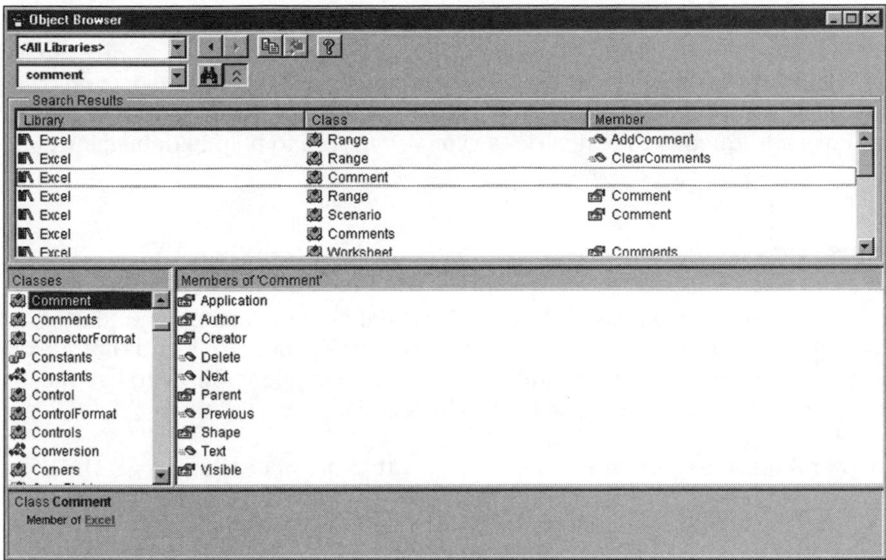

Figure 7-17: The Object Browser is a great reference source.

Your selection in this upper-left drop-down list determines what is displayed in the Classes window, and your selection in the Classes window determines what is visible in the Members of window.

Once you select a library, you can search for a particular text string to get a list of properties and methods that contain the text. You do so by entering the text in the second drop-down list and then clicking the binoculars icon. For example, assume that you're working on a project that manipulates cell comments:

1. Select the library of interest (you probably want to select <All Libraries>).
2. Enter **Comment** in the drop-down list below the library list.
3. Click the binoculars icon to begin the text search.

The Search Results window displays the matching text. Select an object to display its classes in the Classes window. Select a class to display its members (properties, methods, and constants). You can press F1 to go directly to the appropriate help topic.

The Object Browser may seem complex at first, but its usefulness will increase over time.

Experiment with the Immediate window

As I describe in the sidebar earlier in this chapter (see "About the Code Examples"), the Immediate window of the VBE is very useful for testing statements and trying out various VBA expressions. I generally keep the Immediate window visible at all times, and I use it frequently to test various expressions and to help in debugging code.

Summary

In this chapter, I introduced VBA and discussed how VBA compares to other languages. I explained that a VBA module contains procedures and that VBA is based on objects, properties, and methods. I also explained how to use the macro recorder to translate your actions into VBA code.

Chapter 8 discusses programming concepts that are necessary to get the most out of VBA.

✦ ✦ ✦

CHAPTER 8

VBA Programming Fundamentals

✦ ✦ ✦ ✦

In This Chapter

Understanding VBA's language elements, including variables, data types, constants, and arrays

Using VBA's built-in functions

Manipulating objects and collections

Controlling the execution of your procedures

✦ ✦ ✦ ✦

In the preceding chapter, I introduced you to VBA; now it's time to get better acquainted. This chapter discusses some of the key language elements and programming concepts in VBA. If you've used other programming languages, much of this information may sound familiar. VBA has a few unique wrinkles, however, so even experienced programmers may find some new information.

VBA Language Elements: An Overview

In Chapter 7, I presented an overview of objects, properties, and methods. But I didn't tell you much about how to manipulate objects so that they do meaningful things. This chapter gently nudges you in that direction by exploring VBA's *language elements*, the keywords and control structures that you use to write VBA routines.

To get the ball rolling, I'll start by presenting a simple procedure. The following procedure is stored in a VBA module and calculates the sum of the first 100 integers. When done, the procedure displays a message with the result.

```
Sub VBA_Demo()
'   This is a simple VBA Example
    Total = 0
    For i = 1 To 100
        Total = Total + i
    Next i
    MsgBox Total
End Sub
```

This procedure uses some common language elements, including a comment (the line preceded by the apostrophe), a variable (`Total`), two assignment statements (`Total = 0` and `Total = Total + i`), a looping structure (`For-Next`), and a VBA statement (`MsgBox`). All these are discussed in subsequent sections of this chapter.

Note: VBA procedures need not manipulate any objects. The preceding procedure, for example, doesn't do anything with objects.

Entering VBA Code

VBA code, which resides in a VBA module, consists of instructions. The accepted practice is to use one instruction per line. This standard is not a requirement, however; you can use a colon to separate multiple instructions on a single line. The following example combines four instructions on one line:

```
Sub OneLine()
    x= 1: y= 2: z= 3: MsgBox x + y + z
End Sub
```

Most programmers agree that code is easier to read if you use one instruction per line:

```
Sub OneLine()
    x = 1
    y = 2
    z = 3
    MsgBox x + y + z
End Sub
```

Each line can be as long as you like; the VBA module window scrolls to the left when you reach the right side. For lengthy lines, you may want to use VBA's line continuation sequence: an underscore (_) preceded by a space. For example,

```
Sub LongLine()
    SummedValue = _
      Worksheets("Sheet1").Range("A1").Value + _
      Worksheets("Sheet2").Range("A1").Value
End Sub
```

When you record macros, Excel often uses underscores to break long statements into multiple lines.

After you enter an instruction, VBA performs the following actions to improve readability:

✦ It inserts spaces between operators. If you enter `Ans=1+2` (without any spaces), for example, VBA converts it to

```
Ans = 1 + 2
```

✦ VBA adjusts the case of the letters for keywords, properties, and methods. If you enter the following text

```
Result=activesheet.range("a1").value=12
```

VBA converts it to

```
Result = ActiveSheet.Range("a1").Value = 12
```

Notice that text within quotation marks (in this case, `"a1"`) is not changed.

✦ Because VBA variable names are not case sensitive, the interpreter by default adjusts the names of all variables with the same letters so that their case matches the case of letters that you most recently typed. For example, if you first specify a variable as `myvalue` (all lowercase) and then enter the variable as `MyValue` (mixed case), VBA changes all other occurrences of the variable to `MyValue`. An exception occurs if you declare the variable with `Dim` or a similar statement; in this case, the variable name always appears as it was declared.

✦ VBA scans the instruction for syntax errors. If VBA finds an error, it changes the color of the line and may display a message describing the problem. Use the VBE's Tools⇨Options command to display the Options dialog box, where you control the error color (use the Editor Format tab) and whether the error message is displayed (use the Auto Syntax Check option in the Editor tab).

Comments

A *comment* is descriptive text embedded within your code. The text of a comment is completely ignored by VBA. It's a good idea to use comments liberally to describe what you're doing (an instruction's purpose is not always obvious).

You can use a complete line for your comment, or you can insert a comment *after* an instruction on the same line. A comment is indicated by an apostrophe. VBA ignores any text that follows an apostrophe — except when the apostrophe is contained within quotation marks — up until the end of the line. For example, the following statement does not contain a comment, even though it has an apostrophe:

```
Msg = "Can't continue"
```

The following example shows a VBA procedure with three comments:

```
Sub Comments()
'   This procedure does nothing of value
    x = 0   'x represents nothingness
'   Display the result
    MsgBox x
End Sub
```

Although the apostrophe is the preferred comment indicator, you can also use the Rem keyword to mark a line as a comment. For example,

```
Rem — The next statement prompts the user for a filename
```

The Rem keyword is essentially a holdover from old versions of BASIC; it is included in VBA for the sake of compatibility. Unlike the apostrophe, Rem can be written only at the beginning of a line, not on the same line as another instruction.

Using comments is definitely a good idea, but not all comments are equally beneficial. To be useful, comments should convey information that's not immediately obvious from reading the code. Otherwise, you're just chewing up valuable bytes. The following procedure, for example, contains many comments, none of which really adds anything of value:

```
Sub BadComments()
'   Declare variables
    Dim x As Integer
    Dim y As Integer
    Dim z As Integer
'   Start the routine
    x = 100 ' Assign 100 to x
    y = 200 ' Assign 200 to y
'   Add x and y and store in z
    z = x + y
'   Show the result
    MsgBox z
End Sub
```

Following are a few general tips on making the best use of comments:

- ✦ Use comments to describe briefly the purpose of each procedure you write.
- ✦ Use comments to describe changes you make to a procedure.
- ✦ Use comments to indicate that you're using functions or constructs in an unusual or nonstandard manner.
- ✦ Use comments to describe the purpose of variables so that you and other people can decipher otherwise cryptic names.
- ✦ Use comments to describe workarounds that you develop to overcome Excel bugs.
- ✦ Write comments *as* you code rather than after.

You may want to test a procedure without including a particular instruction or group of instructions. Instead of deleting the instruction, simply turn it into a comment by inserting an apostrophe at the beginning. VBA then ignores the instruction(s) when the routine is executed. To convert the comment back to an instruction, delete the apostrophe.

The VB Editor's Edit toolbar contains two very useful buttons. Select a group of instructions and then use the Comment Block button to convert the instructions to comments. The Uncomment Block button converts a group of comments back to instructions. These buttons are very useful, so you may want to copy them to your Standard toolbar.

Variables, Data Types, and Constants

VBA's main purpose in life is to manipulate data. Some data resides in objects, such as worksheet ranges. Other data is stored in variables that you create.

A *variable* is simply a named storage location in your computer's memory. Variables can accommodate a wide variety of *data types*—from simple Boolean values (True or False) to large, double-precision values (see the following section). You assign a value to a variable by using the equal sign operator (more about this later).

You'll make your life easier if you get into the habit of making your variable names as descriptive as possible. VBA does, however, have a few rules regarding variable names:

- ✦ You can use alphabetic characters, numbers, and some punctuation characters, but the first character must be alphabetic.
- ✦ VBA does not distinguish between case. To make variable names more readable, programmers often use mixed case (for example, `InterestRate` rather than `interestrate`).
- ✦ You cannot use spaces or periods. To make variable names more readable, programmers often use the underscore character (`Interest_Rate`).
- ✦ Special type declaration characters (`#`, `$`, `%`, `&`, or `!`) cannot be embedded in a variable name.
- ✦ Variable names may comprise as many as 254 characters—but no one in his right mind would create a variable name that long!

The following list contains some examples of assignment expressions that use various types of variables. The variable names are to the left of the equal sign. Each statement assigns the value to the right of the equal sign to the variable on the left.

```
x = 1
InterestRate = 0.075
LoanPayoffAmount = 243089
DataEntered = False
x = x + 1
MyNum = YourNum * 1.25
UserName = "Bob Johnson"
DateStarted = #3/14/94#
```

VBA has many *reserved words*, which are words that you cannot use for variable or procedure names. If you attempt to use one of these words, you get an error message. For example, although the reserved word `Next` might make a very descriptive variable name, the following instruction generates a syntax error:

```
Next = 132
```

Unfortunately, syntax error messages aren't always very descriptive. The preceding instruction generates this error message: `Compile Error: Expected: variable`. It would be nice if the error message were something like `Reserved word used as a variable`. So if an instruction produces a strange error message, check the online help to make sure your variable name doesn't have a special use in VBA.

Defining data types

VBA makes life easy for programmers because it can automatically handle all the details involved in dealing with data. Not all programming languages make it so easy. For example, some languages are *strictly typed,* which means that the programmer must explicitly define the data type for every variable used.

Data type refers to how data is stored in memory — as integers, real numbers, strings, and so on. Although VBA can take care of data typing automatically, it does so at a cost: slower execution and less efficient use of memory. (There's no such thing as a free lunch.) As a result, letting VBA handle data typing may present problems when you're running large or complex applications. If you need to conserve every last byte of memory, you need to be on familiar terms with data types.

Table 8-1 lists VBA's assortment of built-in data types (note that you can also define custom data types, which I describe later in this chapter).

Table 8-1
VBA's Built-in Data Types

Data Type	***Bytes Used***	***Range of Values***
Byte	1 byte	0 to 255
Boolean	2 bytes	True or False
Integer	2 bytes	–32,768 to 32,767
Long	4 bytes	–2,147,483,648 to 2,147,483,647
Single	4 bytes	–3.402823E38 to –1.401298E–45 (for negative values); 1.401298E–45 to 3.402823E38 (for positive values)

Data Type	*Bytes Used*	*Range of Values*
Double	8 bytes	−1.79769313486232E308 to −4.94065645841247E−324 (negative values); 4.94065645841247E−324 to 1.79769313486232E308 (positive values)
Currency	8 bytes	−922,337,203,685,477.5808 to 922,337,203,685,477.5807
Decimal	14 bytes	+/−79,228,162,514,264,337,593,543,950,335 with no decimal point; +/−7.9228162514264337593543950335 with 28 places to the right of the decimal
Date	8 bytes	January 1, 0100 to December 31, 9999
Object	4 bytes	Any object reference
String (variable-length)	10 bytes + string length	0 to approximately 2 billion
String (fixed-length)	Length of string	1 to approximately 65,400
Variant (with numbers)	16 bytes	Any numeric value up to the range of a double data type
Variant (with characters)	22 bytes + string length	0 to approximately 2 billion
User-defined	Varies	Varies by element

The decimal data type is new to Excel 2000. This is a rather unusual data type because you cannot actually declare it. In fact, it is a "subtype" of a variant. You need to use VBA's `CDec` function to convert a variant to the decimal data type.

Generally, it's best to use the data type that uses the smallest number of bytes yet still can handle all the data assigned to it. When VBA works with data, execution speed is a function of the number of bytes VBA has at its disposal. In other words, the fewer bytes used by data, the faster VBA can access and manipulate the data.

Benchmarking Variant Data Types

To test whether data-typing is important, I developed the following routine, which performs some meaningless calculations in a loop and then displays the procedure's total execution time:

```
Sub TimeTest()
    Dim x As Integer, y As Integer
    Dim A As Integer, B As Integer, C As Integer
    Dim i As Integer, j As Integer
```

Continued

```
    Dim StartTime, EndTime As Date
'   Store the starting time
    StartTime = Timer
'   Perform some calculations
    x = 0
    y = 0
    For i = 1 To 5000
        For j = 1 To 1000
            A = x + y + i
            B = y - x - i
            C = x - y - i
        Next j
    Next i
'   Get ending time
    EndTime = Timer
'   Display total time in seconds
    MsgBox Format(EndTime - StartTime, "0.0")
End Sub
```

On my system, this routine took 7.4 seconds to run (the time will vary, depending on your system's processor speed). I then *commented out* the `Dim` statements, which declare the data types. That is, I turned the `Dim` statements into comments by adding an apostrophe at the beginning of the lines. As a result, VBA used the default data type, variant. I ran the procedure again. It took 15.1 seconds, more than twice as long as before.

The moral is simple: If you want your VBA applications to run as fast as possible, declare your variables!

Declaring variables

If you don't declare the data type for a variable that you use in a VBA routine, VBA uses the default data type, variant. Data stored as a variant acts like a chameleon: It changes type, depending on what you do with it. The procedure below demonstrates how a variable can assume different data types.

```
Sub VariantDemo()
    MyVar = "123"
    MyVar = MyVar / 2
    MyVar = "Answer: " & MyVar
    MsgBox MyVar
End Sub
```

In the VariantDemo procedure, MyVar starts out as a three-character string. Then this "string" is divided by two and becomes a numeric data type. Next, MyVar is appended to a string, converting MyVar back to a string. The MsgBox statement displays the final string: *Answer: 61.5.*

Determining a data type

You can use VBA's TypeName function to determine the data type of a variable. Here's a modified version of the previous procedure. This version displays the data type of MyVar at each step. You'll see that it starts out as a string, then is converted to a double, and finally ends up as a string again.

```
Sub VariantDemo2()
    MyVar = "123"
    MsgBox TypeName(MyVar)
    MyVar = MyVar / 2
    MsgBox TypeName(MyVar)
    MyVar = "Answer: " & MyVar
    MsgBox TypeName(MyVar)
    MsgBox MyVar
End Sub
```

Thanks to VBA, the data type conversion of undeclared variables is automatic. This process may seem like an easy way out, but remember that you sacrifice speed and memory.

Before you use a variable in a procedure, you may want to *declare* it — that is, tell VBA its name and data type. Declaring variables provides two main benefits:

- *Your programs run faster and use memory more efficiently.* The default data type, variant, causes VBA to repeatedly perform time-consuming checks and reserve more memory than necessary. If VBA knows the data type, it doesn't have to investigate, and it can reserve just enough memory to store the data.
- *You avoid problems involving misspelled variable names.* Say that you use an undeclared variable named CurrentRate. At some point in your routine, however, you insert the statement CurentRate = .075. This misspelled variable name, which is very difficult to spot, will likely cause your routine to give incorrect results.

Forcing yourself to declare all variables

To force yourself to declare all the variables that you use, include the following as the first instruction in your VBA module:

```
Option Explicit
```

This statement causes your program to stop whenever VBA encounters a variable name that has not been declared. VBA issues an error message, and you must declare the variable before you can proceed.

To ensure that the `Option Explicit` statement is automatically inserted whenever you insert a new VBA module, enable the Require Variable Declaration option in the Editor tab of the VBE's Options dialog box. I highly recommend doing so.

Scoping variables

A variable's *scope* determines which modules and procedures the variable can be used in. A variable's scope can be any of the following:

Scope	*How a Variable with This Scope Is Declared*
Single procedure	Include a `Dim`, `Static`, or `Private` statement within the procedure.
Modulewide	Include a `Dim` statement before the first procedure in a module.
All modules	Include a Public statement before the first procedure in a module.

I discuss each scope further in the following sections.

A Note about the Examples in This Chapter

This chapter contains many examples of VBA code, usually presented in the form of simple procedures. These examples demonstrate various concepts as simply as possible. Most of these examples do not perform any particularly useful task; in fact, the task can often be performed in a different way. In other words, don't use these examples in your own work. Subsequent chapters provide many more code examples that *are* useful.

Local variables

A *local variable* is a variable declared within a procedure. Local variables can be used only in the procedure in which they are declared. When the procedure ends, the variable no longer exists, and Excel frees up its memory.

If you need the variable to retain its value, declare it as a `Static` variable (see "Static variables" later in this section).

The most common way to declare a local variable is to place a Dim statement between a Sub statement and an End Sub statement (in fact, Dim statements usually are placed right after the Sub statement, before the procedure's code).

If you're curious about this word, Dim is a shortened form of *Dimension.* In old versions of BASIC, this statement was used exclusively to declare the dimensions for an array. In VBA, the Dim keyword is used to declare any variable, not just arrays.

The following procedure uses six local variables declared using Dim statements:

```
Sub MySub()
    Dim x As Integer
    Dim First As Long
    Dim InterestRate As Single
    Dim TodaysDate As Date
    Dim UserName As String * 20
    Dim MyValue
'   - [The procedure's code goes here] -
End Sub
```

Notice that the last Dim statement in the preceding example doesn't declare a data type; it simply names the variable. As a result, that variable becomes a variant.

By the way, you also can declare several variables with a single Dim statement. For example,

```
Dim x As Integer, y As Integer, z As Integer
Dim First As Long, Last As Double
```

Unlike some languages, VBA does not let you declare a group of variables to be a particular data type by separating the variables with commas. For example, the following statement, although valid, does *not* declare all the variables as integers:

```
Dim i, j, k As Integer
```

In VBA, only k is declared to be an integer; the other variables are declared variants. To declare i, j, and k as integers, use this statement:

```
Dim i As Integer, j As Integer, k As Integer
```

If a variable is declared with a local scope, other procedures in the same module can use the same variable name, but each instance of the variable is unique to its own procedure.

In general, local variables are the most efficient because VBA frees up the memory they use when the procedure ends.

Another Way of Data-Typing Variables

Like most other dialects of BASIC, VBA lets you append a character to a variable's name to indicate the data type. For example, you can declare the MyVar variable as an integer by tacking % onto the name:

```
Dim MyVar%
```

Type-declaration characters exist for most of VBA's data types (data types not listed don't have type-declaration characters).

Data Type	*Type-Declaration Character*
Integer	%
Long	&
Single	!
Double	#
Currency	@
String	$

This method of data typing is essentially a holdover from BASIC; it's better to declare your variables using the procedures described in this chapter.

Modulewide variables

Sometimes, you'll want a variable to be available to all procedures in a module. If so, just declare the variable *before* the module's first procedure — outside of any procedures or functions.

In the following example, the Dim statement is the first instruction in the module. Both MySub and YourSub have access to the CurrentValue variable.

```
Dim CurrentValue as Integer

Sub MySub()
'    - [Code goes here] -
End Sub

Sub YourSub()
'    - [Code goes here] -
End Sub
```

The value of a modulewide variable does not change when a procedure ends.

Public variables

To make a variable available to all the procedures in all the VBA modules in a project, declare the variable at the module level by using the `Public` keyword rather than `Dim`. Here's an example:

```
Public CurrentRate as Long
```

The `Public` keyword makes the `CurrentRate` variable available to any procedure in the project (that is, a single workbook), even those in other modules. You must insert this statement before the first procedure in a module. This type of declaration must also appear in a standard VBA module — not in a code module for a sheet or a UserForm.

Static variables

Static variables are a special case. They are declared at the procedure level, and they retain their value when the procedure ends.

You declare static variables using the `Static` keyword:

```
Sub MySub()
    Static Counter as Integer
    - [Code goes here] -
End Sub
```

Variable Naming Conventions

Some programmers name variables so that their data types can be identified just by looking at their names. Personally, I usually don't use this technique because I think it makes the code more difficult to read. But you might find it helpful.

The naming convention involves using a standard lowercase prefix for the variable's name. For example, if you have a Boolean variable that tracks whether a workbook has been saved, you might name the variable `bWasSaved`. That way, it is clear that the variable is a Boolean variable. The following table lists some standard prefixes for data types:

Data Type	***Prefix***	***Data Type***	***Prefix***
Boolean	b	Date/Time	dt
Integer	i	String	str
Long	l	Object	obj
Single	s	Variant	v
Double	d	User-defined	u
Currency	c		

Working with constants

A variable's value may, and often does, change while a procedure is executing (that's why it's called a variable). Sometimes, you need to refer to a named value or string that never changes: a *constant.*

Declaring constants

You declare constants using the Const statement. Here are some examples:

```
Const NumQuarters as Integer = 4
Const Rate = .0725, Period = 12
Const ModName as String = "Budget Macros"
Public Const AppName as String = "Budget Application"
```

The second example doesn't declare a data type. Consequently, the two constants are variants. Because a constant never changes its value, you'll normally want to declare your constants as a specific data type.

Like variables, constants also have a scope. If you want a constant to be available within a single procedure only, declare it after the Sub or Function statement to make it a local constant. To make a constant available to all procedures in a module, declare it before the first procedure in the module. To make a constant available to all modules in the workbook, use the Public keyword, and declare the constant before the first procedure in a module.

Note: If you attempt to change the value of a constant in a VBA procedure, you get an error—which is what you would expect. A constant is a constant, not a variable.

Using constants throughout your code in place of hard-coded values or strings is an excellent programming practice. For example, if your procedure needs to refer to a specific value, such as an interest rate, several times, it's better to declare the value as a constant and use the constant's name rather than its value in your expressions. This technique not only makes your code more readable, it also makes it easier to change should the need arise—you have to change only one instruction rather than several.

Using predefined constants

Excel and VBA contain many predefined constants, which you can use without declaring; in fact, you don't even need to know the value of these constants to use them. The macro recorder generally uses constants rather than actual values. The following procedure uses a built-in constant (xlManual) to change the Calculation property of the Application object (that is, to change Excel's recalculation mode to manual):

```
Sub CalcManual()
    Application.Calculation = xlManual
End Sub
```

I discovered the `xlManual` constant by recording a macro that changed the calculation mode. I also could have looked in the online help under Calculation Property; all the relevant constants for this property are listed there. And if you have the AutoList Members option turned on, VBA lists all the constants that can be assigned to a property. Usually, the names of the constants are self-explanatory.

The actual value of `xlManual` is –4135. The constant that changes Excel's mode to automatic calculation is `xlAutomatic`, and its value is –4105. Obviously, it's easier to use the constant's name than to look up the value.

The Object Browser, which I discussed in Chapter 7, contains a list of all Excel and VBA constants. In the VBE, press F2 to bring up the Object Browser.

Working with strings

Like Excel, VBA can manipulate both numbers and text (strings). There are two types of strings in VBA:

✦ *Fixed-length strings* are declared with a specified number of characters. The maximum length is 65,535 characters.

✦ *Variable-length strings* theoretically can hold up to 2 billion characters.

Each character in a string takes 1 byte of storage, and a small additional amount of storage is used for the header of each string. When you declare a string variable with a `Dim` statement, you can specify the maximum length if you know it (that is, a fixed-length string), or you can let VBA handle it dynamically (a variable-length string). Working with fixed-length strings is slightly more efficient in terms of memory usage.

In the following example, the `MyString` variable is declared to be a string with a maximum length of 50 characters. `YourString` is also declared as a string, but its length is unfixed.

```
Dim MyString As String * 50
Dim YourString As String
```

Working with dates

You can use a string variable to store dates, of course, but you can't perform date calculations on one. Using the date data type is a better way to work with dates.

A variable defined as a date uses 8 bytes of storage and can hold dates ranging from January 1, A.D. 100, to December 31, 9999. That's a span of nearly 10,000 years—more than enough for even the most aggressive financial forecast! The date data type is also useful for storing time-related data. In VBA, you specify dates and times by enclosing them between two pound signs (#), as shown next.

The range of dates that VBA can handle is much larger than Excel's own date range—which begins with January 1, 1900. Therefore, be careful that you don't attempt to use a date in a worksheet that is outside of Excel's acceptable date range.

Here are some examples of declaring variables and constants as date data types:

```
Dim Today As Date
Dim StartTime As Date
Const FirstDay As Date = #1/1/2001#
Const Noon = #12:00:00#
```

Date variables display dates according to your system's short date format, and times appear according to your system's time format (either 12- or 24-hour). You can modify these system settings by using the Regional Settings option in the Windows Control Panel.

Assignment Expressions

An *assignment expression* is a VBA instruction that makes a mathematical evaluation and assigns the result to a variable or an object. Excel's online help defines *expression* as

> a combination of keywords, operators, variables, and constants that yields a string, number, or object. An expression can perform a calculation, manipulate characters, or test data.

I couldn't have said it better myself. Much of the work done in VBA involves developing (and debugging) expressions.

If you know how to create formulas in Excel, you'll have no trouble creating expressions in VBA. With a worksheet formula, Excel displays the result in a cell. A VBA expression, on the other hand, can be assigned to a variable or used as a property value.

VBA uses the equal sign (=) as its assignment operator. The following are examples of assignment statements (the expressions are to the right of the equal sign):

```
x = 1
x = x + 1
x = (y * 2) / (z  * 2)
FileOpen = True
FileOpen = Not FileOpen
Range("TheYear").Value = 1995
```

Expressions can be very complex. You may want to use the continuation sequence (space followed by an underscore) to make lengthy expressions easier to read.

Often, expressions use functions — VBA's built-in functions, Excel's worksheet functions, or custom functions that you develop in VBA. I discuss intrinsic functions later in this chapter.

Operators play a major role in VBA. Familiar operators describe mathematical operations, including addition (+), multiplication (*), division (/), subtraction (-), exponentiation (^), and string concatenation (&). Less-familiar operators are the backslash (\), used in integer division, and the `Mod` operator, used in modulo arithmetic. The `Mod` operator returns the remainder of one number divided by another. For example, the following expression returns 2:

```
17 Mod 3
```

VBA also supports the same comparative operators used in Excel formulas: equal to (=), greater than (>), less than (<), greater than or equal to (>=), less than or equal to (<=), and not equal to (<>).

In addition, VBA provides a full set of logical operators, shown in Table 8-2.

Table 8-2
VBA's Logical Operators

Operator	***What It Does***
`Not`	Performs a logical negation on an expression
`And`	Performs a logical conjunction on two expressions
`Or`	Performs a logical disjunction on two expressions
`XoR`	Performs a logical exclusion on two expressions
`Eqv`	Performs a logical equivalence on two expressions
`Imp`	Performs a logical implication on two expressions

The order of precedence for operators in VBA is exactly the same as in Excel. Of course, you can add parentheses to change the natural order of precedence.

The instruction below uses the `Not` operator to toggle the grid-line display in the active window. The `DisplayGridlines` property takes a value of either True or False. Therefore, using the `Not` operator changes False to True and True to False.

```
ActiveWindow.DisplayGridlines = _
  Not ActiveWindow.DisplayGridlines
```

The expression below performs a logical `And`. The `MsgBox` statement displays True only when Sheet1 is the active sheet *and* the active cell is in row 1.

```
MsgBox ActiveSheet.Name = "Sheet1" And ActiveCell.Row = 1
```

The expression below performs a logical Or. The MsgBox statement displays True when either Sheet1 *or* Sheet2 is the active sheet.

```
MsgBox ActiveSheet.Name = _
  "Sheet1" Or ActiveSheet.Name = "Sheet1"
```

Arrays

An *array* is a group of elements of the same type that have a common name; you refer to a specific element in the array using the array name and an index number. For example, you may define an array of 12 string variables so that each variable corresponds to the name of a different month. If you name the array MonthNames, you can refer to the first element of the array as MonthNames(0), the second element as MonthNames(1), and so on, up to MonthNames(11).

Declaring arrays

You declare an array with a Dim or Public statement, just as you declare a regular variable. You can also specify the number of elements in the array. You do so by specifying the first index number, the keyword To, and the last index number — all inside parentheses. For example, here's how to declare an array comprising exactly 100 integers:

```
Dim MyArray(1 To 100) As Integer
```

When you declare an array, you need specify only the upper index, in which case VBA assumes that 0 is the lower index. Therefore, the two statements below have the same effect:

```
Dim MyArray(0 to 100) As Integer
Dim MyArray(100) As Integer
```

In both these cases, the array consists of 101 elements.

If you would like VBA to assume that 1 is the lower index for all arrays that declare only the upper index, include the following statement before any procedures in your module:

```
Option Base 1
```

Declaring multidimensional arrays

The arrays examples in the preceding section were one-dimensional arrays. VBA arrays can have up to 60 dimensions, although it's rare to need more than three dimensions (a 3D array). The following statement declares a 100-integer array with two dimensions (2D):

```
Dim MyArray(1 To 10, 1 To 10) As Integer
```

You can think of the preceding array as occupying a 10 × 10 matrix. To refer to a specific element in a 2D array, you need to specify two index numbers. For example, here's how you can assign a value to an element in the preceding array:

```
MyArray(3, 4) = 125
```

You can think of a 3D array as a cube, but I can't tell you how to visualize the data layout of an array of more than three dimensions.

A *dynamic array* doesn't have a preset number of elements. You declare a dynamic array with a blank set of parentheses:

```
Dim MyArray() As Integer
```

Before you can use a dynamic array in your code, however, you must use the `ReDim` statement to tell VBA how many elements are in the array (or `ReDim Preserve` if you want to keep the existing values in the array). You can use the `ReDim` statement any number of times, changing the array's size as often as you need to.

Arrays crop up later in this chapter when I discuss looping.

Object Variables

An *object variable* is a variable that represents an entire object, such as a range or a worksheet. Object variables are important for two reasons:

- ✦ They can simplify your code significantly.
- ✦ They can make your code execute more quickly.

Object variables, like normal variables, are declared with the `Dim` or `Public` statement. For example, the statement below declares `InputArea` as a `Range` object.

```
Public InputArea As Range
```

To see how object variables simplify your code, examine the following procedure, which was written without using object variables:

```
Sub NoObjVar()
    Worksheets("Sheet1").Range("A1").Value = 124
    Worksheets("Sheet1").Range("A1").Font.Bold = True
```

```
    Worksheets("Sheet1").Range("A1").Font.Italic = True
End Sub
```

This routine enters a value into cell A1 of Sheet1 on the active workbook and then boldfaces and italicizes the cell's contents. That's a lot of typing. To reduce wear and tear on your fingers, you can condense the routine with an object variable:

```
Sub ObjVar()
    Dim MyCell As Range
    Set MyCell = Worksheets("Sheet1").Range("A1")
    MyCell.Value = 124
    MyCell.Font.Bold = True
    MyCell.Font.Italic = True
End Sub
```

After the variable `MyCell` is declared as a `Range` object, the `Set` statement assigns an object to it. Subsequent statements can then use the simpler `MyCell` reference in place of the lengthy `Worksheets("Sheet1").Range("A1")` reference.

After an object is assigned to a variable, VBA can access it more quickly than it can a normal lengthy reference that has to be resolved. So when speed is critical, use object variables. One way to think about this is in terms of "dot processing." Every time VBA encounters a dot, as in `Sheets(1).Range("A1")`, it takes time to resolve the reference. Using an object variable reduces the number of dots to be processed. The fewer the dots, the faster the processing time. Another way to improve the speed of your code is by using the `With-End With` construct, which also reduces the number of dots to be processed. I discuss this construct later in this chapter.

The true value of object variables will become apparent when I discuss looping later in this chapter.

User-Defined Data Types

VBA lets you create custom, or *user-defined*, data types (a concept much like Pascal records or C structures). A user-defined data type can ease your work with some types of data. For example, if your application deals with customer information, you may want to create a user-defined data type named `CustomerInfo`, as follows:

```
Type CustomerInfo
    Company As String * 25
    Contact As String * 15
    RegionCode As Integer
    Sales As Long
End Type
```

You define custom data types outside of procedures at the top of your module.

After you create a user-defined data type, you use a Dim statement to declare a variable as that type. Usually, you define an array. For example,

```
Dim Customers(1 To 100) As CustomerInfo
```

Each of the 100 elements in this array consists of four components (as specified by the user-defined data type, CustomerInfo). You can refer to a particular component of the record as follows:

```
Customers(1).Company = "Acme Tools"
Customers(1).Contact = "Tim Robertson"
Customers(1).RegionCode = 3
Customers(1).Sales = 150677
```

You can also work with an element in the array as a whole. For example, to copy the information from Customers(1) to Customers(2), use this instruction:

```
Customers(2) = Customers(1)
```

The preceding example is equivalent to the following instruction block:

```
Customers(2).Company = Customers(1).Company
Customers(2).Contact = Customers(1).Contact
Customers(2).RegionCode = Customers(1).RegionCode
Customers(2).Sales = Customers(1).Sales
```

Built-in Functions

Like most programming languages, VBA has a variety of built-in functions that simplify calculations and operations. Often, the functions enable you to perform operations that are otherwise difficult, or even impossible. Many of VBA's functions are similar (or identical) to Excel's worksheet functions. For example, the VBA function UCase, which converts a string argument to uppercase, is equivalent to the Excel worksheet function UPPER.

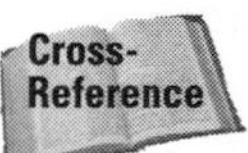

Appendix B contains a complete list of VBA's functions, with a brief description of each. All are thoroughly described in the online help system.

To get a list of VBA functions while you're writing your code, type **VBA** followed by a period (.). The VBE displays a list of all functions (see Figure 8-1). If this doesn't work for you, make sure that the Auto List Members option is selected. Choose Tools⇨Options, and click the Editor tab.

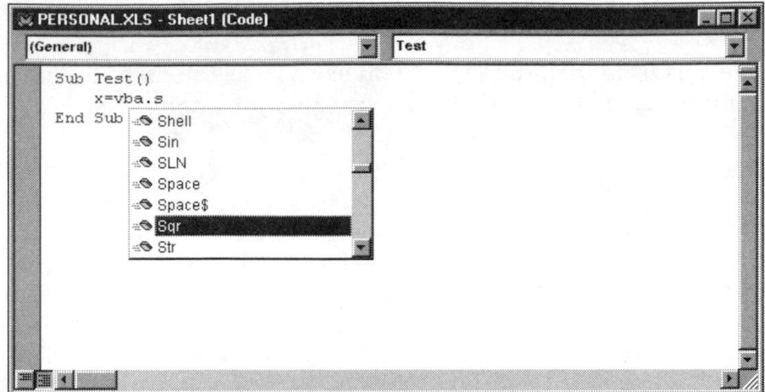

Figure 8-1: Displaying a list of VBA functions in the VBE.

You use functions in VBA expressions in much the same way that you use functions in worksheet formulas. For instance, you can nest VBA functions.

Here's a simple procedure that calculates the square root of a variable using VBA's `Sqr` function, stores the result in another variable, and then displays the result:

```
Sub ShowRoot()
    MyValue = 25
    SquareRoot = Sqr(MyValue)
    MsgBox SquareRoot
End Sub
```

You can use many (but not all) of Excel's worksheet functions in your VBA code. The `WorksheetFunction` object, which is contained in the `Application` object, holds all the worksheet functions that you can call from your VBA procedures.

To use a worksheet function in a VBA statement, just precede the function name with

```
Application.WorksheetFunction
```

The following example demonstrates how to use an Excel worksheet function in a VBA procedure. Excel's infrequently used `ROMAN` function converts a decimal number into a Roman numeral.

```
Sub ShowRoman()
    DecValue = 1999
    RomanValue = Application.WorksheetFunction.Roman(DecValue)
    MsgBox RomanValue
End Sub
```

When you execute this procedure, the `MsgBox` function displays the string `MCMXCIX`. Fans of old movies are often dismayed when they learn that Excel doesn't have a function to convert a Roman numeral to its decimal equivalent.

It's important to understand that you cannot use worksheet functions that have an equivalent VBA function. For example, VBA cannot access Excel's `SQRT` worksheet function because VBA has its own version of that function: `Sqr`. Therefore, the following statement generates an error:

```
MsgBox Application.WorksheetFunction.Sqrt(123)   'error
```

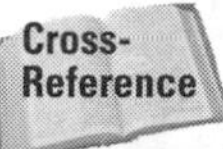

As I describe in Chapter 10, you can use VBA to create custom worksheet functions that work just like Excel's built-in worksheet functions.

The MsgBox Function

The `MsgBox` function is one of the most useful VBA functions. Many of the examples in this chapter use this function to display the value of a variable.

This function often is a good substitute for a simple custom dialog box. It's also an excellent debugging tool because you can insert `MsgBox` functions at any time to pause your code and display the result of a calculation or assignment.

Most functions return a single value, which you assign to a variable. The `MsgBox` function not only returns a value, but also displays a dialog box that the user can respond to. The value returned by the `MsgBox` function represents the user's response to the dialog. You can use the `MsgBox` function even when you have no interest in the user's response but want to take advantage of the message display.

The official syntax of the `MsgBox` function has five arguments (those in square brackets are optional):

```
MsgBox(prompt[, buttons][, title][, helpfile, context])
```

prompt — (Required) The message displayed in the pop-up display.

buttons — (Optional) A value that specifies which buttons and which icon, if any, appear in the message box. Use built-in constants — for example, `vbYesNo`.

title — (Optional) The text that appears in the message box's title bar. The default is `Microsoft Excel`.

helpfile — (Optional) The name of the help file associated with the message box.

context — (Optional) The context ID of the help topic. This represents a specific help topic to display.

Continued

You can assign the value returned to a variable, or you can use the function by itself without an assignment statement. The next example assigns the result to the variable `Ans`.

```
Ans = MsgBox("Continue?", vbYesNo + vbQuestion, "Tell me")
If Ans = vbNo Then Exit Sub
```

Notice that I used the sum of two built-in constants (`vbYesNo + vbQuestion`) for the buttons argument. Using `vbYesNo` displays two buttons in the message box: one labeled Yes and one labeled No. Adding `vbQuestion` to the argument also displays a question mark icon (see the accompanying figure). When the first statement is executed, `Ans` contains one of two values, represented by the constants `vbYes` or `vbNo`. In this example, if the user clicks the No button, the procedure ends.

For more information, refer to the online help, which lists all the constants you can use.

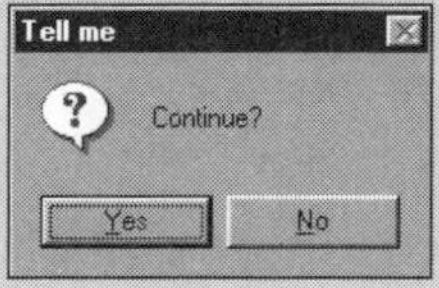

Manipulating Objects and Collections

As an Excel programmer, you'll spend a lot of time working with objects and collections. Therefore, you'll want to know the most efficient ways to write your code to manipulate these objects and collections. VBA offers two important constructs that can simplify working with objects and collections:

- `With-End With` constructs
- `For Each-Next` constructs

With-End With constructs

The `With-End With` instruction construct enables you to perform multiple operations on a single object. To start understanding how the `With-End With` construct works, examine the following procedure, which modifies five properties of a selection's formatting (the selection is assumed to be a `Range` object):

```
Sub ChangeFont1()
    Selection.Font.Name = "Times New Roman"
    Selection.Font.FontStyle = "Bold Italic"
    Selection.Font.Size = 12
```

```
    Selection.Font.Underline = xlSingle
    Selection.Font.ColorIndex = 5
End Sub
```

This procedure can be rewritten using the `With-End With` construct. The following procedure performs exactly like the preceding one:

```
Sub ChangeFont2()
    With Selection.Font
        .Name = "Times New Roman"
        .FontStyle = "Bold Italic"
        .Size = 12
        .Underline = xlSingle
        .ColorIndex = 5
    End With
End Sub
```

Some people think that the second incarnation of the procedure is actually more difficult to read. Remember, though, that the objective is increased speed. Although the first version may be more straightforward and easier to understand, a procedure that uses the `With-End With` construct when changing several properties of an object can be significantly faster than the equivalent procedure that explicitly references the object in each statement.

When you record a VBA macro, Excel uses the `With-End With` construct every chance it gets. To see a good example of this construct, try recording your actions while you change the page setup by choosing the File⇨Page Setup command.

For Each-Next constructs

Recall from the preceding chapter that a *collection* is a group of related objects. For example, the `Workbooks` collection is a collection of all open `Workbook` objects. There are many other collections that you can work with. You don't have to know how many elements are in a collection to use the `For Each-Next` construct.

Suppose that you want to perform some action on all objects in a collection. Or suppose that you want to evaluate all objects in a collection and take action under certain conditions. These are perfect occasions for the `For Each-Next` construct.

The syntax of the `For Each-Next` construct is

```
For Each element In group
    [instructions]
    [Exit For]
    [instructions]
Next [element]
```

The following procedure uses the For Each-Next construct to refer to each of the six single-precision members of a fixed-length array one at a time.

```
Sub Macro1()
    Dim MyArray(5)
    For i = 0 To 5
        MyArray(i) = Rnd
    Next i
    For Each n In MyArray
        Debug.Print n
    Next n
End Sub
```

The next procedure uses the For Each-Next construct with the Sheets collection in the active workbook. When you execute the procedure, the MsgBox function displays each sheet's Name property. (If there are five sheets in the active workbook, the MsgBox function is called five times.)

```
Sub CountSheets()
    Dim Item as WorkSheet
    For Each Item In ActiveWorkbook.Sheets
        MsgBox Item.Name
    Next Item
End Sub
```

In the preceding example, Item is an object variable (more specifically, a Worksheet object). There's nothing special about the name *Item;* you can use any valid variable name in its place.

The next example uses For Each-Next to cycle through all objects in the Windows collection.

```
Sub HiddenWindows()
    AllVisible = True
    For Each Item In Windows
        If Item.Visible = False Then
            AllVisible = False
            Exit For
        End If
    Next Item
    MsgBox AllVisible
End Sub
```

If a window is hidden, the value of AllVisible is changed to False, and the For Each-Next loop is exited. The message box displays True if all windows are visible and False if at least one window is hidden. The Exit For statement is optional. It provides a way to exit the For Each-Next loop early. This is generally used in conjunction with an If-Then statement (described later in this chapter).

Here's an example that closes all workbooks except the active workbook. This procedure uses the If-Then construct to evaluate each workbook in the Workbooks collection.

```
Sub CloseInActive()
    For Each Book In Workbooks
      If Book.Name <> ActiveWorkbook.Name Then Book.Close
    Next Book
End Sub
```

My final example of For Each-Next is designed to be executed after the user selects a range of cells. Here, the Selection object acts as a collection that consists of Range objects because each cell in the selection is a Range object. The procedure evaluates each cell and uses VBA's UCase function to convert its contents to uppercase (numeric cells are not affected).

```
Sub MakeUpperCase()
    For Each Cell In Selection
        Cell.Value = UCase(Cell.Value)
    Next Cell
End Sub
```

Controlling Execution

Some VBA procedures start at the top and progress line by line to the bottom. Macros that you record, for example, always work in this fashion. Often, however, you need to control the flow of your routines by skipping over some statements, executing some statements multiple times, and testing conditions to determine what the routine does next.

The preceding section described the For Each-Next construct, which is a type of loop. This section discusses the additional ways of controlling the execution of your VBA procedures:

- ✦ GoTo statements
- ✦ If-Then constructs
- ✦ Select Case constructs
- ✦ For-Next loops
- ✦ Do While loops
- ✦ Do Until loops

GoTo statements

The most straightforward way to change the flow of a program is to use a `GoTo` statement. This statement simply transfers program execution to a new instruction, which must be preceded by a label (a text string followed by a colon). VBA procedures can contain any number of labels, and a `GoTo` statement cannot branch outside of a procedure.

The following procedure uses VBA's `InputBox` function to get the user's name. If the name is not Howard, the procedure branches to the `WrongName` label and ends. Otherwise, the procedure executes some additional code. The `Exit Sub` statement causes the procedure to end.

```
Sub GoToDemo()
    UserName = InputBox("Enter Your Name:")
    If UserName <> "Howard" Then GoTo WrongName
    MsgBox ("Welcome Howard...")
'   -[More code here] -
    Exit Sub
WrongName:
    MsgBox "Sorry. Only Howard can run this."
End Sub
```

This simple procedure works, but in general you should use the `GoTo` statement only when there is no other way to perform an action. In fact, the only time you *really* need to use a `GoTo` statement in VBA is for error trapping (refer to Chapter 9).

If-Then constructs

Perhaps the most commonly used instruction grouping in VBA is the `If-Then` construct. This common instruction is one way to endow your applications with decision-making capability. Good decision making is the key to writing successful programs. A successful Excel application essentially boils down to making decisions and acting on them.

The basic syntax of the `If-Then` construct is

```
If condition Then true_instructions [Else false_instructions]
```

The `If-Then` construct is used to execute one or more statements conditionally. The `Else` clause is optional. If included, it lets you execute one or more instructions when the condition you're testing is not true.

The following procedure demonstrates an `If-Then` structure without an `Else` clause. The example deals with time. VBA uses the same date-and-time serial number system as Excel. The time of day is expressed as a fractional value — for example, noon is represented as .5. VBA's `Time` function returns a value that represents the time of day, as reported by the system clock. In the example below, a message is displayed if the time is before noon. If the current system time is greater than or equal to .5, the procedure ends and nothing happens.

```
Sub GreetMe()
    If Time < 0.5 Then MsgBox "Good Morning"
End Sub
```

If you want to display a different greeting when the time of day is after noon, add another `If-Then` statement, like so:

```
Sub GreetMe()
    If Time < 0.5 Then MsgBox "Good Morning"
    If Time >= 0.5 Then MsgBox "Good Afternoon"
End Sub
```

Notice that I used `>=` (greater than or equal to) for the second `If-Then` statement. This covers the extremely remote chance that the time is precisely 12:00 noon.

Another approach is to use the `Else` clause of the `If-Then` construct. For example,

```
Sub GreetMe()
    If Time < 0.5 Then MsgBox "Good Morning" Else _
      MsgBox "Good Afternoon"
End Sub
```

Notice that I used the line continuation sequence; `If-Then-Else` is actually a single statement.

If you need to expand a routine to handle three conditions (for example, morning, afternoon, and evening), you can use either three `If-Then` statements or a nested `If-Then-Else` structure. The first approach is the simpler:

```
Sub GreetMe()
    If Time < 0.5 Then MsgBox "Good Morning"
    If Time >= 0.5 And Time < 0.75 Then MsgBox "Good Afternoon"
    If Time >= 0.75 Then MsgBox "Good Evening"
End Sub
```

The value 0.75 represents 6:00 p.m.—three-quarters of the way through the day and a good point at which to call it evening.

The following procedure performs the same action as the previous one but uses the `If-Then-Else` structure:

```
Sub GreetMe()
    If Time < 0.5 Then MsgBox "Good Morning" Else
      If Time >= 0.5 And Time < 0.75 Then MsgBox _
       "Good Afternoon" Else
        If Time >= 0.75 Then MsgBox "Good Evening"
End Sub
```

In both examples, every instruction in the procedure gets executed, even in the morning. A more efficient procedure would include a structure that ends the routine when a condition is found to be true. For example, it might display the `Good Morning` message in the morning and then exit without evaluating the other, superfluous conditions. True, the difference in speed is inconsequential when you design a procedure as small as this routine. But for more complex applications, you need another syntax:

```
If condition Then
    [true_instructions]
[ElseIf condition-n Then
    [alternate_instructions]]
[Else
    [default_instructions]]
End If
```

Here's how you can use this syntax to rewrite the `GreetMe` procedure:

```
Sub GreetMe()
    If Time < 0.5 Then
        MsgBox "Good Morning"
    ElseIf Time >= 0.5 And Time < 0.75 Then
        MsgBox "Good Afternoon"
    ElseIf Time >= 0.75 Then
        MsgBox "Good Evening"
    End If
End Sub
```

With this syntax, when a condition is true, the conditional statements are executed and the `If-Then` construct ends. In other words, the extraneous conditions are not evaluated. Although this syntax makes for greater efficiency, some may find the code to be more difficult to understand. There's always a trade-off.

The following is another example that uses the simple form of the `If-Then` construct. This procedure prompts the user for a value for `Quantity` and then displays the appropriate discount based on that value. If the `InputBox` is cancelled, `Quantity` contains an empty string, and the procedure ends.

```
Sub Discount1()
    Quantity = InputBox("Enter Quantity: ")
    If Quantity = "" Then Exit Sub
    If Quantity >= 0 Then Discount = 0.1
    If Quantity >= 25 Then Discount = 0.15
    If Quantity >= 50 Then Discount = 0.2
    If Quantity >= 75 Then Discount = 0.25
    MsgBox "Discount: " & Discount
End Sub
```

Notice that each If-Then statement in this procedure is always executed, and the value for Discount can change. The final value, however, is the desired value.

The following procedure is the previous one rewritten to use the alternate syntax. In this case, the procedure ends after executing the True instruction block.

```
Sub Discount2()
    Quantity = InputBox("Enter Quantity: ")
    If Quantity = "" Then Exit Sub
    If Quantity >= 0 And Quantity < 25 Then
        Discount = 0.1
    ElseIf Quantity >= 25 And Quantity < 50 Then
        Discount = 0.15
    ElseIf Quantity >= 50 And Quantity < 75 Then
        Discount = 0.2
    ElseIf Quantity >= 75 Then
        Discount = 0.25
    End If
    MsgBox "Discount: " & Discount
End Sub
```

I find nested If-Then structures rather cumbersome. As a result, I usually use the If-Then structure only for simple binary decisions. When you need to choose among three or more alternatives, the Select Case structure is often a better construct to use.

VBA's IIf Function

VBA offers an alternative to the If-Then construct: the IIf function. This function takes three arguments and works much like Excel's IF worksheet function. The syntax is

```
IIf(expr, truepart, falsepart)
```

expr — (Required) Expression to evaluate

truepart — (Required) Value or expression returned if *expr* is True

falsepart — (Required) Value or expression returned if *expr* is False

The instruction below demonstrates the use of the IIf function. The message box displays *Zero* if cell A1 contains a zero or is empty. It displays *Nonzero* if cell A1 contains anything else.

```
MsgBox IIf(Range("A1") = 0, "Zero", "Nonzero")
```

Select Case constructs

The `Select Case` construct is useful for choosing among three or more options. This construct also works with two options and is a good alternative to `If-Then-Else`. The syntax for `Select Case` is as follows:

```
Select Case testexpression
    [Case expressionlist-n
        [instructions-n]]
    [Case Else
        [default_instructions]]
End Select
```

The following example of a `Select Case` construct shows another way to code the `GreetMe` examples presented in the preceding section:

```
Sub GreetMe()
    Select Case Time
        Case Is < 0.5
            Msg = "Good Morning"
        Case 0.5 To 0.75
            Msg = "Good Afternoon"
        Case Else
            Msg = "Good Evening"
    End Select
    MsgBox Msg
End Sub
```

And here's a rewritten version of the `Discount` example, using a `Select Case` construct:

```
Sub Discount3()
    Quantity = InputBox("Enter Quantity: ")
    Select Case Quantity
        Case ""
            Exit Sub
        Case 0 To 24
            Discount = 0.1
        Case 25 To 49
            Discount = 0.15
        Case 50 To 74
            Discount = 0.2
        Case Is >= 75
            Discount = 0.25
    End Select
    MsgBox "Discount: " & Discount
End Sub
```

Any number of instructions can be written below each `Case` statement, and they all are executed if that case evaluates to True. If you use only one instruction per case, as in the preceding example, you may want to put the instruction on the same line as the `Case` keyword (but don't forget VBA's statement-separator character, the colon). This technique makes the code more compact. For example,

```
Sub Discount3()
    Quantity = InputBox("Enter Quantity: ")
    Select Case Quantity
        Case "": Exit Sub
        Case  0 To 24: Discount = 0.1
        Case 25 To 49: Discount = 0.15
        Case 50 To 74: Discount = 0.2
        Case Is >= 75: Discount = 0.25
    End Select
    MsgBox "Discount: " & Discount
End Sub
```

Tip VBA exits a `Select Case` construct as soon as a True case is found. Therefore, for maximum efficiency, you might want to check the most likely case first.

`Select Case` structures can also be nested. The following procedure, for example, tests for Excel's window state (maximized, minimized, or normal) and then displays a message describing the window state. If Excel's window state is normal, the procedure tests for the window state of the active window and then displays another message.

```
Sub AppWindow()
    Select Case Application.WindowState
        Case xlMaximized: MsgBox "App Maximized"
        Case xlMinimized: MsgBox "App Minimized"
        Case xlNormal: MsgBox "App Normal"
            Select Case ActiveWindow.WindowState
                Case xlMaximized: MsgBox "Book Maximized"
                Case xlMinimized: MsgBox "Book Minimized"
                Case xlNormal: MsgBox "Book Normal"
            End Select
    End Select
End Sub
```

You can nest `Select Case` constructs as deeply as you need, but make sure that each `Select Case` statement has a corresponding `End Select` statement.

This procedure demonstrates the value of using indentation in your code to clarify the structure. For example, take a look at the same procedure without the indentations:

```
Sub AppWindow()
Select Case Application.WindowState
Case xlMaximized: MsgBox "App Maximized"
Case xlMinimized: MsgBox "App Minimized"
Case xlNormal: MsgBox "App Normal"
Select Case ActiveWindow.WindowState
```

```
Case xlMaximized: MsgBox "Book Maximized"
Case xlMinimized: MsgBox "Book Minimized"
Case xlNormal: MsgBox "Book Normal"
End Select
End Select
End Sub
```

Fairly incomprehensible, eh?

Looping blocks of instructions

Looping is the process of repeating a block of instructions. You may know the number of times to loop, or it may be determined by the values of variables in your program.

The following code, which enters consecutive numbers into a range, demonstrates what I call a *bad loop*. The procedure starts by prompting the user for two values: a starting value and the total number of cells to fill in (`InputBox` returns a string, so I used the `Val` function to convert the strings to values). This loop uses the `GoTo` statement to control the flow. If the `CellCount` variable, which keeps track of how many cells are filled, is less than the number requested by the user, program control loops back to `DoAnother`.

```
Sub BadLoop()
    StartVal = Val(InputBox("Enter the starting value: "))
    NumToFill = Val(InputBox("How many cells? "))
    ActiveCell.Value = StartVal
    CellCount = 1
DoAnother:
    ActiveCell.Offset(CellCount, 0).Value = StartVal _
     + CellCount
    CellCount = CellCount + 1
    If CellCount < NumToFill Then GoTo DoAnother Else Exit Sub
End Sub
```

This procedure works as intended, so why is it an example of bad looping? Programmers generally frown on using a `GoTo` statement when not absolutely necessary. Using `GoTo` statements to loop is contrary to the concept of structured coding (see the "What is Structured Programming?" sidebar). In fact, a `GoTo` statement makes the code much more difficult to read because it's almost impossible to represent a loop using line indentations. In addition, this type of unstructured loop makes the procedure more susceptible to error. Furthermore, using lots of labels results in *spaghetti code* — code that appears to have little or no structure and flows haphazardly.

Because VBA has several structured looping commands, you almost never have to rely on `GoTo` statements for your decision making.

For-Next loops

The simplest type of *good loop* is a `For-Next` loop, which I've already used in a few previous examples. Its syntax is

```
For counter = start To end [Step stepval]
    [instructions]
    [Exit For]
    [instructions]
Next [counter]
```

What Is Structured Programming?

Hang around with programmers, and sooner or later you'll hear the term *structured programming*. You'll also discover that structured programs are considered superior to unstructured programs.

So what is structured programming? And can you do it with VBA?

The basic premise is that a routine or code segment should have only one entry point and one exit point. In other words, a body of code should be a stand-alone unit, and program control should not jump into or exit from the middle of this unit. As a result, structured programming rules out the `GoTo` statement. When you write structured code, your program progresses in an orderly manner and is easy to follow—as opposed to spaghetti code, where a program jumps around.

A structured program is easier to read and understand than an unstructured one. More important, it's also easier to modify.

VBA is a structured language. It offers standard structured constructs, such as `If-Then-Else` and `Select Case`, and the `For-Next`, `Do Until`, and `Do While` loops. Furthermore, VBA fully supports modular code construction.

If you're new to programming, it's a good idea to form good structured programming habits early.

Following is an example of a `For-Next` loop that doesn't use the optional `Step` value or the optional `Exit For` statement. This routine executes the `Sum = Sum + Sqr(Count)` statement 100 times and displays the result—that is, the sum of the square roots of the first 100 integers.

```
Sub SumSquareRoots()
    Sum = 0
    For Count = 1 To 100
        Sum = Sum + Sqr(Count)
    Next Count
    MsgBox Sum
End Sub
```

In this example, Count (the loop counter variable) started out as 1 and increased by 1 each time the loop repeated. The Sum variable simply accumulates the square roots of each value of Count.

When you use For-Next loops, it's important to understand that the loop counter is a normal variable—nothing special. As a result, it's possible to change the value of the loop counter within the block of code executed between the For and Next statements. This is, however, a *ba-a-ad* practice and can cause unpredictable results. In fact, you should take special precautions to ensure that your code does not change the loop counter.

You can also use a Step value to skip some values in the loop. Here's the same procedure rewritten to sum the square roots of the odd numbers between 1 and 100:

```
Sub SumOddSquareRoots()
    Sum = 0
    For Count = 1 To 100 Step 2
        Sum = Sum + Sqr(Count)
    Next Count
    MsgBox Sum
End Sub
```

In this procedure, Count starts out as 1 and then takes on values of 3, 5, 7, and so on. The final value of Count is 99.

The following procedure performs the same task as the BadLoop example found at the beginning of the "Looping blocks of instructions" section. I eliminated the GoTo statement, however, converting a bad loop into a good loop that uses the For-Next structure.

```
Sub GoodLoop()
    StartVal = Val(InputBox("Enter the starting value: "))
    NumToFill = Val(InputBox("How many cells? "))
    ActiveCell.Value = StartVal
    For CellCount = 0 To NumToFill - 1
      ActiveCell.Offset(CellCount, 0).Value = StartVal + _
       CellCount
    Next CellCount
End Sub
```

For-Next loops can also include one or more Exit For statements within the loop. When this statement is encountered, the loop terminates immediately, as the following example demonstrates. This procedure determines which cell has the largest value in column A of the active worksheet.

```
Sub ExitForDemo()
    MaxVal = Application.WorksheetFunction.Max(Range("A:A"))
    For Row = 1 To 65536
        Set TheCell = Range("A1").Offset(Row - 1, 0)
        If TheCell.Value = MaxVal Then
```

```
            MsgBox "Max value is in Row " & Row
            TheCell.Activate
            Exit For
        End If
    Next Row
End Sub
```

The maximum value in the column is calculated by using Excel's `MAX` function. This value is then assigned to the `MaxVal` variable. The `For-Next` loop checks each cell in the column. If the cell being checked is equal to `MaxVal`, the `Exit For` statement ends the procedure. Before terminating the loop, though, the procedure informs the user of the row location and then activates the cell.

The previous examples use relatively simple loops. But you can have any number of statements in the loop, and you can even nest `For-Next` loops inside other `For-Next` loops. Here's an example that uses nested `For-Next` loops to initialize a 10 × 10 × 10 array with the value –1. When the procedure is finished, each of the 1,000 elements in `MyArray` will contain –1.

```
Sub NestedLoops()
    Dim MyArray(1 to 10, 1 to 10, 1 to 10)
    For i = 1 To 10
        For j = 1 To 10
            For k = 1 To 10
                MyArray(i, j, k) = -1
            Next k
        Next j
    Next i
End Sub
```

Do While loops

A `Do While` loop is another type of looping structure available in VBA. Unlike a `For-Next` loop, a `Do While` loop executes while a specified condition is met. A `Do While` loop can have either of two syntaxes:

```
Do [While condition]
    [instructions]
    [Exit Do]
    [instructions]
Loop
```

or

```
Do
    [instructions]
    [Exit Do]
    [instructions]
Loop [While condition]
```

As you can see, VBA lets you put the `While` condition at the beginning or the end of the loop. The difference between these two syntaxes involves the point in time when the condition is evaluated. In the first syntax, the contents of the loop may never be executed. In the second syntax, the contents of the loop are always executed at least one time.

The example below uses a `Do While` loop with the first syntax.

```
Sub DoWhileDemo()
    Do While Not IsEmpty(ActiveCell)
        ActiveCell.Value = 0
        ActiveCell.Offset(1, 0).Select
    Loop
End Sub
```

This procedure uses the active cell as a starting point and then travels down the column, inserting a zero into the active cell. Each time the loop repeats, the next cell in the column becomes the active cell. The loop continues until VBA's `IsEmpty` function determines that the active cell is not empty.

The procedure below uses the second `Do While` loop syntax. The loop will always be executed at least one time, even if the initial active cell is not empty.

```
Sub DoWhileDemo2()
    Do
        ActiveCell.Value = 0
        ActiveCell.Offset(1, 0).Select
    Loop While Not IsEmpty(ActiveCell)
End Sub
```

The following is another `Do While` loop example. This procedure opens a text file, reads each line, converts the text to upper case, and then stores it in the active sheet, beginning with cell A1 and continuing down the column. The procedure uses VBA's `EOF` function, which returns True when the end of the file has been reached. The final statement closes the text file.

```
Sub DoWhileDemo1()
    Open "c:\data\textfile.txt" For Input As #1
    LineCt = 0
    Do While Not EOF(1)
      Input #1, LineOfText
      Range("A1").Offset(LineCt, 0) = UCase(LineOfText)
      LineCt = LineCt + 1
    Loop
    Close #1
End Sub
```

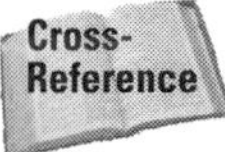

For additional information about reading and writing text files using VBA, see Chapter 26.

`Do While` loops can also contain one or more `Exit Do` statements. When an `Exit Do` statement is encountered, the loop ends immediately.

Do Until loops

The Do Until loop structure is very similar to the Do While structure. The difference is evident only when the condition is tested. In a Do While loop, the loop executes *while* the condition is true. In a Do Until loop, the loop executes *until* the condition is true.

Do Until also has two syntaxes:

```
Do [Until condition]
    [instructions]
    [Exit Do]
    [instructions]
Loop
```

or

```
Do
    [instructions]
    [Exit Do]
    [instructions]
Loop [Until condition]
```

The following example was originally presented for the Do While loop but has been rewritten to use a Do Until loop. The only difference is the line with the Do statement. This example makes the code a bit clearer because it avoids the negative required in the Do While example.

```
Sub DoUntilDemo1()
    Open "c:\data\textfile.txt" For Input As #1
    LineCt = 0
    Do Until EOF(1)
        Input #1, LineOfText
        Range("A1").Offset(LineCt, 0) = UCase(LineOfText)
        LineCt = LineCt + 1
    Loop
    Close #1
End Sub
```

Summary

In this chapter, I discussed the fundamentals of programming in VBA, including variables, constants, data types, arrays, and VBA's built-in functions. I also discussed techniques for manipulating objects and controlling the execution of your procedures.

Chapter 9 focuses on one of the two types of procedures you can write in VBA.

✦ ✦ ✦

Working with VBA Sub Procedures

✦ ✦ ✦ ✦

In This Chapter

Declaring and creating VBA Sub procedures

Executing procedures

Passing arguments to a procedure

Using error-handling techniques

An example of developing a useful procedure

✦ ✦ ✦ ✦

A *procedure* holds a group of VBA statements that accomplishes a desired task. Most VBA code is contained in procedures. This chapter focuses on *Sub procedures*, which perform tasks but do not return discrete values. VBA also supports Function procedures, which I discuss in Chapter 10.

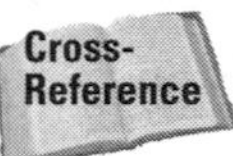

Chapter 11 has many additional examples of procedures that you can incorporate into your work.

About Procedures

A *procedure* is a series of VBA statements that resides in a VBA module, which you access in the VB Editor. A module can hold any number of procedures.

You have a number of ways to *call*, or execute, procedures. A procedure is executed from beginning to end (but it can also be ended prematurely).

A procedure can be any length, but it's usually considered good programming practice to avoid creating extremely long procedures that perform many different operations. You may find it easier to write several smaller procedures, each with a single purpose. Then design a main procedure that calls those other procedures. This approach can make your code easier to maintain.

Some procedures are written to receive arguments. An *argument* is simply information that is used by the procedure that is "passed" to the procedure when it is executed. Procedure arguments work much like the arguments you use in Excel worksheet functions. Instructions within the procedure generally perform logical operations on these arguments, and the results of the procedure are usually based on those arguments.

Declaring a Sub procedure

A procedure declared with the `Sub` keyword must adhere to the following syntax:

```
[Private | Public][Static] Sub name [(arglist)]
    [instructions]
    [Exit Sub]
    [instructions]
End Sub
```

`Private`	(Optional) Indicates that the procedure is accessible only to other procedures in the same module.
`Public`	(Optional) Indicates that the procedure is accessible to all other procedures in all other modules in the workbook. If used in a module that contains an `Option Private` statement, the procedure is not available outside the project.
`Static`	(Optional) Indicates that the procedure's variables are preserved when the procedure ends.
`Sub`	(Required) The keyword that indicates the beginning of a procedure.
name	(Required) Any valid procedure name.
arglist	(Optional) Represents a list of variables, enclosed in parentheses, that receive arguments passed to the procedure. Use a comma to separate arguments.
instructions	(Optional) Represents valid VBA instructions.
`Exit Sub`	(Optional) A statement that forces an immediate exit from the procedure prior to its formal completion.
`End Sub`	(Required) Indicates the end of the procedure.

With a few exceptions, all VBA instructions in a module must be contained in procedures. Exceptions include module-level variable declarations, user-defined data type definitions, and a few other instructions that specify module-level options (for example, `Option Explicit`).

Naming Procedures

Every procedure must have a name. The rules governing procedure names are generally the same as for variable names. The exception is that a procedure name cannot be like a cell address. For example, you can't name a procedure J34, because J34 is a cell address.

Ideally, a procedure's name should describe what its contained processes do. A good rule of thumb is to use a name that includes a verb and a noun (for example, `ProcessDate`, `PrintReport`, `Sort_Array`, or `CheckFilename`). Avoid meaningless names such as `DoIt`, `Update`, and `Fix`.

Some programmers use sentence-like names that describe the procedure (for example, `WriteReportToTextFile` and `Get_Print_Options_ and_Print_Report`). Although long names are very descriptive and unambiguous, they are also more difficult to type.

Scoping a procedure

In the preceding chapter, I noted that a variable's scope determines the modules and procedures in which the variable can be used. Similarly, a procedure's scope determines which other procedures can call it.

Public procedures

By default, procedures are *public* — that is, they can be called by other procedures in any module in the workbook. It's not necessary to use the `Public` keyword, but programmers often include it for clarity. The following two procedures are both public:

```
Sub First()
'    ... [code goes here] ...
End Sub

Public Sub Second()
'    ... [code goes here] ...
End Sub
```

Private procedures

Private procedures can be called by other procedures in the same module, but not by procedures in other modules.

Note

When you choose Excel's Tools ➪ Macro ➪ Macros command, the Macro dialog box displays only the public procedures. Therefore, if you have procedures that are designed to be called only by other procedures in the same module, you should make sure that the procedure is declared as `Private`. This prevents the user from running the procedure from the Macro dialog box.

The following example declares a private procedure, named `MySub`:

```
Private Sub MySub()
'    ... [code goes here] ...
End Sub
```

You can force all procedures in a module to be private — even those declared with the `Public` keyword — by including the following statement before your first `Sub` statement:

```
Option Private Module
```

If you write this statement in a module, you can omit the `Private` keyword from your `Sub` declarations.

Excel's macro recorder normally creates new Sub procedures called `Macro1`, `Macro2`, and so on. These procedures are all public procedures, and they will never use any arguments.

Executing Procedures

In this section, I describe the many ways to *execute*, or call, a VBA Sub procedure:

✦ With the Run ➪ Run Sub/UserForm command (in the VB Editor). Or you can press the F5 shortcut key. Excel executes the procedure at the cursor position. This method doesn't work if the procedure requires one or more arguments.

✦ From Excel's Macro dialog box (which you open by choosing Tools ➪ Macro ➪ Macros). Or you can press the Alt+F8 shortcut key.

✦ Using the Ctrl key shortcut assigned to the procedure (assuming you assigned one).

✦ By clicking a button or a shape on a worksheet. The button or shape must have the procedure assigned to it.

✦ From another procedure you write.

✦ From a Toolbar button.

✦ From a custom menu that you develop.

✦ When an event occurs. These events include opening the workbook, saving the workbook, closing the workbook, making a change to a cell, activating a sheet, and many other things.

✦ From the Immediate window in the VB Editor. Just type the name of the procedure, write any arguments that may apply, and press Enter.

Excel 5 and Excel 95 made it very easy to assign a macro to a new menu item on the Tools menu. For some reason, this feature was removed beginning with Excel 97.

I discuss these methods of executing procedures in the following sections.

In many cases, a procedure will not function properly unless it is in the appropriate context. For example, if a procedure is designed to work with the active worksheet, it will fail if a chart sheet is active. A good procedure incorporates code that checks for the appropriate context and exits gracefully if it can't proceed.

Executing a procedure with the Run ➪ Run Sub/UserForm command

The Run Sub/UserForm menu command is used primarily to test a procedure while you are developing it. You would never expect a user to have to activate the VB Editor to execute a procedure. Use the Run ➪ Run Sub/UserForm command (or F5) in the VB Editor to execute the current procedure (in other words, the procedure that contains the cursor).

If the cursor is not located within a procedure when you issue the Run ➪ Run Sub/UserForm command, the VB Editor displays its Macro dialog box so that you can select a procedure to execute.

Executing a procedure from the Macro dialog box

Choosing Excel's Tools ➪ Macro ➪ Macros command displays the Macro dialog box, shown in Figure 9-1 (you can also press Alt+F8 to access this dialog box). The Macro dialog box lists all available procedures. Use the Macros in drop-down to limit the scope of the macros displayed (for example, show only the macros in the active workbook). The Macro dialog box does not display procedures declared with the `Private` keyword, procedures that require one or more arguments, or procedures contained in add-ins.

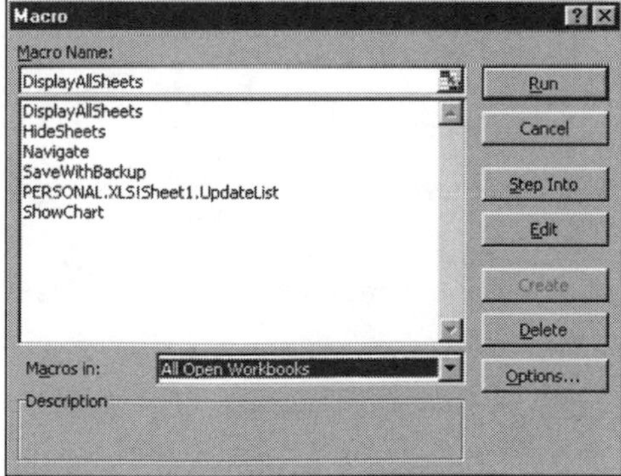

Figure 9-1: The Macro dialog box lists all available procedures.

Executing a procedure using a Ctrl+shortcut key combination

You can assign a Ctrl+shortcut key combination to any procedure that doesn't use any arguments. If you assign the Ctrl+U key combo to a procedure named `Update`, for example, pressing Ctrl+U executes the `Update` procedure.

When you begin recording a macro, the Record Macro dialog box gives you the opportunity to assign a shortcut key. However, you can assign a shortcut key at any time. To assign a Ctrl shortcut key to a procedure (or change a procedure's shortcut key), follow these steps:

1. Activate Excel and choose the Tools ➪ Macro ➪ Macros command.
2. Select the appropriate procedure from the list box in the Macro dialog box.
3. Click the Options button to display the Macro Options dialog box (see Figure 9-2).

Figure 9-2: The Macro Options dialog box lets you assign a Ctrl key shortcut and an optional description to a procedure.

4. Enter a character into the text box labeled Ctrl+.

   The character that you enter into the text box labeled Ctrl+ is case-sensitive. If you enter a lowercase *s*, the shortcut key combo is Ctrl+S. If you enter an uppercase *S*, the shortcut key combo is Ctrl+Shift+S.

5. Enter a description (optional). If you enter a description for a macro, it is displayed in the Macro dialog box.
6. Click OK to close the Macro Options dialog box, and click Close to close the Macro dialog box.

If you assign one of Excel's predefined shortcut key combinations to a procedure, your key assignment takes precedence over the predefined key assignment. For example, Ctrl+S is Excel's predefined shortcut key for saving the active workbook. But if you assign Ctrl+S to a procedure, pressing Ctrl+S no longer saves the active workbook.

The following Ctrl+key combinations are *not* used by Excel: E, J, L, M, Q, and T. Excel doesn't use too many Ctrl+Shift+key combinations. In fact, you can safely use any of them *except* F, O, and P.

Executing a procedure from a custom menu

As I describe in Chapter 22, Excel provides two ways for you to customize its menus: using the View ➪ Toolbars ➪ Customize command or writing VBA code. The latter method is preferable, but you can use either technique to assign a macro to a new menu item.

Note

Excel 5 and Excel 95 include a menu editor—which was removed beginning with Excel 97.

Following are the steps required to display a new menu item on a menu and to assign a macro to the menu item. It assumes that the new menu item is on the **Data** menu, that the menu item text is **Open Customer File**, and that the procedure is named `OpenCustomerFile`.

1. Choose the View ➪ Toolbars ➪ Customize command. Excel displays the Customize dialog box.

   When the Customize dialog box is displayed, Excel is in a special "customization" mode. The menus and toolbars are not active, but they can be customized.

2. Click the Commands tab in the Customize dialog box.
3. Scroll down and click Macros in the Categories list.
4. In the Commands list, drag the first item (labeled Custom Menu Item) to the bottom of the Data menu (after the Refresh Data item). The Data menu drops down when you click it.
5. Right-click the new menu item (which is labeled Custom Menu Item) to display a shortcut menu.
6. Enter a new name for the menu item: **&Open Customer File** in the text box labeled Name (See Figure 9-3).
7. Click Assign Macro on the shortcut menu.
8. In the Assign Macro dialog box, select the `OpenCustomerFile` procedure from the list of macros.
9. Click OK to close the Assign Macro dialog box, and click Close to close the Customize dialog box.

After you follow the process mentioned above, the new menu item always appears on the menu—even when the workbook that contains the macro is not open. In other words, changes you make using the View ➪ Toolbars ➪ Customize command are "permanent." Selecting the new menu item opens the workbook if it's not already open.

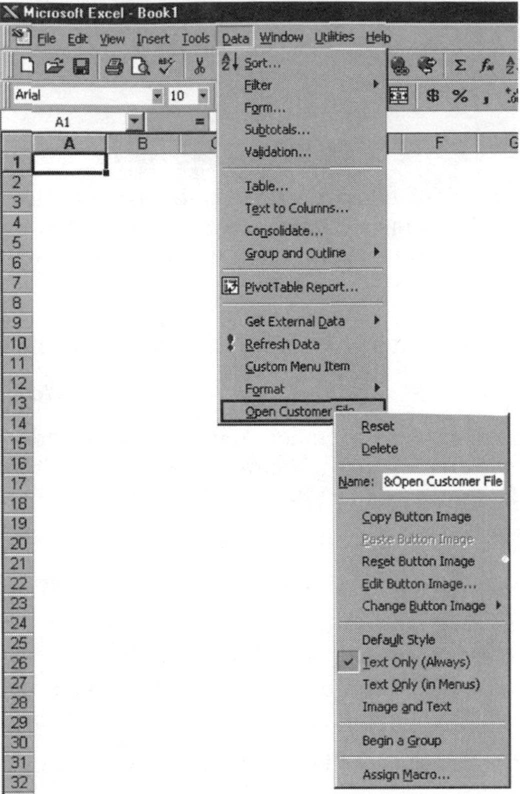

Figure 9-3: Changing the text for a menu item.

Refer to Chapter 22 to learn how to use VBA to create menu items that are displayed only when a particular workbook is open.

Executing a procedure from another procedure

One of the most common ways to execute a procedure is from another procedure. You have three ways to do this:

- ✦ Enter the procedure's name followed by its arguments (if any) separated by commas.
- ✦ Use the `Call` keyword followed by the procedure's name and then its arguments (if any) enclosed in parentheses and separated by commas.
- ✦ Use the `Run` method of the `Application` object. You can use this method to execute other VBA procedures or XLM macros. The `Run` method is also useful when you need to run a procedure and the procedure's name is assigned to a variable. You can then pass the variable as an argument to the `Run` method.

The following example demonstrates the first method. In this case, the `MySub` procedure processes some statements (not shown), executes the `UpdateSheet` procedure, and then executes the rest of the statements.

```
Sub MySub()
'    ... [code goes here] ...
     UpdateSheet
'    ... [code goes here] ...
End Sub

Sub UpdateSheet()
'    ... [code goes here] ...
End Sub
```

The following example demonstrates the second method. The `Call` keyword executes the `Update` procedure, which requires one argument; the calling procedure passes the argument to the called procedure. I discuss procedure arguments later in this chapter.

```
Sub MySub()
     MonthNum = InputBox("Enter the month number: ")
     Call UpdateSheet(MonthNum)
'    ... [code goes here] ...
End Sub

Sub UpdateSheet(MonthSeq)
'    ... [code goes here] ...
End Sub
```

Even though it's optional, some programmers always use the `Call` keyword just to make it perfectly clear that another procedure is being called.

The next example uses the `Run` method to execute the `UpdateSheet` procedure, and passes `MonthNum` as the argument.

```
Sub MySub()
     MonthNum = InputBox("Enter the month number: ")
     Result = Application.Run("UpdateSheet", MonthNum)
'    ... [code goes here] ...
End Sub

Sub UpdateSheet(MonthSeq)
'    ... [code goes here] ...
End Sub
```

The `Run` method is also useful when the procedure name is assigned to a variable. In fact, it's the only way to execute a procedure in such a way. The example below demonstrates this. The `Main` procedure determines the day of the week (an integer between 0 and 6, beginning with Sunday). The `SubToCall` variable is assigned a string that represents a procedure name. The `Run` method then calls the appropriate procedure (either `WeekEnd` or `Daily`).

```
Sub Main()
    Select Case WeekDay(Now)
        Case 0: SubToCall = "WeekEnd"
        Case 6: SubToCall = "WeekEnd"
        Case Else: SubToCall = "Daily"
    End Select
        Application.Run SubToCall
End Sub

Sub WeekEnd()
    MsgBox "Today is a weekend"
'   Code to execute on the weekend
'   goes here
End Sub

Sub Daily()
    MsgBox "Today is not a weekend"
'   Code to execute on the weekdays
'   goes here
End Sub
```

You can also use the `Run` method to execute a procedure located in a different workbook. See "Calling a procedure in a different workbook" later in this chapter.

Calling a procedure in a different module

If VBA can't locate a called procedure in the current module, it looks for public procedures in other modules in the same project.

If you need to call a private procedure from another procedure, both procedures must reside in the same module.

You can't have two procedures with the same name in the same module, but you can have identically named procedures in different modules. You can persuade VBA to execute an *ambiguously named* procedure — that is, another procedure in a different module that has the same name. To do so, precede the procedure name with the module name and a dot. For example, say that you define procedures named `MySub` in `Module1` and `Module2`. If you want a procedure in `Module2` to call the `MySub` in `Module1`, you can use either of the following statements:

```
Module1.MySub
Call Module1.MySub
```

If you do not differentiate between procedures that have the same name, you get an `Ambiguous name detected` error message.

Calling a procedure in a different workbook

In some cases, you may need your procedure to execute another procedure defined in a different workbook. To do so, you have two options: Establish a reference to the other workbook, or use the `Run` method and specify the workbook name explicitly.

To add a reference to another workbook, select the VB Editor's Tools ➪ References command. Excel displays the References dialog box (see Figure 9-4), which lists all available references, including all open workbooks. Simply check the box that corresponds to the workbook that you want to add as a reference and click OK. After you establish a reference, you can call procedures in the workbook as if they were in the same workbook as the calling procedure.

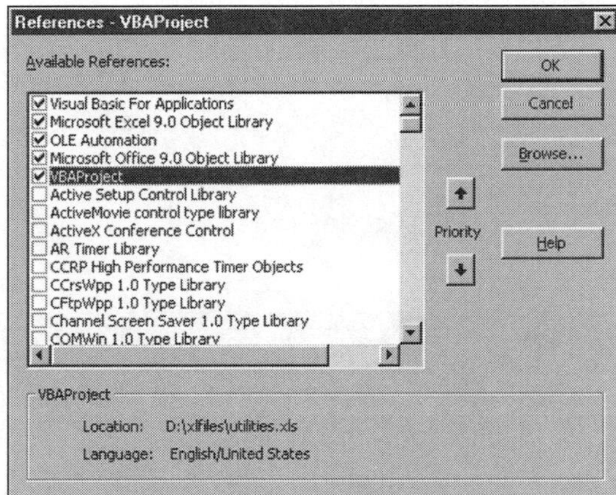

Figure 9-4: The References dialog box lets you establish a reference to another workbook.

A referenced workbook does not have to be open; it is treated like a separate object library. Use the Browse button in the References dialog box to establish a reference to a workbook that isn't open. The workbook names that appear in the list of references are listed by their VB Editor project names. By default, every project is initially named *VBAProject*. Therefore, the list may contain several identically named items. To distinguish a project, change its name in Properties window of the VB Editor. The list of references displayed in the References dialog box also includes object libraries and ActiveX controls that are registered on your system. Your Excel 2000 workbooks always include references to the following object libraries (and you can't unreference them, because they are essential):

✦ Visual Basic for Applications

✦ Microsoft Excel 9.0 Object Library

✦ OLE Automation

✦ Microsoft Office 9.0 Object Library

If you've established a reference to a workbook that contains the procedure `YourSub`, for example, you can use either of the following statements to call `YourSub`:

```
YourSub
Call YourSub
```

To precisely identify a procedure in a different workbook, specify the project name, module name, and procedure name using the following syntax:

```
MyProject.MyModule.MySub
```

Alternatively, you can use the `Call` keyword:

```
Call MyProject.MyModule.MySub
```

Another way to call a procedure in a different workbook is to use the `Run` method of the `Application` object. This technique does not require that you establish a reference. The statement below executes the `Consolidate` procedure located in a workbook named `budget macros.xls`:

```
Application.Run "'budget macros.xls'!Consolidate"
```

Why Call Other Procedures?

If you're new to programming, you may wonder why anyone would ever want to call a procedure from another procedure. You may ask, "Why not just put the code from the called procedure into the calling procedure and keep things simple?"

One reason is to clarify your code. The simpler your code, the easier it is to modify. Smaller routines are easier to decipher and then debug. Examine the accompanying procedure, which does nothing but call other procedures. This procedure is so easy to read, it acts like an outline.

```
Sub Main()
    Call GetUserOptions
    Call ProcessData
    Call CleanUp
    Call CloseItDown
End Sub
```

Calling other procedures also eliminates redundancy. Suppose that you need to perform an operation at ten different places in your routine. Rather than enter the code ten times, you can write a procedure to perform the operation and then simply call the procedure ten times.

Also, you may have a series of general purpose procedures that you use frequently. If you store these in a separate module, you can import the module to your current project and then call these procedures as needed—which is much easier than copying and pasting the code into your new procedures.

Remember, creating several small procedures rather than a single large one is simply good programming practice. A modular approach not only makes your job easier, but also makes life easier for the people who wind up working with your code.

Executing a procedure from a toolbar button

You can customize Excel's toolbars to include buttons that execute procedures when clicked. The procedure for assigning a macro to a toolbar button is virtually identical to the procedure for assigning a macro to a menu item.

Assume that you want to assign a procedure to a toolbar button on a toolbar. Here are the steps required to do so:

1. Choose the View ➪ Toolbars ➪ Customize command. Excel displays the Customize dialog box.

   When the Customize dialog box is displayed, Excel is in a special "customization" mode. The menus and toolbars are not active, but they can be customized.
2. Click the Commands tab in the Customize dialog box.
3. Scroll down and click Macros in the Categories list.
4. In the Commands list, drag the second item (labeled Custom Button) to the desired toolbar
5. Right-click the new button to display a shortcut menu.
6. Enter a new name for the button in the text box labeled Name. This is the "tooltip" text that appears when the mouse pointer moves over the button. This step is optional; if you omit it, the tooltip displays *Custom*.
7. Right-click the new button, and select Assign Macro from the shortcut menu.

   Excel displays its Assign Macro dialog box.
8. Select the procedure from the list of macros.
9. Click OK to close the Assign Macro dialog box.
10. Click Close to close the Customize dialog box.

After you follow the process above, the new toolbar button always appears on the assigned toolbar — even when the workbook that contains the macro is not open. In other words, changes you make using the View ➪ Toolbars ➪ Customize command are "permanent." Clicking the new toolbar button item opens the workbook if it's not already open.

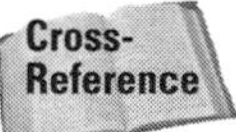

I cover custom toolbars in Chapter 21.

Executing a procedure by clicking an object

Excel has a variety of objects that you can place on a worksheet or chart sheet, and you can attach a macro to any of these objects. These objects are available from three toolbars:

✦ The Drawing toolbar

✦ The Forms toolbar

✦ The Control Toolbox toolbar

The Control Toolbox toolbar contains ActiveX controls — the same controls that you use in a custom dialog box. The Forms toolbar, included for compatibility purposes, contains similar controls (which are not ActiveX controls). The controls on the Forms toolbar were designed for Excel 5 and Excel 95. However, they can still be used in later versions (and may be preferable in some cases). The discussion that follows applies to the Button control on the Forms toolbar. Refer to Chapter 12 for information about using ActiveX controls on worksheets.

To assign a procedure to a `Button` object (which is on the Forms toolbar), follow these steps:

1. Make sure the Forms toolbar is displayed.
2. Click the Button tool on the Forms toolbar.
3. Drag in the worksheet to create the button.

Excel jumps right in and displays the Assign Macro dialog box. Select the macro you want to assign to the button, and click OK.

To assign a macro to a shape, create a shape using the Drawing toolbar. Right-click the shape and choose Assign Macro from the shortcut menu.

Executing a procedure when an event occurs

You might want a procedure to be executed when a particular event occurs. Examples of events include opening a workbook, entering data into a worksheet, saving a workbook, and many others. A procedure that is executed when an event occurs is known as an *event-handler* procedure. Event-handler procedures are characterized by the following:

✦ They have special names that are made up of an object, an underscore, and the event name. For example, the procedure that is executed when a workbook is opened is called `Workbook_Open`.

✦ They are stored in the code window for the particular object.

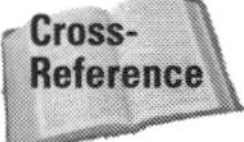

Chapter 18 is devoted to event-handler procedures.

Executing a procedure from the Immediate window

You also can execute a procedure by entering its name in the Immediate window of the VB Editor. If the Immediate window is not visible, press Ctrl+G. The Immediate window executes VBA statements as you enter them. To execute a procedure, simply enter the name of the procedure in the Immediate window and press Enter.

This method can be quite useful when you're developing a procedure because you can insert commands to display results in the Immediate window. The following procedure demonstrates this technique:

```
Sub ChangeCase()
    MyString = "This is a test"
    MyString = UCase(MyString)
    Debug.Print MyString
End Sub
```

Figure 9-5 shows what happens when you enter **ChangeCase** in the Immediate window: The `Debug.Print` statement displays the result immediately.

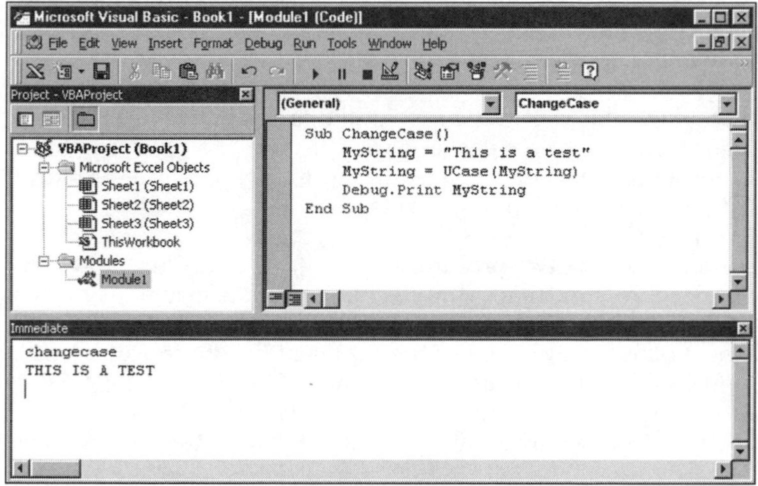

Figure 9-5: Executing a procedure by entering its name in the Immediate window.

Passing Arguments to Procedures

A procedure's *arguments* provide it with data that it uses in its instructions. The data that's *passed* by an argument can be any of the following:

- ✦ A variable
- ✦ A constant
- ✦ A literal
- ✦ An array
- ✦ An object

With regard to arguments, procedures are very similar to worksheet functions in the following respects:

- ✦ A procedure may not require any arguments.
- ✦ A procedure may require a fixed number of arguments.
- ✦ A procedure may accept an indefinite number of arguments.
- ✦ A procedure may require some arguments, leaving others optional.
- ✦ A procedure may have all optional arguments.

For example, a few of Excel's worksheet functions such as `RAND` use no arguments. Others, such as `COUNTIF`, require two arguments. Others still, such as `SUM` can use an indefinite number of arguments — up to 30. Still other worksheet functions have optional arguments. The `PMT` function, for example, can have five arguments (three are required, two are optional).

Most of the procedures that you've seen so far in this book have been declared without any arguments. They were declared with just the `Sub` keyword, the procedure's name, and a set of empty parentheses. Empty parentheses indicate that the procedure does not accept arguments.

The following example shows two procedures. The `Main` procedure calls the `ProcessFile` procedure three times (the `Call` statement is in a `For-Next` loop). Before calling `ProcessFile`, however, a three-element array is created. Inside the loop, each element of the array becomes the argument for the procedure call. The `ProcessFile` procedure takes one argument (named `TheFile`) — notice that the argument goes inside parentheses in the `Sub` statement. When `ProcessFile` finishes, program control continues with the statement after the `Call` statement.

```
Sub Main()
    File(1) = "dept1.xls"
    File(2) = "dept2.xls"
    File(3) = "dept3.xls"
    For i = 1 To 3
        Call ProcessFile(File(i))
    Next i
End Sub

Sub ProcessFile(TheFile)
    Workbooks.Open FileName:=TheFile
'   ...[more code here]...
End Sub
```

You can also, of course, pass literals (that is, not variables) to a procedure. For example,

```
Sub Main()
    Call ProcessFile("budget.xls")
End Sub
```

You can pass an argument to a procedure in two ways: by reference and by value. Passing an argument by reference (the default method) simply passes the memory address of the variable. Passing an argument by value, on the other hand, passes a *copy* of the original variable. Consequently, changes to the argument within the procedure are not reflected in the original variable.

The following example demonstrates this concept. The argument for the Process procedure is passed by reference (the default method). After the `Main` procedure assigns a value of 10 to `MyValue`, it calls the `Process` procedure and passes `MyValue` as the argument. The `Process` procedure multiplies the value of its argument (named `YourValue`) by 10. When `Process` ends and program control passes back to `Main`, the `MsgBox` function displays `MyValue: 100`.

```
Sub Main()
    MyValue = 10
    Call Process(MyValue)
    MsgBox MyValue
End Sub

Sub Process(YourValue)
    YourValue = YourValue * 10
End Sub
```

If you don't want the called procedure to modify any variables passed as arguments, you can modify the called procedure's argument list so that arguments are passed to it *by value* rather than *by reference*. To do so, precede the argument with the `ByVal` keyword. This technique causes the called routine to work with a copy of the passed variable's data, not the data itself. In the following procedure, for example, the changes made to `YourValue` in the `Process` procedure do not affect the `MyValue` variable in `Main`. As a result, the `MsgBox` function displays `10`, not `100`.

```
Sub Process(ByVal YourValue)
    YourValue = YourValue * 10
End Sub
```

In most cases, you'll be content to use the default reference method of passing arguments. However, if your procedure needs to use data passed to it in an argument — and you absolutely must keep the original data intact — you'll want to pass the data by value.

A procedure's arguments can mix and match by value and by reference. Arguments preceded with `ByVal` are passed by value; all others are passed by reference.

Note

If you pass a variable defined as a user-defined data type to a procedure, it must be passed by reference. Attempting to pass it by value generates an error.

Because I didn't declare a data type for any of the arguments in the preceding examples, all the arguments have been of the variant data type. But a procedure that uses arguments can define the data types directly in the argument list. The following is a Sub statement for a procedure with two arguments of different data types. The first is declared as an integer, and the second is declared as a string.

```
Sub Process(Iterations As Integer, TheFile As String)
```

When you pass arguments to a procedure, it's important that the data that is passed as the argument matches the argument's data type. For example, if you call Process in the preceding example and pass a string variable for the first argument, you get a *type mismatch* error.

Arguments are relevant to both Sub procedures and Function procedures. In Chapter 10, where I focus on Function procedures, I provide more examples of using arguments with your routines, including how to handle optional arguments.

Public Variables versus Passing Arguments to a Procedure

In Chapter 8, I pointed out how a variable declared as Public is available to all procedures in the module. In some cases, you may want to access a Public variable rather than pass the variable as an argument when calling another procedure.

For example, the procedure that follows passes the value of MonthVal to the ProcessMonth procedure:

```
Sub MySub()
    Dim MonthVal as Integer
'   ... [code goes here]
    MonthVal = 4
    Call ProcessMonth(MonthVal)
'   ... [code goes here]
End Sub
```

An alternative approach is

```
Public MonthVal as Integer

Sub MySub()
'   ... [code goes here]
    MonthVal = 4
    Call ProcessMonth
'   ... [code goes here]
End Sub
```

In the revised code, because MonthVal is a public variable, the ProcessMonth procedure can access it, eliminating the need for an argument for the ProcessMonth procedure.

Error-Handling Techniques

When a VBA procedure is running, errors can occur — as you undoubtedly know. These include either syntax errors (which you must correct before you can execute a procedure) or run-time errors (which occur while the procedure is running). This section deals with run-time errors.

For error-handling procedures to work, the Break on All Errors setting *must* be turned off. In the VB Editor, select Tools ➪ Options and click the General tab in the Options dialog box. If Break on All Errors is selected, VBA ignores your error-handling code. You'll usually want to use the Break on Unhandled Errors option.

Normally, a run-time error causes VBA to stop, and the user sees a dialog box that displays the error number and a description of the error. A good application doesn't make the user deal with these messages. Rather, it incorporates error-handling code to trap errors and take appropriate actions. At the very least, your error-handling code can display a more meaningful error message than the one popped up by VBA.

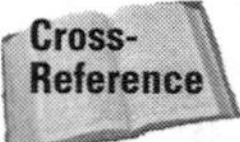

Appendix C lists all the VBA error codes and descriptions.

Trapping errors

You can use the `On Error` statement to specify what happens when an error occurs. Basically, you have two choices:

✦ Ignore the error, and let VBA continue. You can later poll the `Err` object to determine what the error was, and take action if necessary.

✦ Jump to a special error-handling section of your code to take action. This section is placed at the end of the procedure, and marked by a label.

To cause the VBA program to continue when an error occurs, insert the following statement in your code:

```
On Error Resume Next
```

Some errors are inconsequential, and can simply be ignored. But you may want to determine what the error was. When an error occurs, you can use the `Err` object to determine the error number. VBA's `Error` function can be used to display the text for `Err.Value`, which defaults to just `Err`. For example, the following statement displays the same information as the normal Visual Basic error dialog box (the error number and the error description):

```
MsgBox "Error" & Err & ": " & Error(Err)
```

Figure 9-6 shows a VBA error message, and Figure 9-7 shows the same error displayed in a message box. You can, of course, make the error message a bit more meaningful to your end users by using more descriptive text.

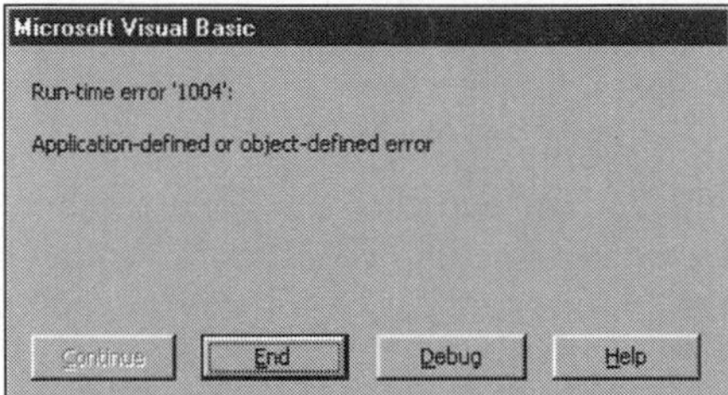

Figure 9-6: VBA's error messages aren't always user friendly.

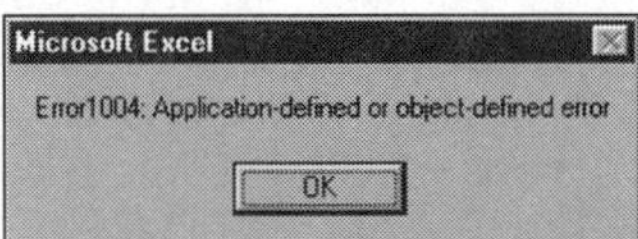

Figure 9-7: You can create a message box to display the error code and description.

You also use the `On Error` statement to specify a location in your procedure to jump to when an error occurs. You use a label to mark the location. For example,

```
On Error GoTo ErrorHandler
```

Error-handling examples

The first example demonstrates an error that can safely be ignored. The `SpecialCells` method selects cells that meet a certain criteria. (This method is equivalent to selecting the Edit ➪ Go To command and clicking the Special button to select, for example, cells that contain formulas.)

In the example that follows, the `SpecialCells` method selects all the cells in the current range selection that contain a formula that returns a number. Normally, if no cells in the selection qualify, VBA generates an error message. Using the `On Error Resume Next` statement simply prevents the error message from appearing.

```
Sub SelectFormulas()
    On Error Resume Next
    Selection.SpecialCells(xlFormulas, xlNumbers).Select
End Sub
```

The procedure below uses an additional statement to determine if an error did occur.

```
Sub SelectFormulas2()
    On Error Resume Next
    Selection.SpecialCells(xlFormulas, xlNumbers).Select
    If Err <> 0 Then MsgBox "No formula cells were found."
End Sub
```

If the value of `Err` is not equal to 0, an error occurred, and a message box displays a notice to the user.

The next example demonstrates error handling by jumping to a label.

```
Sub ErrorDemo()
    On Error GoTo Handler
    Selection.Value = 123
    Exit Sub
Handler:
    MsgBox "Cannot assign a value to the selection."
End Sub
```

The procedure attempts to assign a value to the current selection. If a range is not selected or the sheet is protected, the assignment statement results in an error. The `On Error` statement specifies a jump to the `Handler` label if an error occurs. Notice the use of the `Exit Sub` statement before the label. This prevents the error-handling code from being executed if no error occurs.

Sometimes, you can take advantage of an error to get information. The example that follows simply checks to see whether a particular workbook is open.

```
Sub CheckForFile1()
    FileName = "BUDGET.XLS"
    FileExists = False

'   Cycle through all workbooks
    For Each book In Workbooks
        If UCase(book.Name) = FileName Then
            FileExists = True
        End If
    Next book

'   Display appropriate message
    If FileExists Then _
        MsgBox FileName & " is open." Else _
            MsgBox FileName & " is not open."
End Sub
```

Here, a For Each-Next loop cycles through all objects in the Workbooks collection. If the workbook is open, the FileExists variable is set to True. Finally, a message is displayed that tells the user whether the workbook is open.

The preceding routine can be rewritten to use error handling to determine whether the file is open. In the example that follows, the On Error Resume Next statement causes VBA to ignore any errors. The next instruction attempts to reference the workbook and assign its name to a variable. If the workbook is not open, an error occurs. The If-Then-Else structure checks the value property of Err and displays the appropriate message.

```
Sub CheckForFile()
    FileName = "BUDGET.XLS"
    On Error Resume Next
    x = UCase(Workbooks(FileName).Name)
    If Err = 0 Then
        MsgBox FileName & " is open."
    Else
        MsgBox FileName & " is not open."
    End If
End Sub
```

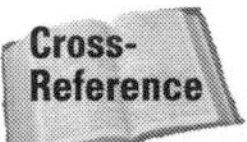

Chapter 11 presents several additional examples that use error handling.

A Realistic Example

In this chapter, I have provided you with a foundation for creating procedures. Most of the previous examples, I will admit, have been rather wimpy. The remainder of this chapter is a real-life exercise that demonstrates many of the concepts covered in this and the preceding two chapters.

This section describes the development of a useful utility that qualifies as an application as defined in Chapter 5. More important, I demonstrate the *process* of analyzing a problem and then solving it with VBA. A word of warning to the more experienced users in the audience: I wrote this section with VBA newcomers in mind. As a result, I don't simply present the code, but I show how to find out what you need to know to develop the code.

The completed application can be found on the companion CD-ROM.

The goal

The goal of this exercise is to develop a utility that rearranges a workbook by alphabetizing its sheets. If you tend to create workbooks that consist of many sheets, you know that it can be difficult to locate a particular sheet. If the sheets are ordered alphabetically, though, it's much easier to find a desired sheet.

Project requirements

Where to begin? One way to get started is to list the requirements for your application. As you develop your application, you can check your list to ensure that you're covering all the bases.

Here's the list of requirements that I compiled for this example application:

1. It should sort the sheets in the active workbook in ascending order.
2. It should be easy to execute.
3. It should always be available. In other words, the user shouldn't have to open a workbook to use this utility.
4. It should work properly for any open workbook.
5. It should not display any VBA error messages.

What you know

Often, the most difficult part of a project is figuring out where to start. In this case, I started by listing things that I know about Excel that may be relevant to the project requirements:

- ✦ Excel doesn't have a command that sorts sheets.
- ✦ I can move a sheet easily by dragging its sheet tab.

  Mental note: Turn on the macro recorder and drag a sheet to a new location to find out what kind of code this action generates.
- ✦ I'll need to know how many sheets are in the active workbook. I can get this information with VBA.
- ✦ I'll need to know the names of all the sheets. Again, I can get this information with VBA.
- ✦ Excel has a command that sorts data in worksheet cells.

  Mental note: Maybe I can transfer the sheet names to a range and use this feature. Or, maybe VBA has a sorting method that I can take advantage of.
- ✦ Thanks to the Macro Options dialog box, it's easy to assign a shortcut key to a macro.
- ✦ If a macro is stored in the Personal Macro Workbook, it will always be available.
- ✦ I need a way to test the application as I develop it. For certain, I don't want to be testing it using the same workbook in which I'm developing the code.

  Mental note: Create a dummy workbook for testing purposes.
- ✦ If I develop the code properly, VBA won't display any errors.

  Mental note: Wishful thinking . . .

The approach

Although I still didn't know exactly how to proceed, I could devise a preliminary, skeleton plan that describes the general tasks required:

1. Identify the active workbook.
2. Get a list of all the sheet names in the workbook.
3. Count the sheets.
4. Sort them (somehow).
5. Rearrange the sheets in the sorted order.

What you need to know

I saw a few holes in the plan. I knew that I had to determine the following:

- How to identify the active workbook
- How to count the sheets in the active workbook
- How to get a list of the sheet names
- How to sort the list
- How to rearrange the sheets according to the sorted list

When you lack critical information about specific methods or properties, you can consult this book or the online help. You may eventually discover what you need to know. Your best bet, however, is to turn on the macro recorder and see what it spits out when you perform some relevant actions.

Some preliminary recording

Here's an example of using the macro recorder to learn about VBA. I started with a workbook that contained three worksheets. Then I turned on the macro recorder and specified my Personal Macro Workbook as the destination for the macro. With the macro recorder running, I dragged the third worksheet to the first sheet position. Here's what the macro recorder spat out:

```
Sub Macro1()
    Sheets("Sheet3").Select
    Sheets("Sheet3").Move Before:=Sheets(1)
End Sub
```

I searched the online help for *Move,* and discovered that it's a method that moves a sheet to a new location in the workbook. It also takes an argument that specifies the location for the sheet. Very relevant to the task at hand.

Next I needed to find out how many sheets were in the active workbook. I searched for the word *Count* and found out that it's a property of a collection. I activated the Immediate window in the VB Editor and typed the following statement:

```
? ActiveWorkbook.Sheets.Count
```

Figure 9-8 shows the result. More useful information.

Figure 9-8: Using the VB Editor's Immediate window to test a statement.

What about the sheet names? Time for another test. I entered the following statement in the Immediate window:

```
? ActiveWorkbook.Sheets(1).Name
```

This told me that the name of the first sheet is `Sheet3`, which is correct. More good information to keep in mind.

Then I remembered something about the `For Each-Next` construct: It is useful for cycling through each member of a collection. After checking out the online help, I created a short procedure to test it out:

```
Sub Test()
    For Each Item In ActiveWorkbook.Sheets
        MsgBox Item.Name
    Next Item
End Sub
```

Another success. This macro displayed three message boxes, each displaying a different sheet name.

Finally, it was time to think about sorting options. From the online help, I learned that the `Sort` method applies to a range or a pivot table. So one option was to transfer the sheet names to a range and then sort the range, but that seemed like overkill for this application. I thought a better option was to dump the sheet names into an array of strings and then sort the array by using VBA code.

Initial set-up

Now I knew enough to get started writing some serious code. Before doing so, however, I need to do some initial set-up work. To recreate my steps, follow the instructions below.

1. Create an empty workbook with five worksheets, named **Sheet1**, **Sheet2**, **Sheet3**, **Sheet4**, and **Sheet5**.
2. Move the sheets around randomly so that they aren't in any particular order.
3. Save the workbook as **Test.xls**.
4. Activate the VB Editor and select the Personal.xls project in the Project Window.

   If Personal.xls doesn't appear in the Project window in the VB Editor, you haven't used the Personal Macro Workbook. To have Excel create this workbook for you, simply record a macro (any macro) and specify the Personal Macro Workbook as the destination for the macro.
5. Insert a new VBA module (use the Insert ➪ Module command).
6. Create an empty procedure called **SortSheets** (see Figure 9-9).

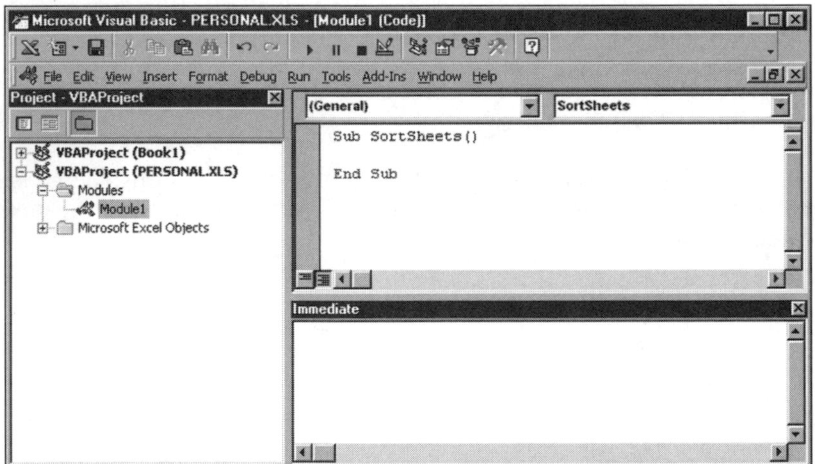

Figure 9-9: An empty procedure in a module located in the Personal Macro Workbook.

   Actually, you can store this macro in any module in the Personal Macro Workbook. However, it's a good idea to keep each macro in a separate module That way, you can easily export the module and import it into a different project later on.

7. Activate Excel. Use the Tools ➪ Macro ➪ Macros command (Options button) to assign a shortcut key to this macro. The Ctrl+Shift+S key combination is a good choice.

Code writing

Now it's time to write some code. I knew that I needed to put the sheet names into an array of strings. Because I won't know yet how many sheets are in the active workbook, I used a `Dim` statement with empty parentheses to declare the array. I knew that I could use `ReDim` afterward to redimension the array for the proper number of elements.

I entered the following code, which inserts the sheet names into the `SheetNames` array. I also added a `MsgBox` function within the loop just to assure me that the sheets' names were indeed being entered into the array.

```
Sub SortSheets()
    Dim SheetNames()
    SheetCount = ActiveWorkbook.Sheets.Count
    ReDim SheetNames(1 To SheetCount)
    For i = 1 To SheetCount
        SheetNames(i) = ActiveWorkbook.Sheets(i).Name
        MsgBox SheetNames(i)
    Next i
End Sub
```

To test the preceding code, I activated the Text.xls workbook and pressed Ctrl+Shift+S. Five message boxes appeared, each displaying the name of a corresponding sheet.

I'm a major proponent of testing your work as you go. When you're convinced that your code is working correctly, remove the `MsgBox` statement (these message boxes become annoying after a while).

Rather than use the `MsgBox` function to test your work, you can use the `Print` method of the `Debug` object to display information in the Immediate window. For this example, use the following statement in place of the `MsgBox` statement:

```
Debug.Print SheetNames(i)
```

You may find this technique less intrusive than using `MsgBox` statements.

At this point, the `SortSheets` procedure simply creates an array of sheet names in the active workbook. Two steps remain: Sort the values in the `SheetNames` array, and then rearrange the sheets to correspond to the sorted array.

Sort procedure writing

It was time to sort the `SheetNames` array. I could have stuck the sorting code in the `SortSheets` procedure, but I thought a better approach was to write a general-purpose sorting procedure that I could reuse with other projects (sorting arrays is a common operation).

You may be a bit daunted by the thought of writing a sorting procedure. The good news is that it's relatively easy to find commonly used routines that you can use or adapt. The Internet, of course, is a great source for such information.

You can sort an array in many ways. I chose the *bubble sort* method; although it's not a particularly fast technique, it's easy to code. The bubble sort method uses a nested `For-Next` loop to evaluate each array element. If the array element is greater than the next element, the two elements swap positions. This evaluation is repeated for every pair of items (that is, n–1 times).

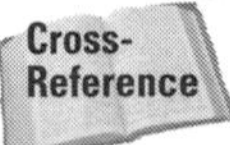

In Chapter 11, I present some other sorting routines and compare them in terms of speed.

Here's the sorting procedure I developed:

```
Sub BubbleSort(List())
'   Sorts the List array in ascending order
    Dim First As Integer, Last As Integer
    Dim i As Integer, j As Integer
    Dim Temp
    First = LBound(List)
    Last = UBound(List)
    For i = First To Last - 1
        For j = i + 1 To Last
            If List(i) > List(j) Then
                Temp = List(j)
                List(j) = List(i)
                List(i) = Temp
            End If
        Next j
    Next i
End Sub
```

This procedure accepts one argument: a one-dimensional array named `List`. An array passed to a procedure can be of any length. I use the `LBound` and `UBound` functions to define the lower bound and upper bound of the array to the variables `First` and `Last`, respectively.

After I was satisfied that this procedure worked reliably, I modified `SortSheets` by adding a call to the `BubbleSort` procedure, passing the `SheetNames` array as an argument. At this point, my module looked like this:

```
Sub SortSheets()
    Dim SheetNames()
    SheetCount = ActiveWorkbook.Sheets.Count
    ReDim SheetNames(1 To SheetCount)
    For i = 1 To SheetCount
        SheetNames(i) = ActiveWorkbook.Sheets(i).Name
    Next i
    Call BubbleSort(SheetNames)
End Sub
```

```
Sub BubbleSort(List() As String)
'   Sorts the List array in ascending order
    Dim First As Integer, Last As Integer
    Dim i As Integer, j As Integer
    Dim Temp

    First = LBound(List)
    Last = UBound(List)
    For i = First To Last - 1
        For j = i + 1 To Last
            If List(i) > List(j) Then
                Temp = List(j)
                List(j) = List(i)
                List(i) = Temp
            End If
        Next j
    Next i
End Sub
```

At this point, when the `SheetSort` procedure ends, it contains an array that consists of the sorted sheet names in the active workbook. So far, so good. Now I merely had to write some code to rearrange the sheets to correspond to the sorted items in the `SheetNames` array.

The code that I recorded earlier, again proved useful. Remember the instruction that was recorded when I moved a sheet to the first position in the workbook?

```
Sheets("Sheet1").Move Sheets(1)
```

After a little thought, I was able to write a `For-Next` loop that would go through each sheet and move it to its corresponding sheet location, specified in the `SheetNames` array.

```
For i = 1 To SheetCount
    Sheets(SheetNames(i)).Move Sheets(i)
Next i
```

For example, the first time through the loop, the loop counter (i) is 1. The first element in the SheetNames array is (in this example) Sheet1. Therefore, the expression for the `Move` method within the loop evaluates to

```
Sheets("Sheet1").Move Sheets(1)
```

The second time through the loop, the expression evaluates to

```
Sheets("Sheet2").Move Sheets(2)
```

I then added the new code to the `SortSheets` procedure:

```
Sub SortSheets()
    SheetCount = ActiveWorkbook.Sheets.Count
```

```
    ReDim SheetNames(1 To SheetCount)
    For i = 1 To SheetCount
        SheetNames(i) = ActiveWorkbook.Sheets(i).Name
    Next i
    Call BubbleSort(SheetNames)
    For i = 1 To SheetCount
        ActiveWorkbook.Sheets(SheetNames(i)).Move _
            ActiveWorkbook.Sheets(i)
    Next i
End Sub
```

I did some testing, and it seemed to work just fine for the Test.xls workbook.

Time to clean things up. I declared all the variables used and then added a few comments and blank lines to make the code easier to read. The `SortSheets` procedure now looked like the following:

```
Sub SortSheets()
'   This routine sorts the sheets of the
'   active workbook in ascending order.

    Dim SheetNames() As String
    Dim SheetCount As Integer
    Dim i As Integer

    SheetCount = ActiveWorkbook.Sheets.Count
    ReDim SheetNames(1 To SheetCount)

'   Fill array with sheet names
    For i = 1 To SheetCount
        SheetNames(i) = ActiveWorkbook.Sheets(i).Name
    Next i

'   Sort the array in ascending order
    Call BubbleSort(SheetNames)

'   Move the sheets
    For i = 1 To SheetCount
        ActiveWorkbook.Sheets(SheetNames(i)).Move _
            ActiveWorkbook.Sheets(i)
    Next i
End Sub
```

Everything seemed to be working. To test the code further, I added a few more sheets to Test.xls and changed some of the sheet names. It works like a charm!

More testing

I was tempted to call it a day. However, the fact that the procedure worked with the Test.xls workbook didn't mean that it would work with all workbooks. To test it further, I loaded a few other workbooks and retried the routine. I soon discovered that the application was not perfect. In fact, it was far from perfect. I identified the following problems:

✦ Workbooks with many sheets took a long time to sort because the screen was continually updated during the move operations.

✦ The sorting didn't always work. For example, in one of my tests, a sheet named SUMMARY (all uppercase) appeared before a sheet named Sheet1. This problem was caused by the BubbleSort procedure (an uppercase U is "greater than" a lower case H).

✦ If there were no visible workbook windows, pressing the Ctrl+Shift+S shortcut key combo caused the macro to fail.

✦ If the workbook's structure was protected, the `Move` method failed.

✦ After sorting, the last sheet in the workbook became the active sheet. Changing the active sheet is not a good practice; it's better to keep the original sheet active.

✦ If I interrupted the macro by pressing Ctrl+Break, VBA displayed an error message.

Screen updating problems

Fixing the screen-updating problem was a breeze. I inserted the following instruction at the beginning of `SortSheets` to turn screen updating off:

```
Application.ScreenUpdating = False
```

It was also easy to fix the problem with the `BubbleSort` procedure: I used VBA's `UCase` function to convert the sheet names to uppercase. That way, all the comparisons were made using uppercase versions of the sheet names. The corrected line read as follows:

```
If UCase(List(i)) > UCase(List(j)) Then
```

Another way to solve the "case" problem is to add the following statement to the top of your module:

```
Option Text Compare
```

This statement causes VBA to perform string comparisons based on a case-insensitive text sort order. In other words, *A* is considered the same as *a*.

To prevent the error message that appears when no workbooks are visible, I added some error checking. If no active workbook exists, an error occurred. I used `On Error Resume Next` to ignore the error, and then checked the value of `Err`. If `Err` is not equal to 0, it means that an error occurred. Therefore, the procedure ends. The error-checking code is

```
On Error Resume Next
SheetCount = ActiveWorkbook.Sheets.Count
If Err <> 0 Then Exit Sub ' No active workbook
```

There's usually a good reason that a workbook's structure is protected. I decided that the best approach was to display a message box to that effect (with a stop sign icon generated by the `vbCritical` constant) and then exit the procedure. (If desired, a user can unprotect the workbook and redo the sheet sorting.) Testing for a protected workbook structure was easy — the `ProtectStructure` property of a `Workbook` object returns True if a workbook is protected. I added the following block of code:

```
'   Check for protected workbook structure
    If ActiveWorkbook.ProtectStructure Then
        MsgBox ActiveWorkbook.Name & " is protected.", _
           vbCritical, "Cannot Sort Sheets."
        Exit Sub
    End If
```

To reactivate the original active sheet after the sorting is performed, I wrote code that assigned the original sheet to an object variable (`OldActive`), and then activated that sheet when the routine was finished.

Pressing Ctrl+Break normally halts a macro, and VBA usually displays an error message. But because one of my goals was to avoid VBA error messages, I needed to insert a command to prevent this situation. From the online help, I discovered that the `Application` object has an `EnableCancelKey` property that can disable Ctrl+Break. So I added the following statement at the top of the routine:

```
Application.EnableCancelKey = xlDisabled
```

Be very careful when you disable the cancel key. If your code gets caught in an infinite loop, there is no way to break out of it. For best results, insert this statement only after you're sure everything is working properly.

After I made all these corrections, the `SortSheets` procedure looked like Listing 9-1.

Listing 9-1: The final build for the SortSheets procedure

```
Sub SortSheets()
'   This routine sorts the sheets of the
'   active workbook in ascending order.

    Dim SheetNames() As String
    Dim i As Integer
    Dim SheetCount As Integer
    Dim VisibleWins As Integer
    Dim Item As Object
    Dim OldActive As Object
```

Continued

```
    On Error Resume Next
    SheetCount = ActiveWorkbook.Sheets.Count
    If Err <> 0 Then Exit Sub ' No active workbook

'   Check for protected workbook structure
    If ActiveWorkbook.ProtectStructure Then
        MsgBox ActiveWorkbook.Name & " is protected.", _
           vbCritical, "Cannot Sort Sheets."
        Exit Sub
    End If

'   Disable Ctrl+Break
    Application.EnableCancelKey = xlDisabled

'   Get the number of sheets
    SheetCount = ActiveWorkbook.Sheets.Count

'   Redimension the array
    ReDim SheetNames(1 To SheetCount)

'   Store a reference to the active sheet
    Set OldActive = ActiveSheet

'   Fill array with sheet names and hidden status
    For i = 1 To SheetCount
        SheetNames(i) = ActiveWorkbook.Sheets(i).Name
    Next i

'   Sort the array in ascending order
    Call BubbleSort(SheetNames)

'   Turn off screen updating
    Application.ScreenUpdating = False

'   Move the sheets
    For i = 1 To SheetCount
        ActiveWorkbook.Sheets(SheetNames(i)).Move _
            ActiveWorkbook.Sheets(i)
    Next i

'   Reactivate the original active sheet
    OldActive.Activate
End Sub
```

Utility availability

Because the `SortSheets` macro is stored in the Personal Macro Workbook, it is available whenever Excel is running. At this point, the macro can be executed by selecting the macro's name from the Macro dialog box (Alt+F8 displays this dialog box), or by pressing Ctrl+Shift+F8.

If you like, you can also assign this macro to a new toolbar button or to a new menu item. Procedures for doing this are described earlier in this chapter.

Evaluating the project

So there you have it. The utility meets all the original project requirements: It sorts all sheets in the active workbook, it can be executed easily, it's always available, it seems to work for any workbook, and I have yet to see it display a VBA error message.

The procedure still has one slight problem: The sorting is strict and may not always be "logical." For example, after sorting, Sheet11 is placed before Sheet2. Most would want Sheet2 to be listed before Sheet11.

The companion CD-ROM contains another version of the sheet sorting utility that overcomes the problem described above — in most cases. This version of the utility parses the sheet names into two components: the left-most text and the right-most numbers (if any). The parsed data is stored on a worksheet, and the procedure uses Excel's built-in sorting to perform the sort using two sort keys. It's still not perfect because it won't properly sort a sheet with a name like Sheet2Part1.

In this exercise, I tried to demonstrate the process of developing VBA procedures — a valuable lesson even if you're not yet a VBA veteran. I communicated the following points:

- ✦ Developing a successful procedure is not necessarily a linear process.
- ✦ It's often useful to use short procedures or the Immediate window to test ideas or approaches before incorporating them into your work.
- ✦ Even though a procedure appears to work correctly, appearances can be deceiving. Therefore, it's important to test your work in a realistic situation.
- ✦ You can learn a lot by recording your actions and studying the code that is recorded. Although I didn't actually use any of the recorded code, I learned several things by examining the code.
- ✦ A project's original requirements aren't always complete. In this example, I didn't think to require that the original active sheet remain the active sheet after the sorting.

Summary

In this chapter, I presented a comprehensive list of ways to execute Sub procedures, and I described how to use arguments. I also gave an example of developing and debugging procedures.

In the next chapter, I focus on the other type of VBA procedures — Function procedures.

✦ ✦ ✦

Creating Function Procedures

In This Chapter

The difference between Sub procedures and Function procedures

How to create custom functions

About Function procedures and function arguments

Examples, examples, examples

How to use the MySum custom function

How to debug functions, deal with the Paste Function dialog box, and use add-ins to store custom functions

How to call the Windows API to perform otherwise impossible feats

VBA enables you to create Sub procedures and Function procedures. I covered Sub procedures in the preceding chapter, and in this chapter I discuss Function procedures.

Chapter 11 has many useful and practical examples of Function procedures. You can incorporate many of those techniques into your work.

Sub Procedures versus Function Procedures

You can think of a Sub procedure as a command that can be executed either by the user or by another procedure. Function procedures, on the other hand, always return a single value—just as Excel's worksheet functions and VBA's built-in functions do. As with built-in functions, your Function procedures can use arguments.

Function procedures are quite versatile and can be used in two situations:

- As part of an expression in a VBA procedure
- In formulas that you create in a worksheet

In fact, you can use a Function procedure anywhere that you can use an Excel worksheet function or a VBA built-in function.

Why Create Custom Functions?

You are undoubtedly familiar with Excel's worksheet functions; even novices know how to use the most common worksheet functions, such as `SUM`, `AVERAGE`, and `IF`. By my count, Excel contains more than 300 predefined worksheet functions, plus additional functions available through the Analysis Toolpak add-in. If that's not enough, however, you can create custom functions by using VBA.

With all the functions available in Excel and VBA, you may wonder why you would ever need to create new functions. The answer: to simplify your work. With a bit of planning, custom functions are very useful in worksheet formulas and VBA procedures.

Often, for example, you can create a custom function that can significantly shorten your formulas. And shorter formulas are more readable and easier to work with. I should also point out, however, that custom functions in your formulas are usually much slower than built-in functions.

As you create applications, you may notice that some procedures repeat calculations. It's often possible to create a custom function that performs a calculation. Then, you can simply call the function from your procedure. A custom function thus can eliminate the need for duplicated code, reducing errors.

Coworkers often can benefit from your specialized functions. And some may be willing to pay you for custom functions that save them time and work.

Although many cringe at the thought of creating custom worksheet functions, the process is not difficult. In fact, I *enjoy* creating custom functions. I especially like how my custom functions appear in the Paste Function dialog box along with Excel's built-in functions, as if I'm reengineering the software in some way.

In this chapter, I tell you what you need to know to start creating custom functions, and I provide lots of examples.

An Introductory Example

Without further ado, here's an example of a VBA Function procedure.

A custom function

The following is a custom function defined in a VBA module. This function, named `Reverse`, uses a single argument. The function reverses its argument so that it reads backwards and returns the result as a string.

```
Function Reverse(InString) As String
'   Returns its argument, reversed
    Reverse = ""
    StringLength = Len(InString)
    For i = StringLength To 1 Step -1
        Reverse = Reverse & Mid(InString, i, 1)
    Next i
End Function
```

I explain how this function works later, in the "Analyzing the custom function" section.

When you create custom functions that will be used in a worksheet formula, make sure that they reside in a normal VBA module. If you place your custom functions in a code module for a Sheet or ThisWorkbook, they will not work in your formulas.

Using the function in a worksheet

When you enter a formula that uses the Reverse function, Excel executes the code to get the value (see Figure 10-1). Actually, the function works just like any built-in worksheet function. You can insert it in a formula by using the Insert ➪ Function command or the Paste Function button on the Standard toolbar (in the Paste Function dialog box, custom functions are located in the User Defined category).

Book1

	A	B	C
1	Excel	lecxE	
2	Reversed Text	txeT desreveR	
3	NAÏVE	EVÏAN	
4	Able was I ere I saw Elba	ablE was I ere I saw elbA	
5	Was it a rat I saw	was I tar a ti saW	
6	12345.401	104.54321	
7	TRUE	eurT	
8			
9			
10			
11			

Sheet1

Figure 10-1: Using a custom function in a worksheet formula.

The following worksheet formula shows the Reverse function in action. As you can see, it returns its single argument, but its characters are in reverse order.

```
=Reverse(A1)
```

You also can nest custom functions and combine them with other elements in your formulas. For example, the following (useless) formula uses the Reverse function twice. The result is the original string:

```
=Reverse(Reverse(A1))
```

Using the function in a VBA procedure

The following VBA procedure, which is defined in the same module as the custom Reverse function, first displays an input box to solicit some text from the user. Then, the procedure uses VBA's built-in MsgBox function to display the user input after it's processed by the Reverse function (see Figure 10-2). The original input appears as the caption in the message box.

```
Sub ReverseIt()
     UserInput = InputBox("Enter some text:")
     MsgBox Reverse(UserInput), , UserInput
End Sub
```

In the example shown in Figure 10-2, the string entered in response to the InputBox function was Babba Booey. The MsgBox function displays the reversed text.

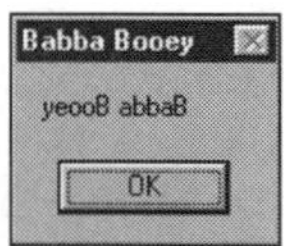

Figure 10-2: Using a custom function in a VBA procedure.

Analyzing the custom function

Function procedures can be as complex as you need. Most of the time, they are more complex and much more useful than this sample procedure. Nonetheless, an analysis of this example may help you understand what is happening.

Here's the code, again:

```
Function Reverse(InString) As String
'   Returns its argument, reversed
    Reverse = ""
    StringLength = Len(InString)
    For i = StringLength To 1 Step -1
        Reverse = Reverse & Mid(InString, i, 1)
    Next i
End Function
```

Notice that the procedure starts with the keyword Function, rather than Sub, followed by the name of the function (Reverse). This custom function uses only one argument (InString), enclosed in parentheses. As String defines the data type of the function's return value. (Excel uses the variant data type if none is specified.)

The second line is simply a comment (optional) that describes what the function does.

What Custom Worksheet Functions Can't Do

As you develop custom functions, it's important to understand a key distinction between functions that you call from other VBA procedures and functions that you use in worksheet formulas. Function procedures used in worksheet formulas must be "passive." For example, code within a function procedure cannot manipulate ranges. An example may make this clear.

You may be tempted to write a custom worksheet function that changes a cell's formatting. For example, it might be useful to have a function that changes the color of text in a cell based on the cell's value. Try as you might, however, such a function is impossible to write. No matter what you do, the function will always return an error. Remember, a function returns a value — it does not perform actions with objects.

Then, the procedure initializes the result as an empty string. Note that I use the function's name as a variable here. When a function ends, it always returns the current value of the variable that corresponds to the function's name.

Next, VBA's `Len` function determines the length of the input string and assigns this value to the `StringLength` variable.

The next three instructions make up a `For-Next` loop. The procedure loops through each character in the input (backwards) and builds the string. Notice that the `Step` value in the `For-Next` loop is a negative number, causing the looping to proceed in reverse. The instruction within the loop uses VBA's `Mid` function to return a single character from the input string. When the loop is finished, `Reverse` consists of the input string, with the characters rearranged in reverse order. This string is the value that the function returns.

The procedure ends with an `End Function` statement.

Function Procedures

A custom Function procedure has a lot in common with a Sub procedure. (For more information on Sub procedures, see Chapter 9.)

Declaring a function

The syntax for declaring a function is as follows:

```
[Public | Private][Static] Function name [(arglist)][As type]
    [instructions]
    [name = expression]
```

```
    [Exit Function]
    [instructions]
    [name = expression]
End Function
```

`Public`	(Optional) Indicates that the Function procedure is accessible to all other procedures in all other modules in all active Excel VBA projects.
`Private`	(Optional) Indicates that the Function procedure is accessible only to other procedures in the same module.
`Static`	(Optional) Indicates that the values of variables declared in the Function procedure are preserved between calls.
`Function`	(Required) Is the keyword that indicates the beginning of a procedure that returns a value or other data.
name	(Required) Represents any valid Function procedure name, which must follow the same rules as a variable name. When the function finishes, the single-value result is assigned to its own name.
arglist	(Optional) Represents a list of one or more variables that represent arguments passed to the Function procedure. The arguments are enclosed in parentheses. Use a comma to separate pairs of arguments.
type	(Optional) Is the data type returned by the Function procedure.
instructions	(Optional) Are any number of valid VBA instructions.
`Exit Function`	(Optional) Is a statement that forces an immediate exit from the Function procedure prior to its completion.
`End Function`	(Required) Is a keyword that indicates the end of the Function procedure.

To coincide with Excel terminology, I'll call a Function procedure simply *function*. The main thing to remember about a custom function written in VBA is that a value is always assigned to its name a minimum of one time, generally when it has completed execution.

To create a custom function, start by inserting a VBA module. (Or you can use an existing module.) Enter the keyword `Function`, followed by the function's name and a list of its arguments (if any) in parentheses. Insert the VBA code that performs the work, and make sure that the appropriate value is assigned to the term corresponding to the function's name at least once within the body of the Function procedure. End the function with an `End Function` statement.

Function names must adhere to the same rules for variable names, and you cannot use a name that looks like a worksheet cell's name (for example, a function named J21 won't work).

A function's scope

In Chapter 9, I discussed the concept of a procedure's scope (public or private). The same discussion applies to functions: A function's scope determines whether it can be called by procedures in other modules or in worksheets.

Here are a few things to keep in mind about a function's scope:

✦ If you don't declare a function's scope, its default is public.

✦ Functions declared `As Private` do not appear in Excel's Paste Function dialog box. Therefore, when you create a function that should be used only in a VBA procedure, you should declare it private so that users don't try to use it in a formula.

✦ If your VBA code needs to call a function that's defined in another workbook, set up a reference to the other workbook by using the VB Editor's Tools ➪ References command.

Executing Function procedures

Although you can execute a Sub procedure in many ways, you can execute a Function procedure in only two ways: Call it from another procedure, or use it in a worksheet formula.

From a procedure

You can call custom functions from a procedure the same way you call built-in functions. For example, after you define a function called `SumArray`, you can enter a statement like the following:

```
Total = SumArray(MyArray)
```

This statement executes the `SumArray` function with `MyArray` as its argument, returns the function's result, and assigns it to the `Total` variable.

In a worksheet formula

Using custom functions in a worksheet formula is like using built-in functions, except that you must ensure that Excel can locate the Function procedure. If the Function procedure is in the same workbook, you don't have to do anything special. If it's in a different workbook, you may have to tell Excel where to find it.

You can do so in three ways:

- *Precede the function's name with a file reference.* For example, if you want to use a function called `CountNames` that's defined in a workbook named `Myfuncs.xls`, you can use the following reference:

  ```
  =Myfuncs.xls!CountNames(A1:A1000)
  ```

  If you insert the function with the Paste Function dialog box, the workbook reference is inserted automatically.

- *Set up a reference to the workbook.* You do so with the VB Editor's Tools ➪ References command. If the function is defined in a referenced workbook, you don't need to use the worksheet name. Even when the dependent workbook is assigned as a reference, the Paste Function dialog box continues to insert the workbook reference (although it's not necessary).

- *Create an add-in.* When you create an add-in from a workbook that has Function procedures, you don't need to use the file reference when you use one of the functions in a formula. The add-in must be installed, however. I discuss add-ins in Chapter 20.

You'll notice that your Function procedures don't appear in the Macro dialog box when you issue the Tools ➪ Macro ➪ Macros command. In addition, you can't choose a function when you issue the VB Editor's Run ➪ Sub/UserForm command (or press F5) if the cursor is located in a Function procedure (you get the Macro dialog box that lets you choose a macro to run). As a result, you need to do a bit of extra up-front work to test your functions as you're developing them. One approach is to set up a simple procedure that calls the function. If the function is designed to be used in worksheet formulas, you'll want to enter a simple formula to test it.

Function Arguments

Keep in mind the following points about Function procedure arguments:

- Arguments can be variables (including arrays), constants, literals, or expressions.
- Some functions do not have arguments.
- Some functions have a fixed number of required arguments (from 1 to 60).
- Some functions have a combination of required and optional arguments.

Note

If your formula uses a custom worksheet function and it returns #VALUE!, there is an error in your function. The error could be caused by logical errors in your code or by passing incorrect arguments to the function. See "Debugging Functions" later in this chapter.

Reinventing the Wheel

Most of Excel's built-in functions are impossible to create in VBA. However, some *can* be duplicated.

Just for fun, I wrote my own version of Excel's UPPER function (which converts a string to all uppercase) and named it UpCase:

```
Function UpCase(InString As String) As String
'   Converts its argument to all uppercase.
    Dim StringLength As Integer
    Dim i As Integer
    Dim ASCIIVal As Integer
    Dim CharVal As Integer

    StringLength = Len(InString)
    UpCase = InString
    For i = 1 To StringLength
        ASCIIVal = Asc(Mid(InString, i, 1))
        CharVal = 0
        If ASCIIVal >= 97 And ASCIIVal <= 122 Then
            CharVal = -32
            Mid(UpCase, i, 1) = Chr(ASCIIVal + CharVal)
        End If
    Next i
End Function
```

I was curious to see how the custom function differed from the built-in function, so I created a worksheet that called the function 10,000 times, using an argument that was 26 characters long. The worksheet took 13 seconds to calculate. I then substituted Excel's UPPER function and ran the test again. The recalculation time was virtually instantaneous.

I don't claim that my UpCase function is the optimal algorithm for this task, but it's fairly obvious that a custom function will never match the speed of Excel's built-in functions.

Function Examples

In this section, I present a series of examples, demonstrating how to use arguments effectively with functions. By the way, this discussion also applies to procedures.

All the function examples in this section are available on the companion CD-ROM.

A function with no argument

Like Sub procedures, Function procedures need not have arguments. Excel, for example, has a few built-in functions that don't use arguments, including RAND(), TODAY(), and NOW(). You can create similar functions.

Here's a simple example of a function that doesn't use an argument. The following function returns the UserName property of the Application object. This name appears in the Options dialog box (General tab) and is stored in the Windows Registry.

```
Function User()
'   Returns the name of the current user
    User = Application.UserName
End Function
```

When you enter the following formula, the cell returns the name of the current user (assuming that it's listed properly in the Registry):

```
=User()
```

Note

When you use a function with no arguments in a worksheet formula, you must include a set of empty parentheses. This requirement is not necessary if you call the function in a VBA procedure, although including the empty parentheses does make it clear that you're calling a function.

To use this function in another procedure, you must assign it to a variable, use it in an expression, or use it as an argument for another function.

The following example uses this function as an argument for the MsgBox statement. The concatenation operator (&) joins the literal string with the result of the User function.

```
Sub ShowUser()
    MsgBox "The user is " & User()
End Sub
```

Another function with no argument

I used to use Excel's RAND() function to quickly fill a range of cells with values. But I didn't like the fact that the random numbers change whenever the worksheet is recalculated. So I usually had to convert the formulas to values by using the Edit ➪ Paste Special command (with the Values option).

Then, I realized that I could create a custom function that returned random numbers that didn't change. I used VBA's built-in Rnd function, which returns a random number between 0 and 1. The custom function is as follows:

```
Function StaticRand()
'    Returns a random number that doesn't
'    change when recalculated
     StaticRand = Rnd
End Function
```

If you want to generate a series of random integers between 0 and 1000, you can use a formula such as this:

```
=INT(StaticRand()*1000)
```

The values produced by this formula never change, unlike those created by the built-in RAND() function.

Controlling Function Recalculation

When you use a custom function in a worksheet formula, when is it recalculated?

Custom functions behave like Excel's built-in worksheet functions. Normally, a custom function is recalculated only when it needs to be—which is only when any of the function's arguments are modified. You can, however, force functions to recalculate more frequently. Adding the following statement to a Function procedure makes the function recalculate whenever any cell is changed:

```
Application.Volatile True
```

The Volatile method of the Application object has one argument (either True or False). Marking a Function procedure as volatile forces the function to be calculated whenever recalculation occurs for any cell in the worksheet.

For example, the custom StaticRand function can be changed to emulate Excel's RAND() function using the Volatile method, as follows:

```
Function NonStaticRand()
'    Returns a random number that
'    doesn't change when recalculated
     Application.Volatile True
     NonStaticRand = Rnd
End Function
```

Using the False argument of the Volatile method causes the function to be recalculated only when one or more of its arguments change as a result of a recalculation (if a function has no arguments, this method has no effect).

A function with one argument

This section describes a function for sales managers who need to calculate the commissions earned by their sales forces. The calculations in this example are based on the following table:

Monthly Sales	*Commission Rate*
0–$9,999	8.0%
$10,000–$19,999	10.5%
$20,000–$39,999	12.0%
$40,000+	14.0%

Note that the commission rate depends on the month's total sales. Employees who sell more earn a higher commission rate.

There are several ways to calculate commissions for various sales amounts entered into a worksheet. If you're not thinking too clearly, you might waste lots of time and come up with a lengthy formula such as this:

```
=IF(AND(A1>=0,A1<=9999.99),A1*0.08,
 IF(AND(A1>=10000,A1<=19999.99),A1*0.105,
 IF(AND(A1>=20000,A1<=39999.99),A1*0.12,
 IF(A1>=40000,A1*0.14,0))))
```

This is a bad approach for a couple of reasons. First, the formula is overly complex, making it difficult to understand. Second, the values are hard-coded into the formula, making the formula difficult to modify.

A better approach is to use a lookup table function to compute the commissions. For example,

```
=VLOOKUP(A1,Table,2)*A1
```

Yet another approach (which eliminates the need to use a lookup table) is to create a custom function such as the following:

```
Function Commission(Sales)
    Const Tier1 = 0.08
    Const Tier2 = 0.105
    Const Tier3 = 0.12
    Const Tier4 = 0.14
'   Calculates sales commissions
```

```
    Select Case Sales
        Case 0 To 9999.99: Commission = Sales * Tier1
        Case 1000 To 19999.99: Commission = Sales * Tier2
        Case 20000 To 39999.99: Commission = Sales * Tier3
        Case Is >= 40000: Commission = Sales * Tier4
    End Select
End Function
```

After you enter this function in a VBA module, you can use it in a worksheet formula or call the function from other VBA procedures.

Entering the following formula into a cell produces a result of 3,000 (the amount, 25,000, qualifies for a commission rate of 12 percent):

```
=Commission(25000)
```

Even if you don't need custom functions in a worksheet, creating Function procedures can make your VBA coding much simpler. For example, if your VBA procedure calculates sales commissions, you can use the exact same function and call it from a VBA procedure. Here's a tiny procedure that asks the user for a sales amount and then uses the `Commission` function to calculate the commission due:

```
Sub CalcComm()
     Sales = InputBox("Enter Sales:")
     MsgBox "The commission is " & Commission(Sales)
End Sub
```

The `CalcComm` procedure starts by displaying an input box that asks for the sales amount. Then, it displays a message box with the calculated sales commission for that amount.

This Sub procedure works, but it is rather crude. Following is an enhanced version that displays formatted values and keeps looping until the user clicks No (see Figure 10-3).

```
Sub CalcComm()
'   Prompt for sales amount
    Sales = Val(InputBox("Enter Sales:", _
     "Sales Commission Calculator"))

'   Build the message
    Message = "Sales Amount:" & vbTab & Format(Sales, "$#,##0")
    Message = Message & vbCrLf & "Commission:" & vbTab
    Message = Message & Format(Commission(Sales), "$#,##0")
    Message = Message & vbCrLf & vbCrLf & "Another?"

'   Display the result and prompt for another
```

```
    Ans = MsgBox(Message, vbYesNo, "Sales Commission
Calculator")
    If Ans = vbYes Then CalcComm
End Sub
```

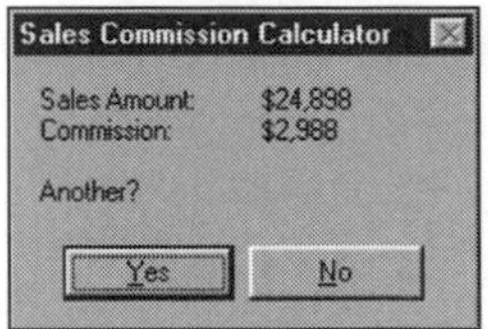

Figure 10-3: Using a function to display the result of a calculation.

This function uses two VBA built-in constants: `vbTab` represents a tab (to space the output) and `vbCrLf` specifies a carriage return and line feed (to skip to the next line). VBA's `Format` function displays a value in a specified format (in this case, with a dollar sign, comma, and no decimal places).

In both of these examples, the `Commission` function must be available in the active workbook; otherwise, Excel displays a message saying that the function is not defined.

A function with two arguments

Imagine that the aforementioned hypothetical sales managers implement a new policy to help reduce turnover: The total commission paid is increased by 1 percent for every year that the salesperson has been with the company.

I modified the custom `Commission` function (defined in the preceding section) so that it takes two arguments. The new argument represents the number of years. Call this new function `Commission2`:

```
Function Commission2(Sales, Years)'    Calculates sales
commissions based on
'    years in service
     Const Tier1 = 0.08
     Const Tier2 = 0.105
     Const Tier3 = 0.12
     Const Tier4 = 0.14
     Select Case Sales
        Case 0 To 9999.99: Commission2 = Sales * Tier1
        Case 1000 To 19999.99: Commission2 = Sales * Tier2
        Case 20000 To 39999.99: Commission2 = Sales * Tier3
        Case Is >= 40000: Commission2 = Sales * Tier4
     End Select
     Commission2 = Commission2 + (Commission2 * Years / 100)
End Function
```

Pretty simple, eh? I just added the second argument (`Years`) to the `Function` statement and included an additional computation that adjusts the commission.

Here's an example of how you can write a formula using this function (it assumes that the sales amount is in cell A1 and the number of years the salesperson has worked is in cell B1):

```
=Commission2(A1,B1)
```

A function with an array argument

A Function procedure also can accept one or more arrays as arguments, process the array(s), and return a single value. The following function accepts an array as its argument and returns the sum of its elements:

```
Function SumArray(List) As Double
    SumArray = 0
    For Each Item In List
        If Application.IsNumber(Item) Then _
            SumArray = SumArray + Item
    Next Item
End Function
```

The `IsNumber` function checks to see whether each element is a number before adding it to the total. Adding this simple error-checking statement eliminates the type mismatch error that occurs when you try to perform arithmetic with a string.

The following procedure demonstrates how to call this function. It creates a 100-element array and assigns a random number to each element. Then, the `MsgBox` function displays the sum of the values in the array by calling the `SumArray` function.

```
Sub MakeList()
    Dim Nums(1 To 100) As Double
    For i = 1 To 100
        Nums(i) = Rnd * 1000
    Next i
    MsgBox SumArray(Nums)
End Sub
```

Because the `SumArray` function doesn't declare the data type of its argument (it's a variant), the function also works in your worksheet formulas. For example, the following formula returns the sum of the values in A1:C10:

```
=SumArray(A1:C10)
```

You may notice that, when used in a worksheet formula, the `SumArray` function works very much like Excel's `SUM` function. One difference, however, is that `SumArray` does not accept multiple arguments (`SUM` accepts up to 30 arguments).

A function with optional arguments

Many of Excel's built-in worksheet functions use optional arguments. An example is the LEFT function, which returns characters from the left side of a string. Its syntax is

```
LEFT(text[,num_chars])
```

The first argument is required, but the second is optional. If the optional argument is omitted, Excel assumes a value of 1. Therefore, the following two formulas return the same result:

```
=LEFT(A1,1)
=LEFT(A1)
```

The custom functions that you develop in VBA also can have optional arguments. You specify an optional argument by preceding the argument's name with the keyword Optional.

The following is an example of a custom function that uses an optional argument. This function randomly chooses one cell from an input range and returns the cell's contents. If the second argument is True, the selected value changes whenever the worksheet is recalculated (the function is made volatile). If the second argument is False (or omitted), the function is not recalculated unless one of the cells in the input range is modified.

```
Function Draw(InRange As Variant, Optional Recalc As Boolean)
'    Chooses one cell at random from a range

'    Assign default value (False) if 2nd argument is missing
     If IsMissing(Recalc) Then Recalc = False

'    Make function volatile if Recalc is True
     Application.Volatile Recalc

'    Determine a random cell
     Draw = InRange(Int((InRange.Count) * Rnd + 1))
End Function
```

I used VBA's IsMissing function to determine whether the second argument Recalc was supplied. Whenever you use an optional argument, you need to use the IsMissing function to determine whether the argument was omitted.

All the following formulas are valid, and the first two have the same effect:

```
=Draw(A1:A100)
=Draw(A1:A100,False)
=Draw(A1:A100,True)
```

This function might be useful for choosing lottery numbers, picking a winner from a list of names, and so on.

A function that returns a VBA array

VBA includes a useful function called `Array`. The `Array` function returns a variant that contains an array. If you're familiar with array formulas in Excel, you'll have a head start understanding VBA's `Array` function. You enter an array formula into a cell by pressing Ctrl+Shift+Enter. Excel inserts brackets around the formula to indicate that it's an array formula. See Chapter 3 for more details on array formulas.

Note: It's important to understand that the array returned is not the same as a normal array that's made up of elements of the variant data type. In other words, a variant array is not the same as an array of variants.

The `MonthNames` function (refer to the next code example) is designed to be used in a worksheet formula. It has an optional argument that works as follows:

✦ If the argument is missing, the function returns a horizontal array of month names.

✦ If the argument is less than or equal to 0, the function returns a vertical array of month names. It uses the `Transpose` function to convert the array.

✦ If the argument is greater than or equal to 1, it returns the month name that corresponds to the argument value. (The following procedure adds a slight twist, using the `Mod` operator to determine the month value. The `Mod` operator returns the remainder after dividing the first operand by the second. An argument of 13, for example, returns 1. An argument of 24 returns 12, and so on.)

```
Function MonthNames(Optional MIndex)
    Dim AllNames As Variant
    AllNames = Array("Jan", "Feb", "Mar", "Apr", _
      "May", "Jun", "Jul", "Aug", "Sep", "Oct", _
      "Nov", "Dec")
    If IsMissing(MIndex) Then
        MonthNames = AllNames
    Else
        Select Case MIndex
            Case Is >= 1
'             Determine month value (for example, 13=1)
              MonthVal = ((MIndex - 1) Mod 12)
              MonthNames = AllNames(MonthVal)
            Case Is <= 0 ' Vertical array
              MonthNames = Application.Transpose(AllNames)
         End Select
    End If
End Function
```

You can use this function in a number of ways, as illustrated in Figure 10-4.

Book1

	A	B	C	D	E	F	G	H	I	J	K	L
1	Jan	Feb	Mar	Apr	May	Jun	Jul	Aug	Sep	Oct	Nov	Dec
2												
3	1	Jan		Jan								
4	2	Feb		Feb								
5	3	Mar		Mar								
6	4	Apr		Apr								
7	5	May		May								
8	6	Jun		Jun								
9	7	Jul		Jul								
10	8	Aug		Aug								
11	9	Sep		Sep								
12	10	Oct		Oct								
13	11	Nov		Nov								
14	12	Dec		Dec								
15												

Sheet1

Figure 10-4: Different ways of passing an array or a single value to a worksheet.

Range A1:L1 contains the following formula entered as an array. Start by selecting A1:L1, enter the formula, and then end it by pressing Ctrl+Shift+Enter.

```
=MonthNames()
```

Range D3:D14 contains the following formula entered as an array:

```
=MonthNames(-1)
```

Cell B3 contains the following (nonarray) formula, which was copied to the 11 cells below it:

```
=MonthNames(A3)
```

Remember, to enter an array formula, you must press Ctrl+Shift+Enter.

The lower bound of an array created using the `Array` function is always 0. Unlike other types of arrays, it is not affected by the lower bound specified with the `Option Base` statement.

A function that returns an error value

In some cases, you might want your custom function to return a particular error value. Consider the `Reverse` function, which I presented earlier in this chapter.

```
Function Reverse(InString) As String
'   Returns its argument, reversed
    Reverse = ""
    StringLength = Len(InString)
    For i = StringLength To 1 Step -1
        Reverse = Reverse & Mid(InString, i, 1)
    Next i
End Function
```

When used in a worksheet formula, this function reverses the contents of its single-cell argument (which can be text or a value). If the argument is a multicell range, the function returns #VALUE! Assume that you want this function to work only with strings. If the argument doesn't contain a string, you want the function to return an error value (#N/A).

You might be tempted simply to assign a string that looks like an Excel formula error value. For example,

```
Reverse = "#N/A"
```

Although the string *looks* like an error value, it is not treated as such by other formulas that may reference it. To return a *real* error value from a function, use VBA's `CVErr` function, which converts an error number to a real error.

Fortunately, VBA has built-in constants for the errors that you would want to return from a custom function. These errors are Excel formula error values, not VBA run-time error values. These constants are as follows:

- xlErrDiv0
- xlErrNA
- xlErrName
- xlErrNull
- xlErrNum
- xlErrRef
- xlErrValue

To return a #N/A error, you can use a statement like this:

```
Reverse = CVErr(xlErrNA)
```

The revised `Reverse` function is listed below. This function uses Excel's `IsText` function to determine whether the argument contains text. If it does, the function proceeds normally. If the cell doesn't contain text, the function returns the #N/A error.

```
Function Reverse(InString) as Variant
'   If a string, returns its argument, reversed
'   Otherwise returns #N/A error
    If Application.WorksheetFunction.IsText(InString) Then
        Reverse = ""
        StringLength = Len(InString)
        For i = StringLength To 1 Step -1
            Reverse = Reverse & Mid(InString, i, 1)
        Next i
    Else
        Reverse = CVErr(xlErrNA)
    End If
End Function
```

I also had to change the data type for the function's return value. Because the function can now return something other than a string, I changed the data type to variant.

A function with an indefinite number of arguments

Some of Excel's worksheet functions take an indefinite number of arguments. A familiar example is the `SUM` function, which has the following syntax:

```
SUM(number1,number2...)
```

The first argument is required, but you can have as many as 29 additional arguments. Here's an example of a `SUM` function with four range arguments:

```
=SUM(A1:A5,C1:C5,E1:E5,G1:G5)
```

You can mix and match the argument types. For example, the following example uses three arguments: the first is a range, the second is a value, and the third is an expression.

```
=SUM(A1:A5,12,24*3)
```

You can create Function procedures that have an indefinite number of arguments. The trick is to use an array as the last (or only) argument, preceded by the keyword `ParamArray`.

`ParamArray` can apply only to the *last* argument in the procedure's argument list. It is always a variant data type, and it is always an optional argument (although you don't use the `Optional` keyword).

Listed below is a function that can have any number of single-value arguments (it doesn't work with multicell range arguments). It simply returns the sum of the arguments.

```
Function SimpleSum(ParamArray arglist() As Variant) As Double
    For Each arg In arglist
        SimpleSum = SimpleSum + arg
    Next arg
End Function
```

The `SimpleSum` function is certainly not a substitute for Excel's `SUM` function. Try it out using various types of arguments, and you'll see that it fails unless each argument is a value or a reference to a single cell that contains a value.

Emulating Excel's SUM Function

In this section, I present a custom function called `MySum`. Unlike the `SimpleSum` function listed in the previous section, the `MySum` function emulates Excel's `SUM` function perfectly.

Before you look at the code for `MySum`, take a minute to think about Excel's `SUM` function. It is, in fact, very versatile. It can have any number of arguments (even "missing" arguments), and the arguments can be numerical values, cells, ranges, text representations of numbers, logical values, and even embedded functions. For example, consider the following formula:

```
=SUM(B1,5,"6",,TRUE,SQRT(4),A1:A5)
```

This formula — which is a valid formula — contains all of the following types of arguments, listed here in the order of their presentation:

- ✦ A single cell reference
- ✦ A literal value
- ✦ A string that looks like a value
- ✦ A missing argument
- ✦ A logical TRUE value
- ✦ An expression that uses another function
- ✦ A range reference

The `MySum` function (see Listing 10-1) handles all these argument types.

A workbook containing the `MySum` function is available on the companion CD-ROM.

Listing 10-1: MySum function

```
Function MySum(ParamArray arglist() As Variant) As Variant
' Emulates Excel's SUM function

' Variable declarations
  Dim arg As Variant
  Dim TempRange As Range, cell As Range
  Dim ErrCode As String
  MySum = 0

' Process each argument
  For arg = 0 To UBound(arglist)
'   What type of argument is it?
    Select Case TypeName(arglist(arg))
      Case "Range"
'       Create temp range to handle full row or column ranges
        Set TempRange = _
         Intersect(arglist(arg).Parent.UsedRange, _
         arglist(arg))
        For Each cell In TempRange
          If Application.IsErr(cell.Value) Then
            ErrCode = CStr(cell.Value)
            MySum = CVErr(Right(ErrCode, Len(ErrCode) _
             - InStr(ErrCode, " ")))
            Exit Function
          End If
          If cell.Value = True Or cell.Value = False Then
            MySum = MySum + 0
          Else
            If IsNumeric(cell.Value) Then MySum = MySum _
             + cell.Value
          End If
        Next cell
      Case "Null"  'ignore it
      Case "Error" 'return the error
        MySum = arglist(arg)
        Exit Function
      Case Else
'        Check for literal TRUE and compensate
         If arglist(arg) = "True" Then MySum = MySum + 2
         MySum = MySum + arglist(arg)
    End Select
  Next arg
End Function
```

As you study the code for `MySum`, keep the following points in mind:

- ✦ The procedure uses VBA's `TypeName` function to determine the type of argument. Each argument type is handled differently.

- For a range argument, the function loops through each cell in the range and adds its value to a running total.
- The data type for the function is variant because the function needs to return an error if any of its arguments is an error value.
- If an argument contains an error (for example, #DIV0!), the `MySum` function simply returns the error — just like Excel's `SUM` function.
- Excel's `SUM` function considers a text string to have a value of 0 unless it appears as a literal argument (that is, as an actual value, not a variable). Therefore, `MySum` adds the cell's value only if it can be evaluated as a number (I use VBA's `IsNumeric` function for this).
- Dealing with Boolean arguments is tricky. For `MySum` to emulate `SUM` exactly, it needs to test for a literal TRUE in the argument list and compensate for the difference (that is, add 2 to –1 to get 1).
- Testing for a NULL type handles missing arguments.
- For range arguments, I use the `Intersect` function to create a temporary range that consists of the intersection of the range and the sheet's used range. This handles cases in which a range argument consists of a complete row or column, which would take forever to evaluate.

You may be curious about the relative speeds of `SUM` and `MySum`. `MySum`, of course, is much slower, but just how much slower depends on the speed of your system and the formulas themselves. On my system, a worksheet with 1,000 `SUM` formulas recalculated instantly. After I replaced the `SUM` functions with `MySum` functions, it took about 12 seconds. `MySum` may be improved a bit, but it can never come close to `SUM`'s speed.

The point of this example is not to create a new `SUM` function. Rather, it demonstrates how to create custom worksheet functions that look and work like those built into Excel.

Debugging Functions

When you're using a formula in a worksheet to test a Function procedure, run-time errors do not appear in the all-too-familiar pop-up error box. If an error occurs, the formula simply returns an error value (#VALUE!). Luckily, this does not present a problem for debugging functions because you have several possible workarounds:

- *Place `MsgBox` functions at strategic locations to monitor the value of specific variables.* Fortunately, message boxes in Function procedures do pop up when the procedure is executed. But make sure that you have only one formula in the worksheet that uses your function, or message boxes will appear for each formula that is evaluated — a repetition that will quickly become annoying.

✦ *Test the procedure by calling it from a Sub procedure, not from a worksheet formula.* Run-time errors are displayed in the usual manner, and you can either fix the problem (if you know it) or jump right into the debugger.

✦ *Set a breakpoint in the function, and then step through the function.* You then can access all the standard debugging tools.

✦ *Use one or more temporary* `Debug.Print` *statements in your code to write values to the VB Editor's Immediate window.* For example, if you want to monitor a value inside of a loop, use something like the following routine:

```
Function VowelCount(r)
    Count = 0
    For i = 1 To Len(r)
        Ch = UCase(Mid(r, i, 1))
        If Ch Like "[AEIOU]" Then
           Count = Count + 1
           Debug.Print Ch, i
        End If
    Next i
    VowelCount = Count
End Function
```

In this case, the values of two variables, `Ch` and `i`, are printed to the Immediate window whenever the `Debug.Print` statement is encountered. Figure 10-5 shows the result when the function has an argument of `Mississippi`.

Figure 10-5: Using the Immediate window to display results while a function is running.

Dealing with the Paste Function Dialog Box

Excel's Paste Function dialog box is a handy tool that lets you choose a particular worksheet function from a list of functions. These functions are grouped into various categories to make it easier to locate a particular function. The Paste Function dialog box also displays your custom worksheet functions and prompts you for a function's arguments.

Custom Function procedures defined with the `Private` keyword do not appear in the Paste Function dialog box (although they can still be entered into formulas manually). If you develop a function for exclusive use of your other VBA procedures, you should declare it using the `Private` keyword.

By default, custom functions are listed under the User Defined category, but you can have them appear under a different category if you like. You also can add some text to describe the function (I highly recommend this step).

Specifying a function category

Oddly, Excel does not provide a direct way to assign a custom function to a category. If you would like your custom function to appear in a function category other than User Defined, you need to execute some VBA code when the workbook (or add-in) that contains the function definition is opened.

The following procedure, which is located in the code window for `ThisWorkbook`, is executed whenever the workbook is opened. This procedure assigns the function named `Commission` to the Financial category (category number 1).

```
Private Sub Workbook_Open()
    Application.MacroOptions Macro:="Commission", _
     Category:=1
End Sub
```

Table 10-1 lists the category numbers that you can use. Notice that a few of these categories (10–13) are normally not displayed in the Paste Function dialog box. If you assign your function to one of these categories, the category will appear in the dialog box.

Table 10-1
Function Categories

Category Number	*Category Name*
0	All (no specific category)
1	Financial
2	Date & Time
3	Math & Trig
4	Statistical
5	Lookup & Reference
6	Database
7	Text
8	Logical
9	Information
10	Commands

Continued

Table 10-1 (continued)

Category Number	Category Name
11	Customizing
12	Macro Control
13	DDE/External
14	User Defined
15	Engineering

Adding a function description

When you select a function in the Paste Function dialog box, a brief description of the function appears (see Figure 10-6). You can specify a description for your custom function two ways: Use the Macro dialog box, or write VBA code.

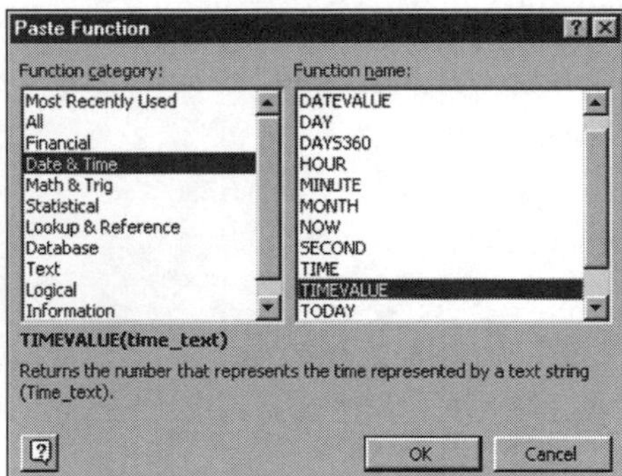

Figure 10-6: Excel's Paste Function dialog box displays brief descriptions of functions.

If you don't provide a description for your custom function, the Paste Function dialog box displays the following text: "Choose the help button for help on this function and its arguments." In most cases, of course, the help description is not accurate.

Describing your function in the Macro dialog box

Follow these steps to provide a description for a custom function:

1. Create the function in the VB Editor.
2. Activate Excel, and select Tools ➪ Macro ➪ Macros (or press Alt+F8).

The Macro dialog box lists available procedures but not functions.

3. Type the name of your function in the Macro Name box.
4. Click the Options button to display the Macro Options dialog box.
5. Enter the function description in the Description box (see Figure 10-7). The Shortcut key field is irrelevant for functions.

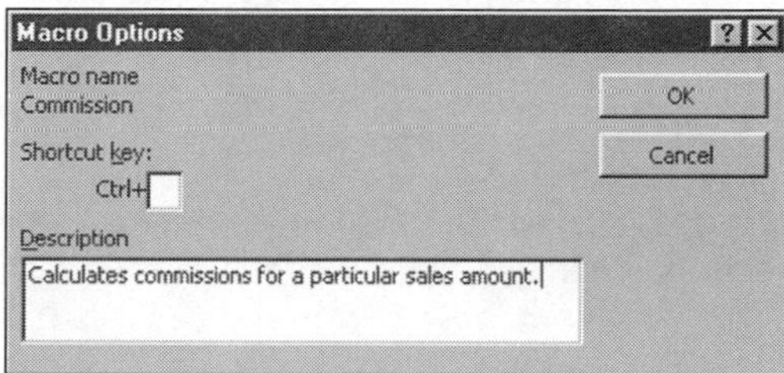

Figure 10-7: Providing a function description in the Macro Options dialog box.

6. Click OK, and then click Cancel.

After you perform the preceding steps, the Paste Function dialog box displays the description you entered in Step 5 when the function is selected.

For information on creating a custom help topic accessible from the Function Wizard, refer to Chapter 23.

When you use the Paste Function dialog box to enter a function, the formula palette kicks in after you click OK. For built-in functions, the formula palette displays a description for each of the function's arguments. Unfortunately, you cannot provide such descriptions for custom function arguments.

Describing your function with VBA code

Another way to provide a description for a custom function is to write VBA code. The following procedure assigns a description for the the function named `Commission`.

```
Sub MakeDescription()
    Application.MacroOptions _
        Macro:= "Commission", _
        Description:= "Calculates sales commissions"
End Sub
```

After you execute this procedure, you can delete it. Alternatively, you can execute the VBA statement in the Immediate window.

Using Add-ins to Store Custom Functions

You might prefer to store custom functions that you use frequently in an add-in file. A primary advantage of doing this is that the functions can be used in formulas without a filename qualifier.

Assume that you have a custom function named `ZapSpaces` and that it's stored in Myfuncs.xls. To use this function in a formula in a workbook other than `Myfuncs.xls`, you need to enter the following formula:

```
=Myfuncs.xls!ZapSpaces(A1:C12)
```

If you create an add-in from `Myfuncs.xls` and the add-in is loaded, you can omit the file reference and enter a formula such as the following:

```
=ZapSpaces(A1:C12)
```

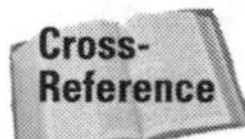

I discuss add-ins in Chapter 20.

Using the Windows API

VBA can borrow methods from other files that have nothing to do with Excel or VBA — for example, the DLL (Dynamic Link Library) files that Windows and other software use. As a result, you can do things with VBA that would otherwise be outside the language's scope.

The Windows API (Application Programming Interface) is a set of functions available to Windows programmers. When you call a Windows function from VBA, you're accessing the Windows API. Many of the Windows resources used by Windows programmers are available in DLLs, which store programs and functions and are linked at run time rather than at compile time.

Excel itself uses several DLLs, for example. The code in many of these DLLs could have been compiled right into the excel.exe executable, but the designers chose to store it in DLLs, which are loaded only when needed. This technique makes Excel's main executable file smaller. In addition, it is a more efficient use of memory because the library is loaded only when it's needed.

DLLs also are used to share code. For example, most Windows programs use dialog boxes to open and save files. Windows comes with a DLL that has the code to generate several standard dialog boxes. Programmers thus can call this DLL rather than write their own routines.

If you're a C programmer, you can produce your own DLLs and use them from VBA. Microsoft's Visual Basic language also has the capability to create DLL files that can be called from Excel.

Windows API examples

Before you can use a Windows API function, you must declare the function at the top of a standard VBA module, above the first procedure. You cannot declare Windows API functions in a code module for ThisWorkbook or a Sheet.

Declaring an API function is a bit tricky; it must be declared precisely. The declaration statement tells VBA

- ✦ Which API function you're using
- ✦ In which library the API function is located
- ✦ The API function's arguments

After you declare an API function, you can use it in your VBA code.

Determining the Windows directory

Following is an example of an API function declaration:

```
Declare Function GetWindowsDirectoryA Lib "kernel32" _
  (ByVal lpBuffer As String, ByVal nSize As Long) As Long
```

This function, which has two arguments, returns the name of the directory in which Windows is installed (something that is not normally possible using VBA). After calling the function, the Windows directory is contained in `lpBuffer`, and the length of the directory string is contained in `nSize`.

After inserting the `Declare` statement at the top of your module, you can access the function by calling the `GetWindowsDirectoryA` function. The following is an example of calling the function and displaying the result in a message box.

```
Sub ShowWindowsDir()
    Dim WinPath As String
    Dim WinDir As String
    WinPath = Space(255)
    WinDir = Left(WinPath, GetWindowsDirectoryA _
      (WinPath, Len(WinPath)))
    MsgBox WinDir, vbInformation, "Windows Directory"
End Sub
```

Executing the `ShowWindowsDir` procedure displays a message box like the one in Figure 10-8. Usually, Windows 95 or Windows 98 is installed in C:\WINDOWS, and Windows NT is often installed in C:\WINNT, but not always.

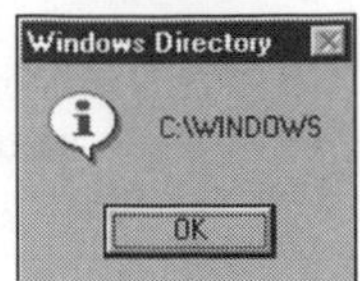

Figure 10-8: Using a Windows API function to display the Windows directory.

Often, you'll want to create a *wrapper* for API functions. In other words, you'll create your own function that uses the API function. This greatly simplifies using the API function. Here's an example of a wrapper VBA function:

```
Function WindowsDir() As String
'   Returns the Windows directory
    Dim WinPath As String
    WinPath = Space(255)
    WindowsDir = Left(WinPath, GetWindowsDirectoryA _
      (WinPath, Len(WinPath)))
End Function
```

After declaring this function, you can call it from another procedure:

```
Msgbox WindowsDir()
```

You can even use the function in a worksheet formula:

```
=WindowsDir()
```

The reason for using API calls is to perform an action that would otherwise be impossible (or at least very difficult). If your application needs to find the path of the Windows directory, you could search all day and not find a function in Excel or VBA to do the trick. But knowing how to access the Windows API may solve your problem.

Detecting the Shift key

Here's another example: Suppose you've written a VBA macro that will be executed from a toolbar button. Furthermore, suppose you want the macro to perform differently if the user presses the Shift key when the button is clicked. Normally, there is no way to detect whether the Shift key is pressed. But you can use the `GetKeyState` API function to find out. The `GetKeyState` function tells you whether a particular key is pressed. It takes a single argument, `nVirtKey`, which represents the code for the key you are interested in.

The following code demonstrates how to detect whether the Shift key is pressed when the `Button_Click` event-handler procedure is executed. Notice that I define a constant for the Shift key (using a hexadecimal value) and then use this constant as the argument for GetKeyState. If GetKeyState returns a value less than zero, it means that the Shift key was pressed; otherwise, the Shift key was not pressed.

```
Declare Function GetKeyState Lib "user32" _
  (ByVal nVirtKey As Long) As Integer

Sub Button_Click()
    Const VK_SHIFT As Integer = &H10
    Dim Shifted As Boolean
    If GetKeyState(VK_SHIFT) < 0 Then
        MsgBox "Shift is pressed"
    Else
        MsgBox "Shift is not pressed"
    End If
End Sub
```

A workbook on the companion CD-ROM demonstrates how to detect the following keys (as well as any combinations): Ctrl, Shift, Alt.

Learning more about API functions

Working with the Windows API functions can be tricky. Many programming reference books list the declarations for common API calls and often provide examples. Usually, you can simply copy the declarations and use the functions without really understanding the details. In reality (at least the reality that I've seen), most Excel programmers take a cookbook approach to API functions. The Internet has hundreds of examples that can be copied and pasted and that work quite reliably.

Chapter 11 has several additional examples of using the Windows API.

The companion CD-ROM includes a file named winapi.txt – a text file that contains Windows API declarations and constants. You can open this file with a text editor and copy the appropriate declarations to a VBA module.

When you work with API calls, system crashes during testing are not uncommon, so save your work often.

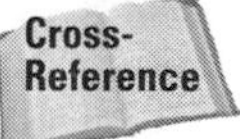

Some potentially serious compatibility issues arise when you use API calls. For example, if you develop an Excel 2000 application that uses API calls, the application will not run with Excel 5 – even if you save the workbook in the Excel 5 format – because Excel 2000 is a 32-bit application (and uses 32-bit API calls) and Excel 5 is a 16-bit application. Refer to Chapter 25 for additional information and tips on how to circumvent this problem.

Summary

In this chapter, I explained how to create and use custom VBA functions. These functions can be used in worksheet formulas and in other VBA procedures. I also described how to call Windows API functions.

The next chapter contains many examples that demonstrate the techniques discussed in this and previous chapters.

✦ ✦ ✦

CHAPTER 11

VBA Programming Examples and Techniques

In This Chapter

Examples of using VBA to work with ranges

Custom functions for use in your VBA procedures and in worksheet formulas

Examples of using Windows API functions

Examples of miscellaneous VBA tricks and techniques

I believe that learning programming concepts is accelerated by a heavy emphasis on examples. And based on the feedback that I've received from readers of previous editions of this book, I have plenty of company. VBA programmers especially benefit from a hands-on approach. A well-thought-out example usually communicates a concept much better than a description of the underlying theory. I decided, therefore, not to write a reference book that painstakingly describes every nuance of VBA. Rather, I prepared numerous examples to demonstrate useful Excel programming techniques.

The previous chapters in this section provide enough information to get you started. The online help system provides all the details I left out. In this chapter, I pick up the pace and present examples that solve practical problems while furthering your knowledge of VBA.

I've categorized this chapter's examples into six groups:

- Working with ranges
- VBA techniques
- Functions useful in your VBA procedures
- Functions you can use in worksheet formulas
- Windows API calls
- Miscellaneous techniques

Subsequent chapters in this book present additional feature specific examples: charts, pivot tables, events, UserForms, and so on.

Using the Examples in This Chapter

Not all the examples in this chapter are intended to be stand-alone programs. They are, however, set up as executable procedures that you can adapt for your own applications.

I urge you to follow along on your computer as you read this chapter. Better yet, modify the examples, and see what happens. I guarantee that this hands-on experience will help more than reading a reference book.

Working with Ranges

The examples in this section demonstrate how to manipulate worksheet ranges with VBA.

Copying a range

Excel's macro recorder is useful not so much for generating usable code as for discovering the names of relevant objects, methods, and properties. The code that's generated by the macro recorder isn't always the most efficient, but it can usually provide you lots of useful insights.

For example, recording a simple copy-and-paste operation generates five lines of VBA code:

```
Sub Macro1()
    Range("A1").Select
    Selection.Copy
    Range("B1").Select
    ActiveSheet.Paste
    Application.CutCopyMode = False
End Sub
```

But in VBA, it's not necessary to select an object to work with it. You would never learn this important point by mimicking the preceding recorded macro code, where two lines incorporate the `Select` method. This procedure can be replaced with the following much simpler routine, which takes advantage of the fact that the `Copy` method can use an argument that represents the destination for the copied range.

```
Sub CopyRange()
    Range("A1").Copy Range("B1")
End Sub
```

Both these macros assume that a worksheet is active and that the operation takes place on the active worksheet. To copy a range to a different worksheet or workbook, simply qualify the range reference for the destination. The following example copies a range from Sheet1 in File1.xls to Sheet2 in File2.xls. Because the references are fully qualified, this example works regardless of which workbook is active.

```
Sub CopyRange2()
    Workbooks("File1.xls").Sheets("Sheet1").Range("A1").Copy _
      Workbooks("File2.xls").Sheets("Sheet2").Range("A1")
End Sub
```

Another way to approach this task is to use object variables to represent the ranges, as the following example demonstrates.

```
Sub CopyRange3()
    Set Rng1 = Workbooks("File1.xls"). _
      Sheets("Sheet1").Range("A1")
    Set Rng2 = Workbooks("File2.xls"). _
      Sheets("Sheet2").Range("A1")
    Rng1.Copy Rng2
End Sub
```

Moving a range

The VBA instructions for moving a range are very similar to those for copying a range, as the following example demonstrates. The difference is that you use the `Cut` method instead of the `Copy` method. Note that you need to specify only the upper-left cell for the destination range.

```
Sub MoveRange1()
   Range("A1:C6").Cut Range("A10")
End Sub
```

Copying a variably sized range

In many cases, you need to copy a range of cells, but you don't know the exact row and column dimensions. For example, you might have a workbook that tracks weekly sales. The number of rows changes weekly as you add new data.

Figure 11-1 shows a range on a worksheet. This range consists of several rows, and the number of rows changes each week. Because you don't know the exact range address at any given time, writing a macro to copy the range requires some additional coding.

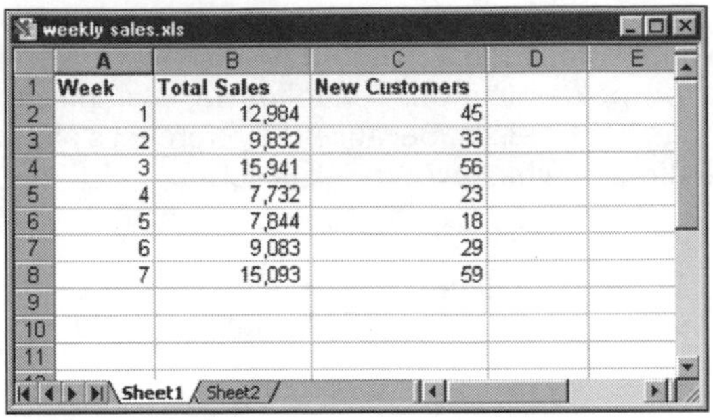

weekly sales.xls

	A	B	C	D	E
1	Week	Total Sales	New Customers		
2	1	12,984	45		
3	2	9,832	33		
4	3	15,941	56		
5	4	7,732	23		
6	5	7,844	18		
7	6	9,083	29		
8	7	15,093	59		
9					
10					
11					

Sheet1 / Sheet2

Figure 11-1: This range can consist of any number of rows.

The following macro demonstrates how to copy this range from Sheet1 to Sheet2 (beginning at cell A1). It uses the `CurrentRegion` property, which returns a `Range` object that corresponds to the block of cells around a particular cell (in this case, A1).

```
Sub CopyCurrentRegion2()
    Range("A1").CurrentRegion.Copy Sheets("Sheet2").Range("A1")
End Sub
```

Tips for Working with Ranges

When you work with ranges, keep the following points in mind:

- ✦ Your code doesn't need to select a range to work with it.
- ✦ If your code does select a range, its worksheet must be active.
- ✦ The macro recorder doesn't always generate the most efficient code. Often, you can create your macro by using the recorder and then edit the code to make it more efficient.
- ✦ It's a good idea to use named ranges in your VBA code. For example, `Range("Total")` is better than `Range("D45")`. In the latter case, if you add a row above row 45, you need to modify the macro so it uses the correct range address (D46).
- ✦ The macro recorder doesn't record keystrokes used to select a range. For example, if you press Ctrl+Shift+⇨ to select to the end of a row, Excel records the actual range selected.
- ✦ When running a macro that works on the current range selection, the user might select entire columns or rows. In most cases, you don't want to loop through every cell in the selection. Your macro should create a subset of the selection consisting of only the nonblank cells.
- ✦ Excel allows multiple selections. For example, you can select a range, press Ctrl, and select another range. You can test for this in your macro and take appropriate actions.

Using the `CurrentRegion` property is equivalent to choosing the Edit⇨Go To command, clicking the Special button, and selecting the Current Region option. To see how this works, record your actions while you issue that command. Generally, the `CurrentRegion` property setting consists of a rectangular block of cells surrounded by one or more blank rows or columns.

Selecting or otherwise identifying various types of ranges

Much of the work you will do in VBA will involve working with ranges — either selecting a range or identifying a range so you can do something with the cells.

Recording your actions while selecting cells usually doesn't generate the code you need. For example, you might be surprised at how keystroke combinations such as Ctrl+Shift+Right Arrow and Ctrl+Shift+Down Arrow are recorded by the macro recorder. In normal use, these key combinations extend the selected range to the right or down to the edge of the worksheet. The macro records the address of the range selected. Usually, this is not what you want; instead, you'll want your macro to be more general and work with any size range.

Well, you can't *record* a macro that simulates these key combinations, but you can *write* one. The trick is to use the `End` method of the `Range` object. The `End` method takes one argument, which determines the direction in which the selection is extended. The following statement selects a range from the active cell to the last nonempty cell:

```
Range(ActiveCell, ActiveCell.End(xlDown)).Select
```

As you may expect, three other constants simulate key combinations in the other directions: `xlUp`, `xlToLeft`, and `xlToRight`.

The companion CD-ROM includes a workbook that demonstrates several common types of range selections relative to the active cell. When you open this workbook, you'll see a new menu command, Selection Demo. This menu contains commands that enable the user to make various types of selections, as shown in Figure 11-2.

The following macro is in the example workbook. The `SelectCurrentRegion` macro simulates pressing Ctrl+Shift+*.

```
Sub SelectCurrentRegion()
    ActiveCell.CurrentRegion.Select
End Sub
```

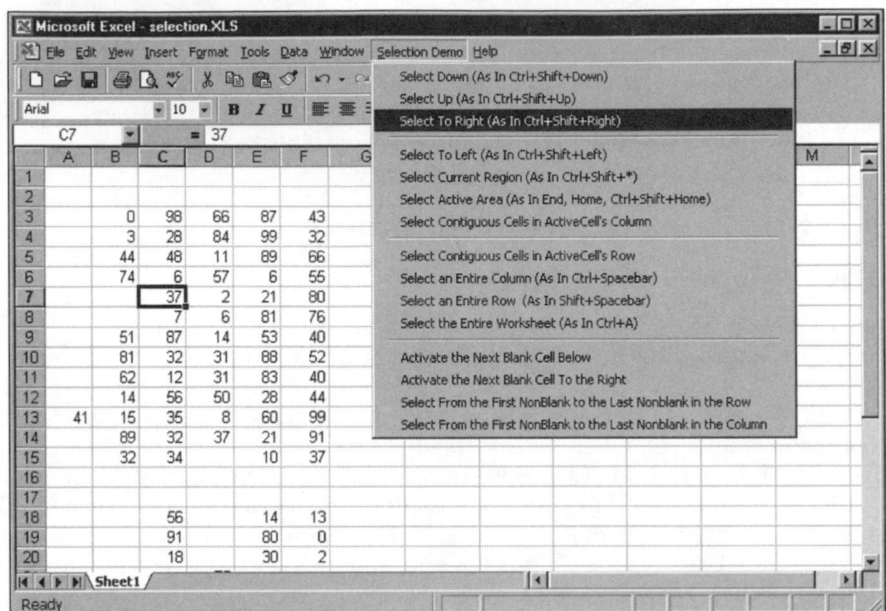

Figure 11-2: This workbook demonstrates how to select variably sized ranges using VBA.

Often, you won't want to actually select the cells. Rather, you'll want to work with them in some way (for example, format them). The cell-selecting procedures can easily be adapted. The following procedure was adapted from `SelectCurrentRegion`. This procedure doesn't select cells; it creates a `Range` object and then applies formatting to the range. The other procedures in the example workbook can also be adapted in this manner.

```
Sub FormatCurrentRegion()
    Set WorkRange = ActiveCell.CurrentRegion
    WorkRange.Font.Bold = True
End Sub
```

Prompting for a cell value

The following procedure demonstrates how to ask the user for a value and then insert it into cell A1 of the active worksheet:

```
Sub GetValue1()
    Range("A1").Value = InputBox("Enter the value")
End Sub
```

Figure 11-3 shows how the input box looks.

Figure 11-3: The `InputBox` function gets a value from the user to be inserted into a cell.

If the user clicks the Cancel button in the input box, the procedure essentially clears the cell. The following procedure checks for the Cancel button clicks and takes no action.

```
Sub GetValue2()
    UserEntry = InputBox("Enter the value")
    If UserEntry <> "" Then Range("A1").Value = UserEntry
End Sub
```

In many cases, you'll need to validate the user's entry. For example, you may require a number between 1 and 12. The following example demonstrates one way to validate the user's entry. In this example, an invalid entry is ignored and the input box is displayed again. This cycle keeps repeating until the user enters a valid number or clicks Cancel.

```
Sub GetValue3()
    MinVal = 1
    MaxVal = 12
    Msg = "Enter a value between 1 and 12"
    ValidEntry = False
    Do
        UserEntry = InputBox(Msg)
        If IsNumeric(UserEntry) Then
            If UserEntry >= 1 And UserEntry <= 12 Then
                ValidEntry = True
            Else
                Msg = "Your previous entry was INVALID."
                Msg = Msg & vbCrLf
                Msg = Msg & "Enter a value between 1 and 12"
            End If
        End If
        If UserEntry = "" Then Exit Sub
    Loop Until ValidEntry
    ActiveSheet.Range("A1").Value = UserEntry
End Sub
```

As you can see in Figure 11-4, the code also changes the message displayed if the user makes an invalid entry.

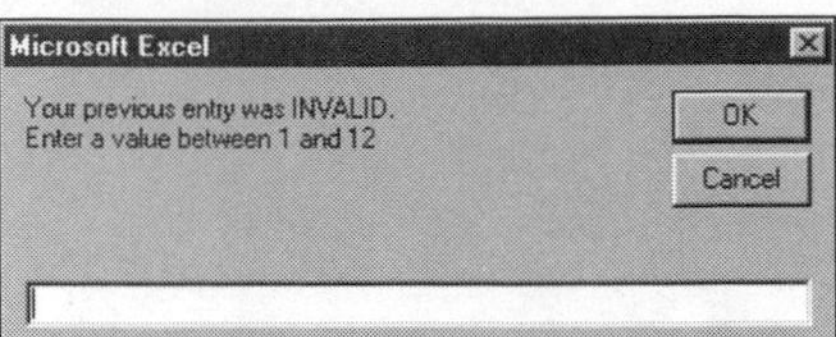

Figure 11-4: Validating a user's entry using the VBA `InputBox` function.

Entering a value in the next empty cell

A common requirement is to enter a value into the next empty cell in a column or row. The following example prompts the user for a name and a value and then enters the data into the next empty row (see Figure 11-5).

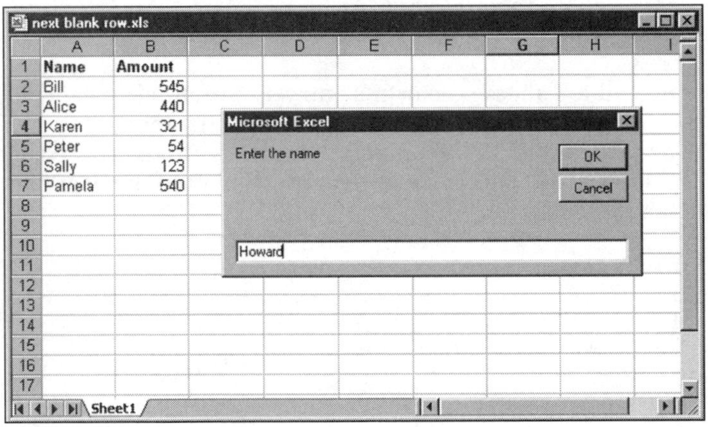

Figure 11-5: A macro for inserting data into the next empty row in the table.

```
Sub GetData()
  Do
    NextRow = _
     Application.WorksheetFunction.CountA(Range("A:A")) + 1
    Entry1 = InputBox("Enter the name")
    If Entry1 = "" Then Exit Sub
    Entry2 = InputBox("Enter the amount")
    If Entry2 = "" Then Exit Sub
    Cells(NextRow, 1) = Entry1
    Cells(NextRow, 2) = Entry2
  Loop
End Sub
```

Notice that the loop continues "forever." I use `Exit Sub` statements to get out of the loop when the user clicks Cancel.

Note

To keep things simple, this procedure doesn't perform any validation.

I used Excel's `COUNTA` function to count the number of entries in column A and then incremented this value by one to get the next empty row. Note that this technique works only when the data range begins in cell A1 and doesn't contain any blank cells.

If the data range begins in a cell other than A1, you'll need to use a different method to determine the next blank cell. For example, if the data range begins in cell B3, you can use a statement like this to determine the next blank row:

```
NextRow = Range("B3").Row + Range("B3") _
  .CurrentRegion.Rows.Count
```

Entering an AutoSum-like formula

When you click the AutoSum toolbar button, Excel analyzes the context of the active cell and attempts to determine which cells you want to sum in your formula.

The `EnterAvg` procedure shown in Listing 11-1 inserts a formula that averages the contents of the cells above the active cell. The code, which uses Excel's `AVERAGE` function, works only when at least two cells are directly above the active cell. Like the preceding example, this example uses the `End` method to determine the range to use for the `AVERAGE` function's argument.

Listing 11-1: Averaging the values of the contents above the currently active cell

```
Sub EnterAvg()
'   Check for invalid conditions
    If TypeName(Selection) <> "Range" Then Exit Sub
    If ActiveCell.Row = 1 Then Exit Sub
    If ActiveCell.Offset(-1, 0).Value = "" Then Exit Sub
    If ActiveCell.Offset(-2, 0).Value = "" Then Exit Sub

'   Determine address of first and last cell in the range
    FirstCell = ActiveCell.Offset(-1, 0).End(xlUp).Address _
     (rowabsolute:=False, columnabsolute:=False)
    LastCell = ActiveCell.Offset(-1, 0).Address _
     (rowabsolute:=False, columnabsolute:=False)
```

Continued

Listing 11-1 *(continued)*

```
'    Build the formula
     TheFormula = "=AVERAGE(" & FirstCell & ":" & LastCell _
      & ")"

'    Assign the formula
     ActiveCell.Formula = TheFormula
End Sub
```

The formula is constructed as a string (the ampersand [&] is VBA's string concatenation operator). The procedure is similar to Excel's `AutoSum` feature, but it has one key difference: It doesn't display the "guessed range" and give you an opportunity to change it. As far as I know, doing such a thing with a macro is impossible.

Although the formula is constructed by using the A1 reference style, the routine works correctly when the user uses the R1C1 reference style; Excel automatically converts the formula before inserting it into the cell.

The `EnterAvg` procedure can easily be adapted to work with horizontal ranges or to use other worksheet functions such as `MIN` or `MAX`.

This example can be found on the companion CD-ROM. When this workbook is open, you can execute the procedure with the Tools⇨Enter Average Formula command.

Counting selected cells

You can use the `Count` property of the `Range` object to determine how many cells are contained in a particular range or range selection. For example, the following statement displays a message box that contains the number of cells in the current selection:

```
MsgBox Selection.Count
```

If the active sheet contains a range named `data`, the following statement assigns the number of cells in the `data` range to a variable named `CellCount`:

```
CellCount = Range("data").Count
```

You can also determine how many rows or columns are contained in a range. The following expression calculates the number of columns in the currently selected range:

```
Selection.Columns.Count
```

And, of course, you can also use the Rows property to determine the number of rows in a range. The following statement counts the number of rows in a range named data and assigns the number to a variable named RowCount:

```
RowCount = Range("data").Rows.Count
```

Determining the type of selected range

Excel supports several types of range selections:

- A single cell
- A contiguous range of cells
- One or more entire columns
- One or more entire rows
- The entire worksheet
- Any combination of the above (that is, a multiple selection)

As a result, when your VBA procedure processes a selected range, you can't make any presumptions about what that range might be.

In the case of a multiple range selection, the Range object comprises separate areas. To process all the cells in a multiple selection, you need to loop through the cells in each of these areas. You can do so with the Areas method, which returns an Areas collection. This collection represents all the ranges in a multiple range selection.

You can use an expression like the following to determine whether a selected range has multiple areas:

```
NumAreas = Selection.Areas.Count
```

If the NumAreas variable contains a value greater than one, the selection is a multiple selection.

The AboutRangeSelection procedure uses the AreaType custom function listed here:

```
Function AreaType(RangeArea As Range) As String
'   Returns the type of a range in an area
    Select Case True
        Case RangeArea.Count = 1
            AreaType = "Cell"
        Case RangeArea.Count = Cells.Count
            AreaType = "Worksheet"
        Case RangeArea.Rows.Count = Cells.Rows.Count
            AreaType = "Column"
        Case RangeArea.Columns.Count = Cells.Columns.Count
```

```
                AreaType = "Row"
            Case Else
                AreaType = "Block"
        End Select
    End Function
```

This function accepts a `Range` object as its argument and returns one of five strings that describe the area: `Cell`, `Worksheet`, `Column`, `Row`, or `Block`. The function uses a `Select Case` construct to determine which of four comparison expressions is True. For example, if the range consists of a single cell, the function returns `Cell`. If the number of cells in the range is equal to the number of cells in the worksheet, it returns `Worksheet`. If the number of rows in the range equals the number of rows in the worksheet, it returns `Column`. If the number of columns in the range equals the number of columns in the worksheet, the function returns `Row`. If none of the `Case` expressions is True, the function returns `Block`.

Notice that the comparison doesn't involve absolute numbers. For example, rather than use 65,536 to determine whether the range is a column, it uses `Cells.Count`. Because of this, the function works properly even with earlier versions of Excel (which contain only 16,384 rows).

A workbook on the companion CD-ROM contains a procedure (named AboutRangeSelection) that uses the AreaType function to display a message box that describes the current range selection. Figure 11-6 shows an example. Understanding how this routine works will give you a good foundation for working with Range objects.

Figure 11-6: The `AboutRangeSelection` procedure analyzes the currently selected range.

You may be surprised to discover that Excel allows multiple selections to be identical. For example, if you hold down Ctrl and click five times in cell A1, the selection will have five identical areas. The `AboutRangeSelection` procedure takes this into account.

Looping through a selected range efficiently

A common task is to create a macro that evaluates each cell in a range and performs an operation if the cell meets a certain criterion. Listing 11-2 provides an example of such a macro. In this example, the `SelectiveColor1` procedure applies a red background to all cells in the selection that have a negative value. The background of other cells is reset.

Listing 11-2: Coloring all negative cells' backgrounds red

```
Sub SelectiveColor1()
'   Makes cell background red if the value is negative
    If TypeName(Selection) <> "Range" Then Exit Sub
    Const REDINDEX = 3
    Application.ScreenUpdating = False
    For Each cell In Selection
        If cell.Value < 0 Then
          cell.Interior.ColorIndex = REDINDEX
        Else
          cell.Interior.ColorIndex = xlNone
        End If
    Next cell
End Sub
```

The `SelectiveColor1` procedure certainly works, but it has a serious flaw. For example, what if the selection consists of an entire column? Or ten columns? Or the entire worksheet? The user would probably give up before all the cells were evaluated. A better solution (`SelectiveColor2`) is shown in Listing 11-3.

Listing 11-3: Improving this procedure to include wider, multiple-column ranges

```
Sub SelectiveColor2()
'   Makes cell background red if the value is negative

    Dim FormulaCells As Range
    Dim ConstantCells As Range

    Const REDINDEX = 3
```

Continued

Listing 11-3 *(continued)*

```
'   Ignore errors
    On Error Resume Next

    Application.ScreenUpdating = False

'   Create subsets of original selection
    Set FormulaCells = Selection.SpecialCells _
      (xlFormulas, xlNumbers)
    Set ConstantCells = Selection.SpecialCells _
       (xlConstants, xlNumbers)

'   Process the formula cells
    For Each cell In FormulaCells
        If cell.Value < 0 Then _
          cell.Font.ColorIndex = REDINDEX
    Next cell

'   Process the constant cells
    For Each cell In ConstantCells
        If cell.Value < 0 Then
           cell.Interior.ColorIndex = REDINDEX
        Else
           cell.Interior.ColorIndex = xlNone
        End If
    Next cell
End Sub
```

This procedure performs some extra steps that make it very efficient. I used the `SpecialCells` method to generate two subsets of the selection: One subset includes only the cells with numeric constants; the other subset includes only the cells with numeric formulas. Then, I processed the cells in these subsets by using two `For Each-Next` constructs. The net effect: Only nonblank cells are evaluated, speeding up the macro considerably.

The `On Error` statement is necessary because the `SpecialCells` method generates an error if no cells qualify. This statement also handles situations in which a range is not selected when the procedure is executed.

Deleting all empty rows

The following procedure deletes all empty rows in the active worksheet. This routine is fast and efficient because it doesn't check all rows. It checks only the rows in the "used range," which is determined using the `UsedRange` property of the `Worksheet` object.

```
Sub DeleteEmptyRows()
    LastRow = ActiveSheet.UsedRange.Rows.Count
    Application.ScreenUpdating = False
    For r = LastRow To 1 Step -1
        If Application.WorksheetFunction.CountA(Rows(r)) = 0 _
          Then Rows(r).Delete
    Next r
End Sub
```

The procedure uses Excel's `COUNTA` worksheet function to determine whether a row is empty. Notice that the procedure uses a negative step value in the `For-Next` loop. This is necessary because deleting rows causes all subsequent rows to "move up" in the worksheet, which causes a problem with the counter within the loop.

Determining whether a range is contained in another range

The following `InRange` function accepts two arguments, both `Range` objects. The function returns True if the first range is contained in the second range. Notice that the function checks to make sure that the two range arguments are contained in the same sheet and in the same workbook.

```
Function InRange(rng1, rng2) As Boolean
'   Returns True if rng1 is a subset of rng2
    InRange = False
    If rng1.Parent.Parent.Name = rng2.Parent.Parent.Name Then
        If rng1.Parent.Name = rng2.Parent.Name Then
            If Union(rng1, rng2).Address = rng2.Address Then
                InRange = True
            End If
        End If
    End If
End Function
```

The `InRange` function may appear a bit more complex than it need be because the code needs to ensure that the two ranges are in the same worksheet and workbook. Notice that the procedure uses the `Parent` property, which returns an object's own container object. For example, the following expression returns the name of the worksheet for the `rng1` object reference:

```
rng1.Parent.Name
```

The following expression returns the name of the workbook for `rng1`:

```
rng1.Parent.Parent.Name
```

Determining a cell's data type

Excel provides a number of built-in functions that can help determine the type of data contained in a cell. These include ISTEXT, ISLOGICAL, and ISERROR. In addition, VBA includes functions such as IsEmpty, IsDate, and IsNumeric.

The following CellType function accepts a range argument and returns a string (Blank, Text, Logical, Error, Date, Time, or Value) that describes the data type of the upper-left cell in the range. You can use this function in a worksheet formula or from another VBA procedure.

```
Function CellType(Rng)
'   Returns the cell type of the upper left
'   cell in a range
    Application.Volatile
    Set Rng = Rng.Range("A1")
    Select Case True
        Case IsEmpty(Rng)
            CellType = "Blank"
        Case WorksheetFunction.IsText(Rng)
            CellType = "Text"
        Case WorksheetFunction.IsLogical(Rng)
            CellType = "Logical"
        Case WorksheetFunction.IsErr(Rng)
            CellType = "Error"
        Case IsDate(Rng)
            CellType = "Date"
        Case InStr(1, Rng.Text, ":") <> 0
            CellType = "Time"
        Case IsNumeric(Rng)
            CellType = "Value"
    End Select
End Function
```

Notice that the CellType function accepts a range argument of any size but operates on only the upper-left cell in the range.

Reading and writing ranges

Many spreadsheet tasks involve transferring the values from an array to a range or from a range to an array. For some reason, Excel reads from ranges much faster than it writes to ranges. The WriteReadRange procedure shown in Listing 11-4 demonstrates the relative speeds of writing and reading a range. This procedure creates an array and then uses For-Next loops to write the array to a range and then read the range back into the array. It calculates the time required for each operation.

Listing 11-4: Benchmarking read and write operations involving ranges

```
Sub WriteReadRange()
    Dim MyArray()
    Dim Time1 As Date
    NumElements = 60000
    ReDim MyArray(1 To NumElements)

'   Fill the array
    For i = 1 To NumElements
        MyArray(i) = i
    Next i

'   Write the array to a range
    Time1 = Timer
    For i = 1 To NumElements
        Cells(i, 1) = i
    Next i
    WriteTime = Format(Timer - Time1, "00:00")

'   Read the range into the array
    Time1 = Timer
    For i = 1 To NumElements
        MyArray(i) = Cells(i, 1)
    Next i
    ReadTime = Format(Timer - Time1, "00:00")

'   Show results
    Msg = "Write: " & WriteTime
    Msg = Msg & vbCrLf
    Msg = Msg & "Read: " & ReadTime
    MsgBox Msg, vbOKOnly, NumElements & " Elements"
End Sub
```

On my system, it took 32 seconds to write a 60,000-element array to a range but only 6 seconds to read the range into an array.

A better way to write to a range

The example in the previous section uses a `For-Next` loop to transfer the contents of an array to a worksheet range. In this section, I demonstrate a more efficient way to accomplish this.

The example in Listing 11-5 illustrates the most obvious way to fill a range: Loop through each cell in the range, and insert its value.

Listing 11-5: Filling a range by brute force

```
Sub LoopFillRange()
'   Fill a range by looping through cells

    Dim CurrRow As Long, CurrCol As Integer
    Dim CurrVal As Long

'   Get the dimensions
    CellsDown = Val(InputBox("How many cells down?"))
    CellsAcross = Val(InputBox("How many cells across?"))

'   Record starting time
    StartTime = Timer

'   Loop through cells and insert values
    CurrVal = 1
    Application.ScreenUpdating = False
    For CurrRow = 1 To CellsDown
        For CurrCol = 1 To CellsAcross
            ActiveCell.Offset(CurrRow - 1, _
            CurrCol - 1).Value = CurrVal
            CurrVal = CurrVal + 1
        Next CurrCol
    Next CurrRow

'   Display elapsed time
    Application.ScreenUpdating = True
    MsgBox Format(Timer - StartTime, "00.00") & " seconds"
End Sub
```

The example in Listing 11-6 demonstrates a faster way to produce the same result. This code inserts the values into an array and then uses a single statement to transfer the contents of an array to the range.

Listing 11-6: Borrowing arrays to fill ranges faster

```
Sub ArrayFillRange()
'   Fill a range by transferring an array

    Dim TempArray() As Integer
    Dim TheRange As Range

'   Get the dimensions
    CellsDown = Val(InputBox("How many cells down?"))
    CellsAcross = Val(InputBox("How many cells across?"))

'  Record starting time
```

```
    StartTime = Timer

'   Redimension temporary array
    ReDim TempArray(1 To CellsDown, 1 To CellsAcross)

'   Set worksheet range
    Set TheRange = ActiveCell.Range(Cells(1, 1), _
        Cells(CellsDown, CellsAcross))

'   Fill the temporary array
    CurrVal = 0
    Application.ScreenUpdating = False
    For i = 1 To CellsDown
        For j = 1 To CellsAcross
            TempArray(i, j) = CurrVal + 1
            CurrVal = CurrVal + 1
        Next j
    Next i

'   Transfer temporary array to worksheet
    TheRange.Value = TempArray

'   Display elapsed time
    Application.ScreenUpdating = True
    MsgBox Format(Timer - StartTime, "00.00") & " seconds"
End Sub
```

On my system, using the loop method to fill a 500 × 256 cell range (128,000 cells) took 58.66 seconds. The array transfer method took only 1.27 seconds to generate the same results — nearly 50 times faster!

Transferring one-dimensional arrays

The example in the preceding section involves a two-dimensional array, which works out nicely for row-and-column-based worksheets.

When transferring a one-dimensional array to a range, the range must be horizontal — that is, one row with multiple *columns*. If you have to use a vertical range instead, you must first transpose the array to make it vertical. You can use Excel's TRANSPOSE function to do this. The following example transfers a 100-element array to a vertical worksheet range (A1:A100):

```
Range(A1:A100).Value = _
    Application.WorksheetFunction.Transpose(MyArray)
```

Selecting the maximum value in a range

The GoToMax procedure in Listing 11-7 activates the worksheet cell that contains the maximum value. The procedure determines the maximum value in the selected range; but if a single cell is selected, it determines the maximum value for the entire worksheet. Next, it uses the Find method to locate the value and select the cell.

Listing 11-7: Moving the pointer to the cell containing the greatest value

```
Sub GoToMax()
'   Activates the cell with the largest value
    Dim WorkRange as Range

'   Exit if a range is not selected
    If TypeName(Selection) <> "Range" Then Exit Sub

'   If one cell is selected, search entire worksheet;
'   Otherwise, search the selected range
    If Selection.Count = 1 Then
        Set Workrange = Cells
    Else
        Set Workrange = Selection
    End If

'   Determine the maximum value
    MaxVal = Application.Max(Workrange)

'   Find it and select it
    On Error Resume Next
    Workrange.Find(What:=MaxVal, _
        After:=Workrange.Range("A1"), _
        LookIn:=xlValues, _
        LookAt:=xlPart, _
        SearchOrder:=xlByRows, _
        SearchDirection:=xlNext, MatchCase:=False _
        ).Select
    If Err <> 0 Then MsgBox "Max value was not found: " _
     & MaxVal
End Sub
```

VBA Techniques

The examples in this section illustrate common VBA techniques that you may be able to adapt to your own projects.

Toggling a Boolean property

A Boolean property is one that is either True or False. The easiest way to toggle a Boolean property is to use the Not operator, as shown in the following example, which toggles the WrapText property of a selection.

```
Sub ToggleWrapText()
'   Toggles text wrap alignment for selected cells
    If TypeName(Selection) = "Range" Then
      Selection.WrapText = Not ActiveCell.WrapText
    End If
End Sub
```

Note that the active cell is used as the basis for toggling. When a range is selected and the property values in the cells are inconsistent (for example, some cells are bold and others are not), it is considered *mixed*, and Excel uses the active cell to determine how to toggle. If the active cell is bold, for example, all cells in the selection are made not bold when you click the Bold toolbar button. This simple procedure mimics the way Excel works — which is usually the best practice.

Note also that this procedure uses the TypeName function to check whether the selection is a range. If it isn't, nothing happens.

You can use the Not operator to toggle many other properties. For example, to toggle the display of row and column borders in a worksheet, use the following code:

```
ActiveWindow.DisplayHeadings = Not _
  ActiveWindow.DisplayHeadings
```

To toggle the display of grid lines in the active worksheet, use the following code:

```
ActiveWindow.DisplayGridlines = Not _
  ActiveWindow.DisplayGridlines
```

Determining the number of printed pages

If you need to determine the number of printed pages for a worksheet printout, you can use Excel's print preview feature and view the page count displayed at the bottom of the screen. But if you would like to know how to determine the page count using VBA, you can search the online help forever and not find the answer.

As far as I know, the only way to determine the page count programmatically is to use the Excel 4 (XLM) Get.Document macro function. You can execute this macro function from VBA, as follows:

```
PgCnt = ExecuteExcel4Macro("Get.Document(50)")
```

In the preceding statement, the number of printed pages in the active sheet is assigned to the PgCnt variable.

The following VBA procedure loops through all worksheets in the active workbook and displays the total number of printed pages.

```
Sub ShowPageCount()
    PageCount = 0
    For Each sht In Worksheets
        sht.Activate
        Pages = ExecuteExcel4Macro("Get.Document(50)")
        PageCount = PageCount + Pages
    Next sht
    MsgBox "Total Pages = " & PageCount
End Sub
```

Displaying the date and time

If you understand the serial number system that Excel uses to store dates and times, you won't have any problems using dates and times in your VBA procedures.

The DateAndTime procedure displays a message box with the current date and time, as depicted in Figure 11-7. This example also displays a personalized message in the message box's title bar.

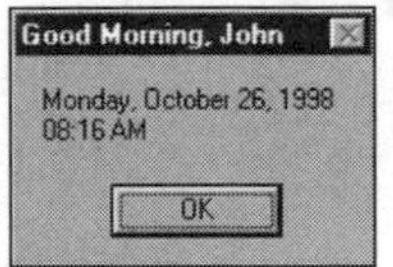

Figure 11-7: A message box displaying the date and time.

The procedure shown in Listing 11-8 uses the Date function as an argument for the Format function. The result is a string with a nicely formatted date. I used the same technique to get a nicely formatted time.

Listing 11-8: Displaying the current date and time in a cell

```
Sub DateAndTime()
    TheDate = Format(Date, "Long Date")
    TheTime = Format(Time, "Medium Time")

'   Determine greeting based on time
    Select Case Time
        Case Is < 0.5:      Greeting = "Good Morning, "
        Case Is >= 0.7083:  Greeting = "Good Evening, "
        Case Else:          Greeting = "Good Afternoon, "
    End Select

'   Append user's first name to greeting
```

```
    FullName = Application.UserName
    SpaceInName = InStr(1, FullName, " ", 1)

'   Handle situation when name has no space
    If SpaceInName = 0 Then SpaceInName = Len(FullName)
    FirstName = Left(FullName, SpaceInName)
    Greeting = Greeting & FirstName

'   Show the message
    MsgBox TheDate & vbCrLf & TheTime, vbOKOnly, Greeting
End Sub
```

In the preceding example, I used named formats (“Long Date” and “Medium Time”) to ensure that the macro will work properly regardless of the user’s international settings. You can, however, use other formats. For example, to display the date in mm/dd/yy format, you can use a statement like the following:

```
TheDate = Format(Date, "mm/dd/yy")
```

I used a `Select Case` construct to base the greeting displayed in the message box’s title bar on the time of day. VBA time values work just as they do in Excel. If the time is less than .5 (noon), it’s morning. If it’s greater than .7083 (5 p.m.), it’s evening. Otherwise, it’s afternoon.

The next series of statements determines the user’s first name, as recorded in the General tab in the Options dialog box. I used VBA’s `InStr` function to locate the first space in the user’s name. When I first wrote this procedure, I didn’t consider a user name that has no space. So when I ran this procedure on a machine with a user’s name of *Nobody*, the code failed — which goes to show you that I can’t think of everything, and even the simplest procedures can run aground. (By the way, if the user’s name is left blank, Excel always substitutes the name *User*.) The solution to this problem was to use the length of the full name for the `SpaceInName` variable so the `Left` function extracts the full name.

The `MsgBox` function concatenates the date and time but uses the built-in `vbCrLf` constant to insert a line break between them. `vbOKOnly` is a predefined constant that returns 0, causing the message box to appear with only an OK button. The final argument is the `Greeting`, constructed earlier in the procedure.

Sorting an array

Although Excel has a built-in command to sort worksheet ranges, VBA doesn’t offer a method to sort arrays. One viable, but cumbersome, workaround is to transfer your array to a worksheet range, sort it using Excel’s commands, and then return the result to your array. But if speed is essential, it’s better to write a sorting routine in VBA.

In this section, I describe four different sorting techniques:

✦ *Worksheet Sort* transfers an array to a worksheet range, sorts it, and transfers it back to the array. This procedure accepts an array as its only argument and is limited to arrays with no more than 65,536 elements — the number of rows in a worksheet.

✦ *Bubble Sort* is a simple sorting technique (also used in the Chapter 9 sheet-sorting example). Although easy to program, the bubble-sorting algorithm is not the fastest sorting technique.

✦ *Quick Sort* is a much faster sorting routine than Bubble Sort, but it is also more difficult to understand.

✦ *Counting Sort* is lightning fast but also difficult to understand.

The companion CD-ROM includes a workbook application that demonstrates these sorting methods. This workbook is useful for comparing the techniques with arrays of varying sizes.

Figure 11-8 shows the dialog box for this project. I tested the sorting procedures with seven different array sizes, ranging from 100 to 100,000 elements (random numbers).

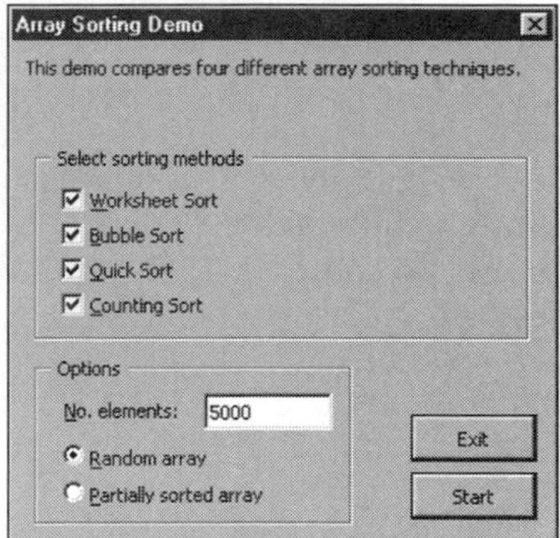

Figure 11-8: Comparing the time required to perform sorts of various array sizes.

Table 11-1 shows the results of my tests. A 0.00 entry means that the sort was virtually instantaneous (less than .01 second).

Table 11-1
Sorting Times in Seconds for Four Sort Algorithms Using Randomly Filled Arrays

Array Elements	*Excel Worksheet Sort*	*VBA Bubble Sort*	*VBA Quick Sort*	*VBA Counting Sort*
100	0.11	0.00	0.06	0.00
500	0.22	0.22	0.16	0.00
1,000	0.22	0.88	0.27	0.00
5,000	0.93	19.61	1.98	0.05
10,000	2.14	71.74	4.07	0.05
50,000	11.37	N/A	24.28	0.42
100,000	N/A	N/A	50.97	0.71

I then performed a second series of tests using an array that was almost sorted. These results are shown in Table 11-2.

Table 11-2
Sorting Times in Seconds for Four Sort Algorithms Using Nearly Sorted Arrays

Array Elements	*Excel Worksheet Sort*	*VBA Bubble Sort*	*VBA Quick Sort*	*VBA Counting Sort*
100	.11	0.00	0.06	0.00
500	0.17	0.16	0.11	0.00
1,000	0.22	0.55	0.17	0.00
5,000	0.61	14.12	1.37	0.05
10,000	1.37	58.27	3.24	0.11
50,000	6.54	N/A	24.22	0.44
100,000	N/A	N/A	73.43	0.77

The Worksheet Sort algorithm is amazingly fast, especially when you consider that the array is transferred to the sheet, sorted, and then transferred back to the array. If the array is almost sorted, the Worksheet Sort technique is even faster.

The Bubble Sort algorithm is reasonably fast with small arrays, but for larger arrays (more than 5,000 elements), forget it. The Quick Sort algorithm seems like a winner. If the array is almost sorted, however, the speed drops significantly. Overall, Counting Sort wins by a long shot.

Processing a series of files

One reason for using macros, of course, is to repeat an operation a number of times. The example in Listing 11-9 demonstrates how to execute a macro on a series of files stored on disk. This example — which may help you set up your own routine for this type of task — prompts the user for a file specification and then processes all matching files. In this case, processing consists of importing the file and entering a series of summary formulas that describe the data in the file.

Listing 11-9: A macro that processes multiple stored files

```
Sub BatchProcess()
    Dim Files() As String
    Dim FileSpec As String

'   Get file spec
    DefaultPath = ThisWorkbook.Path & "\text??.txt"
    FileSpec = InputBox("Enter path and file spec:", _
      "File Import", DefaultPath)

'   Extract the path and change directory
    NewPath = ExtractPath(FileSpec)
    If NewPath <> "" Then _
        ChDir NewPath _
            Else Exit Sub

'   See if any files exist
    FoundFile = Dir(FileSpec)
    If FoundFile = "" Then
        MsgBox "Cannot find file:" & vbCrLf & FileSpec
        Exit Sub
    End If

'   Get first file name
    FileCount = 1
    ReDim Preserve Files(FileCount)
    Files(FileCount) = FoundFile

'   Get other file names, if any
    Do While FoundFile <> ""
        FoundFile = Dir()
        If FoundFile <> "" Then
            FileCount = FileCount + 1
            ReDim Preserve Files(FileCount)
            Files(FileCount) = FoundFile
```

```
        End If
    Loop

'   Loop through all files and process them
    For i = 1 To FileCount
        Application.StatusBar = "Processing " & Files(i)
        Call ProcessFiles(Files(i))
    Next i
    Application.StatusBar = False
End Sub
```

This example uses three additional files, which are also provided on the CD-ROM: Text01.txt, Text02.txt, and Text03.txt. You'll need to modify the routine to import other text files.

The BatchProcess procedure uses a For-Next loop to process the files. Within the loop, the status bar text is changed to display the name of the file being processed, and the actual processing is done by calling the following ProcessFiles procedure. This simple procedure uses the OpenText method to import the file and then inserts five formulas. You may, of course, substitute your own routine in place of this one:

```
Sub ProcessFiles(FileName As String)
'   Import the file
    Workbooks.OpenText FileName:=FileName, _
        Origin:=xlWindows, _
        StartRow:=1, _
        DataType:=xlFixedWidth, _
        FieldInfo:= _
        Array(Array(0, 1), Array(3, 1), Array(12, 1))
'   Enter summary formulas
    Range("D1").Value = "A"
    Range("D2").Value = "B"
    Range("D3").Value = "C"
    Range("E1:E3").Formula = "=COUNTIF(B:B,D1)"
    Range("F1:F3").Formula = "=SUMIF(B:B,D1,C:C)"
End Sub
```

The BatchProcess procedure uses a custom function, ExtractPath, to extract the path from the file specification:

```
Function ExtractPath(Spec As String) As String
    SpecLen = Len(Spec)
    For i = SpecLen To 1 Step -1
        If Mid(Spec, i, 1) = "\" Then
            ExtractPath = Left(Spec, i - 1)
            Exit Function
        End If
    Next i
    ExtractPath = ""
End Function
```

The following version of the function is much better. However, it won't work with Excel 97 because that version of VBA doesn't support `InStrRev`.

```
Function ExtractPath(Spec As String) As String
    ExtractPath = Left(Spec, InStrRev(Spec, "\"))
End Function
```

Some Useful Custom Functions

In this section, I present some custom "utility" functions that you may find useful in your own applications and that may provide inspiration for creating similar functions. These functions are most useful when called from another VBA procedure. Therefore, they are declared using the `Private` keyword and thus will not appear in Excel's Paste Function dialog box.

The FileExists function

This function takes one argument — a path with filename — and returns True if the file exists.

```
Private Function FileExists(fname) As Boolean
'   Returns TRUE if the file exists
    Dim x As String
    x = Dir(fname)
    If x <> "" Then FileExists = True _
        Else FileExists = False
End Function
```

The FileNameOnly function

This function accepts one argument — a path with filename — and returns only the filename. In other words, it strips out the path.

```
Private Function FileNameOnly(pname) As String
'   Returns the filename from a path/filename string
    Dim i As Integer, length As Integer, temp As String
    length = Len(pname)
    temp = ""
    For i = length To 1 Step -1
        If Mid(pname, i, 1) = Application.PathSeparator Then
            FileNameOnly = temp
            Exit Function
        End If
        temp = Mid(pname, i, 1) & temp
    Next i
    FileNameOnly = pname
End Function
```

The PathExists function

This function accepts one argument — a path — and returns True if the path exists.

```
Private Function PathExists(pname) As Boolean
'   Returns TRUE if the path exists
    Dim x As String
    On Error Resume Next
    x = GetAttr(pname) And 0
    If Err = 0 Then PathExists = True _
      Else PathExists = False
End Function
```

The RangeNameExists function

This function accepts a single argument — a range name — and returns True if the range name exists in the active workbook.

```
Private Function RangeNameExists(nname) As Boolean
'   Returns TRUE if the range name exists
    Dim n As Name
    RangeNameExists = False
    For Each n In ActiveWorkbook.Names
        If UCase(n.Name) = UCase(nname) Then
            RangeNameExists = True
            Exit Function
        End If
    Next n
End Function
```

The SheetExists function

This function accepts one argument — a worksheet name — and returns True if the worksheet exists in the active workbook.

```
Private Function SheetExists(sname) As Boolean
'   Returns TRUE if sheet exists in the active workbook
    Dim x As Object
    On Error Resume Next
    Set x = ActiveWorkbook.Sheets(sname)
    If Err = 0 Then SheetExists = True _
        Else SheetExists = False
End Function
```

The WorkbookIsOpen function

This function accepts one argument — a workbook name — and returns True if the workbook is open.

```
Private Function WorkbookIsOpen(wbname) As Boolean
'   Returns TRUE if the workbook is open
    Dim x As Workbook
    On Error Resume Next
    Set x = Workbooks(wbname)
    If Err = 0 Then WorkbookIsOpen = True _
        Else WorkbookIsOpen = False
End Function
```

Some Useful Worksheet Functions

The examples in this section are custom functions that can be used in worksheet formulas.

These functions are available on the companion CD-ROM.

Understanding object parents

As you know, Excel's object model is a hierarchy: Objects are contained in other objects. At the top of the hierarchy (beneath the `Excel` term, which is generally omitted) is the `Application` object. Excel contains other objects, and these objects contain other objects, and so on. The following hierarchy depicts how a `Range` object fits into this scheme.

`Application` Object

`Workbook` Object

`Worksheet` Object

`Range` Object

In the lingo of object-oriented programming, a `Range` object's parent is the `Worksheet` object that contains it. A `Worksheet` object's parent is the `Workbook` object that contains the worksheet, and a `Workbook` object's parent is the `Application` object.

How can this information be put to use? Examine the following VBA function. This function, which can be used in a VBA procedure or in a worksheet formula, accepts a single argument (a range) and returns the name of the worksheet that contains the range. It uses the `Parent` property of the `Range` object. The `Parent` property returns an object: the object that contains the `Range` object.

```
Function SheetName(ref) As String
    SheetName = ref.Parent.Name
End Function
```

The next function, `WorkbookName`, returns the name of the workbook for a particular cell. Notice that it uses the `Parent` property twice. The first `Parent` property returns a Worksheet object, and the second Parent property returns a Workbook object.

```
Function WorkbookName(ref) As String
    WorkbookName = ref.Parent.Parent.Name
End Function
```

The following function carries this exercise to the next logical level, accessing the Parent property three times. This function returns the name of the Application object for a particular cell. It will, of course, always return Excel.

```
Function AppName(ref) As String
    AppName = ref.Parent.Parent.Parent.Name
End Function
```

Counting cells between two values

The following function, named COUNTBETWEEN, returns the number of values in a range (first argument) that fall between values represented by the second and third arguments.

```
Function COUNTBETWEEN(InRange, num1, num2) As Integer
'   Counts number of values between num1 and num2
    Dim TheCount As Integer
    Dim cell As Range
    Set InRange = Intersect(InRange.Parent.UsedRange, InRange)
    TheCount = 0
    For Each cell In InRange
        If cell.Value >= num1 And _
          cell.Value <= num2 Then TheCount = TheCount + 1
    Next cell
    COUNTBETWEEN = TheCount
End Function
```

Following is an example formula that uses this function. The formula returns the number of cells in A1:A100 that are greater than or equal to 10 and less than or equal to 20.

```
=COUNTBETWEEN(A1:A100,10,20)
```

Note

Excel's COUNTIF function can't handle this type of comparison.

Determining the last nonempty cell in a column or row

In this section, I present two useful functions: LASTINCOLUMN returns the contents of the last nonempty cell in a column; LASTINROW returns the contents of the last nonempty cell in a row. Each function accepts a range as its single argument. The range argument can be a complete column (for LASTINCOLUMN) or a complete row (for LASTINROW). If the supplied argument is not a complete column or row, the function uses the column or row of the upper-left cell in the range. For example, the following formula returns the last value in column B:

```
=LASTINCOLUMN(B5)
```

The following formula returns the last value in row 7:

```
=LASTINROW(C7:D9)
```

You'll find that these functions are quite fast because they examine only the cells in the intersection of the specified column or row and the worksheet's used range.

The LASTINCOLUMN function

The LASTINCOLUMN function is listed below.

```
Function LASTINCOLUMN(rngInput As Range)
    Dim WorkRange As Range
    Dim i As Integer, CellCount As Integer
    Application.Volatile
    Set WorkRange = rngInput.Columns(1).EntireColumn
    Set WorkRange = Intersect(WorkRange.Parent.UsedRange, _
       WorkRange)
    CellCount = WorkRange.Count
    For i = CellCount To 1 Step -1
        If Not IsEmpty(WorkRange(i)) Then
            LASTINCOLUMN = WorkRange(i).Value
            Exit Function
        End If
    Next i
End Function
```

The LASTINROW function

The LASTINROW function is listed below.

```
Function LASTINROW(rngInput As Range) As Variant
    Dim WorkRange As Range
    Dim i As Integer, CellCount As Integer
    Application.Volatile
    Set WorkRange = rngInput.Rows(1).EntireRow
    Set WorkRange = Intersect(WorkRange.Parent.UsedRange, _
      WorkRange)
    CellCount = WorkRange.Count
    For i = CellCount To 1 Step -1
        If Not IsEmpty(WorkRange(i)) Then
            LASTINROW = WorkRange(i).Value
```

```
            Exit Function
        End If
    Next i
End Function
```

Does a string match a pattern?

The ISLIKE function returns True if a text string matches a specified pattern. This function takes two arguments:

text	A text string or a reference to a cell that contains a text string
pattern	A string that contains wildcard characters according to the following list

Character(s) in pattern	Matches in *text*
?	Any single character
*	Zero or more characters
#	Any single digit (0–9)
[*charlist*]	Any single character in *charlist*
[!*charlist*]	Any single character not in *charlist*

This function, shown below, is remarkably simple. As you can see, the function is essentially a "wrapper" that lets you take advantage of VBA's powerful Like operator in your formulas.

```
Function ISLIKE(text As String, pattern As String) As Boolean
'   Returns true if the first argument is like the second
    If text Like pattern Then ISLIKE = True _
        Else ISLIKE = False
End Function
```

The following formula returns True because * matches any number of characters. It returns True if the first argument is any text that begins with "g".

```
=ISLIKE("guitar","g*")
```

The following formula returns True because ? matches any single character. If the first argument were "Unit12", the function would return False.

```
=ISLIKE("Unit1","Unit?")
```

The next formula returns True because the first argument is a single character in the second argument.

```
=ISLIKE("a","[aeiou]")
```

The following formula returns True if cell A1 contains *a, e, i, o, u, A, E, I, O,* or *U*. Using the UPPER function for the arguments makes the formula not case sensitive.

```
=ISLIKE(UPPER(A1),UPPER ("[aeiou]"))
```

The following formula returns True if cell A1 contains a value that begins with 1 and has exactly three digits (that is, any integer between 100 and 199).

```
=ISLIKE(A1,"1##")
```

Extracting the nth element from a string

ExtractElement is a custom worksheet function (which can also be called from a VBA procedure) that extracts an element from a text string. For example, if a cell contains the following text, you can use the ExtractElement function to extract any of the substrings between the hyphens.

```
123-456-789-0133-8844
```

The following formula, for example, returns 0133, which is the fourth element in the string. The string uses a hyphen (-) as the separator.

```
=ExtractElement("123-456-789-0133-8844",4,"-")
```

The ExtractElement function uses three arguments:

Txt	The text string from which you're extracting. This can be a literal string or a cell reference
n	An integer that represents the element to extract.
Separator	A single character used as the separator.

If you specify a space as the Separator character, multiple spaces are treated as a single space, which is almost always what you want. If n exceeds the number of elements in the string, the function returns an empty string.

The VBA code for the ExtractElement function is listed below.

```
Function ExtractElement(Txt, n, Separator) As String
'   Returns the nth element of a text string, where the
'   elements are separated by a specified separator character

    Dim Txt1 As String, temperament As String
    Dim ElementCount As Integer, i As Integer

    Txt1 = Txt
'   If space separator, remove excess spaces
```

```
    If Separator = Chr(32) Then Txt1 = Application.Trim(Txt1)

'   Add a separator to the end of the string
    If Right(Txt1, Len(Txt1)) <> Separator Then _
        Txt1 = Txt1 & Separator

'   Initialize
    ElementCount = 0
    TempElement = ""

'   Extract each element
    For i = 1 To Len(Txt1)
        If Mid(Txt1, i, 1) = Separator Then
            ElementCount = ElementCount + 1
            If ElementCount = n Then
'               Found it, so exit
                ExtractElement = TempElement
                Exit Function
            Else
                TempElement = ""
            End If
        Else
            TempElement = TempElement & Mid(Txt1, i, 1)
        End If
    Next i
    ExtractElement=""
End Function
```

A multifunctional function

This example describes a technique that may be helpful in some situations: making a single worksheet function act like multiple functions. For example, the following VBA listing is for a custom function called `StatFunction`. It takes two arguments: the range (`rng`) and the operation (`op`). Depending on the value of `op`, the function returns a value computed using any of the following worksheet functions: `AVERAGE`, `COUNT`, `MAX`, `MEDIAN`, `MIN`, `MODE`, `STDEV`, `SUM`, or `VAR`.

For example, you can use this function in your worksheet as follows:

```
=STATFUNCTION(B1:B24,A24)
```

The result of the formula depends on the contents of cell A24, which should be a string such as Average, Count, Max, and so on. You can adapt this technique for other types of functions.

```
Function STATFUNCTION(rng, op)
    Select Case UCase(op)
        Case "SUM"
            STATFUNCTION = WorksheetFunction.Sum(rng)
```

```
        Case "AVERAGE"
            STATFUNCTION = WorksheetFunction.Average(rng)
        Case "MEDIAN"
            STATFUNCTION = WorksheetFunction.Median(rng)
        Case "MODE"
            STATFUNCTION = WorksheetFunction.Mode(rng)
        Case "COUNT"
            STATFUNCTION = WorksheetFunction.Count(rng)
        Case "MAX"
            STATFUNCTION = WorksheetFunction.Max(rng)
        Case "MIN"
            STATFUNCTION = WorksheetFunction.Min(rng)
        Case "VAR"
            STATFUNCTION = WorksheetFunction.Var(rng)
        Case "STDEV"
            STATFUNCTION = WorksheetFunction.StDev(rng)
        Case Else
            STATFUNCTION = CVErr(xlErrNA)
    End Select
End Function
```

The SHEETOFFSET function: Take 1

You probably know that Excel's support for "3D workbooks" is limited. For example, if you need to refer to a different worksheet in a workbook, you must include the worksheet's name in your formula. This is not a big problem . . . until you attempt to copy the formula across other worksheets. The copied formulas continue to refer to the original worksheet name, and the sheet references are not adjusted as they would be in a true 3D workbook.

The example discussed in this section is a VBA function (named `SHEETOFFSET`) that enables you to address worksheets in a relative manner. For example, you can refer to cell A1 on the previous worksheet using this formula:

```
=SHEETOFFSET(-1,A1)
```

The first argument can be positive, negative, or zero. The second argument must be a reference to a single cell. You can copy this formula to other sheets, and the relative referencing will be in effect in all the copied formulas.

The VBA code for the `SHEETOFFSET` function is listed below.

```
Function SHEETOFFSET(offset, Ref)
'   Returns cell contents at Ref, in sheet offset
    Application.Volatile
    SHEETOFFSET = Sheets(Application.Caller.Parent.Index _
      + offset).Range(Ref.Address)
End Function
```

This function works fine in most cases. However, if your worksheet contains Chart sheets, the function will fail if it attempts to reference a cell on a Chart sheet.

The SHEETOFFSET function: Take 2

The following SHEETOFFSET function is a bit more complex, but it eliminates the problem described in the preceding section. This version of SHEETOFFSET essentially ignores any non-Worksheet sheets in the workbook.

```
Function SHEETOFFSET2(offset, Ref)
'   Returns cell contents at Ref, in sheet offset
    Dim WBook As Workbook
    Dim WksCount As Integer, i As Integer
    Dim CallerSheet As String, CallerIndex As Integer
    Application.Volatile

'   Create an array consisting only of Worksheets
    Set WBook = Application.Caller.Parent.Parent
    Dim Wks() As Worksheet
    WksCount = 0
    For i = 1 To WBook.Sheets.Count
        If TypeName(WBook.Sheets(i)) = "Worksheet" Then
            WksCount = WksCount + 1
            ReDim Preserve Wks(1 To WksCount)
            Set Wks(WksCount) = WBook.Sheets(i)
        End If
    Next i

'   Determine the position of the calling sheet
    CallerSheet = Application.Caller.Parent.Name
    For i = 1 To UBound(Wks)
        If CallerSheet = Wks(i).Name Then CallerIndex = i
    Next i

'   Get the value
    SHEETOFFSET2 = Wks(CallerIndex + _
      offset).Range(Ref.Address)
End Function
```

Windows API Calls

One of VBA's most important features is the capability to use functions that are stored in Dynamic Link Libraries (DLLs). The examples in this section use common Windows API calls.

The API declarations that you can use depend on your version of Excel. If you attempt to use a 32-bit API function with 16-bit Excel 5, you'll get an error. Similarly, if you attempt to use a 16-bit API function with 32-bit Excel 95 or later, you'll get an error. The examples in this section are for 32-bit Excel.

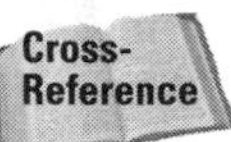

I discuss this and other compatibility issues in detail in Chapter 25.

Getting disk information

In some cases, you might need to know about the disk drives attached to the system that's running your application. The examples in this section make use of the API function to determine a variety of useful information about storage devices.

The companion CD-ROM contains a workbook with six custom VBA functions that use Windows API calls. The functions can be referenced by VBA code or worksheet functions.

The workbook on the CD-ROM contains a procedure called `ShowDriveInfo`. Executing this routine creates a table on a worksheet with information about each drive. Figure 11-9 shows an example of `ShowDriveInfo` output.

diskinfo.xls

Create a table displaying information for all drives...

Drive	Type	Bytes Free	Total Bytes
A:\	Removable	663,552	1,457,664
C:\	Local	79,134,720	2,146,467,840
D:\	Local	1,039,073,280	2,146,467,840
E:\	Local	1,588,789,248	2,146,467,840
F:\	CD-ROM	0	10,485,760

Figure 11-9: `ShowDriveInfo` creates a table with information about each disk drive.

The API functions

These functions use three API calls. The declarations are listed here:

```
Private Declare Function GetDriveType32 Lib "kernel32" _
  Alias "GetDriveTypeA" (ByVal nDrive As String) As Long
```

`GetDriveType32` accepts a drive letter as an argument and returns a code that represents the type of drive (such as removable, CD-ROM, or fixed).

```
Private Declare Function GetLogicalDriveStrings _
  Lib "kernel32" Alias "GetLogicalDriveStringsA" (ByVal _
  nBufferLength As Long, ByVal lpBuffer As String) As Long
```

`GetLogicalDriveStrings` returns a string that contains the names of all drives. Each drive is followed by a null character. Therefore, to get the drive names, you must parse this string.

```
Private Declare Function GetDiskFreeSpace Lib "kernel32" _
  (ByVal lpRootPathName As String, lpSectorsPerCluster As _
  Long, lpBytesPerSector As Long, lpNumberOfFreeClusters As _
  Long, lpTotalNumberOfClusters As Long) As Long
```

GetDiskFreeSpace returns four values for a specified drive: the number of sectors per cluster, the number of bytes per sector, the number of free clusters, and the total clusters. This information can be used to determine the total drive capacity and the amount of free space.

The VBA Function procedures that use these API functions are listed in the sections that follow.

The DriveExists function

This function takes one argument (a drive letter) and returns True if the specified drive exists.

```
Function DriveExists(DriveLetter As String) As Boolean
'   Returns True if a specified drive letter exists

    Dim Buffer As String * 255
    Dim BuffLen As Long

    DLetter = Left(DriveLetter, 1)
    BuffLen = GetLogicalDriveStrings(Len(Buffer), Buffer)

    DriveExists = False
'   Search for the string
    For i = 1 To BuffLen
        If UCase(Mid(Buffer, i, 1)) = UCase(DLetter) Then
'           Found it
            DriveExists = True
            Exit Function
        End If
    Next i
End Function
```

The DriveName function

This function takes one argument (an index number) and returns the corresponding drive letter.

```
Function DriveName(index As Integer) As String
'   Returns the drive letter using an index
'   Returns an empty string if index > number of drives

    Dim Buffer As String * 255
    Dim BuffLen As Long
    Dim TheDrive As String
```

```
    Dim DriveCount As Integer

    BuffLen = GetLogicalDriveStrings(Len(Buffer), Buffer)

'   Search thru the string of drive names
    TheDrive = ""
    DriveCount = 0
    For i = 1 To BuffLen
        If Asc(Mid(Buffer, i, 1)) <> 0 Then _
          TheDrive = TheDrive & Mid(Buffer, i, 1)
        If Asc(Mid(Buffer, i, 1)) = 0 Then
 '          null separates drives
            DriveCount = DriveCount + 1
            If DriveCount = index Then
                DriveName = UCase(Left(TheDrive, 1))
                Exit Function
            End If
            TheDrive = ""
        End If
    Next i
End Function
```

The DriveType function

This function takes one argument (a drive letter) and returns one of the following strings that describe the type of drive: `"Local"`, `"Removable"`, `"Fixed"`, `"Remote"`, `"CD-ROM"`, `"RAM Disk"`, or `"Unknown Drive Type"`.

```
Function DriveType(DriveLetter As String) As String
'   Returns a string that describes the drive type

    DLetter = Left(DriveLetter, 1) & ":"
    DriveCode = GetDriveType32(DLetter)

    Select Case DriveCode
        Case 1: DriveType = "Local"
        Case 2: DriveType = "Removable"
        Case 3: DriveType = "Fixed"
        Case 4: DriveType = "Remote"
        Case 5: DriveType = "CD-ROM"
        Case 6: DriveType = "RAM Disk"
        Case Else: DriveType = "Unknown Drive Type"
    End Select
End Function
```

The NumberofDrives() function

This function returns a value that indicates the number of drives on the system. It does not take any arguments.

```
Function NumberofDrives() As Integer
'   Returns the number of drives

    Dim Buffer As String * 255
```

```
    Dim BuffLen As Long
    Dim DriveCount As Integer

    BuffLen = GetLogicalDriveStrings(Len(Buffer), Buffer)
    DriveCount = 0
'   Search for a null - which separates the drives
    For i = 1 To BuffLen
        If Asc(Mid(Buffer, i, 1)) = 0 Then _
          DriveCount = DriveCount + 1
    Next i
    NumberofDrives = DriveCount
End Function
```

The TotalDiskSpace function

This function takes one argument (a drive letter) and returns the total capacity (in bytes) for the specified drive.

```
Function TotalDiskSpace(DriveLetter As String) As Long
'   Returns the total storage capacity for a drive

    Dim SectorsPerCluster As Long
    Dim BytesPerSector As Long
    Dim NumberofFreeClusters As Long
    Dim TotalClusters As Long

    DLetter = Left(DriveLetter, 1) & ":\"
    x = GetDiskFreeSpace(DLetter, SectorsPerCluster, _
      BytesPerSector, NumberofFreeClusters, TotalClusters)

    If x = 0 Then 'Error occurred
        TotalDiskSpace = -99 'Assign an arbitrary error value
        Exit Function
    End If
    TotalDiskSpace = _
      SectorsPerCluster * BytesPerSector * TotalClusters
End Function
```

The FreeDiskSpace function

This function takes one argument (a drive letter) and returns the free space (in bytes) for the specified drive.

```
Function FreeDiskSpace(DriveLetter As String) As Long
'   Returns the number of free bytes for a drive

    Dim SectorsPerCluster As Long
    Dim BytesPerSector As Long
    Dim NumberofFreeClusters As Long
    Dim TotalClusters As Long

    DLetter = Left(DriveLetter, 1) & ":\"
    x = GetDiskFreeSpace(DLetter, SectorsPerCluster, _
      BytesPerSector, NumberofFreeClusters, TotalClusters)
```

```
    If x = 0 Then 'Error occurred
        FreeDiskSpace = -99 'Assign an arbitrary error value
        Exit Function
    End If
    FreeDiskSpace = _
      SectorsPerCluster * BytesPerSector * NumberofFreeClusters
End Function
```

Determining file associations

In Windows, many file types are associated with a particular application. This association makes it possible to double-click the file to load it into its associated application.

The following function, named `GetExecutable`, uses a Windows API call to get the full path to the application associated with a particular file. For example, your system has many files with a .txt extension — one named Readme.txt is probably in your Windows directory right now. You can use the `GetExecutable` function to determine the full path of the application that opens when the file is double-clicked.

```
Private Declare Function FindExecutableA Lib "shell32.dll" _
    (ByVal lpFile As String, ByVal lpDirectory As String, _
    ByVal lpResult As String) As Long

Function GetExecutable(strFile As String) As String
    Dim strPath As String
    Dim intLen As Integer
    strPath = String(255, 0)
    intLen = FindExecutableA(strFile, "\", strPath)
    If intLen > 32 Then
        GetExecutable = Left(strPath, intLen)
     Else
        GetExecutable = ""
     End If
End Function
```

Figure 11-10 shows the result of executing this procedure.

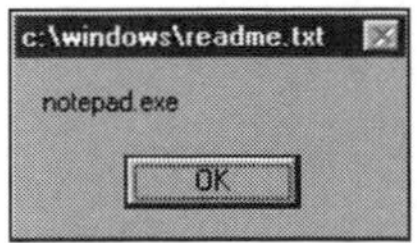

Figure 11-10: Determining the path of the application associated with a particular file.

Determining default printer information

The example in this section uses a Windows API function to return information about the active printer. The information is contained in a single text string. The example parses the string and displays the information in a more readable format.

```
Private Declare Function GetProfileStringA Lib "kernel32" _
  (ByVal lpAppName As String, ByVal lpKeyName As String, _
  ByVal lpDefault As String, ByVal lpReturnedString As _
  String, ByVal nSize As Long) As Long

Sub DefaultPrinterInfo()
    Dim strLPT As String * 255
    Dim Result As String
    Call GetProfileStringA _
      ("Windows", "Device", "", strLPT, 254)

    Result = Application.Trim(strLPT)
    ResultLength = Len(Result)

    Comma1 = Application.Find(",", Result, 1)
    Comma2 = Application.Find(",", Result, Comma1 + 1)

'   Gets printer's name
    Printer = Left(Result, Comma1 - 1)

'   Gets driver
    Driver = Mid(Result, Comma1 + 1, Comma2 - Comma1 - 1)

'   Gets last part of device line
    Port = Right(Result, ResultLength - Comma2)

'   Build message
    Msg = "Printer:" & Chr(9) & Printer & Chr(13)
    Msg = Msg & "Driver:" & Chr(9) & Driver & Chr(13)
    Msg = Msg & "Port:" & Chr(9) & Port

'   Display message
    MsgBox Msg, vbInformation, "Default Printer Information"
End Sub
```

The `ActivePrinter` property of the `Application` object returns the name of the active printer (and lets you change it), but there's no direct way to determine what printer driver or port is being used. That's why this function is useful.

Figure 11-11 shows a sample message box returned by this procedure.

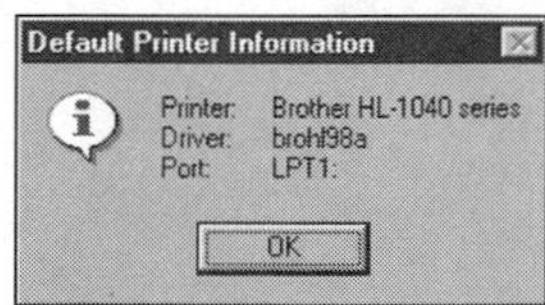

Figure 11-11: Getting information about the active printer using a Windows API call.

Determining the current video mode

The example in this section uses Windows API calls to determine a system's current video mode. If your application needs to display a certain amount of information on one screen, knowing the display size helps you scale the text accordingly.

```
'32-bit API declaration
Declare Function GetSystemMetrics Lib "user32" _
  (ByVal nIndex As Long) As Long

Public Const SM_CXSCREEN = 0
Public Const SM_CYSCREEN = 1

Sub DisplayVideoInfo()
    vidWidth = GetSystemMetrics(SM_CXSCREEN)
    vidHeight = GetSystemMetrics(SM_CYSCREEN)

    Msg = "The current video mode is: "
    Msg = Msg & vidWidth & " X " & vidHeight
    MsgBox Msg
End Sub
```

Figure 11-12 shows the message box returned by this procedure in standard VGA mode.

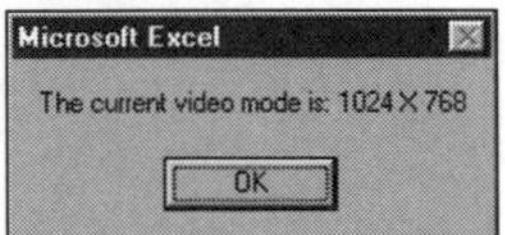

Figure 11-12: Using a Windows API call to determine the video display mode.

Reading from and writing to the Registry

Most Windows applications use the Windows Registry database to store settings (see Chapter 4 for some additional information about the Registry). Your VBA procedures can read values from the Registry and write new values to the Registry. Doing so requires the following Windows API declarations:

```
Private Declare Function RegOpenKeyA Lib "ADVAPI32.DLL" _
    (ByVal hKey As Long, ByVal sSubKey As String, _
    ByRef hkeyResult As Long) As Long

Private Declare Function RegCloseKey Lib "ADVAPI32.DLL" _
    (ByVal hKey As Long) As Long

Private Declare Function RegSetValueExA Lib "ADVAPI32.DLL" _
    (ByVal hKey As Long, ByVal sValueName As String, _
```

```
    ByVal dwReserved As Long, ByVal dwType As Long, _
    ByVal sValue As String, ByVal dwSize As Long) As Long

Private Declare Function RegCreateKeyA Lib "ADVAPI32.DLL" _
    (ByVal hKey As Long, ByVal sSubKey As String, _
    ByRef hkeyResult As Long) As Long

Private Declare Function RegQueryValueExA Lib "ADVAPI32.DLL" _
    (ByVal hKey As Long, ByVal sValueName As String, _
    ByVal dwReserved As Long, ByRef lValueType As Long, _
    ByVal sValue As String, ByRef lResultLen As Long) As Long
```

I developed two "wrapper" functions that simplify the task of working with the Registry: `GetRegistry` and `WriteRegistry`. These functions are available on the companion CD-ROM. This workbook includes a procedure that demonstrates reading from the Registry and writing to the Registry.

Reading from the Registry

The `GetRegistry` function returns a setting from the specified location in the Registry. It takes three arguments:

`RootKey` A string that represents the branch of the Registry to address. This string may be one of the following:

HKEY_CLASSES_ROOT
HKEY_CURRENT_USER
HKEY_LOCAL_MACHINE
HKEY_USERS
HKEY_CURRENT_CONFIG
HKEY_DYN_DATA

`Path` The full path of the Registry category being addressed.

`RegEntry` The name of the setting to retrieve.

Here's an example. If you'd like to find the path and filename for the file that stores the user's AutoCorrect entries, you can call `GetRegistry` as follows (notice that the arguments are not case sensitive):

```
RootKey = "hkey_current_user"
Path = "software\microsoft\office\9.0\common\autocorrect"
RegEntry = "path"
MsgBox GetRegistry(RootKey, Path, RegEntry), _
  vbInformation, Path & "\RegEntry"
```

Figure 11-13 shows that the AutoCorrect file is named John.acl, and it's in the C:\WINDOWS directory. If the registration entry does not exist, the function returns "Not Found."

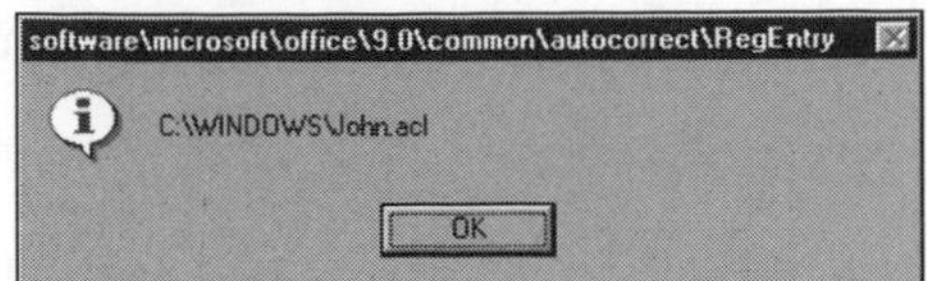

Figure 11-13: This value was retrieved from the Windows Registry.

Writing to the Registry

The `WriteRegistry` function writes a value to the Registry at a specified location. If the operation is successful, the function returns True; otherwise, it returns False. `WriteRegistry` takes the following arguments (all of them are strings):

`RootKey` A string that represents the branch of the Registry to address. This string may be one of the following:

HKEY_CLASSES_ROOT
HKEY_CURRENT_USER
HKEY_LOCAL_MACHINE
HKEY_USERS
HKEY_CURRENT_CONFIG
HKEY_DYN_DATA

`Path` The full path in the Registry. If the path doesn't exist, it is created.

`RegEntry` The name of the Registry category to which the value will be written. If it doesn't exist, it is added.

`RegVal` The value that you are writing.

Here's an example that writes a value representing the time and date Excel was started to the Registry. The information is written in the area that stores Excel's settings.

```
Sub Auto_Open()
    RootKey = "hkey_current_user"
    Path = "software\microsoft\office\9.0\excel\LastStarted"
    RegEntry = "DateTime"
    RegVal = Now()
    If WriteRegistry(RootKey, Path, RegEntry, RegVal) Then
        msg = RegVal & " has been stored in the registry."
          Else msg = "An error occurred"
    End If
    MsgBox msg
End Sub
```

If you store this routine in your personal macro workbook, the setting is automatically updated whenever you start Excel.

An Easier Way to Access the Registry

If you want to use the Windows Registry to store and retrieve settings for your Excel applications, you don't have to bother with the Windows API calls. Rather, you can use VBA's `GetSetting` and `SaveSetting` functions.

These two functions are described in the online help, so I won't cover the details here. However, it's important to understand that these functions work only with the following key name:

```
HKEY_CURRENT_USER\Software\VB and VBA Program Settings
```

In other words, you can't use these functions to access *any* key in the Registry. Rather, these functions are most useful for storing information about your Excel application that you need to maintain between sessions.

Miscellaneous Techniques

The examples in this section cover some additional techniques that demonstrate various aspects of VBA.

Adding sound to your applications

By itself, Excel doesn't have much to offer in the area of sound — VBA's `Beep` command is about as good as it gets. However, with a few simple API calls, your application can play WAV or MIDI files.

Not all systems support sound. To determine whether a system supports sound, use the `CanPlaySounds` method. Here's an example:

```
If Not Application.CanPlaySounds Then
    MsgBox "Sorry, sound is not supported on your system."
    Exit Sub
End If
```

Playing a WAV file

The following example contains the API function declaration plus a simple procedure to play a sound file called dogbark.wav, which is presumed to be in the same directory as the workbook.

```
Private Declare Function PlaySound Lib "winmm.dll" _
  Alias "PlaySoundA" (ByVal lpszName As String, _
  ByVal hModule As Long, ByVal dwFlags As Long) As Long

Const SND_SYNC = &H0
Const SND_ASYNC = &H1
```

```
Const SND_FILENAME = &H20000

Sub PlayWAV()
    WAVFile = "dogbark.wav"
    WAVFile = ThisWorkbook.Path & "\" & WAVFile
    Call PlaySound(WAVFile, 0&, SND_ASYNC Or SND_FILENAME)
End Sub
```

In the preceding example, the WAV file is played asynchronously. This means execution continues while the sound is playing. To stop code execution while the sound is playing, use this statement instead:

```
    Call PlaySound(WAVFile, 0&, SND_SYNC Or SND_FILENAME)
```

Playing a MIDI file

If the sound file is a MIDI file, you'll need to use a different API call. The `PlayMIDI` procedure starts playing a MIDI file. Executing the `StopMIDI` procedure stops playing the MIDI file. This example uses a file named xfiles.mid.

```
Private Declare Function mciExecute Lib "winmm.dll" _
  (ByVal lpstrCommand As String) As Long

Sub PlayMIDI()
    MIDIFile = "xfiles.mid"
    MIDIFile = ThisWorkbook.Path & "\" & MIDIFile
    mciExecute ("play " & MIDIFile)
End Sub

Sub StopMIDI()
    MIDIFile = "xfiles.mid"
    MIDIFile = ThisWorkbook.Path & "\" & MIDIFile
    mciExecute ("stop " & MIDIFile)
End Sub
```

Summary

In this chapter, I presented dozens of examples to help you better understand the capabilities of VBA.

The next chapter is the first of three chapters that deal with UserForms.

✦ ✦ ✦

P A R T

IV

Working with UserForms

The three chapters in this part cover custom dialog boxes (also known as UserForms). In Chapter 12, you'll learn how to determine whether you need to develop a custom dialog box — and what the alternatives are. You'll also be exposed to the various controls you can use. Chapters 13 and 14 present many examples of custom dialog boxes, ranging from basic to advanced.

✦ ✦ ✦ ✦

In This Part

✦ ✦ ✦ ✦

CHAPTER 12

Introducing UserForms

Dialog boxes are, perhaps, the most important user interface element in Windows programs. Virtually every Windows program uses them. And most users understand how they work. Excel makes it relatively easy to create custom dialog boxes for your applications. In fact, you can duplicate the look and feel of all Excel's dialog boxes.

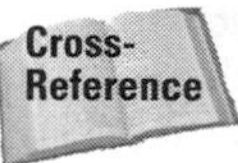

A spreadsheet application that you develop using Excel can consist of any number of elements, or user interface controls, as discussed in Chapter 5. If your application depends on user input, you'll probably want to design custom dialog boxes.

Beginning with Excel 97, things changed substantially with regard to custom dialog boxes. UserForms replaced the clunky old dialog sheets and gave you much more control over your custom dialog boxes. However, for compatibility purposes, Excel 97 and Excel 2000 still support Excel 5/95 dialog sheets. The good news is that it's much easier to work with UserForms, and they offer lots of new capabilities.

How Excel Handles Custom Dialog Boxes

A custom dialog box is created on a UserForm, and you access UserForms in the Visual Basic Editor.

Following is the typical sequence of steps you perform when you create a custom dialog box:

1. Insert a new UserForm into your workbook.

✦ ✦ ✦ ✦

In This Chapter

Custom dialog boxes handled by Excel

How to create, show, and add controls to UserForms

UserForm controls available to you

How to adjust dialog box controls and a control's properties

The control of custom dialog boxes with VBA procedures

A hands-on example of creating UserForms

Types of events relevant to UserForms and controls

How to reference UserForm controls

How to customize your control Toolbox and create UserForm templates

A handy checklist for creating custom dialog boxes

Alternatives to custom dialog boxes

Displaying Excel's built-in dialog boxes

✦ ✦ ✦ ✦

2. Write a procedure that displays the UserForm. This procedure is located in a VBA module — not in the code module for the UserForm.
3. Add controls to the UserForm.
4. Adjust some of the properties of the controls you added.
5. Write event-handler procedures for the controls. These procedures, which are located in the code window for the UserForm, are executed when various events (such as a button click) occur.

Inserting a New UserForm

To insert a new UserForm, activate the VBE (Alt+F11), select your workbook's project from the Project window, and select Insert⇨UserForm. UserForms have names like `UserForm1`, `UserForm2`, and so on.

You can change the name of a UserForm to make it easier to identify. Select the form and use the Properties window to change the `Name` property (press F4 if the Properties window is not displayed). Figure 12-1 shows the Properties window when an empty UserForm is selected.

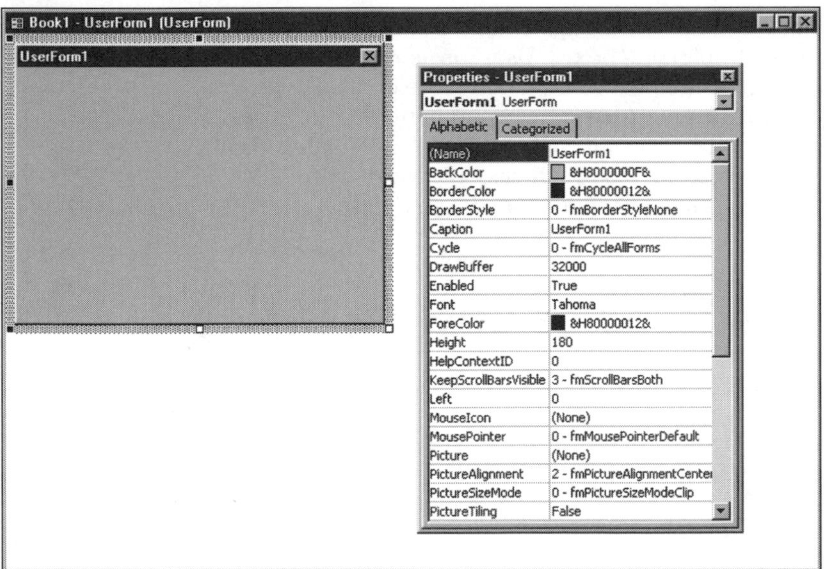

Figure 12-1: The Properties window for an empty UserForm.

A workbook can have any number of UserForms, and each UserForm holds a single custom dialog box.

Displaying a UserForm

To display a UserForm, use the `Show` method of the UserForm object. The following procedure, which is contained in a normal VBA module, displays `UserForm1`.

```
Sub ShowForm
    UserForm1.Show
End Sub
```

When the UserForm is displayed, it remains visible on-screen until it is dismissed. Usually, you'll add a CommandButton to the UserForm that executes a procedure that dismisses the UserForm. The procedure can either unload the UserForm (with the `Unload` statement) or hide the UserForm (with the `Hide` method of the UserForm object). This concept becomes clearer later in the chapter.

Adding Controls to a UserForm

To add controls to a custom dialog box, use the Toolbox (the VBE does not have menu commands that add controls). If the Toolbox is not displayed, select View➪Toolbox. Figure 12-2 shows the Toolbox.

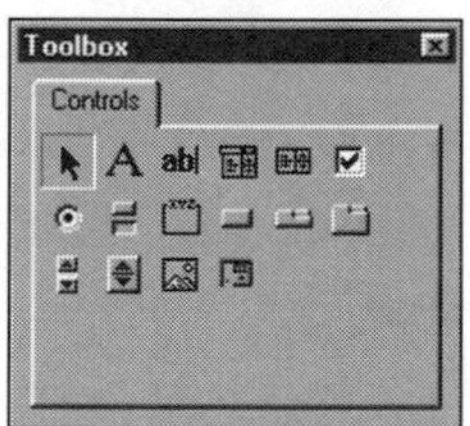

Figure 12-2: Use the Toolbox to add controls to a UserForm.

Just click the Toolbox button that corresponds to the control you want to add, and then click inside the dialog box. Or, you can click the control and then drag the mouse pointer in the dialog box to specify the dimensions for the control.

When you add a new control, it is assigned a name that combines the control type with the numeric sequence for that type of control. For example, if you add a CommandButton control to an empty dialog box, it is named `CommandButton1`. If you then add a second CommandButton, it is named `CommandButton2`.

It's a good idea to rename all the controls that you will be manipulating with your VBA code. Doing so enables you to refer to meaningful names (such as `ProductListBox`), rather than generic names such as `ListBox1`. To change the name of a control, use the Properties window in the VBA. Just select the object and enter a new name.

Controls Available to You

In the sections that follow, I briefly describe the controls available to you in the Toolbox.

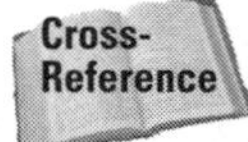

Your UserForms can also use other ActiveX controls. See "Customizing the Toolbox" later in this chapter.

CheckBox

A CheckBox control is useful for giving the user a binary choice: yes or no, true or false, on or off, and so on. When a CheckBox is checked, it has a value of True; when it's not checked, the CheckBox's value is False.

ComboBox

A ComboBox control is similar to a ListBox control. A ComboBox, however, is a drop-down box, and it displays only one item at a time. Another difference is that the user may be able to enter a value that does not appear in the given list of items.

CommandButton

Every dialog box that you create will probably have at least one CommandButton. Usually, you'll want to have one CommandButton labeled OK and another labeled Cancel.

Frame

A Frame control is used to enclose other controls. You do this either for aesthetic purposes or to logically group a set of controls. A frame is particularly useful when the dialog box contains more than one set of OptionButton controls.

Image

An Image control is used to display a graphic image, which can come from a file or can be pasted from the clipboard. You might want to use an Image control to display your company's logo in a dialog box. The graphics image is stored in the workbook. That way, if you distribute your workbook to someone else, it is not necessary to include a copy of the graphics file.

Some graphics files are very large, and using such images can make your workbook increase dramatically in size. For best results, use a file that's as small as possible.

Label

A Label control simply displays text in your dialog box.

ListBox

A ListBox control presents a list of items from which the user can select an item (or multiple items). ListBox controls are very flexible. For example, you can specify a worksheet range that holds the ListBox items, and this range can consist of multiple columns. Or you can fill the ListBox with items using VBA.

MultiPage

A MultiPage control enables you to create tabbed dialog boxes, such as the one that appears when you choose the Tools ➪ Options command. By default, a MultiPage control has two pages. To add additional pages, right-click a tab and select New Page from the shortcut menu.

OptionButton

OptionButtons are useful when the user needs to select from a small number of items. OptionButtons are always used in groups of at least two. When one OptionButton is selected, the other OptionButtons in its group are unselected.

If your dialog box contains more than one set of OptionButtons, each set of OptionButtons must have the same `GroupName` property value. Otherwise, all OptionButtons become part of the same set. Alternately, you can enclose the OptionButtons in a Frame control, which automatically groups the OptionButtons contained in the frame.

RefEdit

A RefEdit control is used when you need to enable the user to select a range in a worksheet.

ScrollBar

A ScrollBar control is similar to a SpinButton control. The difference is that the user can drag the ScrollBar's button to change the control's value in larger increments. The ScrollBar control is most useful for selecting a value that extends across a wide range of possible values.

SpinButton

A SpinButton control enables the user to select a value by clicking one of two arrows; one arrow increases the value and the other arrow decreases the value. A SpinButton is often used in conjunction with a TextBox control or a Label control, both of which display the current value of the SpinButton.

TabStrip

A TabStrip control is similar to a MultiPage control, but it's not as easy to use. In fact, I'm not sure why this control is even included, as the MultiPage control is much more versatile.

TextBox

A TextBox control enables the user to input text.

ToggleButton

A ToggleButton control has two states: on and off. Clicking the button toggles between these two states, and the button changes its appearance. Its value is either True (pressed) or False (not pressed). This is not exactly a "standard" control, and using two OptionButtons is often a better choice.

Using Controls on a Worksheet

Many of the UserForm controls can be embedded directly into a worksheet. These controls are accessible from the Control Toolbox toolbar in Excel (not VBE). Adding such controls to a worksheet requires much less effort than creating a dialog box. In addition, you may not have to create any macros, because you can link a control to a worksheet cell. For example, if you insert a CheckBox control on a worksheet, you can link it to a particular cell by setting its `LinkedCell` property. When the CheckBox is checked, the linked cell displays TRUE. When the CheckBox is unchecked, the linked cell displays FALSE.

The accompanying figure shows a worksheet that contains some embedded controls.

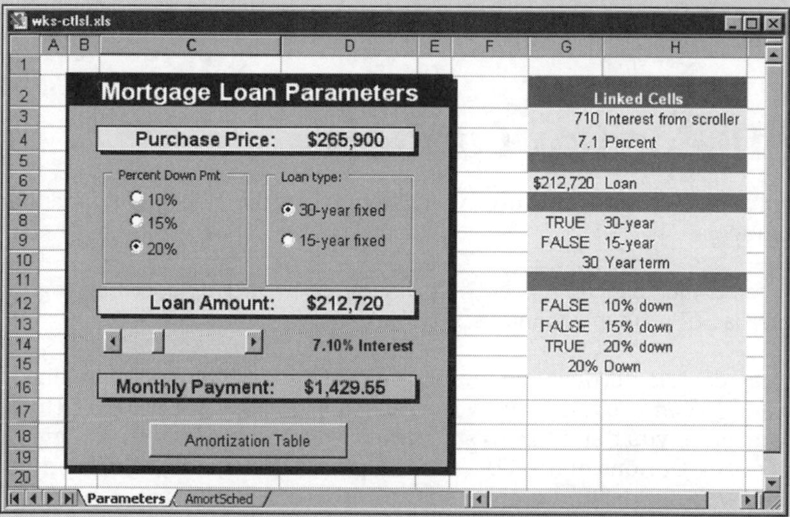

Adding controls to a worksheet can be a bit confusing because controls can come from either of two toolbars:

- ✦ *Forms toolbar.* These controls are insertable objects (and are compatible with Excel 5 and Excel 95).
- ✦ *Control Toolbox toolbar.* These are ActiveX controls. These controls are a subset of those that are available for use on UserForms. These controls work only with Excel 97 and Excel 2000, and are not compatible with Excel 5 and Excel 95.

You can use the controls from either of these toolbars, but it's important that you understand the distinctions between them. The controls from the Forms toolbar work much differently than the ActiveX controls.

When you add a control to a worksheet, Excel goes into *design mode.* In this mode, you can adjust the properties of any controls on your worksheet, add or edit event-handler procedures for the control, or change its size or position. To display the Properties window for an ActiveX control, right-click the control and select Properties from the shortcut menu.

Continued

(continued)

For simple buttons, I often use the Button control on the Forms toolbar because it enables me to attach any macro to it. If I use a CommandButton control from the Control Toolbox, clicking it executes its event-handler procedure (for example, `CommandButton1_Click`) in the code module for the `Sheet` object—you can't attach just any macro to it.

When Excel is in design mode, you can't try out the controls. To test the controls, you must exit design mode by clicking the Exit Design Mode button on the Control Toolbox toolbar.

This workbook, plus another that demonstrates all worksheet controls, is available on the companion CD-ROM.

Adjusting Dialog Box Controls

After a control is placed in a dialog box, you can move and resize it using standard mouse techniques.

You can select multiple controls by Shift-clicking, or by clicking and dragging the pointer to "lasso" a group of controls.

A UserForm may contain vertical and horizontal grid lines which help you align the controls you add. When you add or move a control, it *snaps* to the grid to help you line up the controls. If you don't like to see these grid lines, you can turn them off by choosing Tools ➪ Options in the VBE. In the Options dialog box, select the General tab and set your desired options in the Form Grid Settings section.

The Format menu in the VBE window provides several commands to help you precisely align and space the controls in a dialog box. Before you use these commands, select the controls you want to work with. These commands work just as you would expect, so I don't explain them here. Figure 12-3 shows a dialog box with several OptionButton controls about to be aligned.

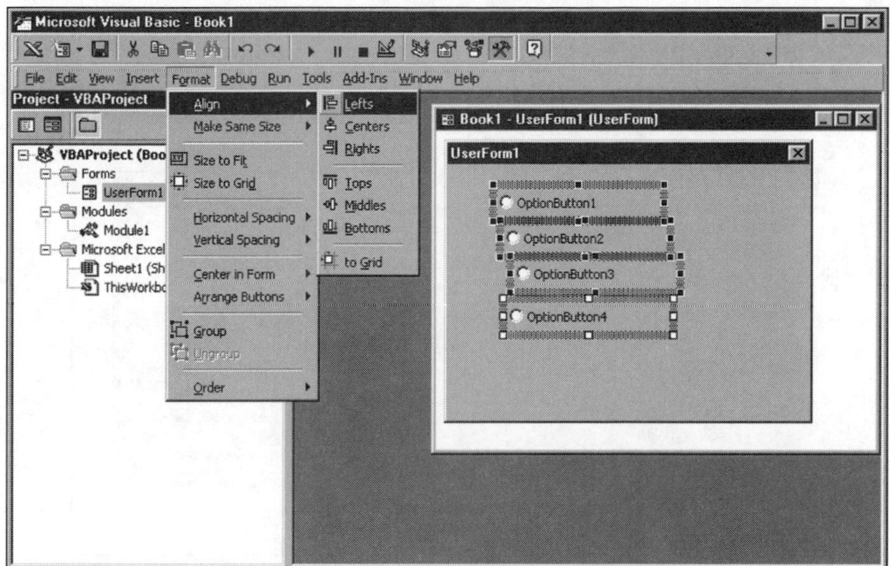

Figure 12-3: Using the Format ➪ Align command to change the alignment of controls.

When you select multiple controls, the last control you select appears with white handles rather than the normal black handles. The control with the white handles is used as the model against which the other black-handle controls are compared for size or position.

Adjusting a Control's Properties

You can change a control's properties at *design time* with the Properties window while you're developing the dialog box or during *run time* when the dialog box is being displayed for the user. You use VBA instructions to change a control's properties at run time.

Using the Properties window

In the VBE, the Properties window adjusts to display the properties of the selected item, which can be a control or the UserForm itself. In addition, you can select a control using the drop-down list at the top of the Properties window (see Figure 12-4).

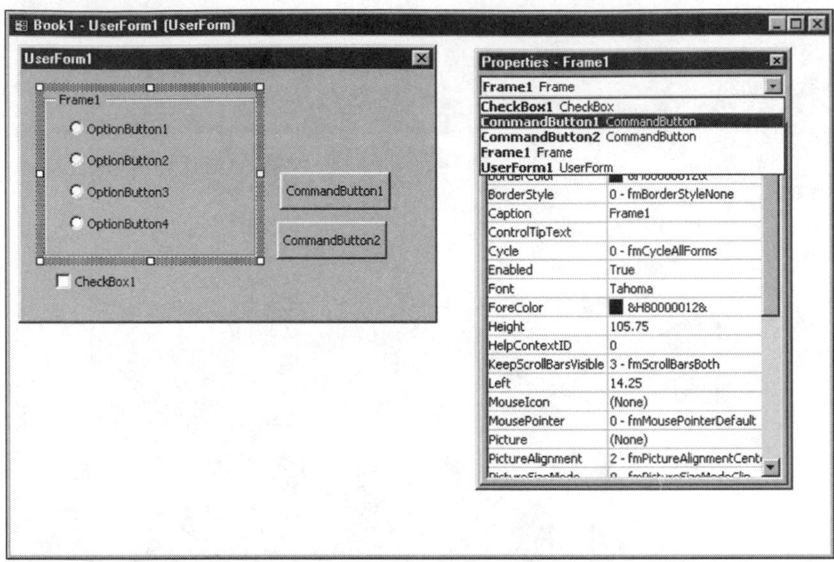

Figure 12-4: Selecting a control from the drop-down list at the top of the Properties window.

The Properties window has two tabs. The Alphabetic tab displays the properties for the selected object in alphabetical order. The Categorized tab displays them grouped into logical categories. Both tabs contain the same properties, but in a different order.

To change a property, just click it and specify the new property. Some properties can take on a finite number of values, selectable from a list. If so, the Properties window displays a button with a downward-pointing arrow. Click the button and you'll be able to select the property's value from the list. For example, the `TextAlign` property can have any of the following values: 1 - fmTextAlignLeft, 2 - fmTextAlignCenter, or 3 - fmTextAlignRight.

A few properties (for example, `Font` and `Picture`) display a small button with an ellipsis when selected. Click the button to display a dialog box associated with the property.

The Image control's `Picture` property is worth mentioning because you can either select a graphic file that contains the image or paste an image from the clipboard. When pasting an image, first copy it to the clipboard, and then select the `Picture` property for the Image control and press Ctrl+V to paste the clipboard contents.

If you select two or more controls at once, the Properties window displays only the properties that are common to the selected controls.

Common properties

Although each control has its own unique set of properties, many of those properties have the same name, and often share a common purpose. For example, every control has a `Name` property and properties that determine its size and position (`Height`, `Width`, `Left`, and `Right`).

If you're going to manipulate a control using VBA, you may prefer to provide a meaningful name for the control. For example, the first OptionButton that you add to a UserForm has a default name of `OptionButton1`. You refer to this object in your code using a statement such as

```
OptionButton1.Value = True
```

But if you give the OptionButton a more meaningful name (such as `obLandscape`), you can use a statement such as

```
obLandscape.Value = True
```

Many people find it helpful to use a name that also identifies the type of object. In the preceding example, I use *ob* as the prefix to identify the fact that this control is an OptionButton.

Learning more about properties

The best way to learn about the various properties for a control is to use the online help. Simply click a property in the Properties window and press F1. Figure 12-5 shows an example of the type of help provided for a property.

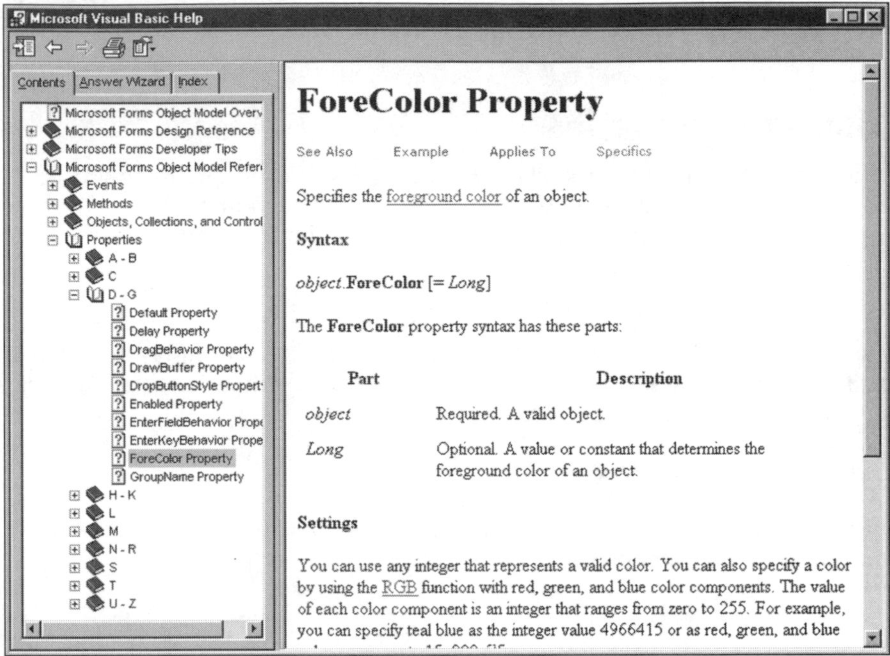

Figure 12-5: The online help provides information about each property for every control.

Accommodating keyboard users

Many users prefer to navigate through a dialog box using the keyboard. The Tab and Shift+Tab keystrokes cycle through the controls, and pressing a hot key operates the control. To make sure that your dialog box works properly for keyboard users, you must be mindful of two issues: tab order and accelerator keys.

Changing the tab order

The tab order determines the sequence in which the controls are activated when the user presses Tab or Shift+Tab. It also determines which control has the initial *focus*. If a user enters text into a TextBox control, for example, the TextBox has the focus. If the user clicks an OptionButton, the OptionButton has the focus. The control that's first in the tab order has the focus when a dialog box is first displayed.

To set the tab order of your controls, choose View ➪ Tab Order. You can also right-click the dialog box and choose Tab Order from the shortcut menu. In either case, Excel displays the Tab Order dialog box shown in Figure 12-6. The Tab Order dialog box lists all the controls, the sequence of which corresponds to the order in which controls pass the focus between each other in the UserForm. To move a control, select it and click the arrow keys up or down. You can choose more than one control (click while pressing Shift or Ctrl) and move them all at once.

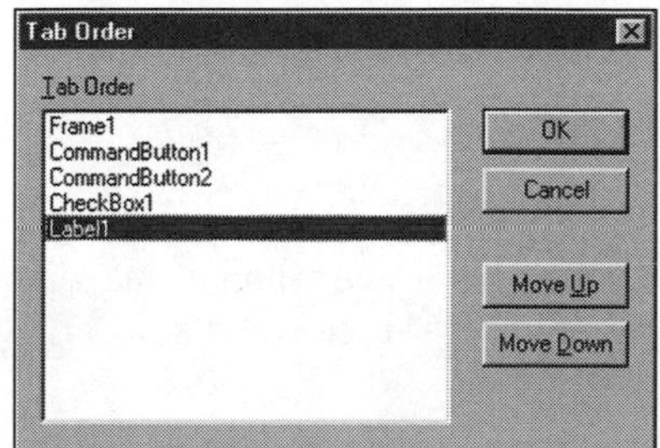

Figure 12-6: Use the Tab Order dialog box to specify the tab order of the controls.

Alternately, you can set an individual control's position in the tab order using the Properties window. The first control in the tab order has a `TabIndex` property of 0. Changing the `TabIndex` property for a control may also affect the `TabIndex` property of other controls. These adjustments are made automatically to ensure that no control has a `TabIndex` setting that is greater than the total number of controls in the UserForm. If you want to remove a control from the tab order, set its `TabStop` property to False.

Some controls, such as Frame and MultiPage, act as containers for other controls. The controls inside a container have their own tab order. To set the tab order for a group of OptionButtons inside a Frame control, select the Frame control before you choose the View➪Tab Order command.

Setting hot keys

You can assign an accelerator key, or *hot key,* to most dialog box controls. This enables the user to access the control by pressing Alt+the hot key. Use the `Accelerator` property in the Properties window for this purpose.

Some controls, such as a TextBox, don't have an `Accelerator` property because they don't display a Caption. You still can enable direct keyboard access to these controls using a Label control. Assign an accelerator key to the Label, and put it ahead of the TextBox in the tab order.

Testing a UserForm

There are three ways you can test a UserForm without actually calling it from a VBA procedure:

✦ Choose the Run➪Run Sub/UserForm command.

✦ Press F5.

✦ Click the Run Sub/UserForm button on the Standard toolbar.

These three techniques all trigger the UserForm's `Initialize` event. When a dialog box is displayed in this test mode, you can try out the tab order and the accelerator keys.

Manipulating UserForms with VBA

In this section I provide an overview of using VBA to work with custom dialog boxes.

Displaying a UserForm

To display a dialog box from VBA, you create a procedure that uses the `Show` method of the UserForm object. You cannot display a dialog box without using at least one line of VBA code. If your UserForm is named `UserForm1`, the following procedure displays the dialog box on that form:

```
Sub ShowDialog()
    UserForm1.Show
End Sub
```

This procedure must be located in a standard VBA module, not in the code module for the UserForm.

VBA also has a `Load` statement. Loading a UserForm loads it into memory, but it is not visible until you use the `Show` method. To load a UserForm, use a statement like this:

```
Load UserForm1
```

If you have a complex UserForm, you might want to load it into memory before it is needed so it appears more quickly when you use the `Show` method. In the majority of situations, however, it's not necessary to use the `Load` statement.

Closing a UserForm

To close a UserForm, use the `UnLoad` statement. For example,

```
Unload UserForm1
```

Or, you can use the following:

```
Unload Me
```

Normally, your VBA code should include the `Unload` statement after the dialog box has performed its actions. For example, your dialog box may have a CommandButton that serves as an OK button. Clicking this button executes a macro. One of the statements in the macro unloads the UserForm. The UserForm remains visible on the screen until the macro that contains the `Unload` statement finishes.

When a UserForm is unloaded, its controls are reset to their original values. In other words, your code will not be able to access the user's choices after the UserForm is unloaded. If the user's choice must be used later on (after the UserForm is unloaded), you need to store the value in a global variable.

A UserForm is automatically unloaded by default when the user clicks the close button (the big *X*) in the upper-right corner. No `Unload` statement is necessary for the UserForm to start unloading itself. With a CommandButton marked Cancel, it's generally convenient to have an event-handler procedure that contains the `Unload` statement, plus whatever other instructions are necessary to perform the business of the UserForm and clean up after itself. But the close button has no event of its own. So clicking the big *X* stops VBA execution of the UserForm module, and any cleanup instructions associated with the Cancel button are skipped over. The solution to this problem is to place your cleanup instructions within the `UserForm_Terminate` event hander. This way, both the Cancel button and the close button initiate the cleanup process. You can then keep your `Unload` statement within the `_Click` event handler for the Cancel button. You'll see more about event-handler procedures in just a few paragraphs.

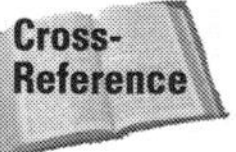

The next chapter presents an example that effectively disables the close button.

UserForms also have a `Hide` method. When you invoke this method, the dialog box disappears, but it remains loaded in memory, so your code can still access the various properties of the controls. Here's an example of a statement that hides a UserForm:

```
UserForm1.Hide
```

Or, you can use the following:

```
Me.Hide
```

If for some reason you would like your UserForm to disappear immediately while its macro is executing, use the `Hide` method at the top of the procedure, and follow it with a `DoEvents` command. For example, in the following procedure, the UserForm disappears immediately when `CommandButton1` is clicked. The last statement in the procedure unloads the UserForm.

```
Private Sub CommandButton1_Click()
    Me.Hide
    DoEvents
    For r = 1 To 10000
        Cells(r, 1) = r
    Next r
    Unload Me
End Sub
```

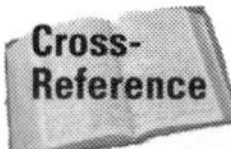

In Chapter 14, I describe how to display a progress indicator, which takes advantage of the fact that a UserForm remains visible while the macro executes.

About event-handler procedures

In official terminology, when the user interacts with the dialog box by selecting an item from a ListBox, clicking a CommandButton, and so on, he causes an *event* to occur. For example, clicking a CommandButton raises the `Click` event for the CommandButton. Your application needs procedures that are executed when these events occur. These procedures are sometimes known as *event-handler* procedures.

Event-handler procedures must be located in the code window for the UserForm. However, your event-handler procedure can call another procedure that's located in a standard VBA module.

Your VBA code can change the properties of the controls while the dialog box is displayed — that is, at run time. For example, you may assign to a ListBox control a procedure that changes the text in a Label when an item is selected. This type of manipulation becomes clearer later in this chapter.

Creating a UserForm: An Example

If you've never created a custom dialog box, you may want to walk through the example in this section. The example includes step-by-step instructions for creating a simple dialog box and developing a VBA procedure to support the dialog box.

This example uses a custom dialog box to get two pieces of information: a person's name and sex. The dialog box uses a TextBox control to get the name, and three OptionButtons to get the sex (Male, Female, or Unknown). The information collected in the dialog box is then sent to the next blank row in a worksheet.

Creating the dialog box

Figure 12-7 shows the finished custom dialog box for this example.

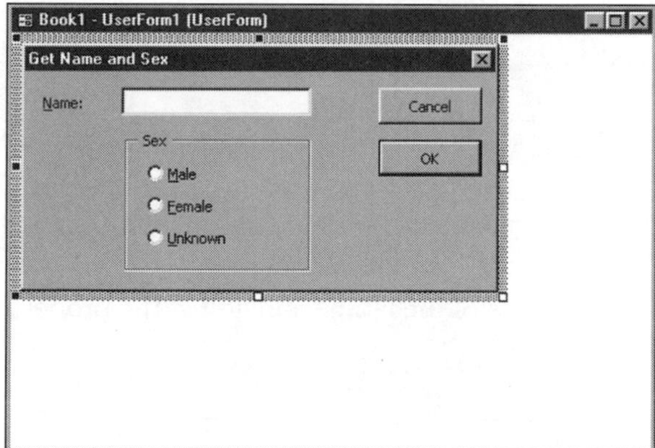

Figure 12-7: This dialog box asks the user to enter a name and a sex.

For best results, start with a new workbook with only one worksheet in it. Then follow these steps:

1. Press Alt+F11 to activate the VBE.
2. In the Project window, select the workbook's project, and choose Insert⇨UserForm to add an empty UserForm.
3. If the Properties window isn't visible, press F4.
4. Use the Properties window to change the UserForm's `Caption` property to **Get Name and Sex.**
5. Add a Label control and adjust the properties as follows:

Property	***Value***
`Accelerator`	N
`Caption`	Name:
`TabIndex`	0

6. Add a TextBox control and adjust the properties as follows:

Property	Value
Name	TextName
TabIndex	1

7. Add a Frame control and adjust the properties as follows:

Property	Value
Caption	Sex
TabIndex	2

8. Add an OptionButton control inside of the Frame and adjust the properties as follows:

Property	Value
Accelerator	M
Caption	Male
Name	OptionMale
TabIndex	0

9. Add another OptionButton control inside of the Frame and adjust the properties as follows:

Property	Value
Accelerator	F
Caption	Female
Name	OptionFemale
TabIndex	1

10. Add yet another Option Button control inside the Frame and adjust the properties as follows:

Property	*Value*
`Accelerator`	U
`Caption`	Unknown
`Name`	OptionUnknown
`TabIndex`	2
`Value`	True

11. Add a CommandButton control outside the frame and adjust the properties as follows:

Property	*Value*
`Caption`	OK
`Default`	True
`Name`	OKButton
`TabIndex`	3

12. Add another CommandButton control and adjust the properties as follows:

Property	*Value*
`Caption`	Cancel
`Cancel`	True
`Name`	CancelButton
`TabIndex`	4

In some cases, you may find it easier to copy an existing control rather than create a new one. To copy a control, press Ctrl while you drag the control.

Writing code to display the dialog box

Next, you add a CommandButton to the worksheet. This button executes a procedure that displays the UserForm. Here's how:

1. Activate Excel.
2. Right-click any toolbar, and select Control Toolbox from the shortcut menu. Excel displays its Control Toolbox toolbar, which closely resembles the VBE Toolbox.
3. Use the Control Toolbox toolbar to add a CommandButton to the worksheet. Click the CommandButton tool, and then drag in the worksheet to create the button.

   If you like, you can change the caption for the worksheet CommandButton. To do so, right-click the button and select CommandButton Object⇨Edit from the shortcut menu.
4. Double-click the button.

   This activates the VBE—specifically, the code module for the worksheet is displayed, with an empty event-handler procedure for the worksheet's CommandButton.
5. Enter a single statement in the `CommandButton1_Click` procedure (see Figure 12-8). This short procedure uses the `Show` method of an object (`UserForm1`) to display the dialog box.

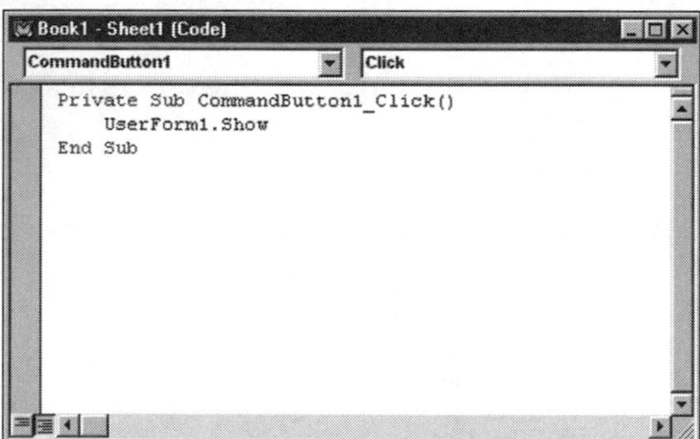

Figure 12-8: The `CommandButton1_Click` procedure is executed when the button is clicked.

Trying it out

The next step is to try out the procedure that displays the dialog box.

When you click the CommandButton on the worksheet, you'll find that nothing happens. Rather, the button is selected because Excel is still in design mode, which happens automatically when you enter a control using the Control Toolbox toolbar. To exit design mode, click the button labeled Exit Design Mode.

When you exit design mode, clicking the button displays the dialog box (see Figure 12-9).

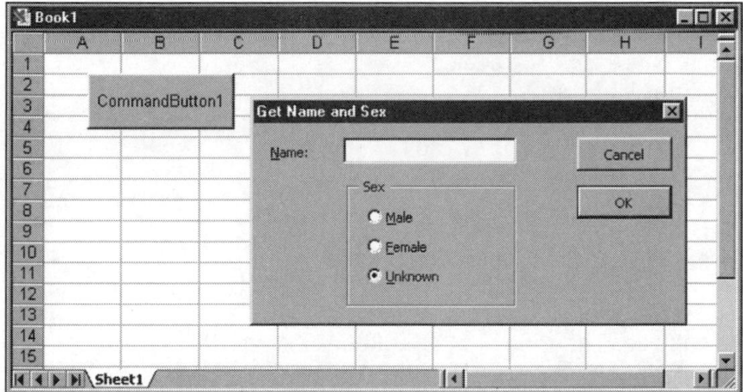

Figure 12-9: The CommandButton's `Click` event procedure displays the dialog box.

When the dialog box is displayed, enter some text into one of the TextBoxes and click OK. You'll find that nothing happens — this is understandable because you haven't created any event-handler procedures yet.

Click the Close button in the dialog box's title bar to get rid of the dialog box.

Adding event-handler procedures

In this section I explain how to write the procedures that handle the events that occur when the dialog box is displayed. To continue our example, do the following:

1. Press Alt+F11 to activate the VBE.
2. Make sure the UserForm is displayed, and double-click the Cancel button. The VBE activates the Code window for the UserForm and provides an empty procedure named `CancelButton_Click`.
3. Modify the procedure as follows (this is the event handler for the CancelButton's `Click` event):

```
Private Sub CancelButton_Click()
    Unload UserForm1
End Sub
```

This procedure, which is executed when the user clicks the Cancel button, simply unloads the dialog box.

4. Press Shift+F7 to redisplay `UserForm1`.

5. Double-click the OK button and enter the following procedure (this is the event handler for the OKButton's `Click` event):

```
Private Sub OKButton_Click()
'   Make sure Sheet1 is active
    Sheets("Sheet1").Activate

'   Determine the next empty row
    NextRow = _
      Application.WorksheetFunction.CountA(Range("A:A")) + 1
'   Transfer the name
    Cells(NextRow, 1) = TextName.Text

'   Transfer the sex
    If OptionMale Then Cells(NextRow, 2) = "Male"
    If OptionFemale Then Cells(NextRow, 2) = "Female"
    If OptionUnknown Then Cells(NextRow, 2) = "Unknown"

'   Clear the controls for the next entry
    TextName.Text = ""
    OptionUnknown = True
    TextName.SetFocus
End Sub
```

6. Activate Excel and click the CommandButton again to display the UserForm.

   You'll find that the dialog box controls now function correctly. Figure 12-10 shows how this looks in action.

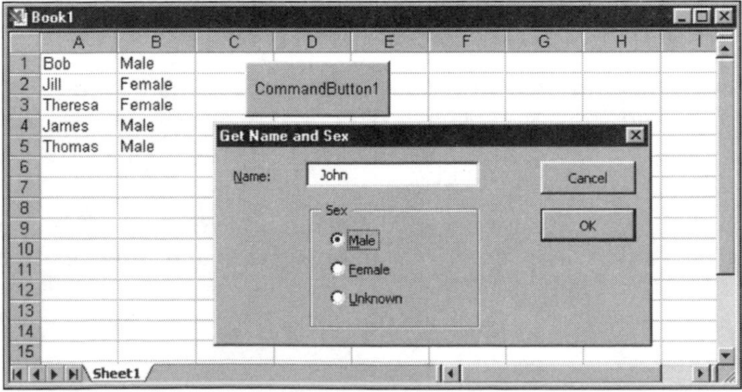

Figure 12-10: Using the custom dialog box.

Here's how the OKButton_Click procedure works: First, the procedure makes sure that the proper worksheet (Sheet1) is active. It then uses Excel's COUNTA function to determine the next blank cell in column A. Here, column A is represented by the numeral 1 in the second parameter of the Cells collection; the first parameter refers to the row number. (Column B is later represented by the numeral 2 at the same position.) Next, the procedure transfers the text from the TextBox to column A. It then uses a series of If statements to determine which OptionButton was selected, and writes the appropriate text (Male, Female, or Unknown) to column B. Finally, the dialog box is reset to make it ready for the next entry. Notice that clicking OK doesn't close the dialog box. To end data entry and unload the UserForm, click the Cancel button.

Validating the data

Play around with this example some more, and you'll find that it has a small problem: It doesn't ensure that the user actually enters a name into the TextBox. The following code is inserted in the OKButton_Click procedure before the text is transferred to the worksheet. It ensures that the user enters a name (well, at least some text) in the TextBox. If the TextBox is empty, a message appears and the routine stops.

```
'   Make sure a name is entered
    If TextName.Text = "" Then
        MsgBox "You must enter a name."
        Exit Sub
    End If
```

Now it works

After making all these modifications, you'll find that the dialog box works flawlessly. In real life, you probably need to collect more information than just name and sex. However, the same basic principles apply. You just have to deal with more dialog box controls.

UserForm Events

Each UserForm control (as well as the UserForm itself) is designed to respond to certain types of events, and these events can be triggered by a user or by Excel. For example, clicking a button generates a CommandButton Click event. You can write code that is executed when a particular event occurs.

Some actions generate multiple events. For example, clicking the upward-pointing arrow of a SpinButton control generates a SpinUp event and also a Change event.

When a UserForm is loaded using the `Show` method, Excel generates an `Initialize` event and an `Activate` event.

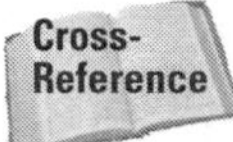

Excel also supports events associated with a `Sheet` object, a `Chart` object, and the `ThisWorkbook` object. I discuss these types of events in Chapter 18.

Learning about events

To find out which events are supported by a particular control, perform the following steps:

1. Add a control to a UserForm.
2. Double-click the control to activate the code module for the UserForm. The VBE inserts an empty event-handler procedure for the control.
3. Click the drop-down list in the upper-right corner of the module window, and you'll see a complete list of events for the control (see Figure 12-11).

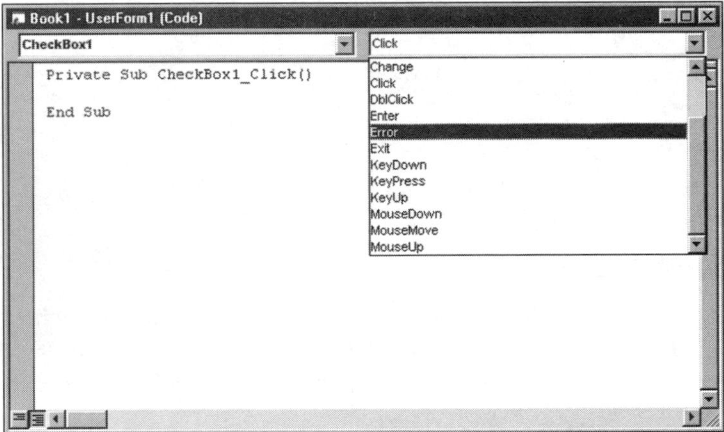

Figure 12-11: The event list for a CheckBox control.

4. Select an event from the list, and the VBE creates an empty event-handler procedure for you.

To find out specific details about an event, consult the online help. The help system also lists the events available for each control.

Event-handler procedures incorporate the name of the object in the procedure's name. Therefore, if you change the name of a control, you also need to make the appropriate changes to the control's event-handler procedure(s). The name changes are not performed automatically! To make things easy on yourself, it's a good idea to provide names for your controls before you begin creating event-handler procedures.

UserForm events

Several events are associated with showing and unloading a UserForm:

`Initialize`	Occurs before a UserForm is loaded or shown
`Activate`	Occurs when a UserForm is activated
`Deactivate`	Occurs when a UserForm is deactivated
`QueryClose`	Occurs before a UserForm is unloaded
`Terminate`	Occurs after the UserForm is unloaded

Often, it's critical that you choose the appropriate event for your event-handler procedure and that you understand the order in which the events occur. Using the `Show` method invokes the `Initialize` and `Activate` events (in that order). Using the `Load` command invokes only the `Initialize` event. Using the `Unload` command triggers the `QueryClose` and `Terminate` events (in that order). Using the `Hide` method doesn't trigger either of these events.

The companion CD-ROM contains a workbook that monitors all these events and displays a message box when an event occurs. If you're confused about UserForm events, studying the code in this example should clear things up.

Example: SpinButton events

To help clarify the concept of events, this section takes a close look at the events associated with a SpinButton control.

The companion CD-ROM contains a workbook that demonstrates the sequence of events that occur for a SpinButton and the UserForm that contains it. The workbook contains a series of event-handler procedures – one for each SpinButton and UserForm event. Each of these procedures simply displays a message box that tells you the event that just fired.

Table 12-1 lists all the events for the SpinButton control.

Table 12-1
SpinButton Events

Event	*Description*
`AfterUpdate`	Occurs after the control is changed through the user interface
`BeforeDragOver`	Occurs when a drag-and-drop operation is in progress
`BeforeUpdate`	Occurs before the control is changed
`Change`	Occurs when the `Value` property changes
`Enter`	Occurs before the control actually receives the focus from a control on the same UserForm
`Error`	Occurs when the control detects an error and cannot return the error information to a calling program
`Exit`	Occurs immediately before a control loses the focus to another control on the same form
`KeyDown`	Occurs when the user presses a key and the object has the focus
`KeyPress`	Occurs when the user presses any key that produces a typeable character
`KeyUp`	Occurs when the user releases a key and the object has the focus
`SpinDown`	Occurs when the user clicks the lower (or left) SpinButton arrow
`SpinUp`	Occurs when the user clicks the upper (or right) SpinButton arrow

A user can operate a SpinButton control by clicking it with the mouse, or (if the control has the focus) using the up-arrow or down-arrow keys.

Mouse-initiated events

When the user clicks the upper SpinButton arrow, the following events occur in this precise order:

1. `Enter` (triggered only if the SpinButton did not already have the focus)
2. `Change`
3. `SpinUp`

Keyboard-initiated events

The user can also press Tab to set the focus to the SpinButton, and then use the up-arrow key to increment the control. If so, the following events occur (in order):

1. `Enter`
2. `KeyDown`
3. `Change`
4. `SpinUp`

What about changes via code?

The SpinButton control can also be changed by VBA code, which also triggers the appropriate event(s). For example, the following instruction sets `SpinButton1`'s `Value` property to zero, and also triggers the `Change` event for the SpinButton control.

```
SpinButton1.Value = 0
```

You might think that you could disable events by setting the `EnableEvents` property of the `Application` object to False. Unfortunately, this property applies only to events that involve true Excel objects: `Workbooks`, `Worksheets`, and `Charts`.

Pairing a SpinButton with a TextBox

A SpinButton has a `Value` property, but this control doesn't have a caption in which to display its value. In many cases, however, you will want the user to see the SpinButton's value. And sometimes you'll want the user to be able to change the SpinButton's value directly instead of clicking the SpinButton repeatedly.

The solution is to pair a SpinButton with a TextBox, which enables the user to specify a value by typing it into the TextBox directly, or by clicking the SpinButton to increment or decrement the value in the TextBox.

Figure 12-12 shows a simple example. The SpinButton's `Min` property is 1, and its `Max` property is 100. Therefore, clicking the SpinButton's arrows changes its `Value` property setting to an integer between 1 and 100.

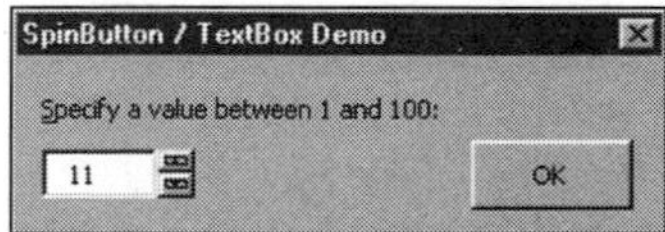

Figure 12-12: This SpinButton is paired with a TextBox.

This workbook is available on the companion CD-ROM.

The code required to "link" a SpinButton with a TextBox is relatively simple. It's basically a matter of writing event-handler procedures to ensure that the SpinButton's `Value` property is in sync with the TextBox's `Text` property.

The following procedure is executed whenever the SpinButton's `Change` event is triggered. That is, the procedure is executed when the user clicks the SpinButton, or changes its value by pressing the up arrow or the down arrow.

```
Private Sub SpinButton1_Change()
    TextBox1.Text = SpinButton1.Value
End Sub
```

The procedure simply assigns the SpinButton's `Value` to the `Text` property of the TextBox control. Here, the controls have their default names (`SpinButton1` and `TextBox1`). If the user enters a value directly into the TextBox, its `Change` event is triggered and the following procedure is executed:

```
Private Sub TextBox1_Change()
    NewVal = Val(TextBox1.Text)
    If NewVal >= SpinButton1.Min And _
        NewVal <= SpinButton1.Max Then _
        SpinButton1.Value = NewVal
End Sub
```

This procedure starts by using VBA's `Val` function to convert the text in the TextBox to a value (if the TextBox contains a string, the `Val` function returns 0). The next statement determines if the value is within the proper range for the SpinButton. If so, the SpinButton's `Value` property is set to the value entered in the TextBox.

The example is set up so that clicking the OK button (which is named `OKButton`) transfers the SpinButton's value to the active cell. The event handler for this CommandButton's `Click` event is as follows:

```
Private Sub OKButton_Click()
'   Enter the value into the active cell
    If CStr(SpinButton1.Value) = TextBox1.Text Then
        ActiveCell = SpinButton1.Value
        Unload Me
    Else
        MsgBox "Invalid entry.", vbCritical
        TextBox1.SetFocus
        TextBox1.SelStart = 0
```

```
        TextBox1.SelLength = Len(TextBox1.Text)
    End If
End Sub
```

This procedure does one final check: It makes sure that the text entered in the TextBox matches the SpinButton's value. This is necessary in the case of an invalid entry. For example, should the user enter **3r** into the TextBox, the SpinButton's value would not be changed, and the result placed in the active cell would not be what the user intended. Notice that the SpinButton's `Value` property is converted to a string using the `CStr` function. This ensures that the comparison does not generate an error if a value is compared to text. If the SpinButton's value does not match the TextBox's contents, a message box is displayed. Notice that the focus is set to the TextBox object, and the contents are selected (using the `SelStart` and `SelLength` properties). This makes it very easy for the user to correct the entry.

About the Tag Property

Every UserForm and control has a `Tag` property. This property doesn't represent anything specific, and, by default, is empty. You can use the `Tag` property to store information for your own use.

For example, you may have a series of TextBox controls in a UserForm. The user may be required to enter text into some, but not all of them. You can use the `Tag` property to identify (for your own use) which fields are required. In this case, you can set the `Tag` property to a string such as **Required.** Then, when you write code to validate the user's entries, you can refer to the `Tag` property.

The following example is a function that examines all TextBox controls on `UserForm1` and returns the number of "required" TextBox controls that are empty.

```
Function EmptyCount()
  EmptyCount= 0
  For Each ctl In UserForm1.Controls
    If TypeName(ctl) = "TextBox" Then
      If ctl.Tag = "Required" Then
        If ctl.Text = "" Then
           EmptyCount = EmptyCount + 1
        End If
      End If
   End If
 Next ctl
End Function
```

You can probably think of lots of other uses for the `Tag` property.

Referencing UserForm Controls

When working with controls on a UserForm, the VBA code is usually contained in the code window for the UserForm. You can also refer to dialog box controls from a general VBA module. To do so, you need to *qualify* the reference to the control by specifying the UserForm name. For example, consider the following procedure, which is located in a VBA module. It simply displays the UserForm named UserForm1.

```
Sub GetData()
    UserForm1.Show
End Sub
```

Assume that you wanted to provide a default value for the text box named TextName. You could modify the procedure as follows:

```
Sub GetData()
    UserForm1.TextName.Value = "John Doe"
    UserForm1.Show
End Sub
```

Another way to set the default value is to take advantage of the UserForm's Initialize event. You can write code in the UserForm_Initialize procedure, which is located in the code module for the UserForm. Here's an example:

```
Private Sub UserForm_Initialize()
    TextName.Value = "John Doe"
End Sub
```

Notice that when the control is referenced in the code module for the UserForm, there is no need to qualify the references with the UserForm name.

Understanding the Controls Collection

The controls on a UserForm compose a collection. For example, the following statement displays the number of controls on UserForm1:

```
MsgBox UserForm.Controls.Count
```

There is *not* a collection of each control type. For example, there is no collection of CommandButton controls. However, you can determine the type of control using the TypeName function. The following procedure uses a For Each-Next structure to loop through the Controls collection and then displays the number of CommandButton controls on UserForm1:

```
Sub CountButtons()
    cbCount = 0
```

```
    For Each ctl In UserForm1.Controls
        If TypeName(ctl) = "CommandButton" Then _
          cbCount = cbCount + 1
    Next ctl
    MsgBox cbCount
End Sub
```

Customizing the Toolbox

When a UserForm is active in the VBE, the Toolbox (see Figure 12-13) displays the controls that you can add to the UserForm. This section describes ways to customize the Toolbox.

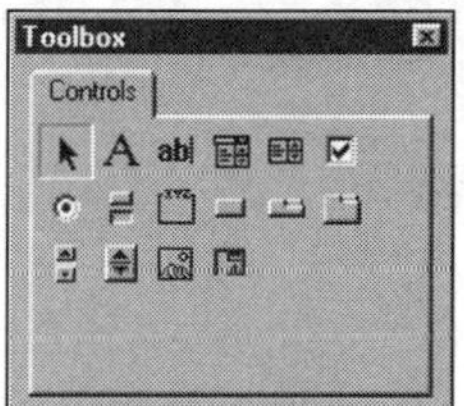

Figure 12-13: The Toolbox contains the controls that you can add to a UserForm.

Changing icons or tip text

If you would prefer a different icon or different tip text for a particular tool, right-click the tool and select Customize *xxx* from the shortcut menu (where *xxx* is the control's name). This brings up a new dialog box that enables you to change the Tool Tip Text, edit the icon, or load a new icon image from a file.

Adding new pages

The Toolbox initially contains a single tab. Right-click this tab and select New Page to add a new tab to the Toolbox. You can also change the text displayed on the tab by selecting Rename from the shortcut menu.

Customizing or combining controls

A very handy feature enables you to customize a control and then save it for future use. You can, for instance, create a CommandButton control that's set up to serve an OK button. You can set the following properties: `Width`, `Height`, `Caption`,

`Default`, and `Name`. Then, drag the customized CommandButton to the Toolbox. This creates a new control. Right-click the new control to rename it or change its icon.

You can also create a new Toolbox entry that consists of multiple controls. For example, you can create two CommandButtons that represent a UserForm's OK and Cancel buttons. Customize them as you want and then select them both and drag them to the Toolbox. In this case, you can use this new Toolbox control to add two customized buttons in one fell swoop.

This also works with controls that act as containers. For example, create a Frame control and add four customized OptionButtons, neatly spaced and aligned. Then drag the Frame to the Toolbox to create a customized Frame control.

You might want to place your customized controls on a separate page in the Toolbox. This enables you to export the entire page so you can share it with other Excel users. To export a Toolbox page (so that it may be reloaded into a later instance of the Toolbox), right-click the tab and select Export Page.

The companion CD-ROM contains a PAG file that contains some customized controls. You can import this file as a new page in your Toolbox. Right-click a tab and select Import Page. Then locate the PAG file.

Adding new ActiveX controls

UserForms can use some other ActiveX controls developed by Microsoft or other vendors. To add an additional ActiveX control to the Toolbox, right-click the page of the Toolbox where you want the new controls to appear, and select Additional Controls. This displays the dialog box shown in Figure 12-14.

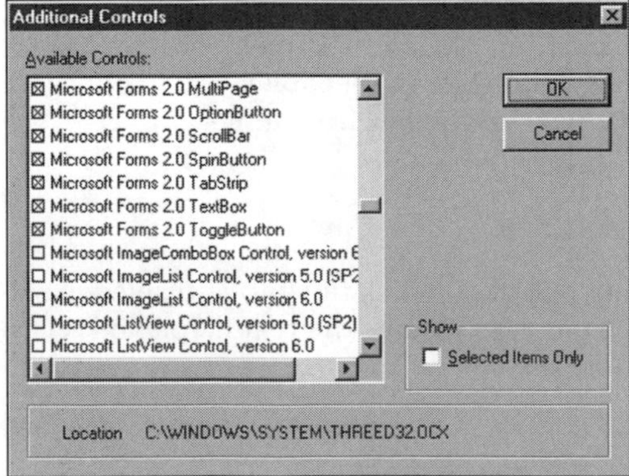

Figure 12-14: The Additional Controls dialog box enables you to add other ActiveX controls.

The Additional Controls dialog box lists all ActiveX controls that are installed on your system. Select the control(s) that you want to add, and then click OK to add an icon for each selected control.

Not all ActiveX controls that are installed on your system will work in Excel UserForms. In fact, most of them probably won't work. Moreover, you need a license to use some controls in an application. If you aren't licensed to use a particular control, you'll receive an error message to that effect.

Creating UserForm "Templates"

You might find that when you design a new UserForm, you tend to add the same controls each time. For example, every UserForm might have two CommandButtons that serve as OK and Cancel buttons. In the previous section, I described how to create a new control that combines these two (customized) buttons into a single control. Another option is to create your UserForm "template" and then export it so it can be imported into other projects.

Start by creating a UserForm that contains all the controls and customizations that you would need to reuse in other projects. Then, make sure the UserForm is selected and choose File⇨Export File (or press Ctrl+E). You are prompted for a filename. When you start your next project, select File⇨Import File to load the saved UserForm.

Emulating Excel's Dialog Boxes

The look and feel of Windows dialog boxes differ from program to program. When developing applications for Excel, it's best to try to mimic Excel's dialog box style whenever possible.

In fact, a good way to learn how to create effective dialog boxes is to try to copy one of Excel's dialog boxes down to the smallest detail. For example, make sure that you get all the hot keys defined and that the tab order is the same. To recreate one of Excel's dialog boxes, you need to test it under various circumstances and see how it behaves. I guarantee that your analysis of Excel's dialog boxes will improve your own dialog boxes.

Prior to Excel 97, it was impossible to duplicate some of Excel's dialog boxes. But the new capabilities introduced in Excel 97 enable you to duplicate virtually every one of them. An exception is the range selector control found (for example) in the Goal Seek dialog box. The RefEdit control, however, is a close substitute.

A Dialog Box Checklist

Before you unleash a custom dialog box on end users, make sure that everything is working correctly. The following checklist should help you identify potential problems.

- Are similar controls the same size?
- Are the controls evenly spaced?
- Is the dialog box too overwhelming? If so, you may want to group the controls using a MultiPage control.
- Can every control be accessed with a hot key?
- Are any of the hot keys duplicated?
- Is the tab order set correctly?
- If the dialog box will be stored in an add-in, did you test it thoroughly after creating the add-in? It's important to remember that an add-in will never be the active workbook.
- Will your VBA code take appropriate action if the dialog box is canceled or the user presses Esc?
- Are there any misspellings in the text?
- Does the dialog box have an appropriate caption?
- Will the dialog box display properly at all video resolutions? Sometimes labels that display properly with a high-resolution display appear cut off in VGA display mode.
- Are the controls grouped logically (by function)?
- Do ScrollBar and SpinButton controls allow valid values only?
- Are ListBoxes set properly (Single, Multi, or Extended)?

Custom Dialog Box Alternatives

In some cases, you can save yourself the trouble of creating a custom dialog box by using one of several prebuilt dialog boxes:

- An input box
- A message box
- A dialog box for selecting a file to open

Converting Dialog Sheets to UserForms

If you open an Excel 5/95 workbook that contains custom dialog boxes, they are displayed in dialog sheets in the workbook. Usually, it's not necessary to convert these dialog sheets to UserForms because Excel 97 and Excel 2000 both support dialog sheets.

Excel doesn't provide a way to convert a dialog sheet to a UserForm, but I developed a utility to do so. A copy of my DialogSheet-to-UserForm wizard is available on the companion CD-ROM. Note that this utility simply creates the UserForm. It's up to you to write the VBA code to make it function correctly.

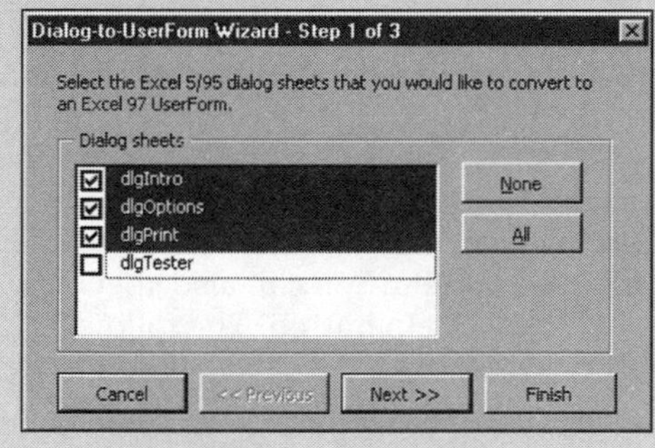

✦ A dialog box for specifying a filename and location for a save operation

✦ A dialog box for specifying a directory (requires a Windows API call)

I describe these dialog boxes in the following sections.

Using an input box

There are actually two `InputBox` functions: one from Excel and one from VBA.

VBA's InputBox function

The syntax for VBA's `InputBox` function is

```
InputBox(prompt[,title][,default][,xpos][,ypos][,helpfile,
context])
```

prompt	(Required) The text displayed in the input box
title	(Optional) The caption of the input box window
default	(Optional) The default value to be displayed in the dialog box
xpos, ypos	(Optional) The screen coordinates at the upper-left corner of the window
helpfile, context	(Optional) The help file and help topic

The `InputBox` function prompts the user for a single bit of information. The function always returns a string, so it may be necessary to convert the results to a value.

The prompt may consist of about 1,024 characters (more or less, depending on the width of the characters used). In addition, you can provide a title for the dialog box, a default value, and specify its position on the screen. You can also specify a custom help topic; if you do, the input box includes a Help button. The following example, whose output is shown in Figure 12-15, uses VBA's `InputBox` function to ask the user for his full name.

Figure 12-15: VBA's `InputBox` function at work.

```
Sub GetName()
    Do Until UserName <> ""
        UserName = InputBox("Enter your full name: ", _
            "Identify Yourself")
    Loop
    FirstSpace = InStr(UserName, " ")
    If FirstSpace <> 0 Then
        UserName = Left(UserName, FirstSpace)
    End If
    MsgBox "Hello " & UserName
End Sub
```

Notice that this `InputBox` function is written in a `Do Until` loop to ensure that something is entered when the input box appears. If the user clicks Cancel or doesn't enter any text, UserName contains an empty string and the input box reappears. The procedure then attempts to extract the first name by searching for the first space character (using the `InStr` function), and then using the `Left` function to extract all characters before the first space. If a space character is not found, the entire name is used as entered.

As I mentioned, the `InputBox` function always returns a string. If the string returned by the `InputBox` function looks like a number, you can convert it to a value using VBA's `Val` function. Or, you can use Excel's `InputBox` method, which is described in the next section.

Excel's InputBox method

One advantage of using Excel's `InputBox` method rather than VBA's is that with Excel's you can specify the data type returned. In addition, the `InputBox` method enables the user to specify a worksheet range by dragging in the worksheet. The method's syntax is

```
object.InputBox(prompt,title,default,left,top,helpfile,context,
type)
```

prompt	(Required) The text displayed in the input box
title	(Optional) The caption in the input box window
default	(Optional) The default value to be returned by the function, if the user enters nothing
left, top	(Optional) The screen coordinates at the upper-left corner of the window
helpfile, context	(Optional) The help file and help topic
type	(Optional) A code for the data type returned, as listed in Table 12-2

Table 12-2
Codes to Determine the Data Type Returned by Excel's InputBox Method

Code	*Meaning*
0	A formula
1	A number
2	A string (text)

Continued

Table 12-2 (continued)

Code	*Meaning*
4	A logical value (True or False)
8	A cell reference, as a `Range` object
16	An error value, such as #N/A
64	An array of values

To specify more than one data type to be returned, use the sum of the pertinent codes. For example, to display an input box that can accept text or numbers, set type equal to 3 (that is, 1 + 2, or "number" plus "text").

Excel's `InputBox` method is quite versatile. For example, if you use 8 for the type argument, the user can point to a range in the worksheet. In the following code, the `InputBox` method returns a `Range` object (note the `Set` keyword) and then clears the values from the selected cells. The default value displayed in the input box is the current selection's address. The `On Error` statement ends the procedure if the input box is canceled.

```
Sub GetRange()
    Dim UserRange As Range
    Default = Selection.Address
    On Error GoTo Canceled
    Set UserRange = Application.InputBox _
        (Prompt:="Range to erase:", _
        Title:="Range Erase", _
        Default:=Default, _
        Type:=8)
    UserRange.Clear
    UserRange.Select
Canceled:
End Sub
```

Yet another advantage of using Excel's `InputBox` method instead of VBA's is that Excel performs input validation automatically. In the `GetRange` example, if you enter something other than a range address, Excel displays an informative message and enables the user to try again.

VBA's MsgBox function

I use VBA's `MsgBox` function in many of this book's examples as an easy way to display a variable's value. The official syntax for `MsgBox` is as follows:

```
MsgBox(prompt[,buttons][,title][,helpfile, context])
```

prompt	(Required) The text displayed in the message box
buttons	(Optional) A numeric expression that determines which buttons and icon is displayed in the message box (see Table 12-3)
title	(Optional) The caption in the message box window
helpfile, context	(Optional) The help file and help topic

You can easily customize your message boxes because of the flexibility of the *buttons* argument. (Table 12-3 lists the many constants that you can use for this argument.) You can specify which buttons to display, whether an icon appears, and which button is the default.

Table 12-3
Constants Used for Buttons in the MsgBox Function

Constant	Value	Description
`VbOKOnly`	0	Display OK button only
`VbOKCancel`	1	Display OK and Cancel buttons
`VbAbortRetryIgnore`	2	Display Abort, Retry, and Ignore buttons
`VbYesNoCancel`	3	Display Yes, No, and Cancel buttons
`VbYesNo`	4	Display Yes and No buttons
`VbRetryCancel`	5	Display Retry and Cancel buttons
`VbCritical`	16	Display Critical Message icon
`VbQuestion`	32	Display Warning Query icon
`VbExclamation`	48	Display Warning Message icon
`VbInformation`	64	Display Information Message icon
`VbDefaultButton1`	0	First button is default
`VbDefaultButton2`	256	Second button is default
`VbDefaultButton3`	512	Third button is default
`VbDefaultButton4`	768	Fourth button is default
`VbSystemModal`	4096	All applications are suspended until the user responds to the message box (may not work under all conditions)

You can use the MsgBox function by itself (to simply display a message) or assign its result to a variable. When MsgBox does return a result, it represents the button clicked by the user. The following example displays a message and does not return a result:

```
Sub MsgBoxDemo()
    MsgBox "Click OK to continue"
End Sub
```

To get a response from a message box, you can assign the results of the MsgBox function to a variable. In the following code, I use some built-in constants (described in Table 12-3) to make it easier to work with the values returned by MsgBox:

```
Sub GetAnswer()
    Ans = MsgBox("Continue?", vbYesNo)
    Select Case Ans
        Case vbYes
'           ...[code if Ans is Yes]...
        Case vbNo
'           ...[code if Ans is No]...
    End Select
End Sub
```

Actually, it's not even necessary to use a variable to use the result of a message box. The following procedure displays a message box with Yes and No buttons. If the user doesn't click the Yes button, the procedure ends.

```
Sub GetAnswer2()
    If MsgBox("Continue?", vbYesNo) <> vbYes Then Exit Sub
'   ...[code if Yes button is not clicked]...
End Sub
```

The following function example uses a combination of constants to display a message box with a Yes button, a No button, and a question mark icon. The second button is designated as the default button (see Figure 12-16). For simplicity, I assigned these constants to the Config variable.

```
Function ContinueProcedure() as Boolean
    Config = vbYesNo + vbQuestion + vbDefaultButton2
    Ans = MsgBox("An error occurred. Continue?", Config)
    If Ans = vbYes Then ContinueProcedure = True _
        Else ContinueProcedure = False
End Function
```

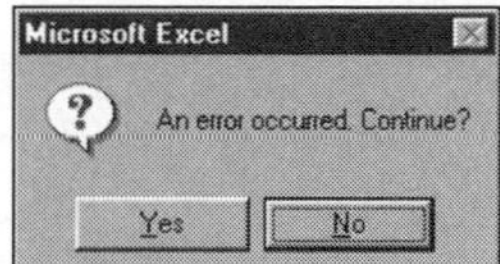

Figure 12-16: The buttons argument of the MsgBox function determines which buttons appear.

If you would like to force a line break in the message, use the vbCrLf constant in the text. The following example displays the message in three lines:

```
Sub MultiLine()
    Msg = "This is the first line" & vbCrLf
    Msg = Msg & "Second line" & vbCrLf
    Msg = Msg & "Last line"
    MsgBox Msg
End Sub
```

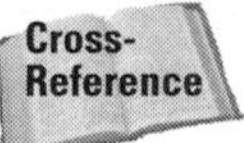

Chapter 14 includes a VBA example that emulates the MsgBox function.

Excel's GetOpenFilename method

If your application needs to ask the user for a filename, you can use the InputBox function. But this approach often leads to typographical errors. A better approach is to use the GetOpenFilename method of the Application object, which ensures that your application gets a valid filename as well as its complete path.

The GetOpenFilename method displays the normal Open dialog box (displayed when you select the File➪Open command), but does not actually open the file specified. Rather, the method returns a string that contains the path and filename selected by the user. Then you can do whatever you want with the filename. The syntax for this method is as follows (all arguments are optional):

```
object.GetOpenFilename(FileFilter, FilterIndex, Title,
ButtonText, MultiSelect)
```

The *FileFilter* argument determines what appears in the dialog box's Files of type drop-down list. The argument consists of pairs of file filter strings followed by the wildcard file filter specification, with each part and each pair separated by commas. If omitted, this argument defaults to the following:

```
"User (*.*),*.*"
```

Notice that the first part of this string (User (*.*)) is the text displayed in the Files of type drop-down list. The second part (*.*) actually determines which files are displayed.

The *FilterIndex* argument specifies which FileFilter is the default, and the title argument is text that is displayed in the title bar. If the *MultiSelect* argument is True, the user can select multiple files, all of which are returned in an array. The *ButtonText* argument is not used in Excel for Windows.

The following instruction assigns a string to a variable named `Filt`. This string can then be used as a `FileFilter` argument for the `GetOpenFilename` method. In this case, the dialog box enables the user to select from four different file types, plus an "all files" option.

```
Filt = "Text Files (*.txt),*.txt," & _
       "Lotus Files (*.prn),*.prn," & _
       "Comma Separated Files (*.csv),*.csv," & _
       "ASCII Files (*.asc),*.asc," & _
       "All Files (*.*),*.*"
```

The following example prompts the user for a filename. It defines five file filters. Notice that I used VBA's line continuation sequence to set up the `Filter` variable; doing so makes it much easier to work with this rather complicated argument.

```
Sub GetImportFileName()
'   Set up list of file filters
    Filt = "Text Files (*.txt),*.txt," & _
           "Lotus Files (*.prn),*.prn," & _
           "Comma Separated Files (*.csv),*.csv," & _
           "ASCII Files (*.asc),*.asc," & _
           "All Files (*.*),*.*"

'   Display *.* by default
    FilterIndex = 5

'   Set the dialog box caption
    Title = "Select a File to Import"

'   Get the file name
    FileName = Application.GetOpenFilename _
        (FileFilter:=Filt, _
         FilterIndex:=FilterIndex, _
         Title:=Title)

'   Exit if dialog box canceled
    If FileName = False Then
        MsgBox "No file was selected."
        Exit Sub
    End If

'   Display full path and name of the file
    MsgBox "You selected " & FileName
End Sub
```

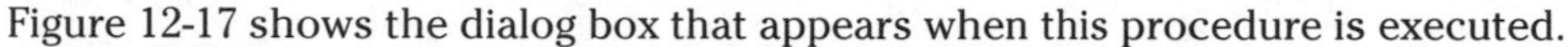

Figure 12-17 shows the dialog box that appears when this procedure is executed.

Figure 12-17: The GetOpenFilename method displays a customizable dialog box.

The following example is similar to the previous example. The difference is that the user can press Ctrl or Shift and select multiple files when the dialog box is displayed. Notice that I check for the Cancel button click by determining if `FileName` is an array. If the user doesn't click Cancel, the result is an array that consists of at least one element. In this example, a list of the selected files is displayed in a message box.

```
Sub GetImportFileName2()
'   Set up list of file filters
    Filt  = "Text Files (*.txt),*.txt," & _
            "Lotus Files (*.prn),*.prn," & _
            "Comma Separated Files (*.csv),*.csv," & _
            "ASCII Files (*.asc),*.asc," & _
            "All Files (*.*),*.*"

'   Display *.* by default
    FilterIndex = 5

'   Set the dialog box caption
    Title = "Select a File to Import"

'   Get the file name
    FileName = Application.GetOpenFilename _
        (FileFilter:=Filt, _
         FilterIndex:=FilterIndex, _
```

```
            Title:=Title, _
            MultiSelect:=True)

'   Exit if dialog box canceled
    If Not IsArray(FileName) Then
        MsgBox "No file was selected."
        Exit Sub
    End If

'   Display full path and name of the files
    For i = LBound(FileName) To UBound(FileName)
        Msg = Msg & FileName(i) & vbCrLf
    Next i
    MsgBox "You selected:" & vbCrLf & Msg
End Sub
```

Excel's GetSaveAsFilename method

Like the `GetOpenFilename` method, Excel's `GetSaveAsFilename` method returns a filename and path but doesn't take any action. The syntax for this method is

```
object.GetSaveAsFilename(InitialFilename, FileFilter,
FilterIndex, Title, ButtonText)
```

All the arguments are optional.

Prompting for a directory

If you need to get a filename, use the `GetOpenFileName` method, as described previously. But if you need to get only a directory name, you'll find that there is no direct way to do so. However, you can use a Windows API call to display a dialog box that returns a drive and directory name.

In this section I present a function named `GetDirectory` that displays the dialog box shown in Figure 12-18, and returns a string that represents the selected directory. If the user clicks Cancel, the function returns an empty string.

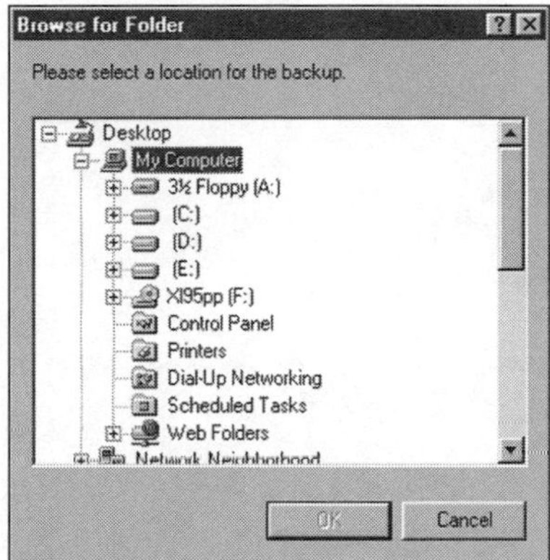

Figure 12-18: Use an API function to display this dialog box.

The `GetDirectory` function takes one argument, which is optional. This argument is a string that will be displayed in the dialog box. If the argument is omitted, the dialog box displays `Select a folder` as the message.

On the CD-ROM

The companion CD-ROM contains a workbook that demonstrates this procedure.

Following are the API declarations required at the beginning of the workbook module. This function also uses a custom data type, called `BROWSEINFO`.

```
'32-bit API declarations
Declare Function SHGetPathFromIDList Lib "shell32.dll" _
  Alias "SHGetPathFromIDListA" (ByVal pidl As Long, ByVal _
  pszPath As String) As Long

Declare Function SHBrowseForFolder Lib "shell32.dll" _
  Alias "SHBrowseForFolderA" (lpBrowseInfo As BROWSEINFO) _
  As Long

Public Type BROWSEINFO
    hOwner As Long
    pidlRoot As Long
    pszDisplayName As String
    lpszTitle As String
    ulFlags As Long
    lpfn As Long
    lParam As Long
    iImage As Long
End Type
```

The `GetDirectory` function is as follows:

```
Function GetDirectory(Optional Msg) As String
    Dim bInfo As BROWSEINFO
    Dim path As String
    Dim r As Long, x As Long, pos As Integer

'   Root folder = Desktop
    bInfo.pidlRoot = 0&

'   Title in the dialog
    If IsMissing(Msg) Then
        bInfo.lpszTitle = "Select a folder."
    Else
        bInfo.lpszTitle = Msg
    End If

'   Type of directory to return
    bInfo.ulFlags = &H1

'   Display the dialog
    x = SHBrowseForFolder(bInfo)

'   Parse the result
    path = Space$(512)
    r = SHGetPathFromIDList(ByVal x, ByVal path)
    If r Then
        pos = InStr(path, Chr$(0))
        GetDirectory = Left(path, pos - 1)
    Else
        GetDirectory = ""
    End If
End Function
```

The following simple procedure demonstrates how to use the `GetDirectory` function in your code. Executing this procedure displays the dialog box. When the user clicks OK or Cancel, the `MsgBox` function displays the full path of the selected directory.

```
Sub GetAFolder()
    Dim Msg As String
    Msg = "Please select a location for the backup."
    MsgBox GetDirectory(Msg)
End Sub
```

Displaying Excel's Built-In Dialog Boxes

Code that you write in VBA can execute Excel's menu commands. And, if the command leads to a dialog box, your code can "make choices" in the dialog box— although the dialog box itself isn't displayed. For example, the following statement is equivalent to selecting the Edit⇨Go To command, specifying a range named `InputRange`, and clicking OK. However, the Go To dialog box never appears.

```
Application.Goto Reference:="InputRange"
```

In some cases, however, you may *want* to display one of Excel's built-in dialog boxes so the end user can make the choices. This is easy to do, using the `Dialogs` method of the `Application` object. Here's an example:

```
Result = Application.Dialogs(xlDialogFormulaGoto).Show
```

This statement, when executed, displays the GoTo dialog box (`xlDialogFormulaGoto` is a predefined constant). The user can specify a named range or enter a cell address to go to. This dialog box works exactly as it does when you choose the Edit ⇨ Go To command (or press F5).

Contrary to what you might think, the `Result` variable does not hold the range that is selected. Rather, the value assigned to `Result` is True if the user clicked OK, and False if the user clicked Cancel or pressed Esc.

You can get a list of all the dialog box constants using the Object Browser. Follow these steps:

1. In a VBA module, press F2 to bring up the Object Browser.
2. In the Object Browser dialog box, select Excel from the top list.
3. Type **xlDialog** in the second list.
4. Click the binoculars button.

Attempting to display a built-in dialog box in an incorrect context results in an error. For example, if you select a series in a chart and then attempt to display the `xlDialogFormatFont` dialog box, you'll get an error message because that dialog box is not appropriate for that selection.

The companion CD-ROM contains a workbook with a looping macro that displays every possible built-in dialog box that can be displayed when a worksheet is active.

Most of the built-in dialog boxes also accept arguments, which correspond to the controls on the dialog box. You can specify arguments that correspond to the defaults for the dialog box. For example, the `xlDialogCellProtection` dialog box uses two arguments: locked and hidden. If you want to display that dialog box with both of these options checked, use the following statement:

```
Application.Dialogs(xlDialogCellProtection).Show True, True
```

Normally, the dialog box used to protect cells is one “tab” in the Format Cells dialog box. If you use the preceding statement, however, the Protection tab appears in its own dialog box with no other tabs.

The arguments for each of the built-in dialog boxes are listed in the online help. To locate the help topic, search for *Built-In Dialog Box Argument Lists.*

Summary

In this chapter, I introduced you to custom dialog boxes and provided an overview of the controls you can use in your dialog boxes. I also presented several examples, illustrating how to create custom dialog boxes and use them with VBA.

In the next chapter, I offer many more examples of VBA procedures and dialog boxes.

✦ ✦ ✦

CHAPTER 13

UserForm Examples

✦ ✦ ✦ ✦

In This Chapter

Using a dialog box for a simple menu

Selecting ranges from a dialog box

Using a UserForm as a splash screen

Changing the size of a dialog box while it's displayed

Zooming and scrolling a sheet from a UserForm

Understanding various techniques that involve a ListBox control

Using the MultiPage control

✦ ✦ ✦ ✦

This chapter presents lots of useful and informative examples that introduce you to some additional techniques that involve UserForms. You may be able to adapt these techniques to your own work. All the examples are available on the CD-ROM that accompanies this book.

Creating a Dialog Box "Menu"

Sometimes, you may want to use a dialog box as a type of menu. For example, you can present a dialog box that contains a number of buttons. Clicking a button executes a macro. Or you can use a ListBox to hold your "menu" items.

Figure 13-1 shows an example of a dialog box that uses CommandButton controls as a simple menu. Figure 13-2 shows another example that uses a ListBox as a menu.

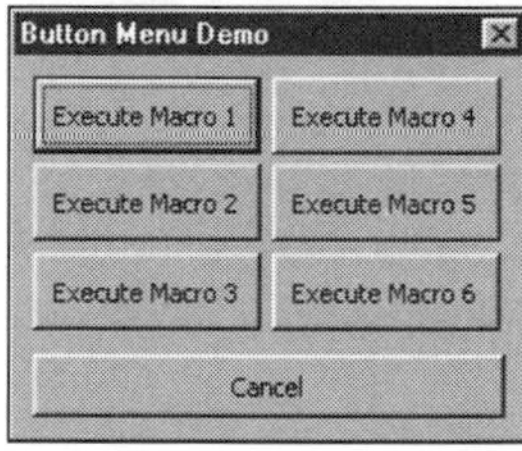

Figure 13-1: This dialog box uses CommandButtons as a menu.

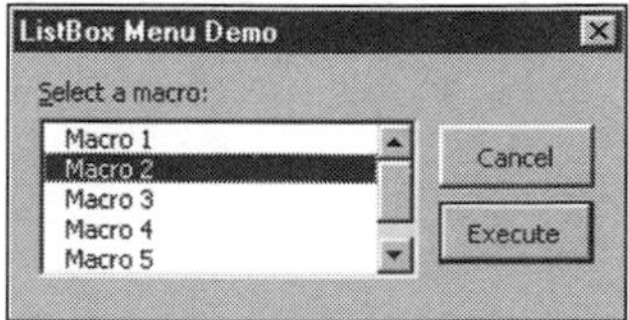

Figure 13-2: This dialog box uses a ListBox as a menu.

Setting up this sort of thing is easy, and the code behind these UserForms is very straightforward. For the CommandButton menu, each CommandButton has its own event-handler procedure. For example, the following procedure is executed when `CommandButton1` is clicked:

```
Private Sub CommandButton1_Click()
    Call Macro1
    Unload Me
End Sub
```

This procedure simply calls `Macro1` and closes the UserForm. The other buttons have similar event-handler procedures.

Excel, of course, also enables you to create "real" menus and toolbars. Refer to Chapters 21 and 22 for details.

Selecting Ranges

Several of Excel's built-in dialog boxes enable the user to specify a range by pointing and clicking in a sheet. For example, the Goal Seek dialog box asks the user to select two ranges.

Your custom dialog boxes can also provide this type of functionality, thanks to the RefEdit control. The RefEdit control doesn't look exactly like the range selection control used in Excel's built-in dialog boxes, but it works the same. If the user clicks the small button on the right side of the control, the dialog box disappears temporarily and a small range selector is displayed — this is exactly what happens with Excel's built-in dialog boxes.

Figure 13-3 shows a custom dialog box that contains a RefEdit control. This dialog box performs a simple mathematical operation on all nonformula (and nonempty) cells in the selected range.

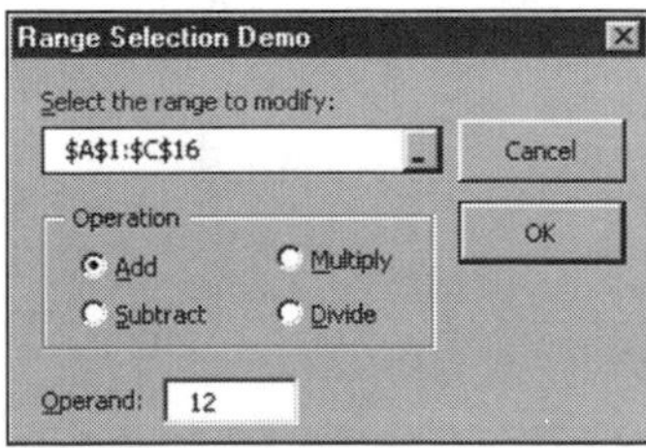

Figure 13-3: The RefEdit control seen here enables the user to select a range.

Following are a few things to keep in mind when using a RefEdit control:

✦ The RefEdit control returns a text string that represents a range address. You can convert this string to a `Range` object using a statement such as this:

```
Set UserRange = Range(RefEdit1.Text)
```

✦ It's a good practice to initialize the RefEdit control to display the current range selection. You can do so in the `UserForm_Initialize` procedure using a statement such as this:

```
RefEdit1.Text = ActiveWindow.RangeSelection.Address
```

✦ Don't assume that RefEdit will always return a valid range address. Pointing to a range isn't the only way get text into this control. The user can type any text, and edit or delete the displayed text. Therefore, you need to make sure the range is valid. The following code snippet is an example of a way to check for a valid range:

```
On Error Resume Next
Set UserRange = Range(RefEdit1.Text)
If Err <> 0 Then
    MsgBox "Invalid range selected"
    RefEdit1.SetFocus
    On Error GoTo 0
    Exit Sub
End If
```

✦ The user can also click the worksheet tabs while selecting a range with the RefEdit control. Therefore, you can't assume that the selection is on the active sheet. However, if a different sheet is selected, the range address is preceded by a sheet name. For example,

```
Sheet2!$A$1:$C:4
```

✦ If you need to get a single cell selection from the user, you can pick out the upper-left cell of a selected range by using a statement such as this:

```
Set OneCell = Range(RefEdit1.Text).Range("A1")
```

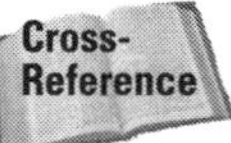

As I discussed in Chapter 12, you can also use VBA's `InputBox` function to enable the user to select a range.

Creating a Splash Screen

Some developers like to display some introductory information when the application is opened. This is commonly known as a *splash screen*. You are undoubtedly familiar with Excel's splash screen, which appears for a few seconds as Excel is loading. You can create a splash screen for your Excel application with a UserForm. Follow these instructions to create a splash screen for your project:

1. Create your workbook.
2. Activate the Visual Basic Editor and insert a new UserForm into the project. The code in this example assumes this form is named `UserForm1`.
3. Place any controls you like on `UserForm1`. For example, you may want to insert an Image control that has your company's logo. Figure 13-4 shows an example.

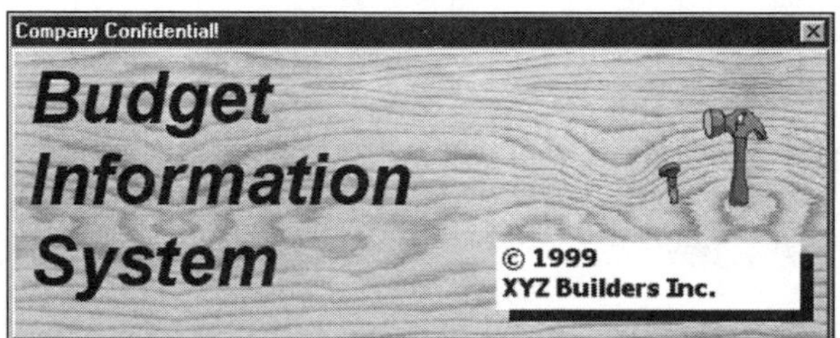

Figure 13-4: This splash screen is displayed briefly when the workbook is opened.

4. Insert the following procedure into the code module for the `ThisWorkbook` object:

```
Private Sub Workbook_Open()
    UserForm1.Show
End Sub
```

5. Insert the following procedure into the code module for `UserForm1` (this assumes a five-second delay):

```
Private Sub UserForm_Activate()
    Application.OnTime Now + _
      TimeValue("00:00:05"), "KillTheForm"
End Sub
```

6. Insert the following procedure into a general VBA module:

```
Private Sub KillTheForm()
    Unload UserForm1
End Sub
```

When the workbook is opened, the `Workbook_Open` procedure is executed. This procedure displays the UserForm. At that time, its `Activate` event occurs, which triggers the `UserForm_Activate` procedure. This procedure uses the `OnTime` method of the `Application` object to execute a procedure named `KillTheForm` at a particular time. In this case, the time is five seconds from the current time. The `KillTheForm` procedure simply unloads the UserForm.

7. As an option, you can add a small CommandButton named `CancelButton`, set its `Cancel` property to True, and insert the following event-handler procedure in the UserForm's code module:

```
Private Sub CancelButton_Click()
    KillTheForm
End Sub
```

   Doing so enables the user to cancel the splash screen before the time has expired by pressing Esc. You can stash this small button behind another object so it won't be visible.

Keep in mind that the splash screen is not displayed until the workbook is entirely loaded. In other words, if you would like to display the splash screen to give the user something to look at while the workbook is loading, this technique won't fill the bill.

Disabling a UserForm's Close Button

When a UserForm is displayed, clicking the close button (the *X* in the upper-right corner) unloads the form. You might have a situation in which you don't want this to happen. For example, you may require that the UserForm be closed only by clicking a particular CommandButton.

Although you can't physically disable the close button, you can prevent the user from closing a UserForm by clicking it. You can do this by monitoring the UserForm's `QueryClose` event.

The procedure that follows, which is located in the code module for the UserForm, is executed before the form is closed (that is, when the `QueryClose` event occurs).

```
Private Sub UserForm_QueryClose _
  (Cancel As Integer, CloseMode As Integer)
    If CloseMode = vbFormControlMenu Then
        MsgBox "Click the OK button to close the form."
        Cancel = True
    End If
End Sub
```

The `UserForm_QueryClose` procedure uses two arguments. The `CloseMode` argument contains a value that indicates the cause of the `QueryClose` event. If `CloseMode` is equal to `vbFormControlMenu` (a built-in constant), that means the user clicked the close button. In such a case a message is displayed, the `Cancel` argument is set to True, and the form is not actually closed.

Changing a Dialog Box's Size

Many applications use dialog boxes that change their own size. For example, Excel's AutoFormat dialog box (displayed when you select Format⇨AutoFormat) increases its height when the user clicks the Options button.

The example in this section demonstrates how to get a custom dialog box to change its size dynamically. Changing a dialog box's size is done by altering the `Width` or `Height` property of the UserForm object.

Figure 13-5 shows the dialog box as it is first displayed, and Figure 13-6 shows it after the user clicks the Options button. Notice that the button's caption changes, depending on the size of the UserForm.

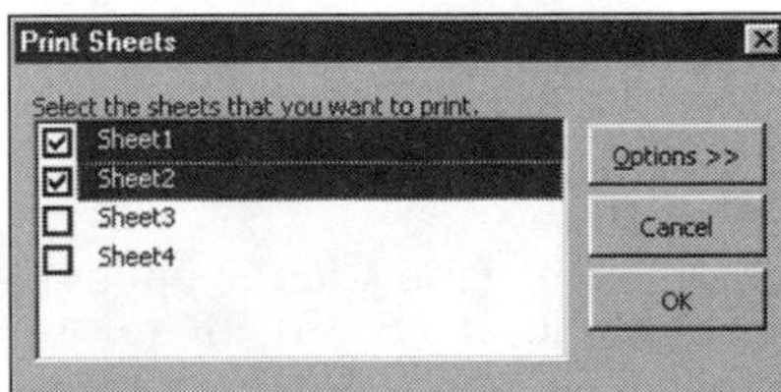

Figure 13-5: A sample dialog box in its standard mode.

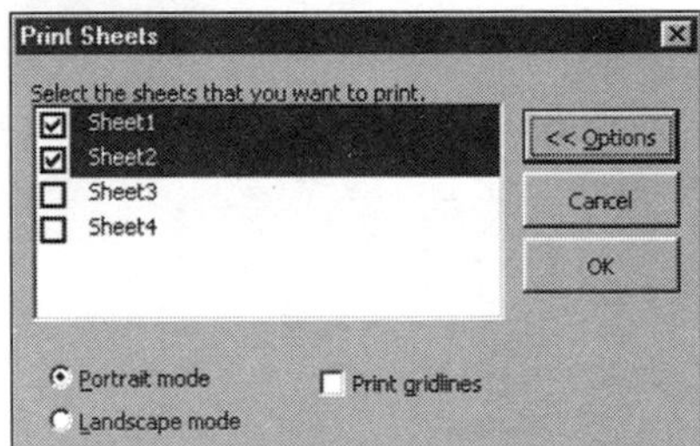

Figure 13-6: The same dialog box enlarged to show some options.

This workbook is available on the companion CD-ROM.

As you're creating the UserForm, set it to its largest size to enable you to work with the controls. Then use the `UserForm_Initialize` procedure to set it to its default size.

This example displays a list of worksheets in the active workbook, and enables the user to select which sheets to print. Following is the event handler that's executed when the CommandButton named `OptionsButton` is clicked:

```
Private Sub OptionsButton_Click()
    If OptionsButton.Caption = "Options >" Then
        UserForm1.Height = 164
        OptionsButton.Caption = "<< Options"
    Else
        UserForm1.Height = 128
        OptionsButton.Caption = "Options >"
    End If
End Sub
```

This procedure examines the `Caption` of the CommandButton, and sets the UserForm's `Height` property accordingly.

When controls are not displayed because they are outside of the visible portion of the UserForm, the accelerator keys for such controls continue to function. In the example on the CD-ROM, the user can press the Alt+L hot key (to select the Landscape mode option) even if that option is not visible. To block access to nondisplayed controls, you can write code to disable the controls when they are not displayed.

Zooming and Scrolling a Sheet from a UserForm

When you display a dialog box, it's often helpful if the user can scroll through the worksheet to examine various ranges. Normally, this is impossible while a dialog box is displayed.

The example in this section demonstrates how to use ScrollBar controls to enable sheet scrolling and zooming while a dialog box is displayed. Figure 13-7 shows how the example dialog box is set up.

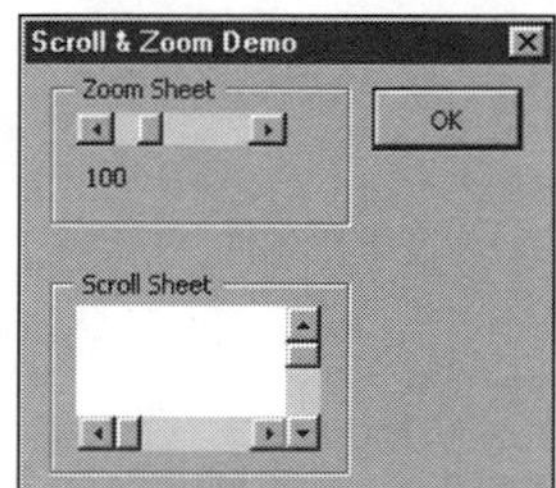

Figure 13-7: Here, ScrollBar controls enable zooming and scrolling of the worksheet.

If you look at the code for this example, you'll see that it's remarkably simple. The controls are initialized in the `UserForm_Initialize` procedure.

```
Private Sub UserForm_Initialize()
    LabelZoom.Caption = ActiveWindow.Zoom
'   Zoom
    With ScrollBarZoom
        .Min = 10
        .Max = 400
        .SmallChange = 1
        .LargeChange = 10
        .Value = ActiveWindow.Zoom
    End With

'   Horizontally scrolling
    With ScrollBarColumns
        .Min = 1
        .Max = 256
        .Value = ActiveWindow.ScrollColumn
        .LargeChange = 25
        .SmallChange = 1
    End With

'   Vertically scrolling
    With ScrollBarRows
        .Min = 1
        .Max = ActiveSheet.Rows.Count
        .Value = ActiveWindow.ScrollRow
        .LargeChange = 25
        .SmallChange = 1
    End With
End Sub
```

This procedure sets various properties of the ScrollBar controls using values based on the active window.

When the ScrollBarZoom control is used, the `ScrollBarZoom_Change` procedure is executed. This procedure sets the ScrollBar control's `Value` property to the ActiveWindow's `Zoom` property value. It also changes a label to display the current zoom factor.

```
Private Sub ScrollBarZoom_Change()
    With ActiveWindow
        .Zoom = ScrollBarZoom.Value
        LabelZoom = .Zoom & "%"
    End With
End Sub
```

Worksheet scrolling is accomplished by the following two procedures. These procedures set the `ScrollRow` or `ScrollColumns` property of the ActiveWindow object equal to the appropriate ScrollBar control value.

```
Private Sub ScrollBarColumns_Change()
    ActiveWindow.ScrollColumn = ScrollBarColumns.Value
End Sub

Private Sub ScrollBarRows_Change()
    ActiveWindow.ScrollRow = ScrollBarRows.Value
End Sub
```

ListBox Techniques

The ListBox control is extremely versatile, but it can be a bit tricky to work with. This section consists of a number of simple examples that demonstrate common techniques involving the ListBox control.

In most cases, the techniques described in this section also work with a ComboBox control.

About the ListBox control

Following are a few points to keep in mind when working with ListBox controls. Examples in the sections that follow demonstrate many of these points.

- The items in a ListBox can be retrieved from a range of cells (specified by the `RowSource` property), or they can be added using VBA code (using the `AddItem` method).
- A ListBox can be set up to enable a single selection, or a multiple selection. This is determined by the `MultiSelect` property.
- It's possible to display a ListBox with no items selected (the `ListIndex` property is -1). However, once an item is selected, it's not possible to unselect all items.
- A ListBox can contain multiple columns (controlled by the `ColumnCount` property), and even a descriptive header (controlled by the `ColumnHeads` property).
- The vertical height of a ListBox displayed in a UserForm window isn't always the same as the vertical height when the UserForm is actually displayed.
- The items in a ListBox can be displayed as check boxes if multiple selection is allowed or as option buttons if a single selection is allowed. This is controlled by the `ListStyle` property.

For complete details on the properties and methods for a ListBox control, consult the online help.

Adding items to a ListBox control

Before displaying a UserForm that uses a ListBox control, you probably need to fill the ListBox with items. You can fill a ListBox at design time using items stored in a worksheet range, or at run time using VBA to add the items to the ListBox.

The two examples in this section presume that

- ✦ You have a dialog box on a UserForm named `UserForm1`.
- ✦ This dialog box contains a ListBox control named `ListBox1`.
- ✦ The workbook contains a sheet named `Sheet1`, and range A1:A12 contains the items to be displayed in the ListBox.

Adding items to a ListBox at design time

To add items to a ListBox at design time, the ListBox items must be stored in a worksheet range. Use the `RowSource` property to specify the range that contains the ListBox items. Figure 13-8 shows the Properties window for a ListBox control. The `RowSource` property is set to `Sheet1A!:A12`. When the UserForm is displayed, the ListBox contains the 12 items in this range. The items appear in the ListBox at design time, as soon as you specify the range for the `RowSource` property.

Make sure that you include the worksheet name when you specify the `RowSource` property. Otherwise, the ListBox uses the specified range on the active worksheet.

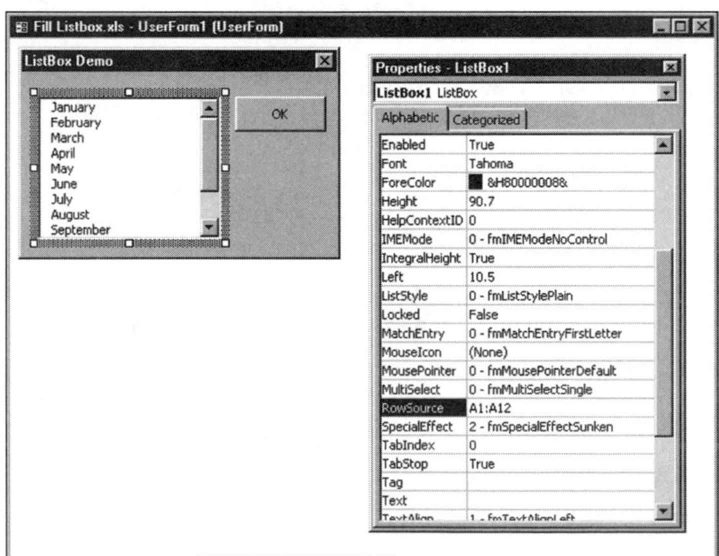

Figure 13-8: Setting the RowSource property at design time.

Adding items to a ListBox at run time

To add ListBox items at run time, you have two choices:

- ✦ Set the RowSource property to a range address using code.
- ✦ Write code that uses the AddItem method to add the ListBox items.

As you might expect, you can set the RowSource property via code rather than with the Properties window. For example, the following procedure sets the RowSource property for a ListBox before displaying the UserForm. In this case, the items consist of the cell entries in a range named Categories on the Budget worksheet.

```
UserForm1.ListBox1.RowSource = "Budget!Categories"
UserForm1.Show
```

If the ListBox items are not contained in a worksheet range, you can write VBA code to fill the ListBox before the dialog box appears. The procedure fills the ListBox with the names of the months using the AddItem method.

```
Sub ShowUserForm2()
'   Fill the list box
    With UserForm2.ListBox1
        .RowSource=""
        .AddItem "January"
        .AddItem "February"
        .AddItem "March"
        .AddItem "April"
        .AddItem "May"
        .AddItem "June"
        .AddItem "July"
        .AddItem "August"
        .AddItem "September"
        .AddItem "October"
        .AddItem "November"
        .AddItem "December"
    End With
    UserForm2.Show
End Sub
```

In the preceding code, notice that I set the RowSource property to an empty string. This is to avoid a potential error that occurs if the Properties window has a nonempty RowSource setting. If you try to add items to a ListBox that has a non-null RowSource setting, you'll get a "permission denied" error.

You can also use the AddItem method to retrieve ListBox items from a range. Here's an example that fills a ListBox with the contents of A1:A12 on Sheet1.

```
For Row = 1 To 12
  UserForm1.ListBox1.AddItem Sheets("Sheet1").Cells(Row, 1)
Next Row
```

If your data is stored in a one-dimensional array, you can assign the array to the ListBox with a single instruction. For example, assume you have an array named `dData` that contains 50 elements. The following statement creates a 50-item list in `ListBox1`:

```
ListBox1.List = dData
```

Adding only unique items to a ListBox

In some cases, you may need to fill a ListBox with unique (nonduplicated) items from a list. For example, assume you have a worksheet that contains customer data. One of the columns might contain the state name of each customer (see Figure 13-9). You would like to fill a ListBox with the state name of your customers, but you don't want to include duplicate state names.

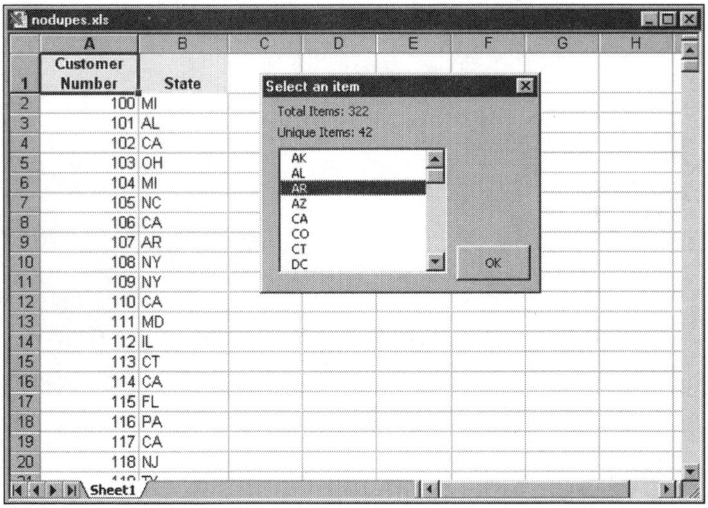

Figure 13-9: A Collection object is used to fill a ListBox with the unique items from Column B.

One technique involves using a `Collection` object. You can add items to a `Collection` object with the following syntax:

```
object.Add item, key, before, after
```

The *key* argument, if used, must be a unique text string that specifies a separate key that can be used to access a member of the collection. The important word here is *unique*. If you attempt to add a nonunique key to a collection, an error occurs and the item is not added. You can take advantage of this situation and use it to create a collection that consists only of unique items.

The following procedure demonstrates how to fill a ListBox with unique items. It starts by declaring a new `Collection` object named `NoDupes`. It assumes that range B1:B100 contains a list of items, some of which may be duplicated. The code loops through the cells in the range and attempts to add the cell's value to the `NoDupes` collection. It also uses the cell's value (converted to a string) for the *key* argument. Using the `On Error Resume Next` statement causes VBA to ignore the error that occurs if the key is not unique. When an error occurs, the item is not added to the collection, which is just what you want. The procedure then transfers the items in the `NoDupes` collection to the ListBox.

```
Sub RemoveDuplicates1()
    Dim AllCells As Range, Cell As Range
    Dim NoDupes As New Collection

 On Error Resume Next
    For Each Cell In Range("B1:B100")
        NoDupes.Add Cell.Value, CStr(Cell.Value)
    Next Cell
    On Error GoTo 0

'   Add the non-duplicated items to a ListBox
    For Each Item In NoDupes
        UserForm1.ListBox1.AddItem Item
    Next Item

'   Show the UserForm
    UserForm1.Show
End Sub
```

A slightly more sophisticated version of this example is available on the CD-ROM.

Determining the selected item

The examples in preceding sections merely display a UserForm with a ListBox filled with various items. These procedures omit a key point: how to determine which item or items were selected by the user.

This discussion assumes a "single selection" ListBox object—one whose `MultiSelect` property is set to 0.

To determine which item was selected, access the ListBox's `Value` property. The following statement, for example, displays the text of the selected item in `ListBox1`:

```
MsgBox ListBox1.Value
```

If you need to know the position of the selected item in the list (rather than the content of that item) you can access the ListBox's `ListIndex` property. The next example uses a message box to display the item number of the selected ListBox item.

```
MsgBox "You selected item #" & ListBox1.ListIndex
```

The numbering of items in a ListBox begins with 0, not 1. Therefore, the `ListIndex` of the first item is 0, and the `ListIndex` of the last item is equivalent to the value of the `ListCount` property minus 1.

Determining multiple selections

Normally, a ListBox's `MultiSelect` property is zero, which means that the user can select only one item in the ListBox.

If the ListBox allows multiple selections (that is, if its `MultiSelect` property is either 1 or 2), trying to access the `ListIndex`, `Value`, or `List` properties results in an error. Instead, you need to use the `Selected` property, which returns an array whose first item has an index of 0. For example, the following statement displays True if the first item in the ListBox list is selected:

```
MsgBox ListBox1.Selected(0)
```

The companion CD-ROM contains a workbook that demonstrates how to identify the selected item(s) in a ListBox. It works for single selection and multiple selection ListBoxes.

The following code from the example workbook on the CD-ROM loops through each item in the ListBox. If the item was selected, it appends the item's text to a variable called `Msg`. Finally, the names of all the selected items are displayed in a message box.

```
Private Sub OKButton_Click()
    Msg = ""
    For i = 0 To ListBox1.ListCount - 1
        If ListBox1.Selected(i) Then _
          Msg = Msg & ListBox1.List(i) & vbCrLf
    Next i
    MsgBox "You selected: " & vbCrLf & Msg
    Unload Me
End Sub
```

Figure 13-10 shows the result when multiple ListBox items are selected.

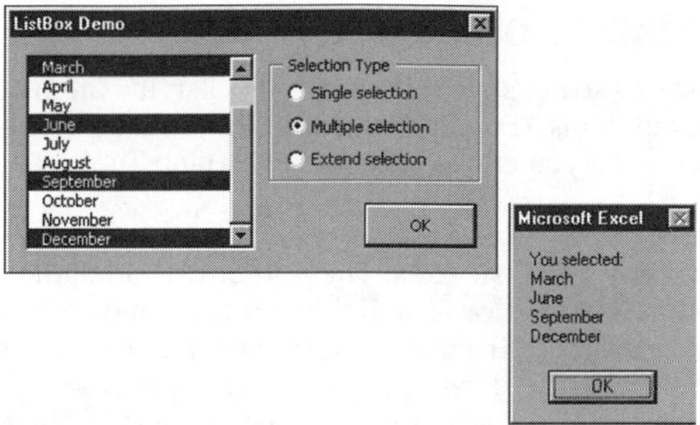

Figure 13-10: This message box displays a list of items selected in a ListBox.

Creating a ListBox with changing contents

This example demonstrates how to create a ListBox in which the contents change depending on the user's selection from a group of OptionButtons.

Figure 13-11 shows the sample dialog box. The ListBox gets its items from a worksheet range. The procedures that handle the `Click` event for the OptionButton controls simply set the ListBox's `RowSource` property to a different range. One of these procedures is as follows:

```
Private Sub obMonths_Click()
    ListBox1.RowSource = "Sheet1!Months"
End Sub
```

Clicking the OptionButton named `obMonths` changes the `RowSource` property of the ListBox to use a range named `Months` on `Sheet1`.

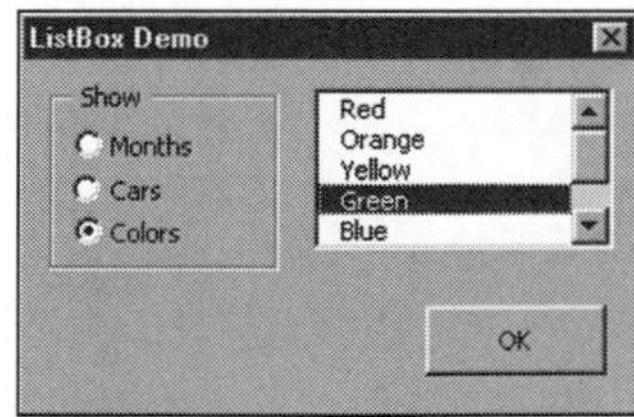

Figure 13-11: The contents of this ListBox depend on the OptionButton selected.

Building a ListBox from another list

Some applications require a user to select several items from a list. It's often useful to create a new list of the selected items. (For an example of this situation, check out the dialog box that appears when you choose the Tools⇨Attach Toolbars command in a VBA module.)

Figure 13-12 shows a dialog box with two ListBoxes. The Add button adds the item selected in the left ListBox to the right ListBox. The Delete button removes the selected item from the list on the right. A CheckBox determines the behavior when a duplicate item is added to the list. If the Allow duplicates CheckBox is not checked, a message box appears if the user attempts to add an item that's already on the list.

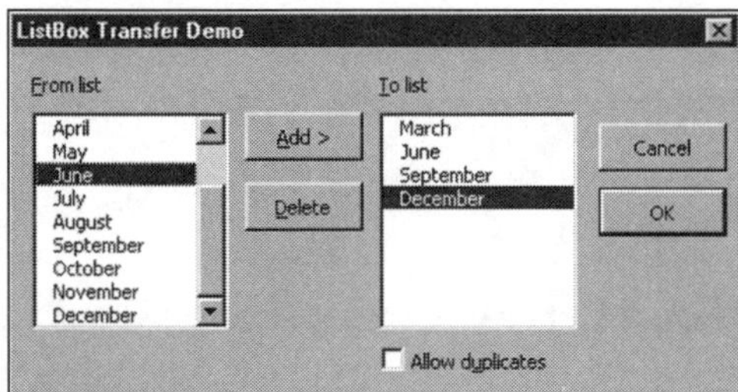

Figure 13-12: Building a list from another list.

The code for this example is relatively simple. Here's the procedure that is executed when the user clicks the Add button:

```
Private Sub AddButton_Click()
    If ListBox1.ListIndex = -1 Then Exit Sub
    If Not cbDuplicates Then
'       See if item already exists
        For i = 0 To ListBox2.ListCount - 1
            If ListBox1.Value = ListBox2.List(i) Then
                Beep
                Exit Sub
            End If
        Next i
    End If
    ListBox2.AddItem ListBox1.Value
End Sub
```

The code for the Delete button is even simpler:

```
Private Sub DeleteButton_Click()
    If ListBox2.ListIndex = -1 Then Exit Sub
    ListBox2.RemoveItem ListBox2.ListIndex
End Sub
```

Notice that both routines check to make sure that an item is actually selected. If the ListBox's `ListIndex` property is -1, no items are selected and the procedure ends.

Moving items in a ListBox

The example in this section demonstrates how to enable the user to move the location of items up or down in a ListBox. The VB Editor uses this type of technique itself to enable you to control the tab order of the items in a UserForm.

Figure 13-13 shows a dialog box that contains a ListBox and two CommandButtons. Clicking the Move Up button moves the selected item up in the ListBox; clicking the Move Down button moves the selected item down.

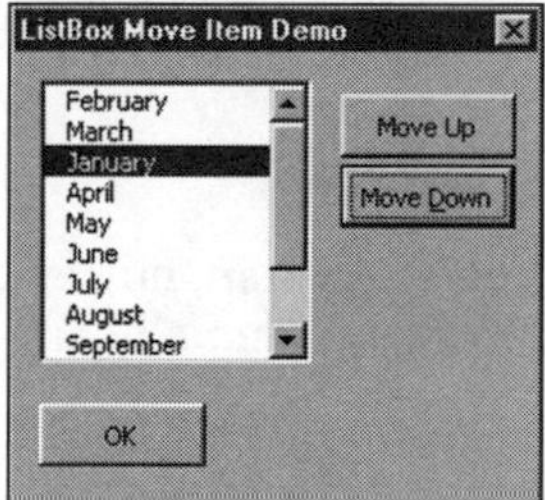

Figure 13-13: The buttons enable the user to move items up or down in the ListBox.

The event-handler procedures for the two CommandButtons are as follows:

```
Private Sub MoveUpButton_Click()
    With ListBox1
        ItemNum = .ListIndex
        If ItemNum > 0 Then
            TempItem = .List(ItemNum - 1)
            .List(ItemNum - 1) = .List(ItemNum)
            .List(ItemNum) = TempItem
            .ListIndex = .ListIndex - 1
        End If
    End With
End Sub

Private Sub MoveDownButton_Click()
    With ListBox1
        ItemNum = .ListIndex
        If ItemNum < .ListCount - 1 And ItemNum <> -1 Then
            TempItem = .List(ItemNum + 1)
            .List(ItemNum + 1) = .List(ItemNum)
            .List(ItemNum) = TempItem
            .ListIndex = .ListIndex + 1
        End If
    End With
End Sub
```

These procedures work fairly well, but you'll find that for some reason, relatively rapid clicking doesn't always register. For example, you may click the Move Down button three times in quick succession, but the item moves only one or two positions. The solution is to add a new `DblClick` event handler for each CommandButton. These procedures, which simply call the `Click` procedures, are as follows:

```
Private Sub MoveUpButton_DblClick _
  (ByVal Cancel As MSForms.ReturnBoolean)
    Call MoveUpButton_Click
End Sub

Private Sub MoveDownButton_DblClick _
  (ByVal Cancel As MSForms.ReturnBoolean)
    Call MoveDownButton_Click
End Sub
```

Working with multicolumn ListBox controls

A normal ListBox has a single column for its contained items. You can, however, create a ListBox that displays multiple columns and, optionally, column headers. Figure 13-14 shows an example.

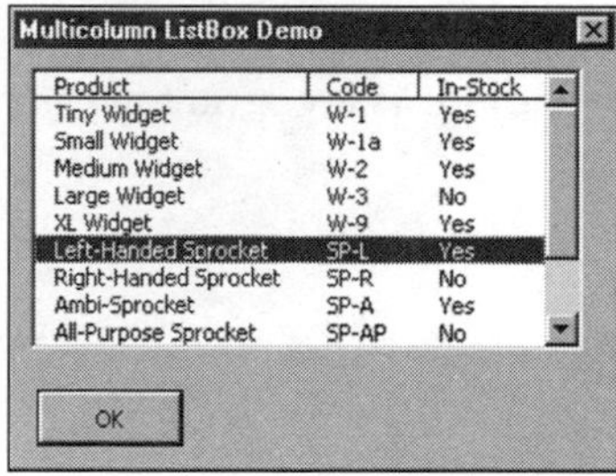

Figure 13-14: This ListBox displays a three-column list, with column headers.

To set up a multicolumn ListBox that uses data stored in a worksheet range, follow these steps:

1. Make sure the ListBox's `ColumnCount` property is set to the correct number of columns.
2. Specify the correct multicolumn range in the Excel worksheet as the ListBox's `RowSource` property.
3. To display column heads like the ListBox in Figure 13-14, set the `ColumnHeads` property to True. Do not include the column headings on the worksheet in the range setting for the `RowSource` property. VBA instead automatically uses the row directly above the first row of the `RowSource` range.

4. Adjust the column widths by assigning a series of values, specified in points (1/72 of one inch) separated by semicolons, to the `ColumnWidths` property. For example, for a three-column ListBox, the `ColumnWidths` property might be set to the following text string:

```
100.;40;30
```

5. Specify the appropriate column as the `BoundColumn` property. The bound column specifies which column is referenced when an instruction polls the ListBox's `Value` property.

Note

To fill a ListBox with multicolumn data without using a range, you first create a two-dimensional array, and then assign the array to the ListBox's `List` property. The following statements demonstrate this technique using a 50 row by 2 column array. The result is a 50-item ListBox that has two columns.

```
Dim Data(1 To 50, 1 To 2)
' Code to fill the array goes here
ListBox1.List = Data
```

Note

There appears to be no way to specify column headers for the `ColumnHeads` property when the list source is a VBA array.

Using a ListBox to select rows

The example in this section is actually a useful utility. It displays a ListBox that consists of the entire used range of the active worksheet (see Figure 13-15). The user can select multiple items in the ListBox. Clicking the All button selects all items, and clicking the None button deselects all items. Clicking OK selects those corresponding rows in the worksheet. You can, of course, select multiple noncontiguous rows directly in the worksheet by pressing Ctrl as you click the row borders. However, you may find that selecting rows is easier using this method.

Row Selector

Row 3

	Calif	Tex	Wash
January	18,357	8,448	3,296
February	21,472	6,191	3,707
March	9,008	9,176	17,053
Qtr-1	48,837	23,815	24,056
April	3,052	1,332	15,836
May	10,044	21,324	11,497
June	23,215	6,362	22,154
Qtr-2	36,311	29,018	49,487
July	1,138	17,505	6,541
August	8,230	22,909	3,024

All None Cancel OK

Figure 13-15: This ListBox makes it easy to select rows in a worksheet.

Selecting multiple items is possible because the ListBox's MultiSelect property is set to 1 - fmMultiSelectMulti. The "check boxes" on each item are displayed because the ListBox's ListStyle property is set to 1 - fmListStyleOption.

The UserForm's Initialize procedure is as follows. This procedure creates a Range object named rng that consists of the active sheet's used range—or more accurately, the narrowest rectangular range on the active worksheet containing data. Additional code sets the ListBox's ColumnCount and RowSource properties, and adjusts the ColumnWidths property such that the ListBox columns are proportional to the column widths in the worksheet.

```
Private Sub UserForm_Initialize()
    ColCnt = ActiveSheet.UsedRange.Columns.Count
    Set rng = ActiveSheet.UsedRange
    With ListBox1
        .ColumnCount = ColCnt
        .RowSource = rng.Address
        cw = ""
        For c = 1 To .ColumnCount
            cw = cw & rng.Columns(c).Width & ";"
        Next c
        .ColumnWidths = cw
        .ListIndex = 0
    End With
End Sub
```

The All and None buttons (named SelectAllButton and SelectNoneButton, respectively) have simple event-handler procedures and are listed here:

```
Private Sub SelectAllButton_Click()
    For r = 0 To ListBox1.ListCount - 1
        ListBox1.Selected(r) = True
    Next r
End Sub

Private Sub SelectNoneButton_Click()
    For r = 0 To ListBox1.ListCount - 1
        ListBox1.Selected(r) = False
    Next r
End Sub
```

The OKButton_Click procedure is listed next. This procedure creates a Range object named RowRange that consists of the rows that correspond to the selected items in the ListBox. To determine if a row was selected, the code examines the Selected property of the ListBox control. Notice that it uses the Union function to add additional ranges to the RowRange object.

```
Private Sub OKButton_Click()
    Dim RowRange As Range
    RowCnt = 0
    For r = 0 To ListBox1.ListCount - 1
        If ListBox1.Selected(r) Then
            RowCnt = RowCnt + 1
            If RowCnt = 1 Then
                Set RowRange = ActiveSheet.Rows(r + 1)
            Else
                Set RowRange = _
                  Union(RowRange, ActiveSheet.Rows(r + 1))
            End If
        End If
    Next r
    If Not RowRange Is Nothing Then RowRange.Select
    Unload Me
End Sub
```

Using a ListBox to activate a sheet

The example in this section is just as useful as it is instructive. This example uses a multicolumn ListBox to display a list of sheets within the active workbook. The columns represent

- ✦ The sheet's name
- ✦ The type of sheet (worksheet, chart, or Excel 5/95 dialog sheet)
- ✦ The number of nonempty cells in the sheet
- ✦ Whether the sheet is visible

Figure 13-16 shows an example of the dialog box.

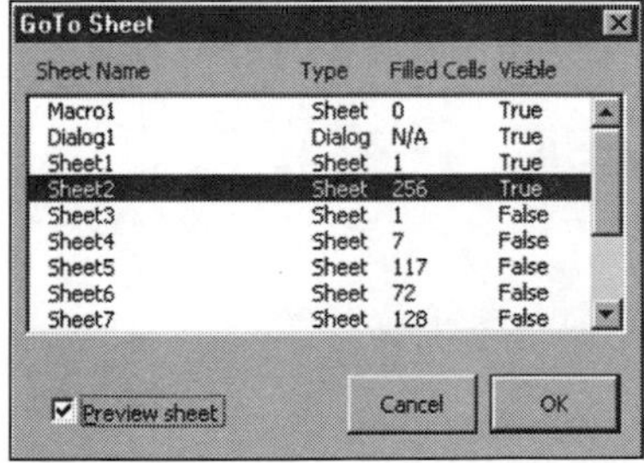

Figure 13-16: This dialog box enables the user to activate a sheet.

The code in the following UserForm_Initialize procedure creates a two-dimensional array, and collects the information by looping through the sheets in the active workbook. It then transfers this array to the ListBox named ListBox1.

```
Private Sub UserForm_Initialize()
    Dim SheetData() As String
    Set OriginalSheet = ActiveSheet
    ShtCnt = ActiveWorkbook.Sheets.Count
    ReDim SheetData(1 To ShtCnt, 1 To 4)
    ShtNum = 1
    For Each Sht In ActiveWorkbook.Sheets
        If Sht.Name = ActiveSheet.Name Then _
          ListPos = ShtNum - 1
        SheetData(ShtNum, 1) = Sht.Name
        Select Case TypeName(Sht)
            Case "Worksheet"
                SheetData(ShtNum, 2) = "Sheet"
                SheetData(ShtNum, 3) = _
                  Application.CountA(Sht.Cells)
            Case "Chart"
                SheetData(ShtNum, 2) = "Chart"
                SheetData(ShtNum, 3) = "N/A"
            Case "DialogSheet"
                SheetData(ShtNum, 2) = "Dialog"
                SheetData(ShtNum, 3) = "N/A"
        End Select
        If Sht.Visible Then
            SheetData(ShtNum, 4) = "True"
        Else
            SheetData(ShtNum, 4) = "False"
        End If
        ShtNum = ShtNum + 1
    Next Sht
    With ListBox1
        .ColumnWidths = "100 pt;30 pt;40 pt;50 pt"
        .List = SheetData
        .ListIndex = ListPos
    End With
End Sub
```

The ListBox1_Click procedure is as follows:

```
Private Sub ListBox1_Click()
    If cbPreview Then _
        Sheets(ListBox1.Value).Activate
End Sub
```

The value of the CheckBox control named cbPreview determines if the selected sheet is previewed when the user clicks an item in the ListBox.

Clicking the OK button named OKButton executes the OKButton_Click procedure, which is as follows:

```
Private Sub OKButton_Click()
    Dim UserSheet As Object
    Set UserSheet = Sheets(ListBox1.Value)
    If UserSheet.Visible Then
        UserSheet.Activate
    Else
        If MsgBox("Unhide sheet?", _
          vbQuestion + vbYesNoCancel) = vbYes Then
            UserSheet.Visible = True
            UserSheet.Activate
        Else
            OriginalSheet.Activate
        End If
    End If
    Unload Me
End Sub
```

The OKButton_Click procedure creates an object variable that represents the selected sheet. If the sheet is visible, it is activated. If it's not visible, the user is presented with a message box asking if it should be unhidden. If the user responds in the affirmative, the sheet is unhidden and activated. Otherwise, the original sheet (stored in an object variable named OriginalSheet) is activated.

Double-clicking an item in the ListBox has the same result as clicking the OK button. The following ListBox1_DblClick procedure simply calls the OKButton_Click procedure.

```
Private Sub ListBox1_DblClick(ByVal Cancel As _
 MSForms.ReturnBoolean)
    Call OKButton_Click
End Sub
```

Using the MultiPage Control

The MultiPage control is very useful for custom dialog boxes that must display many controls. The MultiPage control enables you to group the choices and place each group on a separate "tab."

Figure 13-17 shows several examples of a UserForm that contains a MultiPage control. In this case, the control has three pages, each with its own tab. As you can see, the MultiPage control is very versatile, giving you a great deal of control over its appearance and functionality. The figure shows the result of the four settings for the MultiPage's TabOrientation property.

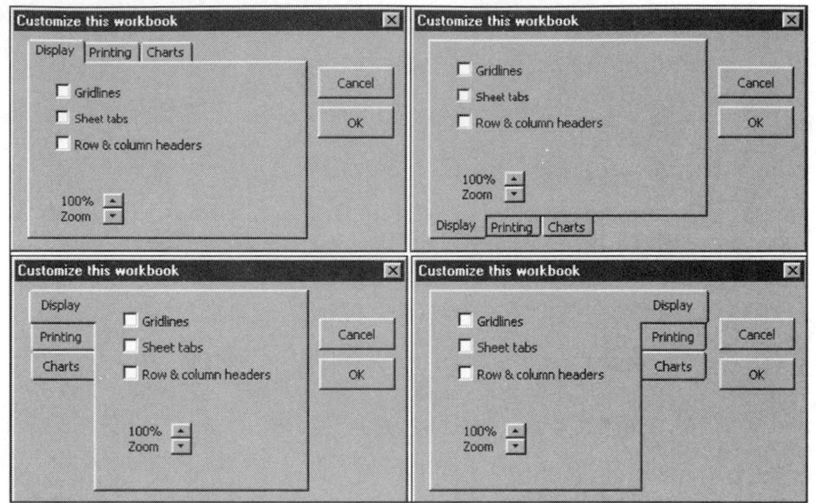

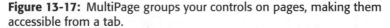

Figure 13-17: MultiPage groups your controls on pages, making them accessible from a tab.

Note

The Toolbox also contains a control named TabStrip. As far as I can tell, the MultiPage control is much more versatile, and I can't think of a single reason to use the TabStrip control.

Using a MultiPage control can be a bit tricky. Following are some things to keep in mind when using this control:

✦ The tab (or page) that's displayed up front is determined by the control's `Value` function. A value of 0 displays the first tab, a value of 1 displays the second tab, and so on.

✦ By default, a MultiPage control has two pages. To add a new page, right-click a tab and select New Page from the shortcut menu.

✦ When you're working with a MultiPage control, just click a tab to set the properties for that particular page. The Properties window displays the properties that you can adjust.

✦ You may find it difficult to select the actual MultiPage control because clicking the control selects a page within the control. To select the control itself, you can use the Tab key to cycle among all the controls. Or you can select the MultiPage control from the drop-down list in the Properties window.

✦ If your MultiPage control has lots of tabs, you can set its `MultiRow` property to True to display the tabs in more than one row.

✦ If you prefer, you can display buttons instead of tabs. Just change the `Style` property to 1. If the `Style` property value is 0, the MultiPage control won't display tabs or buttons.

✦ The `TabOrientation` property determines the location of the tabs on the MultiPage control. Figure 13-17 shows the result of each of the four `TabOrientation` property settings.

✦ For each page, you can set a transition effect by changing the `TransitionEffect` property. For example, clicking a tab can cause the new page to "push" the former page out of the way. Use the `TransitionPeriod` property to set the speed of the transition effect.

The next chapter contains several examples that use the MultiPage control.

Summary

In this chapter, I provided several UserForm examples that demonstrate common techniques. I also included many examples using the ListBox control.

The next chapter contains additional, more advanced examples of UserForms.

✦ ✦ ✦

Advanced UserForm Techniques

✦ ✦ ✦ ✦

In This Chapter

Displaying a progress indicator (two techniques)

Using a third-party Timer control to provide simple animation in a UserForm

Displaying a "live" chart in a UserForm

Creating a wizard

Creating a function that emulates VBA's `MsgBox` function

Using modal dialog boxes

Handling multiple objects with a single event handler

Using a dialog box to select a color

Using an enhanced data form

✦ ✦ ✦ ✦

This chapter presents some additional UserForm techniques, most of which are a bit more complex than those discussed in the previous chapters. All the examples are available on the CD-ROM that accompanies this book.

Displaying a Progress Indicator

One of the most common requests among Excel developers involves progress indicators. A progress indicator is a graphical thermometer-type display that shows the progress of a task such as a lengthy macro.

Before Excel 97, creating a progress indicator was a difficult task. But now, it's relatively easy. In this section, I describe how to create two types of progress indicators for

- ✦ A macro that's not initiated by a dialog box (a stand-alone progress indicator)
- ✦ A macro that is initiated by a dialog box (using a MultiPage control)

Using a progress indicator requires that you are (somehow) able to gauge how far along your macro may be in completing its given task. How you do this varies depending on the macro. For example, if your macro writes data to cells (and you know the number of cells that will be written to), it's a simple matter to write code that calculates the percentage completed.

It's important to understand that a progress indicator slows down your macro a bit due to the extra overhead of having to update it. If speed is absolutely critical, you may prefer to forgo a progress indicator.

Displaying Progress in the Status Bar

Excel's status bar is a good place to display the progress of a macro. The advantage is that it's very easy to program. The disadvantage is that most users aren't accustomed to watching the status bar, and would prefer a more visual display.

To write text to the status bar, use a statement such as this:

```
Application.StatusBar = "Please wait..."
```

You can, of course, update the status bar as your macro progresses. For example, if you have a variable named `Pct` that represents the percentage completed, you can write code that periodically executes a statement such as this:

```
Application.StatusBar = "Processing... " & Pct & "% Completed"
```

When your macro finishes, reset the status bar to its normal state with the following statement:

```
Application.StatusBar = False
```

Creating a stand-alone progress indicator

This section describes how to set up a custom dialog box to display the progress of a macro.

This example is available on the companion CD-ROM.

Building the UserForm

Follow these steps to create the UserForm that you will use to display the progress of your task:

1. Insert a new UserForm and change its `Caption` property setting to `Progress`.
2. Add a Frame control and name it `FrameProgress`.
3. Add a Label control inside of the Frame and name it `LabelProgress`. Remove the Label's caption, and make its background color (`BackColor` property) red. The Label's size and placement do not matter for now.
4. Add another label above the frame to describe what's going on (optional).
5. Adjust the UserForm and controls so they look something like Figure 14-1.

You can, of course, apply any other type of formatting to the controls. For example, I changed the `SpecialEffect` property for the Frames shown in Figure 14-1.

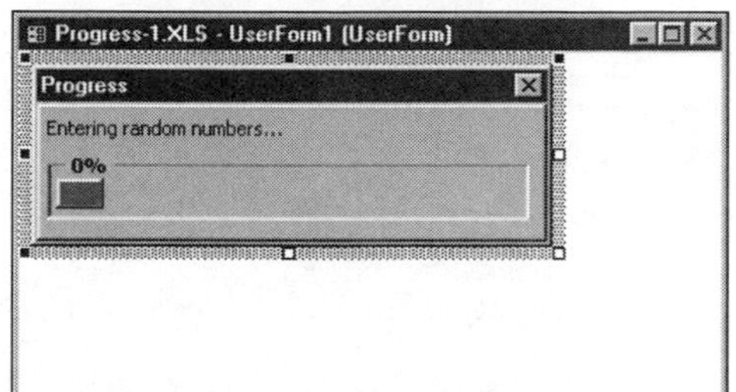

Figure 14-1: This UserForm will serve as a progress indicator.

Creating the event-handler procedures

The trick here involves running a procedure automatically when the UserForm is displayed. One option is to use the `Initialize` event. However, this event occurs *before* the UserForm is actually displayed so it's not appropriate. The `Activate` event, on the other hand, is triggered at the time the UserForm is displayed — so it's perfect for this application. Insert the following procedure in the code window for the UserForm. This procedure simply calls the `Main` procedure (stored in a VBA module) when the UserForm is displayed.

```
Private Sub UserForm_Activate()
    Call Main
End Sub
```

The `Main` procedure is as follows. This demo routine simply inserts random numbers into the active worksheet. As it does so, it changes the width of the Label control and displays the percentage completed in the Frame's caption. This procedure is just for exercising the progress bar; you may, of course, substitute your own for more meaningful purposes.

```
Sub Main()
'   Inserts random numbers on the active worksheet
    Cells.Clear
    Counter = 1
    RowMax = 200
    ColMax = 25
    For r = 1 To RowMax
        For c = 1 To ColMax
            Cells(r, c) = Int(Rnd * 1000)
            Counter = Counter + 1
        Next c
        PctDone = Counter / (RowMax * ColMax)
        Call UpdateProgress(PctDone)
    Next r
    Unload UserForm1
End Sub
```

The Main procedure contains a loop (two loops, actually). Inside of the loop is a call to the UpdateProgress procedure. This procedure takes one argument: a value between 0 and 100 that represents the progress of the macro.

```
Sub UpdateProgress(Pct)
    With UserForm1
      .FrameProgress.Caption = Format(Pct, "0%")
      .LabelProgress.Width = Pct * (.FrameProgress.Width - 10)
      .Repaint
    End With
End Sub
```

Creating the startup procedure

All that's missing is a procedure to display the dialog box. Enter the following procedure in a VBA module:

```
Sub ShowDialog()
    UserForm1.LabelProgress.Width = 0
    UserForm1.Show
End Sub
```

How it works

When you execute the ShowDialog procedure, the Label object's width is set to 0. Then the Show method of the UserForm1 object displays the dialog box. When the dialog box is displayed, its Activate event is triggered, which executes the Main procedure. The Main procedure periodically updates the width of the Label. Notice that the procedure uses the Repaint method of the UserForm1 object. Without this statement, the changes to the Label are not updated. Before the procedure ends, the last statement unloads the UserForm object.

To customize this technique, you'll need to figure out how to determine the progress complete and assign it to the PctDone variable.

Showing progress using a MultiPage control

In the preceding example, the macro was not initiated by a dialog box. If your lengthy macro is kicked off by presenting a UserForm, the technique described in this section is a better solution. It assumes the following:

- ✦ Your project is completed.
- ✦ It uses a dialog box (without a MultiPage control) to initiate a lengthy macro.
- ✦ You have a way to gauge the progress of your macro.

The companion CD-ROM contains an example that demonstrates this technique.

Modifying your UserForm

This step assumes that you have a UserForm all set up. You'll add a MultiPage control. The first page of the MultiPage control will contain your original controls; the second page will contain the controls that display the progress indicator.

The first step is to add a MultiPage control to your UserForm. Then, cut all the existing controls on the UserForm and paste them to Page1 of the MultiPage control.

Next, activate Page2 of the MultiPage control and set it up as in Figure 14-2. This is essentially the same combination of controls used in the example in the previous section.

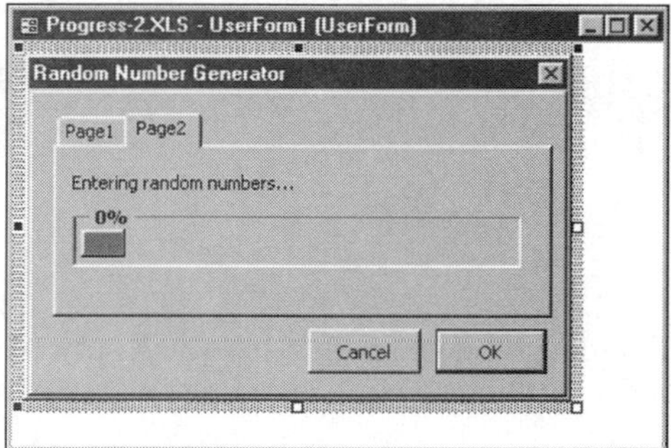

Figure 14-2: Page2 of the MultiPage control displays the progress indicator.

1. Add a Frame control and name it `FrameProgress`.
2. Add a Label control inside of the Frame and name it `LabelProgress`. Remove the Label's caption, and make its background color red.
3. Add another label to describe what's going on (optional).
4. Next, activate the MultiPage control itself (not a page on the control) and set its `Style` property to 2 - fmTabStyleNone (this hides the tabs). The easiest way to select the MultiPage control is to use the drop-down list in the Properties window. You'll probably need to adjust the size of the MultiPage control to account for the fact that the tabs are not displayed.

Inserting the UpdateProgress procedure

Insert the following procedure in the code module for the UserForm:

```
Sub UpdateProgress(Pct)
    With UserForm1
      .FrameProgress.Caption = Format(Pct, "0%")
      .LabelProgress.Width = Pct * (.FrameProgress.Width - 10)
      .Repaint
    End With
End Sub
```

This procedure is called from the main macro and does the actual updating of the progress indicator.

Modifying your procedure

You'll need to modify the procedure that is executed when the user clicks the OK Button — the `Click` event-handler procedure for the button. First, insert the following statement at the top of your procedure:

```
MultiPage1.Value = 1
```

This statement activates Page2 of the MultiPage control, which is the page that displays the progress indicator.

In the next step, you're pretty much on your own. You'll need to write code to calculate the percent completed, and assign this value to a variable named `PctDone`. Most likely, this calculation will be performed inside of a loop. Then insert the following statement, which updates the progress indicator:

```
Call UpdateProgress(PctDone)
```

How it works

This technique is very straightforward and, as you've seen, it involves only one UserForm. The code switches pages of the MultiPage control and converts your normal dialog box into a progress indicator.

Animated Controls in a UserForm

In certain situations, it might be useful to provide some type of simple animation in a UserForm — for example, flashing text or a moving marquee. I've tried everything I can think of to program these types of effects, with no success.

You might think that you could take advantage of the `Application.OnTime` event to trigger a procedure repeatedly at a specified time interval. That works quite well . . . except when a UserForm is displayed.

I discuss the `OnTime` event, as well as lots of other events, in Chapter 18.

One solution that *does* work is to use a third-party ActiveX timer control. One control that I found that works great is called the `ccrpTimer` control, developed by Karl E. Peterson as part of the Common Controls Replacement Project (CCRP).

Using the ccrpTimer control

The `ccrpTimer` control is free and does not require a license for you to use it. This control is one of several available in a single file named ccrptmr.dll. To use this control with Excel, you must establish a reference to the DLL file. You can do so in two ways:

✦ In the VB Editor, select Tools ➪ References to display the References dialog box (see Figure 14-3). Click the Browse button and locate the library file (in this case, ccrpTmr.dll).

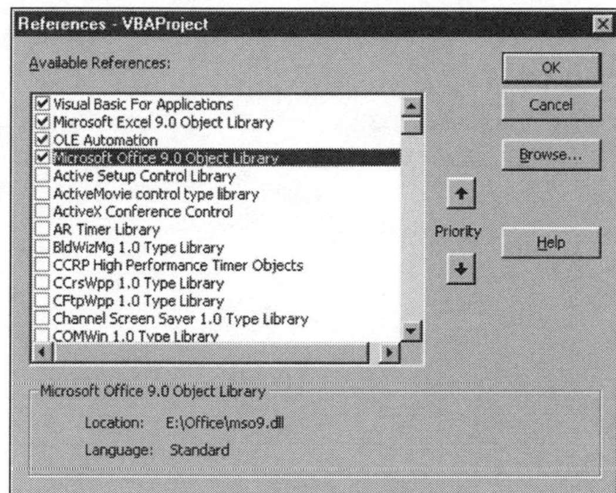

Figure 14-3: The References dialog box lists all references for a particular project.

✦ Add the reference dynamically when the workbook loads. To do so, you must know the path of the library file, or the library file must be registered on the system.

Once a reference is established, your code can access the objects defined in the library file. The `ccrpTimer` control has its own properties and methods. For example, the `Enabled` property determines if the timer is running, and the `Interval` property contains the timer's frequency (in milliseconds).

For complete details on the `ccrpTimer` control, point your Web browser to `http://www.mvps.org/ccrp`. You'll find complete documentation there, and you can try out other controls.

I developed two simple examples that use the ccrpTimer control with a UserForm, both of which are on the companion CD-ROM.

Scrolling text

The first example scrolls a TextBox from right to left, similar to a marquee. The code assumes that the ccrpTmr.dll file is in the same directory as the workbook. The `Workbook_Open` procedure (which is executed when the workbook is opened) adds the reference.

Figure 14-4 shows the UserForm in this workbook. The Label control scrolls from right to left at a speed determined by the OptionButton controls.

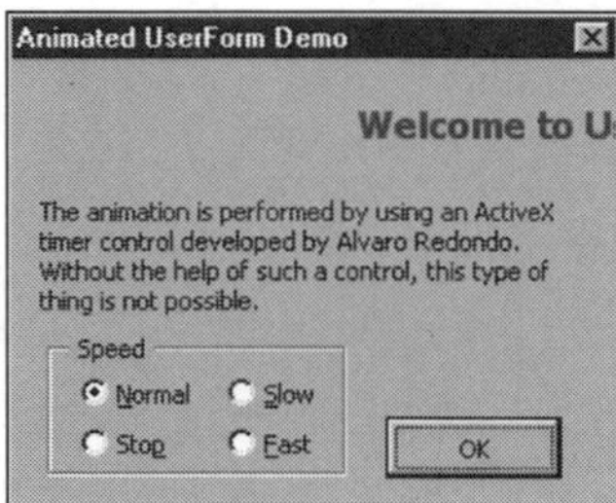

Figure 14-4: The `ccrpTimer` control causes the Label control to scroll across the dialog box.

The following code, located in the code module for the UserForm, creates a new object named `Timer1`. It then sets the `Interval` property to 40 (milliseconds) and starts the timer by setting its `Enabled` property to True.

```
Private WithEvents Timer1 As ccrpTimer

Private Sub UserForm_Initialize()
    Set Timer1 = New ccrpTimer
    Timer1.Interval = 40
    Timer1.Enabled = True
End Sub
```

After these statements are executed, the `ccrpTimer` object generates a `Timer` event every 40 milliseconds. What's needed is a procedure to handle this event. Here's an event-handler procedure:

```
Private Sub Timer1_Timer(ByVal Milliseconds As Long)
    Label1.Left = Label1.Left - 1
    If Label1.Left + Label1.Width < 0 _
      Then Label1.Left = Me.Width
End Sub
```

This procedure decrements the Label control's `Left` property by one unit, causing it to scroll to the left. It also checks the position; if the Label is off of the form, it resets the `Left` property so the scrolling begins again.

Each of the four OptionButtons (named `obStop`, `obNormal`, `obSlow`, and `obFast`) has a procedure to handle its `Click` event. These procedures are as follows:

```
Private Sub obStop_Click()
    Timer1.Enabled = False
End Sub

Private Sub obNormal_Click()
    Timer1.Interval = 40
    Timer1.Enabled = True
End Sub

Private Sub obSlow_Click()
    Timer1.Interval = 300
    Timer1.Enabled = True
End Sub

Private Sub obFast_Click()
    Timer1.Interval = 5
    Timer1.Enabled = True
End Sub
```

The `obStop_Click` procedure simply sets the `Enabled` property of the `Timer1` object to False, which disables `Timer1` so it doesn't generate any `Timer` events.

The other three procedures change the `Interval` property to a different value (smaller values increase the frequency of the `Timer` events; larger values decrease the frequency of the events). These procedures also set the `Enabled` property, just in case it was disabled by the Stop OptionButton.

Flashing text in a UserForm

Figure 14-5 shows the UserForm for another example that uses the `ccrpTimer` control. In this case, the control causes the labels to flash. Obviously, you can't see the flashing effect by looking at the figure, so open the file from the CD-ROM and take a look. This example creates two Timers that are independent of each other.

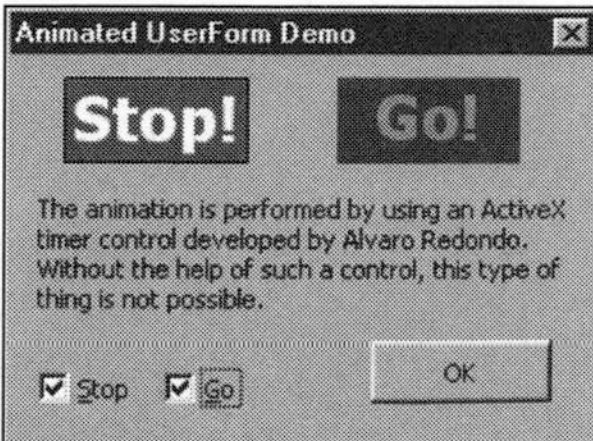

Figure 14-5: This UserForm uses two `ccrpTimer` controls to make the Label controls flash.

Here's a listing of the code that creates the controls:

```
Private WithEvents Timer1 As ccrpTimer
Private WithEvents Timer2 As ccrpTimer

Private Sub UserForm_Initialize()
    Set Timer1 = New ccrpTimer
    Set Timer2 = New ccrpTimer
End Sub
```

The CheckBox controls affect the `Enabled` property of each timer. For example, here's the event-handler procedure for the Stop CheckBox named `cbStop`:

```
Private Sub cbStop_Click()
    Timer1.Interval = 500
    Timer1.Enabled = cbStop
End Sub
```

If `cbStop` is checked (True), then `Timer1`'s `Enabled` property is True; if `cbStop` is not checked (True), then `Timer1`'s `Enabled` property is False.

The event-handler procedure for the `cbGo` CheckBox is shown next and works like the `cbStop_Click` procedure.

```
Private Sub cbGo_Click()
    Timer2.Interval = 10
    Timer2.Enabled = cbGo
End Sub
```

Each Timer has its own `Timer` event handler. Here's the code for `Timer1`:

```
Private Sub Timer1_Timer(ByVal Milliseconds As Long)
    With LabelStop
        Temp = .ForeColor
        .ForeColor = .BackColor
        .BackColor = Temp
    End With
End Sub
```

This procedure swaps the foreground and background colors of the Label control every time `Timer1` fires (which is twice per second, or every 500 milliseconds).

The `Timer2_Timer` procedure is as follows:

```
Private Sub Timer2_Timer(ByVal Milliseconds As Long)
    With LabelGo
        .ForeColor = RGB(Int(256 * Rnd), _
           Int(256 * Rnd), Int(256 * Rnd))
        .BackColor = RGB(Int(256 * Rnd), _
            Int(256 * Rnd), Int(256 * Rnd))
    End With
End Sub
```

This procedure uses VBA's `RGB` and `Rnd` functions to set the `ForeColor` and `BackColor` properties of the `LabelGo` label.

Displaying a Chart in a UserForm

With Excel 5 or Excel 95, it was very easy to display a "live" chart in a custom dialog box (using a dialog sheet). You just copied a chart and pasted it into your dialog sheet.

Oddly, there is no direct way to display a chart in a UserForm. You can, of course, copy the chart and paste it to the `Picture` property of an Image control, but this creates a static image of the chart and does not display any changes to the chart. Although UserForms are vastly superior to the old dialog sheets, this is one area that Microsoft seems to have overlooked.

You can still use dialog sheets in Excel 97 or Excel 2000.

Just because Microsoft doesn't allow a live chart to be displayed in a UserForm, that doesn't mean it can't be done! Figure 14-6 shows a UserForm with a chart displayed in an Image object. The chart actually resides on a worksheet, and the UserForm always displays the current chart. This technique works by copying the chart to a temporary graphics file, and then setting the Image control's `Picture` property to the temporary file.

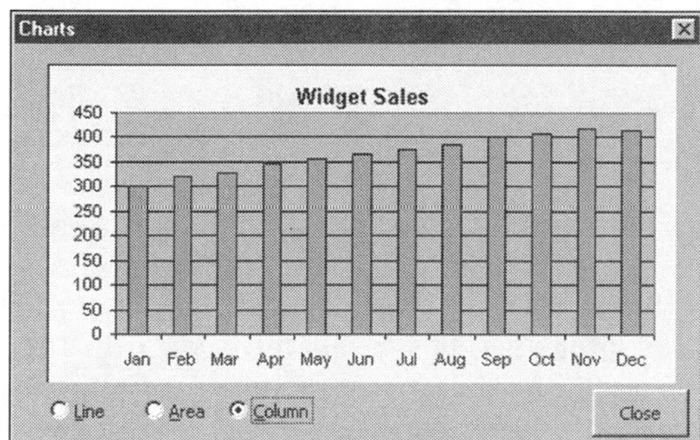

Figure 14-6: With a bit of trickery, a UserForm can display "live" charts.

General steps

To display a chart in a UserForm, follow these general steps:

1. Create your chart or charts as usual.

2. Insert a UserForm and then add an Image control.
3. Write VBA code to save the chart as a GIF file, and then set the Image control's `Picture` property to the GIF file. You need to use VBA's `LoadPicture` function to do this.
4. Add other bells and whistles as desired. For example, the UserForm in the demo file contains controls that enable you to change the chart type. Alternately, you could write code to display multiple charts.

Saving a chart as a GIF file

The code that follows demonstrates how to create a GIF file named TEMP.GIF from a chart — in this case, the first chart object on the sheet named `Data`.

```
Set CurrentChart = Sheets("Data").ChartObjects(1).Chart
Fname = ThisWorkbook.Path & "\temp.gif"
CurrentChart.Export FileName:=Fname, FilterName:="GIF"
```

Changing the Image control's Picture property

If the Image control on the UserForm is named `Image1`, the following statement loads the image (represented by the `Fname` variable) into the Image control:

```
Image1.Picture = LoadPicture(Fname)
```

This technique works fine, but you may notice a slight delay as the chart is saved and then retrieved. On a fast system, however, this delay is barely noticeable.

Creating Wizards

Many applications incorporate wizards to guide users through an operation. Excel's Text Import Wizard is a good example. A *wizard* is essentially a series of dialog boxes that solicit information from the user. Often, the user's choices in earlier dialog boxes influence the contents of later dialog boxes. In most wizards, the user is free to go forward or backward through the dialog box sequence, or click the Finish button to accept all defaults.

You can, of course, create wizards using VBA and a series of UserForms. However, I've found that the most efficient way to create a wizard is to use a single UserForm and a MultiPage control.

Figure 14-7 shows an example of a simple four-step wizard, which consists of a single UserForm that contains a MultiPage control. Each step of the wizard displays a different page in the MultiPage control.

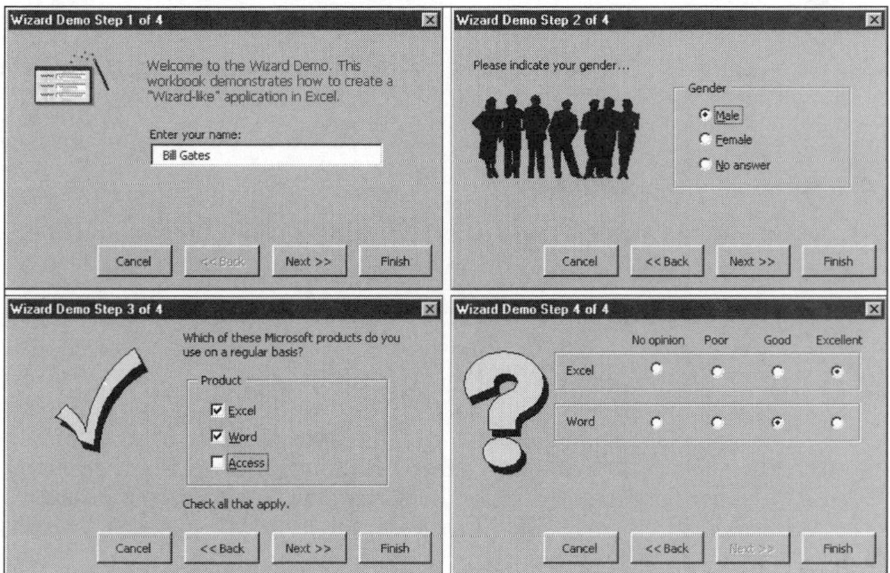

Figure 14-7: This four-step wizard uses a MultiPage control.

If you need to create a wizard, the example workbook on the CD-ROM serves as a good starting point. This is a four-step wizard that collects information and inserts it into a worksheet.

The sections that follow describe how I created the example wizard.

Setting up the MultiPage control

Start with a new UserForm, and add a MultiPage control. By default, this control contains two pages. Right-click the MultiPage tab and insert enough new pages to handle your wizard — one page for each wizard step. The example on the CD-ROM is a four-step wizard, so the MultiPage control has four pages.

The names of the MultiPage tabs are irrelevant. The MultiPage control's `Style` property will eventually be set to 2 - fmTabStyleNone. While working on the UserForm, you'll want to keep the tabs visible to make it easier to access various pages.

Add the desired controls to each page of the MultiPage control. The number of controls varies, of course, depending on your application. You may need to resize the MultiPage control as you work to have room for the controls.

Adding the buttons

Next, add the buttons that control the progress of the wizard. These buttons are placed outside of the MultiPage control because they are used while any of the pages are displayed. Most wizards have four buttons:

- *Cancel* cancels the wizard.
- *Back* returns to the previous step. During Step 1, this button should be disabled.
- *Next* advances to the next step. During the last step, this button should be disabled.
- *Finish* finishes the wizard.

In some cases, the user is enabled to click the Finish button at any time and accept the defaults for items that were skipped over. In other cases, the wizard requires user response for some items. If this is the case, the Finish button is disabled until all required input is made. The example on the CD-ROM requires an entry in the TextBox in Step 1.

In the example, these CommandButtons are named CancelButton, BackButton, NextButton, and FinishButton.

Programming the buttons

Each of the four wizard buttons requires a procedure to handle its Click event. The following event-handler procedure for CancelButton uses a MsgBox function (see Figure 14-8) to verify that the user really wants to exit. If the user clicks the Yes button, the UserForm is unloaded with no action taken. This type of verification is optional, of course.

```
Private Sub CancelButton_Click()
    Msg = "Cancel the wizard?"
    Ans = MsgBox(Msg, vbQuestion + vbYesNo, APPNAME)
    If Ans = vbYes Then Unload Me
End Sub
```

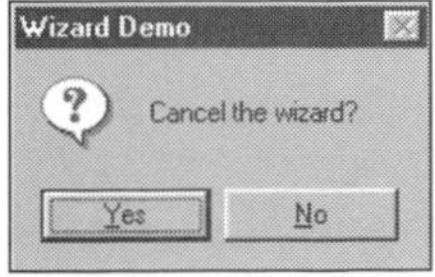

Figure 14-8: Clicking the Cancel button displays a message box.

Following are the event-handler procedures for the Back and Next buttons:

```
Private Sub BackButton_Click()
    MultiPage1.Value = MultiPage1.Value - 1
    UpdateControls
End Sub

Private Sub NextButton_Click()
    MultiPage1.Value = MultiPage1.Value + 1
    UpdateControls
End Sub
```

These two procedures are very simple. They change the `Value` property of the MultiPage control, and then call another procedure named `UpdateControls`.

The `UpdateControls` procedure in Listing 14-1 is responsible for enabling and disabling the `BackButton` and `NextButton` controls.

Listing 14-1: These procedures enable the key controls in the wizard

```
Sub UpdateControls()
    Select Case MultiPage1.Value
        Case 0
            BackButton.Enabled = False
            NextButton.Enabled = True
        Case MultiPage1.Pages.Count - 1
            BackButton.Enabled = True
            NextButton.Enabled = False
        Case Else
            BackButton.Enabled = True
            NextButton.Enabled = True
    End Select

'   Update the caption
    Me.Caption = APPNAME & " Step " _
      & MultiPage1.Value + 1 & " of " _
      & MultiPage1.Pages.Count

'   The Name field is required
    If tbName.Text = "" Then
        FinishButton.Enabled = False
    Else
        FinishButton.Enabled = True
    End If
End Sub
```

The procedure changes the UserForm's caption to display the current step and the total number of steps (APPNAME is a public constant, defined in Module1). It then examines the name field on the first page (a TextBox named tbName). This is a required field, so the Finish button can't be clicked if it's empty. If the TextBox is empty, the FinishButton is disabled; otherwise it's enabled.

Programming dependencies

In most wizards, a user's response to a particular step may affect what's displayed in a subsequent step. In the CD-ROM example, the user indicates which products he or she uses in Step 3, and then rates those products in Step 4. The OptionButtons for a product's rating are visible only if the user has indicated a particular product.

Programmatically, this is accomplished by monitoring the MultiPage's Change event. Whenever the Value of the MultiPage is changed (by clicking the Back or Next button), the MultiPage1_Change procedure is executed. If the MultiPage control is on the last tab (Step 4), the procedure examines the values of the CheckBox controls in Step 3, and makes the appropriate adjustments in Step 4.

In this example, the code uses two arrays of controls: one for the product CheckBox controls (Step 3) and one for the Frame controls (Step 4). The code uses a For-Next loop to hide the Frames for the products that are not used and to adjust their vertical positioning. If none of the CheckBoxes in Step 3 is checked, everything in Step 4 is hidden except a TextBox that displays *Click Finish to exit* (if a name is entered in Step 1) or *A name is required in Step 1* (if a name is not entered in Step 1). The MultiPage1_Change procedure is shown in Listing 14-2.

Listing 14-2: Bringing up the page corresponding to the user's choice

```
Private Sub MultiPage1_Change()
'   Set up the Ratings page?
    If MultiPage1.Value = 3 Then
'       Create an array of CheckBox controls
        Dim ProdCB(1 To 3) As MSForms.CheckBox
        Set ProdCB(1) = cbExcel
        Set ProdCB(2) = cbWord
        Set ProdCB(3) = cbAccess

'       Create an array of Frame controls
        Dim ProdFrame(1 To 3) As MSForms.Frame
        Set ProdFrame(1) = FrameExcel
        Set ProdFrame(2) = FrameWord
        Set ProdFrame(3) = FrameAccess
```

```
        TopPos = 22
        FSpace = 8
        AtLeastOne = False

        Loop through all products
        For i = 1 To 3
            If ProdCB(i) Then
                ProdFrame(i).Visible = True
                ProdFrame(i).Top = TopPos
                TopPos = TopPos + ProdFrame(i).Height + FSpace
                AtLeastOne = True
            Else
                ProdFrame(i).Visible = False
            End If
        Next i

        Uses no products?
        If AtLeastOne Then
            lblHeadings.Visible = True
            Image4.Visible = True
            lblFinishMsg.Visible = False
        Else
            lblHeadings.Visible = False
            Image4.Visible = False
            lblFinishMsg.Visible = True
            If tbName = "" Then
                lblFinishMsg.Caption = _
                  "A name is required in Step 1."
            Else
                lblFinishMsg.Caption = _
                  "Click Finish to exit."
             End If
        End If
    End If
End Sub
```

Performing the task

When the user clicks the Finish button, the wizard performs its task: it transfers the information from the UserForm to the next empty row in the worksheet. This procedure, shown in Listing 14-3, is very straightforward. It starts by determining the next empty worksheet row and assigns this value to a variable (`r`). The remainder of the procedure simply translates the values of the controls and enters data into the worksheet.

Listing 14-3: Inserting the acquired data into the worksheet

```
Private Sub FinishButton_Click()
    r = Application.WorksheetFunction. _
      CountA(Range("A:A")) + 1

'   Insert the name
    Cells(r, 1) = tbName.Text

'   Insert the gender
    Select Case True
        Case obMale: Cells(r, 2) = "Male"
        Case obFemale: Cells(r, 2) = "Female"
        Case obNoAnswer: Cells(r, 2) = "Unknown"
    End Select

'   Insert usage
    If cbExcel Then Cells(r, 3) = True Else _
     Cells(r, 3) = False
    If cbWord Then Cells(r, 4) = True Else Cells(r, 4) = False
    If cbAccess Then Cells(r, 5) = True Else _
     Cells(r, 5) = False

'   Insert ratings
    If obExcel1 Then Cells(r, 6) = ""
    If obExcel2 Then Cells(r, 6) = 0
    If obExcel3 Then Cells(r, 6) = 1
    If obExcel4 Then Cells(r, 6) = 2
    If obWord1 Then Cells(r, 7) = ""
    If obWord2 Then Cells(r, 7) = 0
    If obWord3 Then Cells(r, 7) = 1
    If obWord4 Then Cells(r, 7) = 2
    If obAccess1 Then Cells(r, 8) = ""
    If obAccess2 Then Cells(r, 8) = 0
    If obAccess3 Then Cells(r, 8) = 1
    If obAccess4 Then Cells(r, 8) = 2

'   Unload the form
    Unload Me
End Sub
```

Final steps

Once you've tested your wizard and everything seems to be working, you can then set the MultiPage control's `Style` property to 2 - fmTabStyleNone.

Emulating the MsgBox Function

VBA's MsgBox function is a bit unusual because, unlike most functions, it displays a dialog box. But, like other functions, it also returns a *value* — an integer that represents which button the user clicked.

This example discusses a custom function I created that emulates VBA's MsgBox function. On first thought, creating such a function might seem rather easy. Think again! The MsgBox function is extraordinarily versatile, due to the arguments it accepts. Consequently, creating a function to emulate MsgBox is no small feat.

The point of this exercise is not to create an alternative messaging function. Rather, it's to demonstrate how to develop a relatively complex function that also incorporates a UserForm. However, some people might like the idea of being able to customize their messages. If so, you'll find that this function is very easy to customize. For example, you can change the font, colors, button text, and so on.

I named my pseudo-MsgBox function MyMsgBox. The emulation is not perfect. MyMsgBox has the following limitations:

✦ It does not support the Helpfile argument, which adds a Help button that, when clicked, opens a Help file.

✦ It does not support the Context argument, which specifies the context ID for the Help file.

✦ It does not support the "system modal" option, which puts everything in Windows on hold until you respond to the dialog box.

The syntax for MyMsgBox is

```
MyMsgBox(prompt[, buttons] [, title])
```

This syntax is exactly the same as the MsgBox syntax, except that it doesn't use the last two optional arguments (Helpfile and Context). MyMsgBox also uses the same predefined constants as MsgBox: vbOKOnly, vbQuestion, vbDefaultButton1, and so on.

You might want to examine the MsgBox listing in the online help to become familiar with its arguments.

MyMsgBox code

The MyMsgBox function makes use of a UserForm named MyMsgBoxForm. The function itself is very short, as you can see from the following listing. The bulk of the work is done in the UserForm_Initialize procedure.

```
Public Prompt1 As String
Public Buttons1 As Integer
Public Title1 As String
Public UserClick As Integer

Function MyMsgBox(ByVal Prompt As String, _
  Optional ByVal Buttons As Integer, _
  Optional ByVal Title As String) As Integer
    Prompt1 = Prompt
    Buttons1 = Buttons
    Title1 = Title
    MyMsgBoxForm.Show
    MyMsgBox = UserClick
End Function
```

The complete code for the MyMsgBox module is too lengthy to list here, but it's available in a workbook on the companion CD-ROM.

Figure 14-9 shows `MyMsgbox` in action (I used a different font for the message text).

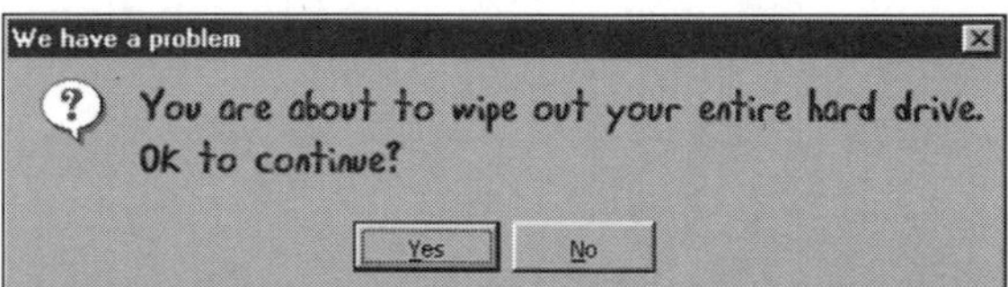

Figure 14-9: The result of the `MsgBox` emulation function (using a different font).

Here's the code I used to execute the function:

```
Prompt = "You are about to wipe out your entire hard drive."
Prompt = Prompt & vbCrLf & "OK to continue?"
Buttons = vbQuestion + vbYesNo
Title = "We have a problem"
Ans = MyMsgBox(Prompt, Buttons, Title)
```

How it works

Notice the use of four `Public` variables. The first three (`Prompt1`, `Buttons1`, and `Title1`) represent the arguments that are passed to the function. The other variable (`UserClick`) represents the values returned by the function. The `UserForm_Initialize` procedure needs a way to get this information and send it back to the function, and using `Public` variables is the only way to accomplish that.

The UserForm (shown in Figure 14-10) contains four Image controls (one for each of the four possible icons), three CommandButton controls, and a TextBox control.

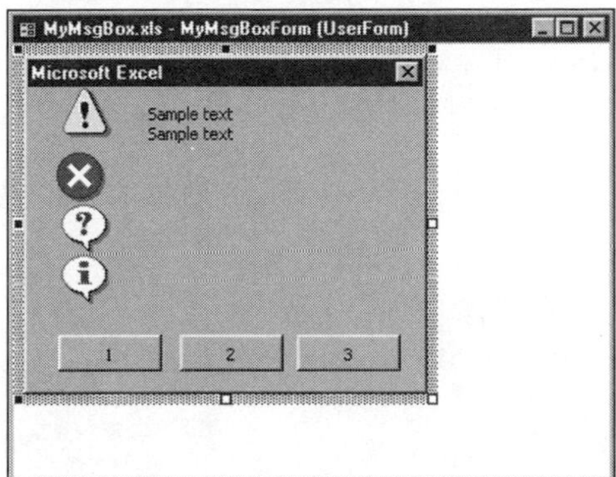

Figure 14-10: The UserForm for the `MyMsgBox` function.

The code in the `UserForm_Initialize` procedure examines the arguments and does the following:

- ✦ Determines which, if any, image to display (and hides the others)
- ✦ Determines which button(s) to display (and hides the others)
- ✦ Determines which button is the default button
- ✦ Centers the buttons in the dialog box
- ✦ Determines the captions for the CommandButtons
- ✦ Determines the position of the text within the dialog box
- ✦ Determines how wide to make the dialog box (it uses an API call to get the video resolution)
- ✦ Determines how tall to make the dialog box
- ✦ Displays the UserForm

Three additional event-handler procedures are included (one for each CommandButton). These routines determine which button was clicked, and return a value for the function by setting a value for the `UserClick` variable.

Interpreting the second argument (*buttons*) is a bit challenging. This argument can consist of a number of constants added together. For example, the second argument can be something like this:

```
VbYesNoCancel + VbQuestion + VbDefaultButton3
```

This argument creates a three-button `MsgBox` (Yes, No, and Cancel), displays the Question icon, and makes the third button the default button. The actual argument is 547 (3 + 32 + 512). The challenge was pulling three pieces of information from a single number. The solution involves converting the argument to a binary number, and then having the interpreter examine specific bits. For example, 547 in binary is 1000100011. Binary digits 4 through 6 determine which image to display, digits 8 through 10 determine which buttons to display, and digits 1 and 2 determine which button is the default button.

The MyMsgBox function

To use this function in your own project, export the `MyMsgBoxMod` module and the `MyMsgBoxForm` UserForm. Then import these two files into your project.

A Modeless Dialog Box

Most dialog boxes you encounter are *modal* dialog boxes, which must be dismissed from the screen before the user can do anything with the underlying application. Some dialog boxes, however, are *modeless,* which means the user may continue to work in the application while the dialog box is displayed.

In Excel 2000, a UserForm can be *modeless.* This means that the user doesn't have to dismiss the UserForm before activating the workbook and doing other work in Excel. The `Show` method of the UserForm object defaults to displaying a *modal* form, meaning that the rest of Excel is suspended while the UserForm is visible. To display a modeless UserForm, use an instruction such as this:

```
UserForm1.Show vbModeless
```

The word `vbModeless` is a built-in constant that has a value of 0. Therefore, the effect of the following statement is identical to that of the preceding statement:

```
UserForm1.Show 0
```

Figure 14-11 shows a modeless dialog box that displays information about the active cell. When the dialog box is displayed, the user is free to move the cell cursor and activate other sheets.

This example is available on the companion CD-ROM.

The trick here is determining when to update the information in the dialog box. To do so, the example monitors two workbook events: `SheetSelectionChange` and `SheetActivate`. These event-handler procedures are located in the code module for the `ThisWorkbook` object.

Refer to Chapter 18 for additional information about events.

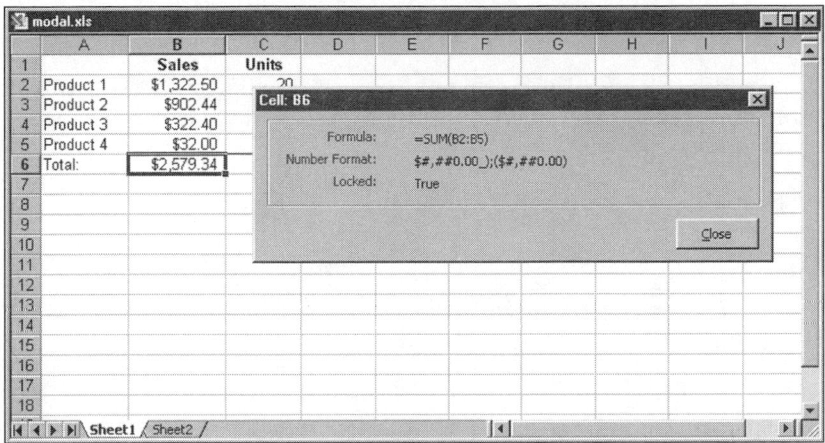

Figure 14-11: This modeless dialog box remains visible while the user continues working.

The event-handler procedures are as follows:

```
Private Sub Workbook_SheetSelectionChange _
  (ByVal Sh As Object, ByVal Target As Range)
    Call UpdateBox
End Sub

Private Sub Workbook_SheetActivate(ByVal Sh As Object)
    Call UpdateBox
End Sub
```

These procedures call the `UpdateBox` procedure, listed here:

```
Sub UpdateBox()
    With UserForm1
        .Caption = "Cell: " & ActiveCell.Address(False, False)
'       Formula
        If ActiveCell.HasFormula Then
            .lblFormula.Caption = ActiveCell.Formula
        Else
            .lblFormula.Caption = "(none)"
        End If
'       Number format
        .lblNumFormat.Caption = ActiveCell.NumberFormat
'       Locked
        .lblLocked.Caption = ActiveCell.Locked
    End With
End Sub
```

The `UpdateBox` procedure changes the UserForm's caption to show the active cell's address, and then it updates the three Label controls (`lblFormula`, `lblNumFormat`, and `lblLocked`).

Multiple Buttons, One Event Handler

Every CommandButton on a UserForm must have its own event-handler procedure. For example, if you have two CommandButtons, you need at least two event-handler procedures:

```
Private Sub CommandButton1_Click()
' Code goes here
End Sub

Private Sub CommandButton2_Click()
' Code goes here
End Sub
```

In other words, you cannot assign a macro to execute when *any* CommandButton is clicked. Each `Click` event handler is "hardwired" to its CommandButton. You can, however, have each event handler call another all-inclusive macro in the event-handler procedures, but you need to pass an argument to indicate which button was clicked. In the following examples, clicking either `CommandButton1` or `CommandButton2` executes the `ButtonClick` procedure, and the single argument tells the `ButtonClick` procedure which button was clicked.

```
Private Sub CommandButton1_Click()
Call ButtonClick(1)
End Sub

Private Sub CommandButton2_Click()
Call ButtonClick(2)
End Sub
```

If your UserForm has many CommandButtons, setting up all these event handlers can get tedious. You might prefer to have a single procedure that could determine which button was clicked, and take the appropriate action.

This section describes a way around this limitation by using a class module to define a new class.

This example is available on the companion CD-ROM.

Using a Class module

The steps that follow describe how to recreate the example workbook.

1. Create your UserForm as usual, and add several CommandButtons (the example on the CD contains 16 CommandButtons). This example assumes the form is named `UserForm1`.

2. Insert a class module into your project (use Insert➪Class Module), give it the name `BtnClass`, and enter the following code. You will need to customize the `ButtonGroup_Click` procedure.

```
Public WithEvents ButtonGroup As MsForms.CommandButton

Private Sub ButtonGroup_Click()
    Msg = "You clicked " & ButtonGroup.Name & vbCrLf _
     & vbCrLf
    Msg = Msg & "Caption: " & ButtonGroup.Caption _
     & vbCrLf
    Msg = Msg & "Left Position: " & ButtonGroup.Left _
     & vbCrLf
    Msg = Msg & "Top Position: " & ButtonGroup.Top
    MsgBox Msg, vbInformation, ButtonGroup.Name
End Sub
```

3. Insert a normal VBA module and enter the following code. This routine simply displays the UserForm.

```
Sub ShowDialog()
    UserForm1.Show
End Sub
```

In the code module for the UserForm, enter the code in Listing 14-4. This procedure is kicked off by the UserForm's `Initialize` event. Notice that the code excludes a button named `OKButton` from the "button group." Therefore, clicking the OK Button does not execute the `ButtonGroup_Click` procedure.

Listing 14-4: Establishing the Buttons() object array

```
Dim Buttons() As New BtnClass

Private Sub UserForm_Initialize()
    Dim ButtonCount As Integer
    Dim ctl As Control

'   Create the Button objects
    ButtonCount = 0
    For Each ctl In UserForm1.Controls
        If TypeName(ctl) = "CommandButton" Then
            If ctl.Name <> "OKButton" Then 'Skip the OKButton
                ButtonCount = ButtonCount + 1
                ReDim Preserve Buttons(1 To ButtonCount)
                Set Buttons(ButtonCount).ButtonGroup = ctl
            End If
        End If
    Next ctl
End Sub
```

After performing these steps, you can execute the ShowDialog procedure to display the UserForm. Clicking any of the CommandButtons (except the OKButton) executes the ButtonGroup_Click procedure. Figure 14-12 shows an example of the message displayed when a button is clicked.

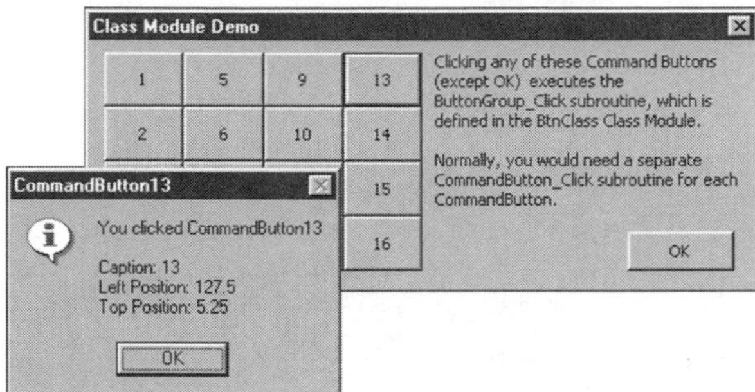

Figure 14-12: The ButtonGroup_Click procedure describes the button that was clicked.

Adapting this technique

You can adapt this technique to work with other types of controls. You need to change the type name in the Public WithEvents declaration. For example, if you have OptionButtons instead of CommandButtons, use a declaration statement like this:

```
Public WithEvents ButtonGroup As MsForms.OptionButton
```

A Color Picker Dialog Box

This example is similar to the example in the previous section, but a bit more complex. The example workbook demonstrates a technique to display a UserForm that enables the user to select a color from the workbook's color palette (which consists of 56 colors).

The example, which is available on the companion CD-ROM, is actually a function (named GetAColor) that displays a UserForm and returns a color value. The GetAColor function is as follows:

```
Public ColorValue As Variant
Dim Buttons(1 To 56) As New ColorButtonClass

Function GetAColor() As Variant
'   Displays a UserForm and returns a
'   color value - or False if no color is selected
    Dim ctl As Control
```

```
    Dim ButtonCount As Integer
    ButtonCount = 0
    For Each ctl In UserForm1.Controls
'       The 56 color buttons have their '
'       Tag property set to "ColorButton"
        If ctl.Tag = "ColorButton" Then
            ButtonCount = ButtonCount + 1
            Set Buttons(ButtonCount).ColorButton = ctl
'           Get colors from the active workbook's palette
            Buttons(ButtonCount).ColorButton.BackColor = _
                ActiveWorkbook.Colors(ButtonCount)
        End If
    Next ctl
    UserForm1.Show
    GetAColor = ColorValue
End Function
```

The UserForm contains 56 CommandButton controls, which are colored using the colors in the active workbook's palette.

You can access the `GetAColor` function with a statement such as the following:

```
UserColor = GetAColor()
```

Executing this statement displays the UserForm and assigns a color value to the `UserColor` variable. The color corresponds to the color selected by the user.

Figure 14-13 shows the UserForm (it looks better in color), which contains 56 CommandButton controls. The `BackColor` property of each button corresponds to one of the colors in the workbook's color palette. Clicking a button unloads the UserForm and provides a value for the function to return.

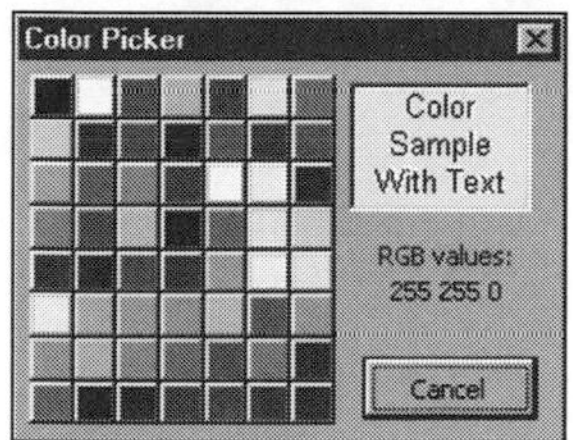

Figure 14-13: This dialog box enables the user to select a color by clicking a button.

The example file on the accompanying CD-ROM contains the following:

- ✦ A UserForm (`UserForm1`) that contains a dialog box with 56 CommandButtons (plus a few other accoutrements)
- ✦ A class module (`ColorButtonClass`) that defines a `ColorButton` class
- ✦ A VBA module (`Module1`) that contains a Function procedure (`GetAColor`)
- ✦ Two examples that demonstrate the `GetAColor` Function procedure

The `GetAColor` procedure sets up the UserForm and displays it. It later returns the color value of the selected button. If the user clicks Cancel, `GetAColor` returns False. As the user moves the mouse pointer over the color buttons, the Color Sample image displays the color.

An Enhanced Data Form

Next, here is one of the more complex UserForms you'll encounter. I designed it as a replacement for Excel's Data Form, which is shown in Figure 14-14. You'll recall this is the dialog box that appears when you select Data➪Form.

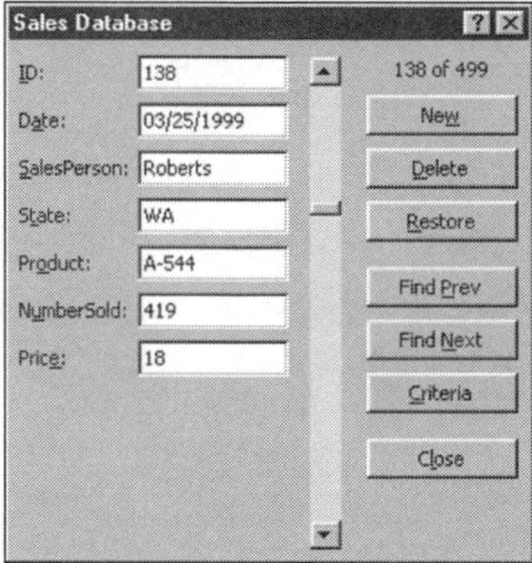

Figure 14-14: Excel's Data Form.

Like Excel's Data Form, my Enhanced Data Form works with a list in a worksheet. But as you can see in Figure 14-15, it has a dramatically different appearance and offers several advantages.

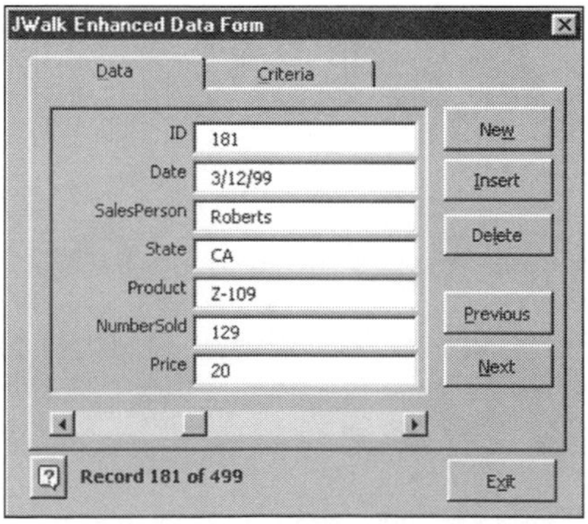

Figure 14-15: The author's Enhanced Data Form.

The Enhanced Data Form features the following enhancements:

- ✦ It handles any number of records and fields. Excel's Data Form is limited to 32 fields.
- ✦ The dialog box is always the same size, with scrollable fields. Excel's Data Form's dialog box isn't scrollable, and can take up the entire screen.
- ✦ The record displayed in the dialog box is always visible on-screen and is highlighted so you know exactly where you are. Excel's Data Form doesn't scroll the screen for you and does not highlight the current record.
- ✦ At startup, the dialog box always displays the record in the row of the active cell. Excel's Data Form always starts with the first record in the database.
- ✦ When you close the dialog box, the current record is selected for you. Excel's Data Form doesn't change your selection when you exit.
- ✦ It enables you to insert a new record at any position in the database. Excel's Data Form adds new records only at the end of the database.
- ✦ It includes an Undo button for Data Entry, Insert Record, Delete Record, and New Record. Excel's Data Form includes only a Restore button.
- ✦ Search criteria are stored in a separate panel, so you always know exactly what you're searching for. The search criteria are not always apparent in Excel's Data Form.
- ✦ It supports approximate matches while searching (*, ?, and #). Excel's Data Form does not.
- ✦ The complete VBA source code is available, so you can customize it to your needs. Excel's Data Form is not written in VBA and cannot be customized.

The Enhanced Data Form is a commercial product (sort of). It can be used and distributed freely, but access to the complete VBA source code is available for a modest fee.

Installing the add-in

To try out the Enhanced Data Form, install the add-in:

1. Copy the **dataform.xla** file from the CD-ROM to a directory on your hard drive.
2. In Excel, select Tools ➪ Add-Ins.
3. In the Add-Ins dialog box, click Browse and locate the **dataform.xla** in the directory from Step 1.

Using the Enhanced Data Form

When the Enhanced Data Form add-in is installed, a new menu command is available: Data➪JWalk Enhanced Data Form. You can use the Enhanced Data Form to work with any worksheet database.

Summary

This chapter provided several more advanced examples of UserForm. Studying the provided code will help you become a master of UserForms.

This chapter concludes Part IV. Subsequent chapters include additional UserForm examples.

✦ ✦ ✦

PART V

Advanced Programming Techniques

The six chapters in this part cover additional topics that are often considered advanced. The first three chapters discuss how to develop utilities and how to use VBA to work with pivot tables and charts. Chapter 18 covers the topic of event handling, which enables you to execute procedures automatically when certain events occur. Chapter 19 describes how to work with other applications, and Chapter 20 discusses the topic of add-ins.

✦ ✦ ✦ ✦

In This Part

✦ ✦ ✦ ✦

Developing Excel Utilities with VBA

✦ ✦ ✦ ✦

In This Chapter

About Excel utilities and utilities in general

Why use VBA to develop utilities

What you need to know to develop good utilities

Step-by-step details for developing a useful Excel utility to manipulate text in cells

Where to go for more Excel utilities

✦ ✦ ✦ ✦

This chapter is about Excel utilities. In general, a *utility* is something that enhances software, adding useful features or making existing features more accessible. As you'll see, creating utilities for Excel is an excellent way to make a great product even better.

About Excel Utilities

A utility isn't an end product, such as a quarterly report. Rather, it's a tool that helps you produce an end product (such as a quarterly report). Symantec's Norton Utilities is an example of a popular utilities package for Windows. An Excel utility is (almost always) an add-in that enhances Excel with new features or capabilities.

Excel is an extraordinary program that gets better with every release. But as good as Excel is, many users soon develop a wish list of features that they would like to see added to the software. For example, some users who turn off the grid-line display want a feature that toggles this attribute so that they don't have to go through the tedious Tools➪Options command. Users who work with dates might want a pop-up calendar feature. And some users desire an easier way to export a range of data to a separate file.

Utilities don't need to be complicated. Some of the most useful ones are actually very simple. For example, the following VBA procedure is a utility that toggles the worksheet grid-line display.

```
Sub ToggleGridDisplay()
    ActiveWindow.DisplayGridlines = _
        Not ActiveWindow.DisplayGridlines
End Sub
```

You can store this macro in your Personal Macro Workbook so that it's always available. Even better, you can assign it to a toolbar button, a right-click shortcut menu, or a keystroke combination.

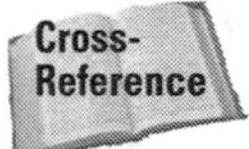

Several of the examples in Part IV are actually utilities—or at least they easily can be turned into utilities.

Using VBA to Develop Utilities

When I received the beta version of Excel 5, I was blown away by VBA's potential. VBA was light-years ahead of Excel's powerful XLM macro language, and it made Excel the clear leader among spreadsheets in terms of programming.

In an effort to learn VBA, I wrote a collection of Excel utilities using only VBA. I figured that I would learn the language more quickly if I gave myself a tangible goal. The result was a product I call the Power Utility Pak for Excel, which is available to you at no charge as a benefit of buying this book. Use the coupon in the back of the book to order your copy.

I learned several things from my initial efforts on this project.

- VBA can be difficult to grasp at first, but it becomes easier with practice.
- Experimentation is the key to mastering VBA. Every project usually involves dozens of small coding experiments that eventually lead to a finished product.
- VBA enables you to extend Excel in a way that is entirely consistent with Excel's look and feel, including menus, toolbars, and dialog boxes.
- Excel can do almost anything. When you reach a dead end, chances are there's another path that leads to a solution.

The bottom line: Few other software packages include such an extensive set of tools that enable the end user to extend the software.

What Makes a Good Utility?

An Excel utility, of course, should add something that makes your job easier or more efficient. But if you're developing utilities for other users, what makes an

Excel utility valuable? I've put together a list of elements that are common to good utilities:

✦ *It adds something to Excel.* This may be a new feature, a way to combine existing features, or just a way to make an existing feature easier to use.

✦ *It's general in nature.* Ideally, a utility should be useful under a wide variety of conditions. Of course, it's more difficult to write a general-purpose utility than it is to write one that works in a highly defined environment.

✦ *It's flexible.* The best utilities provide many options to handle various situations.

✦ *It looks, works, and feels like an Excel command.* Although it's tempting to add your own special touch to utilities, other users will find them easier to use if they look and act like familiar Excel commands.

✦ *It provides help for the user when needed.* In other words, it requires documentation that's thorough and accessible.

✦ *It traps errors.* An end user should never see a VBA error message. Any error messages that appear should be ones that you write.

✦ *Its effects are undoable.* Users who don't like the result caused by your utility should be able to reverse their path.

Text Tools: The Anatomy of a Utility

In this section, I describe an Excel utility that I developed (and that is part of my Power Utility Pak). The Text Tools utility enables the user to perform a number of manipulations of text in a selected range of cells. Specifically, this utility enables the user to do the following:

✦ Change the case of the text (uppercase, lowercase, or proper case)

✦ Add new text to the beginning or the end, or at a specific character position

✦ Remove text from the beginning or the end, or at the start of a specific character position

✦ Remove excess spaces (or all spaces)

Background

Excel has many text functions that can manipulate text strings in useful ways. For example, you can uppercase the text in a cell, delete characters from text, remove spaces, and so on. But to perform any of these operations, you have to write formulas, copy them, convert the formulas to values, and paste the values over the original text. In other words, Excel doesn't make it particularly easy to modify text. Wouldn't it be nice if Excel had some text manipulation tools that didn't require formulas?

By the way, many good utility ideas come from statements that begin, "Wouldn't it be nice if . . ."

Project goals for Text Tools

The first step in designing a utility is to envision exactly how you want the utility to work. Here's my original plan, stated in the form of ten goals:

- ✦ It will have the same look and feel of other Excel commands. In other words, it will have a dialog box that looks like Excel's dialog boxes.
- ✦ It will be accessible from the Tools menu.
- ✦ It will operate with the current selection of cells (including multiple selections), and it will enable the user to modify the range selection while the dialog box is displayed.
- ✦ Its main features will consist of tools to change the case of text, add new text to the strings, delete a fixed number of characters from the text, and remove spaces from the text in each cell.
- ✦ It also will enable the user to display key statistics about selected cells.
- ✦ It will enable the user to request the preceding types of changes to nontext cells as well as text cells.
- ✦ It will have no effect on cells that contain formulas.
- ✦ It will be fast and efficient. For example, if the user selects an entire range, the utility should ignore empty cells.
- ✦ It will enable the user to undo the changes.
- ✦ It will have online help available.

How it works

When the Text Tools workbook opens, it creates a new menu command: Tools⇨Text Tools. Selecting this item executes the `StartTextTools` procedure, which checks to make sure that Excel is in the proper context (a worksheet is active and not protected) and then displays the main Text Tools dialog box.

The user can specify various modifications and click the Apply button to perform them. The changes are visible in the worksheet, and the dialog box remains displayed. Each operation can be undone, or the user can perform additional text modifications. Clicking the Help button displays a help dialog box, and clicking the Exit button dismisses the dialog box.

Figure 15-1 shows an example of the Text Tools utility in use.

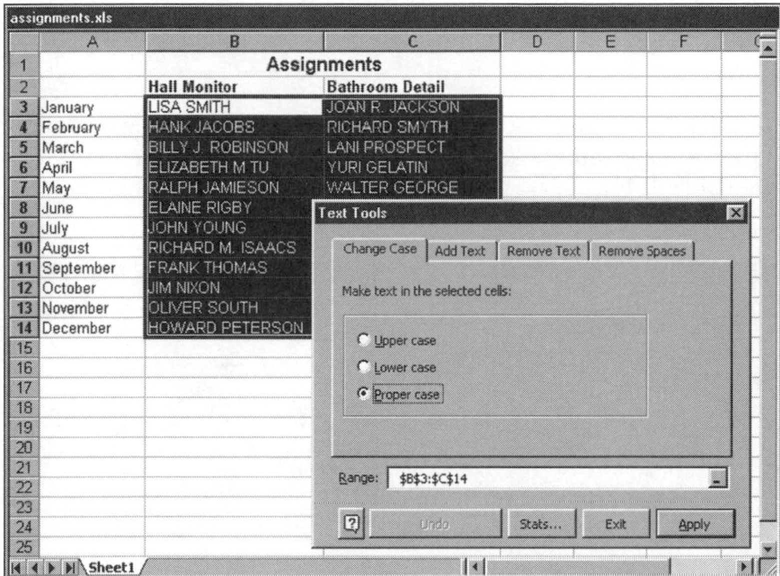

Figure 15-1: Using the Text Tools utility to change text to proper case.

The Text Tools workbook

The Text Tools workbook consists of the following components:

✦ *One worksheet.* Every workbook must have at least one worksheet. I take advantage of this fact and use the worksheet named `HelpSheet` to store user help text.

✦ *Two VBA modules.* One (`modMenus`) contains the code to create and delete the menu item; the other (`modMain`) contains the code to display the main UserForm. The code that does the actual work is stored in the code modules for the UserForms.

✦ *Two UserForms.* One (`FormMain`) is the main dialog box; the other (`FormMenus`) is used to display help.

The Text Tools utility is available on the CD-ROM that accompanies this book. This is a stand-alone version of the tool that is included with Power Utility Pak.

The FormMain UserForm

When I create a utility, I usually begin by designing the user interface, which in this case is the main dialog box. Creating the dialog box forces me to think through the project one more time.

The MainForm UserForm contains a MultiPage control, with four pages that correspond to the main features in the utility. Figure 15-2 shows the four pages of the MultiPage control.

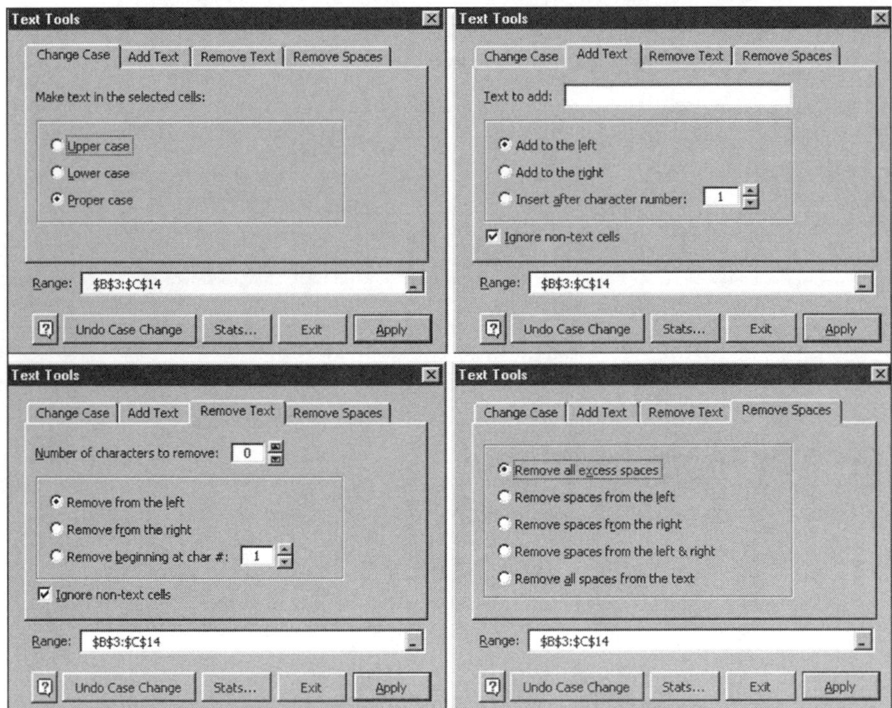

Figure 15-2: The FormMain UserForm contains a MultiPage control with four pages.

The controls contained in the MultiPage control are very straightforward, so I won't explain them (you can refer to the code for details). The MainForm dialog box also contains additional controls outside of the MultiPage control.

- *A RefEdit control.* The UserForm_Initialize procedure displays the address of the current range selection. And, of course, the user can select a different range at any time.
- *Help button.* This is a CommandButton control that displays an image. Clicking the button displays the FormHelp UserForm.
- *Undo button.* Clicking this button reverses the effect of the most recent text manipulation.
- *Stats button.* Clicking this CommandButton displays a message box that shows key statistics for the text in the selected cells.
- *Exit button.* Clicking this CommandButton unloads the UserForm.
- *Apply button.* Clicking this CommandButton applies the text manipulation options specified in the current page of the MultiPage control.

You may notice that this utility violates one of my design "rules" outlined earlier in this chapter (see "What Makes a Good Utility?"). Unlike most of Excel's built-in dialog boxes, the MainForm dialog box does not have an OK or Cancel button, and clicking the Apply button does *not* dismiss the dialog box. The original version of Text Tools had an OK button and was designed so that clicking OK performed the task and closed the dialog box. User feedback, however, convinced me to change the design. Many people, it turns out, like to perform several different manipulations at one time. Invoking the Text Tools dialog box multiple times was not efficient.

The modMain module

The modMain module contains a simple procedure that kicks off the utility.

Declarations

Listed below are the declarations at the top of the modMain module.

```
Public Const APPNAME As String = "Text Tools"

'Custom data type for undoing
Type OrigData
    OldText As Variant
    Address As String
End Type
```

I declare a public constant containing a string that stores the name of the application. This string is used in the message boxes and is also used as the Caption for the menu item that's created (see "Create menu and delete menu procedures" later in this chapter).

I also create a custom data type named OrigData. As you'll see, this data type is used to store information so an operation can be undone.

The StartTextTools procedure

The StartTextTools procedure is listed below.

```
Sub StartTextTools()
  If ValidContext(True, True, False, False, False, True) Then _
     FormMain.Show
End Sub
```

As you can see, it's rather simple. It calls a custom function Boolean (ValidContext) that determines whether the current context is appropriate for the utility. If ValidContext returns True, then the FormMain UserForm appears.

This function takes six arguments (each Boolean):

- VisWin. If True, the function determines whether at least one window is visible.
- Wksht. If True, the function determines whether a worksheet is active.
- RngSel. If True, the function determines whether a range is selected.
- MultSel. If True, the function determines whether the selected range is a multiple selection.
- Chart. If True, the function determines whether a chart or Chart sheet is selected.
- Prot. If True, the function determines whether the contents of the active sheet are protected.

The values of these arguments determine what gets checked by the ValidContext function. For example, if the first argument (VisWin) is True, the function checks to see whether at least one window is visible. If the second argument (Wksht) is True, the function checks to see whether a worksheet is active. If any of these requested checks come up negative, the ValidContext function does two things: It displays a message box that describes the problem (see Figure 15-3) and returns False to the calling procedure.

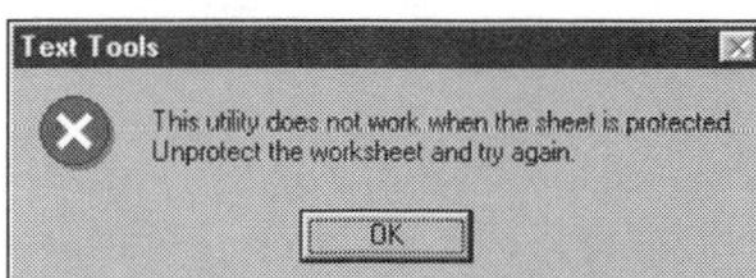

Figure 15-3: The ValidContext function displays this message if the worksheet is protected.

The Text Tools utility requests the following checks from the ValidContext function:

✦ VisWin. At least one window must be visible.

✦ Wksht. A worksheet must be active.

✦ Prot. The sheet may not be protected.

The Text Tools utility doesn't require a range selection; it uses the RangeSelection property to determine the selected range in the UserForm_Initialize procedure for FormMain. It also works well with a multiple range selection.

I wrote the ValidContext function to be a "general purpose" function that can be used in other applications. In other words, there is nothing in the function that makes it specific to the Text Tools utility.

The ValidContext function is shown in Listing 15-1.

Listing 15-1: Certifying that the utility can run in the current context of the worksheet

```
Function ValidContext(VisWin, Wksht, RngSel, MultSel, _
 Chart, Prot) As Boolean
    Dim VisWinCnt As Integer
    Dim Win As Window

    Const MsgVisWin As String = _
      "A workbook must be active in order to use this utility."
    Const MsgWksht As String = _
    "A worksheet must be active in order to use this utility."
    Const MsgRngSel As String = _
       "This utility requires a range selection." & vbCrLf & _
       "Select a range and try again."
    Const MsgMultSel As String = _
   "This utility does not allow a multiple range selection." _
       & vbCrLf & "Select a single range and try again."
    Const MsgChart As String = _
    "Select a chart or Chart sheet before using this utility."
    Const MsgProt As String = _
   "This utility does not work when the sheet is protected." _
     & vbCrLf & "Unprotect the worksheet and try again."

    ValidContext = True

'   Check for a visible window?
```

Continued

Listing 15-1 *(continued)*

```
    If VisWin Then
        VisWinCnt = 0
        For Each Win In Application.Windows
            If Win.Visible Then VisWinCnt = VisWinCnt + 1
        Next
        If VisWinCnt = 0 Then
            MsgBox MsgVisWin, vbCritical, APPNAME
            ValidContext = False
            Exit Function
        End If
    End If

'   Check for a worksheet?
    If Wksht Then
        If TypeName(ActiveSheet) <> "Worksheet" Then
            MsgBox MsgWksht, vbCritical, APPNAME
            ValidContext = False
            Exit Function
        End If
    End If

'   Check for a range selection?
    If RngSel Then
        If TypeName(Selection) <> "Range" Then
            MsgBox MsgRngSel, vbCritical, APPNAME
            ValidContext = False
            Exit Function
        End If
    End If

'   Check for multiple selection?
    If MultSel Then
        If TypeName(Selection) = "Range" Then
            If Selection.Areas.Count > 1 Then
                MsgBox MsgMultSel, vbCritical, APPNAME
                Exit Function
            End If
        End If
    End If

'   Check for a chart selection?
    If Chart Then
        If TypeName(ActiveSheet) <> "Chart" Then
            If TypeName(Selection) <> "Chart" Then
                If TypeName(Selection.Parent) <> "Chart" Then
                    If TypeName(Selection.Parent.Parent) <> _
                     "Chart" Then
                       MsgBox MsgChart, vbCritical, APPNAME
```

```
                        ValidContext = False
                        Exit Function
                    End If
                End If
            End If
        End If
    End If

'   Check for protected sheet?
    If Prot Then
        If ActiveSheet.ProtectContents Then
            MsgBox MsgProt, vbCritical, APPNAME
            ValidContext = False
            Exit Function
        End If
    End If
End Function
```

The ApplyButton_Click procedure

All work done by the Text Tools utility is performed by code contained in the code module for the `FormMain` object. The `ApplyButton_Click` procedure in Listing 15-2 is executed when the user clicks the Apply button.

Listing 15-2: Applying the chosen changes without dismissal of the dialog box

```
Private Sub ApplyButton_Click()
'   Perform the selected operation
    Dim i As Integer
    Dim WorkRange As Range

'   Validate Range reference
    If Not ValidReference(RefEdit1.Text) Then
        MsgBox "Invalid range.", vbInformation, APPNAME
        Application.ScreenUpdating = True
        With RefEdit1
            .SelStart = 0
            .SelLength = 100
            .SetFocus
        End With
        Exit Sub
    End If

'   Figure out what to do
```

Continued

Listing 15-2 *(continued)*

```
    Application.ScreenUpdating = False
    Select Case MultiPage1.Value
        Case 0: Call ChangeCaseTab
        Case 1: Call AddTextTab
        Case 2: Call RemoveTextTab
        Case 3: Call RemoveSpacesTab
    End Select
    Application.ScreenUpdating = True
End Sub
```

The `ApplyButton_Click` procedure is relatively simple. First, it calls a custom function (`ValidReference`) to determine whether the RefEdit control contains a valid range address. If not, it displays a message, selects the text in the RefEdit control, and makes a quick exit.

The `ValidReference` function is listed below. This function returns True if its single argument contains a valid range reference. It relies on the fact that VBA generates an error when you try to create an invalid `Range` object.

```
Function ValidReference(ref)
'   Returns True if ref is a valid range reference
    Dim x As Range
    On Error Resume Next
    Set x = Range(ref)
    If Err = 0 Then ValidReference = True _
       Else ValidReference = False
End Function
```

The reason that the `ApplyButton_Click` procedure is so short is because it calls other procedures, depending on the value of the MultiPage control. And, the value of the MultiPage control determines which task the user is requesting. (Remember, the first page of a MultiPage control has a value of 0, not 1.) These "task" procedures are described and listed in the following section.

Notice that the `ApplyButton_Click` procedure does not unload the UserForm. Therefore, the user can perform other text manipulations. Clicking the Exit button is the only way to unload the form. The Click event handler for this button is listed below.

```
Private Sub ExitButton_Click()
    Unload Me
End Sub
```

The "task" procedures

In this section, I describe the four procedures that actually perform the work for the Text Tools utility.

Changing the case of text

The first page of the MultiPage control (see Figure 15-4) enables the user to change the case of text in the selected cells. The text can be converted to *UPPERCASE, lowercase,* or *Proper Case.*

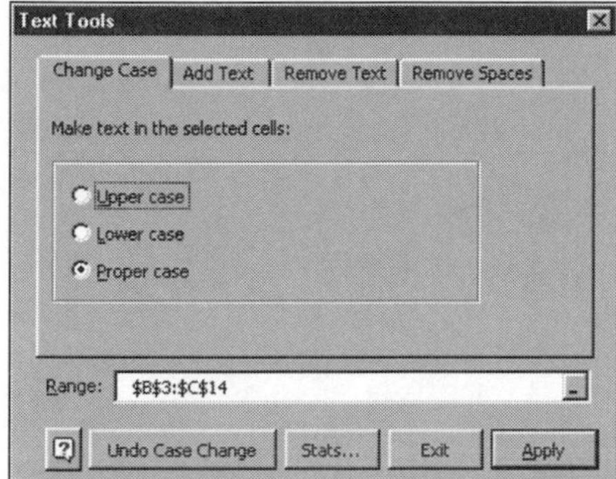

Figure 15-4: This page enables the user to change the case of text.

The `ApplyButton_Click` procedure calls the `ChangeCaseTab` procedure if the MultiPage's `Value` property is 0 (that is, the first page is active). Listing 15-3 shows the complete `ChangeCaseTab` procedure.

Listing 15-3: Altering the case of text in cells

```
Sub ChangeCaseTab()
    Dim WorkRange As Range
    Dim Cell As Range
    Dim CellCount As Long

    Set WorkRange = CreateWorkRange(Range(RefEdit1.Text), _
     True)
    If WorkRange Is Nothing Then Exit Sub

    CellCount = 0
```

Continued

Listing 15-3 *(continued)*

```
    ReDim LocalUndo(CellCount)

'   Process the cells
    For Each Cell In WorkRange
'       Store info for undoing
        CellCount = CellCount + 1
        ReDim Preserve LocalUndo(CellCount)
        LocalUndo(CellCount).OldText = Cell.Value
        LocalUndo(CellCount).Address = Cell.Address

'       Change the case
        Select Case True
            Case ChangeCaseProper
                Cell.Value = Application.Proper(Cell.Value)
            Case ChangeCaseUpper
                Cell.Value = UCase(Cell.Value)
            Case ChangeCaseLower
                Cell.Value = LCase(Cell.Value)
            End Select
    Next Cell

'   Update the Undo button
    UndoButton.Enabled = True
    UndoButton.Caption = "Undo Case Change"
End Sub
```

A key element in this procedure is the creation of a `Range` object named `WorkRange`. The `WorkRange` object contains a subset of the user's range selection that consists of only the nonempty cells that contain text and not a formula. If no cell qualifies, the function returns `Nothing`.

If the Ignore nontext cells `CheckBox` is not checked, then WorkRange also includes the cells that contain values.

The `CreateWorkRange` function (which creates and returns a `Range` object) accepts two arguments.

`r`	A `Range` object. In this case, it's the range selected by the user and displayed in the RefEdit control.
`TextOnly`	If True, the created object excludes nontext cells.

The `CreateWorkRange` function in Listing 15-4 is a general purpose function that is not specific to the Text Tools utility.

Listing 15-4: Blocking off a segment of text-only cells

```
Function CreateWorkRange(r As Range, TextOnly As Boolean) As
Range
'   Creates a range object that consists of nonempty and
'   nonformula cells. If TextOnly is True, the object
'   excludes numeric cells

    Set CreateWorkRange = Nothing
    Select Case r.Count
        Case 1 ' one cell is selected
            If r.HasFormula Then Exit Function
            If TextOnly Then
                If IsNumeric(r.Value) Then
                    Exit Function
                Else
                    Set CreateWorkRange = r
                End If
            Else
                If Not IsEmpty(r) Then Set CreateWorkRange = r
            End If

        Case Else 'More than one cell is selected
            On Error Resume Next
            If TextOnly Then
                Set CreateWorkRange = _
                  r.SpecialCells(xlConstants, xlTextValues)
                If Err <> 0 Then Exit Function
            Else
                Set CreateWorkRange = _
                  r.SpecialCells(xlConstants, xlTextValues _
                    + xlNumbers)
                If Err <> 0 Then Exit Function
            End If
    End Select
End Function
```

The `CreateWorkRange` function makes heavy use of the `SpecialCells` property. To learn more about the `SpecialCells` property, try recording a macro while making various selections in Excel's Go To Special dialog box. You can display this dialog box by pressing F5 and then clicking the Special button in the Go To dialog box.

You'll notice a quirk when you use the Go To Special dialog box. Normally, it operates on the current range selection. For example, if an entire column is selected, then the result is a subset of that column. But if a single cell is selected, it operates on the entire worksheet. Because of this, the CreateWorkRange function checks the number of cells in the range passed to it.

Once the WorkRange object is created, the ChangeCaseTab procedure continues to process each cell in the WorkRange. Before the procedure ends, it enables the Undo button and adds a descriptive caption.

Later in this chapter, I discuss how the Undo feature works.

Adding text

The second page of the MultiPage control (see Figure 15-5) enables the user to add text to the contents of the selected cells. The text can be added at the beginning, at the end, or after a specified character position.

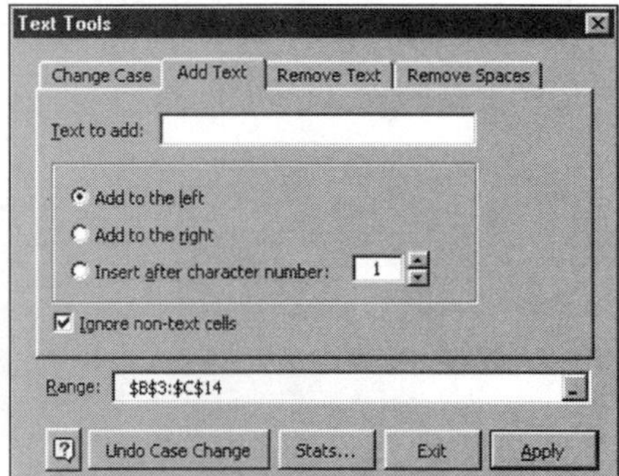

Figure 15-5: This page enables the user to add text to the contents of the selected cells.

The ApplyButton_Click procedure calls the AddTextTab procedure if the MultiPage's Value is 1 (that is, the second page is active). Listing 15-5 presents the complete AddTextTab procedure.

Listing 15-5: Inserting properly filtered text into cells by way of the dialog box

```
Sub AddTextTab()
   Dim WorkRange As Range
    Dim Cell As Range
    Dim NewText As String
    Dim InsPos As Integer
```

```
    Dim CellCount As Long

    Set WorkRange = _
      CreateWorkRange(Range(RefEdit1.Text), cbIgnoreNonText1)
    If WorkRange Is Nothing Then Exit Sub

    NewText = TextToAdd.Text
    If NewText = "" Then Exit Sub

'   Check for potential invalid formulas
    If OptionAddToLeft And Left(NewText, 1) Like "[=+-]" _
     Then MsgBox _
     "Adding that text would create an invalid formula.", _
     vbInformation, APPNAME
        With TextToAdd
            .SelStart = 0
            .SelLength = Len(.Text)
            .SetFocus
        End With
        Exit Sub
    End If

'   Add text to the middle?
    If OptionAddToMiddle Then
        InsPos = Val(InsertPos.Caption)
        If InsPos = 0 Then Exit Sub
    End If

'   Loop through the cells
    CellCount = 0
    ReDim LocalUndo(CellCount)
    For Each Cell In WorkRange
      With Cell
'       Store info for undoing
        CellCount = CellCount + 1
        ReDim Preserve LocalUndo(CellCount)
        With LocalUndo(CellCount)
            .OldText = Cell.Value
            .Address = Cell.Address
        End With

        If OptionAddToLeft Then .Value = NewText & .Value
        If OptionAddToRight Then .Value = .Value & NewText
        If OptionAddToMiddle Then
            If InsPos > Len(.Value) Then
                .Value = .Value & NewText
            Else
                .Value = Left(.Value, InsPos) & NewText & _
                   Right(.Value, Len(.Value) - InsPos)
```

Continued

Listing 15-5 *(continued)*

```
                End If
            End If
          End With
        Next Cell

'       Update the Undo button
        UndoButton.Enabled = True
        UndoButton.Caption = "Undo Add Text"
    End Sub
```

This procedure is similar in structure to `ChangeCaseTab`. Notice that this procedure catches an error that would occur if the user tries to insert a plus (+), minus (–), or equal (=) sign as the first character of a cell. Such an insertion would cause Excel to interpret the cell contents as an invalid formula.

Removing text

The third page of the MultiPage control (see Figure 15-6) enables the user to remove text from the selected cells. A specific number of characters can be removed from the beginning or end, or starting at a specified character position.

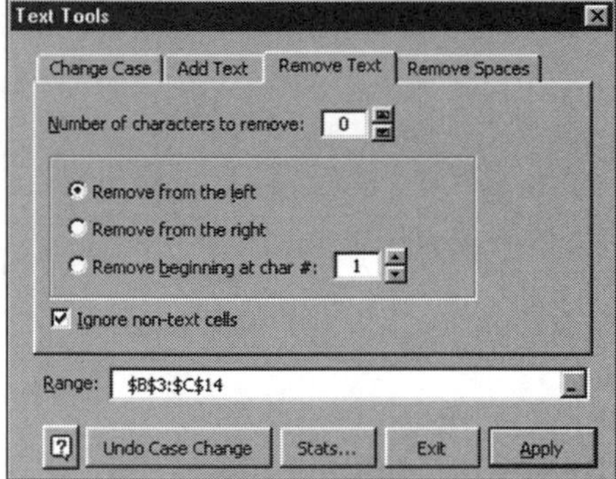

Figure 15-6: This page enables the user to remove characters from the selected text.

The `ApplyButton_Click` procedure calls the `RemoveTextTab` procedure if the MultiPage's `Value` property is 2 (that is, the third page is active). Listing 15-6 presents the complete `RemoveTextTab` procedure.

Listing 15-6: Removing text from cells by way of the dialog box

```
Sub RemoveTextTab()
    Dim WorkRange As Range
    Dim Cell As Range
    Dim NumToDel As Integer
    Dim CellCount As Long

    Set WorkRange = _
      CreateWorkRange(Range(RefEdit1.Text), cbIgnoreNonText2)
    If WorkRange Is Nothing Then Exit Sub

    NumToDel = Val(CharstoDelete.Caption)
    If NumToDel = 0 Then Exit Sub

'   Process the cells
    ReDim LocalUndo(0)
    CellCount = 0
    For Each Cell In WorkRange
      With Cell
'       Store info for undoing
        CellCount = CellCount + 1
        ReDim Preserve LocalUndo(CellCount)
        LocalUndo(CellCount).OldText = .Value
        LocalUndo(CellCount).Address = .Address

        If Len(Cell.Value) <= NumToDel Then
          NumToDel = Len(.Value)
        Select Case True
            Case OptionDeleteFromLeft
                .Value = Right(.Value, Len(.Value) - NumToDel)
            Case OptionDeleteFromRight
                .Value = Left(.Value, Len(.Value) - NumToDel)
            Case OptionDeleteFromMiddle
                .Value = RemoveChars(.Value, _
                 CInt(BeginChar.Caption), NumToDel)
        End Select
      End With
    Next Cell

'   Update the Undo button
    UndoButton.Enabled = True
    UndoButton.Caption = "Undo Remove Text"
End Sub
```

The RemoveTextTab procedure is, again, similar in structure to the other procedures called by ApplyButton_Click. If the characters are to be removed from the middle of the text, it calls a Function procedure, RemoveChars, to do the work.

The RemoveChars Function procedure is shown below. This procedure removes a specified number of characters (n), beginning at a specified character position (b) from a string (t).

```
Private Function RemoveChars(t, b, n) As String
    Dim k As Integer
    Dim Temp As String
    Temp = ""
    For k = 1 To Len(t)
        If k < b Or k >= b + n Then
            Temp = Temp & Mid(t, k, 1)
        End If
    Next k
    RemoveChars = Temp
End Function
```

Removing spaces

The fourth page of the MultiPage control (see Figure 15-7) enables the user to remove spaces from the selected cells.

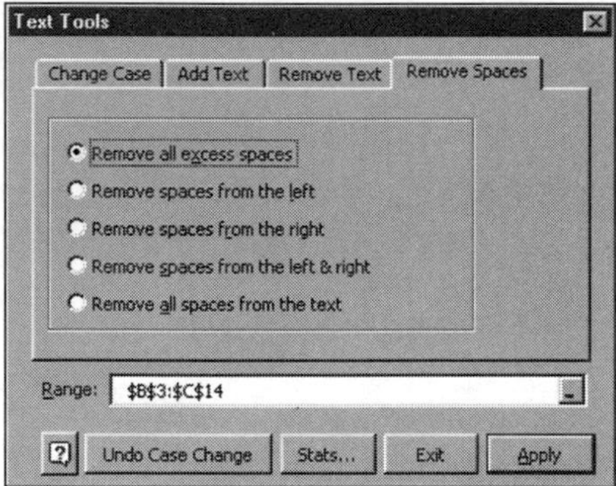

Figure 15-7: This page enables the user to remove spaces from the selected text.

The ApplyButton_Click procedure calls the RemoveSpacesTab procedure if the MultiPage's value is 3 (that is, the fourth page is active). Listing 15-7 shows the complete RemoveSpacesTab procedure.

Listing 15-7: Filtering unnecessary spaces from textual cells

```
Sub RemoveSpacesTab()
    Dim WorkRange As Range
    Dim Cell As Range
    Dim CellCount As Long

    Set WorkRange = CreateWorkRange _
     (Range(RefEdit1.Text), True)
    If WorkRange Is Nothing Then Exit Sub

'   Process the cells
    CellCount = 0
    ReDim LocalUndo(CellCount)

    For Each Cell In WorkRange
      With Cell
'       Store info for undoing
        CellCount = CellCount + 1
        ReDim Preserve LocalUndo(CellCount)
        LocalUndo(CellCount).OldText = .Value
        LocalUndo(CellCount).Address = .Address
        Select Case True
            Case OptionRemoveExcess
                .Value = _
                 Application.WorksheetFunction.Trim(.Value)
            Case OptionRemoveLeft
                .Value = LTrim(.Value)
            Case OptionRemoveRight
                .Value = RTrim(.Value)
            Case OptionRemoveBoth
                .Value = Trim(.Value)
            Case OptionRemoveAllSpaces
                .Value = RemoveSpaces(.Value)
        End Select
      End With
    Next Cell

'   Update the Undo button
    UndoButton.Enabled = True
    UndoButton.Caption = "Undo Remove Spaces"
```

Notice that the first option (Remove all excess spaces) uses an Excel worksheet function. The second and third options use VBA functions. The final option (Remove all spaces from the text) uses a custom function, listed next.

```
Private Function RemoveSpaces(t) As String
'   Removes all spaces from a string
    Dim NumChars As Integer
    Dim i As Integer
    NumChars = Len(t)
    RemoveSpaces = ""
    For i = 1 To NumChars
        If Mid(t, i, 1) <> " " Then _
          RemoveSpaces = RemoveSpaces & Mid(t, i, 1)
    Next i
End Function
```

The undo technique

Unlike Excel's Undo feature, the undo technique used in the Text Tools utility is a single level. In other words, the user can undo only the most recent operation. Refer to the sidebar "Undoing a VBA Procedure" for additional information about using Undo with your applications.

In the Text Tools utility, recall that the `modMain` VBA module declared a custom data type named OrigData. This declaration is as follows:

```
Type OrigData
    OldText As Variant
    Address As String
End Type
```

The OrigData data type consists of two elements: `OldText` (contains the previous cell contents) and `Address` (the range address of the cell).

Each of the four "task" procedures creates an array (named `LocalUndo`) of type OrigData. Then before each cell is modified, the following code is executed:

```
'   Store info for undoing
    CellCount = CellCount + 1
    ReDim Preserve LocalUndo(CellCount)
    LocalUndo(CellCount).OldText = .Value
    LocalUndo(CellCount).Address = .Address
```

The last step in each of these four procedures updates the Undo button on the `FormMain` UserForm. For example, the code in the `RemoveTextTab` procedures is as follows:

```
'   Update the Undo button
    UndoButton.Enabled = True
    UndoButton.Caption = "Undo Remove Text"
```

When each of these procedures finishes, the LocalUndo array is filled with data that contains, for each cell, its previous contents and its address. If the user clicks the Undo button, the UndoButton_Click procedure is executed. This procedure is listed below.

```
Private Sub UndoButton_Click()
    Dim i As Integer
    Application.ScreenUpdating = False

'   Restore the previous contents
    For i = 1 To UBound(LocalUndo)
        Range(LocalUndo(i).Address).Value =
LocalUndo(i).OldText
    Next i
    Application.ScreenUpdating = True

'   Update the Undo button
    UndoButton.Caption = "Undo"
    UndoButton.Enabled = False
End Sub
```

This procedure simply loops through the LocalUndo array and inserts the previous contents of each cell.

Undoing a VBA Procedure

Computer users have become accustomed to the ability to "undo" an operation. Almost every operation you perform in Excel can be undone. Even better, beginning with Excel 97, the program features multiple levels of undo.

If you program in VBA, you may have wondered whether it's possible to undo the effects of a procedure. The answer is *yes*. The qualified answer is *it's not always easy.*

Making the effects of your procedures undoable isn't automatic. Your procedure needs to store the previous state so that it can be restored if the user chooses the Edit⇨Undo command. How you do this can vary depending on what the procedure does. In extreme cases, you might need to save an entire worksheet. If your procedure modifies a range, for example, you need to save only the contents of that range.

The Application object contains an OnUndo method, which lets the programmer specify text to appear on the Edit⇨Undo menu, and a procedure to execute if the user selects Edit⇨Undo. For example, the statement below causes the Undo menu item to display "Undo my cool macro." If the user selects Edit⇨Undo my cool macro, the UndoMyMacro procedure is executed.

```
Application.OnUndo "Undo my cool macro", "UndoMyMacro"
```

The companion CD-ROM contains an example that demonstrates how to enable the Edit⇨Undo command after a VBA procedure is executed.

The ShowStats procedure

Clicking the Stats button displays a message box that contains information about the contents of the selected cells. Figure 15-8 shows an example.

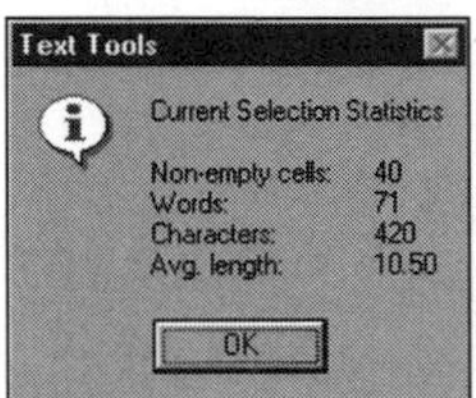

Figure 15-8: Clicking the Status button shows a message box like this one.

Listing 15-8 shows the complete event handler for the statistics procedure.

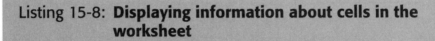

Listing 15-8: Displaying information about cells in the worksheet

```
Private Sub StatsButton_Click()
'   Displays statistics about the selection
    Dim WorkRange As Range
    Dim NumWords As Integer
    Dim NumChars As Integer
    Dim CellLength As Integer
    Dim NonBlanks As Integer
    Dim Cell As Range
    Dim Msg As String
    Dim Words As Integer
    Dim Contents As String
    Dim i As Integer

'   Validate range reference
    If Not ValidReference(RefEdit1.Text) Then
        MsgBox "Invalid range.", vbInformation, APPNAME
        With RefEdit1
            .SelStart = 0
            .SelLength = 100
            .SetFocus
        End With
        Exit Sub
    End If
```

```
        Set WorkRange = CreateWorkRange(Range(RefEdit1.Text), _
         True)
        If WorkRange Is Nothing Then
            MsgBox _
           "The range contains no nonformula cells with text.", _
             vbInformation, APPNAME
            Exit Sub
        End If

        NonBlanks = WorkRange.Count
        NumWords = 0
        NumChars = 0
        For Each Cell In WorkRange
            CellLength = Len(Cell.Value)
            NumChars = NumChars + CellLength
            Contents = Application.Trim(Cell.Value)
            Words = 1
            For i = 1 To Len(Contents)
                If Mid(Contents, i, 1) = " " Then _
                 Words = Words + 1
            Next i
            If Len(Contents) = 0 Then Words = 0 'Accounts for
                                                ' empty cells
            NumWords = NumWords + Words
        Next Cell
        Msg = "Current Selection Statistics" & vbCrLf & vbCrLf
        Msg = Msg & "Nonempty cells:" & Chr(9) & NonBlanks _
         & Chr(13)
        Msg = Msg & "Words:" & Chr(9) & Chr(9) & NumWords _
         & Chr(13)
        Msg = Msg & "Characters:" & Chr(9) & NumChars & Chr(13)
        Msg = Msg & "Avg. length:" & Chr(9) & Format(NumChars _
         / NonBlanks, "#.00")
        MsgBox Msg, vbInformation, APPNAME
        Exit Sub
    End Sub
```

The `ShowStats` procedure is lengthy but quite straightforward. Notice that this procedure validates the range reference (displayed in the RefEdit control) and displays an error if it contains an invalid range.

User help technique

There are many ways to provide online help. The Text Tools utility uses a simple technique that reads text stored in a worksheet. Column A contains the help topics, and column B contains the help text. The help topics are read into a ComboBox control, and the help topics are displayed in a Label control.

Chapter 23 describes this method (and others) of providing user help.

Figure 15-9 shows how the help dialog box (contained in `FormHelp`) looks when the user clicks the Help button on the `FormMain` UserForm.

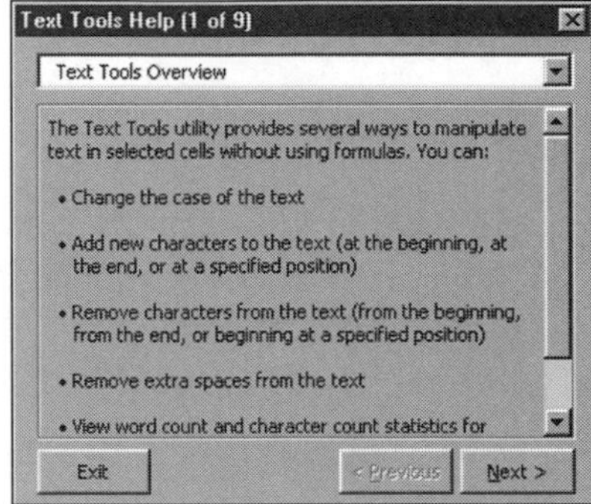

Figure 15-9: User help is displayed in a UserForm with a ComboBox and a Label control.

Create menu and delete menu procedures

The only element of Text Tools that I haven't discussed is the menu item used to invoke the utility. When the workbook opens, its `Workbook_Open` procedure (located in the `ThisWorkbook` object module) is executed. This procedure is very simple:

```
Private Sub Workbook_Open()
    Call CreateMenu
End Sub
```

The `Workbook_BeforeClose` procedure is equally simple:

```
Private Sub Workbook_BeforeClose(Cancel As Boolean)
    Call DeleteMenu
End Sub
```

The `CreateMenu` and `DeleteMenu` procedures are located in the `modMenus` VBA module. `CreateMenu` adds a new menu item to the Tools menu, and the `DeleteMenu` procedure removes that menu item. You can examine this code on your own.

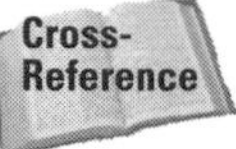

Refer to Chapter 22 for detailed information on menu manipulation techniques.

Evaluation of the project

The previous sections described each component of the Text Tools utility. At this point, it's useful to revisit the original project goals to see whether they were met. The original goals, along with my comments, appear below.

- ✦ *It will have the same look and feel of other Excel commands. In other words, it will have a dialog box that looks like Excel's dialog boxes.* As I noted earlier, the Text Tools utility deviates from Excel's normal look and feel by using an Apply button rather than an OK button. In light of the enhanced usability, I think this is quite reasonable.
- ✦ *It will be accessible from the Tools menu.* Accomplished.
- ✦ *It will operate with the current selection of cells (including multiple selections), and it will enable the user to modify the range selection while the dialog box is displayed.* Accomplished.
- ✦ *Its main features will consist of tools to change the case of text, add new text to the strings, delete a fixed number of characters from the text, and remove spaces from the text in each cell.* Accomplished.
- ✦ *It also will enable the user to display key statistics about the selected cells.* Accomplished.
- ✦ *It will enable the user to request the preceding types of changes on nontext cells as well as text cells.* Accomplished.
- ✦ *It will have no effect on cells that contain formulas.* Accomplished.
- ✦ *It will be fast and efficient. For example, if the user selects an entire range, the utility should ignore empty cells.* Accomplished.
- ✦ *It will enable the user to undo the changes.* Accomplished, but in a nonstandard way.
- ✦ *It will have online help available.* Accomplished, but in a nonstandard way.

Understand the Text Tools utility

If you don't fully understand how this utility works, I urge you to load the workbook and use the Debugger to step through the code. Try it out with different types of selections, including an entire worksheet. You will see that, regardless of the size of the original selection, only the appropriate cells are processed and empty cells are completely ignored. If a worksheet has only one cell with text in it, the utility operates just as quickly whether you select that cell or the entire worksheet.

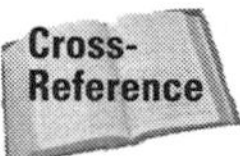

For the best results, you might want to convert the Text Tools utility workbook to an add-in. Refer to Chapter 20 for more information about creating add-ins.

More About Excel Utilities

I wrap up this chapter with a few closing words about Excel utilities.

Acquiring more utilities

You can use the coupon in the back of this book to order a free copy of my Power Utility Pak (see Figure 15-10). This product includes several dozen useful utilities (plus many custom worksheet functions). The complete VBA source code also is available for a small fee. You can get a feel for how the product works by installing the shareware version, available on the companion CD-ROM.

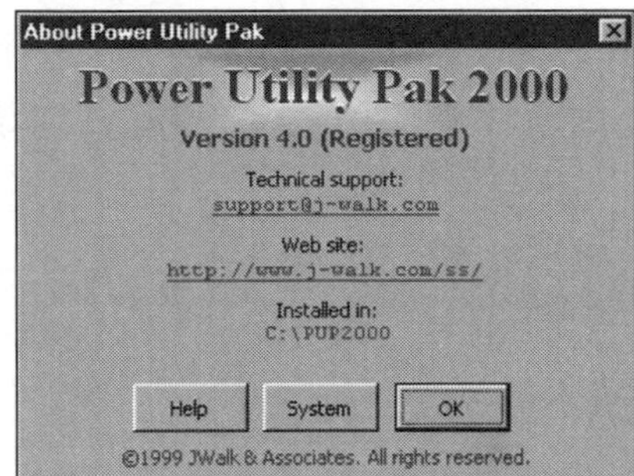

Figure 15-10: The author's Power Utility Pak contains many useful Excel utilities.

In addition to Power Utility Pak, several other utility packages exist, and they can be downloaded from the Internet. A good starting point for locating additional Web utilities is my Web site. Visit The Spreadsheet Page at `http://www.j-walk.com/ss`.

Summary

In this chapter, I discussed why you might want to develop Excel utilities with VBA. I also presented and explained the VBA code for my Text Tools utility. As you gain more experience with programming Excel, you'll probably have some ideas for creating your own utilities. This chapter should provide you with enough background information to give you a jump-start.

In the next chapter, I discuss various ways to use VBA to create and manipulate pivot tables.

✦ ✦ ✦

Working with Pivot Tables

In This Chapter

What you need to know to create pivot tables with VBA

Examples of VBA procedures that create pivot tables

One example of how to use VBA to modify an existing pivot table

Excel's pivot table feature is, arguably, its most innovative and powerful feature. Pivot tables first appeared in Excel 5, and the feature remains unique to Excel — no other spreadsheet has anything that comes close to it. As you probably know, creating a pivot table from a database or list enables you to summarize data in ways that otherwise would not be possible — and it's amazingly fast. You also can write VBA code to generate and modify pivot tables.

New Feature

Excel's pivot table feature has been significantly enhanced in Excel 2000. It uses more efficient data caching, and it also supports PivotCharts. A PivotChart is a chart linked to a pivot table. Therefore, if you develop applications for both Excel 97 and Excel 2000, make sure you don't use any of the new pivot table features.

This chapter assumes that you're familiar with pivot tables and understand how to create and modify them manually.

An Introductory Example

This section gets the ball rolling with a simple example of using VBA to create a pivot table.

Figure 16-1 shows a very simple worksheet database. It contains four fields: `SalesRep`, `Region`, `Month`, and `Sales`. Each record describes the sales for a particular sales representative in a particular month.

SalesRep	Region	Month	Sales
Amy	North	Jan	33,488
Amy	North	Feb	47,008
Amy	North	Mar	32,128
Bob	North	Jan	34,736
Bob	North	Feb	92,872
Bob	North	Mar	76,128
Chuck	South	Jan	41,536
Chuck	South	Feb	23,192
Chuck	South	Mar	21,736
Doug	South	Jan	44,834
Doug	South	Feb	32,002
Doug	South	Mar	23,932

Figure 16-1: This simple database is a good candidate for a pivot table.

Creating a pivot table

Figure 16-2 shows a pivot table created from the data. This pivot table summarizes the sales by sales representative and month. This pivot table is set up with the following fields.

`Region`	A page field in the pivot table
`SalesRep`	A row field in the pivot table
`Month`	A column field in the pivot table
`Sales`	A data field in the pivot table that uses the `SUM` function

Region	(All)			
Sum of Sales	Month			
SalesRep	Jan	Feb	Mar	Grand Total
Amy	33488	47008	32128	112624
Bob	34736	92872	76128	203736
Chuck	41536	23192	21736	86464
Doug	44834	32002	23932	100768
Grand Total	154594	195074	153924	503592

Figure 16-2: A pivot table created from the data in Figure 16-1.

I had the macro recorder turned on as I created this pivot table. The code that I generated is listed here.

```
Sub Macro1()
    Range("A1").Select
    ActiveWorkbook.PivotCaches.Add(SourceType:=xlDatabase, _
     SourceData:="Sheet1!R1C1:R13C4").CreatePivotTable _
     TableDestination:="", _
     TableName:="PivotTable1"
    ActiveSheet.PivotTableWizard _
     TableDestination:=ActiveSheet.Cells(3, 1)
    ActiveSheet.Cells(3, 1).Select
    ActiveSheet.PivotTables("PivotTable1").SmallGrid = False
    With ActiveSheet.PivotTables("PivotTable1") _
      .PivotFields("Region")
        .Orientation = xlPageField
        .Position = 1
    End With
    With ActiveSheet.PivotTables("PivotTable1") _
      .PivotFields("Month")
        .Orientation = xlColumnField
        .Position = 1
    End With
    With ActiveSheet.PivotTables("PivotTable1") _
      .PivotFields("SalesRep")
        .Orientation = xlRowField
        .Position = 1
    End With
    With ActiveSheet.PivotTables("PivotTable1") _
      .PivotFields("Sales")
        .Orientation = xlDataField
        .Position = 1
    End With
End Sub
```

How the macro recorder generates code for you depends on how you built the pivot table. In the preceding example, I created a pivot table, which was empty until I dragged in the fields from the PivotTable toolbar. The alternate method is to click the Layout button in the second step of the PivotTable Wizard and lay out the pivot table before it's created.

You can, of course, execute the recorded macro to create another *identical* pivot table. If you do this, make sure the sheet with the data is active when you execute the macro.

Examining the recorded code

VBA code that works with pivot tables can be confusing. To make any sense of the recorded macro, you need to know about a few relevant objects, all of which are thoroughly explained in the online help.

`PivotCaches`	A collection of `PivotCache` objects in a `Workbook` object
`PivotTables`	A collection of `PivotTable` objects in a `Worksheet` object
`PivotTableFields`	A collection of fields in a `PivotTable` object
`CreatePivotTable`	A `PivotCache` object method that creates a pivot table using the data in a pivot cache
`PivotTableWizard`	A `Worksheet` object method that creates a pivot table. As you'll see in the next section, this method isn't necessary.

Cleaning up the recorded code

As with most recorded macros, the preceding example is not as efficient as it could be. It can be simplified to make it more understandable. Listing 16-1 generates the same pivot table as the procedure previously listed.

Listing 16-1: A more efficient way to generate a pivot table in VBA

```
Sub CreatePivotTable()
    Dim PTCache As PivotCache
    Dim PT As PivotTable

    Set PTCache = ActiveWorkbook.PivotCaches.Add _
        (SourceType:=xlDatabase, _
         SourceData:=Range("A1").CurrentRegion.Address)

    Set PT = PTCache.CreatePivotTable _
        (TableDestination:="", _
         TableName:="PivotTable1")

    With PT
        .PivotFields("Region").Orientation = xlPageField
        .PivotFields("Month").Orientation = xlColumnField
        .PivotFields("SalesRep").Orientation = xlRowField
        .PivotFields("Sales").Orientation = xlDataField
    End With
End Sub
```

The `CreatePivotTable` procedure is simplified (and may be easier to understand) because it declares two object variables: `PTCache` and `PT`. These take the place of the indexed references to `ActiveSheet.PivotCaches` and `ActiveSheet.PivotTables`. A new `PivotCache` object is created using the `Add` method. Then a new `PivotTable` object is created using the `CreatePivotTable` method of the `PivotCaches` collection. The last section of the code adds the fields to the pivot table and specifies their location within it (page, column, row, or data field).

Notice that the original macro "hard coded" the data range used to create the `PivotCache` object. In the `CreatePivotTable` procedure, the pivot table is based on the current region surrounding Cell A1. This ensures that the macro will continue to work properly when more data is added.

The code also could be more general through the use of indices rather than literal strings for the `PivotFields` collections. This way, if the user changes the column headings, the code will still work.

As always, the best way to master this topic is to record your actions within a macro to find out its relevant objects, methods, and properties. Then study the online help topics to understand how everything fits together. In almost every case you'll need to modify the recorded macros. Or, once you understand how to work with pivot tables, you can write code from scratch and avoid the macro recorder.

Creating a More Complex Pivot Table

In this section, I present VBA code to create a relatively complex pivot table.

The data

Figure 16-3 shows the first portion of the pivot table. The worksheet that contains this table holds 15,840 rows containing hierarchical budget data for a corporation. There are five divisions, and each division contains eleven departments. Each department has four budget categories, and each budget category contains several budget items. Budgeted and actual amounts are included for each of the twelve months.

This workbook is available on the companion CD-ROM.

The pivot table

Figure 16-4 shows a pivot table created from the data. Notice that the pivot table contains a calculated field named `Variance`, plus four calculated items, Q1, Q2, Q3, and Q4, which calculate quarterly totals.

budget.xls

	A	B	C	D	E	F	G
1	DIVISION	DEPARTMENT	CATEGORY	ITEM	MONTH	BUDGET	ACTUAL
2	N. America	Data Processing	Compensation	Salaries	Jan	2583	3165
3	N. America	Data Processing	Compensation	Benefits	Jan	4496	2980
4	N. America	Data Processing	Compensation	Bonuses	Jan	3768	3029
5	N. America	Data Processing	Compensation	Commissions	Jan	3133	2815
6	N. America	Data Processing	Compensation	Payroll Taxes	Jan	3559	3770
7	N. America	Data Processing	Compensation	Training	Jan	3099	3559
8	N. America	Data Processing	Compensation	Conferences	Jan	2931	3199
9	N. America	Data Processing	Compensation	Entertainment	Jan	2632	2633
10	N. America	Data Processing	Facility	Rent	Jan	2833	2508
11	N. America	Data Processing	Facility	Lease	Jan	3450	2631
12	N. America	Data Processing	Facility	Utilities	Jan	4111	3098
13	N. America	Data Processing	Facility	Maintenance	Jan	3070	2870
14	N. America	Data Processing	Facility	Telephone	Jan	3827	4329
15	N. America	Data Processing	Facility	Other	Jan	3843	3322
16	N. America	Data Processing	Supplies & Services	General Office	Jan	2642	3218
17	N. America	Data Processing	Supplies & Services	Computer Supplies	Jan	3052	4098
18	N. America	Data Processing	Supplies & Services	Books & Subs	Jan	4346	3361
19	N. America	Data Processing	Supplies & Services	Outside Services	Jan	2869	3717
20	N. America	Data Processing	Supplies & Services	Other	Jan	3328	3116
21	N. America	Data Processing	Equipment	Computer Hardware	Jan	3088	2728
22	N. America	Data Processing	Equipment	Software	Jan	4226	2675
23	N. America	Data Processing	Equipment	Photocopiers	Jan	3780	3514
24	N. America	Data Processing	Equipment	Telecommunications	Jan	3893	3664
25	N. America	Data Processing	Equipment	Other	Jan	2851	4380
26	N. America	Human Resources	Compensation	Salaries	Jan	3604	3501
27	N. America	Human Resources	Compensation	Benefits	Jan	2859	4493

Sheet1

Figure 16-3: The data in this workbook will be summarized in a pivot table.

budget.xls

	A	B	C	D	E	F	G	H	I
1	DIVISION	(All)							
2									
3			MONTH						
4	DEPARTMENT	Data	Jan	Feb	Mar	Q1	Apr	May	Jun
5	Accounting	Budget ($)	422455	433317	420522	1276294	417964	411820	414
6		Actual ($)	422662	413163	416522	1252347	420672	431303	429
7		Variance ($)	-207	20154	4000	23947	-2708	-19483	-15
8	Advertising	Budget ($)	424590	419331	417949	1261870	420324	427150	424
9		Actual ($)	416008	420828	425437	1262273	417310	419996	428
10		Variance ($)	8582	-1497	-7488	-403	3014	7154	-4
11	Data Processing	Budget ($)	422197	422057	419659	1263913	417260	422848	421
12		Actual ($)	414743	438990	430545	1284278	424214	411775	421
13		Variance ($)	7454	-16933	-10886	-20365	-6954	11073	-
14	Human Resources	Budget ($)	422053	425313	418634	1266000	423038	423514	419
15		Actual ($)	424934	429275	407053	1261262	429187	410258	421
16		Variance ($)	-2881	-3962	11581	4738	-6149	13256	-2
17	Operations	Budget ($)	413530	427975	419527	1261032	422299	415298	414
18		Actual ($)	415819	406592	426827	1249238	418223	431307	413
19		Variance ($)	-2289	21383	-7300	11794	4076	-16009	1
20	Public Relations	Budget ($)	424896	414507	415179	1254582	417100	426223	408
21		Actual ($)	413526	414084	415476	1243086	414040	396652	416
22		Variance ($)	11370	423	-297	11496	3060	29571	-7
23	R&D	Budget ($)	417771	429880	424066	1271717	421539	417440	421
24		Actual ($)	432019	426644	419595	1278258	427567	412038	425
25		Variance ($)	-14248	3236	4471	-6541	-6028	5402	-4
26	Sales	Budget ($)	420659	421962	417814	1260435	420302	422409	426
27		Actual ($)	431565	421251	408661	1261477	408912	425620	428

PivotSheet Sheet1

Figure 16-4: A pivot table created from the data in Figure 16-3.

The code that created the pivot table

The VBA code that created the pivot table is shown in Listing 16-2.

Listing 16-2: Creating a compartmentalized pivot table

```
Sub CreatePivotTable()
    Dim PTCache As PivotCache
    Dim PT As PivotTable

    Application.ScreenUpdating = False

'   Delete PivotSheet if it exists
    On Error Resume Next
    Application.DisplayAlerts = False
    Sheets("PivotSheet").Delete
    On Error GoTo 0

'   Create a Pivot Cache
    Set PTCache = ActiveWorkbook.PivotCaches.Add( _
      SourceType:=xlDatabase, _
      SourceData:=Range("A1").CurrentRegion.Address)

'   Add new worksheet
    Worksheets.Add
    ActiveSheet.Name = "PivotSheet"

'   Create the Pivot Table from the Cache
    Set PT = PTCache.CreatePivotTable( _
      TableDestination:=Sheets("PivotSheet").Range("A1"), _
      TableName:="BudgetPivot")

    With PT
'       Add fields
        .PivotFields("DEPARTMENT").Orientation = xlRowField
        .PivotFields("MONTH").Orientation = xlColumnField
        .PivotFields("DIVISION").Orientation = xlPageField
        .PivotFields("BUDGET").Orientation = xlDataField
        .PivotFields("ACTUAL").Orientation = xlDataField

'       Add a calculated field to compute variance
        .CalculatedFields.Add "Variance", "=BUDGET-ACTUAL"
        .PivotFields("Variance").Orientation = xlDataField

'       Add calculated items
        .PivotFields("MONTH").CalculatedItems.Add _
          "Q1", "= Jan+Feb+Mar"
```

Continued

Listing 16-2 *(continued)*

```
        .PivotFields("MONTH").CalculatedItems.Add _
          "Q2", "= Apr+May+Jun"
        .PivotFields("MONTH").CalculatedItems.Add _
          "Q3", "= Jul+Aug+Sep"
        .PivotFields("MONTH").CalculatedItems.Add _
          "Q4", "= Oct+Nov+Dec"

'       Move the calculated items
        .PivotFields("MONTH").PivotItems("Q1").Position = 4
        .PivotFields("MONTH").PivotItems("Q2").Position = 8
        .PivotFields("MONTH").PivotItems("Q3").Position = 12
        .PivotFields("MONTH").PivotItems("Q4").Position = 16

'       Change the captions
        .PivotFields("Sum of BUDGET").Caption = "Budget ($)"
        .PivotFields("Sum of ACTUAL").Caption = "Actual ($)"
        .PivotFields("Sum of Variance").Caption = "Variance
($)"

    End With
    Application.ScreenUpdating = True
End Sub
```

How it works

The second `CreatePivotTable` procedure in Listing 16-2 starts by deleting the `PivotSheet` worksheet if it already exists. It then creates a `PivotCache` object, inserts a new worksheet named `PivotSheet`, and creates the pivot table. The code then adds the following fields to the pivot table.

`Department`	A row field
`Month`	A column field
`Division`	A page field
`Budget`	A data field
`Actual`	A data field

Next, the procedure uses the `Add` method of the `CalculatedFields` collection to create the calculated field `Variance`, which subtracts the `Actual` amount from the `Budget` amount. The code then adds four calculated items to compute the quarterly totals. By default, the calculated items are added to the right side of the pivot table, so additional code is required to move them adjacent to the months to which they refer (for example, Q1 is placed after March). Finally, the code changes the captions displayed in the pivot table. For example Sum of Budget is replaced by Budget ($).

I created this procedure by recording my actions while I created and modified the pivot table. Then I cleaned up the code to make it more readable and efficient.

Creating a Pivot Table from an External Database

In the preceding example, the source data was in a worksheet. As you probably know, Excel also enables you to use an external data source to create a pivot table. The example in this section demonstrates how to write VBA code to create a pivot table based on data stored in an Access 2000 database file (see Figure 16-5).

Microsoft Access - [Budget : Table]

File Edit View Insert Format Records Tools Window Help

DIVISION	DEPARTMENT	CATEGORY	ITEM	MONTH	BUDGET	ACTUAL
N. America	Data Processing	Compensation	Salaries	Jan	2583	3165
N. America	Data Processing	Compensation	Benefits	Jan	4496	2980
N. America	Data Processing	Compensation	Bonuses	Jan	3768	3029
N. America	Data Processing	Compensation	Commissions	Jan	3133	2815
N. America	Data Processing	Compensation	Payroll Taxes	Jan	3559	3770
N. America	Data Processing	Compensation	Training	Jan	3099	3559
N. America	Data Processing	Compensation	Conferences	Jan	2931	3199
N. America	Data Processing	Compensation	Entertainment	Jan	2632	2633
N. America	Data Processing	Facility	Rent	Jan	2833	2508
N. America	Data Processing	Facility	Lease	Jan	3450	2631
N. America	Data Processing	Facility	Utilities	Jan	4111	3098
N. America	Data Processing	Facility	Maintenance	Jan	3070	2870
N. America	Data Processing	Facility	Telephone	Jan	3827	4329
N. America	Data Processing	Facility	Other	Jan	3843	3322
N. America	Data Processing	Supplies & Serv	General Office	Jan	2642	3218
N. America	Data Processing	Supplies & Serv	Computer Supp	Jan	3052	4098
N. America	Data Processing	Supplies & Serv	Books & Subs	Jan	4346	3361
N. America	Data Processing	Supplies & Serv	Outside Service	Jan	2869	3717
N. America	Data Processing	Supplies & Serv	Other	Jan	3328	3116
N. America	Data Processing	Equipment	Computer Hardv	Jan	3088	2728
N. America	Data Processing	Equipment	Software	Jan	4226	2675
N. America	Data Processing	Equipment	Photocopiers	Jan	3780	3514

Record: 1 of 15840

Datasheet View

Figure 16-5: A pivot table will be created from this Access database table.

The database consists of a single table that is identical to the data used in the previous example.

The code that creates the pivot table is shown in Listing 16-3. It assumes that the budget.mdb database file is stored in the same directory as the workbook.

Listing 16-3: Generating a pivot table from an external database

```
Sub CreatePivotTableFromDB()
    Dim PTCache As PivotCache
    Dim PT As PivotTable

'   Delete PivotSheet if it exists
    On Error Resume Next
    Application.DisplayAlerts = False
    Sheets("PivotSheet").Delete
    On Error GoTo 0

'   Create a Pivot Cache
    Set PTCache = ActiveWorkbook.PivotCaches.Add _
      (SourceType:=xlExternal)

'   Connect to database, and do query
    DBFile = ThisWorkbook.Path & "\budget.mdb"
    ConString = "ODBC;DSN=MS Access Database;DBQ=" & DBFile

    QueryString = "SELECT * FROM `" & ThisWorkbook.Path & _
      "\BUDGET`.Budget Budget"
    With PTCache
        .Connection = ConString
        .CommandText = QueryString
    End With

'   Add new worksheet
    Worksheets.Add
    ActiveSheet.Name = "PivotSheet"

'   Create pivot table
    Set PT = PTCache.CreatePivotTable( _
      TableDestination:=Sheets("PivotSheet").Range("A1"), _
      TableName:="BudgetPivot")

'   Add fields
    With PT
'       Add fields
        .PivotFields("DEPARTMENT").Orientation = xlRowField
        .PivotFields("MONTH").Orientation = xlColumnField
```

```
        .PivotFields("DIVISION").Orientation = xlPageField
        .PivotFields("BUDGET").Orientation = xlDataField
        .PivotFields("ACTUAL").Orientation = xlDataField
    End With
End Sub
```

Notice that the `SourceType` argument for the `Add` method of the `PivotCaches` collection is specified as `xlExternal`. In the example in the previous section (which used data in a worksheet database), the `SourceType` argument was `xlDatabase`.

The `PivotCache` object needs the following information to retrieve the data from the external file.

✦ *A connection string.* This describes the type of data source and the filename. In this example, the connection string specifies an ODBC data source that is a Microsoft Access file named budget.mdb.

✦ *A query string.* This is a Structured Query Language (SQL) statement that determines which records and fields are returned. In this example, the entire `Budget` table is selected.

This information is passed to the `PivotCache` object by setting the `Connection` and `CommandText` properties. Once the data is stored in the pivot cache, the pivot table is created using the `CreatePivotTable` method.

SQL is a standard language for performing database queries. For more information, consult the online help. Better yet, you might want to purchase a book that deals exclusively with SQL. Several such books are available from IDG Books Worldwide.

Creating Multiple Pivot Tables

The final example creates a series of pivot tables that summarize data collected in a customer survey. That data is stored in a worksheet database (see Figure 16-6) and consists of 100 rows. Each row contains the respondent's sex, plus a numerical rating using a 1-to-5 scale for each of the 14 survey items.

surveydata.xls

	A	B	C	D	E	F	G	H	I
1	Name	Sex	Store locations are convenient	Store hours are convenient	Stores are well-maintained	You are easy to reach by phone	I like your web site	Employees are friendly	Employees are helpful
2	Subject1	Male	1	4	4	4	1	1	2
3	Subject2	Female	2	5	1	1	4	2	4
4	Subject3	Male	1	1	4	2	3	3	2
5	Subject4	Male	2	1	3	5	1	2	3
6	Subject5	Female	2	2	5	5	4	2	1
7	Subject6	Female	2	4	3	3	1	1	4
8	Subject7	Female	2	4	5	4	5	3	2
9	Subject8	Male	3	2	1	2	3	4	3
10	Subject9	Female	3	4	4	4	5	1	4
11	Subject10	Male	2	1	5	5	5	1	4
12	Subject11	Male	4	3	3	2	1	2	4
13	Subject12	Female	2	1	4	5	5	5	3
14	Subject13	Female	4	3	4	3	2	5	3
15	Subject14	Female	2	3	4	2	1	1	4
16	Subject15	Female	1	3	5	1	2	2	4
17	Subject16	Male	1	4	1	3	4	3	4
18	Subject17	Female	3	4	3	5	5	4	4
19	Subject18	Male	1	5	5	3	5	3	4

SurveyData

Figure 16-6: Creating a series of pivot tables will summarize this survey data.

Figure 16-7 shows a few of the resulting pivot tables. Each pivot table provides a frequency distribution of a survey item, broken down by sex.

surveydata.xls

	A	B	C	D	E	F	G
1		Sex	Data				
2		Female		Male		Total Freq	Total Pct
3	Store locations are convenient	Freq	Pct	Freq	Pct		
4	Strongly Disagree	20	10.05%	26	13.07%	46	23.12%
5	Disagree	26	13.07%	22	11.06%	48	24.12%
6	Undecided	30	15.08%	18	9.05%	48	24.12%
7	Agree	12	6.03%	40	20.10%	52	26.13%
8	Strongly Agree	5	2.51%		0.00%	5	2.51%
9	Grand Total	93	46.73%	106	53.27%	199	100.00%
10							
11							
12		Sex	Data				
13		Female		Male		Total Freq	Total Pct
14	Store hours are convenient	Freq	Pct	Freq	Pct		
15	Strongly Disagree	6	1.99%	9	2.99%	15	4.98%
16	Disagree	10	3.32%	16	5.32%	26	8.64%
17	Undecided	57	18.94%	48	15.95%	105	34.88%
18	Agree	60	19.93%	60	19.93%	120	39.87%
19	Strongly Agree	10	3.32%	25	8.31%	35	11.63%
20	Grand Total	143	47.51%	158	52.49%	301	100.00%
21							

Summary / SurveyData

Figure 16-7: A VBA procedure created these pivot tables.

The VBA code that created the pivot tables is presented in Listing 16-4.

Listing 16-4: Creating multiple pivot tables from a complex external database

```
Sub MakePivotTables()
'   This procedure creates 14 pivot tables
    Dim PTCache As PivotCache
    Dim PT As PivotTable
    Dim SummarySheet As Worksheet
    Dim ItemName As String
    Dim Row As Integer, i As Integer

    Application.ScreenUpdating = False

'   Delete Summary sheet if it exists
    On Error Resume Next
    Application.DisplayAlerts = False
    Sheets("Summary").Delete
    On Error GoTo 0

'   Add Summary sheet
    Set SummarySheet = Worksheets.Add
    ActiveSheet.Name = "Summary"

'   Create Pivot Cache
    Set PTCache = ActiveWorkbook.PivotCaches.Add( _
      SourceType:=xlDatabase, _
      SourceData:=Sheets("SurveyData").Range("A1"). _
      CurrentRegion.Address)

    Row = 1
    For i = 1 To 14
        ItemName = Sheets("SurveyData").Cells(1, i + 2)
'       Create pivot table
        Set PT = PTCache.CreatePivotTable _
          (TableDestination:=SummarySheet.Cells(Row, 1), _
           TableName:=ItemName)
        Row = Row + 11

'       Add the fields
        With PT.PivotFields(ItemName)
            .Orientation = xlDataField
            .Name = "Freq"
        End With

        With PT.PivotFields(ItemName)
            .Orientation = xlDataField
            .Name = "Pct"
            .Calculation = xlPercentOfTotal
```

Continued

Listing 16-4 *(continued)*

```
          End With

          PT.AddFields RowFields:=Array(ItemName, "Data")
          PT.PivotFields("Sex").Orientation = xlColumnField
          PT.PivotFields("Data").Orientation = xlColumnField
       Next i

'   Replace numbers with descriptive text
    SummarySheet.Activate
    With Columns("A:A")
        .Replace "1", "Strongly Disagree"
        .Replace "2", "Disagree"
        .Replace "3", "Undecided"
        .Replace "4", "Agree"
        .Replace "5", "Strongly Agree"
    End With

'   Adjust column widths
    Columns("A:G").EntireColumn.AutoFit
End Sub
```

Notice that the pivot tables are created within a loop, and all come from a single `PivotCache` object. The `Row` variable keeps track of the start of each pivot table. After the pivot tables are created, the code replaces the numeric categories in the first column with text (for example, *1* is replaced with Strongly Agree). Finally, the column widths are adjusted.

Modifying Pivot Tables

An Excel pivot table is designed to be flexible. For example, users can easily change a row field to a column field and hide certain items in the pivot table that are not relevant to their current needs. You may want to provide your own interface to make it even easier for the user to make certain pivot table changes. The example in this section presents a pivot table that can be controlled by a series of OptionButtons and two CheckBox controls, as shown in Figure 16-8.

The pivot table contains four additional calculated items (Q1, Q2, Q3, and Q4), which compute quarterly totals. The VBA code that's executed when `OptionButton1` (Months Only) is clicked is shown in Listing 16-5. The procedure is straightforward and similar to the event-handler procedures for the other OptionButtons.

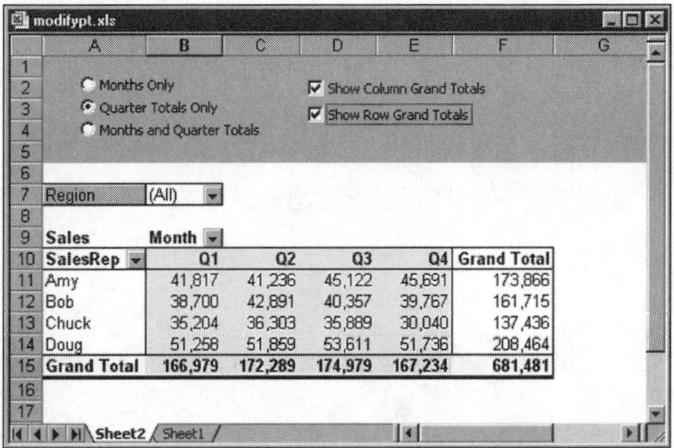

Sales	Month				
SalesRep	Q1	Q2	Q3	Q4	Grand Total
Amy	41,817	41,236	45,122	45,691	173,866
Bob	38,700	42,891	40,357	39,767	161,715
Chuck	35,204	36,303	35,889	30,040	137,436
Doug	51,258	51,859	53,611	51,736	208,464
Grand Total	166,979	172,289	174,979	167,234	681,481

Figure 16-8: The user can use the controls to adjust the pivot table.

Listing 16-5: Responding to a user request to adjust a pivot table option

```
Private Sub OptionButton1_Click()
'   Months only
    Application.ScreenUpdating = False
    With ActiveSheet.PivotTables(1).PivotFields("Month")
        .PivotItems("Jan").Visible = True
        .PivotItems("Feb").Visible = True
        .PivotItems("Mar").Visible = True
        .PivotItems("Apr").Visible = True
        .PivotItems("May").Visible = True
        .PivotItems("Jun").Visible = True
        .PivotItems("Jul").Visible = True
        .PivotItems("Aug").Visible = True
        .PivotItems("Sep").Visible = True
        .PivotItems("Oct").Visible = True
        .PivotItems("Nov").Visible = True
        .PivotItems("Dec").Visible = True
        .PivotItems("Q1").Visible = False
        .PivotItems("Q2").Visible = False
        .PivotItems("Q3").Visible = False
        .PivotItems("Q4").Visible = False
    End With
End Sub
```

The CheckBox controls simply toggle the display of the grand totals. These event-handler procedures are shown below.

```
Private Sub CheckBox1_Click()
'    Column Grand Totals
     Application.ScreenUpdating = False
     ActiveSheet.PivotTables(1).ColumnGrand = CheckBox1.Value
End Sub

Private Sub CheckBox2_Click()
'    Row Grand Totals
     Application.ScreenUpdating = False
     ActiveSheet.PivotTables(1).RowGrand = CheckBox2.Value
End Sub
```

Pivot tables, of course, can be modified in many other ways. As I've mentioned, the easiest way to create VBA code that modifies pivot tables is to turn on the macro recorder while you make the changes manually. Then adjust the code and copy it to the event-handler procedures for your controls.

Summary

This chapter provided several examples of how to create and modify pivot tables using VBA code.

In the next chapter, I present VBA techniques to manipulate charts.

✦ ✦ ✦

CHAPTER 17

Working with Charts

✦ ✦ ✦ ✦

In This Chapter

Essential background information on Excel charts

The difference between embedded charts and chart sheets

Understanding the `Chart` class object model

Using the macro recorder to help you learn about `Chart` class objects

Examples of common charting tasks using VBA

Examples of more complex charting macros

Some interesting (and useful) chart-making tricks

✦ ✦ ✦ ✦

When you think about it, Excel's charting feature is pretty awesome. A chart displays data of virtually any type that's stored in a worksheet. Excel supports more than 100 different chart types, and you have almost complete control over nearly every aspect of each chart.

About Charts

Due to its richness, a chart is simply packed with objects, each of which has its own properties and methods. Because of this, manipulating charts with VBA can be a bit of a challenge. In this chapter, I discuss the key concepts that you need to understand to write VBA code that generates or manipulates charts. The secret is a good understanding of the object hierarchy for charts. First, a bit of background about Excel charts.

Chart locations

In Excel, a chart can be located in one of two places within a workbook:

- ✦ As an embedded object on a worksheet (a worksheet can contain any number of embedded charts)
- ✦ In a separate chart sheet (a chart sheet holds a single chart)

An embedded chart can also reside on an Excel 5/95 dialog sheet. And, as I discuss later in this chapter (see "Storing multiple charts on a chart sheet"), you can also store embedded charts on a chart sheet.

Most charts are created manually using the ChartWizard. But, as you'll see, you can also create charts using VBA. And, of course, you can use VBA to modify existing charts.

Tip

The fastest way to create a chart on a new sheet is to select your data and press F11. Excel creates a new chart sheet and uses the default chart type.

A key concept when working with charts is the *active chart.* When the user clicks an embedded chart or actives a chart sheet, a `Chart` class object is activated. In VBA, the `ActiveChart` property returns the activated `Chart` class object (if any). You can write code to work with this `Chart` class object, much as you can write code to work with the `Workbook` object returned by the `ActiveWorkbook` property.

Here's an example. If a chart is activated, the following statement displays the `Name` property for the `Chart` class object:

```
MsgBox ActiveChart.Name
```

If a chart is not activated, the preceding statement generates an error.

Note

As you'll see later in this chapter, it's not necessary to activate a chart to manipulate it with VBA.

The Chart object model

To get a feel for the number of objects involved when working with charts, turn on the macro recorder, create a chart, and perform some routine chart editing tasks. You might be surprised by the amount of code Excel generates. When you first start exploring the object model for the `Chart` class, you'll probably be very confused . . . which is not surprising, because the object model *is* very confusing. It's also very deep.

For example, assume that you want to change the title displayed in an embedded chart. The top-level object (not counting `Excel`, the name of the library, which is generally omitted) is the `Application` object. The `Application` object contains a `Workbook` object, and the `Workbook` object contains a `Worksheet` object. The `Worksheet` object contains a `ChartObject` class object, which contains a `Chart` class object. The `Chart` class object has a `ChartTitle` object, and the `ChartTitle` object contains a `Characters` object. The `Text` property of the `Characters` object stores the text that's displayed as the chart's title. In other words, the `Characters` object is at the seventh hierarchical object level.

Here's another way to look at this hierarchy for an embedded chart:

```
Application
  Workbook
    Worksheet
       ChartObject
         Chart
               ChartTitle
                  Characters
```

Your VBA code must, of course, follow this object model precisely. For example, to set a chart's title to *YTD Sales,* you could write a VBA instruction such as this:

```
WorkSheets("Sheet1").ChartObjects(1).Chart.ChartTitle. _
  Characters.Text = "YTD Sales"
```

This statement assumes the active workbook is the `Workbook` object. The instruction works with the first item in the `ChartObjects` collection on the worksheet named `Sheet1`. The `Chart` property returns the actual `Chart` class object. The `ChartTitle` property returns the `ChartTitle` object, and the `Characters` property returns the `Characters` object. What you're really interested in is the `Text` property of this `Characters` object.

For a chart sheet, the object hierarchy is a bit different because it doesn't involve the `Worksheet` object or the `ChartObject` object. For example, here's the hierarchy for the `Characters` object for a chart in a chart sheet:

```
Application
  Workbook
    Chart
          ChartTitle
             Characters
```

In terms of VBA, you could use the following instruction to set the chart title to *YTD Sales:*

```
Sheets("Chart1").ChartTitle.Characters.Text = "YTD Sales"
```

In other words, a chart sheet is actually a `Chart` class object, and it has no containing `ChartObject` class object. Put another way, the parent object for an embedded chart is a `ChartObject` class object and the parent object for a chart on a separate chart sheet is a `Workbook` object.

Both of the following instructions display a message box with the word *Chart* in it:

```
MsgBox TypeName(Sheets("Sheet1").ChartObjects(1).Chart)

Msgbox TypeName(Sheets("Chart1"))
```

When you create a new embedded chart, you're adding to the `ChartObjects` collection contained in a particular worksheet (there is no `Charts` collection for a worksheet). When you create a new chart sheet, you're adding to the `Charts` collection and the `Sheets` collection for a particular workbook.

Recording Chart Macros

Perhaps the best way to become familiar with the `Chart` class object model is to turn on the macro recorder while you create and manipulate charts. Even though the macro recorder tends to spit out lots of extraneous and inefficient code, the recorded code still gives you information regarding the object, properties, and methods you need to know about.

Excel's macro recorder always activates a chart and then uses the `ActiveChart` property to return the actual `Chart` class object. In Excel, it's not necessary to select an object (or activate a chart) to work with it in VBA. And, as I mentioned, the macro recorder generates lots of extraneous code. Therefore, if efficiency is among your goals, you should *never* actually use unedited recorded macros — especially those that manipulate charts.

Macro recorder output

I turned on the macro recorder while I created a chart (shown in Figure 17-1) and then performed some simple customizations to it.

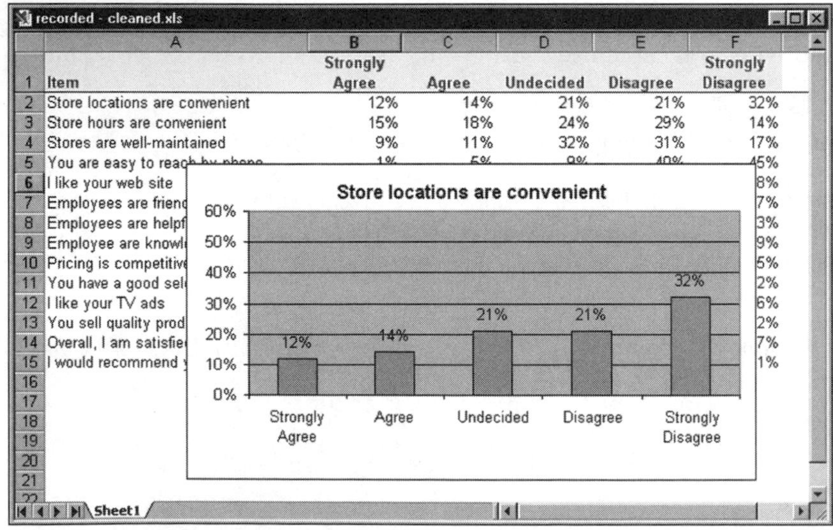

Figure 17-1: This chart was created while Excel's macro recorder was turned on.

Following is a listing of what the macro recorder spit out:

```
Sub Macro1()
    Range("A1:F2").Select
    Charts.Add
    ActiveChart.ChartType = xlColumnClustered
    ActiveChart.SetSourceData _
      Source:=Sheets("Sheet1").Range("A1:F2"), _
      PlotBy:=xlRows
    ActiveChart.Location _
      Where:=xlLocationAsObject, _
      Name:="Sheet1"
    ActiveChart.HasLegend = False
    ActiveChart.ApplyDataLabels _
      Type:=xlDataLabelsShowValue, LegendKey:=False
    ActiveChart.HasDataTable = False
    ActiveChart.Axes(xlCategory).Select
    Selection.TickLabels.Orientation = xlHorizontal
    ActiveChart.ChartTitle.Select
    Selection.Font.Bold = True
    Selection.AutoScaleFont = True
    With Selection.Font
        .Name = "Arial"
        .Size = 12
        .Strikethrough = False
        .Superscript = False
        .Subscript = False
        .OutlineFont = False
        .Shadow = False
        .Underline = xlUnderlineStyleNone
        .ColorIndex = xlAutomatic
        .Background = xlAutomatic
    End With
    ActiveChart.PlotArea.Select
    Selection.Top = 18
    Selection.Height = 162
    ActiveChart.ChartArea.Select
    ActiveChart.Axes(xlValue).Select
    With ActiveChart.Axes(xlValue)
        .MinimumScaleIsAuto = True
        .MaximumScale = 0.6
        .MinorUnitIsAuto = True
        .MajorUnitIsAuto = True
        .Crosses = xlAutomatic
        .ReversePlotOrder = False
        .ScaleType = xlLinear
    End With
End Sub
```

The "cleaned up" macro

Much of the code generated for the macro in the previous section is not necessary; it sets values for properties that really don't need to be set. Following is a listing for my edited macro. This performs exactly like the macro in the previous section, but it's significantly shorter and more efficient. Setting the `ScreenUpdating` property to False eliminates the screen refreshing.

```
Sub CleanedMacro()
    Application.ScreenUpdating = False
    Charts.Add
    ActiveChart.Location _
      Where:=xlLocationAsObject, Name:="Sheet1"
    With ActiveChart
        .SetSourceData Range("A1:F2")
        .HasTitle = True
        .ChartType = xlColumnClustered
        .HasLegend = False
        .ApplyDataLabels Type:=xlDataLabelsShowValue
        .Axes(xlCategory).TickLabels.Orientation = _
         xlHorizontal
        .ChartTitle.Font.Bold = True
        .ChartTitle.Font.Size = 12
        .PlotArea.Top = 18
        .PlotArea.Height = 162
        .Axes(xlValue).MaximumScale = 0.6
    End With
    ActiveWindow.Visible = False
    ActiveWindow.RangeSelection.Activate
    Application.ScreenUpdating = True
End Sub
```

When you create a chart using the `Add` method of the `Charts` collection, the created chart is always a chart sheet. In the preceding code, the `Location` method moves the chart to a worksheet.

The `Location` method of the `Chart` class object is interesting because it essentially creates a new object rather than relocating an existing object. To demonstrate, execute the following code:

```
Sub Test()
    Charts.Add
    MsgBox ActiveChart.Name
    ActiveChart.Location _
      Where:=xlLocationAsObject, Name:="Sheet1"
    MsgBox ActiveChart.Name
End Sub
```

This procedure adds a chart (a chart sheet) and then displays a message box that shows the name of the active chart. Then the `Location` method moves the chart to a worksheet. The next message box displays the name of the active chart, which is different from the previous active chart. The original `Chart` class object ceases to exist, and is replaced with a new `Chart` class object contained in a `ChartObject` class object.

A workbook that contains both the recorded macro and the "cleaned up" macro is included on the companion CD-ROM so you can compare their performance.

Common VBA Charting Techniques

In this section I describe how to perform some common tasks that involve charts.

Activating a chart

Your VBA code can activate an embedded chart using the `Activate` method. Here's an example:

```
ActiveSheet.ChartObjects("Chart 1").Activate
```

If the chart is on a chart sheet, use a statement such as this:

```
Sheets("Chart1").Activate
```

Once a chart is activated, you can refer to it in your code with `ActiveChart`. For example, the following instruction displays the name of the active chart. If there is no active chart, the statement generates an error.

```
MsgBox ActiveChart.Name
```

To modify a chart with VBA, it's not necessary to activate it. The following two procedures have exactly the same effect (they change the embedded chart named `Chart 1` to an area chart). The first procedure activates the chart before performing the manipulations; the second one doesn't.

```
Sub ModifyChart1()
    ActiveSheet.ChartObjects("Chart 1").Activate
    ActiveChart.Type = xlArea
    ActiveWindow.Visible = False
End Sub

Sub ModifyChart2()
    ActiveSheet.ChartObjects("Chart 1").Chart.Type = xlArea
End Sub
```

A chart embedded on a worksheet can easily be converted to a chart sheet. To do so manually, just activate the embedded chart and select Chart ➪ Location. In the Chart Location dialog box, select the As new sheet option and specify a name. This action essentially copies the `Chart` class object (contained in a `ChartObject` class object) to a chart sheet and then destroys its containing `ChartObject` class object.

You can also convert an embedded chart to a chart sheet with VBA. Here's an example that converts the first `ChartObject` on a worksheet named `Sheet1` to a chart sheet named `MyChart`:

```
Sub ConvertChart1()
    Sheets("Sheet1").ChartObjects(1).Chart. _
      Location xlLocationAsNewSheet, "MyChart"
End Sub
```

The next example does just the opposite of the previous procedure: It converts the chart on a chart sheet named `MyChart` to an embedded chart on the worksheet named `Sheet1`.

```
Sub ConvertChart2()
    Charts("MyChart") _
      .Location xlLocationAsObject, "Sheet1"
End Sub
```

The `Location` method also activates the relocated chart.

When you activate a chart contained in a `ChartObject`, the chart actually is contained in a window that is normally *invisible*. To see an embedded chart in its own window, right-click the `ChartObject` and select Chart Window from the shortcut menu. The embedded chart remains on the worksheet, but the chart also appears in its own floating window (see Figure 17-2). You can move and resize this window (but you can't maximize it). If you move the window, you'll notice that the embedded chart is still displayed in its original location. Activating any other window makes the `ChartObject` window invisible again.

The following VBA code displays the window for the first `ChartObject` on the active sheet:

```
ActiveSheet.ChartObjects(1).Activate
ActiveChart.ShowWindow = True
```

For a practical application of using a window to display an embedded chart, see "Printing embedded charts on a full page" later in this chapter.

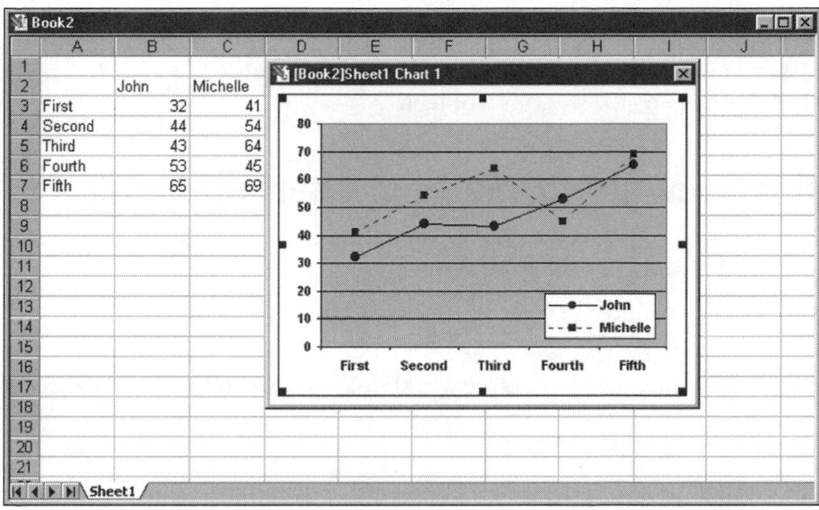

Figure 17-2: Displaying an embedded chart in a window.

Determining whether a chart is activated

A common type of macro performs some manipulations on the active chart — for example, it changes the chart's type, applies colors, or changes the font size.

The question is, how can your VBA code determine whether the user has actually selected a chart? By selecting a chart, I mean activating a chart sheet, or activating an embedded chart by clicking it. Your first inclination might be to check the `TypeName` property of the `Selection`, as in this expression:

```
TypeName(Selection) = "Chart"
```

The preceding expression evaluates to True if a chart sheet is active, but it *will not* be True if an embedded chart is selected. Rather, when an embedded chart is selected, the actual selection will be an object within the `Chart` class object. For example, the selection might be a `Series` object, a `ChartTitle` object, a `Legend` object, a `PlotArea` object, and so on.

The following `ChartIsSelected` function returns True if a chart sheet is active or if an embedded chart is activated, and returns False if a chart is not activated:

```
Private Function ChartIsSelected() As Boolean
    Dim x As String
    ChartIsSelected = False
    On Error Resume Next
    x = ActiveChart.Name
    If Err = 0 Then ChartIsSelected = True
End Function
```

This function attempts to access the Name property of the ActiveChart object. If there is no ActiveChart, an error is generated (but is ignored due to the On Error Resume Next statement). If an error did not occur, the value of Err is 0, which means that there is an ActiveChart object.

Deleting from ChartObjects or Charts

To delete all ChartObject class objects on a worksheet, you can simply use the Delete method of the ChartObjects collection:

```
ActiveSheet.ChartObjects.Delete
```

To delete all chart sheets in the active workbook, use the following statement:

```
ActiveWorkbook.Charts.Delete
```

Normally, deleting sheets causes Excel to display a warning such as the one shown in Figure 17-3. The user must reply to this prompt for the macro to continue. To eliminate this prompt, use the following series of statements:

```
Application.DisplayAlerts = False
ActiveWorkbook.Charts.Delete
Application.DisplayAlerts = False
```

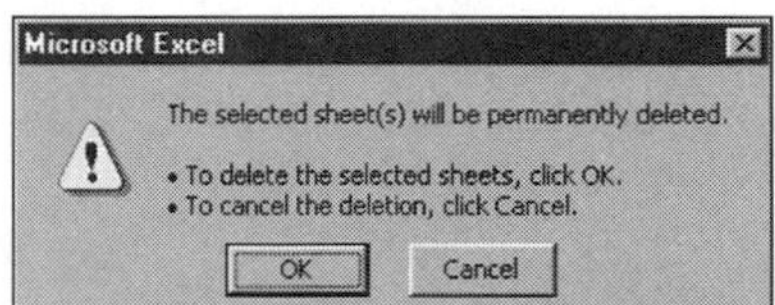

Figure 17-3: Attempting to delete one or more chart sheets results in this message.

Applying chart formatting

The following example applies several different types of formatting to the active chart:

```
Sub ChartMods1()
    With ActiveChart
        .Type = xlArea
        .ChartArea.Font.Name = "Arial"
        .ChartArea.Font.FontStyle = "Regular"
        .ChartArea.Font.Size = 9
        .PlotArea.Interior.ColorIndex = xlNone
        .Axes(xlValue).TickLabels.Font.Bold = True
        .Axes(xlCategory).TickLabels.Font.Bold = True
        .HasLegend = True
```

```
        .Legend.Position = xlBottom
    End With
End Sub
```

A chart must be active, or this routine generates an error. Notice also that the code sets the `HasLegend` property to True. This is to avoid an error that would occur if you tried to set the `Position` property of the `Legend` object if the chart had no legend.

The next example is another version of the `ChartMods` procedure. In this case, it works on a particular chart: the one contained in a `ChartObject` named `Chart 1`, located on `Sheet1`. Notice that the chart is never activated.

```
Sub ChartMods2()
    With Sheets("Sheet1").ChartObjects("Chart 1").Chart
        .Type = xlArea
        .ChartArea.Font.Name = "Arial"
        .ChartArea.Font.FontStyle = "Regular"
        .ChartArea.Font.Size = 9
        .PlotArea.Interior.ColorIndex = xlNone
        .Axes(xlValue).TickLabels.Font.Bold = True
        .Axes(xlCategory).TickLabels.Font.Bold = True
        .HasLegend = True
        .Legend.Position = xlBottom
    End With
End Sub
```

Looping through all charts

In some cases, you may need to perform an operation on all charts. The following example changes the chart type of every embedded chart on the active sheet. The procedure uses a `For-Next` loop to cycle through each object in the `ChartObjects` collection and then accesses the `Chart` class object in each and changes its `Type` property. An `Area` chart is specified by using the predefined constant `xlArea`. Consult the online help for other chart type constants.

```
Sub ChangeChartType()
    For Each cht In ActiveSheet.ChartObjects
        cht.Chart.Type - xlArea
    Next cht
End Sub
```

The macro that follows performs the same operation as the preceding procedure but works on all the chart sheets in the active workbook:

```
Sub ChangeChartType2()
    For Each cht In ActiveWorkbook.Charts
        cht.Type = xlArea
    Next cht
End Sub
```

The following example changes the legend font for all charts on the active sheet. It uses a For-Next loop to process all ChartObject class objects.

```
Sub LegendMod()
    For Each cht In ActiveSheet.ChartObjects
        With cht.Chart.Legend.Font
            .Name = "Arial"
            .FontStyle = "Bold"
            .Size = 12
        End With
    Next cht
End Sub
```

Aligning and sizing ChartObjects

A ChartObject class object has standard positional and sizing properties that you can access with your VBA code. The following example resizes all ChartObject class objects on Sheet1 so they match the dimensions of the ChartObject named Chart 1. It also arranges the ChartObject class objects so they appear one after the other along the left side of the worksheet.

```
Sub ResizeAndArrangeChartObjects()
    W = ActiveSheet.ChartObjects("Chart 1").Width
    H = ActiveSheet.ChartObjects("Chart 1").Height
    TopPos = 0
    For Each chtObj In ActiveSheet.ChartObjects
        With chtObj
            .Width = W
            .Height = H
            .Left = 0
            .Top = TopPos
        End With
        TopPos = TopPos + H
    Next chtObj
End Sub
```

The TopPos variable keeps track of the vertical location for the next chart. Each time the loop cycles, this variable is incremented by the value of H (the height of each ChartObject).

More Charting Examples

In this section, I describe some additional charting techniques. I discuss two examples that demonstrate how to use VBA to change the data used by a chart.

Working with PivotCharts

Excel 2000 introduced a new facet to charting: PivotCharts. This handy feature enables you to create a dynamic chart that's attached to a PivotTable. The PivotChart displays the current layout of the PivotTable graphically. When you create a PivotTable, you have the option of creating a PivotTable alone or creating a PivotChart (which includes an associated PivotTable). To create a PivotChart from an existing PivotTable, activate the PivotTable and click the ChartWizard button. The chart is created on a new chart sheet. By default, a new PivotChart always appears on a chart sheet, but you can use the Chart ⇨ Location command to convert it to an embedded chart (see the accompanying figure).

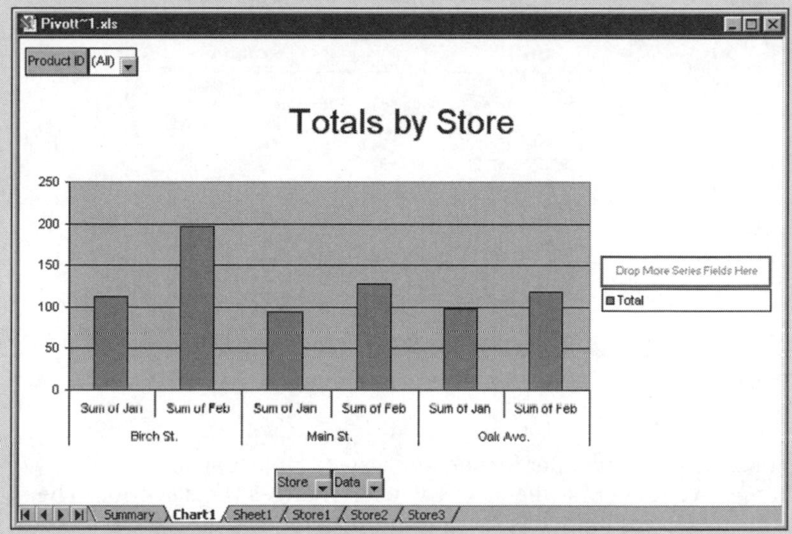

When Microsoft adds a new feature to Excel, it also needs to augment Excel's object model so the new feature is exposed and can be controlled by VBA. In the case of PivotCharts, you'll find a new `PivotLayout` object as a member of the `Chart` class. The best way to become familiar with this object is to record your actions as you modify a PivotChart and examine the code produced. Then you can learn more about the objects, properties, and methods by consulting the online help.

Specifying the data used by a chart

As you know, a chart can consist of any number of series, and the data used by each series is determined by the range references in its SERIES formula. For more about this topic, see the sidebar titled "Understanding a Chart's SERIES Formula."

Changing chart data based on the active cell

Figure 17-4 displays a chart based on the data in the row of the active cell. As the user moves the cell pointer, the chart is updated automatically.

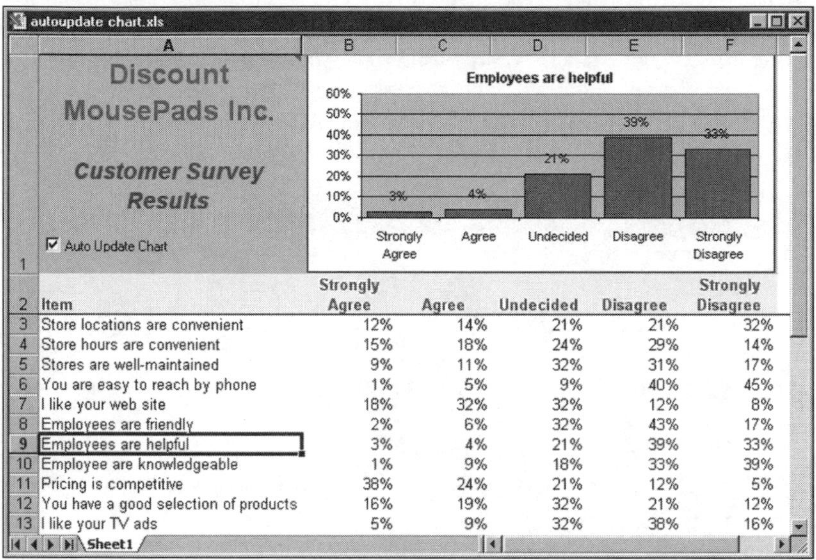

	Item	Strongly Agree	Agree	Undecided	Disagree	Strongly Disagree
3	Store locations are convenient	12%	14%	21%	21%	32%
4	Store hours are convenient	15%	18%	24%	29%	14%
5	Stores are well-maintained	9%	11%	32%	31%	17%
6	You are easy to reach by phone	1%	5%	9%	40%	45%
7	I like your web site	18%	32%	32%	12%	8%
8	Employees are friendly	2%	6%	32%	43%	17%
9	Employees are helpful	3%	4%	21%	39%	33%
10	Employee are knowledgeable	1%	9%	18%	33%	39%
11	Pricing is competitive	38%	24%	21%	12%	5%
12	You have a good selection of products	16%	19%	32%	21%	12%
13	I like your TV ads	5%	9%	32%	38%	16%

Figure 17-4: This chart always displays the data from the row of the active cell.

This example uses an event handler for the `Worksheet` object. The `SelectionChange` event occurs whenever the user changes the selection. The event handler for this event (which is located in the code module for the `Sheet1` object) is as follows:

```
Private Sub Worksheet_SelectionChange(ByVal Target _
  As Excel.Range)
    Call UpdateChart
End Sub
```

In other words, every time the user moves the cell cursor, the `Worksheet_SelectionChange` procedure is executed, which in turn calls the following `UpdateChart` procedure:

```
Sub UpdateChart()
    If Sheets("Sheet1").CheckBox1 Then
        Set TheChartObj = ActiveSheet.ChartObjects(1)
        Set TheChart = TheChartObj.Chart
        UserRow = ActiveCell.Row
        If UserRow < 3 Or IsEmpty(Cells(UserRow, 1)) Then
```

```
            TheChartObj.Visible = False
        Else
            Set CatTitles = Range("A2:F2")
            Set SrcRange = Range(Cells(UserRow, 1), _
             Cells(UserRow, 6))
            Set SourceData = Union(CatTitles, SrcRange)
            TheChart.SetSourceData _
              Source:=SourceData, PlotBy:=xlRows
            TheChartObj.Visible = True
        End If
    End If
End Sub
```

The first step is to determine whether the Auto Update Chart check box is checked. If this check box is checked, nothing happens. The `UserRow` variable contains the row number of the active cell. The `If` statement checks to make sure that the active cell is in a row that has data (the data starts in row 3). If the cell cursor is in a row that doesn't have data, the `ChartObject` class object is hidden. Otherwise, the code creates a `Range` object (`CatTitle`) that holds the category titles, and another `Range` object (`SrcRange`) that contains the data for the row. These two `Range` objects are joined using VBA's `Union` function and assigned to a `Range` object named `SourceData`. Finally, the `SourceData` range is assigned to the chart using the `SetSourceData` method of the `Chart` class object.

Changing chart data with a ComboBox

The next example uses a ComboBox control on a chart sheet to enable the user to select a chart (see Figure 17-5).

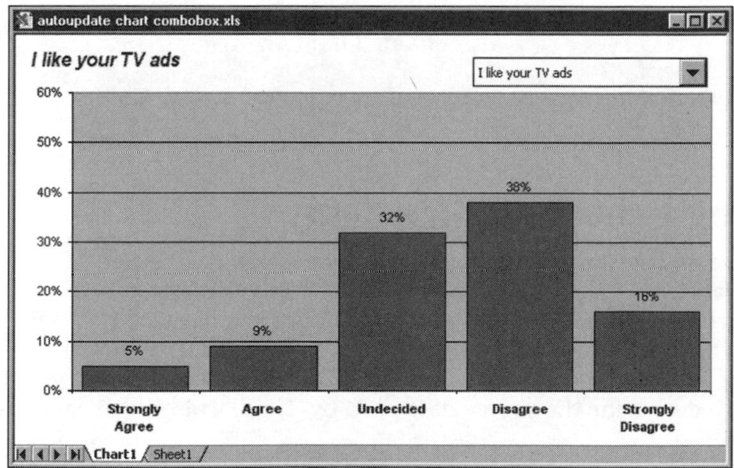

Figure 17-5: Selecting from the ComboBox changes the source data for the chart.

Note

The ComboBox used in this example is from the Forms toolbar (not the Control Toolbox toolbar). For some reason, Excel does not enable you to add ActiveX controls to a chart sheet.

When the user makes a selection from the ComboBox, the following procedure is executed:

```
Sub DropDown1_Change()
    ListIndex = Charts(1).DropDowns(1).Value
    Call UpdateChart(ListIndex)
End Sub
```

This procedure calls the `UpdateChart` procedure, and passes an integer that represents the user's choice. Following is the listing of the `UpdateChart` procedure. This is very similar to the `UpdateChart` procedure in the previous section.

```
Sub UpdateChart(Item)
'   Updates the chart using the selected dropdown item
    Set TheChart = Sheets("Chart1")
    Set DataSheet = Sheets("Sheet1")

    With DataSheet
        Set CatTitles = .Range("A1:F1")
        Set SrcRange = .Range(.Cells(Item + 1, 1), _
          .Cells(Item + 1, 6))
    End With
    Set SourceData = Union(CatTitles, SrcRange)

    With TheChart
        .SetSourceData Source:=SourceData, PlotBy:=xlRows
        .ChartTitle.Left = TheChart.ChartArea.Left
        .Deselect
    End With
End Sub
```

Determining a chart's source data

Assume you have an embedded chart such as the one shown in Figure 17-6. This chart displays data for three months. You would like to write a VBA procedure that extends the chart's source data to use the three additional months. If your VBA code created the chart and is "aware" of the chart's data source, it's fairly simple to extend the range. But if your code needs to work with any arbitrary chart, you'll find that using VBA to determine the source data used by the chart is not an easy task.

Understanding a Chart's SERIES Formula

The data used in each series in a chart is determined by its SERIES formula. When you select a data series in a chart, the SERIES formula appears in the formula bar. This is not a "real" formula. In other words, you can't use it in a cell, and you can't use worksheet functions within the SERIES formula. You can, however, edit the arguments in the SERIES formula.

A SERIES formula has the following syntax:

```
=SERIES(name, category_labels, values, order)
```

name – (Optional) The name used in the legend. If the chart has only one series, the name argument is used as the title.

category_labels – (Optional) The range that contains the labels for the category axis. If omitted, Excel uses consecutive integers beginning with 1.

values – (Required) The range that contains the values.

order – (Required) An integer that specifies the plotting order of the series (relevant only if the chart has more than one series).

Range references in a SERIES formula are always absolute, and they always include the sheet name. For example,

```
=SERIES(Sheet1!$B$1,,Sheet1!$B$2:$B$7,1)
```

A range reference can consist of a noncontiguous range. If so, each range is separated by a comma and the argument is enclosed in parentheses. In the following SERIES formula, the values range consists of B2:B3 and B5:B7:

```
=SERIES(,,(Sheet1!$B$2:$B$3,Sheet1!$B$5:$B$7),1)
```

You can substitute range names for the range references. If you do so, Excel changes the reference in the SERIES formula to include the workbook. For example,

```
=SERIES(Sheet1!$B$1,,budget.xls!MyData,1)
```

The Series object

It's my opinion that Excel's object model has a serious flaw: There is no direct way to determine the ranges used in a chart. Let's look at what the object model *does* provide.

The `Series` object is contained in a `Chart` class object. The `SeriesCollection` is a collection of `Series` objects for a particular `Chart` class object. If a chart plots two data series, it has two `Series` objects. You can refer to a particular `Series` object by its index number. The following expression, for example, creates an object variable that represents the first `Series` object in the active chart:

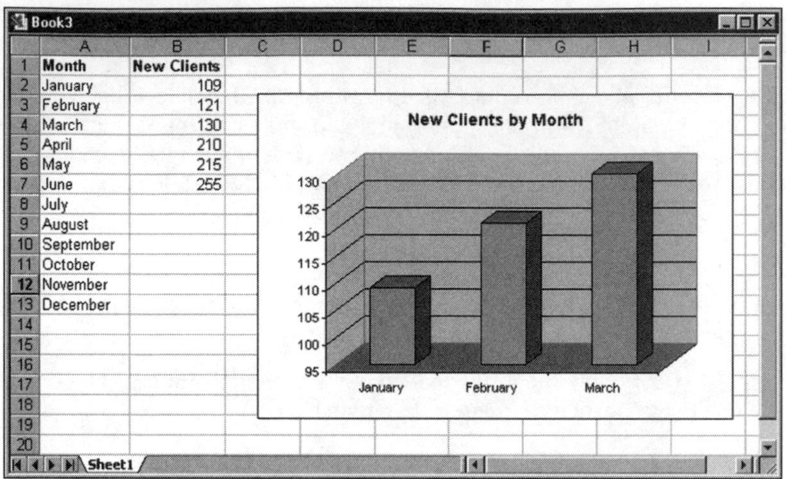

Figure 17-6: What's the best way to determine which ranges are used by this chart?

```
Set MySeries = ActiveChart.SeriesCollection(1)
```

A `Series` object has many properties, but here is a list of three that seem relevant to this discussion:

`Formula`	Returns or sets the SERIES formula for the `Series` object. When you select a series in a chart, its SERIES formula is displayed in the formula bar. The `Formula` property returns this formula as a string.
`Values`	Returns or sets a collection of all the values in the series. This can be a range on a worksheet or an array of constant values, but not a combination of both.
`XValues`	Returns or sets an array of *x* values for a chart series. The `XValues` property can be set to a range on a worksheet or to an array of values — but it can't be a combination of both.

So if your code needs to determine the data range used by a particular chart series, it's obvious that the `Values` property of the `Series` object is just the ticket. And, you can use the `XValues` property to get the range that contains the *x* values (or category labels). In theory, that certainly seems correct . . . but in practice, it doesn't work.

A simple demonstration

To demonstrate why accessing the `Value` property doesn't produce the results you need, start with a new workbook and create the simple chart shown in Figure 17-7. The chart uses A1:A3 as its `Values` range.

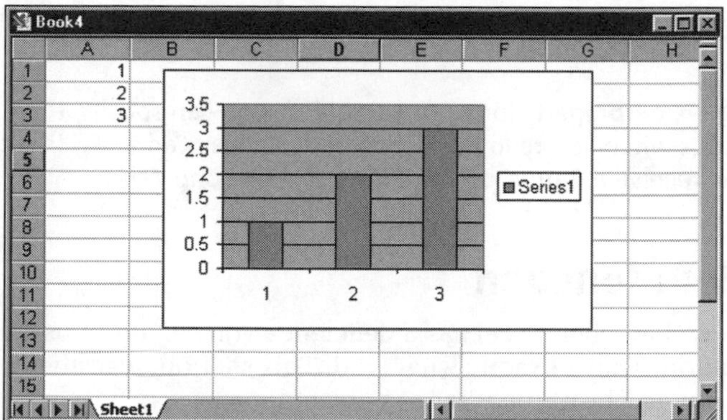

Figure 17-7: Use this chart to discover why `Values` and `XValues` don't work as they should.

Create a VBA general module, and enter the following procedure:

```
Sub Test1()
    Dim DataRange As Range
    Set DataRange = ActiveSheet.Range("A1:A2")
    ActiveSheet.ChartObjects(1). _
      Chart.SeriesCollection(1).Values = DataRange
End Sub
```

This procedure changes the source data for the chart's series to use the data in A1:A2. Execute the procedure, and you find that the chart now displays only two columns.

Next, try running the following procedure:

```
Sub Test2()
    Dim DataRange As Range
    Set DataRange = Sheets("Sheet1").ChartObjects(1). _
      Chart.SeriesCollection(1).Values
End Sub
```

This procedure attempts to create a `Range` object named `DataRange` from the chart's series. When you execute this procedure, you get an error: `Object required`. The problem is that the `Values` property for the `Series` object (the member of the collection named `SeriesCollection`) always returns an array—never a `Range` object. If you don't believe me, execute this statement, which uses VBA's `IsArray` function to determine whether its argument is an array:

```
MsgBox IsArray(Sheets("Sheet1").ChartObjects(1). _
  Chart.SeriesCollection(1).Values)
```

Specifically, the Values property returns a variant array. Unfortunately, there is no direct way to get a Range object for a Series object.

When you set the Values property for a Series object, you can specify a Range object or an array. But when you read this property, it is always an array. In other words, a variant can receive a Range object, but it can't give one back.

Creating a custom function

By now, you should know that when Excel has a deficiency you can often use VBA to create your own solution. That's exactly what I did. This section describes a VBA function that returns a Range object for a Series object.

The function, named GetChartRange, takes three arguments:

cht	A Chart class object
series	An integer that corresponds to the Series number in the SeriesCollection object
ValsOrX	A string, either "values" or "xvalues" (not case-sensitive)

The following statements demonstrate how to use the GetChartRange Function:

```
Set MyChart = ActiveSheet.ChartObjects(1).Chart
Set DataRange = GetChartRange(MyChart, 1, "values")
MsgBox DataRange.Address
```

The first statement creates an object variable for the Chart class object of interest. The second statement creates a Range object by calling the GetChartRange Function procedure. The Range returned by the DataRange function contains the data plotted in the first Series on the chart. The third statement simply displays the address for the range.

The GetChartRange procedure works by parsing the SERIES formula (a text string) and extracting the range addresses. The GetChartRange does have one limitation: It does not work if the chart series uses a noncontiguous range. When a series uses a noncontiguous range, the range references in the SERIES formula are enclosed in parentheses and separated by a comma. GetChartRange parses the SERIES formula by searching for commas. If the SERIES formula contains more than three commas, it's using a noncontiguous range and the parsing algorithm doesn't work.

The GetChartRange procedure is available on the companion CD-ROM. The workbook also contains procedures to demonstrate the function, as shown in Figure 17-8.

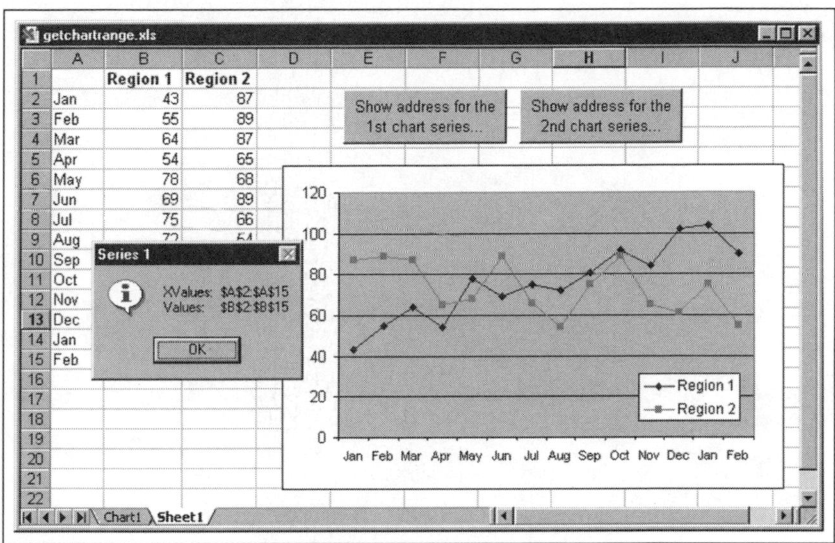

Figure 17-8: The `GetChartRange` procedure determines the ranges used by a chart.

The `GetChartRange` procedure is provided here in Listing 17-1.

Listing 17-1: Parsing Excel's SERIES function to find a chart's source range

```
Function GetChartRange(cht As Chart, series As Integer, _
 ValOrX As String) As Range
'   cht: A Chart class object
'   series: Integer representing the Series
'   ValOrX: String, either "values" or "xvalues"

    Dim Sf As String
    Dim CommaCnt As Integer
    Dim Commas() As Integer
    Dim ListSep As String * 1
    Dim Temp As String

    Set GetChartRange = Nothing
    On Error Resume Next

'   Get the SERIES formula
    Sf = cht.SeriesCollection(series).Formula

'   Check for noncontiguous ranges by counting commas
'   Also, store the character position of the commas
    CommaCnt = 0
```

Continued

Listing 17-1 *(continued)*

```
    ListSep = Application.International(xlListSeparator)
    For i = 1 To Len(Sf)
        If Mid(Sf, i, 1) = ListSep Then
            CommaCnt = CommaCnt + 1
            ReDim Preserve Commas(CommaCnt)
            Commas(CommaCnt) = i
        End If
    Next i
    If CommaCnt > 3 Then Exit Function

'   XValues or Values?
    Select Case UCase(ValOrX)
        Case "XVALUES"
'           Text between 1st and 2nd commas in SERIES Formula
            Temp = Mid(Sf, Commas(1) + 1, Commas(2) - _
             Commas(1) - 1)
            Set GetChartRange = Range(Temp)
        Case "VALUES"
'       Text between the 2nd and 3rd commas in SERIES Formula
            Temp = Mid(Sf, Commas(2) + 1, Commas(3) - _
             Commas(2) - 1)
            Set GetChartRange = Range(Temp)
    End Select
End Function
```

Using names in a SERIES formula

In some cases, using range names in the SERIES formulas in a chart can greatly simplify things if you need to change the chart's source data using VBA. For example, consider the following SERIES formula:

```
=SERIES(,Sheet1!$A$1:$A$6,Sheet1!$B$1:$B$6,1)
```

You can define range names for the two ranges (for example, `Categories` and `Data`), and then edit the SERIES formula so it uses the range names instead of the range references. The edited formula would be as follows:

```
=SERIES(,Sheet1!Categories,Sheet1!Data,1)
```

Once you've defined the names and edited the SERIES formula, your VBA code can work with the names, and the changes will be reflected in the chart. For example, the following instruction redefines the "refers to" range as `Data`:

```
Range("B1:B12").Name = "Data"
```

After executing this statement, the chart updates itself and uses the new definition of Data.

The Resize method of the Range object is useful for resizing a named range. For example, the following code expands the range named Data to include one additional row:

```
With Range("Data")
    .Resize(.Rows.Count + 1, 1).Name = "Data"
End With
```

Displaying arbitrary data labels on a chart

One of the most frequent complaints about Excel's charting is its inflexible data labeling feature. For example, consider the XY chart in Figure 17-9. It might be useful to display the associated name for each data point. However, you can search all day and never find the Excel command that enables you to do this automatically. Data labels are limited to the values only . . . unless you want to edit each data label manually and replace it with text of your choice.

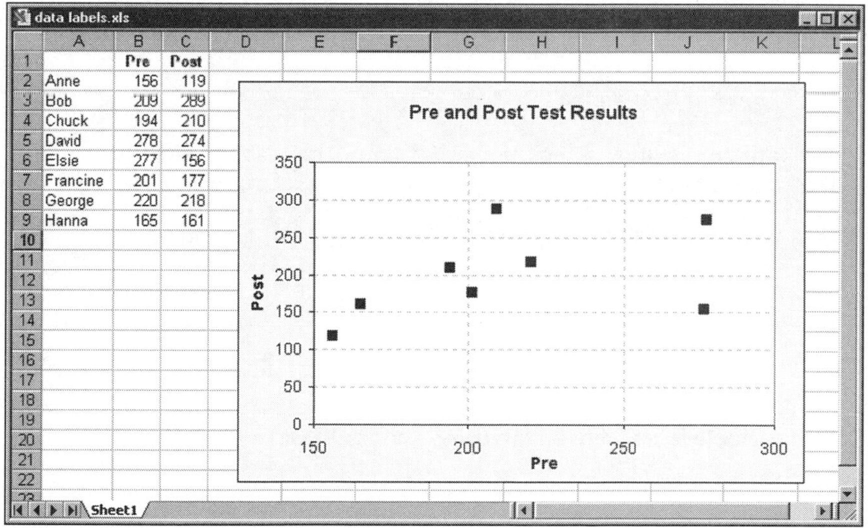

Figure 17-9: An XY chart with no data labels.

Listing 17-2 presents a simple procedure that works with the first chart on the active sheet. It prompts the user for a range and then loops through the `Points` collection and changes the `Text` property to the values found in the range.

Listing 17-2: Retrieving data point labels from field names in the worksheet

```
Sub DataLabelsFromRange()
    Dim DLRange As Range
    Dim Cht As Chart
    Dim i As Integer

'   Specify chart
    Set Cht = ActiveSheet.ChartObjects(1).Chart

'   Prompt for a range
    On Error Resume Next
    Set DLRange = Application.InputBox _
      (prompt:="Range for data labels?", Type:=8)
    If DLRange Is Nothing Then Exit Sub
    On Error GoTo 0

'   Add data labels
    Cht.SeriesCollection(1).ApplyDataLabels _
      Type:=xlDataLabelsShowValue, _
      AutoText:=True, _
      LegendKey:=False

'   Loop through the Points, and set the data labels
    Pts = Cht.SeriesCollection(1).Points.Count
    For i = 1 To Pts
        Cht.SeriesCollection(1). _
          Points(i).DataLabel.Characters.Text = DLRange(i)
    Next i
End Sub
```

This example is available on the companion CD-ROM.

Figure 17-10 shows the chart after running the `DataLabelsFromRange` procedure and specifying A2:A9 as the data range.

Note: The preceding procedure is rather crude, and does very little error checking. In addition, it works only with the first `Series` object. The Power Utility Pak (available by using the coupon in the back of the book) includes a much more sophisticated data labeling utility.

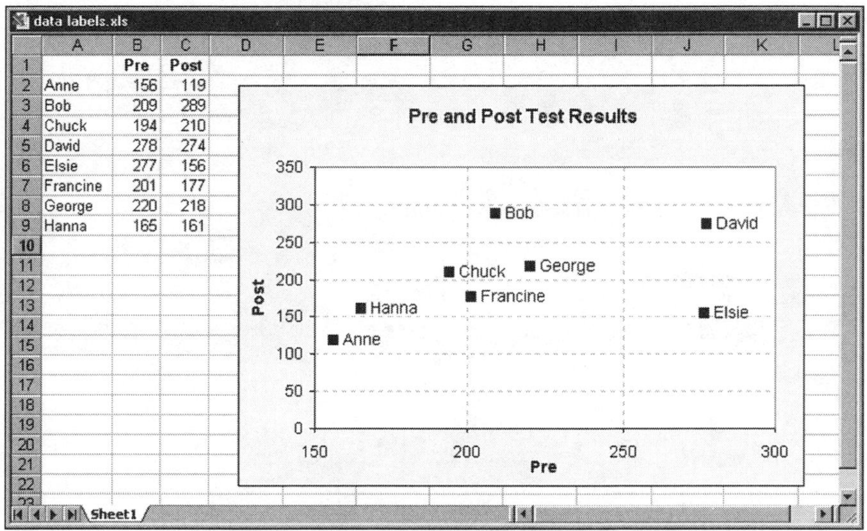

Figure 17-10: This XY chart has data labels, thanks to a VBA procedure.

Displaying a chart in a UserForm

In Chapter 14, I described a way to display a chart in a UserForm. The technique saves the chart as a GIF file and then loads the GIF file into an Image control on the UserForm.

The example in this section uses the same technique but adds a new twist: The chart is created on the fly and uses the data in the row of the active cell. Figure 17-11 shows an example.

The UserForm for this example is very simple. It contains an Image control and a CommandButton (Close). The worksheet that contains the data has a button that executes the following procedure:

```
Sub ShowChart()
    UserRow = ActiveCell.Row
    If UserRow < 2 Or IsEmpty(Cells(UserRow, 1)) Then
        MsgBox _
          "Move the cell cursor to a row that contains data."
```

```
        Exit Sub
    End If
    CreateChart (UserRow)
    UserForm1.Show
End Sub
```

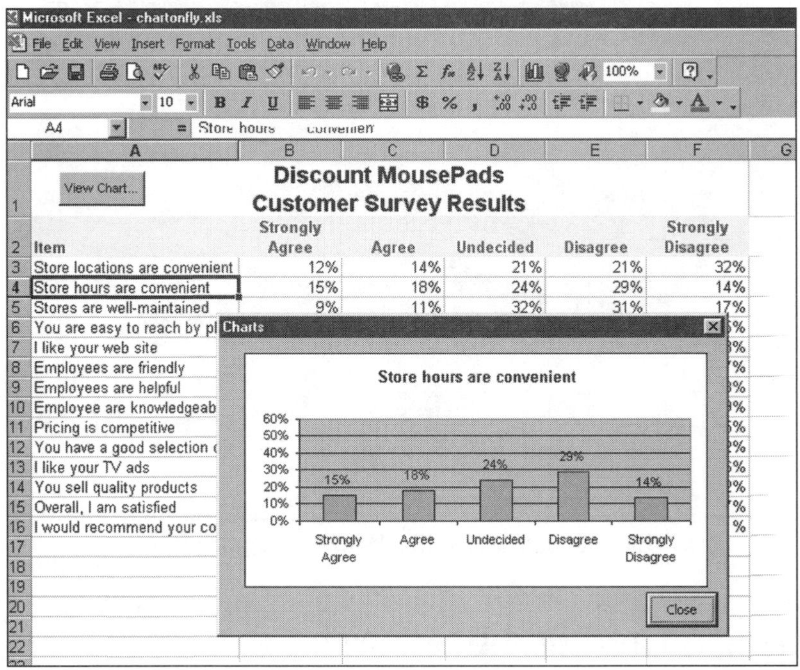

Figure 17-11: The chart in this UserForm is created on the fly using the data in the active row.

Because the chart is based on the data in the row of the active cell, the procedure warns the user if the cell cursor is in an invalid row. If the active cell is appropriate, `ShowChart` calls the `CreateChart` procedure to create the chart, and then displays the UserForm.

The `CreateChart` procedure shown in Listing 17-3 accepts one argument, which represents the row of the active cell. This procedure originated from a macro recording that I cleaned up to make more general.

Listing 17-3: Automatically generating a chart without user interaction

```
Sub CreateChart(r)
    Dim TempChart As Chart
    Application.ScreenUpdating = False

    Set CatTitles = ActiveSheet.Range("A2:F2")
    Set SrcRange = ActiveSheet.Range(Cells(r, 1), Cells(r, 6))
    Set SourceData = Union(CatTitles, SrcRange)

'   Add a chart
    Set TempChart = Charts.Add

'   Fix it up
    With TempChart
        .ChartType = xlColumnClustered
        .SetSourceData Source:=SourceData, PlotBy:=xlRows
        .HasLegend = False
        .ApplyDataLabels Type:=xlDataLabelsShowValue, _
         LegendKey:=False
        .ChartTitle.Font.Size = 14
        .ChartTitle.Font.Bold = True
        .Axes(xlValue).MaximumScale = 0.6
        .Axes(xlCategory).TickLabels.Font.Size = 10
        .Axes(xlCategory).TickLabels.Orientation = _
         xlHorizontal
        .Location Where:=xlLocationAsObject, Name:="Sheet1"
    End With

'   Adjust the ChartObject's size size
    With ActiveSheet.ChartObjects(1)
        .Width = 300
        .Height = 150
        .Visible = False
    End With
End Sub
```

When the CreateChart procedure ends, the worksheet contains a ChartObject with a chart of the data in the row of the active cell. However, the ChartObject is not visible, because ScreenUpdating was turned off.

The final instruction of the ShowChart procedure loads the UserForm. Following is a listing of the UserForm_Initialize procedure. This procedure saves the chart as a GIF file, deletes the ChartObject, and loads the GIF file into the Image control.

```
Private Sub UserForm_Initialize()
    Set CurrentChart = ActiveSheet.ChartObjects(1).Chart
```

```
'    Save chart as GIF
     Fname = ThisWorkbook.Path & Application.PathSeparator _
       & "temp.gif"
     CurrentChart.Export FileName:=Fname, FilterName:="GIF"
     Sheets("Sheet1").ChartObjects(1).Delete

'    Show the chart
     Image1.Picture = LoadPicture(Fname)
     Application.ScreenUpdating = True
End Sub
```

Understanding Chart Events

Excel supports several events associated with charts. For example, when a chart is activated, it generates an `Activate` event. The `Calculate` event occurs after the chart receives new or changed data. You can, of course, write VBA code that gets executed when a particular event occurs.

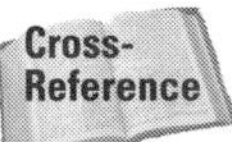

Refer to Chapter 18 for additional information about events.

Table 17-1 lists all the chart events supported by Excel 97 and Excel 2000.

Table 17-1
Events Recognized by the Chart Class

Event	***Action that triggers the event***
`Activate`	A chart sheet or embedded chart is activated.
`BeforeDoubleClick`	An embedded chart is double-clicked. This event occurs before the default double-click action.
`BeforeRightClick`	An embedded chart is right-clicked. This event occurs before the default right-click action.
`Calculate`	New or changed data is plotted on a chart.
`Deactivate`	A chart is deactivated.
`DragOver`	A range of cells is dragged over a chart.
`DragPlot`	A range of cells is dragged and dropped onto a chart.
`MouseDown`	A mouse button is pressed while the pointer is over a chart.

Event	*Action that triggers the event*
`MouseMove`	The position of the mouse pointer changes over a chart.
`MouseUp`	A mouse button is released while the pointer is over a chart.
`Resize`	A chart is resized.
`Select`	A chart element is selected.
`SeriesChange`	The value of a chart data point is changed.

An example of using Chart events

To program an event handler for a event taking place on a chart sheet, your VBA code must reside in the code module for the `Chart` class object. To activate this code module, double-click the Chart item in the Project window. Then, in the code module, select Chart from the Object drop-down list on the left, and select the event from the Procedure drop-down list on the right (see Figure 17-12).

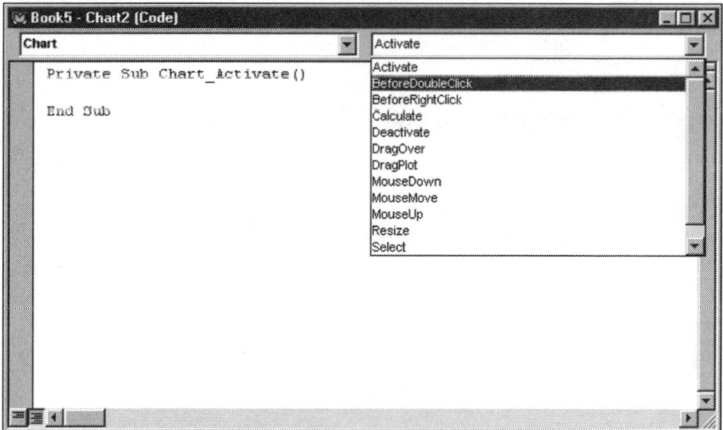

Figure 17-12: Selecting an event in the code module for a `Chart` class object.

Because there is not a code module for embedded charts, the procedure described in this section works only for chart sheets. You can also handle events for embedded charts, but you must do some initial setup work that involves creating a class module. This procedure is described in the next section, "Enabling events for an embedded chart."

To demonstrate, I created a workbook with a chart sheet. Then I wrote three event-handler procedures named as follows:

`Chart_Activate`	Executed when the chart sheet is activated
`Chart_Deactivate`	Executed when the chart sheet is deactivated
`Chart_Select`	Executed when an element on the chart sheet is selected

The `Chart_Activate` procedure is as follows:

```
Private Sub Chart_Activate()
    msg = "Hello " & Application.UserName & vbCrLf & vbCrLf
    msg = msg & "You are now viewing the six-month sales "
    msg = msg & "summary for Products 1-3." & vbCrLf & vbCrLf
    msg = msg & _
      "Click on items in the chart to find out what they are."
    MsgBox msg, vbInformation, ActiveWorkbook.Name
End Sub
```

This procedure simply displays a message whenever the chart is activated (see Figure 17-13).

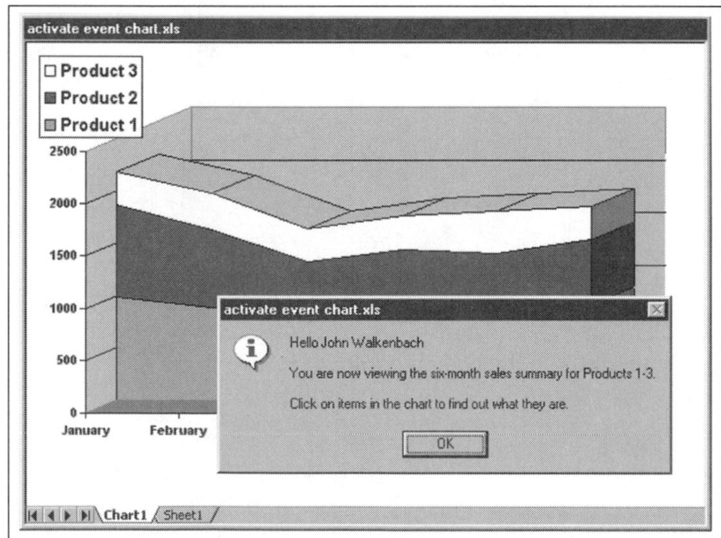

Figure 17-13: Activating the chart causes `Chart_Activate` to display this message.

The following `Chart_Deactivate` procedure also displays a message only when the chart sheet is deactivated:

```
Private Sub Chart_Deactivate()
    msg = "Thanks for viewing the chart."
    MsgBox msg, , ActiveWorkbook.Name
End Sub
```

The `Chart_Select` procedure listed next is executed whenever an item on the chart is selected:

```
Private Sub Chart_Select(ByVal ElementID As Long, _
  ByVal Arg1 As Long, ByVal Arg2 As Long)
    Select Case ElementID
        Case xlChartArea: Id = "ChartArea"
        Case xlChartTitle: Id = "ChartTitle"
        Case xlPlotArea: Id = "PlotArea"
        Case xlLegend: Id = "Legend"
        Case xlFloor: Id = "Floor"
        Case xlWalls: Id = "Walls"
        Case xlCorners: Id = "Corners"
        Case xlDataTable: Id = "DataTable"
        Case xlSeries: Id = "Series"
        Case xlDataLabel: Id = "DataLabel"
        Case xlTrendline: Id = "Trendline"
        Case xlErrorBars: Id = "ErrorBars"
        Case xlXErrorBars: Id = "XErrorBars"
        Case xlYErrorBars: Id = "YErrorBars"
        Case xlLegendEntry: Id = "LegendEntry"
        Case xlLegendKey: Id = "LegendKey"
        Case xlAxis: Id = "Axis"
        Case xlMajorGridlines: Id = "MajorGridlines"
        Case xlMinorGridlines: Id = "MinorGridlines"
        Case xlAxisTitle: Id = "AxisTitle"
        Case xlUpBars: Id = "UpBars"
        Case xlDownBars: Id = "DownBars"
        Case xlSeriesLines: Id = "SeriesLines"
        Case xlHiLoLines: Id = "HiLoLines"
        Case xlDropLines: Id = "DropLines"
        Case xlRadarAxisLabels: Id = "RadarAxisLabels"
        Case xlShape: Id = "Shape"
        Case xlNothing: Id = "Nothing"
        Case Else: Id = "Some unknown thing"
    End Select
    MsgBox "Selection type:" & Id
End Sub
```

This procedure simply displays a message box that contains a description of the selected item. When the `Select` event occurs, the `ElementID` argument contains an integer that corresponds to what was selected. The `Arg1` and `Arg2` arguments provide additional information about the selected item (see the online help for details). The Select Case structure converts the built-in constants to descriptive strings.

Enabling events for an embedded chart

As I noted in the previous section, Chart class events are automatically enabled for chart sheets, but not for embedded charts. To use events with an embedded chart, you need to perform the following steps:

Create a class module

In the VB Editor window, select your project in the Project window and select Insert ➪ Class Module. This adds a new (empty) class module to your project. If you like, you can use the Properties window to give the class module a more descriptive name.

Declare a public Chart class object

The next step is to declare a Public variable that will be used as the class name. The variable should be of type Chart, and it must be declared using the WithEvents keyword. If you omit the WithEvents keyword, the object will not respond to events. Following is an example of such a declaration:

```
Public WithEvents myChartClass As Chart
```

Connect the declared object with your chart

Before your event-handler procedures will run, you must connect the declared object in the class module with your embedded chart. You do this by declaring an object of type Class1 (or whatever your class module is named). Here's an example:

```
Dim MyChart As New Class1
```

Then, you must write code to actually instantiate the object, such as this instruction:

```
Set MyChart.myChartClass = ActiveSheet.ChartObjects(1).Chart
```

After the preceding statement is executed, the myChartClass object in the class module points to the first embedded chart on the active sheet. Consequently, the event-handler procedures in the class module execute when the events occur.

The event-handler procedures for the new object must be written in the class module, not a general module.

Write event-handler procedures for the chart class

In this section I describe how to write event-handler procedures in the class module. Recall that the class module must contain a declaration such as `Public WithEvents myChartClass As Chart`.

After this new object has been declared using the `WithEvents` keyword, it appears in the Object drop-down list box in the class module. When you select the new object in the Object box, the valid events for that object are listed in the Procedure drop-down box on the right (see Figure 17-14).

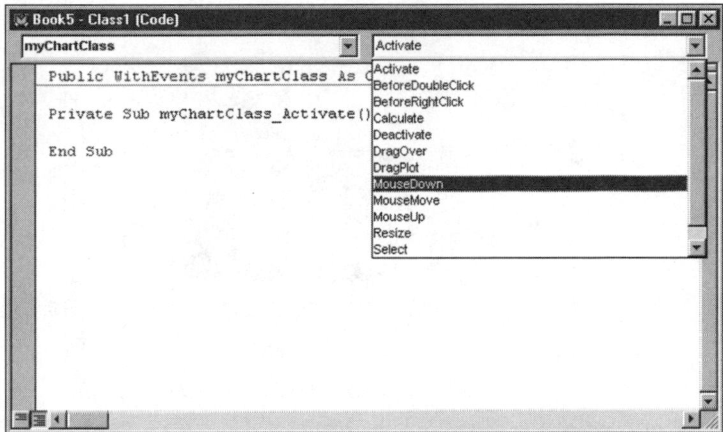

Figure 17-14: The Procedure list displays valid events for the new `Chart` class object.

The following example is a simple event-handler procedure that is executed when the embedded chart is activated. This procedure simply pops up a message box that displays the name of the `Chart` class object's parent (which is a `ChartObject` class object).

```
Private Sub myChartClass_Activate()
    MsgBox myChartClass.Parent.Name & " was activated!"
End Sub
```

Example: Using Chart events with an embedded chart

The example in this section provides a practical demonstration of the information presented in the previous section. The example shown in Figure 17-15 consists of an embedded chart that functions as a clickable image map. Clicking one of the chart columns activates a worksheet that shows detailed data for the region.

The workbook is set up with four worksheets. The one that contains the embedded chart is named `Main`. The others are named `North`, `South`, and `West`. Formulas in B1:B4 sum the data in the respective sheets, and this summary data is displayed in the chart. Clicking a column in the chart triggers an event, and the event-handler procedure activates the appropriate sheet so the user can view the details for the desired region.

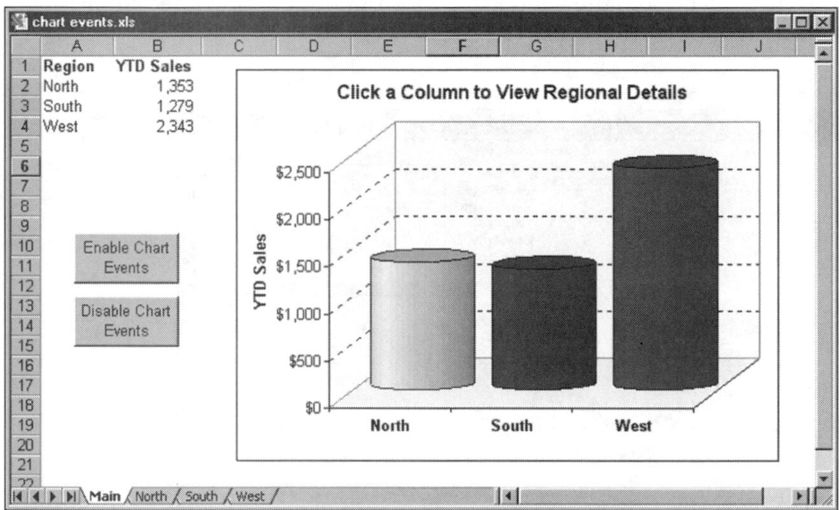

Figure 17-15: This chart has been made interactive.

The workbook contains a class module named `EmbChartClass`, and also a normal VBA module named `Module1`. For demonstration purposes, the `Main` worksheet also contains two buttons: one button executes a procedure named `EnableChartEvents`, and the other button executes a procedure named `DisableChartEvents` (both are located in `Module1`). In addition, each of the other worksheets contains a button that executes a macro that reactivates the Main sheet.

The complete listing of `Module1` is as follows:

```
Dim SummaryChart As New EmbChartClass

Sub EnableChartEvents()
    Range("A1").Select
    Set SummaryChart.myChartClass = _
      Worksheets(1).ChartObjects(1).Chart
End Sub

Sub DisableChartEvents()
    Set SummaryChart.myChartClass = Nothing
```

```
    Range("A1").Select
End Sub

Sub ReturnToMain()
    Sheets("Main").Activate
End Sub
```

The first instruction declares a new object variable `SummaryChart` to be of type `EmbChartClass`, which as you recall is the name of the class module. When the user clicks the Enable Chart Events button, the embedded chart is assigned to the `SummaryChart` class object that, in effect, enables the events for the chart. Listing 17-4 shows the class module for `EmbChartClass`.

Listing 17-4: Reacting to which column has been clicked

```
Public WithEvents myChartClass As Chart

Private Sub myChartClass_MouseDown(ByVal Button As Long, _
  ByVal Shift As Long, ByVal X As Long, ByVal Y As Long)

    Dim IDnum As Long
    Dim a As Long, b As Long

'   The next statement returns values for
'   IDNum, a, and b
    myChartClass.GetChartElement X, Y, IDnum, a, b

'   Was a series clicked?
    If IDnum = xlSeries Then
        Select Case b
            Case 1
                Sheets("North").Activate
            Case 2
                Sheets("South").Activate
            Case 3
                Sheets("West").Activate
        End Select
    End If
    Range("A1").Select
End Sub
```

Clicking the chart generates a `MouseDown` event, which executes the `myChartClass_MouseDown` procedure. This procedure uses the `GetChartElement` method to determine what element of the chart was clicked.

Charting Tricks

I conclude this chapter by sharing a few charting tricks that I've discovered over the years. Some of these techniques may be useful in your applications, and others are simply for fun. At the very least, studying them may give you some new insights into the object model for charts.

Printing embedded charts on a full page

As I noted earlier in this chapter (see "Activating a chart"), an embedded chart can be displayed in a window by right-clicking the chart and selecting Chart Window from the shortcut menu.

When an embedded chart's window is visible, you can print the chart by right-clicking its title bar and selecting Print from the shortcut menu. The result? Your embedded chart is printed on a full page by itself (just as if it were on a chart sheet), yet it remains an embedded chart.

The following macro prints all embedded charts on the active sheet, and each chart is printed on a full page:

```
Sub PrintEmbeddedCharts()
    For Each chtObj In ActiveSheet.ChartObjects
        chtObj.Activate
        ActiveChart.ShowWindow = True
        ActiveWindow.SelectedSheets.PrintOut
        ActiveWindow.Visible = False
    Next chtObj
End Sub
```

Creating a "dead chart"

Normally, an Excel chart uses data stored in a range. Change the data in the range, and the chart is updated automatically. In some cases, you may want to "unlink" the chart from its data ranges and produce a *dead chart*—a chart that never changes. For example, if you plot data generated by various what-if scenarios, you may want to save a chart that represents some baseline so you can compare it with other scenarios.

There are two ways to create such a chart:

✦ *Paste it as a picture:* Activate the chart and choose Edit ➪ Copy. Then, press the Shift key and select Edit ➪ Paste Picture (the Paste Picture command is available only if you press Shift when you select the Edit menu). The result is a picture of the copied chart.

✦ *Convert the range references to arrays:* Click a chart series and then click the formula bar. Press F9 to convert the ranges to an array. Repeat this for each series in the chart.

The xl8galry.xls file uses this technique. This file is a special workbook used by Excel to store its custom chart formats. If you open this workbook, you'll find 20 chart sheets. Each chart sheet has "dummy" data, which uses an array rather than a range as its source.

Note

Another way to create a dead chart is to use VBA to assign an array rather than a range to the `XValue` or `Value` property of the `Series` object.

Controlling a data series by hiding data

Figure 17-16 shows a chart that displays daily data for 365 days. What if you want to plot, say, only the data for February? You could, of course, redefine the chart's data range. Or, you could take advantage of Excel's AutoFilter command.

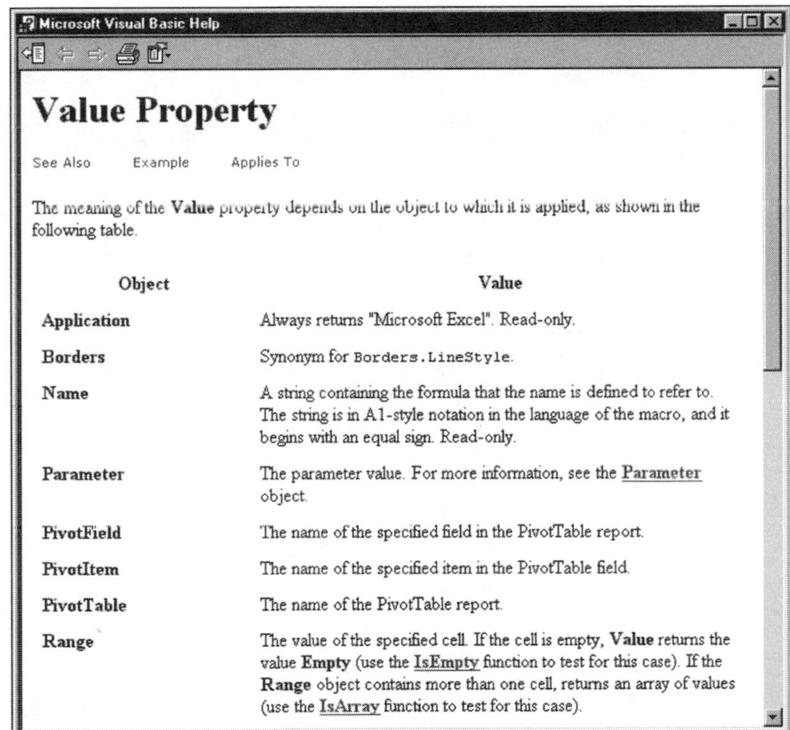

Microsoft Visual Basic Help

Value Property

See Also Example Applies To

The meaning of the **Value** property depends on the object to which it is applied, as shown in the following table.

Object	Value
Application	Always returns "Microsoft Excel". Read-only.
Borders	Synonym for `Borders.LineStyle`.
Name	A string containing the formula that the name is defined to refer to. The string is in A1-style notation in the language of the macro, and it begins with an equal sign. Read-only.
Parameter	The parameter value. For more information, see the Parameter object.
PivotField	The name of the specified field in the PivotTable report.
PivotItem	The name of the specified item in the PivotTable field.
PivotTable	The name of the PivotTable report.
Range	The value of the specified cell. If the cell is empty, **Value** returns the value **Empty** (use the IsEmpty function to test for this case). If the **Range** object contains more than one cell, returns an array of values (use the IsArray function to test for this case).

Figure 17-16: You can use Excel's AutoFilter feature to plot only a subset of the data.

By default, a chart does not display data that's hidden. Because Excel's AutoFilter feature works by hiding rows that don't meet your criteria, it's a simple solution.

Select Data ⇨ Filter ⇨ AutoFilter to turn on the AutoFilter mode. Each row heading in the filtered list displays a drop-down arrow. Click the arrow and select Custom from the list. Then, enter your filter criteria that selects the dates you want to plot. The setting shown in Figure 17-17, for example, hides all rows except those that have a date in February.

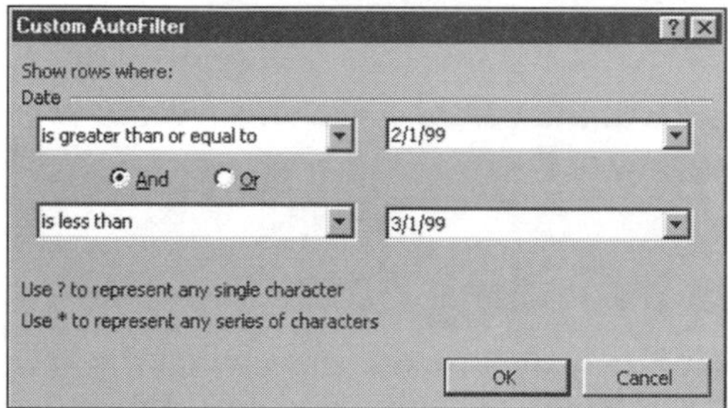

Figure 17-17: Use the Custom AutoFilter dialog box to filter a list.

The resulting chart is shown in Figure 17-18.

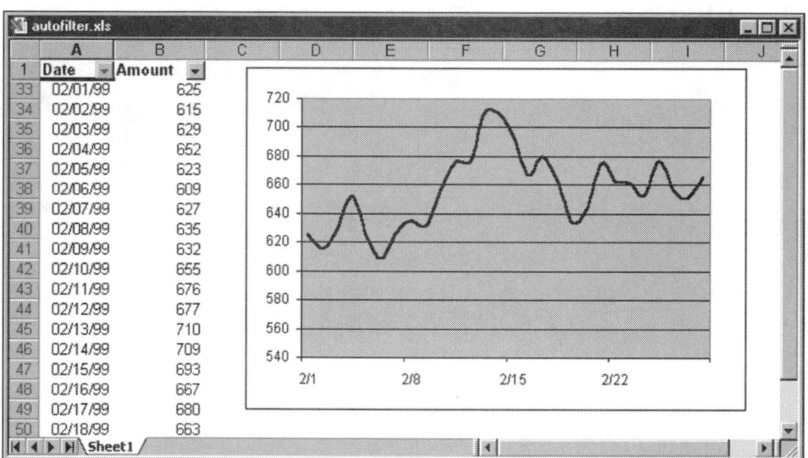

Figure 17-18: Only visible cells are displayed in a chart.

If this technique doesn't seem to be working, you need to change a setting for the chart. Activate the chart, then choose Tools ⇨ Options. In the Options dialog box, click the Chart tab and place a check mark next to *Plot visible cells only.*

A workbook that demonstrates this technique is available on the companion CD-ROM.

Storing multiple charts on a chart sheet

Most Excel users would agree that a chart sheet holds a single chart. Most of the time, that's a true statement. However, it's certainly possible to store multiple charts on a single chart sheet. In fact, Excel enables you to do this directly. If you activate an embedded chart and then select Chart ⇨ Location, Excel displays its Chart Location dialog box. If you select the As new sheet option and specify an existing chart sheet as the location, you see the dialog box shown in Figure 17-19. Click OK and the chart appears on top of the chart in the chart sheet.

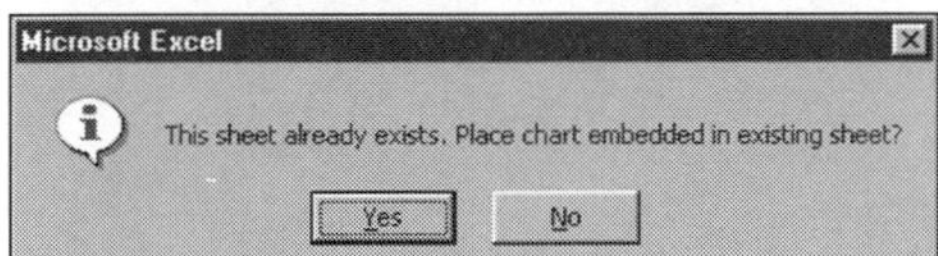

Figure 17-19: Excel enables you to relocate an embedded chart to an existing chart sheet.

Most of the time, you'll want to add embedded charts to an *empty* chart sheet. To create an empty chart sheet, select a single blank cell and press F11.

One advantage of storing multiple charts on a chart sheet is that you can take advantage of the View ⇨ Sized with Window command to automatically scale the charts to the window size and dimensions. Figure 17-20 shows an example of a chart sheet that contains six embedded charts.

Using linked pictures in a chart

Excel has a feature that enables you to display a data table inside of a chart. You can select this option in Step 3 of the ChartWizard. The data table option displays a table that shows the values used in a chart. This is a handy feature, but it's not very flexible. For example, you can't apply formatting, and you have no control over the position of the data table (it always appears below the chart).

An alternative to the data table is a linked picture of a range (see Figure 17-21 for an example).

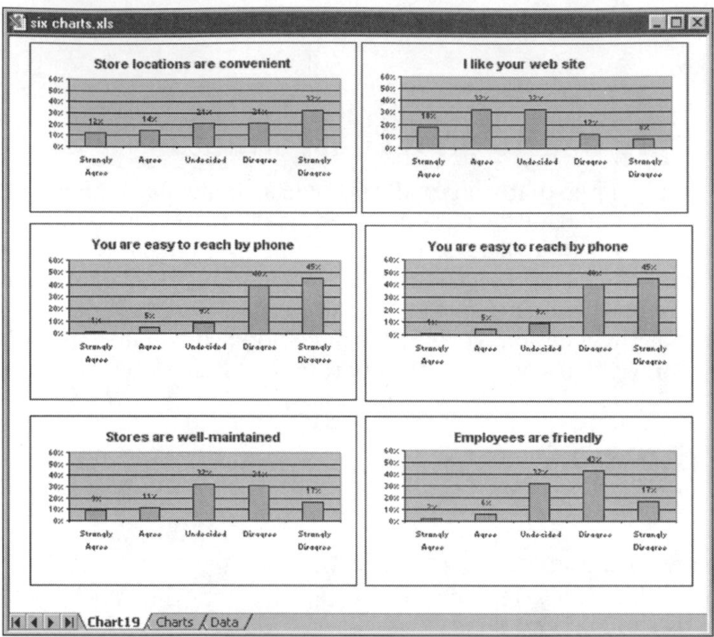

Figure 17-20: This chart sheet contains six embedded charts.

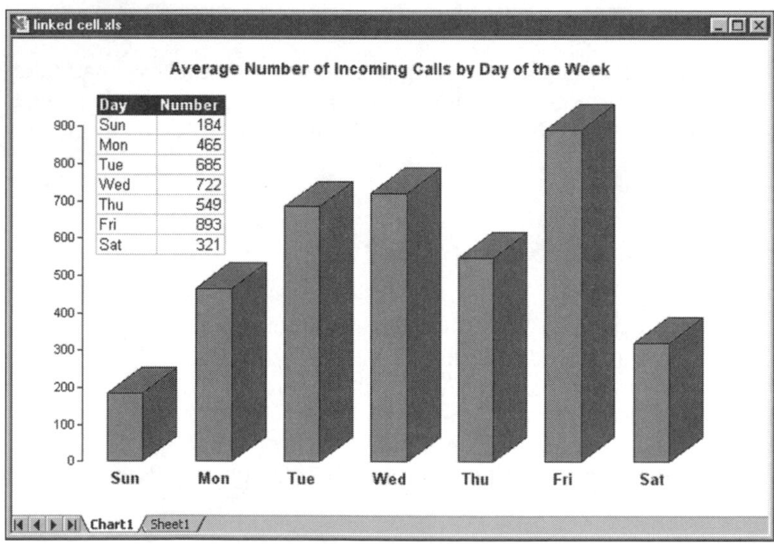

Figure 17-21: This chart contains a linked picture of a range.

To create a linked picture in a chart, first create the chart as you normally would. Then perform the following steps:

1. Select the range that you would like to include in the chart.
2. Select Edit ➪ Copy.
3. Activate the chart.
4. Press Shift, and then select Edit ➪ Paste Picture. This pastes an unlinked picture of the range.
5. To create the link, select the picture and then type a reference to the range in the formula bar. The easiest way to do this is to type an equal sign and then reselect the range.

The picture now contains a live link to the range. If you change the values or cell formatting, they will be reflected in the linked picture.

Animated charts

Most people don't realize it, but Excel is capable of performing simple animations. For example, you can animate shapes and charts. Consider the XY chart shown in Figure 17-22.

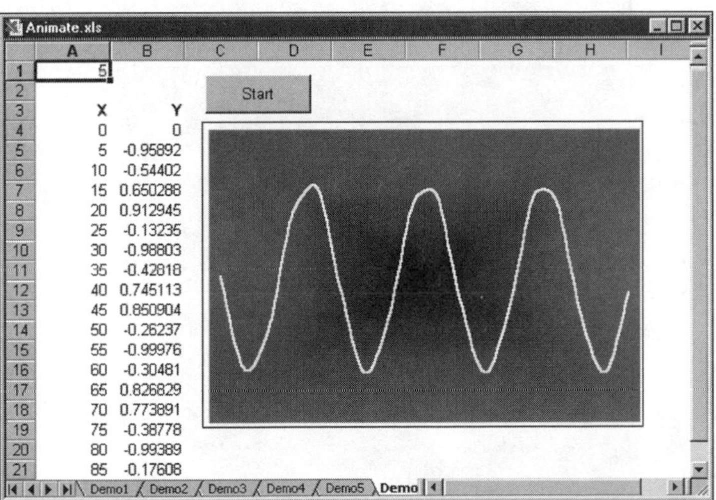

Figure 17-22: A simple VBA procedure turns this graph into an interesting animation.

The X values (column A) depend on the value in cell A1. The value in each row is the previous row's value, plus the value in A1. Column B contains formulas that calculate the SIN of the corresponding value in column A. The following simple procedure produces an interesting animation. It simply changes the value in cell A1, which causes the values in the X and Y ranges to change.

```
Sub AnimateChart()
    Range("A1") = 0
    For i = 1 To 150
        Range("A1") = Range("A1") + 0.035
    Next i
    Range("A1") = 0
End Sub
```

The companion CD-ROM contains a workbook that features this animated chart, plus several other animation examples.

Plotting trigonometric functions

You can waste lots of time creating formulas that use various trigonometric functions . . . and come up with some very interesting charts! Figure 17-23 shows an example of such a chart produced with various trigonometric functions.

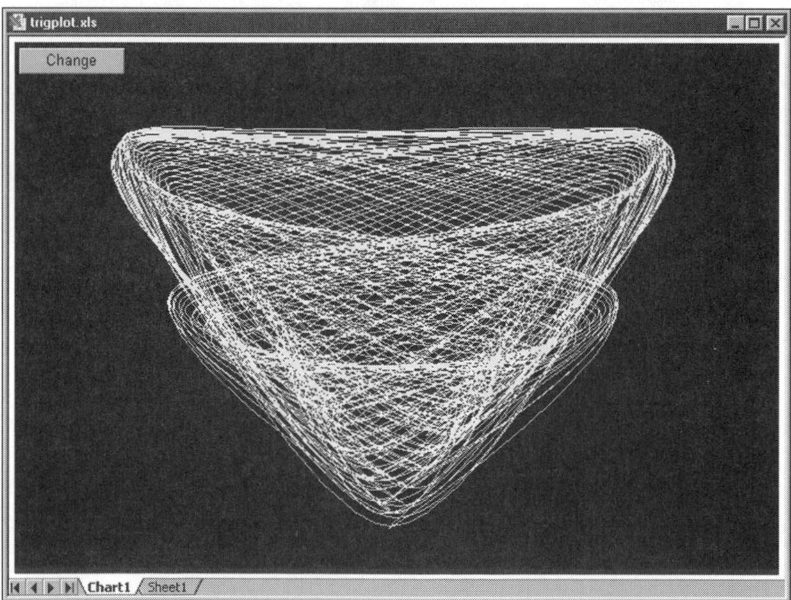

Figure 17-23: Plotting trigonometric functions can generate some attractive charts.

Two columns of numbers (the X and Y ranges) generate this chart. The first column (column B) consists of the following formula:

```
=SIN(A2)*COS(A2)*COS(TAN(A2))
```

The formula in the second column (column C) is as follows:

```
=SIN(B2)*COS(B2)*SIN(A2+B2)*COS(A2-B2)+SQRT(ABS(B2))
```

The look of the chart is highly dependent on the increment used for the values in column A.

Creating a "clock" chart

Figure 17-24 shows an XY chart formatted to look like a clock. It not only *looks* like a clock, but also functions like a clock. I can't think of a single reason why anyone would need to display a clock such as this on a worksheet, but creating the workbook was challenging, and you may find it instructive.

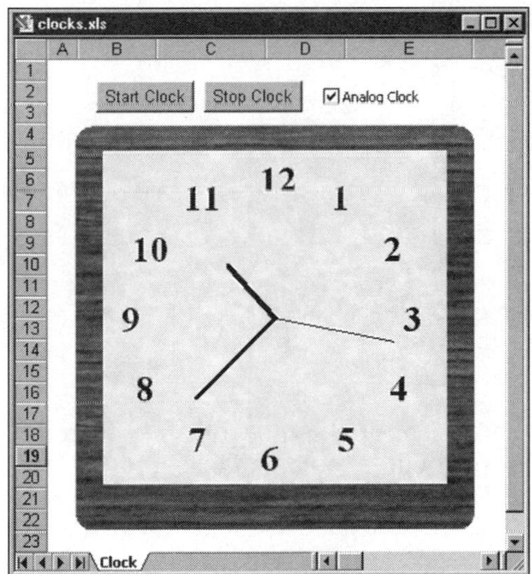

Figure 17-24: This clock is fully functional and is actually an XY chart in disguise.

This workbook is available on the companion CD-ROM.

Besides the clock chart, the workbook contains a text box that displays the time as a normal string, as shown in Figure 17-25. Normally this is hidden, but it can be displayed by deselecting the Analog clock check box.

As you explore this workbook from the CD-ROM, here are a few things to keep in mind:

✦ The `ChartObject` is named `ClockChart`, and it covers up a range named `DigitalClock`, which is used to display the time digitally.

✦ The two buttons on the worksheet are from the Forms toolbar, and each has a macro assigned to it (`StartClock` and `StopClock`).

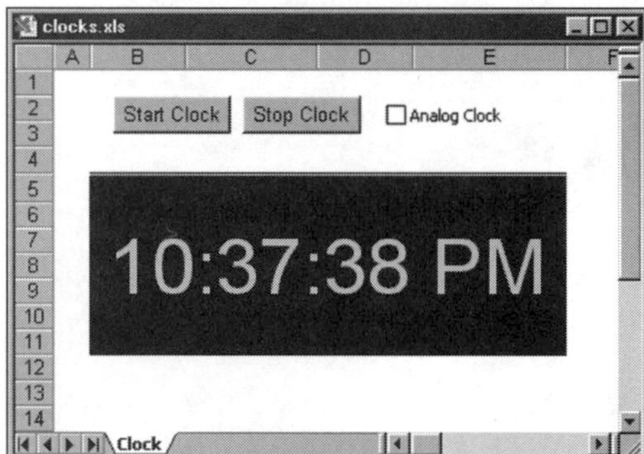

Figure 17-25: Displaying a digital clock in a worksheet is much easier, but not as fun to create.

✦ The CheckBox control (named `cbClockType`) on the worksheet is from the Forms toolbar, not from the Control Toolbox toolbar. Clicking the object executes a procedure named `cbClockType_Click`, which simply toggles the `Visible` property of the `ChartObject`. When it's invisible, the digital clock is revealed.

✦ The chart is an XY chart with four `Series` objects. These series represent the hour hand, the minute hand, the second hand, and the 12 numbers.

✦ The `UpdateClock` procedure is executed when the Start Clock button is clicked. This procedure determines which clock is visible and performs the appropriate updating.

✦ The `UpdateClock` procedure uses the `OnTime` method of the `Application` object. This method enables you to execute a procedure at a specific time.

Before the `UpdateClock` procedure ends, it sets up a new `OnTime` event that will occur in one second. In other words, the `UpdateClock` procedure is called every second.

✦ The `UpdateClock` procedure uses some basic trigonometry to determine the angles at which to display the hands on the clock.

✦ Unlike most charts, this one does not use any worksheet ranges for its data. Rather, the values are calculated in VBA and transferred directly to the `Values` and `Xvalues` properties of the chart's `Series` object.

Drawing with an XY chart

The final example has absolutely no practical value, but you may find it interesting (and maybe even a bit entertaining). The worksheet consists of an embedded XY chart, along with a number of controls (these are controls from the Forms toolbar and are not ActiveX controls).

This workbook is available on the companion CD-ROM.

Clicking one of the arrow buttons draws a line in the chart, the size of which is determined by the step value, which is set with one of the Spin controls. With a little practice (and patience) you can create simple sketches. Figure 17-26 shows an example.

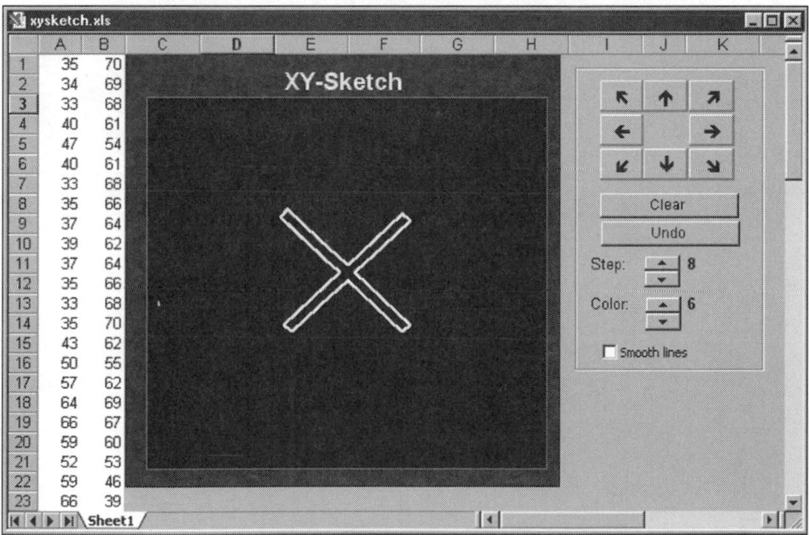

Figure 17-26: This drawing is actually an embedded XY chart.

Clicking an arrow button executes a macro that adds two values to a range: an X value and a Y value. It then redefines two range names (`XRange` and `YRange`) that are used in the chart's SERIES formula. Particularly handy is the multilevel Undo button. Clicking this button simply erases the last two values in the range and then redefines the range names. Additional accouterments include the capability to change the color of the lines and the capability to display "smoothed" lines.

Summary

In this chapter, I introduced the object model for charts and showed how to write VBA code to create and manipulate charts. This chapter included several examples that made use of events.

In the next chapter, I cover the concept of events in detail.

✦ ✦ ✦

CHAPTER 18

Understanding Excel's Events

✦ ✦ ✦ ✦

In This Chapter

An overview of the types of events that Excel can monitor

Essential background information for working with events

Examples of `Workbook`, `Worksheet`, `Chart`, and `UserForm` events

Using Application events to monitor all open workbooks

Examples of processing time-based and keystroke events

✦ ✦ ✦ ✦

In several previous chapters in this book I presented examples of VBA event-handler procedures, which are specially named procedures executed when specific events occur. A simple example is the `CommandButton1_Click` procedure executed when a user clicks a CommandButton on a UserForm.

Excel is capable of monitoring a wide variety of events and executing your VBA code when a particular event occurs. The following are just a few examples of the types of events that Excel can recognize:

- A workbook is opened or closed.
- A window is activated.
- A worksheet is activated or deactivated.
- Data is entered into a cell, or the cell is edited.
- A workbook is saved.
- A worksheet is calculated.
- An object is clicked.
- The data in a chart is updated.
- A particular key or key combination is pressed.
- A cell is double-clicked.
- A particular time of day occurs.
- An error occurs.

This chapter provides comprehensive coverage of the concept of Excel events, and I include many examples that you can adapt to meet your own needs. As you'll see, understanding and implementing events can give your Excel applications a powerful edge.

Event Types That Excel Can Monitor

Excel is programmed to monitor many different events. These events can be classified in the following way:

✦ *Workbook events.* These occur for a particular workbook. Examples include `Open` (the workbook is opened or created), `BeforeSave` (the workbook is about to be saved), and `NewSheet` (a new sheet is added).

✦ *Worksheet events.* These occur for a particular worksheet. Examples include `Change` (a cell on the sheet is changed), `SelectionChange` (the cell pointer is moved), and `Calculate` (the worksheet is recalculated).

✦ *Chart events.* These occur for a particular chart. Examples include `Select` (a chart object is selected) and `SeriesChange` (a data point value in a series is changed). To monitor events for an embedded chart, use a class module as demonstrated in Chapter 17.

✦ *Application events.* These occur for the application (Excel). Examples include `NewWorkbook` (a new workbook is created), `WorkbookBeforeClose` (any workbook is about to be closed), and `SheetChange` (a cell in any open workbook is altered).

✦ *UserForm events.* These occur for a particular UserForm or object contained on the UserForm. For example, a UserForm has an `Initialize` event (which occurs before the UserForm is displayed); and a CommandButton on a UserForm has a `Click` event (which occurs when the button is clicked).

✦ *Events not associated with objects.* The final category consists of two useful Application-level events that I call "On-" events: `OnTime` and `OnKey`. These work differently than other events.

This chapter is organized according to the preceding list. Within each section, I provide examples to demonstrate some events.

What You Should Know about Events

This section provides essential information relevant to working with events and writing event-handler procedures.

Understanding event sequences

As you'll see, some actions trigger multiple events. For example, when you insert a new worksheet into a workbook, this triggers several events at the Application level:

1. `SheetDeactivate` event. This occurs when the active worksheet is deactivated.

2. `SheetActivate` event. This occurs when the newly added worksheet is activated.

3. `WorkbookNewSheet` event. This occurs when a new worksheet is added.

Event sequencing is more complicated than you might think. The preceding events are Application-level events. When you add a new worksheet, additional events occur at the `Workbook` and `Worksheet` levels.

These three events occur in the order listed. Event sequences are not always logical. For example, you might think that the `WorkbookNewSheet` event occurs before the `SheetActivate` event, but it doesn't.

At this point, just keep in mind that events fire in a particular sequence, and knowing what the sequence is can be critical when writing event-handler procedures. Later in this chapter, I describe how to determine the order of the events that occur for a particular action (see "Monitoring Application-level events").

Where to put event-handler procedures

Newcomers often wonder why their event-handler procedures aren't executing when events occur. The answer almost always is that these procedures are in the wrong place.

In the Visual Basic Editor (VB Editor) window, each project is listed in the Project window. The project components are arranged in a collapsible list, as shown in Figure 18-1.

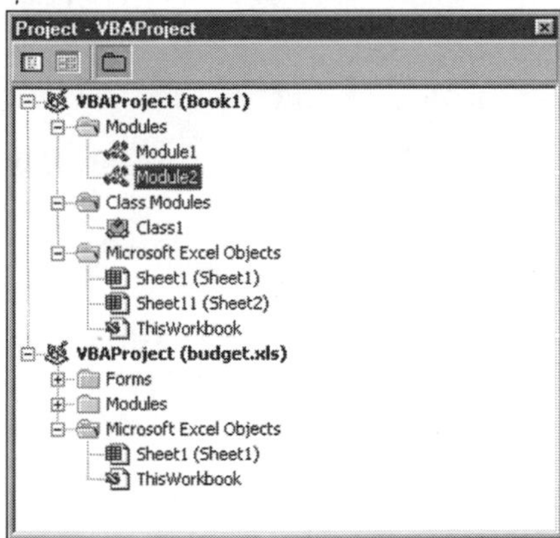

Figure 18-1: The components of each VBA project are listed in the Project window.

Each of the following components has its own code module:

✦ `Sheet` objects.

✦ `Chart` objects.

✦ `ThisWorkbook` object.

✦ General VBA modules. Never put event-handler procedures in a general (that is, nonobject) module.

✦ Class modules.

Even though the event-handler procedure must be located in the correct module, the procedure can call other standard procedures stored in other modules. For example, the following procedure, located in the module for the `ThisWorkbook` object, calls a procedure named `WorkbookSetup` stored in a general VBA module.

```
Private Sub Workbook_Open()
    Call WorkbookSetup
End Sub
```

Disabling events

Be default, all events are enabled. To disable all events, execute the following VBA instruction:

```
Application.EnableEvents = False
```

Programming Events in Older Versions of Excel

Versions of Excel prior to Office 97 also supported events, but the programming protocols required to take advantage of them were different from those described in this chapter.

For example, if you have a procedure named `Auto_Open` stored in a general VBA module, this procedure executes when the workbook opens. In Excel 97, the `Auto_Open` procedure was supplemented with the `Workbook_Open` event-handler procedure, which was stored in the code module for the `ThisWorkbook` object and executed prior to `Auto_Open`.

With prior versions, it often was necessary to explicitly set up events. For example, if you needed to execute a procedure whenever data was entered into a cell, you had to execute a statement such as this:

```
Sheets("Sheet1").OnEntry = "ValidateEntry"
```

This statement instructed Excel to execute the procedure named `ValidateEntry` whenever data was entered into a cell. In Excel 97 or later versions, you simply create a procedure named `Worksheet_Change` and store it in the code module for the `Sheet1` object.

For compatibility reasons, Excel 97 and Excel 2000 still support the older event mechanism. However, if you're developing applications for use with Excel 97 or later versions, use the techniques described in this chapter.

To enable events, use this instruction:

```
Application.EnableEvents = True
```

Why do you need to disable events? The main reason is to prevent an infinite loop of cascading events from occurring.

For example, assume you've written code that executes whenever data is entered into a cell (this particular cell must contain a text string). In this case you use a procedure named `Worksheet_Change` to monitor the `Change` event for a `Worksheet`. Your procedure validates the user's entry, and if that entry is not a string, it displays a message and then clears the entry. The problem is that clearing the entry with your VBA code generates a new `Change` event, so your event-handler procedure executes again. This is not the intention, so you must disable events before you clear the cell, and then enable events again so you can monitor the user's next entry.

Another way to prevent an infinite loop of cascading events is to declare a `Static Boolean` variable at the beginning of your event-handler procedure, such as this:

```
Static AbortProc As Boolean
```

Whenever the procedure must make its own changes, set the `AbortProc` variable to True; otherwise, make sure it is set to False. Insert the following statement as the first instruction in the procedure:

```
If AbortProc Then Exit Sub
```

The event procedure is reentered, but the True state of `AbortProc` trips `Exit Sub`, sending VBA back to the previous iteration (at the end of which `AbortProc` resets to False). `AbortProc` becomes a kind of "guard lock" mechanism.

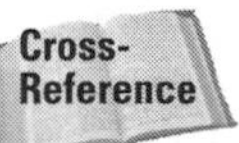

For a practical example of validating data, see "Validating data entry" later in this chapter.

Disabling events in Excel applies to all workbooks. For example, if you disable events in your procedure and then open another workbook that has, say, a `Workbook_Open` procedure, that procedure will not execute.

Entering event-handler code

Every event-handler procedure has a predetermined name. You can declare the procedure by typing it, but a much better approach is to let the VB Editor do it for you.

Figure 18-2 shows the code module for the `ThisWorkbook` object. To insert a procedure declaration, select `Workbook` from the objects list on the left. Then select the event from the procedures list on the right. When you do this, you get a procedure "shell" that contains the procedure declaration line and an `End Sub` statement.

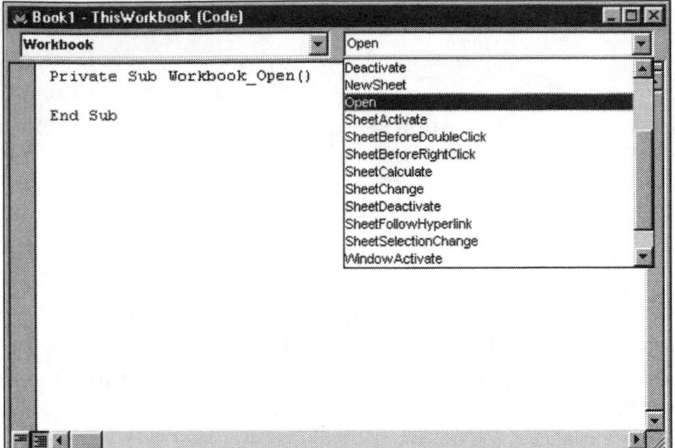

Figure 18-2: The best way to create an event procedure is to let the VB Editor do it for you.

For example, if you select `Workbook` from the objects list and `Open` from the procedures list, the VB Editor inserts the following (empty) procedure:

```
Private Sub Workbook_Open()

End Sub
```

Your code, of course, goes between these two lines.

Event-handler procedures that use arguments

Some event-handler procedures contain an argument list. For example, you may need to create an event-handler procedure to monitor the `SheetActivate` event for a workbook. If you use the technique described in the previous section, the VB Editor creates the following procedure:

```
Private Sub Workbook_SheetActivate(ByVal Sh As Object)

End Sub
```

This procedure uses one argument (`Sh`), which represents the activated sheet. In this case, `Sh` is declared as an Object data type rather than a Worksheet data type because the activated sheet also can be a Chart sheet.

Your code can, of course, make use of data passed as an argument. The following example displays the name of the activated sheet by accessing the argument's `Name` property. The argument becomes either a `Worksheet` object or a `Chart` object.

```
Private Sub Workbook_SheetActivate(ByVal Sh As Object)
    MsgBox Sh.Name & " was activated."
End Sub
```

Several event-handler procedures use a `Boolean` argument named `Cancel`. For example, the declaration for a Workbook's `BeforePrint` event is

```
Private Sub Workbook_BeforePrint(Cancel As Boolean)
```

The value of `Cancel` passed to the procedure is True. However, your code can set `Cancel` to False, which cancels the printing. The following example demonstrates this.

```
Private Sub Workbook_BeforePrint(Cancel As Boolean)
    Msg = "Have you loaded the 5164 label stock?"
    Ans = MsgBox(Msg, vbYesNo, "About to print...")
    If Ans = vbNo Then Cancel = True
End Sub
```

The `Workbook_BeforePrint` procedure executes before the workbook prints. This procedure displays the message box shown in Figure 18-3. If the user clicks the No button, `Cancel` is set to False and nothing prints.

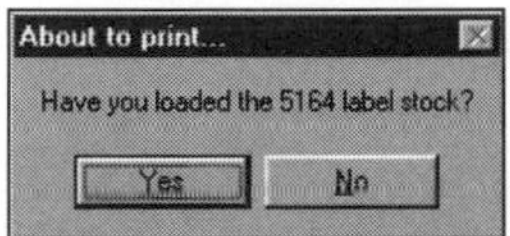

Figure 18-3: You can cancel an operation by changing the `Cancel` argument.

Workbook-Level Events

`Workbook`-level events occur for a particular workbook. Table 18-1 lists the `Workbook` events, along with a brief description of each. `Workbook` event-handler procedures are stored in the code module for the `ThisWorkbook` object.

If you need to monitor events for *any* workbook, you must work with Application-level events (see "Monitoring Application-level events" later in this chapter).

The remainder of this section presents examples of using `Workbook`-level events.

All the example procedures that follow must be located in the code module for the `ThisWorkbook` object. If you put them into any other type of code module, they will not work.

Table 18-1
Workbook Events

Event	Action That Triggers the Event
Activate	A workbook is activated.
AddinInstall	A workbook is installed as an add-in.
AddinUninstall	A workbook is uninstalled as an add-in.
BeforeClose	A workbook is about to be closed.
BeforePrint	A workbook (or anything in it) is about to be printed.
BeforeSave	A workbook is about to be saved.
Deactivate	A workbook is deactivated.
NewSheet	A new sheet is created in a workbook.
Open	A workbook is opened.
SheetActivate	Any sheet is activated.
SheetBeforeDoubleClick	Any worksheet is double-clicked. This event occurs before the default double-click action.
SheetBeforeRightClick	Any worksheet is right-clicked. This event occurs before the default right-click action.
SheetCalculate	Any worksheet is calculated (or recalculated).
SheetChange	Any worksheet is changed by the user or an external link.
SheetDeactivate	Any sheet is deactivated.
SheetSelectionChange	The selection on any worksheet is changed.
WindowActivate	Any workbook window is activated.
WindowDeactivate	Any workbook window is deactivated.
WindowResize	Any workbook window is resized.

Open event

One of the most common monitored events is a workbook's `Open` event. This event is triggered when the workbook (or add-in) opens, and executes the `Workbook_Open` procedure. A `Workbook_Open` procedure can do almost anything and often is used for the following tasks:

- ✦ Displaying welcome messages
- ✦ Opening other workbooks

✦ Setting up custom menus or toolbars

✦ Activating a particular sheet

✦ Ensuring that certain conditions are met. For example, a workbook may require that a particular add-in is installed.

✦ Setting up certain automatic features. For example, you can define a key combination (see "The OnKey event" later in this chapter)

✦ Setting a worksheet's `ScrollArea` property (which isn't stored with the workbook)

If the user holds down the Shift key while opening a workbook, the workbook's `Workbook_Open` procedure will not execute.

The following is a simple example of a `Workbook_Open` procedure. It uses VBA's `Weekday` function to determine the day of the week. If it's Friday, a message box appears to remind the user to perform a file backup. If it's not Friday, nothing happens.

```
Private Sub Workbook_Open()
  If Weekday(Now) = 5 Then
      Msg = "Today is Friday. Make sure that you "
      Msg = Msg & "do your weekly backup!"
      MsgBox Msg, vbInformation
  End If
End Sub
```

Activate event

The following procedure executes whenever the workbook is activated. This procedure simply maximizes the active window.

```
Private Sub Workbook_Activate()
    ActiveWindow.WindowState = xlMaximized
End Sub
```

SheetActivate event

The following procedure executes whenever the user activates any sheet in the workbook. The code simply selects Cell A1. Writing `On Error Resume Next` causes the procedure to ignore the error that occurs if the activated sheet is a Chart sheet.

```
Private Sub Workbook_SheetActivate(ByVal Sh As Object)
    On Error Resume Next
    Range("A1").Select
End Sub
```

An alternative method to handle the case of a Chart sheet is to check the sheet type. Use the Sh argument, which is passed to the procedure.

```
Private Sub Workbook_SheetActivate(ByVal Sh As Object)
    If TypeName(Sh) = "Worksheet" Then Range("A1").Select
End Sub
```

NewSheet event

The following procedure executes whenever a new sheet is added to the workbook. The sheet is passed to the procedure as an argument. Because a new sheet can be either a worksheet or a Chart sheet, this procedure determines the sheet type. If it's a worksheet, it inserts a date and time stamp in Cell A1.

```
Private Sub Workbook_NewSheet(ByVal Sh As Object)
    If TypeName(Sh) = "Worksheet" Then _
      Range("A1") = "Sheet added " & Now()
End Sub
```

BeforeSave event

The BeforeSave event occurs before the workbook is actually saved. As you know, using the File ➪ Save command sometimes brings up the Save As dialog box. This happens if the file has never been saved or was opened in read-only mode.

When the Workbook_BeforeSave procedure executes, it receives an argument that enables you to identify whether the Save As dialog box will appear. The following example demonstrates this.

```
Private Sub Workbook_BeforeSave _
  (ByVal SaveAsUI As Boolean, Cancel As Boolean)
    If SaveAsUI Then
        MsgBox "Click OK to display the Save As dialog box."
    End If
End Sub
```

When the user attempts to save the workbook, the Workbook_BeforeSave procedure executes. If the save operation brings up the Save As dialog box, the SaveAsUI variable is True. The preceding procedure checks this variable and displays a message only if the Save As dialog box is displayed. If the procedure sets the Cancel argument to True, the file is not saved.

Deactivate event

The following example demonstrates the Deactivate event. This procedure executes whenever the workbook is deactivated, and essentially does not enable the user to deactivate the workbook. When the Deactivate event occurs, the code reactivates the workbook and displays a message.

```
Private Sub Workbook_Deactivate()
    Me.Windows(1).Activate
    MsgBox "Sorry, you may not leave this workbook"
End Sub
```

I do not recommend using procedures – such as this one – that attempt to "take over" Excel. It can be very frustrating and confusing for the user. Rather, I recommend training the user on how to use your application correctly.

This example illustrates the importance of understanding event sequences. When you try this procedure you'll see that it works well if the user attempts to activate another workbook. However, it's important to understand that the following actions also trigger the `Workbook_Deactivate` event:

✦ Closing the workbook

✦ Opening a new workbook

✦ Minimizing the workbook

In other words, this procedure might not perform as intended. The user may not activate a different workbook, but he or she can close the workbook, open a new workbook, or minimize the workbook. The message box still appears, but the actions occur anyway.

BeforePrint event

The `BeforePrint` event takes place when the user requests a printout or print preview, but before the printing or previewing occurs. The event uses a `Cancel` argument, so your code can cancel the printing or previewing by setting the `Cancel` variable to True.

One of Excel's deficiencies (that Microsoft seems unwilling to fix) is the incapability to print a workbook's full path name in the page header or footer. The following simple example accomplishes this feat:

```
Private Sub Workbook_BeforePrint(Cancel As Boolean)
    For Each sht In ThisWorkbook.Sheets
        sht.PageSetup.LeftFooter = _
          "&8" & ThisWorkbook.FullName
    Next sht
End Sub
```

This procedure loops through each sheet in the workbook and sets the `LeftFooter` property of the `PageSetup` object to the `FullName` property of the workbook (which is the filename and path name). It also sets the font size to 8 points.

This example exposes an inconsistency in Excel's object model. To change the font size of header or footer text, you must use a string that contains a special formatting code. In the preceding example, "&8" is the code for 8-point font. Ideally, there should be a `Font` object available for page headers and footers. To find out what other formatting codes are available, consult the online help (or record a macro while you access the Page Setup dialog box).

When testing `BeforePrint` event handlers, save time (and paper) by previewing rather than actually printing.

BeforeClose event

The `BeforeClose` event occurs before a workbook is closed. This event often is used in conjunction with a `Workbook_Open` event handler. For example, use the `Workbook_Open` procedure to initialize items in your workbook, and use the `Workbook_BeforeClose` procedure to "clean up" or restore settings to normal before the workbook closes.

As you know, if you attempt to close a workbook that hasn't been saved, Excel displays a prompt that asks if you want to save the workbook before it closes. This is shown in Figure 18-4.

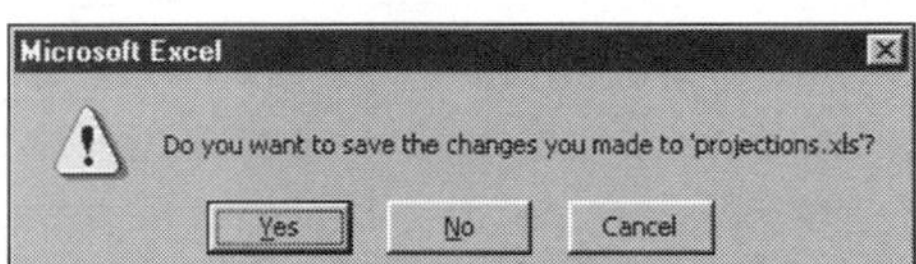
Microsoft Excel
Do you want to save the changes you made to 'projections.xls'?
Yes
No
Cancel

Figure 18-4: Once this message appears, `Workbook_BeforeClose` has done its deed.

A problem can arise from this event. By the time the user sees this message, the `BeforeClose` event has already occurred. This means the `Workbook_BeforeClose` procedure has already executed.

Consider this scenario: You need to display a custom menu when a particular workbook is open. Therefore, your workbook uses a `Workbook_Open` procedure to create the menu when the workbook opens, and it uses a `Workbook_BeforeClose` procedure to remove the menu when the workbook closes. These two event-handler procedures are listed below.

```
Private Sub Workbook_Open()
    Call CreateMenu
End Sub

Private Sub Workbook_BeforeClose(Cancel As Boolean)
    Call DeleteMenu
End Sub
```

As I noted above, Excel's "save workbook before closing" prompt occurs after the `Workbook_BeforeClose` event handler runs. So when the user clicks `Cancel`, the workbook remains open, but the custom menu item is already deleted!

One solution to this problem is to bypass Excel's prompt and write your own code in the `Workbook_BeforeClose` procedure, asking the user to save the workbook. The following code demonstrates this.

```
Private Sub Workbook_BeforeClose(Cancel As Boolean)
    If Not Me.Saved Then
        Msg = "Do you want to save the changes you made to "
        Msg = Msg & Me.Name & "?"
        Ans = MsgBox(Msg, vbQuestion + vbYesNoCancel)
        Select Case Ans
            Case vbYes
                Me.Save
            Case vbNo
                Me.Saved = True
            Case vbCancel
                Cancel = True
                Exit Sub
        End Select
    End If
    Call DeleteMenu
End Sub
```

This procedure determines whether the workbook has been saved. If it has, no problem: the `DeleteMenu` procedure executes and the workbook closes. If the workbook has not been saved, the procedure displays a message box that duplicates the one Excel normally shows. If the user clicks Yes, the menu is deleted and the workbook closes. If the user clicks No, the code sets the `Saved` property of the `Workbook` object to True (but doesn't actually save the file) and deletes the menu. If the user clicks `Cancel`, the `BeforeClose` event is canceled, and the procedure ends without deleting the menu.

Worksheet Events

The events for a `Worksheet` object are some of the most useful. As you'll see, monitoring these events can make your applications perform feats that otherwise would be impossible.

The events in this section apply to worksheets only. There are no specific trappable events for Excel 5/95 dialog sheets or XLM macro sheets. However, you may be able to work with some relevant events by using `Workbook`-level events.

Table 18-2 lists the worksheet events, with a brief description of each.

Table 18-2
Worksheet Events

Event	Action That Triggers the Event
Activate	A worksheet is activated.
BeforeDoubleClick	A worksheet is double-clicked.
BeforeRightClick	A worksheet is right-clicked.
Calculate	A worksheet is calculated (or recalculated).
Change	Cells on a worksheet are changed by the user or an external link.
Deactivate	A worksheet is deactivated.
SelectionChange	The selection on a worksheet is changed.

Change event

The Change event is triggered when any cell in a worksheet is changed by the user or an external link. The Change event is not triggered when a calculation generates a different value for a formula, or when an object is added to the sheet.

When the Worksheet_Change procedure executes, it receives a Range object as its Target argument. This Range object represents the changed cell or range that triggered the event. The following example displays a message box that shows the address of the Target range.

```
Private Sub Worksheet_Change(ByVal Target As Excel.Range)
    MsgBox "Range " & Target.Address & " was changed."
End Sub
```

To get a feel for the types of actions that generate the Change event for a worksheet, enter the preceding procedure into the code module for a Worksheet object. After entering this procedure, activate Excel and, using various techniques, make changes to the worksheet. Every time the Change event occurs, a message box displays the address of the range that changed.

I discovered some interesting quirks when I ran this procedure. Actions that should trigger the event don't, and actions that should not trigger the event do!

- ✦ Changing the formatting of a cell does not trigger the Change event (as expected), but using the Edit ➪ Clear Formats command *does.*
- ✦ Filling a range using the Edit ➪ Fill command does not generate the Change event, but using AutoFill to fill the range *does.*
- ✦ Using the Edit ➪ Delete command does not generate the Change event, but pressing the Del key does. In fact, pressing Del generates an event even if the cell is empty at the start.

✦ Cells changed via Excel commands do not trigger the Change event. These commands include Data ➪ Form, Data ➪ Sort, Tools ➪ Spelling, and Edit ➪ Replace.

✦ If your VBA procedure changes a cell, it *does* trigger the Change event.

As you can see, it's not a good idea to rely on the Change event to detect cell changes for critical applications.

Monitoring a specific range for changes

The Change event occurs when any cell on the worksheet changes. In most cases all that matters are changes made to a specific cell or range. When the Worksheet_Change event-handler procedure is called, it receives a Range object as its argument. This Range object represents the cell or cells that changed.

Assume your worksheet has a range named InputRange, and you want to monitor changes to this range only. There is no Change event for a Range object, but you can perform a quick check within the Worksheet_Change procedure. The following procedure demonstrates this.

```
Private Sub Worksheet_Change(ByVal Target As Excel.Range)
    Dim VRange As Range
    Set VRange = Range("InputRange")
    If Union(Target, VRange).Address = VRange.Address Then
       Msgbox "The changed cell is in the input range."
    End if
End Sub
```

This example creates a range object named VRange, which represents the worksheet range that you want to monitor for changes. The procedure uses VBA's Union function to determine if VRange contains the Target range (passed to the procedure in its argument). The Union function returns an object that consists of all the cells in both of its arguments. If the range address is the same as the VRange address, then Vrange contains Target, and a message box appears. Otherwise, the procedure ends and nothing happens.

The preceding procedure has a flaw. Target may consist of a cell or a range. For example, if the user changes more than one cell at a time, Target becomes a multicell range. Therefore, the procedure requires modification to loop through all the cells in Target. The following procedure checks each changed cell and displays a message box if the cell is within the desired range.

```
Private Sub Worksheet_Change(ByVal Target As Excel.Range)
    Set VRange = Range("InputRange")
    For Each cell In Target
        If Union(cell, VRange).Address = VRange.Address Then
           Msgbox "The changed cell is in the input range."
        End if
    Next cell
End Sub
```

Tracking cell changes in a comment

The following example adds a notation to the cell's comment each time the cell changes (as determined by the `Change` event). The state of a `CheckBox`, embedded in the worksheet, determines whether the change is added to the comment.

Because the object passed to the `Worksheet_Change` procedure can consist of a multicell range, the procedure loops through each cell in the `Target` range. If the cell doesn't contain a comment, one is added. Then, new text is appended to the existing comment text (if applicable).

```
Private Sub Worksheet_Change(ByVal Target As Excel.Range)
  If CheckBox1 Then
    For Each cell In Target
        With cell
            On Error Resume Next
            OldText = .Comment.Text
            If Err <> 0 Then .AddComment
            NewText = OldText & "Changed by " & _
              Application.UserName & " at " & Now & vbLf
            .Comment.Text NewText
            .Comment.Visible = True
            .Comment.Shape.Select
             Selection.AutoSize = True
            .Comment.Visible = False
        End With
    Next cell
  End If
End Sub
```

Figure 18-5 shows a cell comment that has changed several times.

This example is primarily for instructional purposes. If you really need to track changes in a worksheet, Excel's Tools ➪ Track Changes feature does a much better job.

Validating data entry

Excel's Data Validation feature is a useful tool, but it suffers from a potentially serious problem. When you paste data to a cell that uses data validation, the pasted value not only fails to receive validation, but also deletes the validation rules associated with the cell!

In this section, I demonstrate how to use a worksheet's `Change` event to create your own data validation procedure.

Listing 18-1 presents a procedure that executes when a user changes a cell. The validation is restricted to the range named `InputRange`. Values entered into this range must be integers between 1 and 12.

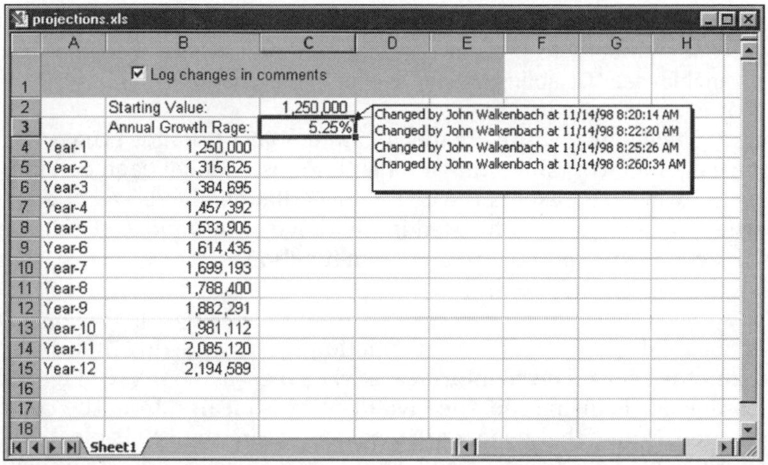

Figure 18-5: The `Worksheet_Change` procedure appends the comment with each cell change.

Listing 18-1: **Determining whether a cell entry will be validated**

```
Private Sub Worksheet_Change(ByVal Target As Excel.Range)
    Dim VRange As Range, cell As Range
    Dim Msg As String
    Dim ValidateCode As Variant
    Set VRange = Range("InputRange")
    For Each cell In Target
        If Union(cell, VRange).Address = VRange.Address Then
            ValidateCode = EntryIsValid(cell)
            If ValidateCode = True Then
                Exit Sub
            Else
                Msg = "Cell " & cell.Address(False, False) _
                  & ":"
                Msg = Msg & vbCrLf & vbCrLf & ValidateCode
                MsgBox Msg, vbCritical, "Invalid Entry"
                Application.EnableEvents = False
                cell.ClearContents
                cell.Activate
                Application.EnableEvents = True
            End If
        End If
    Next cell
End Sub
```

The companion CD-ROM contains two versions of this example. One uses the `EnableEvents` property to prevent cascading `Change` events, the other uses a `Static` variable (see "Disabling events" earlier in this chapter).

The `Worksheet_Change` procedure creates a `Range` object (`VRange`) that represents the validated worksheet range. Then it loops through each cell in the `Target` argument, which represents the cell or cells that changed. The code determines whether each cell is contained in the range to be validated. If it is, the code passes the cell as an argument to a custom function (`EntryIsValid`), which returns True if the cell is a valid entry.

If the entry is not valid, the `EntryIsValid` function returns a string that describes the problem, and the user receives information via a message box (see Figure 18-6). When the message box is dismissed, the invalid entry is cleared from the cell and the cell is activated. Notice that events are disabled before the cell is cleared. If events were not disabled, clearing the cell would produce a `Change` event, which causes an endless loop.

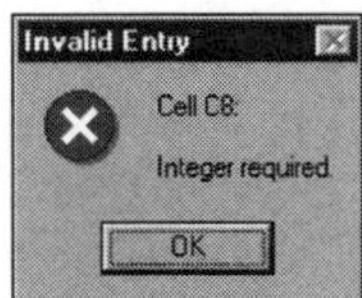

Figure 18-6: This message box describes the problem when the user makes an invalid entry.

The `EntryIsValid` Function procedure is presented in Listing 18-2.

Listing 18-2: Validating an entry that was just made into a restricted range

```
Private Function EntryIsValid(cell) As Variant
'   Returns True if cell is an integer between 1 and 12
'   Otherwise it returns a string that describes the problem

'   Blank
    If cell = "" Then
        EntryIsValid = True
        Exit Function
    End If

'   Numeric?
    If Not IsNumeric(cell) Then
        EntryIsValid = "Non-numeric entry."
        Exit Function
    End If

'   Integer?
    If CInt(cell) <> cell Then
```

```
        EntryIsValid = "Integer required."
        Exit Function
    End If

'   Between 1 and 12?
    If cell < 1 Or cell > 12 Then
        EntryIsValid = "Valid values are between 1 and 12."
        Exit Function
    End If

'   It passed all the tests
    EntryIsValid = True
End Function
```

SelectionChange event

The following procedure demonstrates the `SelectionChange` event. It executes whenever the user makes a new selection on the worksheet.

```
Private Sub Worksheet_SelectionChange(ByVal Target _
  As Excel.Range)
    Cells.Interior.ColorIndex = xlNone
    With ActiveCell
        .EntireRow.Interior.ColorIndex = 36
        .EntireColumn.Interior.ColorIndex = 36
    End With
End Sub
```

This procedure shades the row and column of an active cell, making it easy to identify. The first statement removes the background color of all cells. Next, the entire row and column of the active cell is shaded light yellow. Figure 18-7 shows the shading; trust me, it's yellow.

You won't want to use this procedure if your worksheet contains background shading, because it will be wiped out.

BeforeRightClick event

When the user right-clicks in a worksheet, a shortcut menu appears. If, for some reason, you want to prevent the shortcut menu from appearing, you can trap the `RightClick` event. The following procedure sets the `Cancel` argument to True, which cancels the `RightClick` event and, thus, the shortcut menu. Instead, a message box appears.

```
Private Sub Worksheet_BeforeRightClick _
  (ByVal Target As Excel.Range, Cancel As Boolean)
    Cancel = True
    MsgBox "The shortcut menu is not available."
End Sub
```

Selection Change.xls

	A	B	C	D	E	F	G	H	I	J
1		Project-1	Project-2	Project-3	Project-4	Project-5	Project-6	Project-7	Project-8	Project-9
2	Jan-99	5,052	21,790	21,596	2,192	13,454	9,027	21,026	15,510	6,172
3	Feb-99	10,963	20,640	20,167	15,494	3,923	12,527	15,164	6,440	2,510
4	Mar-99	18,240	22,263	21,042	11,558	17,472	20,923	17,277	15,182	2,778
5	Apr-99	18,148	16,567	10,752	7,882	521	20,624	19,376	19,314	7,396
6	May-99	14,825	12,675	17,949	16,783	19,120	15,011	21,759	13,238	2,397
7	Jun-99	13,207	13,942	10,558	15,133	6,704	5,639	2,575	18,755	13,944
8	Jul-99	21,920	19,380	12,938	3,653	5,045	16,965	7,856	22,798	5,469
9	Aug-99	7,894	12,473	6,367	1,942	18,370	10,960	5,784	4,071	19,675
10	Sep-99	5,664	16,666	22,508	8,525	17,401	10,708	13,205	22,184	1,030
11	Oct-99	594	746	3,540	3,301	19,652	19,346	2,641	5,517	8,975
12	Nov-99	981	7,465	20,315	19,330	3,428	7,332	1,370	12,027	1,109
13	Dec-99	4,329	15,135	21,320	20,972	7,085	17,556	16,703	14,478	11,662
14	Jan-00	21,325	16,679	8,950	4,193	20,096	14,158	15,810	7,465	3,437
15	Feb-00	1,412	15,580	20,393	5,359	18,192	13,523	15,352	11,855	7,550
16	Mar-00	9,485	21,571	8,378	14,995	9,031	12,172	15,356	8,641	5,422
17	Apr-00	8,971	1,560	9,739	2,921	20,444	4,097	17,599	262	10,965
18	May-00	20,691	22,318	8,184	4,293	7,645	20,278	4,947	19,267	10,031
19	Jun-00	8,748	6,278	22,746	17,344	10,664	180	4,954	18,559	21,338
20	Jul-00	18,673	8,234	12,133	2,073	10,814	19,123	1,287	22,540	2,573
21	Aug-00	16,772	3,421	9,165	22,794	10,319	15,110	5,803	10,552	3,313

Sheet1

Figure 18-7: Moving the cell cursor causes the active cell's row and column to become shaded.

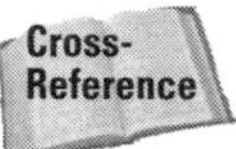

Chapter 22 describes other ways to disable shortcut menus.

Chart Events

By default, events are enabled only for charts that reside on a Chart sheet. To work with events for an embedded chart, you must create a class module.

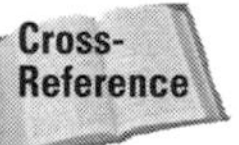

Refer to Chapter 17 for examples that deal with `Chart` events. Chapter 17 also describes how to create a class module that enables events for embedded charts.

Table 18-3 lists the `Chart` events, and a brief description of each.

Table 18-3
Events Recognized by a Chart Sheet

Event	*Action That Triggers the Event*
`Activate`	A Chart sheet or embedded chart is activated.
`BeforeDoubleClick`	An embedded chart is double-clicked. This event occurs before the default double-click action.

Event	*Action That Triggers the Event*
`BeforeRightClick`	An embedded chart is right-clicked. The event occurs before the default right-click action.
`Calculate`	New or changed data is plotted on a chart.
`Deactivate`	A chart is deactivated.
`DragOver`	A range of cells is dragged over a chart.
`DragPlot`	A range of cells is dragged and dropped onto a chart.
`MouseDown`	A mouse button is pressed while the pointer is over a chart.
`MouseMove`	The position of the mouse pointer is changed over a chart.
`MouseUp`	A mouse button is released while the pointer is over a chart.
`Resize`	A chart is resized.
`Select`	A chart element is selected.
`SeriesChange`	The value of a chart data point is changed.

Application Events

In previous sections, I discussed `Workbook` and `Worksheet` events. These events are monitored for a particular workbook. If you want to monitor events for all open workbooks or all worksheets, use Application events.

Table 18-4 lists the Application events, with a brief description of each.

Enabling Application-level events

To make use of Application-level events, do the following:

1. Create a new class module.
2. Set a name for this class module in the Properties window under *Name.*

   By default, VBA gives each new class module a name and a number; but trying to remember which module was `Class21` and which `Class22` can quickly become cumbersome.
3. In the class module, declare a public `Application` object, using the `WithEvents` keyword.

Using the Object Browser to Locate Events

The Object Browser is a useful tool that can help you learn about objects and their properties and methods. It also can help you find out which objects support a particular event. For example, say you want to find out which objects support the `MouseMove` event. Activate the VB Editor and press F2 to display the Object Browser window. Make sure <All Libraries> is selected and then type **MouseMove** and click the binoculars icon (see the accompanying figure).

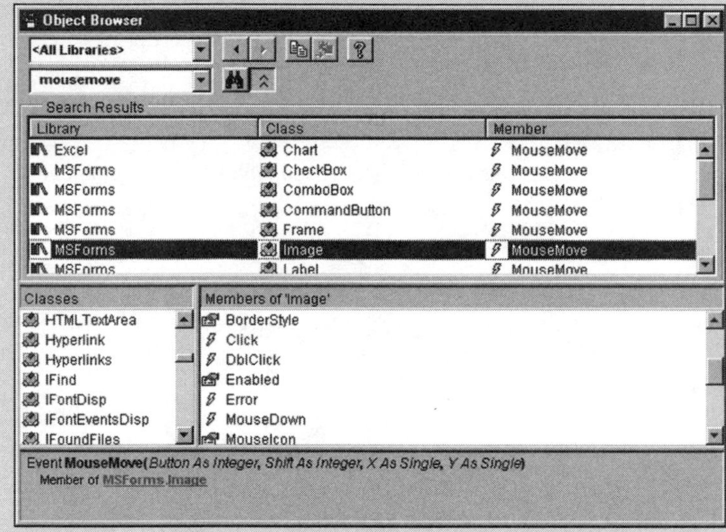

The Object Browser displays a list of matching items. Events are indicated with a small yellow lightning bolt. From this list, you can see which objects support the `MouseMove` event. Most of the objects are controls in the `MSForms` library, home of the UserForm control. But you also can see that Excel's `Chart` object supports the `MouseMove` event.

Notice how the list here is divided into three columns: Library, Class, and Member. The match for the item you're searching for may appear in any of these columns. This brings up a crucial point: The name of an event or term belonging to one library or class may be the same as that for another belonging to a different library or class, though they may not share the same meaning or functionality. In fact, you can probably bet on them being different. So be sure to click each item in the Object Browser list and check the status bar at the bottom of the list for the syntax. You might find, for instance, that one class or library treats the `MouseMove` event differently.

Table 18-4
Events Recognized by the Application Object

Event	*Action That Triggers the Event*
NewWorkbook	A new workbook is created.
SheetActivate	Any sheet is activated.
SheetBeforeDoubleClick	Any worksheet is double-clicked. This event occurs before the default double-click action.
SheetBeforeRightClick	Any worksheet is right-clicked. This event occurs before the default right-click action.
SheetCalculate	Any worksheet is calculated (or recalculated).
SheetChange	Cells in any worksheet are changed by the user or an external link.
SheetDeactivate	Any sheet is deactivated.
SheetFollowHyperlink	A hyperlink is clicked.
SheetSelectionChange	The selection is changed on any worksheet except a Chart sheet.
WindowActivate	Any workbook window is activated.
WindowDeactivate	Any workbook window is deactivated.
WindowResize	Any workbook window is resized.
WorkbookActivate	Any workbook is activated.
WorkbookAddinInstall	A workbook is installed as an add-in.
WorkbookAddinUninstall	Any add-in workbook is uninstalled.
WorkbookBeforeClose	Any open workbook is closed.
WorkbookBeforePrint	Any open workbook is printed.
WorkbookBeforeSave	Any open workbook is saved.
WorkbookDeactivate	Any open workbook is deactivated.
WorkbookNewSheet	A new sheet is created in any open workbook.
WorkbookOpen	A workbook is opened.

4. Create a variable that you will use to refer to the declared object in the class module.
5. Write event-handler procedures in the class module.

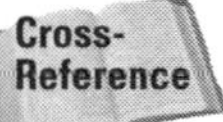

This procedure is virtually identical to the one required to use events with an embedded chart. See Chapter 17.

Determining when a workbook is opened

The example in this section stores information in a text file in order to keep track of every workbook that is opened. I start by inserting a new class module, naming it `AppClass`. The code in the class module is

```
Public WithEvents AppEvents As Application

Private Sub AppEvents_WorkbookOpen _
  (ByVal Wb As Excel.Workbook)
    Call UpdateLogFile(Wb)
End Sub
```

This declares `AppEvents` as an `Application` object with events. The `AppEvents_WorkbookOpen` procedure is called whenever a workbook is opened. This event-handler procedure calls `UpdateLogFile` and passes the `Wb` variable, which represents the Workbook that opened. I then add a VBA module and insert the following code:

```
Dim AppObject As New AppClass

Sub Init()
'   Called by Workbook_Open
    Set AppObject.AppEvents = Application
End Sub

Sub UpdateLogFile(Wb)
    txt = Wb.FullName
    txt = txt & "," & Date & "," & Time
    txt = txt & "," & Application.UserName
    Fname = ThisWorkbook.Path & "\logfile.txt"
    Open Fname For Append As #1
    Write #1, txt
    Close #1
    MsgBox txt
End Sub
```

Notice at the top that the `AppObject` variable is declared as type `AppClass`, that is, the name of the class module. The call to `Init` is in the `Workbook_Open` procedure, which is in the code module for `ThisWorkbook`. This procedure is shown below.

```
Private Sub Workbook_Open()
    Call Init
End Sub
```

The `UpdateLogFile` procedure opens a text file, or creates it if it doesn't exist. It then writes key information about the workbook that opened: filename, full path name, date, time, and username.

The `Workbook_Open` procedure calls the `Init` procedure. Therefore, when the workbook opens, the `Init` procedure instigates the object variable.

The text file is written to the same directory as the workbook. There is no error handling, so the code fails when the workbook is stored on a CD-ROM drive.

Monitoring Application-level events

To get a feel for the event generation process, you might find it helpful to see a list of events that are generated as you go about your work.

The companion CD-ROM contains a workbook that displays each Application-level event as it occurs. Actually, there are two versions of this workbook. The version for Excel 2000 displays the events in a modeless UserForm, as shown in Figure 18-8. The version for Excel 97 displays each event in a message box.

Figure 18-8: This workbook uses a class module to monitor all Application-level events.

The workbook contains a class module with 21 defined procedures, one for each Application-level event. Here's an example.

```
Private Sub XL_NewWorkbook(ByVal Wb As Excel.Workbook)
    LogEvent "NewWorkbook: " & Wb.Name
End Sub
```

Each of these procedures calls the `LogEvent` procedure and passes an argument that consists of the event name and object. The `LogEvent` procedure is listed below.

```
Sub LogEvent(txt)
    EventNum = EventNum + 1
    With UserForm1
        With .lblEvents
            .AutoSize = False
            .Caption = .Caption & vbCrLf & txt
            .Width = UserForm1.FrameEvents.Width - 20
            .AutoSize = True
        End With
        .FrameEvents.ScrollHeight = .lblEvents.Height + 20
        .FrameEvents.ScrollTop = EventNum * 20
    End With
End Sub
```

The `LogEvent` procedure updates the UserForm by modifying the `Caption` property of the `Label` control named `lblEvents`. The procedure also adjusts the `ScrollHeight` and `ScrollTop` properties of the frame named FrameEvents, which contains `Label`. Adjusting these properties causes the most recently added text to show up while older text scrolls out of view.

UserForm Events

A UserForm supports many events, and each control placed on a UserForm has its own set of events. Table 18-5 lists the UserForm events that you can trap.

Table 18-5
Events Recognized by a UserForm

Event	*Action That Triggers the Event*
`Activate`	The UserForm is activated.
`AddControl`	A control is added at run time.
`BeforeDragOver`	A drag-and-drop operation is in progress while the pointer is over the form.
`BeforeDropOrPaste`	Data is about to be dropped or pasted; that is, the mouse button has been released.
`Click`	A mouse is clicked while the pointer is over the form.
`DblClick`	A mouse is double-clicked while the pointer is over the form.
`Deactivate`	The UserForm is deactivated.
`Initialize`	The UserForm is about to be shown.

Event	*Action That Triggers the Event*
`KeyDown`	A key is pressed.
`KeyPress`	Any ANSI key is pressed.
`KeyUp`	A key is released.
`Layout`	The size of a UserForm is changed.
`MouseDown`	A mouse button is pressed.
`MouseMove`	The mouse is moved.
`QueryClose`	This occurs before a UserForm is closed.
`RemoveControl`	A control is removed from the UserForm at run time.
`Scroll`	The UserForm is scrolled.
`Terminate`	The UserForm is terminated.
`Zoom`	The UserForm is zoomed.

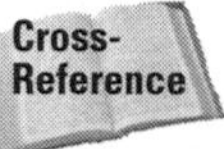

Many of the examples in Chapters 12 through 14 demonstrate event handling for UserForms and UserForm controls.

Events Not Associated with an Object

The events discussed in this chapter are associated with an object (`Application`, `Workbook`, `Sheet`, and so on). In this section I discuss two additional "rogue" events: `OnTime` and `OnKey`. These events are not associated with an object. Rather, they are accessed using methods of the `Application` object.

Unlike the other events discussed in this chapter, you use a general VBA module to program the "On-" events in this section.

OnTime event

The `OnTime` event occurs at a specified time. The following example demonstrates how to program Excel to beep and then display a message at 3:00 p.m.

```
Sub SetAlarm()
    Application.OnTime 0.625, "DisplayAlarm"
End Sub

Sub DisplayAlarm()
    Beep
    MsgBox "Wake up. It's time for your afternoon break!"
End Sub
```

In this example, the `SetAlarm` procedure uses the `OnTime` method of the `Application` object to set up the `OnTime` event. This method takes two arguments: the time (`0.625`, or 3:00 p.m., in the example) and the procedure to execute when the time occurs (`DisplayAlarm` in the example). In the example, after `SetAlarm` executes, the `DisplayAlarm` procedure is called at 3:00 p.m., bringing up the message in Figure 18-9.

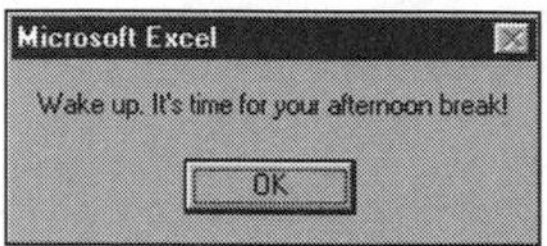

Figure 18-9: This message box was programmed to appear at a particular time.

Compensating for Excel's fractional time values

Most people (myself included) find it difficult to think of time in terms of Excel's time numbering system. Therefore, you might want to use VBA's `TimeValue` function to represent the time. `TimeValue` converts a string that looks like a time into a value that Excel can handle. The following statement shows an easier way to program an event for 3:00 p.m.:

```
Application.OnTime TimeValue("3:00:00 pm"), "DisplayAlarm"
```

If you want to schedule an event that's relative to the current time—for example, 20 minutes from now—you can write an instruction like this:

```
Application.OnTime Now + TimeValue("00:20:00"), "DisplayAlarm"
```

You also can use the `OnTime` method to schedule a procedure on a particular day. Of course, you must keep your computer running and the workbook with the procedure open. The following statement runs the `DisplayAlarm` procedure at 12:01 a.m. on January 1, 2000 (assuming, of course, that no year 2000 glitches occur):

```
Application.OnTime DateValue("1/1/2000 12:01 am"), _
  "MilleniumSub"
```

The `OnTime` method has two additional arguments. If you plan to use this method, refer to the online help for complete details.

The analog clock example in Chapter 17 uses the `OnTime` event to cause a procedure to execute each second.

OnKey event

While you work, Excel constantly monitors what you type. Because of this, you can set up a keystroke or a key combination that, when pressed, executes a particular procedure.

The following example uses the OnKey method to set up an OnKey event. This event essentially reassigns the PgDn and PgUp keys. After the Setup_OnKey procedure executes, pressing PgDn executes the PgDn_Sub procedure, and pressing PgUp executes the PgUp_Sub procedure. The next effect is that pressing PgDn moves down one row and pressing PgUp moves up one row.

```
Sub Setup_OnKey()
    Application.OnKey "{PgDn}", "PgDn_Sub"
    Application.OnKey "{PgUp}", "PgUp_Sub"
End Sub

Sub PgDn_Sub()
    On Error Resume Next
    ActiveCell.Offset(1, 0).Activate
End Sub

Sub PgUp_Sub()
    On Error Resume Next
    ActiveCell.Offset(-1, 0).Activate
End Sub
```

Note

Notice that the key codes are enclosed in brackets, not parentheses. For a complete list of the keyboard codes, consult the online help. Search for OnKey.

In the preceding examples, I used On Error Resume Next to ignore any errors generated. For example, if the active cell is in the first row, trying to move up one row causes an error. Furthermore, if the active sheet is a Chart sheet, an error occurs because there is no such thing as an active cell in a Chart sheet.

By executing the following procedure, you cancel the OnKey events, and the keys return to their normal functions.

```
Sub Cancel_OnKey()
    Application.OnKey "{PgDn}"
    Application.OnKey "{PgUp}"
End Sub
```

Contrary to what you might expect, using an empty string as the second argument for the OnKey method does *not* cancel the OnKey event. Rather, it causes Excel to ignore the keystroke and do nothing at all. For example, the following instruction tells Excel to ignore Alt+F4 (the percent sign represents the Alt key):

```
    Application.OnKey "%{F4}", ""
```

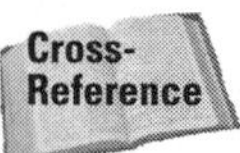

Although you can use the OnKey method to assign a shortcut key for executing a macro, it's better to use the Macro Options dialog box for this task. For more details, see "Executing a procedure using a Ctrl+shortcut key combination" in Chapter 9.

Summary

In this chapter, I described how to write code that executes when a particular event occurs.

In the next chapter, I discuss some VBA techniques that you can use to control other applications from Excel.

✦ ✦ ✦

CHAPTER 19

Interacting with Other Applications

◆ ◆ ◆ ◆

In This Chapter

Starting or activating another application from Excel

Displaying Windows Control Panel dialogs

Using Automation to control another application

Using `SendKeys` as a last resort

◆ ◆ ◆ ◆

In the early days of personal computing, interapplication communication was rare. In the pre-multitasking era, users had no choice but to use one program at a time. Interapplication communication usually was limited to importing files; even copying information and pasting it into another application — something that virtually every user now takes for granted — was impossible.

Nowadays, most software is designed to support at least some type of communication with other applications. At the very least, most Windows programs support the clipboard for copy-and-paste operations between applications. Many Windows products support Dynamic Data Exchange (DDE), and leading-edge products support Automation. In this chapter, I outline the types of true multitasking operations that your Excel applications support. Of course, I also provide several examples.

Starting Another Application

It's often useful to start up another application from Excel. For example, you may want to execute a communications program or even a DOS batch file from Excel. Or, as an application developer, you may want to make it easy for a user to access the Windows Control Panel.

VBA's `Shell` function makes launching other programs relatively easy. Listing 19-1 presents a procedure that starts the Windows Character Map application, which enables the user to insert a special character.

Listing 19-1: Launching a Windows utility application

```
Sub RunCharMap()
    On Error Resume Next
    Program = "Charmap.exe"
    TaskID = Shell(Program, 1)
    If Err <> 0 Then
        MsgBox "Cannot start " & Program, vbCritical, "Error"
    End If
End Sub
```

You'll recognize the application this procedure launches in Figure 19-1.

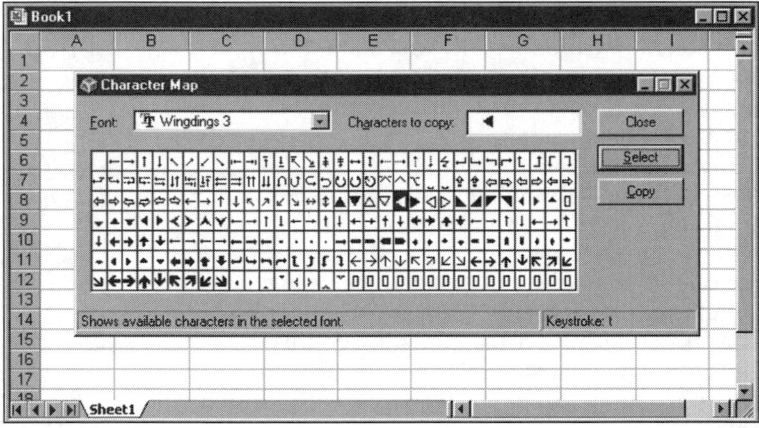

Figure 19-1: Running the Windows Character Map program from Excel.

The `Shell` function returns a task identification number for the application. You can use this number later to activate the task. The second argument for the `Shell` function determines how the application is displayed (`1` is the code for a normal size window, with the focus).

If the `Shell` function is not successful, it generates an error. So this procedure uses an `On Error` statement to display a message if the file cannot be found or some other error occurs.

It's important to understand that VBA does not pause while the application that was started with the `Shell` function is running. In other words, the `Shell` function runs the application *asynchronously*. If the procedure has more instructions after the `Shell` function is executed, they are executed concurrently with the newly loaded program. If any instruction requires user intervention (for example, displaying a message box), Excel's title bar flashes while the other application is active.

In some cases, you may want to launch an application with the Shell function, but you need your VBA code to "pause" until the application is closed. For example, the launched application may generate a file used later in your code. Although you can't pause the execution of your code, you *can* create a loop that does nothing except monitor the application's status. Listing 19-2 shows an example that displays a message box when the application launched by the Shell function has ended.

Listing 19-2: Waiting for an application to end

```
Declare Function OpenProcess Lib "kernel32" _
    (ByVal dwDesiredAccess As Long, _
    ByVal bInheritHandle As Long, _
    ByVal dwProcessId As Long) As Long

Declare Function GetExitCodeProcess Lib "kernel32" _
    (ByVal hProcess As Long, _
    lpExitCode As Long) As Long

Sub RunCharMap2()
    Dim TaskID As Long
    Dim hProc As Long
    Dim lExitCode As Long

    ACCESS_TYPE = &H400
    STILL_ACTIVE = &H103

    Program - "Charmap.exe"

'   Shell the task
    TaskID = Shell(Program, 1)

'   Get the process handle
    hProc = OpenProcess(ACCESS_TYPE, False, TaskID)

    If Err <> 0 Then
        MsgBox "Cannot start " & Program, vbCritical, "Error"
        Exit Sub
    End If

    Do  'Loop continuously
'       Check on the process
        GetExitCodeProcess hProc, lExitCode
'       Allow event processing
        DoEvents
    Loop While lExitCode = STILL_ACTIVE

'   Task is finished, so show message
    MsgBox Program & " is finished"
End Sub
```

While the launched program is running, this procedure continually calls the `GetExitCodeProcess` function from within a `Do-Loop` structure, testing for its returned value (`lExitCode`). When the program is finished, `lExitCode` returns a different value, the loop ends, and the VBA code resumes executing.

Both of the preceding examples are available on the companion CD-ROM.

The Windows 95 and Windows 98 operating systems provide a `Start` command, which also can be used as an argument for the `Shell` function. The `Start` command is a string literal that starts a Windows application from a DOS window. When using the `Start` command, you need to specify only the name of a *document* file—not the executable file. The program associated with that document file's extension is executed, and the file is automatically loaded. For example, the following instructions start up the installed Web browser application—that is, the application associated with the .htm extension—and load an HTML document named homepage.htm.

```
WebPage = "c:\web\homepage.htm"
Shell ("Start " & WebPage)
```

If the application that you want to start is one of several Microsoft applications, you can use the `ActivateMicrosoftApp` method of the Application object. For example, the following procedure starts Word 2000:

```
Sub StartWord()
    Application.ActivateMicrosoftApp xlMicrosoftWord
End Sub
```

If Word is already running when the preceding procedure is executed, it is activated. The other constants available for this method are `xlMicrosoftPowerPoint`, `xlMicrosoftMail`, `xlMicrosoftAccess`, `xlMicrosoftFoxPro`, `xlMicrosoftProject`, and `xlMicrosoftSchedulePlus` (but no constant for Outlook).

Activating Another Application

Beware of a potential problem: You may find that if an application is already running, using the `Shell` function could start another instance of it. In most cases, you'll want to activate the instance that's running, not start another instance of it.

The `StartCalculator` procedure, listed below, uses the `AppActivate` statement to activate an application that's already running (in this case, the Windows Calculator). The argument for `AppActivate` is the caption of the application's title bar. If the `AppActivate` statement generates an error, it means the Calculator is not running. Therefore, the routine starts the application.

```
Sub StartCalculator()
    AppFile = "Calc.exe"
    On Error Resume Next
    AppActivate ("Calculator")
    If Err <> 0 Then
        Err = 0
        CalcTaskID = Shell(AppFile, 1)
        If Err <> 0 Then MsgBox ("Can't start Calculator")
    End If
End Sub
```

This example is available on the companion CD-ROM.

The preceding example works only if you supply the exact caption of the application's window title as the argument for `AppActivate`. If a window caption includes a hyphen followed by a filename (such as *Microsoft Word - testfile.doc*), you need to supply only the text prior to the hyphen.

Running Control Panel Dialog Boxes and Wizards

Windows provides quite a few system dialog boxes and wizards, most of which are accessible from the Windows Control Panel. You may need to display one or more of these from your Excel application. For example, you may want to display the Windows Date/Time Properties dialog box shown in Figure 19-2.

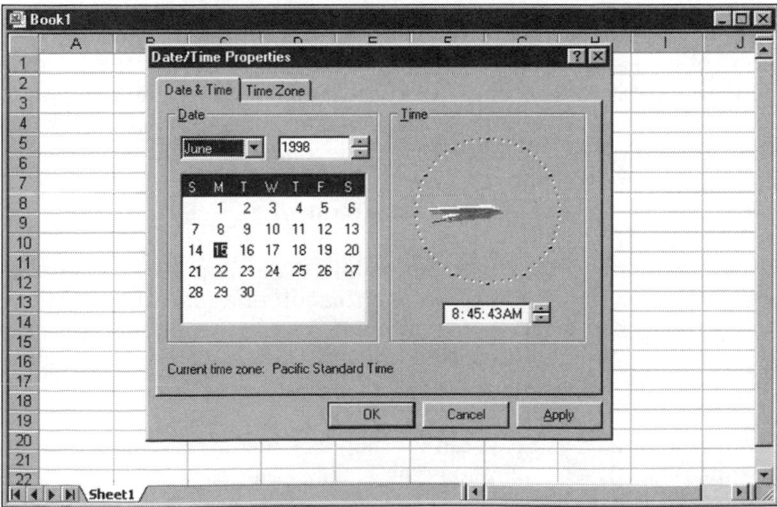

Figure 19-2: Using VBA to display a Control Panel dialog box.

The key to running other system dialog boxes is knowing the argument for the Shell function. The following procedure happens to know the argument for the Date/Time dialog box.

```
Sub ShowDateTimeDlg()
  Arg = "rundll32.exe shell32.dll,Control_RunDLL timedate.cpl"
  On Error Resume Next
  TaskID = Shell(Arg)
  If Err <> 0 Then
      MsgBox ("Cannot start the application.")
  End If
End Sub
```

A workbook, depicted in Figure 19-3, that demonstrates 50 arguments is available on the companion CD-ROM.

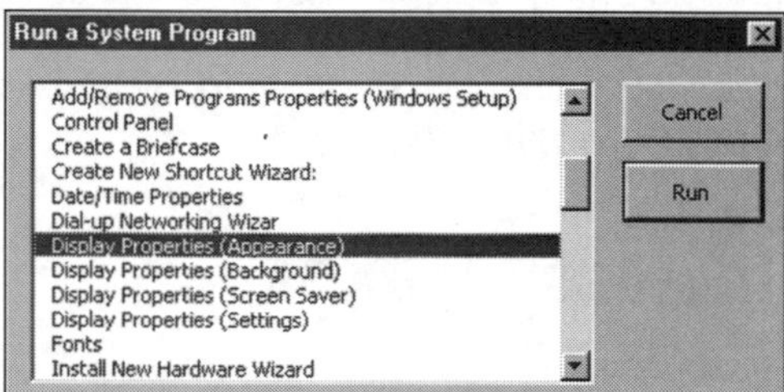

Figure 19-3: This workbook demonstrates how to run system dialog boxes from Excel.

Automation

You can write an Excel macro to control Microsoft Word. More accurately, the Excel macro will control the most important component of Word: its so-called *automation server*. In such circumstances, Excel is called the *native* application and Word the *remote* application. Or you can write a Visual Basic application to control Excel. The process of one application's controlling another is sometimes known as OLE Automation and other times known as ActiveX Automation (Microsoft has a tendency to change its own terminology quite frequently).

The concept behind Automation is quite appealing. A developer who needs to generate a chart, for example, can just reach into another application's grab bag of objects, fetch a Chart object, and then manipulate its properties and use its methods. Automation, in a sense, blurs the boundaries between applications. An end user may be working with an Access object and not even realize it.

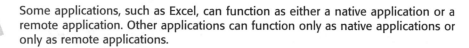

Some applications, such as Excel, can function as either a native application or a remote application. Other applications can function only as native applications or only as remote applications.

In this section, I demonstrate how to use VBA to access and manipulate the objects exposed by other applications. The examples use Microsoft Word, but the concepts apply to any application that exposes its objects for Automation — which accounts for an increasing number of applications.

Working with foreign objects

As you know, you can use Excel's Insert ➪ Object command to embed an object such as a Word document in a worksheet. In addition, you can create an object and manipulate it with VBA. (This action is the heart of Automation.) When you do so, you usually have full access to the object. For developers, this technique is generally more beneficial than embedding the object in a worksheet. When an object is embedded, the user must know how to use the Automation object's application. But when you use VBA to work with the object, you can program the object so that the user can manipulate it by an action as simple as a button click.

Early versus late binding

Before you can work with an external object, you must create an instance of the object. This can be done in either of two ways: early binding or late binding.

Early binding

At design time, you create a reference to the object library using the Tools ➪ References command in the VBE, which brings up the dialog box shown in Figure 19-4.

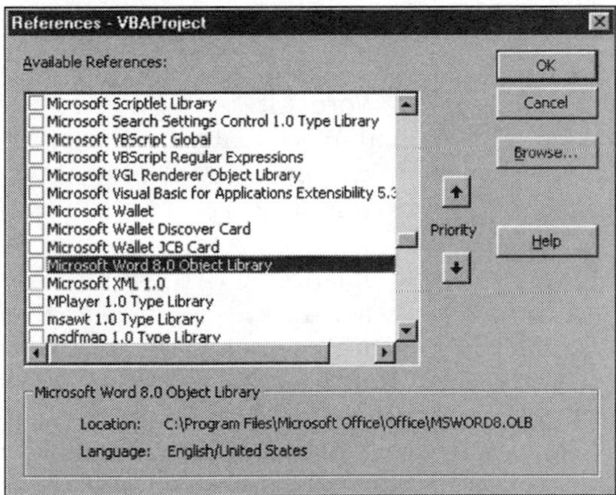

Figure 19-4: Attaching a reference to an object library file.

After the reference to the object library is established, you can use the Object Browser shown in Figure 19-5 to view the object names, methods, and properties.

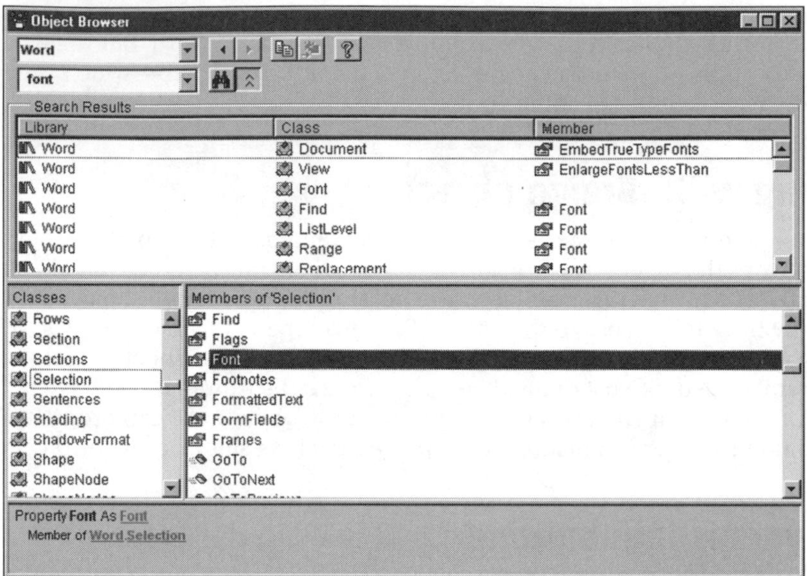

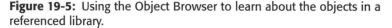

Figure 19-5: Using the Object Browser to learn about the objects in a referenced library.

When you use early binding, you must establish a reference to a version-specific object library (either Microsoft Word 8.0 Object Library or Microsoft Word 9.0 Object Library) within the VBE. Then, you use a statement like the following to create the object:

```
Dim WordApp As New Word.Application
```

Late Binding

At run time, you use either the `CreateObject` function to create the object or the `GetObject` function to obtain a saved instance of the object. Such an object is declared as a generic `Object` type, and its object reference is resolved at run time.

Using early binding to create the object by setting a reference to the object library usually is more efficient and yields better performance. Early binding is an option only if the object that you are controlling has a separate type library or object library file (usually with a .tlb or .olb extension). You also need to ensure that the user of the application actually has a copy of the specific library installed. Early binding also enables you to use constants that are defined in the object library. For example, Word (like Excel) contains many predefined constants that you can use in your VBA code. Another advantage in using early binding is that you can take advantage of the VBE's Object Browser and Auto List Members option to make it easier to access properties and methods; this feature doesn't work when you use late binding.

It is possible to use late binding even when you don't know which version of the application is installed on the user's system. For example, the following code, which works with both Word 97 and Word 2000, creates a `Word` object.

```
Dim WordApp As Object
Set WordApp = CreateObject("Word.Application")
```

If multiple versions of Word are installed, you can create an object for a specific version. The following statement, for example, uses Word 97.

```
Set WordApp = CreateObject("Word.Application.8")
```

The registry key for Word's Automation object and the reference to the `Application` object in VBA just happen to be the same: `Word.Application`. They do not, however, refer to the same thing. When you declare an object `As Word.Application` or `As New Word.Application`, the term refers to the `Application` object in the `Word` library. But when you invoke the function `CreateObject("Word.Application")`, the term refers to the moniker by which the latest version of Word is known in the Windows System Registry. This isn't the case for all Automation objects, although it is true for the main Office 2000 components. If the user replaces Word 97 with Word 2000, `CreateObject("Word.Application")` continues to work properly, referring to the new application. If Word 97 is removed, however, `CreateObject("Word.Application.8")`, which uses the alternate version-specific moniker for Word 97, fails to work.

The `CreateObject` function used on an Automation object such as `Word.Application` or `Excel.Application` always creates a new *instance* of that Automation object—that is, it starts up a new and separate copy of the automation part of the program. Even if an instance of the Automation object is already running, a new instance is started, and then an object of the specified type is created.

To use the current instance, or to start the application and have it load a file, use the `GetObject` function.

A simple example

The following example demonstrates how to create a `Word` object (using late binding). This procedure creates the object, displays the version number, closes the Word application, and then destroys the object (freeing the memory it used).

```
Sub GetWordVersion()
    Dim WordApp As Object
    Set WordApp = CreateObject("Word.Application")
    MsgBox WordApp.Version
    WordApp.Quit
    Set WordApp = Nothing
End Sub
```

The Word object that's created is invisible. If you'd like to see the object while it's being manipulated, set its Visible property to True, as follows:

```
WordApp.Visible = True
```

Controlling Word from Excel

The example in this section demonstrates an Automation session using Word. The MakeMemos procedure creates three customized memos in Word and then saves each document to a file. The information used to create the memos is stored in a worksheet. Figure 19-6 shows these two files.

word automation.xls

	A	B	C	D	E
1	Region1	145	$134,555		Create Word Memos Using Data on This Worksheet
2	Region2	122	$127,883		
3	Region3	203	$288,323		
4					
5					The monthly sales data for your region is listed below. This information was obtained from the central database. Please call if you have any questions.
6					
7					
8					

Sheet1

Figure 19-6: Word automatically generates three memos based on this Excel data.

The MakeMemos procedure, presented in Listing 19-3, starts by creating an object called WordApp. The routine cycles through the three rows of data in Sheet1 and uses Word's properties and methods to create each memo and save it to disk. A range named Message (also on Sheet1) contains the text used in the memo.

Listing 19-3: Generating Word 2000 data from an Excel VBA program

```
Sub MakeMemos()
'   Creates memos in word using Automation
    Dim WordApp As Object

'   Start Word and create an object
```

```
    Set WordApp = CreateObject("Word.Application")

'   Information from worksheet
    Set Data = Sheets("Sheet1").Range("A1")
    Message = Sheets("Sheet1").Range("Message")

'   Cycle through all records in Sheet1
    Records = Application.CountA(Sheets("Sheet1").Range("A:A"))
    For i = 1 To Records
'       Update status bar progress message
        Application.StatusBar = "Processing Record " & i

'       Assign current data to variables
        Region = Data.Offset(i - 1, 0).Value
        SalesAmt = Format(Data.Offset(i - 1, 2).Value, _
         "#,000")
        SalesNum = Data.Offset(i - 1, 1).Value

'       Determine the file name
        SaveAsName = ThisWorkbook.Path & "\" & Region & ".doc"

'       Send commands to Word
        With WordApp
            .Documents.Add
            With .Selection
                .Font.Size = 14
                .Font.Bold = True
                .ParagraphFormat.Alignment = 1
                .TypeText Text:="M E M O R A N D U M"
                .TypeParagraph
                .TypeParagraph
                .Font.Size = 12
                .ParagraphFormat.Alignment = 0
                .Font.Bold = False
                .TypeText Text:="Date:" & vbTab & _
                   Format(Date, "mmmm d, yyyy")
                .TypeParagraph
                .TypeText Text:="To:" & vbTab & Region & _
                 " Manager"
                .TypeParagraph
                .TypeText Text:="From:" & vbTab & _
                  Application.UserName
                .TypeParagraph
                .TypeParagraph
                .TypeText Message
                .TypeParagraph
                .TypeParagraph
                .TypeText Text:="Units Sold:" & vbTab & _
                 SalesNum
                .TypeParagraph
                .TypeText Text:="Amount:" & vbTab & _
                  Format(SalesAmt, "$#,##0")
            End With
```

Continued

Listing 19-3 (continued)

```
                .ActiveDocument.SaveAs FileName:=SaveAsName
                .ActiveWindow.Close
            End With
        Next i

'       Kill the object
        WordApp.Quit
        Set WordApp = Nothing

'       Reset status bar
        Application.StatusBar = ""
        MsgBox Records & " memos were created and saved in " & _
          ThisWorkbook.Path
    End Sub
```

Creating this macro involved several steps. I started by recording a macro in Word. I recorded my actions while creating a new document, adding and formatting some text, and saving the file. That macro provided the information I needed about the appropriate properties and methods. I then copied the macro to an Excel module. Notice that I used `With-End With`. I added a dot before each instruction between `With` and `End With`. For example, the original Word macro contained (among others) the following instruction:

```
Documents.Add
```

I modified the macro as follows:

```
With WordApp
    .Documents.Add
'   more instructions here
End With
```

The macro I recorded in Word used a few of Word's built-in constants. Because this example uses late binding, I had to substitute actual values for those constants. I was able to learn the values by using the Immediate window in Word's VBE.

Controlling Excel from Another Application

You can, of course, also control Excel from another application (such as a Visual Basic program or a Word macro). For example, you may want to perform some calculations in Excel and return the result to a Word document.

You can create any of the following Excel objects with the adjacent functions:

`Application` **object**	`CreateObject("Excel.Application")`
`Workbook` **object**	`CreateObject("Excel.Sheet")`
`Chart` **object**	`CreateObject("Excel.Chart")`

Figure 19-7 shows a document created by the `MakeMemos` procedure.

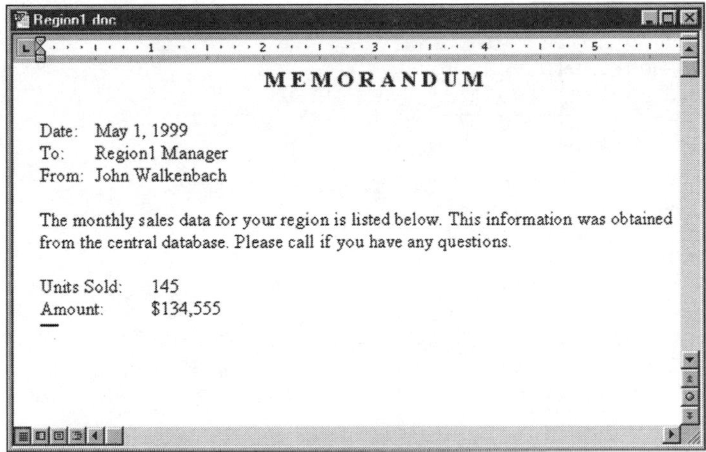

Figure 19-7: An Excel procedure created this document.

Listing 19-4 shows a procedure that is located in a VBA module in a Word 2000 document. This procedure creates an Excel `Worksheet` object—whose moniker is `"Excel.Sheet"`—from an existing workbook.

Listing 19-4: Producing an Excel worksheet on a Word 2000 document

```
Sub MakeExcelChart()
    Dim XLSheet As Object

'   Create a new document
    Documents.Add

'   Prompt for values
    StartVal = InputBox("Starting Value?")
    PctChange = InputBox("Percent Change?")

'   Create Sheet object
```

Continued

Listing 19-4 *(continued)*

```
    Wbook = ThisDocument.Path & "\projections.xls"
    Set XLSheet = GetObject(Wbook, "Excel.Sheet").ActiveSheet

'   Put values in sheet
    XLSheet.Range("StartingValue") = StartVal
    XLSheet.Range("PctChange") = PctChange
    XLSheet.Calculate

'   Insert page heading
    Selection.Font.Size = 14
    Selection.Font.Bold = True
    Selection.TypeText "Monthly Increment: " & _
      Format(PctChange, "0.0%")
    Selection.TypeParagraph
    Selection.TypeParagraph

'   Copy data from sheet & paste to document
    XLSheet.Range("data").Copy
    Selection.Paste

'   Copy chart and paste to document
    XLSheet.ChartObjects(1).Copy
    Selection.PasteSpecial _
        Link:=False, _
        DataType:=wdPasteMetafilePicture, _
        Placement:=wdInLine, DisplayAsIcon:=False

'   Kill the object
    Set XLSheet = Nothing
End Sub
```

The initial workbook is shown in Figure 19-8. The `MakeExcelChart` procedure prompts the user for two values and inserts the values into the worksheet.

Recalculating the worksheet updates a chart. The data and the chart are then copied from the Excel object and pasted into a new document. The results are shown in Figure 19-9.

Using SendKeys

It's possible to control some applications even if they don't support Automation. You can use Excel's `SendKeys` method to send keystrokes to an application, simulating actions that a user might perform.

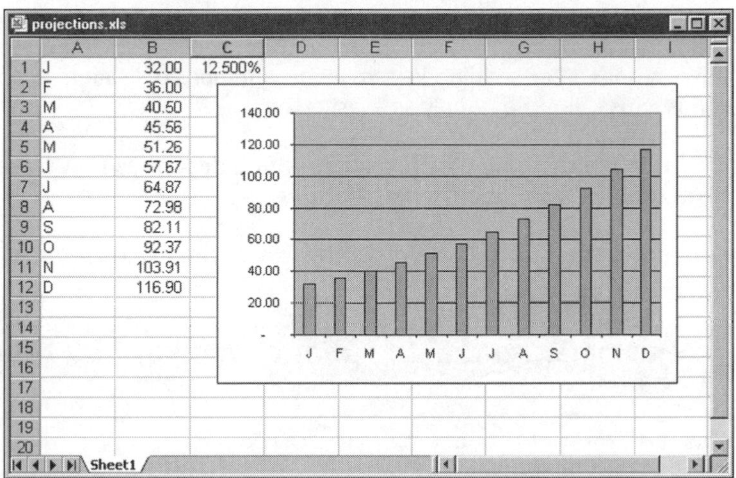

Figure 19-8: A VBA procedure in Word uses this worksheet.

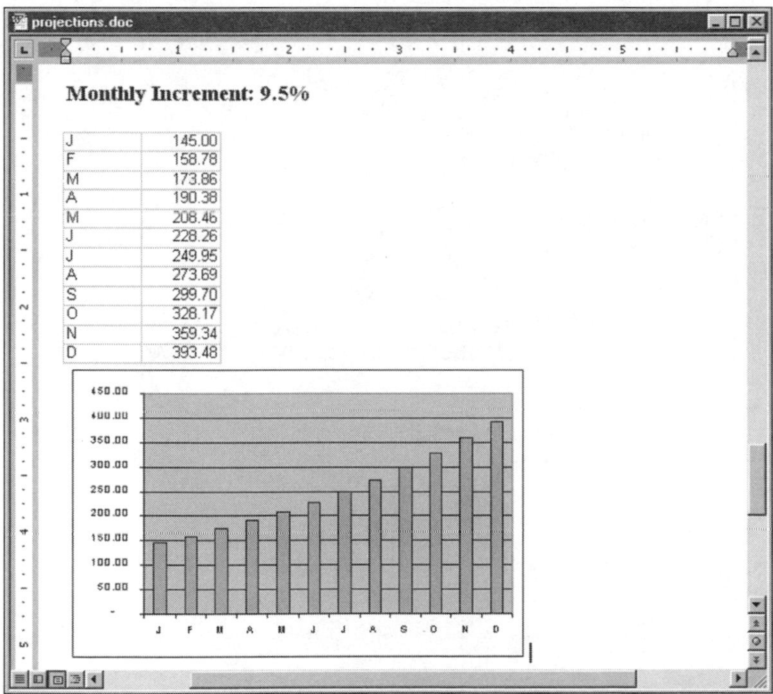

Figure 19-9: The Word VBA procedure uses Excel to create this document.

SendKeys can be quite tricky to use because the keystrokes are not actually sent until VBA is finished executing. For best results, your procedures should not perform any other actions after sending keystrokes to another application. A good rule of thumb is to use SendKeys only as a last resort.

SendKeys is documented in the online help system, which describes how to send nonstandard keystrokes, such as Alt key combinations.

The CellToDialer procedure in Listing 19-5 demonstrates the use of SendKeys.

Listing 19-5: Having Excel dial the phone, one key at a time

```
Sub CellToDialer()
'   Transfers active cell contents to Dialer
'   And then dials the phone

'   Get the phone number
    CellContents = ActiveCell.Value
    If CellContents = "" Then
        MsgBox "Select a cell that contains a phone number."
        Exit Sub
    End If

'   Activate (or start) Dialer
    Appname = "Dialer"
    AppFile = "Dialer.exe"
    On Error Resume Next
    AppActivate (Appname)
    If Err <> 0 Then
        Err = 0
        TaskID = Shell(AppFile, 1)
        If Err <> 0 Then MsgBox "Can't start " & AppFile
    End If

'   Transfer cell contents to Dialer
    Application.SendKeys "%n" & CellContents, True

'   Click Dial button
    Application.SendKeys "%d"
'    Application.SendKeys "{TAB}~", True
End Sub
```

When executed from a worksheet, this procedure starts the Windows Dialer application in Figure 19-10, which dials the phone. If Dialer is not running, it starts Dialer. The macro uses SendKeys to transfer the contents of the active cell to the Windows Dialer application, and then “clicks” the Dial button.

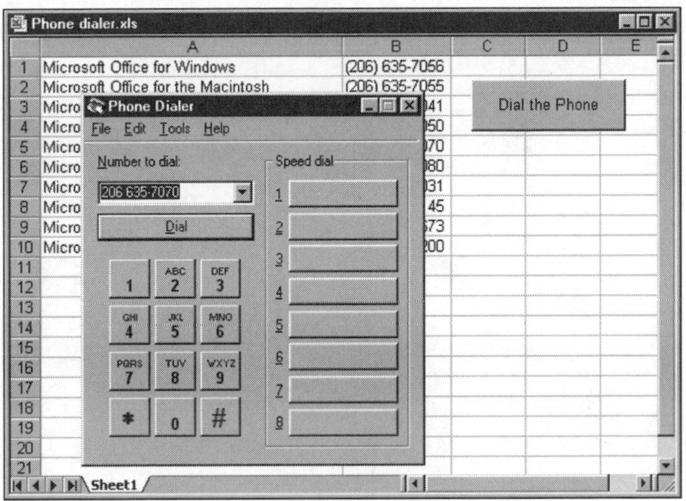

Figure 19-10: SendKeys transfers the phone number in the active cell to Windows Dialer.

Summary

In this chapter, I touched on some of the ways you can automate the process of Excel's working in tandem with other applications. These ways include using Automation to execute and/or activate other applications and using `SendKeys`.

The next chapter describes how to create an add-in from an Excel workbook.

✦ ✦ ✦

CHAPTER 20

Creating and Using Add-Ins

✦ ✦ ✦ ✦

In This Chapter

What an add-in is and why this concept is important for developers

Details about Excel's Add-In Manager

How to create an add-in, including a hands-on example

How XLA files differ from XLS files

Examples of VBA code that manipulates add-ins

How to optimize your add-in for speed and size

✦ ✦ ✦ ✦

One of Excel's most useful features for developers is the capability to create add-ins. Excel is no longer unique among spreadsheets in this respect (current versions of 1-2-3 also support add-ins), but its implementation remains the best. In this chapter, I explain why this feature is so slick, and I show you how to create your own add-ins by using only the tools built into Excel.

What Is an Add-In?

Generally speaking, a spreadsheet add-in is something added to a spreadsheet to give it additional functionality. For example, one of the reasons that 1-2-3 for DOS remained popular for so long was the many add-ins available for it. These add-ins took the form of industry-specific features (for example, the third-party financial forecasting add-ins) or very general features such as on-screen formatting (for example, the WYSIWYG add-in that was included with 1-2-3 for DOS).

Some add-ins provide new worksheet functions that can be used in formulas. The new features usually blend in well with the original interface, so they appear to be part of the program (this is referred to as *seamless integration*).

Add-ins are always spreadsheet-specific. For example, Excel add-ins do not work with 1-2-3.

Comparing an add-in to a standard workbook

Any knowledgeable Excel user can create add-ins from XLS workbooks; no additional programming tools are required.

Any XLS file can be converted to an add-in, but not all XLS files are appropriate for add-ins. An Excel add-in is basically a normal XLS workbook with the following differences:

- ✦ The `IsAddin` property of the `ThisWorkbook` object is True.
- ✦ The workbook window is hidden in such a way that it can't be unhidden using the Window ⇨ Unhide command. This means that you can't display worksheets or chart sheets contained in an add-in (unless you write code to copy the sheet to a standard workbook).
- ✦ The workbook is not a member of the `Workbooks` collection. Rather, it's a member of the `AddIns` collection.
- ✦ Add-ins can be loaded and unloaded using the Tools ⇨ Add-Ins command.
- ✦ The Macro dialog box does not display the macro names in an add-in.
- ✦ A custom worksheet function stored within an add-in can be used in formulas without having to precede its name with the source workbook's filename.

By default, an add-in has an .xla file extension. This is not a requirement, however. An add-in file can have any extension that you like.

Why create add-ins?

You might decide to convert your XLS application into an add-in for any of the following reasons:

- ✦ *To restrict access to your code.* When you distribute an application as an add-in and you protect it with a password, users can't view or modify the sheets or VBA code in the workbook. Therefore, if you use proprietary techniques in your application, you can prevent anyone from copying the code, or at least make it more difficult to do so.
- ✦ *To avoid confusion.* If a user loads your application as an add-in, the file is not visible and is therefore less likely to confuse novice users or get in the way. Unlike a hidden XLS workbook, an add-in can't be unhidden.
- ✦ *To simplify access to worksheet functions.* Custom worksheet functions stored within an add-in don't require the workbook name qualifier. For example, if you store a custom function named `MOVAVG` in a workbook named Newfuncs.xls, you must use a syntax like the following to use this function in a different workbook:

  ```
  =Newfuncs.xls!MOVAVG(A1:A50)
  ```

  But if this function is stored in an add-in file that's open, you can use a much simpler syntax because you don't need to include the file reference:

  ```
  =MOVAVG(A1:A50)
  ```

✦ *To provide easier access for users.* Once you identify the location of your add-in, it appears in the Add-Ins dialog box with a friendly name and a description of what it does.

✦ *To gain better control over loading.* Add-ins can be opened automatically when Excel starts, regardless of the directory in which they are stored.

✦ *To avoid displaying prompts when unloading.* When an add-in is closed, the user never sees the "Save change in *xxx*?" prompt.

Understanding Excel's Add-in Manager

The most efficient way to load and unload add-ins is with Excel's Add-Ins dialog box, which you access by choosing Tools ➪ Add-Ins. This command displays the Add-Ins dialog box, shown in Figure 20-1. The list box contains the names of all add-ins that Excel knows about, and check marks identify add-ins that are open. You can open and close add-ins from this dialog box by checking or unchecking the check boxes.

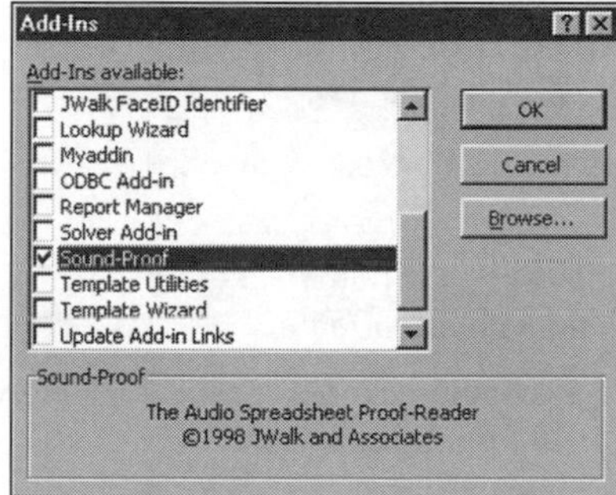

Figure 20-1: The Add-Ins dialog box.

You also can open most add-in files by choosing the File ➪ Open command. Since an add-in is never the active workbook, you can't close an add-in by choosing File ➪ Close. You can remove the add-in only by exiting and restarting Excel or by writing a macro to close the add-in. Opening an add-in with the File ➪ Open command opens the file, but the add-in is not officially "installed."

When you open an add-in, you may or may not notice anything different about Excel. In almost every case, however, the user interface changes in some way: Excel displays either a new menu, one or more new menu items on an existing menu, or a toolbar. For example, when you open the Analysis ToolPak add-in, this add-in gives you a new menu item on the Tools menu: Data Analysis. When you open my Power Utility Pak add-in, you get a new Utilities menu, located between the Data menu and the Window menu. If the add-in contains only custom worksheet functions, the new functions appear in the Paste Function dialog box.

Add-ins Supplied with Excel 2000

You may have used one or more of the add-ins supplied with Excel (maybe without even realizing it). The following table describes the add-ins included with Excel 2000.

Add-In	*Description*
Access Links	Enables you to use Microsoft Access forms and reports with Excel worksheets. (Access must be installed on your system.)
Analysis ToolPak	Contains statistical and engineering tools, plus new worksheet functions.
Analysis ToolPak—VBA	Contains VBA functions for Analysis ToolPak.
AutoSave	Automatically saves your workbook at a time interval that you specify.
MS Query	Works with Microsoft Query to bring external data into a worksheet.
ODBC	Enables you to use ODBC functions to connect directly to external data sources.
Report Manager	Prints reports comprising a set sequence of views and scenarios.
Solver	Helps you use a variety of numeric methods for equation solving and optimization.
Template Utilities	Contains utilities used by the Spreadsheet Solutions templates. This is automatically loaded when you use one of these templates.
Template Wizard with Data Tracking	Helps you create custom templates.
Update Add-in Links	Updates links to Microsoft Excel 4.0 add-ins to access the new built-in functionality directly.
View Manager	Creates, stores, and displays different views of a worksheet.

Creating an Add-In

As I noted earlier, you can convert any workbook to an add-in, but not all workbooks are appropriate candidates for add-ins. Generally, a workbook that benefits most from being converted to an add-in is one that contains macros — especially general-purpose macro procedures. A workbook that consists only of worksheets would be inaccessible as an add-in because worksheets within add-ins are hidden from the user. You can, however, write code that copies all or part of a sheet from your add-in to a visible workbook.

Creating an add-in from a workbook is simple. The following steps describe how to create an add-in from a normal workbook file:

1. Develop your application, and make sure everything works properly.

   Don't forget to include a method for executing the macro or macros. You might want to add a new menu or menu item or to create a custom toolbar. See Chapter 22 for details on customizing menus and Chapter 21 for a discussion of custom toolbars.

2. Test the application by executing it when a *different* workbook is active.

   This simulates the application's behavior when it's used as an add-in because an add-in is never the active workbook.

3. Activate the VBE, and select the workbook in the Project window. Choose Tools ➪ *xxx* Properties, and click the Protection tab. Select the Lock project for viewing check box, and enter a password (twice). Click OK.

   This step is necessary only if you want to prevent others from viewing or modifying your macros or custom dialog boxes.

4. Choose File➪Properties, click the Summary tab, and enter a brief descriptive title in the *Title* field and a longer description in the Comments field.

   This step is not required, but it makes the add-in easier to use by displaying descriptive text in the Add-Ins dialog box.

5. Select File ➪ Save As.

6. In the Save As dialog box, select Microsoft Excel add-in (*.xla) from the Save as type drop-down list.

7. Click Save. A copy of the workbook is saved (with an .xla extension), and the original XLS workbook remains open.

A workbook being converted to an add-in must have at least one worksheet. For example, if your workbook contains only chart sheets or Excel 5/95 dialog sheets, the Microsoft Excel add-in (*.xla) option does not appear in the Save As dialog box.

With previous versions of Excel, to modify an add-in, you had to open the original XLS file, make your changes, and then re-create the add-in. For Excel 97 and later versions, this is no longer necessary. As long as the add-in is not protected, you can make changes to the add-in in the VBE. If the add-in is protected, you must enter the password to unprotect it. Therefore, with Excel 97 or later, keeping an XLS version of your add-in is not necessary.

A Few Words about Security

Microsoft has never promoted Excel as a product that creates applications in which the source code is secure. The password feature provided in Excel is sufficient to prevent casual users from accessing parts of your application that you'd like to keep hidden. But, the truth is, several password-cracking utilities are available. If you must be absolutely sure that no one ever sees your code or formulas, Excel is not your best choice as a development platform.

An Add-in Example

In this section, I discuss the steps involved in creating a useful add-in. The example uses the Text Tools utility that I described in Chapter 15.

The XLS version of the Text Tools utility is available on the companion CD-ROM. You can use this file to create the described add-in.

Setting up the workbook

In this example, you'll be working with a workbook that has already been developed and debugged. The workbook consists of the following items:

✦ A worksheet named `HelpSheet`. This contains the help text that describes the utility.

✦ A UserForm named `FormHelp`. This dialog box is used to display help. The code module for this UserForm contains several event-handler procedures.

✦ A UserForm named `FormMain`. This dialog box serves as the primary user interface. The code module for this UserForm contains several event-handler procedures.

✦ A VBA module named `modMenus`. This contains the code that creates and deletes a menu item (Tools ➪ Text Tools).

✦ A VBA module named `modMain`. This contains several procedures, including a procedure that displays the `FormMain` UserForm.

In addition, the `ThisWorkbook` module contains two event-handler procedures (`Workbook_Open` and `Workbook_BeforeClose`) that call other procedures to create and delete the menu item.

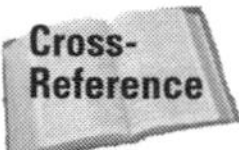

See Chapter 15 for details about how the Text Tools utility works.

Testing the workbook

Before converting this workbook to an add-in, you need to test it. To simulate what happens when the workbook is an add-in, you should test the workbook when a different workbook is active. Remember, an add-in is never the active workbook.

Open a new workbook, and try out the various features in the Text Tools utility. Do everything you can think of to try to make it fail. Better yet, seek the assistance of someone unfamiliar with the application to give it a crash test.

Adding descriptive information

I recommend entering a description of your add-in, but this step is not required. Choose the File ⇨ Properties command, which opens the Properties dialog box. Then, click the Summary tab, as shown in Figure 20-2.

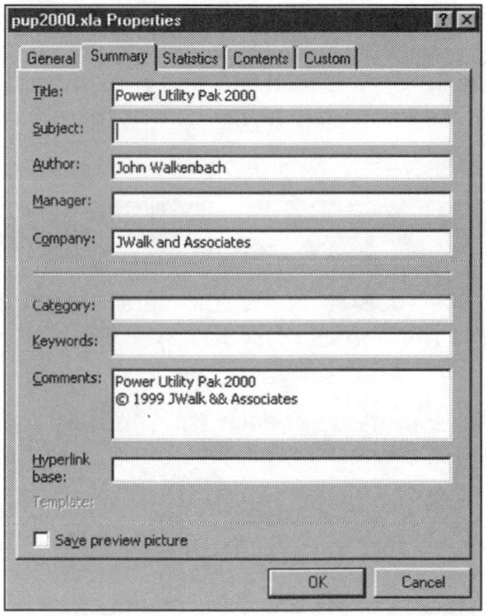

Figure 20-2: Use the Properties dialog box to enter descriptive information about your add-in.

Enter a title for the add-in in the Title field. This text appears in the Add-Ins dialog box. In the Comments field, enter a description. This information appears at the bottom of the Add-Ins dialog box when the add-in is selected.

Creating the add-in

To create the add-in, do the following:

1. Activate the VBE, and select the workbook in the Project window.
2. Choose Tools ➪ *xxx* Properties, and click the Protection tab. Select the Lock project for viewing check box and enter a password (twice). Click OK. If you don't need to protect the project, you can skip this step.
3. Save the workbook.
4. Activate the worksheet, and choose File ➪ Save As. Excel displays its Save As dialog box.
5. In the Save as type drop-down list, select Microsoft Excel add-in (*.xla).
6. Click Save. A new add-in file is created, and the original XLS version remains open.

When you save a file as an add-in, Excel creates the add-in even if it contains syntax errors. Therefore, before converting your workbook to an add-in, you should force a compile of all of your VBA code. To do this, activate the VBE, and select Debug ➪ Compile. This identifies any syntax errors so you can correct them.

About Excel's Add-in Manager

You access Excel's Add-In Manager by selecting the Tools➪Add-Ins command, which displays the Add-Ins dialog box. This dialog box lists the names of all the available add-ins. Those that are checked are open.

In VBA terms, the Add-In dialog box lists the `Title` property of each `AddIn` object in the `AddIns` collection. Each add-in that appears with a check mark has its `Installed` property set to True.

You can install an add-in by checking its box, and you can close an open add-in by removing the check mark from its box. To add an add-in to the list, use the Browse button to locate its file. By default, the Add-In dialog box lists files of the following types:

XLA	An add-in created from an XLS file
XLL	A stand-alone DLL file, written in C and compiled

You can enroll an add-in file into the `AddIns` collection with the `Add` method of VBA's `AddIns` collection, but you can't remove one using VBA. You can also open an add-in using VBA by setting the `AddIn` object's `Installed` property to True. Setting it to False closes the add-in.

The Add-In manager stores the installed status of the add-ins in the Windows Registry when you exit Excel. Therefore, all add-ins that are installed when you close Excel are automatically opened the next time you start Excel.

Opening the add-in

To avoid confusion, close the XLS workbook before opening the add-in created from that workbook.

To open an add-in manually, do the following:

1. Choose the Tools ➪ Add-Ins command. Excel displays the Add-Ins dialog box.
2. Click the Browse button, and locate the add-in you just created. After you find your new add-in, the Add-Ins dialog box displays the add-in in its list. As shown in Figure 20-3, the Add-Ins dialog box also displays the descriptive information you provided in the Properties dialog box.

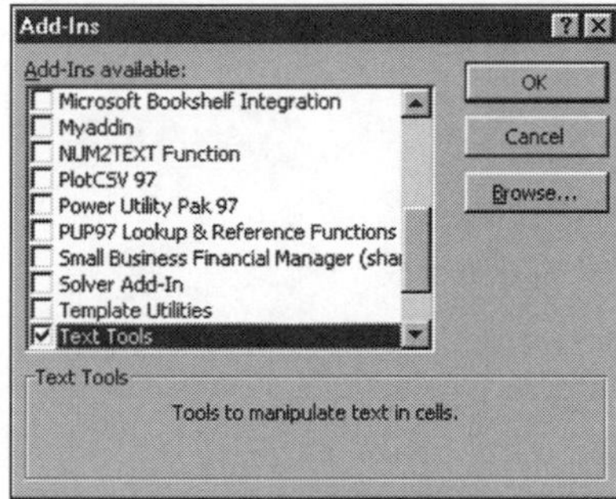

Figure 20-3: The Add-Ins dialog box, with the new add-in selected.

3. Click OK to close the dialog box and open the add-in.

After you open the add-in, the Tools menu displays the new menu item that executes the `StartTextTool` procedure in the add-in.

Distributing the add-in

You can distribute this add-in to other Excel users simply by giving them a copy of the XLA file (they don't need the XLS version) along with instructions on how to install it. If you have the Developer's Edition of Office 2000, you can use the Setup Wizard to create a Setup.exe file that your users can easily make sense of. After they install the add-in, the new Text Tools command appears on the Tools menu. Because you locked the file with a password, your macro code cannot be viewed by others unless they know the password.

Modifying the add-in

If you want to modify an add-in, first open it and then unlock it. To unlock it, activate the VBE, and double-click its project's name in the Project window. You'll be prompted for the password. Make your changes, and then save the file from the VBE (using the File ➪ Save command).

If you create an add-in that stores its information in a worksheet, you must set its workbook's `IsAddIn` property to False before you can view that workbook in Excel. You do this in the Properties window shown in Figure 20-4 when the `ThisWorkbook` object is selected. After you've made your changes, make sure you set the `IsAddIn` property back to True before you save the file. If you leave the `IsAddIn` property set to False, the file is saved as a regular workbook, although it still has the .xla extension. At this point, attempting to install this file by using the Add-Ins dialog box results in an error.

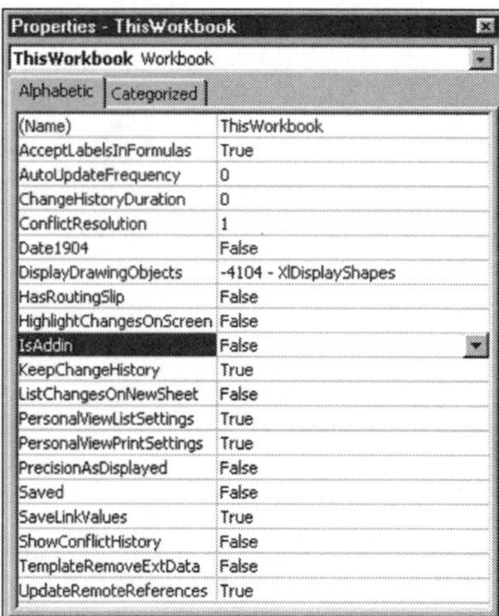

Figure 20-4: Making an add-in not an add-in.

Comparing XLA and XLS Files

This section begins by comparing an add-in XLA file to its XLS source file. Later in this chapter, I discuss methods that you can use to optimize the performance of your add-in. I describe a technique that may reduce its file size, which makes it load more quickly and use less disk space and memory.

File size and structure

An add-in based on an XLS source file is exactly the same size as the original. The VBA code in XLA files is not compressed or optimized in any way, so faster performance is not among the benefits of using an add-in.

Collection membership

An add-in is a member of the AddIns collection but not an "official" member of the Workbooks collection. In other words, you refer to an add-in by referencing the Workbooks collection and supplying the add-in's filename as its index. The following instruction creates an object variable that represents an add-in named Myaddin.xla.

```
Set TestAddin = Workbooks("Myaddin.xla")
```

Add-ins cannot be referenced by an index number in the Workbooks collection. If you use the following code to look through the Workbooks collection, the Myaddin.xla workbook is not displayed:

```
For Each w in Application.Workbooks
    MsgBox w.Name
Next w
```

The following For-Next loop, on the other hand, displays Myaddin.xla — assuming that Excel "knows" about it — in the Add-Ins dialog.

```
For Each a in Application.AddIns
    MsgBox a.Name
Next a
```

Windows

Ordinary XLS workbooks are displayed in one or more windows. For example, the following statement displays the number of windows for the active workbook:

```
MsgBox ActiveWorkbook.Windows.Count
```

You can manipulate the visibility of each window for an XLS workbook by using the Window⇨Hide command or by changing the Visible property. The following code hides all windows for the active workbook:

```
For Each Win In ActiveWorkbook.Windows
    Win.Visible = False
Next Win
```

Add-in files are never visible, and they don't officially have windows, even though they have unseen worksheets. Consequently, they don't appear in the windows list when you select the Window command. If Myaddin.xla is open, the following statement returns 0:

```
MsgBox Workbooks("Myaddin.xla").Windows.Count
```

Sheets

Add-in XLA files, like XLS files, can have any number of worksheets or chart sheets. But, as I noted earlier in this chapter, an XLS file must have at least one worksheet to convert it to an add-in.

When an add-in is open, your VBA code can access its contained sheets as if it were an ordinary workbook. Because add-in files aren't part of the `Workbooks` collection, though, you must reference an add-in by its name, not by an index number. The following example displays the value in cell A1 of the first worksheet in Myaddin.xla, which is assumed to be open:

```
MsgBox Workbooks("Myaddin.xla").Worksheets(1) _
  .Range("A1").Value
```

If your add-in contains a worksheet that you would like the user to see, you can copy it to an open workbook, or create a new workbook from the sheet.

The following code, for example, copies the first worksheet from an add-in and places it in the active workbook (as the last sheet).

```
Sub CopySheetFromAddin()
    Set AddinSheet = Workbooks("Myaddin.xla").Sheets(1)
    NumSheets = ActiveWorkbook.Sheets.Count
    AddinSheet.Copy After:=ActiveWorkbook.Sheets(NumSheets)
End Sub
```

Creating a new workbook from a sheet within an add-in is even simpler:

```
Sub CreateNewWorkbook()
    Workbooks("Myaddin.xla").Sheets(1).Copy
End Sub
```

Accessing VBA procedures in an add-in

Accessing the VBA procedures in an add-in is a bit different from accessing procedures in a normal XLS workbook. First of all, when you issue the Tools ➪ Macro command, the Macro dialog box does not display macro names belonging to open add-ins. It's almost as if Excel is trying to prevent you from accessing them.

Sleuthing a Protected Add-In

The Macro dialog box does not display the names of procedures contained in add-ins. But what if you'd like to run such a procedure, but the add-in is protected so you can't view the code to determine the name of the procedure? Use the Object Browser!

To illustrate, use the Tools⇨Add-Ins command to install the Lookup Wizard add-in. This add-in is distributed with Excel and is protected, so you can't view the code.

1. Activate the VBE, and select the Lookup.xla project in the Project window.
2. Press F2 to activate the Object Browser.
3. In the Libraries drop-down list, select lookup. This displays all the classes in the Lookup.xla add-in, as depicted in the following figure.

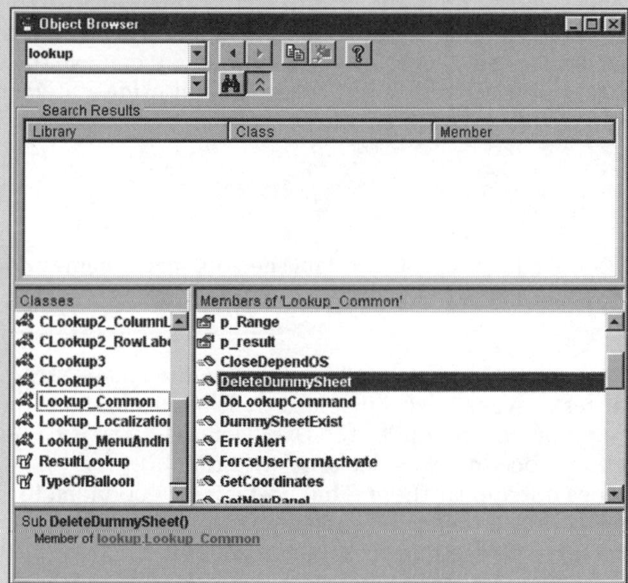

4. Select various items in the Classes list to see what class they are and the members they contain.

In the example above, the `Lookup_Common` class is a module, and its members consist of a number of variables, constants, procedures, and functions. One of these procedures, `DoLookupCommand`, sounds like it may be the main procedure that starts the wizard. To test this theory, activate Excel, and choose Tools⇨Macro⇨Macros. Type `DoLookupCommand` in the Macro Name box, and click Run. Sure enough! You'll see the first dialog box of the Lookup Wizard.

Armed with this information, you can write VBA code to start the Lookup Wizard.

Tip

If you know the name of the procedure, you can enter it directly into the Macros dialog box and click Run to execute it. The Sub procedure must be in a general VBA module, not in a code module for an object.

Because procedures contained in an add-in don't appear in the Macros dialog box, you must provide other means to access them. Your choices include direct methods, such as shortcut keys, custom menus, and custom toolbars, as well as indirect methods, such as event handlers. One such candidate, for example, may be the `OnTime` method, which executes a procedure at a specific time of day.

You can use the `Run` method of the `Application` object to execute a procedure in an add-in. For example,

```
Application.Run "Myaddin.xla"!DisplayNames"
```

If you use the Tools ➪ References command in the VBE to enable references to the add-in, you can refer directly to one of its procedures in your VBA code without the filename qualifier. In fact, you don't need to use the `Run` method; you can call the procedure directly as long as it's not declared as `Private`. The following statement executes a procedure named `DisplayNames` in an add-in that has been added as a reference:

```
Call DisplayNames
```

Note

Even when a reference to the add-in has been established, its macro names do not appear in the Macros dialog box.

Function procedures defined in an add-in work just like those defined in an XLS workbook. They're easy to access because Excel displays their names in the Paste Function dialog box of the Function Wizard, under the User Defined category. The only exception is if the Function procedure was declared with the `Private` keyword; then the function does not appear there. That's why it's a good idea to declare custom functions as `Private` if they will be used only by other VBA procedures and are not designed to be used in worksheet formulas.

Note

To see an add-in that does *not* declare its functions as `Private`, install Microsoft's Lookup Wizard add-in. Then click the Insert Function button. You'll find more than three dozen nonworksheet functions listed in the User Defined category of the Insert Function dialog box.

As I discussed earlier, you can use worksheet functions contained in add-ins without the workbook name qualifier. For example, if you have a custom function named `MOVAVG` stored in the file Newfuncs.xls, you would use the following instruction to address the function from a worksheet belonging to a different workbook:

```
=Newfuncs.xls!MOVAVG(A1:A50)
```

Creating an Add-in: A Checklist

Before you release your add-in to the world, take a few minutes to run through this checklist:

✦ Did you test your add-in with all supported platforms and Excel versions?

✦ Does your add-in make any assumptions about the user's directory structure or directory names?

✦ When you use the Add-Ins dialog box to load your add-in, is its name and description correct and appropriate?

✦ If your add-in uses VBA functions that aren't designed to be used in a worksheet, have you declared the functions as `Private`? If not, these functions will appear in the Paste Function dialog box.

✦ Did you force a recompile of your add-in to ensure that it contains no syntax errors?

✦ Did you account for any international issues? For example, if your add-in creates a new item on the Tools menu, will it fail if the Tools menu has a non-English name?

✦ Is your add-in file optimized for speed? See "Optimizing the Performance of Add-Ins" later in this chapter.

But if this function is stored in an add-in file that's open, you can omit the file reference and write the following instead:

```
=MOVAVG(A1:A50)
```

Manipulating Add-ins with VBA

In this section, I present information that will help you write VBA procedures that manipulate add-ins.

The AddIns collection

The `AddIns` collection consists of all add-ins that Excel knows about. These add-ins can either be installed or not. The Tools➪Add-Ins command displays the Add-Ins dialog box, which lists all members of the `AddIns` collection. Those entries accompanied by a check mark are installed.

Adding an item to the AddIns collection

The add-in files that make up the AddIns collection can be stored anywhere. Excel maintains a list of these files and their locations in the Windows Registry. For Excel 2000, this list is stored at

```
HKEY_CURRENT_USER\Software\Microsoft\Office\9.0\Excel\Add-in
Manager
```

You can use the Windows Registry Editor (Regedit.exe) to view this Registry key.

You can add a new AddIn object to the AddIns collection either manually or programmatically using VBA. To add a new add-in to the collection manually, select Tools⇨Add-Ins, click the Browse button, and locate the add-in.

To enroll a new member of the AddIns collection with VBA, use the collection's Add method. Here's an example:

```
Application.AddIns.Add ("c:\files\newaddin.xla")
```

After the preceding instruction is executed, the AddIns collection has a new member, and the Add-Ins dialog box shows a new item in its list. If the add-in already exists in the collection, nothing happens, and an error is not generated.

If the add-in you're enrolling is on a removable disk (for example, a floppy disk or CD-ROM), you can also copy the file to Excel's library directory with the Add method. The following example copies Myaddin.xla from drive A and adds it to the AddIns collection. The second argument (True, in this case) specifies whether the add-in should be copied. If the add-in resides on a hard drive, the second argument may be ignored.

```
AddIns.Add "a:\Myaddin.xla", True
```

Enrolling a new workbook into the AddIns collection does not install it. To install it, set its Installed property to True.

The Windows Registry does not actually get updated until Excel closes normally. Therefore, if Excel ends abnormally (that is, if it crashes), the add-in's name will not get added to the Registry and the add-in will not be part of the AddIns collection when Excel restarts.

Removing an item from the AddIns collection

Oddly, there is no direct way to remove an add-in from the AddIns collection. The AddIns collection does not have a Delete or Remove method. One way to remove an add-in from the Add-Ins dialog box is to edit the Windows Registry database (using Regedit.exe). After you do this, the add-in will not appear in the Add-Ins dialog box the next time you start Excel.

Another way to remove an add-in from the AddIns collection is to delete or move its XLA file. You'll get a warning like the one in Figure 20-5 the next time you try to install or uninstall the add-in, along with an opportunity to remove it from the AddIns collection.

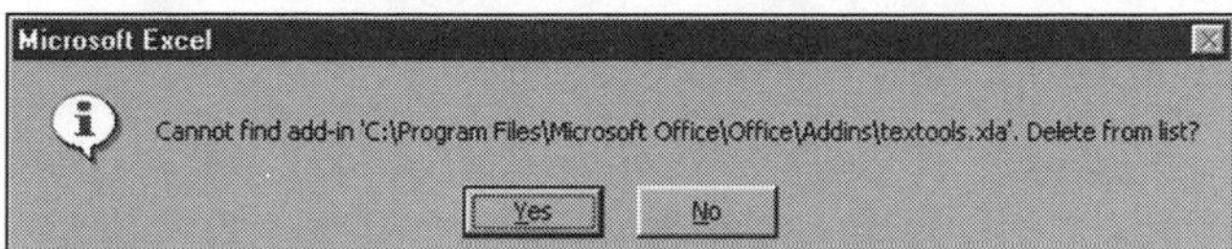

Figure 20-5: One very direct way to remove a member of the AddIns collection.

AddIn object properties

An AddIn object is a single member of the AddIns collection. For example, to display the filename of the first member of the AddIns collection, use the following:

```
Msgbox AddIns(1).Name
```

An AddIn object has twelve properties, which you can read about in the online help. Some of the terminology is a bit confusing, so I'll discuss a few of the more important properties.

Name

This property holds the filename of the add-in. Because Name is a read-only property, you can't change the name of the file by changing the Name property.

Path

This property holds the drive and path where the add-in file is stored. It does not include a final backslash or the filename.

FullName

This property holds the add-in's drive, path, and filename. This property is a bit redundant because this information is also available from the Name and Path properties. The following instructions produce exactly the same message:

```
MsgBox AddIns(1).Path & "\" & AddIns(1).Name
MsgBox AddIns(1).FullName
```

Title

This property holds a descriptive name for the add-in. The Title property is what appears in the Add-Ins dialog box. This property is read-only, and the only way to add or change the Title property of an add-in is to use the File➪Properties command (click the Summary tab, and enter text into the Title field). You must use this menu command with the XLS version of the file before converting it to an add-in.

Most members of collections are addressed by way of their `Name` property settings. The `AddIns` collection is different; it uses the `Title` property instead. The following example displays the filename for the View Manager add-in (that is, Views.xls), whose `Title` property is `"View Manager"`.

```
Sub ShowName()
    MsgBox AddIns("View Manager").Name
End Sub
```

You can, of course, also reference a particular add-in with its index number if you happen to know it.

Comments

This property stores text that is displayed in the Add-Ins dialog box when a particular add-in is selected. `Comments` is a read-only property. The only way to change it is to use the Properties dialog box before you convert the workbook to an add-in. Comments can be as long as 255 characters, but the Add-Ins dialog box can display only about 100 characters.

IsAddIn

You can determine whether a particular workbook is an add-in by accessing its `IsAddIn` property. This is not a read-only property, so you can also convert a workbook to an add-in by setting the `IsAddIn` property to True.

Installed

The `Installed` property is True if the add-in is currently installed — that is, if it is checked in the Add-Ins dialog box. Setting the `Installed` property to True opens the add-in. Setting it to False unloads it. Here's an example of how to install (that is, open) the MS Query add-in with VBA.

```
Sub InstallQuery()
    AddIns("MS Query Add-In").Installed = True
End Sub
```

After this procedure is executed, the Add-Ins dialog box displays a check mark next to MS Query Add-In. If the add-in is already installed, setting its `Installed` property to True has no effect. To remove this add-in (uninstall it), simply set the `Installed` property to False.

Caution: If the add-in was opened with the File ➪ Open command, its `Installed` property is False.

The following procedure displays the number of add-ins in the `AddIns` collection and the number of those that are installed. You'll find that the count does not include add-ins that were opened with the File ➪ Open command.

```
Sub CountInstalledAddIns()
    Count = 0
    For Each Item In AddIns
        If Item.Installed Then Count = Count + 1
    Next Item
    Msg = "Add-ins: " & AddIns.Count & Chr(13)
    Msg = Msg & "Installed: " & Count
    MsgBox Msg
End Sub
```

The next procedure loops through all add-ins in the `AddIns` collection and uninstalls any add-in that's installed. This procedure does not affect add-ins that were opened with the File ➪ Open command.

```
Sub UninstallAll()
    Count = 0
    For Each Item In AddIns
        If Item.Installed Then
            Item.Installed = False
            Count = Count + 1
        End If
    Next Item
    MsgBox Count & " Add-Ins Uninstalled."
End Sub
```

Accessing an add-in as a workbook

As I mentioned earlier, there are two ways to open an add-in file: with the File ➪ Open command and with the Tools ➪ Add-Ins command. The latter method is the preferred method for the following reason: When you open an add-in with the File ➪ Open command, its `Installed` property is *not* set to True. Therefore, you cannot close the file using the Add-Ins dialog box. In fact, the only way to close such an add-in is with a VBA statement such as the following:

```
Workbooks("Myaddin.xla").Close
```

Caution

Using the `Close` method on an installed add-in removes the add-in from memory, but it does *not* set its `Installed` property to False. Therefore, the Add-Ins dialog box still lists the add-in as installed, which can be very confusing. The proper way to remove an installed add-in is to set its `Installed` property to False.

AddIn object events

An `AddIn` object has two events: `AddInInstall` (generated when it is installed) and `AddInUninstall` (generated when it is uninstalled). You can write event-handler procedures for these events in the `ThisWorkbook` object for the add-in.

The following example is displayed as a message when the add-in is installed.

```
Private Sub Workbook_AddinInstall()
    MsgBox ThisWorkbook.Name & _
```

```
        " add-in in has been installed."
End Sub
```

The AddInInstall event occurs before the Open event for the workbook, and the AddInUninstall event occurs before the BeforeClose event for the workbook.

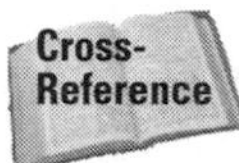

For additional information about events, see Chapter 18.

Optimizing the Performance of Add-Ins

It should be obvious that you want your add-in to be as fast and efficient as possible. In this section, I describe some techniques that you may find helpful.

Code speed

If you ask a dozen Excel programmers to automate a particular task, chances are you'll get a dozen different approaches. Most likely, not all these approaches will perform equally well.

Following are a few tips that you can use to ensure that your code runs as fast as possible:

- ✦ Set the `Application.ScreenUpdating` property to False when writing data to a worksheet.
- ✦ Declare the data type for all variables used, and in your finalized code, avoid variants whenever possible. Use an `Option Explicit` statement at the top of each module to force variable declaration.
- ✦ Create object variables to avoid lengthy object references. For example, if you're working with a `Series` object for a chart, create an object variable using code like this:

  ```
  Dim S1 As Series
  Set S1 = ActiveWorkbook.Sheets(1).ChartObjects(1). _
    Chart.SeriesCollection(1)
  ```

- ✦ Declare object variables as a specific object type, not `As Object`.
- ✦ Use the `With End With` construct, when appropriate, to set multiple properties or call multiple methods for a single object.
- ✦ Remove all extraneous code. This is especially important if you've used the macro recorder to create procedures.
- ✦ If possible, manipulate data with VBA arrays rather than worksheet ranges. Reading and writing to a worksheet takes much longer than manipulating data in memory.

✦ Avoid linking UserForm controls to worksheet cells. Doing so may trigger a recalculation whenever the user changes the UserForm control.

✦ Compile your code before creating the add-in. This may increase the file size, but it eliminates the need for Excel to compile the code before executing the procedures.

File size

Excel workbooks (including add-ins) have always suffered from a serious problem: *bloat.* You may have noticed that the size of your files tends to increase over time, even if you don't add any new content. This is especially true if you delete a lot of code and then replace it with other code.

If you want to make your add-in — or any workbook, for that matter — as small as possible, you'll need to re-create your workbook. Here's how:

1. Make a backup of your application, and keep it in a safe place.
2. Activate the VBE, and export all the components for your project that contain VBA code (modules, code modules, UserForms, and possibly `ThisWorkbook`, worksheet, and chart modules). Make a note of the filenames and the location.
3. Create a new workbook.
4. Copy the contents of all the worksheets from your original application to worksheets in the new workbook. Be especially careful if you used named ranges in your workbook — they must be re-created.
5. Import the components you exported in Step 2.
6. Compile the code.
7. If applicable, reattach any toolbars that were attached to your original workbook.
8. Save the new workbook.
9. Test the new workbook thoroughly to ensure that nothing was lost in the process.

There's an excellent chance that the newly created file will be much smaller than your original. The size reduction depends on many factors, but I've been able to reduce the size of my XLA files by as much as 55 percent with this process.

Special Problems with Add-Ins

Add-ins are great, but you should realize by now that there's no free lunch. Add-ins present their share of problems — or should I say challenges? In this section, I discuss some issues that you need to know about if you'll be developing add-ins for widespread user distribution.

Ensuring that an add-in is installed

In some cases, you may need to ensure that your add-in is installed properly (that is, opened using the Tools➪Add-Ins command, not the File➪Open command). This section describes a technique that determines just that. If it isn't properly installed, VBA installs it (by attaching it to the `AddIns` collection, if necessary) and uses the message shown in Figure 20-6 to tell the user what was done.

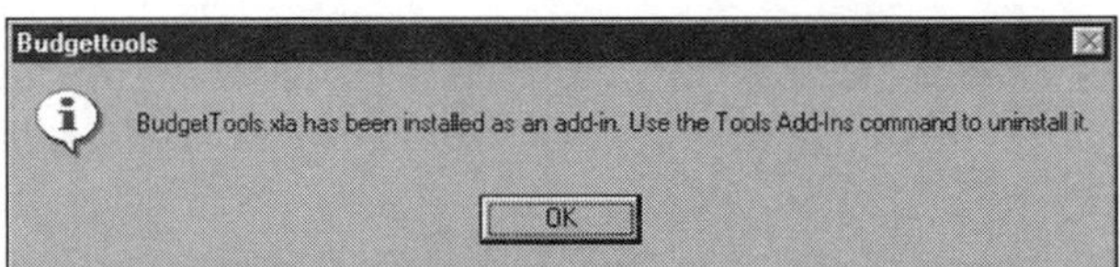

Figure 20-6: When attempting to open the add-in incorrectly, the user sees this message.

Listing 20-1 presents the code module for this example's `ThisWorkbook` object. This technique relies on the fact that the `AddInInstall` event occurs before the `Open` event for the workbook.

Listing 20-1: Ensuring that an accessible add-in is properly installed and workable

```
Dim InstalledProperly As Boolean

Private Sub Workbook_AddinInstall()
    InstalledProperly = True
End Sub

Private Sub Workbook_Open()
    If Not ThisWorkbook.IsAddin Then Exit Sub

    If Not InstalledProperly Then
'       Add it to the AddIns collection
        If Not InAddInCollection(ThisWorkbook) Then _
          AddIns.Add FileName:=ThisWorkbook.FullName

'       Install it
        AddInTitle = GetTitle(ThisWorkbook)
        Application.EnableEvents = False
        AddIns(AddInTitle).Installed = True
        Application.EnableEvents = True

'       Inform user
        Msg = ThisWorkbook.Name & _
          " has been installed as an add-in. "
        Msg = Msg & _
```

```
            "Use the Tools Add-Ins command to uninstall it."
        MsgBox Msg, vbInformation, AddInTitle
    End If
End Sub
```

If the add-in is installed properly, the `Workbook_AddinInstall` procedure is executed. This procedure sets the Boolean variable `InstalledProperly` to True. If the add-in was opened using the File ➪ Open command, the `Workbook_AddinInstall` procedure is not executed, so the `InstalledProperly` variable has its default value (False).

When the `Workbook_Open` procedure is executed, it first checks to make sure the workbook is an add-in. If it isn't, the procedure ends. If the workbook is an add-in, the routine checks the value of `InstalledProperly`. If the add-in was installed properly, the procedure ends. If not, the code executes a custom function to determine whether the add-in is a member of the `AddIns` collection. If it is not in the collection, it is added. The procedure ends by installing the file as an add-in and then informing the user. The net effect is that using File ➪ Open to open the add-in actually installs it properly — and the user receives a brief lesson in the use of add-ins.

The preceding code uses two custom functions, shown in Listing 20-2. The `InAddInCollection` returns True if a workbook passed as an argument is a member of the `AddIns` collection. The `GetTitle` function returns the `Title` property for an add-in workbook.

Listing 20-2: **Filling in for Excel's missing add-in properties**

```
Function InAddInCollection(wb) As Boolean
    For Each item In AddIns
        If item.Name = wb.Name Then
            InAddInCollection = True
        End If
    Next item
End Function

Function GetTitle(wb) As String
    GetTitle = ""
    For Each item In AddIns
        If item.Name = wb.Name Then
            GetTitle = item.Title
        End If
    Next item
End Function
```

Referencing other files

If your add-in uses other files, you need to be especially careful when distributing the application. You can't assume anything about the storage structure of the system that users will run the application on. The easiest approach is to insist that all files for the application be copied to a single directory. Then you can use the `Path` property of your application's workbook to build path references to all other files.

For example, if your application uses a custom help file, be sure that the help file is copied to the same directory as the application itself. Then you can use a procedure like the following to make sure that the help file can be located:

```
Sub GetHelp()
    Path = ThisWorkbook.Path
    Application.Help Path & "\USER.HLP"
End Sub
```

If your application uses API calls to standard Windows DLLs, you can assume that these can be found by Windows. But if you use custom DLLs, the best practice is to make sure that they are installed in the Windows\System directory (which may or may not be named Windows\System). You'll need to use the `GetSystemDirectory` Windows API function to determine the exact path of the System directory.

Specifying the proper Excel version

If your add-in makes use of any features unique to Excel 2000, you'll want to warn users who attempt to open the add-in using Excel 97. The following code does the trick:

```
Sub CheckVersion()
    If Val(Application.Version) < 9 Then
        MsgBox "This works only with Excel 2000 or later"
        ThisWorkbook.Close
    End If
End Sub
```

The `Version` property of the `Application` object returns a string. For example, this might return `9.0a`. This procedure uses VBA's `Val` function, which ignores everything after the first alpha character.

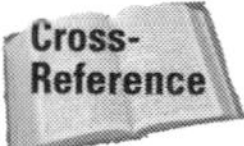

See Chapter 25 for additional information about compatibility.

Summary

In this chapter, I covered add-ins and described what they are, how to create them, and how to manipulate them using VBA.

In the next chapter, I discuss how to create and manipulate toolbars.

✦ ✦ ✦

P A R T

VI

Developing Applications

The chapters in this part deal with important elements of creating user-oriented applications. Chapters 21 and 22 provide information on creating custom toolbars and menus. Chapter 23 presents several different ways to provide online help for your application. In Chapter 24, I present some basic information about developing user-oriented applications, and I describe such an application in detail.

✦ ✦ ✦ ✦

In This Part

✦ ✦ ✦ ✦

CHAPTER 21

Creating Custom Toolbars

✦ ✦ ✦ ✦

In This Chapter

An overview of command bars, which include toolbars

Understanding how Excel keeps track of toolbars

Customizing toolbars manually

Lots of examples that demonstrate how to use VBA to manipulate toolbars

✦ ✦ ✦ ✦

Toolbars, of course, are a pervasive user interface element found in virtually all software these days. Excel is definitely *not* a toolbar-deficient product. It comes with more than three dozen built-in toolbars, and it's easy to construct new toolbars either manually or with VBA. In this chapter, I describe how to create and modify toolbars.

About Command Bars

Beginning with Excel 97, Microsoft introduced a completely new way of handling toolbars. Technically, a toolbar is known as a `CommandBar` object. In fact, what's commonly called a toolbar is actually one of three types of command bars:

Toolbar	A floating bar with one or more clickable controls. This chapter focuses on this type of command bar.
Menu bar	The two built-in menu bars are Worksheet Menu Bar and Chart Menu Bar (see Chapter 22).
Shortcut menu	The menu that pops up when you right-click an object (see Chapter 22).

Because a menu bar is also a command bar, virtually all the information in this chapter also applies to menu bars. In Chapter 22, I discuss the nuances of dealing with custom menus.

Toolbar Manipulations

The following list summarizes the ways in which you can customize toolbars in Excel:

✦ *Remove controls from built-in toolbars.* You can get rid of controls that you never use and free up a few pixels of screen space.

✦ *Add controls to built-in toolbars.* You can add as many controls as you want to any toolbar. These controls can be custom buttons or buttons from other toolbars, or they can come from the stock of controls that Excel provides.

✦ *Create new toolbars.* You can create as many new toolbars as you like, with toolbar controls from any source.

✦ *Change the functionality of built-in toolbar controls.* You do this by attaching your own macro to a built-in control.

✦ *Change the image that appears on any toolbar control.* Excel includes a rudimentary but functional toolbar button editor, although there are several other image-changing techniques.

You can perform these customizations by using the Customize dialog box displayed when you select the View ➪ Toolbars ➪ Customize command or by writing VBA code.

Don't be afraid to experiment with toolbars. If you mess up a built-in toolbar, you can easily reset it to its default state. Just choose View ➪ Toolbars ➪ Customize, select the toolbar in the list, and click the Reset button.

How Excel Handles Toolbars

Before you start working with custom toolbars, it's important to understand how Excel deals with toolbars in general. You may be surprised.

Storing toolbars

Toolbars can be attached to XLS (worksheet) or XLA (add-in) files, which makes it easy to distribute custom toolbars with your applications (see "Distributing toolbars" later in this chapter). You can attach any number of toolbars to a workbook. When the user opens your file, all attached toolbars automatically appear.

Excel stores toolbar information in an XLB file, which resides in Windows's main directory (\WINDOWS or \WINNT). The exact name of this file varies. Why is this

XLB file important? Assume that a colleague gives you an Excel workbook that has a custom toolbar stored in it. When you open the workbook, the toolbar appears. You examine the workbook but decide that you're not interested in it. Nonetheless, when you exit Excel, the custom toolbar is added to your XLB file. If you make *any* toolbar changes — from the minor adjustment of a built-in toolbar to the introduction of a custom toolbar — the XLB file is resaved when you exit Excel. Because the entire XLB file is loaded every time you start Excel, the time it takes to start and exit Excel increases significantly as the XLB file grows in size. Plus, all those toolbars eat up memory and system resources. Therefore, it's in your best interest to delete custom toolbars that you never use. Use the View ➪ Toolbars ➪ Customize command to do this.

When toolbars don't work correctly

Excel's approach to storing toolbars can cause problems. Suppose you've developed an application that uses a custom toolbar, and you've attached that toolbar to the application's workbook. The first time an end user opens the workbook, the toolbar is displayed. When the user closes Excel, your toolbar is saved in the user's XLB file. If the user alters the toolbar in any way — for example, if he accidentally removes a button — the next time your application is opened, the correct toolbar does *not* appear. Rather, the user sees the altered toolbar, which now lacks an important button. In other words, a toolbar attached to a workbook is not displayed if the user already has a toolbar with the same name. In many cases, this is *not* what you want to happen.

Fortunately, you can write VBA code to prevent this scenario. The trick is never to allow your custom toolbar to be added to the user's toolbar collection. The best way to do this is to create the toolbar on the fly every time the workbook is opened and then delete it when your application closes. With this process, the toolbar is never stored in the user's XLB file. You might think that creating a toolbar on the fly would be a slow process. As you'll see later in this chapter, creating toolbars with VBA is amazingly fast.

Manipulating Toolbars and Buttons Manually

Excel makes it easy for you to create new toolbars and modify existing toolbars. In fact, you may not even have to use VBA to work with toolbars, because you can do just about all your toolbar customization without it.

It's important to understand that any customizations you make to a toolbar, either built-in or custom, are "permanent." In other words, the changes remain in effect even when you restart Excel. These toolbar changes are not associated with a particular workbook. To restore a toolbar to its original state, you must reset it.

About command bar customization mode

To perform any type of manual toolbar (or menu) customization, Excel needs to be in what I call *command bar customization mode*. You can put Excel into this mode by using any of these techniques:

- ✦ Select View ➪ Toolbars ➪ Customize.
- ✦ Select Tools ➪ Customize.
- ✦ Right-click any toolbar or menu, and select Customize from the shortcut menu.

When Excel is in command bar customization mode, the Customize dialog box is displayed, and you can manipulate toolbars and menus any way you like. You'll find that you can right-click menus and toolbars to get a handy shortcut menu (see Figure 21-1). After you've made your customization, click the Close button in the Customize dialog box.

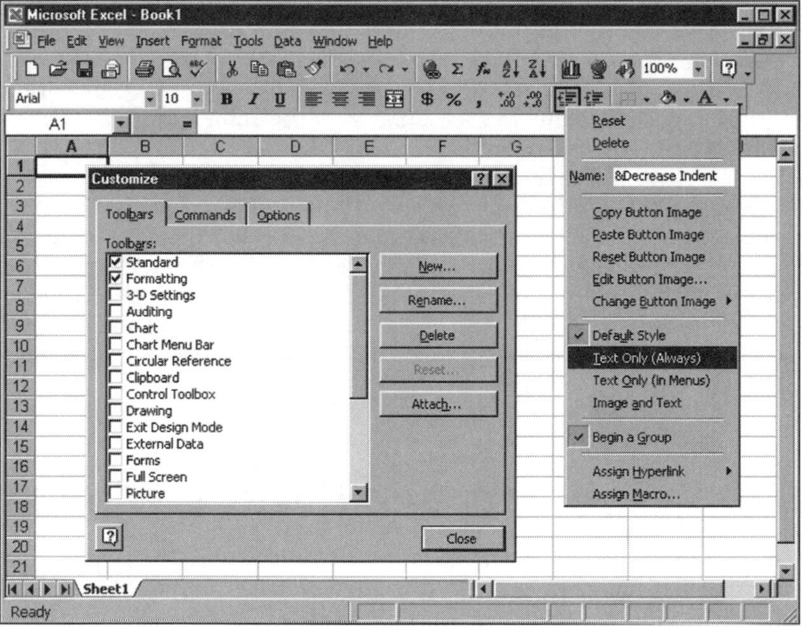

Figure 21-1: In command bar customization mode, you can alter all toolbars and menus.

The Customize dialog box includes three tabs:

Toolbars	Lists all the available toolbars, including custom toolbars you have created. The list box also includes the two menu bars (Worksheet Menu Bar and Chart Menu Bar), plus any other custom menu bars.
Commands	Lists by category all the available built-in commands. Use this tab to add new items to a toolbar or menu bar.
Options	Lets you select various options that relate to toolbars and menus. These include icon size, screen tips, and menu animations.

In the sections that follow, I briefly describe how to perform some common toolbar modifications manually.

Hiding or displaying a toolbar

The Toolbars tab displays every toolbar (built-in toolbars and custom toolbars). Add a check mark to display a toolbar; remove the check mark to hide it. The changes take effect immediately.

Creating a new toolbar

Click the New button, and then enter a name in the New Toolbar dialog box. Excel creates and displays an empty toolbar. You can then add buttons (or menu commands) to the new toolbar.

Figure 21-2 shows a custom toolbar that I created manually. This toolbar, called Custom Formatting, contains the formatting tools that I use most frequently. Notice that this toolbar includes drop-down menus as well as standard toolbar buttons.

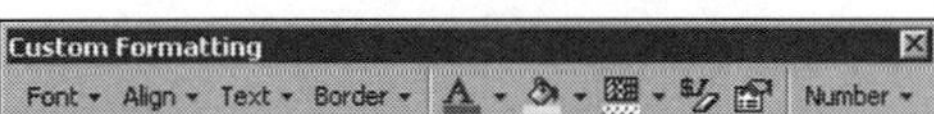

Figure 21-2: A custom toolbar that contains formatting tools.

Renaming a custom toolbar

Select a custom toolbar from the list, and click the Rename button. Enter a new name in the Rename Toolbar dialog box. You cannot rename a built-in toolbar.

Deleting a custom toolbar

Select a custom toolbar from the list, and click the Delete button. You cannot delete a built-in toolbar.

Resetting a built-in toolbar

Select a built-in toolbar from the list, and click the Reset button. The toolbar is restored to its default state. If you've added any custom tools to the toolbar, they are removed. If you've removed any of the default tools, they are restored. The Reset button is disabled when a custom toolbar is selected.

Moving and copying controls

When Excel is in command bar customization mode, you can copy and move toolbar controls freely among any visible toolbars. To move a control, drag it to its new location, either within the current toolbar or on a different toolbar. To copy a control, press Ctrl while you drag that control to another toolbar. You can also copy a control within the same toolbar.

Inserting a new control

To add a new control to a toolbar, use the Commands tab of the Customize dialog box shown in Figure 21-3.

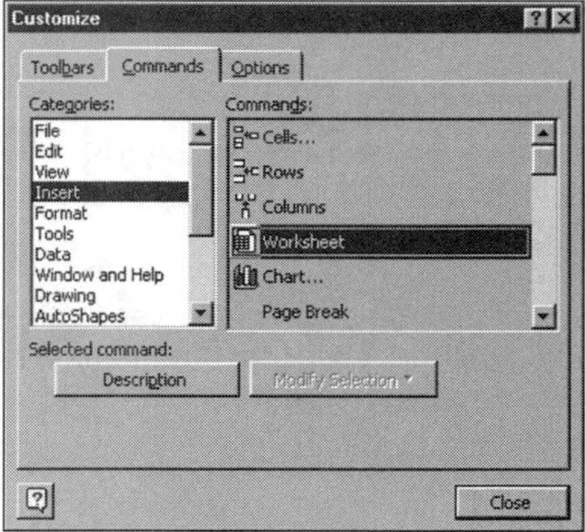

Figure 21-3: The Commands tab contains a list of every available built-in control.

Here, the controls are arranged in 17 categories. When you select a category, the controls in that category appear to the right. To find out what a control does, select it and click the Description button. To add a control to a toolbar, locate it in the Commands list, and then click and drag it to the toolbar.

Adding a toolbar button that executes a macro

To create a new toolbar button to which you will attach a macro, activate the Commands tab of the Customize dialog box, and then choose Macros from the Categories list. Drag the command labeled Custom Button to your toolbar (by default, this button has a smiley face image). After adding the button, right-click it and select your options from the menu shown in Figure 21-4. You'll want to change the name, assign a macro, and (I hope) change the image.

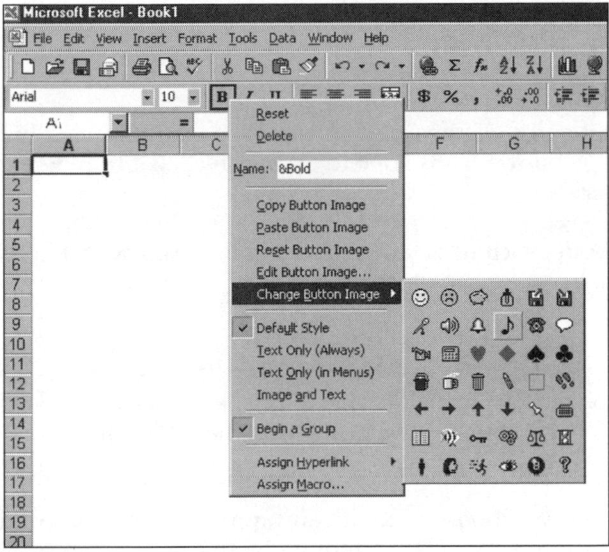

Figure 21-4: Customizing a toolbar button.

Selecting Change Button Image from the shortcut menu displays a list of 42 images. This is a tiny subset of all of the available images you can use. See "Adjusting a toolbar button image" later in this chapter.

Distributing toolbars

In this section, I describe how to distribute custom toolbars to others, and I outline what you need to be aware of to prevent problems.

Attaching a toolbar to a workbook

To store a toolbar in a workbook file, select View ➪ Toolbars ➪ Customize to display the Customize dialog box. Click the Attach button to bring up the Attach Toolbars dialog box, shown in Figure 21-5. This dialog box lists all the custom toolbars in the Toolbars collection in the list box on the left. Toolbars already stored in the workbook are shown in the list box on the right.

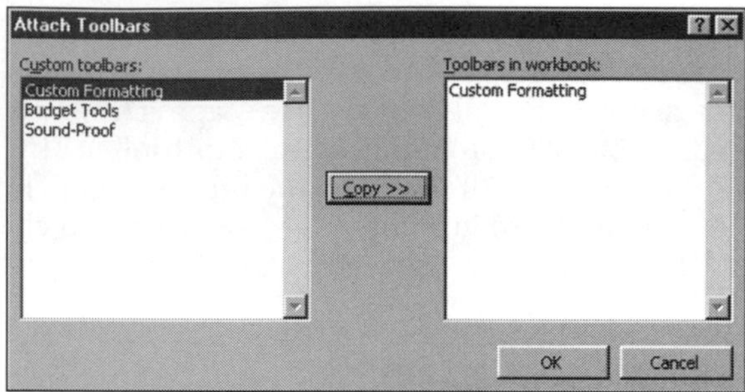

Figure 21-5: The Attach Toolbars dialog box.

To attach a toolbar, select it and click the Copy button. When a toolbar in the right list box is selected, the Copy button reads "Delete"; you can click it to remove a selected toolbar from a workbook.

Oddly, there is no way to attach or detach toolbars from a workbook with VBA. These operations must be performed manually.

The copy of the toolbar stored in the workbook always reflects its contents at the time you attach it. If you modify the toolbar after attaching it, the changed version is not automatically stored in the workbook. You must manually remove the old toolbar and then attach the edited toolbar.

A toolbar that's attached to a workbook automatically appears when the workbook is opened, unless the workspace already has a toolbar by the same name. See "How Excel Handles Toolbars" earlier in this chapter.

Distributing a toolbar with an add-in

As I mentioned in Chapter 20, distributing an application as an add-in is often the preferred method for end users. Not surprisingly, an add-in also can include one or more custom toolbars. But you need to be aware of a potential glitch.

Here's a typical scenario: You create an application that uses a custom toolbar. The buttons on that toolbar execute VBA procedures in the application's workbook. You attach the toolbar to the workbook and save the workbook. You create an add-in from the workbook. You close the XLS version of the application. You install the add-in. You click a button on the custom toolbar *and the XLS file opens!*

Your intent, of course, is to have the toolbar buttons execute procedures in the add-in, *not* the XLS file. But when you attach the toolbar to the workbook, the toolbar is saved in its current state. In that state, the workbook includes references to the macros in the XLS file. Consequently, clicking a button opens the XLS file so that the macro can be executed. You could manually (or via VBA) change the `OnAction` property of each toolbar button so it refers to the add-in. A better approach, though, is to write code to create the toolbar on the fly when the add-in is opened. I discuss this topic in detail later in the chapter.

Manipulating the CommandBars Collection

The `CommandBars` collection—contained in the `Application` object—is a collection of all `CommandBar` objects. Each `CommandBar` object has a collection of `Controls`. All these objects have properties and methods that enable you to control toolbars with VBA procedures.

As you might expect, you can write VBA code to manipulate toolbars and other types of command bars. In this section, I provide some key background information that you should know about before you start mucking around with toolbars. As always, a thorough understanding of the object model will make your task much easier.

You manipulate Excel command bars (including toolbars) by using objects located within the `CommandBars` collection. This collection consists of the following items:

- ✦ All 40 of Excel's built-in toolbars.
- ✦ Any other custom toolbars that you create.
- ✦ A built-in menu bar named Worksheet Menu Bar. This appears when a worksheet is active.
- ✦ A built-in menu bar named Chart Menu Bar. This appears when a chart sheet is active.
- ✦ Any other custom menu bars that you create.
- ✦ All 50 of the built-in shortcut menus.

Command bar types

As I mentioned at the beginning of this chapter, there are actually three types of command bars, each of which is distinguished by its `Type` property. Possible settings for the `Type` property of the `CommandBars` collection are shown in the following table. VBA provides built-in constants for the command bar types.

Type	*Description*	*Constant*
0	Toolbar	`msoBarTypeNormal`
1	Menu Bar	`msoBarTypeMenuBar`
2	Shortcut Menu	`msoBarTypePopUp`

Listing all CommandBar objects

If you're curious about the objects in the `CommandBars` collection, the following procedure should be enlightening. Executing this procedure generates a list (shown in Figure 21-6) of all `CommandBar` objects in the `CommandBars` collection: a total of 92 built-in command bars, plus any custom menu bars or toolbars. For each command bar, the procedure lists its `Index`, `Name`, and `Type` property settings (displayed as *Toolbar, Menu Bar,* or *Shortcut*).

List CommandBars.xls

	A	B	C	D
1	1	Worksheet Menu Bar	Menu Bar	
2	2	Chart Menu Bar	Menu Bar	
3	3	Standard	Toolbar	
4	4	Formatting	Toolbar	
5	5	PivotTable	Toolbar	
6	6	Chart	Toolbar	
7	7	Reviewing	Toolbar	
8	8	Forms	Toolbar	
9	9	Stop Recording	Toolbar	
10	10	External Data	Toolbar	
11	11	Auditing	Toolbar	
12	12	Full Screen	Toolbar	
13	13	Circular Reference	Toolbar	
14	14	Visual Basic	Toolbar	
15	15	Web	Toolbar	
16	16	Control Toolbox	Toolbar	
17	17	Exit Design Mode	Toolbar	
18	18	Refresh	Toolbar	
19	19	Drawing	Toolbar	
20	20	Query and Pivot	Shortcut	
21	21	PivotChart Menu	Shortcut	
22	22	Workbook tabs	Shortcut	
23	23	Cell	Shortcut	
24	24	Column	Shortcut	
25	25	Row	Shortcut	
26	26	Cell	Shortcut	
27	27	Column	Shortcut	
28	28	Row	Shortcut	
29	29	Ply	Shortcut	

Sheet1

Figure 21-6: VBA code produced this list of all `CommandBar` objects.

```
Sub ShowCommandBarNames()
    Cells.Clear
    Row = 1
    For Each cbar In CommandBars
        Cells(Row, 1) = cbar.Index
        Cells(Row, 2) = cbar.Name
        Select Case cbar.Type
            Case msoBarTypeNormal
                Cells(Row, 3) = "Toolbar"
            Case msoBarTypeMenuBar
                Cells(Row, 3) = "Menu Bar"
            Case msoBarTypePopUp
                Cells(Row, 3) = "Shortcut"
        End Select
```

```
        Row = Row + 1
    Next cbar
End Sub
```

When you work with toolbars, you can turn on the macro recorder to see what's happening in terms of VBA code. Most (but not all) of the steps you take while customizing toolbars generate VBA code. By examining this code, you can discover how the object model for toolbars is put together. The object model actually is fairly simple and straightforward.

Creating a command bar

In VBA, you create a new toolbar using the `Add` method of the `CommandBars` collection. The following instruction creates a new toolbar with a default name, such as `Custom 1`. The created toolbar is initially empty (has no controls) and is not visible (its `Visible` property is False).

```
CommandBars.Add
```

More often, you'll want to set some properties when you create a new toolbar. The following example demonstrates one way to do this:

```
Sub CreateAToolbar()
    Dim TBar As CommandBar
    Set TBar = CommandBars.Add
    With TBar
        .Name = "MyToolbar"
        .Top = 0
        .Left = 0
        .Visible = True
    End With
End Sub
```

The `CreateAToolbar` procedure uses the `Add` method of the `CommandBars` collection to add a new toolbar and create an object variable, `Tbar`, that represents this new toolbar. Subsequent instructions provide a name for the toolbar, set its position to the extreme upper-left corner the screen, and make it visible. The `Top` and `Left` properties specify the position of the toolbar. Their settings represent screen coordinates, not Excel's window coordinates.

Referring to command bars

You can refer to a particular `CommandBar` object by its `Index` or its `Name` property. For example, the Standard toolbar has an `Index` property setting of 3, so you can refer to this toolbar in either of the following ways:

```
CommandBars(3)
CommandBars("Standard")
```

Deleting a command bar

To delete a custom toolbar, use the Delete method of the CommandBar object. You can refer to the object by its index number (if you know it) or its name. The following instruction deletes the toolbar named MyToolbar.

```
CommandBars("MyToolbar").Delete
```

If the toolbar doesn't exist, the instruction generates an error. To avoid the error message when you attempt to delete a toolbar that may or may not exist, the simplest solution is to ignore the error. The following code deletes MyToolbar if it exists. If it doesn't exist, no error message is displayed.

```
On Error Resume Next
CommandBars("MyToolbar").Delete
On Error GoTo 0
```

Another approach is to create a custom function that determines whether a particular toolbar is in the CommandBars collection. The following function accepts a single argument (a potential CommandBar object name) and returns True if the command bar exists.

```
Function CommandBarExists(n) As Boolean
    Dim cb As CommandBar
    For Each cb In CommandBars
        If UCase(cb.Name) = UCase(n) Then
            CommandBarExists = True
            Exit Function
        End If
    Next cb
    CommandBarExists = False
End Function
```

Properties of command bars

The following are some of the more useful properties of a CommandBar object:

BuiltIn	True if the object is one of Excel's built-in command bars.
Left	The command bar's left position in pixels.
Name	The command bar's display name.
Position	An integer that specifies the position of the command bar. Possible values are as follows:

	msoBarLeft — The command bar is docked on the left. msoBarTop — The command bar is docked on the top. msoBarRight — The command bar is docked on the right. msoBarBottom — The command bar is docked on the bottom. soBarFloating — The command bar isn't docked. soBarPopup — The command bar is a shortcut menu.
`Protection`	An integer that specifies the type of protection for the command bar. Possible values are as follows: msoBarNoProtection — (Default) Not protected. The command bar can be customized by the user. msoBarNoCustomize — Cannot be customized. msoBarNoResize — Cannot be resized. msoBarNoMove — Cannot be moved. msoBarNoChangeVisible — Its visibility state cannot be changed by the user. msoBarNoChangeDock — Cannot be docked to a different position. msoBarNoVerticalDock — Cannot be docked along the left or right edge of the window. msoBarNoHorizontalDock — Cannot be docked along the top or bottom edge of the window.
`Top`	The command bar's top position in pixels.
`Type`	Returns an integer that represents the type of command bar (a toolbar, a menu, or a shortcut menu).
`Visible`	True if the command bar is visible.

The VBA examples in the following sections demonstrate the use of some of the command bar properties.

Counting custom toolbars

The following function returns the number of custom toolbars. It loops through the CommandBars collection and increments a counter if the command bar represented by cb is a toolbar and if its BuiltIn property is False.

```
Function CustomToolbars()
    Dim cb As CommandBar
    Dim Count As Integer
    Count = 0
    For Each cb In CommandBars
        If cb.Type = msoBarTypeNormal Then
            If Not cb.BuiltIn Then
                Count = Count + 1
            End If
        End If
    Next cb
    CustomToolbars = Count
End Function
```

Preventing a toolbar from being modified

The Protection property of a CommandBar object provides you with many options for protecting a CommandBar. The following instruction sets the Protection property for a toolbar named MyToolbar.

```
CommandBars("MyToolbar").Protection = msoBarNoCustomize
```

After this instruction is executed, the user is unable to customize the toolbar.

The Protection constants are *additive*, which means that you can apply different types of protection with a single command. For example, the following instructions adjust the MyToolbar toolbar so that it cannot be customized or moved:

```
Set cb = CommandBars("MyToolbar")
cb.Protection = msoBarNoCustomize + msoBarNoMove
```

Animating a toolbar

The following example is quite useless, unless you're looking for a way to get the user's attention. But it does demonstrate how your VBA code can change the position of a toolbar. The following MoveToolbar procedure is executed when the user clicks a button on a single-button toolbar named "Mover". The procedure executes a loop and randomly moves the toolbar to a different screen position each time it cycles through the loop until it ends up at its original position.

```
Sub MoveToolbar()
    With CommandBars("Mover")
        OldLeft = .Left
        OldTop = .Top
        For i = 1 To 60
            .Left = Int(vidWidth * Rnd)
            .Top = Int(vidHeight * Rnd)
            DoEvents
        Next i
        .Left = OldLeft
        .Top = OldTop
    End With
End Sub
```

In this procedure, `vidWidth` and `vidHeight` represent the width and height of the video display. These values are calculated by the `DisplayVideoInfo` procedure in Chapter 11, which uses a Windows API function.

Creating an "autosense" toolbar

Many of Excel's built-in toolbars seem to have some intelligence; they appear when you're working in a specific context and disappear when you stop working in that context. For example, the Chart toolbar normally appears when you are working on a chart, and it disappears when you stop working on the chart. At one time, Microsoft referred to this feature as *toolbar autosensing*, but it stopped using that term in later versions. For lack of a better name, I'll continue to use *autosensing* to refer to this automatic toolbar behavior.

To disable autosensing for a particular toolbar, just close the toolbar while you're working in the context in which it normally appears. To reenable it, make the toolbar visible again while you're working in its context.

You may want to program toolbar autosensing for your application. For example, you might want to make a toolbar visible only when a certain worksheet is activated or when a cell in a particular range is activated. Thanks to Excel's support for events, this sort of programming is relatively easy.

The procedure in Listing 2-1 creates a toolbar when the workbook is opened and uses one of its worksheets' `SelectionChange` events to determine whether the active cell is contained in a range named `ToolbarRange`. If so, the toolbar is visible; if not, the toolbar is hidden. In other words, the toolbar is visible only when the active cell is within a specific range of the worksheet.

This procedure, which is called by the `Workbook_Open` procedure, creates a simple toolbar named `AutoSense`. The four toolbar buttons are set up to execute procedures named `Button1`, `Button2`, `Button3`, and `Button4`. The `DeleteToolbar` procedure (not shown) simply deletes the toolbar (if it exists) before creating a new one.

Listing 21-1: This toolbar exists only when the cell pointer falls within a given range

```
Sub CreateToolbar()
'   Creates a demo toolbar named "AutoSense"
    Dim AutoSense As CommandBar
    Dim Button As CommandBarButton

'   Delete the existing toolbar if it exists
    Call DeleteToolbar

'   Create the toolbar
    Set AutoSense = CommandBars.Add
    For i = 1 To 4
        Set Button = AutoSense.Controls.Add(msoControlButton)
        With Button
            .OnAction = "Button" & i
            .FaceId = i + 37
        End With
    Next i
    AutoSense.Name = "AutoSense"
End Sub
```

The event-handler procedure for the `SelectionChange` event is shown below.

```
Private Sub Worksheet_SelectionChange(ByVal Target As _
 Excel.Range)
    If Union(Target, Range("ToolbarRange")).Address = _
      Range("ToolbarRange").Address Then
        CommandBars("AutoSense").Visible = True
    Else
        CommandBars("AutoSense").Visible = False
    End If
End Sub
```

This procedure checks the active cell. If it's contained within a range named `ToolbarRange`, the `AutoSense` toolbar's `Visible` property is set to True; otherwise, it is set to False.

The workbook also contains a `Workbook_BeforeClose` procedure that calls the `DeleteToolbar` procedure (which deletes the `AutoSense` toolbar) when the workbook is closed. This technique, of course, can be adapted to provide autosensing capability based on other criteria.

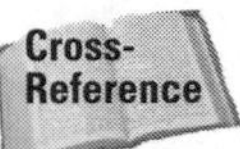

For a comprehensive discussion of the types of events Excel recognizes, see Chapter 18.

Hiding (and later restoring) all toolbars

Some developers like to "take over" Excel when their application is loaded. For example, they like to hide all toolbars, the status bar, and the formula bar. It's only proper, however, for them to clean up when their application is closed. This includes restoring the toolbars that were originally visible.

The example in this section describes a way to hide all toolbars and then restore them when the application is closed. The `HideAllToolbars` procedure is called from the `Workbook_Open` event handler, and the `RestoreToolbars` procedure is called by the `Workbook_BeforeClose` event handler.

The code keeps track of which toolbars were visible by storing their names in a worksheet named `TBSheet`. When the workbook closes, the `RestoreToolbars` subroutine reads these cells and displays the toolbars. Using a worksheet to store the toolbar names is safer than using an array. Both procedures are shown in Listing 21-2.

Listing 21-2: Removing all toolbars and then restoring them

```
Sub HideAllToolbars()
    Dim TB As CommandBar
    Dim TBNum As Integer
    Dim TBSheet As Worksheet
    Set TBSheet = Sheets("TBSheet")
Application.ScreenUpdating = False

'   Clear the sheet
    TBSheet.Cells.Clear

'   Hide all visible toolbars and store
'   their names
    TBNum = 0
    For Each TB In CommandBars
        If TB.Type = msoBarTypeNormal Then
            If TB.Visible Then
                TBNum = TBNum + 1
                TB.Visible = False
                TBSheet.Cells(TBNum, 1) = TB.Name
            End If
        End If
    Next TB
```

Continued

Listing 21-2 *(continued)*

```
    Application.ScreenUpdating = True
End Sub

Sub RestoreToolbars()
    Dim TBSheet As Worksheet
    Set TBSheet = Sheets("TBSheet")
    Application.ScreenUpdating = False

'   Unhide the previously displayed the toolbars
    On Error Resume Next
    For Each cell In TBSheet.Range("A:A") _
      .SpecialCells(xlCellTypeConstants)
        CommandBars(cell.Value).Visible = True
    Next cell
    Application.ScreenUpdating = True
End Sub
```

Referring to controls in a command bar

A `CommandBar` object such as a toolbar contains `Control` objects. These objects are mainly toolbar buttons and menu items.

The following `Test` procedure displays the `Caption` property for the first `Control` object contained in the Standard toolbar, whose index is 3.

```
Sub Test()
    MsgBox CommandBars(3).Controls(1).Caption
End Sub
```

When you execute this procedure, you'll see the message box shown in Figure 21-7. Notice the ampersand (&). The letter following the ampersand is the underlined hot key in the displayed text.

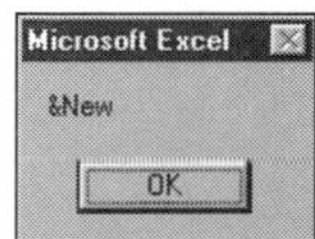

Figure 21-7: Displaying the Caption property for a control.

Rather than use an index number to refer to a control, you can use its `Caption` property setting. The following procedure produces the same result as the previous one.

```
Sub Test2()
```

```
    MsgBox CommandBars("Standard").Controls("New").Caption
End Sub
```

In some cases, Control objects may contain other Control objects. For example, the first control on the Drawing toolbar contains other controls (this also demonstrates that you can include menu items on a toolbar). The concept of Controls within Controls will become clearer in Chapter 22, when I discuss menus.

Listing the controls on a command bar

The following procedure displays the Caption property for each Control object within a CommandBar object. This example uses the Standard toolbar.

```
Sub ShowControlCaptions()
    Dim Cbar as CommandBar
    Set CBar = CommandBars("Standard")
    Cells.Clear
    Row = 1
    For Each ctl In CBar.Controls
        Cells(Row, 1) = ctl.Caption
        Row = Row + 1
    Next ctl
End Sub
```

The output of the ShowControlCaptions procedure is shown in Figure 21-8.

Show Control Captions.xls

	A	B	C
1	&New		
2	Open		
3	&Save		
4	&Mail Recipient		
5	Print (Brother HL-1040 series)		
6	Print Pre&view		
7	&Spelling...		
8	Cu&t		
9	&Copy		
10	&Paste		
11	&Format Painter		
12	&Undo		
13	&Redo		
14	Hyperl&ink...		
15	&AutoSum		
16	Paste Function		
17	Sort &Ascending		
18	Sort Des&cending		
19	&Chart Wizard		
20	M&ap...		
21	&Drawing		
22	&Zoom:		
23	Microsoft Excel &Help		
24			

Sheet1

Figure 21-8: A list of the captions for each control on the Standard toolbar.

Listing all controls on all toolbars

The following procedure loops through all command bars in the collection. If the command bar is a toolbar — that is, if its `Type` property is set to 1 — another loop displays the `Caption` for each toolbar button.

```
Sub ShowAllToolbarControls()
    Cells.Clear
    Row = 1
    For Each Cbar In CommandBars
        If Cbar.Type = msoBarTypeNormal Then
            Cells(Row, 1) = Cbar.Name
            For Each ctl In Cbar.Controls
                Cells(Row, 2) = ctl.Caption
                Row = Row + 1
            Next ctl
        End If
    Next Cbar
End Sub
```

Partial output of the `ShowAllToolbarControls` procedure is shown in Figure 21-9.

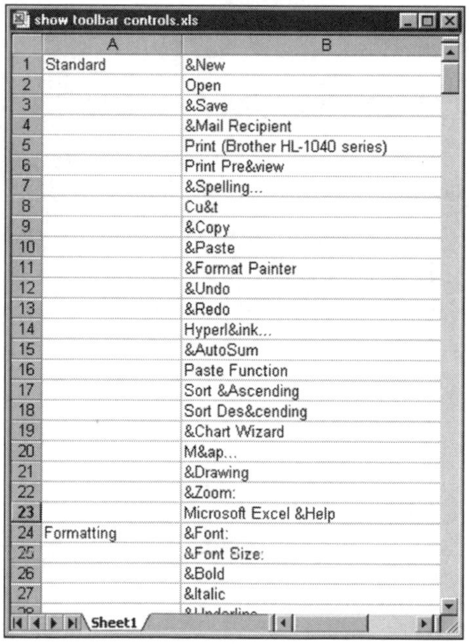

show toolbar controls.xls

	A	B
1	Standard	&New
2		Open
3		&Save
4		&Mail Recipient
5		Print (Brother HL-1040 series)
6		Print Pre&view
7		&Spelling...
8		Cu&t
9		&Copy
10		&Paste
11		&Format Painter
12		&Undo
13		&Redo
14		Hyperl&ink...
15		&AutoSum
16		Paste Function
17		Sort &Ascending
18		Sort Des&cending
19		&Chart Wizard
20		M&ap...
21		&Drawing
22		&Zoom:
23		Microsoft Excel &Help
24	Formatting	&Font:
25		&Font Size:
26		&Bold
27		&Italic

Sheet1

Figure 21-9: A list of the captions for each control on all toolbars.

Adding a control to a command bar

You can add a new control to a CommandBar object by using the Add method of the Controls collection object. The following instruction adds a new control to a toolbar named MyToolbar. Its Type property is set to the msoControlButton constant, which creates a standard button.

```
CommandBars("MyToolbar").Controls.Add _
     Type:=msoControlButton
```

The toolbar button added in the preceding instruction is just a blank button; clicking it has no effect. Most of the time, you'll want to set some properties when you add a new button to a toolbar. The following code adds a new control, gives it an image through the FaceId property, assigns a macro by way of the OnAction property, and specifies a caption.

```
Sub AddButton()
    Set NewBtn = CommandBars("MyToolbar").Controls.Add _
      (Type:=msoControlButton)
    With NewBtn
       .FaceId = 300
       .OnAction = "MyMacro"
       .Caption = "Tooltip goes here"
    End With
End Sub
```

The AddButton procedure creates an object variable (NewBtn) that represents the added control. The With-End With construct then sets the properties for the object.

Deleting a control from a command bar

To delete a control from a CommandBar object, use the Delete method of the Controls collection. The following instruction deletes the first control on a toolbar named MyToolbar.

```
CommandBars("MyToolbar").Controls(1).Delete
```

You can also specify the control by referring to its caption. The following instruction deletes a control that has a caption of SortButton.

```
CommandBars("MyToolbar").Controls("SortButton").Delete
```

Properties of command bar controls

Command bar controls, of course, have a number of properties that determine how the controls look and work. Following is a list of a few of the more useful properties for command bar controls:

`BeginGroup`	True if a separator bar appears before the control.
`BuiltIn`	True if the control is one of Excel's built-in controls.
`Caption`	The text that is displayed for the control. If the control shows only an image, the caption appears when you move the mouse over the control.
`Enabled`	True if the control can be clicked.
`FaceId`	A number that represents a graphic image displayed next to the control's text.
`OnAction`	The name of a VBA procedure to be executed when the user clicks the control.
`Style`	Determines whether the button appears with a caption and/or image.
`ToolTipText`	Text that appears when the user moves the mouse pointer over the control.
`Type`	An integer that determines the type of the control.

Setting a control's Style property

The `Style` property of a command bar control determines its appearance. The `Style` property is usually specified using a built-in constant. For example, to display an image and text, set the `Style` property to `msoButtonIconandCaption`. Refer to the online help for other `Style` constants.

Figure 21-10 shows a toolbar with three controls. The first consists of only text (`msoButtonCaption`), the second has an icon and text (`msoButtonIconandCaption`), and the third has only an icon (`msoButtonIcon`).

Figure 21-10: The three values of the `Style` property for a command bar control.

The text displayed on a control is the control's `Caption` property, and its image is determined by the value of the `FaceId` property.

Adjusting a toolbar button image

When you're in command bar customization mode, you can right-click any toolbar button and select Change Button Image. Doing so displays a list of 42 images from which you can select. Most of the time, none of these images is exactly what you need. Therefore, you must specify the image with VBA.

The image (if any) displayed on a toolbar control is determined by its `FaceId` property. For an image to be displayed, the control's `Style` property must *not* be `msoButtonCaption`.

The following instruction sets the `FaceId` property of the first button on the `MyToolbar` toolbar image to 45, which is the code number for a mailbox icon.

```
CommandBars("MyToolbar").Controls(1).FaceId = 45
```

How does one determine the code number for a particular image? Well, there's trial and error . . . and there's also a free utility that I developed called FaceID Identifier. This add-in makes it easy to determine the `FaceID` value for a particular image. It displays all possible command bar images. When you move the mouse pointer over an image, the `FaceID` value is displayed in a text box (see Figure 21-11).

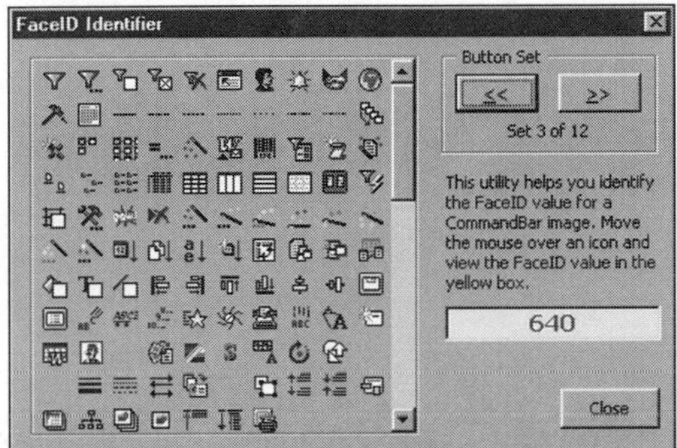

Figure 21-11: My FaceID Identifier add-in shows the FaceID values for built-in toolbar images.

The FaceID Identifier add-in is available on the companion CD-ROM.

Adjusting a control's Visible property

The following procedure — which causes lots of on-screen action — simply reverses the `Visible` property of each toolbar. Hidden toolbars are displayed, and visible toolbars are hidden. To return things to normal, execute the procedure a second time.

```
Sub ToggleAllToolbars()
    For Each cb In CommandBars
        If cb.Type = msoBarTypeNormal Then
            cb.Visible = Not cb.Visible
        End If
    Next cb
End Sub
```

Changing a control's caption dynamically

The procedure in Listing 21-3 creates a toolbar with a single button. The caption on this button displays the number format string for the active cell (see Figure 21-12). The procedure uses `Worksheet` events to monitor when the selection is changed. When a `SelectionChange` event occurs, a procedure is executed that changes the caption in the button.

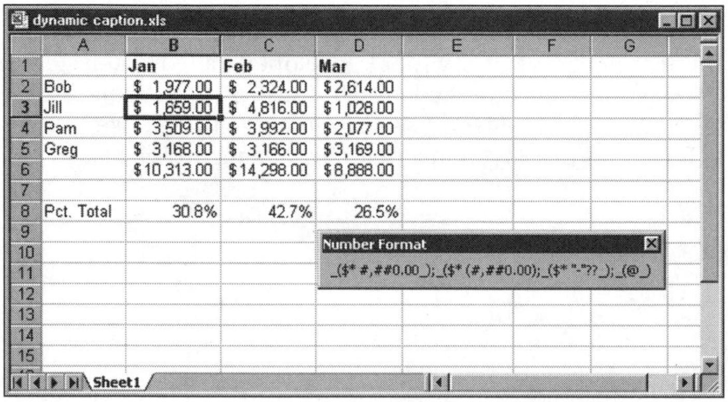

dynamic caption.xls

	A	B	C	D	E	F	G
1		Jan	Feb	Mar			
2	Bob	$ 1,977.00	$ 2,324.00	$2,614.00			
3	Jill	$ 1,659.00	$ 4,816.00	$1,028.00			
4	Pam	$ 3,509.00	$ 3,992.00	$2,077.00			
5	Greg	$ 3,168.00	$ 3,166.00	$3,169.00			
6		$10,313.00	$14,298.00	$8,888.00			
7							
8	Pct. Total	30.8%	42.7%	26.5%			

Number Format

_($* #,##0.00_);_($* (#,##0.00);_($* "-"??_);_(@_)

Sheet1

Figure 21-12: This toolbar button displays the number format for the active cell.

Listing 21-3: Showing the user the current cell's number format

```
Sub MakeNumberFormatDisplay()
    Dim TBar As CommandBar
    Dim NewBtn As CommandBarButton

'   Delete existing toolbar if it exists
    On Error Resume Next
    CommandBars("Number Format").Delete
    On Error GoTo 0

'   Create a new toolbar
    Set TBar = CommandBars.Add
    With TBar
        .Name = "Number Format"
        .Visible = True
    End With

'   Add a button control
    Set NewBtn = CommandBars("Number Format").Controls.Add _
```

```
        (Type:=msoControlButton)
    With NewBtn
        .Caption = ""
        .OnAction = "ChangeNumFormat"
        .Style = msoButtonCaption
    End With
    Call UpdateToolbar
End Sub
```

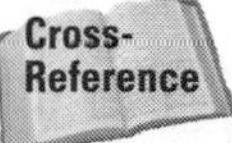

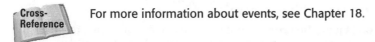

For more information about events, see Chapter 18.

The following UpdateToolbar procedure simply copies the NumberFormat property of the ActiveCell to the Caption property of the button control.

```
Sub UpdateToolbar()
'   Puts the selected month in the active cell
    On Error Resume Next
    CommandBars("Number Format"). _
      Controls(1).Caption = ActiveCell.NumberFormat
    If Err <> 0 Then CommandBars("Number Format"). _
      Controls(1).Caption = ""
End Sub
```

The button's OnAction property is set to a procedure named ChangeNumFormat, which is listed below. This procedure displays the Number tab of Excel's Format Cells dialog box (see Figure 21-13).

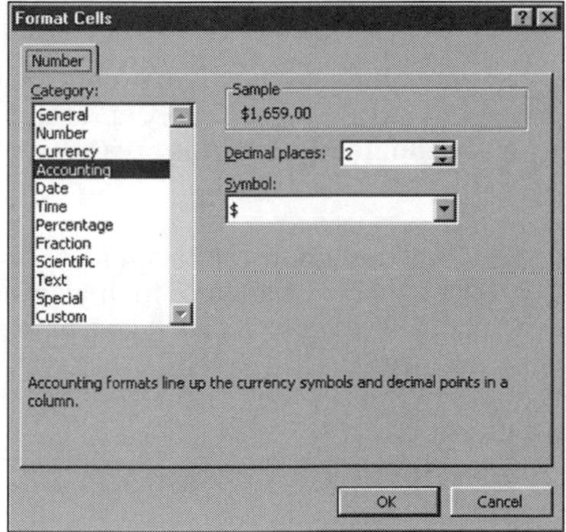

Figure 21-13: Clicking the button enables the user to select a new number format.

```
Sub ChangeNumFormat()
    Application.Dialogs(xlDialogFormatNumber).Show
    Call UpdateToolbar
End Sub
```

The technique described in this section works quite well, but it does have a flaw: If the user changes the number format with a button on the Formatting toolbar, the display in the Number Format is not changed, because changing the number format of a cell does not trigger a trappable event.

Using other types of command bar controls

A standard toolbar button is just one type of control that you can add to a toolbar. The control type is determined by the `Type` property of the control. Besides buttons, the online help lists many other control types. Most of these, however, cannot be added to a command bar. The built-in constants for the control types that you *can* add to a command bar are as follows:

`msoControlButton`	A standard button.
`msoControlEdit`	An edit box.
`msoControlComboBox`	A combo box.
`msoControlDropdown`	A drop-down list.
`msoControlButtonPopup`	A button that, when clicked, displays other controls. Use this control to create a menu with menu items.

The `Type` property for a `Control` object is a read-only property that's set when the control is created. In other words, you can't change a control's type after it has been created.

The online help lists several other `Type` constants for a command bar control. For example, you'll find `msoControlGauge`, `msoControlGraphic Combo`, and others. These controls, however, can't be used. You are limited to controls created with any of the five constants listed above.

The `MakeMonthList` procedure in Listing 21-4 creates a new toolbar, adds a drop-down list control, and fills that control with the names of each month. It also sets the `OnAction` property so that clicking the control executes a procedure named `PasteMonth`. The resulting toolbar is shown in Figure 21-14.

Listing 21-4: Attaching a drop-down list to a command bar

```
Sub MakeMonthList()
    Dim TBar As CommandBar
    Dim NewDD As CommandBarControl
```

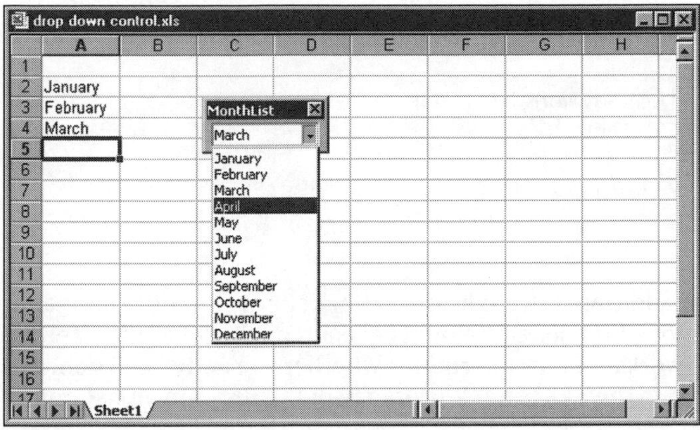

Figure 21-14: This toolbar contains a drop-down list control, with an attached macro.

```
'   Delete existing toolbar if it exists
    On Error Resume Next
    CommandBars("MonthList").Delete
    On Error GoTo 0

'   Create a new toolbar
    Set TBar = CommandBars.Add
    With TBar
        .Name = "MonthList"
        .Visible = True
    End With

'   Add a DropDown control
    Set NewDD = CommandBars("MonthList").Controls.Add _
      (Type:=msoControlDropdown)
    With NewDD
        .Caption = "DateDD"
        .OnAction = "PasteMonth"
        .Style = msoButtonAutomatic

'       Fill it with month name
        For i = 1 To 12
            .AddItem Format(DateSerial(1, i, 1), "mmmm")
        Next i
        .ListIndex = 1
    End With
End Sub
```

The PasteMonth procedure is listed below.

```
Sub PasteMonth()
'   Puts the selected month in the active cell
    On Error Resume Next
    With CommandBars("MonthList").Controls("DateDD")
        ActiveCell.Value = .List(.ListIndex)
    End With
End Sub
```

The workbook has an additional twist: It uses a Worksheet_SelectionChange event handler. This procedure, listed below, is executed whenever the user makes a new selection on the worksheet. It determines whether the active cell contains a month name. If so, it sets the ListIndex property of the drop-down list control in the toolbar.

```
Private Sub Worksheet_SelectionChange(ByVal Target _
 As Excel.Range)
    For i = 1 To 12
        Set ActCell = Target.Range("A1")
        If ActCell.Value = Format(DateSerial(1, i, 1), _
         "mmmm") Then
            CommandBars("MonthList").Controls("DateDD") _
             .ListIndex = i
            Exit Sub
        End If
    Next i
End Sub
```

Summary

In this chapter, I described how to use Excel's built-in toolbars and how to customize toolbars for your applications.

The next chapter discusses two other types of command bars: menus and shortcut menus.

✦ ✦ ✦

Creating Custom Menus

CHAPTER 22

✦ ✦ ✦ ✦

In This Chapter

An overview of Excel's menu system

Types of menu modifications you can make

How to manipulate menus with VBA

Various menu programming techniques used with events

A useful (and very easy) technique for creating custom menus

A procedure for replacing standard menu conventions with your own

How to customize the shortcut menus

✦ ✦ ✦ ✦

Every Windows program has a menu system, which usually serves as the primary user interface element. The Windows standard places the menu bar directly beneath the application's title bar. In addition, many programs now implement another type of menu: shortcut menus. Typically, right-clicking a selection displays a context-sensitive shortcut menu containing commands that enable you to work with the selection.

Excel uses both types of menus, and developers have almost complete control over Excel's entire menu system, including shortcut menus. This chapter tells you everything you need to know about working with Excel's menus.

A Few Words about Excel's Menu Bar

If you've read Chapter 21, you already know that a menu bar (like a toolbar) is a `CommandBar` object. In fact, the techniques described in Chapter 21 also apply to menu bars.

So how does a menu bar differ from a toolbar? In general, a menu bar is displayed at the top of the Excel window, directly below the title bar. When clicked, the top-level controls on a menu bar display a drop-down list of menu items. A menu bar may also contain three window control buttons (Minimize, Restore, and Close) that are displayed only when a workbook window is maximized. Toolbars, on the other hand, usually consist of graphic icons and do not display any control buttons. These rules are definitely not hard and fast. You can, if desired, add traditional toolbar buttons to a menu bar or add traditional menu items to a toolbar. You can even move a menu bar from its traditional location and make it free-floating.

Beginning with Excel 97, the menus in the Microsoft Office applications are not standard Windows menus. This means that they are not affected by settings specified by the user in the Windows Display Properties dialog box, shown in Figure 22-1. For example, you may select a certain text color and highlight color for your Windows menus. These colors choices will have no effect on the menus in Office applications.

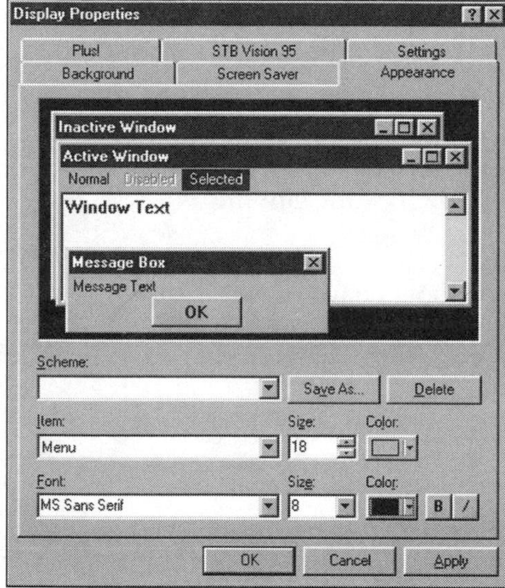

Figure 22-1: Excel's nonstandard Windows menus are not affected by global settings.

What You Can Do with Excel's Menus

Typical Excel users get by just fine with the standard menus. Because you're reading this book, however, you're probably not the typical Excel user. You may want to modify menus to make your life easier and to make life easier for the folks who use the spreadsheets that you develop.

To modify Excel's menus, you can remove elements, add elements, and change elements. In addition, you can temporarily replace Excel's standard menu bar with one of your own creation. You can change Excel's menus two ways: through the Customize dialog box or with VBA code.

When you close Excel, it saves any changes that you've made to the menu system, and these changes appear the next time you open Excel. The information about menu modifications is stored in an XLB file in your Windows directory.

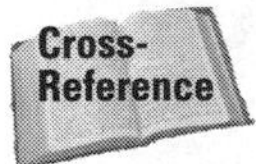

See Chapter 21 for more information about the XLB file.

In most cases, *you won't want your menu modifications to be saved between sessions*. Generally, you'll need to write VBA code to change the menus while a particular workbook is open and then change them back when the workbook closes. Therefore, you'll need VBA code to modify the menu when the workbook is opened and more VBA code to return the menus to normal when the workbook is closed.

Menu terminology

Menu terminology is often a bit confusing at first because many of the terms are similar. The following list presents the official Excel menu terminology that I refer to in this chapter:

✦ *Command bar.* An object that can function as a menu bar, a shortcut menu, or a toolbar. It is represented by the `CommandBar` object in the Office 2000 object library.

✦ *Menu bar.* The row of words that appears directly below the application's title bar. Excel has two menu bars: One is displayed when a worksheet is active, and the other is displayed when a chart sheet is active or when an embedded chart is activated.

✦ *Menu.* A single, top-level element of a menu bar. For example, both of Excel's menu bars have a File menu.

✦ *Menu item.* An element that appears in the drop-down list when you select a menu. For example, the first menu item under the File menu is New. Menu items also appear in submenus and shortcut menus.

✦ *Separator bar.* A horizontal line that appears between two menu items. The separator bar is used to group similar menu items.

✦ *Submenu.* A second-level menu that is under some menus. For example, the Edit menu has a submenu called Clear.

✦ *Submenu item.* A menu item that appears in the list when you select a submenu. For example, the Edit⇨Clear submenu contains the following submenu items: All, Formats, Contents, and Comments.

✦ *Shortcut menu.* The floating list of menu items that appears when you right-click a selection or an object. The shortcut menu that appears depends on the current context.

✦ *Enabled.* A menu item that can be used. If a menu item isn't enabled, its text appears grayed, and it can't be used.

✦ *Checked.* The status of a menu item that represents an on/off or True/False state. A menu item can display a graphical box that is checked or unchecked. The View➪Status Bar menu item is an example.

✦ *Image.* A small graphic icon that appears next to some menu items. This icon is sometimes called a *Face ID*.

✦ *Shortcut key combination.* A keystroke combination that serves as an alternate method to execute a menu item. The shortcut key combination is displayed at the right side of the menu item. For example, Ctrl+S is the shortcut key combination for File➪Save.

Removing menu elements

You can remove any part of Excel's menu system: menu items, menus, and entire menu bars. For example, if you don't want the end users of your application fiddling with the display, you can remove the View menu from the Worksheet Menu Bar. You can also remove one or more menu items from a menu. If you remove the New menu item from the File menu, for example, users can't use the menu to create a new workbook. Finally, you can eliminate Excel's menu bar and replace it with one that you've created. You might do this if you want your application to be completely under the control of your macros.

It's important to remember that simply removing menu bars, menus, or menu items does not affect the alternate method of accomplishing some actions. Specifically, if there are corresponding shortcut keys, toolbar buttons, or shortcut menus that perform the same action as a menu command, those alternate methods still work. For example, if you remove the New menu item from the File menu, the user can still use the New Workbook toolbar button, the Ctrl+N shortcut key, or the Desktop shortcut menu to create a new workbook.

Adding menu elements

You can add your own custom menus to built-in menu bars, and you can add custom menu items to a built-in menu. In fact, you can create an entirely new menu bar if you like. For example, you might develop an application that doesn't require any of Excel's built-in menus. A simple solution is to create a new menu bar that consists of custom menus and custom menu items that execute your macros. You can hide Excel's normal menu bar and replace it with your own.

Changing menu elements

If you get bored with Excel's standard menu text, you can change it to something else — for instance, you can change the Tools menu to the Stuff menu. You can also assign your own macros to built-in menu items. You have many other options for changing menu elements, including rearranging the order of the menus on a menu bar (for example, to make the Help menu appear first instead of last).

The remainder of this chapter focuses on writing VBA code to modify menus.

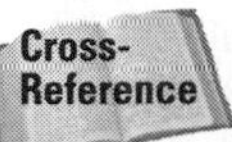

Chapter 21 provides background information about the Customize dialog box.

Moving Up from Excel 5/95?

If you've customized menus using Excel 5 or Excel 95, you can pretty much forget everything you ever learned. Beginning with Excel 97, menu customization has changed significantly in the following respects:

- *A menu bar is actually a toolbar in disguise.* If you don't believe me, grab the vertical bars at the very left of the menu bar and drag the bar away. You'll end up with a floating toolbar. The official (VBA) term for both menus and toolbars is *command bar.*
- *The Excel 5/95 Menu Editor is gone.* To edit a menu manually, you use the View⇨Toolbars⇨Customize command. Understand, however, that Excel 5/95 workbooks that contain menus customized using the old Menu Editor still work in Excel 97 and Excel 2000.
- *Menu items can now have images* (as you've undoubtedly noticed).
- *There is no easy way to assign a VBA macro to a new menu item on the Tools menu.* This was a piece of cake with Excel 5/95. Later in this chapter, however, I provide VBA code that you can use to add a new menu item to the Tools menu.
- *Excel 2000 by default displays only the most recently used menu items.* In my opinion, this is one of the worst ideas Microsoft has come up with. I can't imagine why anyone would want the order of her menu items to be shifting around. Fortunately, this feature can be disabled in the Options panel of the Customize dialog box.

VBA Examples

In this section, I present some practical examples of VBA code that manipulates Excel's menus.

Referencing the CommandBars Collection

The `CommandBars` collection is a member of the `Application` object. When you reference this collection in a regular VBA module, you can omit the reference to the `Application` object (it is assumed). For example, the following statement (contained in a standard VBA module) displays the name of the first element of the `CommandBars` collection:

```
MsgBox CommandBars(1).Name
```

For some reason, when you reference the `CommandBars` collection from a code module for a `ThisWorkbook` object, you must precede it with a reference to the Application object, like this:

```
MsgBox Application.CommandBars(1).Name
```

Listing menu information

The `ListMenuInfo` procedure, listed below, may be instructive. It displays the caption for each item (menu, menu item, and submenu item) on the Worksheet Menu Bar.

```
Sub ListMenuInfo()
    Row = 1
    On Error Resume Next
    For Each Menu In CommandBars(1).Controls
        For Each MenuItem In Menu.Controls
            For Each SubMenuItem In MenuItem.Controls
                Cells(Row, 1) = Menu.Caption
                Cells(Row, 2) = MenuItem.Caption
                Cells(Row, 3) = SubMenuItem.Caption
                Row = Row + 1
            Next SubMenuItem
        Next MenuItem
    Next Menu
End Sub
```

Figure 22-2 shows a portion of the `ListMenuInfo` procedure's output.

A workbook that contains this procedure is available on the companion CD-ROM.

I use `On Error Resume Next` to avoid the error message that appears when the procedure attempts to access a submenu item that doesn't exist.

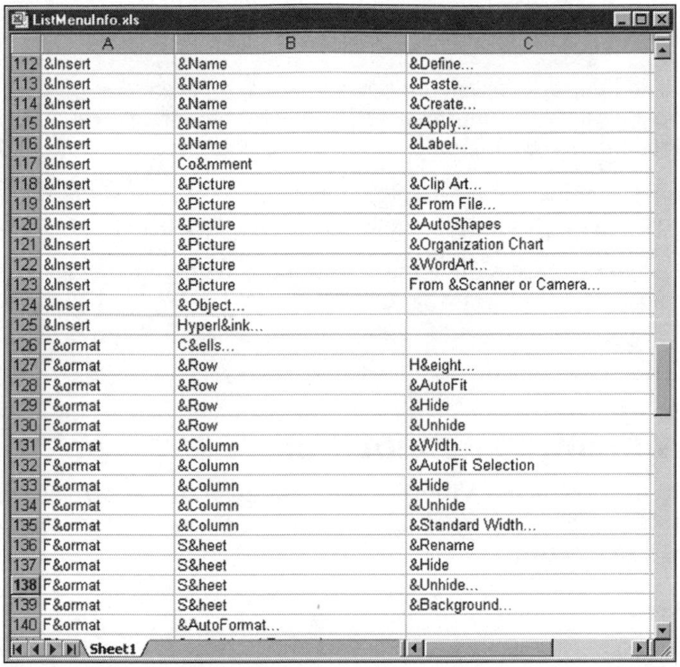

ListMenuInfo.xls

	A	B	C
112	&Insert	&Name	&Define...
113	&Insert	&Name	&Paste...
114	&Insert	&Name	&Create...
115	&Insert	&Name	&Apply...
116	&Insert	&Name	&Label...
117	&Insert	Co&mment	
118	&Insert	&Picture	&Clip Art...
119	&Insert	&Picture	&From File...
120	&Insert	&Picture	&AutoShapes
121	&Insert	&Picture	&Organization Chart
122	&Insert	&Picture	&WordArt...
123	&Insert	&Picture	From &Scanner or Camera...
124	&Insert	&Object...	
125	&Insert	Hyperl&ink...	
126	F&ormat	C&ells...	
127	F&ormat	&Row	H&eight...
128	F&ormat	&Row	&AutoFit
129	F&ormat	&Row	&Hide
130	F&ormat	&Row	&Unhide
131	F&ormat	&Column	&Width...
132	F&ormat	&Column	&AutoFit Selection
133	F&ormat	&Column	&Hide
134	F&ormat	&Column	&Unhide
135	F&ormat	&Column	&Standard Width...
136	F&ormat	S&heet	&Rename
137	F&ormat	S&heet	&Hide
138	F&ormat	S&heet	&Unhide...
139	F&ormat	S&heet	&Background...
140	F&ormat	&AutoFormat...	

Sheet1

Figure 22-2: A portion of the output from the `ListMenuInfo` procedure

Menu-Making Conventions

You may have noticed that menus in Windows programs typically adhere to some established conventions. No one knows where these conventions came from, but you should follow them if you want to give the impression that you know what you're doing. When you modify menus, keep the following points in mind:

- ✦ Tradition dictates that the File menu is always first and the Help menu is always last.
- ✦ Menu text is always proper case. The first letter of each word is uppercase, except for minor words such as *the, a,* and *and.*
- ✦ A menu itself does not cause any action. In other words, each menu must have at least one menu item.
- ✦ Menu items are usually limited to three or fewer words.
- ✦ Every menu item should have a hot key (underlined letter) that's unique to the menu.
- ✦ A menu item that displays a dialog box is followed by an ellipsis (...).

Continued

✦ Menu item lists should be kept relatively short. Sometimes, submenus provide a good alternative to long lists. If you must have a lengthy list of menu items, use separator bars to group items into logical groups.

✦ If possible, disable menu items that are not appropriate in the current context. In VBA terminology, to disable a menu item, set its `Enabled` property to False.

✦ Some menu items serve as toggles. When the option is on, the menu item is preceded by a check mark.

Adding a new menu to a menu bar

In this section, I describe how to use VBA to add a new menu to the Worksheet Menu Bar. The Worksheet Menu Bar is the first item in the `CommandBars` collection, so you can reference it one of two ways:

```
CommandBars("Worksheet Menu Bar")
CommandBars(1)
```

In VBA terms, you use the `Add` method to append a new control to the `CommandBarControls` collection. The new control is a "pop-up control" of type `msoControlPopup`. You can specify the new control's position; if you don't, the new menu is added to the end of the menu.

Adding a new menu is a two-step process:

1. Use the `Add` method to create an object variable that refers to the new control. Arguments for the `Add` method enable you to specify the control's type, its ID (useful only if you're adding a built-in menu item), its position, and whether it's a temporary control that will be deleted when Excel closes.
2. Adjust the properties of the new control. For example, you'll probably want to specify a `Caption` property and an `OnAction` property.

Adding a menu: Take 1

In this example, the objective is to add a new Budgeting menu to the Worksheet Menu Bar and to position this new menu to the left of the Help menu.

```
Sub AddNewMenu()
'   Get Index of Help menu
    HelpIndex = CommandBars(1).Controls("Help").Index

'   Create the menu
```

```
    Set NewMenu = CommandBars(1).Controls.Add _
      (Type:=msoControlPopup, _
       Before:=HelpIndex, _
       Temporary:=True)

'   Add a caption
    NewMenu.Caption = "&Budgeting"
End Sub
```

The preceding code is *not* a good example of how to add a menu, and it may or may not insert the menu at the proper position. It suffers from two problems:

- ✦ It assumes that the Help menu exists, but the user may have removed the Help menu.
- ✦ It assumes that the Help menu has *Help* as its caption, but non-English versions of Excel may have a different caption for their menus.

Adding a menu: Take 2

Listing 22-1 presents a better demonstration. It uses the `FindControl` method to attempt to locate the Help menu. If the Help menu is not found, the code adds the new menu item to the end of the Worksheet Menu Bar.

Listing 22-1: Adding the Budgeting menu to Excel's main menu bar

```
Sub AddNewMenu()
    Dim HelpMenu As CommandBarControl
    Dim NewMenu As CommandBarPopup

'   Find the Help Menu
    Set HelpMenu = CommandBars(1).FindControl(Id:=30010)

    If HelpMenu Is Nothing Then
'       Add the menu to the end
        Set NewMenu = CommandBars(1).Controls _
         .Add(Type:=msoControlPopup, Temporary:=True)
    Else
'      Add the menu before Help
        Set NewMenu = CommandBars(1).Controls _
         .Add(Type:=msoControlPopup, Before:=HelpMenu.Index, _
         Temporary:=True)
    End If

'   Add a caption
    NewMenu.Caption = "&Budgeting"
End Sub
```

The preceding procedure creates an essentially worthless menu — it has no menu items. See "Adding a menu item to the Tools menu" later in this chapter for an example of how to add a menu item to a menu.

To use the `FindControl` method, you must know the `Id` property of the control that you're looking for. Each of Excel's own built-in `CommandBar` controls has a unique `Id` property. For this example, I determined the `Id` property of the Help menu by executing the following statement:

```
MsgBox CommandBars(1).Controls("Help").Id
```

The message box displayed `30010`, which is the value I used as the `Id` argument for the `FindControl` method. Table 22-1 shows the `Id` property settings for the top-level controls in Excel's menu bars.

Table 22-1
Id Property Settings for Excel's Built-in Menus

Menu	*Id Setting*
File	30002
Edit	30003
View	30004
Insert	30005
Format	30006
Tools	30007
Data	30011
Chart	30022
Window	30009
Help	30010

Deleting a menu from a menu bar

To delete a menu, use the `Delete` method. The following example deletes the menu in the Worksheet Menu Bar whose caption is "Budgeting." Notice that I use `On Error Resume Next` to avoid the error message that appears if the menu does not exist.

```
Sub DeleteMenu()
    On Error Resume Next
    CommandBars(1).Controls("Budgeting").Delete
End Sub
```

Adding menu items to a menu

In the example under "Adding a new menu to a menu bar," I demonstrated how to add a menu to a menu bar. Listing 22-2 adds to the original procedure and, in so doing, demonstrates how to add menu items to the new menu.

Listing 22-2: Adding selections and submenu items to the Budgeting menu

```
Sub CreateMenu()
    Dim HelpMenu as CommandBarControl
    Dim NewMenu As CommandBarPopup

'   Delete the menu if it already exists
    Call DeleteMenu

'   Find the Help Menu
    Set HelpMenu = CommandBars(1).FindControl(Id:=30010)

    If HelpMenu Is Nothing Then
'       Add the menu to the end
        Set NewMenu = CommandBars(1).Controls _
          .Add(Type:=msoControlPopup, temporary:=True)
    Else
'      Add the menu before Help
        Set NewMenu = CommandBars(1).Controls _
          .Add(Type:=msoControlPopup, Before:=HelpMenu.Index, _
          temporary:=True)
    End If

'   Add a caption for the menu
    NewMenu.Caption = "&Budgeting"

'   FIRST MENU ITEM
    Set MenuItem = NewMenu.Controls.Add _
      (Type:=msoControlButton)
    With MenuItem
        .Caption = "&Data Entry..."
        .FaceId = 162
        .OnAction = "Macro1"
    End With

'   SECOND MENU ITEM
    Set MenuItem = NewMenu.Controls.Add _
      (Type:=msoControlButton)
    With MenuItem
        .Caption = "&Generate Reports..."
        .FaceId = 590
        .OnAction = "Macro2"
```

Continued

Listing 22-2 *(continued)*

```
    End With
'   THIRD MENU ITEM
    Set MenuItem = NewMenu.Controls.Add _
      (Type:=msoControlPopup)
    With MenuItem
        .Caption = "View &Charts"
        .BeginGroup = True
    End With

'   FIRST SUBMENU ITEM
    Set SubMenuItem = MenuItem.Controls.Add _
      (Type:=msoControlButton)
    With SubMenuItem
        .Caption = "Monthly &Variance"
        .FaceId = 420
        .OnAction = "Macro3"
    End With

'   SECOND SUBMENU ITEM
    Set SubMenuItem = MenuItem.Controls.Add _
      (Type:=msoControlButton)
    With SubMenuItem
        .Caption = "Year-To-Date &Summary"
        .FaceId = 422
        .OnAction = "Macro4"
    End With
End Sub
```

Specifically, the `CreateMenu` procedure builds the menu shown in Figure 22-3. This menu has three menu items, and the last menu item is a submenu with two submenu items.

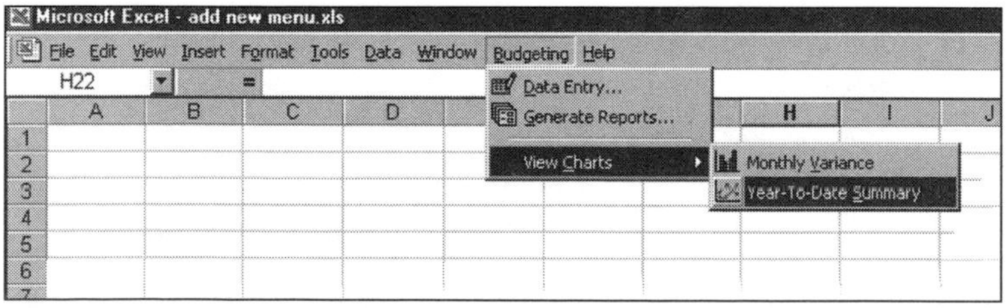

Figure 22-3: A VBA procedure created this menu and its associated menu items.

You might be wondering why the code in the preceding example deletes the menu (if it already exists) and doesn't simply exit the procedure. Rebuilding the menu ensures that the latest version is added to the menu bar. This also makes it much easier on you while you're developing the code because you don't have to delete the menu manually before testing your procedure. As you may have noticed, creating menus is very fast, so the additional time required to rebuild a menu is usually negligible.

When you examine the `CreateMenu` procedure, keep the following points in mind:

✦ The control type for the first two menu items is `msoControlButton`. The type of the third menu item, however, is `msoControlPopup` because the third menu item has submenu items.

✦ There is no `OnAction` property for controls of type `msoControlPopup`.

✦ The `BeginGroup` property of the third menu item is True, which causes a separator bar to appear before the item. The separator bar is purely cosmetic and serves to "group" similar menu items together.

✦ The `FaceID` property determines which image (if any) appears next to the menu text. The `FaceID` number represents a built-in image.

✦ The text for the `Caption` properties uses an ampersand (&) to indicate the "hot key," or accelerator key, for the menu item. The hot key is the underlined letter that provides keyboard access to the menu item.

Adding a menu item to the Tools menu

The example in Listing 22-2 adds several menu items to a custom menu on the Worksheet Menu Bar. Often, you'll simply want to add a menu item to one of Excel's built-in menus, such as the Tools menu.

With Excel 5 and Excel 95, assigning a macro to a new menu item on the Tools menu was easy. For some reason, this feature was removed, beginning with Excel 97. With Excel 97 or later, if you want to assign a macro to a menu item on the Tools menu (or any other menu, for that matter), you must write VBA code to do so.

Listing 22-3 adds the menu item Clear All But Formulas to the Tools menu — whose `Id` property is set to 30007. Clicking this menu item executes a procedure named `ClearAllButFormulas`.

Listing 22-3: Adding a selection to Excel's Tools menu

```
Sub AddMenuItem()
    Dim ToolsMenu As CommandBarPopup
    Dim NewMenuItem As CommandBarButton

'   Delete the menu if it already exists
    Call DeleteMenuItem

'   Find the Tools Menu
    Set ToolsMenu = CommandBars(1).FindControl(Id:=30007)
    If ToolsMenu Is Nothing Then
        MsgBox "Cannot add menu item."
        Exit Sub
    Else
        Set NewMenuItem = ToolsMenu.Controls.Add _
         (Type:=msoControlButton)
        With NewMenuItem
            .Caption = "&Clear All But Formulas"
            .FaceId = 348
            .OnAction = "ClearAllButFormulas"
            .BeginGroup = True
        End With
    End If
End Sub
```

Figure 22-4 shows the Tools menu with the new menu item.

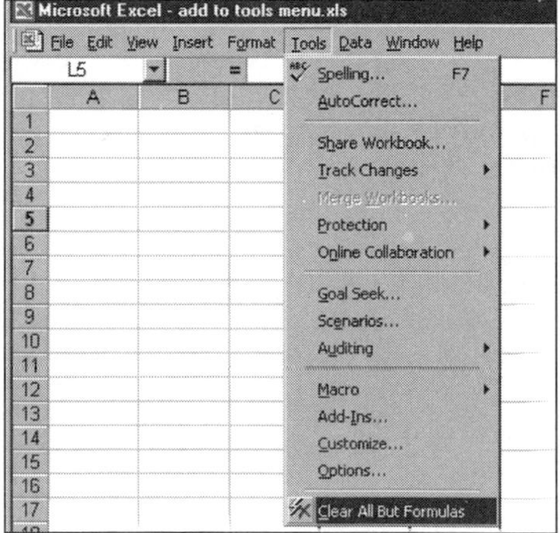

Figure 22-4: A new menu item has been added to the Tools menu.

Deleting a menu item from the Tools menu

To delete a menu item, use the `Delete` method of the `Controls` collection. The following example deletes the Clear All But Formulas menu item on the Tools menu. Note that it uses the `FindControl` method to handle the situation when the Tools menu has a different caption.

```
Sub DeleteMenuItem()
    On Error Resume Next
    CommandBars(1).FindControl(Id:=30007). _
      Controls("&Clear All But Formulas").Delete
End Sub
```

Displaying a shortcut key with a menu item

Some of Excel's built-in menu items also display a shortcut key combination that, when pressed, has the same effect as the menu command. For example, Excel's Edit menu lists several shortcut keys.

To display a shortcut key combination as part of your menu item, use the `ShortcutText` property. Listing 22-4 creates a menu item Clear All But Formulas on the Tools menu. It sets the `ShortcutText` property to the string Ctrl+Shift+C and also uses the `MacroOptions` method to set up the shortcut key.

Listing 22-4: Adding a menu selection that features a shortcut key

```
Sub AddMenuItem()
    Dim ToolsMenu As CommandBarPopup
    Dim NewMenuItem As CommandBarButton

'   Delete the menu if it already exists
    Call DeleteMenuItem

'   Find the Tools Menu
    Set ToolsMenu = CommandBars(1).FindControl(Id:=30007)
    If ToolsMenu Is Nothing Then
        MsgBox "Cannot add a menu item - use Ctrl+Shift+C."
        Exit Sub
    Else
        Set NewMenuItem = ToolsMenu.Controls.Add _
         (Type:=msoControlButton)
        With NewMenuItem
            .Caption = "&Clear All But Formulas"
            .FaceId = 348
            .ShortcutText = "Ctrl+Shift+C"
```

Continued

Listing 22-4 *(continued)*

```
            .OnAction = "ClearAllButFormulas"
            .BeginGroup = True
        End With
    End If

'   Create the shortcut key
    Application.MacroOptions _
      Macro:="ClearAllButFormulas", _
      HasShortcutKey:=True, _
      ShortcutKey:="C"
End Sub
```

After this procedure is executed, the menu item is displayed as shown in Figure 22-5.

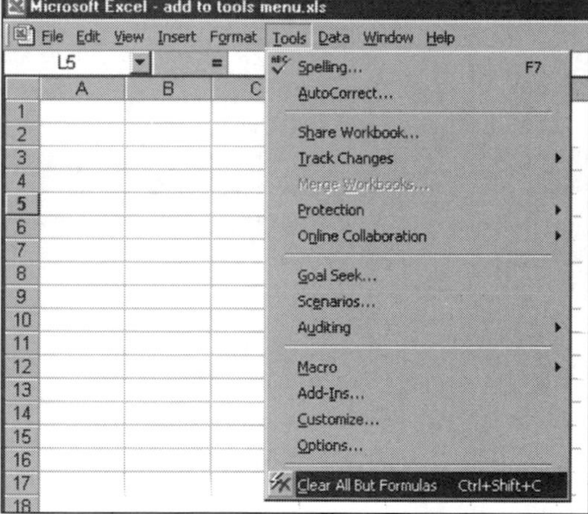

Figure 22-5: The Clear All But Formulas menu item also displays a shortcut key combination.

Fixing a menu that has been reset

Consider this scenario: You write VBA code that creates a new menu when your workbook application is opened. The user opens another workbook containing a macro that resets Excel's menu bar. Or consider this: The user plays around with the Customize dialog box, selects the Workbook Menu Bar from the list on that dialog, and clicks the Reset button. In both cases, your custom menu is zapped.

Your menu-making code is probably triggered by the `Workbook_Open` event, so the only way the user can get your menu back is to close and reopen the workbook. To provide another way, create a key combination that executes the procedure that builds your menu.

Apparently, applications that reset Excel's menu bar are not uncommon. Users of my Power Utility Pak add-in sometimes tell me that the Utilities menu has disappeared for no apparent reason. This is always caused by some other application that feels it must reset the Worksheet Menu Bar. Therefore, I added a key combination (Ctrl+Shift+U) that, when pressed, rebuilds the Utilities menu. The real problem, of course, is getting the user to read the documentation that describes how to recreate the menu.

Working with Events

Suppose you want to create a menu when a workbook opens. You'll also want to delete the menu when the workbook closes because menu modifications remain in effect between Excel sessions. Or suppose you want a menu to be available only when a particular workbook or worksheet is active. These sorts of things are relatively easy to program, thanks to Excel's event handlers.

The examples in this section demonstrate various menu-programming techniques used in conjunction with events.

I discuss event programming in depth in Chapter 18.

Adding and deleting menus automatically

If you need a menu to be created when a workbook is opened, use the `Workbook_Open` event. The following code, stored in the code module for the `ThisWorkbook` object, executes the `CreateMenu` procedure.

```
Private Sub Workbook_Open()
    Call CreateMenu
End Sub
```

To delete the menu when the workbook is closed, use a procedure such as the following. This procedure is executed before the workbook closes, and it executes the `DeleteMenu` procedure.

```
Private Sub Workbook_BeforeClose(Cancel As Boolean)
```

```
    Call DeleteMenu
End Sub
```

A problem may arise, however, if the workbook is not saved when the user closes it. Excel's "save workbook before closing" prompt occurs *after* the `Workbook_BeforeClose` event handler runs. So if the user clicks Cancel, the workbook remains open, but your custom menu has already been deleted!

One solution to this problem is to bypass Excel's prompt and write your own code in the `Workbook_BeforeClose` procedure to ask the user to save the workbook. The following code demonstrates how:

```
Private Sub Workbook_BeforeClose(Cancel As Boolean)
    If Not Me.Saved Then
        Msg = "Do you want to save the changes you made to "
        Msg = Msg & Me.Name & "?"
        Ans = MsgBox(Msg, vbQuestion + vbYesNoCancel)
        Select Case Ans
            Case vbYes
                Me.Save
            Case vbNo
                Me.Saved = True
            Case vbCancel
                Cancel = True
                Exit Sub
        End Select
    End If
    Call DeleteMenu
End Sub
```

This procedure determines whether the workbook has been saved. If it has, no problem; the `DeleteMenu` procedure is executed, and the workbook is closed. But if the workbook has not been saved, the procedure displays a message box that duplicates the one Excel normally shows. If the user clicks Yes, the workbook is saved, the menu is deleted, and the workbook is closed. If the user clicks No, the code sets the `Saved` property of the `Workbook` object to True (without actually saving the file) and deletes the menu. If the user clicks Cancel, the `BeforeClose` event is canceled, and the procedure ends without deleting the menu.

Disabling or hiding menus

When a menu or menu item is disabled, its text appears in a faint shade of gray, and clicking it has no effect. Excel disables its menu items when they are out of context. For example, the Links menu item on the Edit menu is disabled when the active workbook does not contain any links.

You can write VBA code to enable or disable both built-in and custom menus or menu items. Similarly, you can write code to hide menus or menu items. The key, of course, is tapping into the correct event.

The following procedures are stored in the code module for the ThisWorkbook object.

```
Private Sub Workbook_Open()
    Call AddMenu
End Sub

Private Sub Workbook_BeforeClose(Cancel As Boolean)
    Call DeleteMenu
End Sub

Private Sub Workbook_Activate()
    Call UnhideMenu
End Sub

Private Sub Workbook_Deactivate()
    Call HideMenu
End Sub
```

When the workbook is opened, the AddMenu procedure is called. When the workbook is closed, the DeleteMenu workbook is called. Two additional event-handler procedures are executed when the workbook is activated or deactivated. The UnhideMenu procedure is called when the workbook is activated, and the HideMenu procedure is called when the workbook is deactivated.

The HideMenu procedure sets the Visible property of the menu item to False, which effectively removes it from the menu bar. The UnhideMenu procedure does just the opposite. The net effect is that the menu is visible only when the workbook is active. These procedures, which assume that the Caption for the menu is "Budgeting", are listed below.

```
Sub UnhideMenu()
    CommandBars(1).Controls("Budgeting").Visible = True
End Sub

Sub HideMenu()
    CommandBars(1).Controls("Budgeting").Visible = False
End Sub
```

To disable the menu rather than hide it, simply access the Enabled property instead of the Visible property.

This example is available on the companion CD-ROM.

Working with checked menu items

Several of Excel's menu items appear with or without a check mark. For example, the View➪Formula Bar menu item displays a check mark if the formula bar is visible and does not display a check mark if the formula bar is hidden. When you select this menu item, the formula bar's visibility is toggled, and the check mark is either displayed or not.

You can add this type of functionality to your custom menu items. Figure 22-6 shows a menu item that displays a check mark only when the active sheet is displaying grid lines. Selecting this item toggles the grid-line display and also adjusts the check mark. The check mark display is determined by the `State` property of the menu item control.

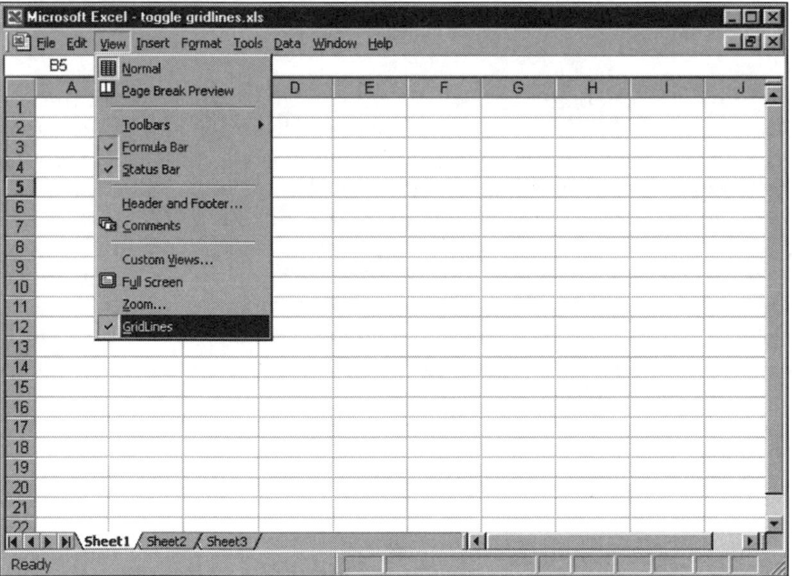

Figure 22-6: The GridLines menu item displays a check mark if the active sheet displays grid lines.

The trick here is keeping the check mark in sync with the active sheet. To do so, it's necessary to update the menu item whenever a new sheet or a new workbook is activated. This is done by setting up application-level events.

Adding the menu item

The AddMenuItem procedure shown in Listing 22-5 is executed when the workbook is opened. It creates a new GridLines menu item on the View menu.

Listing 22-5: Augmenting a built-in Excel menu

```
Dim AppObject As New XLHandler

Sub AddMenuItem()
    Dim ViewMenu As CommandBarPopup
    Dim NewMenuItem As CommandBarButton

'   Delete the menu if it already exists
    Call DeleteMenuItem

'   Find the View Menu
    Set ViewMenu = CommandBars(1).FindControl(ID:=30004)
    If ViewMenu Is Nothing Then
        MsgBox "Cannot add menu item."
        Exit Sub
    Else
        Set NewMenuItem = ViewMenu.Controls.Add _
         (Type:=msoControlButton)
        With NewMenuItem
            .Caption = "&GridLines"
            .OnAction = "ToggleGridlines"
        End With
    End If

'   Set up application event handler
    Set AppObject.AppEvents = Application
End Sub
```

The AddMenuItem procedure adds the new menu item to the Worksheet Menu Bar, not the Chart Menu Bar. Therefore, the new menu item isn't displayed when a chart sheet is active — which is just what we want!

Notice that the final statement in the AddMenuItem procedure sets up the application-level events that will be monitored. These event procedures, which are stored in a class module named XLHandler, are listed below.

```
Public WithEvents AppEvents As Excel.Application

Private Sub AppEvents_SheetActivate(ByVal Sh As Object)
    Call CheckGridlines
End Sub
```

```
Private Sub AppEvents_WorkbookActivate _
  (ByVal Wb As Excel.Workbook)
    Call CheckGridlines
End Sub
```

Toggling the grid-line display

The net effect is that when the user changes worksheets or workbooks, the `CheckGridlines` procedure listed below is executed. This procedure ensures that the check mark displayed on the GridLines menu option is in sync with the sheet.

```
Sub CheckGridlines()
    Dim TG As CommandBarButton
    On Error Resume Next
    Set TG = CommandBars(1).FindControl(Id:=30004). _
      Controls("&GridLines")
    If ActiveWindow.DisplayGridlines Then
        TG.State = msoButtonDown
    Else
        TG.State = msoButtonUp
    End If
End Sub
```

This procedure checks the active window and sets the `State` property of the menu item. If grid lines are displayed, it adds a check mark to the GridLines menu item. If grid lines are not displayed, it removes the check mark from the menu item.

Keeping the menu in sync with the sheet

When the menu item is selected, the `OnAction` property of that menu item triggers the following `ToggleGridlines` procedure:

```
Sub ToggleGridlines()
    On Error Resume Next
    ActiveWindow.DisplayGridlines = _
      Not ActiveWindow.DisplayGridlines
    Call CheckGridlines
End Sub
```

This procedure simply toggles the grid-line display of the active window. I use `On Error Resume Next` to eliminate the error message that is generated if the sheet is not a worksheet.

The Easy Way to Create Custom Menus

When Excel 97 was released, I was a bit frustrated with the code required to create a custom menu, so I developed a technique that simplifies the process considerably. My technique uses a worksheet, shown in Figure 22-7, to store information about the new menu. A VBA procedure reads the data in the workbook and creates the menu, menu items, and submenu items.

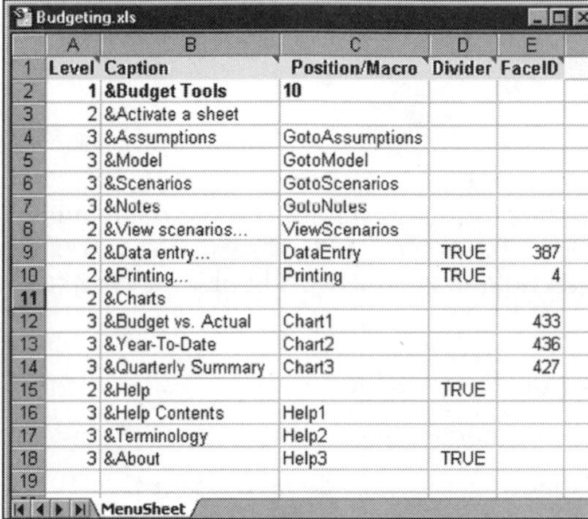
Budgeting.xls

	A	B	C	D	E
1	Level	Caption	Position/Macro	Divider	FaceID
2	1	&Budget Tools	10		
3	2	&Activate a sheet			
4	3	&Assumptions	GotoAssumptions		
5	3	&Model	GotoModel		
6	3	&Scenarios	GotoScenarios		
7	3	&Notes	GotoNotes		
8	2	&View scenarios...	ViewScenarios		
9	2	&Data entry...	DataEntry	TRUE	387
10	2	&Printing...	Printing	TRUE	4
11	2	&Charts			
12	3	&Budget vs. Actual	Chart1		433
13	3	&Year-To-Date	Chart2		436
14	3	&Quarterly Summary	Chart3		427
15	2	&Help		TRUE	
16	3	&Help Contents	Help1		
17	3	&Terminology	Help2		
18	3	&About	Help3	TRUE	
19					

MenuSheet

Figure 22-7: The information in this worksheet is used to create a custom menu.

The worksheet consists of a table with five columns:

✦ *Level.* This is the location of the particular item relative to the hierarchy of the menu system. Valid values are 1, 2, and 3. Level 1 is for a menu; 2 is for a menu item; and 3 is for a submenu item. Normally, you'll have one level 1 item, with level 2 items below it. A level 2 item may or may not have level 3 (submenu) items.

✦ *Caption.* This is the text that appears in the menu, menu item, or submenu. To underline a character, place an ampersand (&) before it.

✦ *Position/Macro.* For level 1 items, this should be an integer that represents the position in the menu bar. For level 2 or level 3 items, this is the macro that executes when the item is selected. If a level 2 item has one or more level 3 items, the level 2 item may not have a macro associated with it.

✦ *Divider.* Enter True if a separator bar should be placed before the menu item or submenu item.

✦ *FaceID.* This optional entry is a code number that represents the built-in graphic images displayed next to an item.

Figure 22-8 shows the menu that was created from the worksheet data.

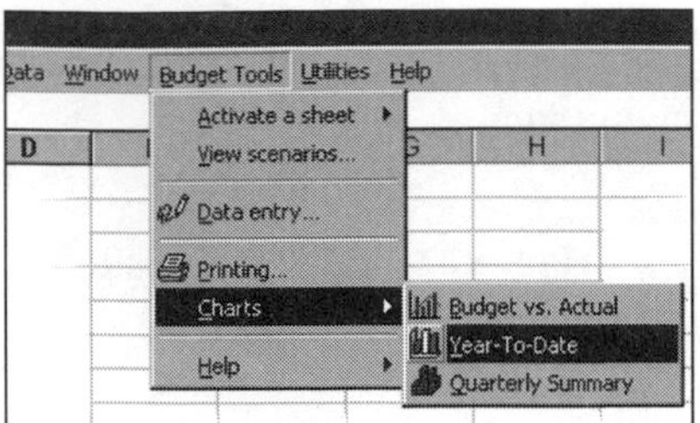

Figure 22-8: This menu was created from the data stored in a worksheet.

A workbook that demonstrates this technique is available on the companion CD-ROM. This workbook contains the VBA procedure that reads the worksheet data and creates the menu. To use this technique in your workbook or add-in, follow these general steps:

1. Open the example workbook from the CD-ROM.
2. Copy all the code in `Module1` to a module in your project.
3. Add procedures such as the following to the code module for the `ThisWorkbook` object:

```
Private Sub Workbook_Open()
    Call CreateMenu
End Sub

Private Sub Workbook_BeforeClose(Cancel As Boolean)
    Call DeleteMenu
End Sub
```

4. Insert a new worksheet, and name it `MenuSheet`. Better yet, copy the `MenuSheet` from the example file.
5. Customize the `MenuSheet` to correspond to your custom menu.

There is no error handling in the example workbook, so it's up to you to make sure that everything works.

Creating a Substitute Worksheet Menu Bar

In some cases, you may want to hide Excel's standard Worksheet Menu Bar and replace it with your own.

The `MakeMenuBar` procedure in Listing 22-6 creates a new menu bar named `MyMenuBar`. This menu bar consists of two menus. The first menu is the standard File menu, copied from the Worksheet Menu Bar. The second menu contains two items: Restore Normal Menu and Help.

Listing 22-6: Replacing Excel's built-in menu with your own

```
Sub MakeMenuBar()
    Dim NewMenuBar As CommandBar

'   Delete menu bar if it exists
    Call DeleteMenuBar

'   Add a menu bar
    Set NewMenuBar = CommandBars.Add(MenuBar:=True)
    With NewMenuBar
        .Name = "MyMenuBar"
        .Visible = True
    End With

'   Copy the File menu from Worksheet Menu Bar
    CommandBars("Worksheet Menu Bar") _
     .Controls(1).Copy Bar:=CommandBars("MyMenuBar")

'   Add a new menu
    Set NewMenu = NewMenuBar.Controls.Add _
      (Type:=msoControlPopup)
    NewMenu.Caption = "&Commands"

'   Add a new menu item
    Set NewItem = NewMenu.Controls.Add(Type:=msoControlButton)
    With NewItem
        .Caption = "&Restore Normal Menu"
        .OnAction = "DeleteMenuBar"
    End With

'   Add a new menu item
    Set NewItem = NewMenu.Controls.Add(Type:=msoControlButton)
    With NewItem
        .Caption = "&Help"
        .OnAction = "ShowHelp"
    End With
End Sub
```

Figure 22-9 shows the new menu bar.

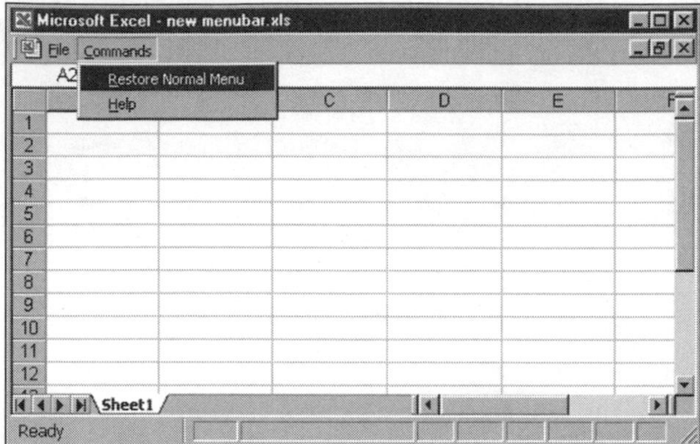

Figure 22-9: A custom menu bar replaces the standard Worksheet Menu Bar.

Notice that nothing in this procedure hides the Worksheet Menu Bar. The instruction `Set NewMenuBar = CommandBars.Add(MenuBar:=True)` adds the new command bar, and the `MenuBar` argument makes it the active menu bar. Only one menu bar can be active at a time.

Deleting the custom toolbar displays the Worksheet Menu Bar and makes it the active menu bar. The following `DeleteMenuBar` procedure returns things to normal.

```
Sub DeleteMenuBar()
    On Error Resume Next
    CommandBars("MyMenuBar").Delete
    On Error GoTo 0
End Sub
```

Working with Shortcut Menus

A *shortcut menu* is a pop-up menu that appears when you right-click virtually anything in Excel. You can't use Excel's Customize dialog box to remove or modify shortcut menus. The only way to customize shortcut menus is through VBA.

Menu Shenanigans

Here's a good April Fools' Day trick to play on an office mate (one with a sense of humor, that is). Create a procedure that cycles through all the menus, menu items, and submenu items and changes their captions so that they are *backwards.* Set things up so the routine is executed when the workbook is opened, and save the workbook in the victim's XLStart directory. The next time Excel is started, the menus look as if they're in a strange language.

For lazy pranksters, use the workbook on the CD-ROM that accompanies this book. The `ReverseMenuText` procedure performs its mischief by calling a custom function that reverses the text in the captions (except for the ellipses), converts the new text to proper case, and maintains the original hot keys. The net effect, as you can see in the accompanying figure, is a worksheet menu system that works exactly like the original (and is even keystroke compatible) but looks very odd.

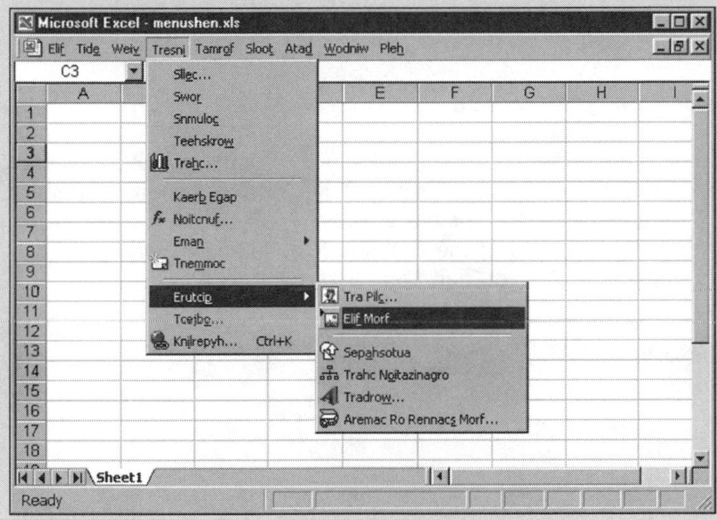

Before exiting, the routine adds an escape route: a new (legible) menu item to the Pleh menu (formerly the Help menu). This new item calls a procedure that returns the menus to normal.

Actually, this trick can be rather instructive. For example, I found out that Excel automatically resets some of the menu items when a menu is accessed; for example, the New, Save, and Save As menu items on the File menu appear as they normally do. Go figure.

Excel has lots of shortcut menus — 44 in Excel 97 and 52 in Excel 2000. To work with a shortcut menu, you need to know its `Caption` property setting. You can use the following procedure to generate a list of all shortcut menus and the `Index` and `Caption` settings for each:

```
Sub ListShortCutMenus()
    Row = 1
    For Each cbar In CommandBars
        If cbar.Type = msoBarTypePopup Then
            Cells(Row, 1) = cbar.Index
            Cells(Row, 2) = cbar.Name
            For col = 1 To cbar.Controls.Count
                Cells(Row, col + 2) = _
                 cbar.Controls(col).Caption
            Next col
            Row = Row + 1
        End If
    Next cbar
End Sub
```

Figure 22-10 shows a portion of the output.

Although you can refer to a shortcut menu by its `Index` property, this is not recommended. For some reason, `Index` values have not remained consistent between Excel 97 and Excel 2000. For example, in Excel 97 the `CommandBar` object with an `Index` value of 21 is the Cell shortcut menu. In Excel 2000, an `Index` value of 21 refers to the PivotChart Menu shortcut menu.

list shortcut menus.xls

	A	B	C	D	E
1	20	Query and Pivot	Forma&t Report...	Pivot&Chart	&Wizard...
2	21	PivotChart Menu	Fi&eld Settings...	&Options...	&Refresh Data
3	22	Workbook tabs	Sheet1	&Sheet List	&Sheet List
4	23	Cell	Cu&t	&Copy	&Paste
5	24	Column	Cu&t	&Copy	&Paste
6	25	Row	Cu&t	&Copy	&Paste
7	26	Cell	Cu&t	&Copy	&Paste
8	27	Column	Cu&t	&Copy	&Paste
9	28	Row	Cu&t	&Copy	&Paste
10	29	Ply	&Ungroup Sheets	&Insert...	&Delete
11	30	XLM Cell	Cu&t	&Copy	&Paste
12	31	Document	&Save	Save &As...	&Print...
13	32	Desktop	&New...	&Open...	Save &Workspace...
14	33	Nondefault Drag and Drop	&Move Here	&Copy Here	Copy Here as &Values Onl
15	34	AutoFill	&Copy Cells	Fill &Series	Fill &Formats
16	35	Button	Cu&t	&Copy	&Paste
17	36	Dialog	&Paste	Ta&b Order...	&Run Dialog
18	37	Series	&Selected Object	Chart &Type...	&Source Data...
19	38	Plot Area	&Selected Object	Chart &Type...	&Source Data...
20	39	Floor and Walls	&Selected Object	3-D &View...	Cle&ar
21	40	Trendline	&Selected Object	Cle&ar	
22	41	Chart	&Selected Object	Cle&ar	
23	42	Format Data Series	&Set Print Area	&Clear Print Area	
24	43	Format Axis			
25	44	Format Legend Entry	&Mail Recipient	M&ail Recipient (as Attachment)...	&Routing Recipient...
26	45	Formula Bar	Cu&t	&Copy	&Paste
27	46	PivotTable Context Menu	&Format Cells...	Forma&t Report...	Pivot&Chart
28	47	Query	Cu&t	&Copy	&Paste

Sheet1

Figure 22-10: A listing of all shortcut menus, plus the menu items in each.

Adding menu items to shortcut menus

Adding a menu item to a shortcut menu works just like adding a menu item to a regular menu. The following example demonstrates how to add a menu item to the Cell shortcut menu that appears when you right-click a cell or a row or column border. This menu item is added to the end of the shortcut menu, with a separator bar above it.

```
Sub AddItemToShortcut()
    Set NewItem = CommandBars("Cell").Controls.Add
    With NewItem
        .Caption = "Toggle Word Wrap"
        .OnAction = "ToggleWordWrap"
        .BeginGroup = True
    End With
End Sub
```

Selecting the new menu item executes a procedure named `ToggleWordWrap`. Figure 22-11 shows the new shortcut menu in action.

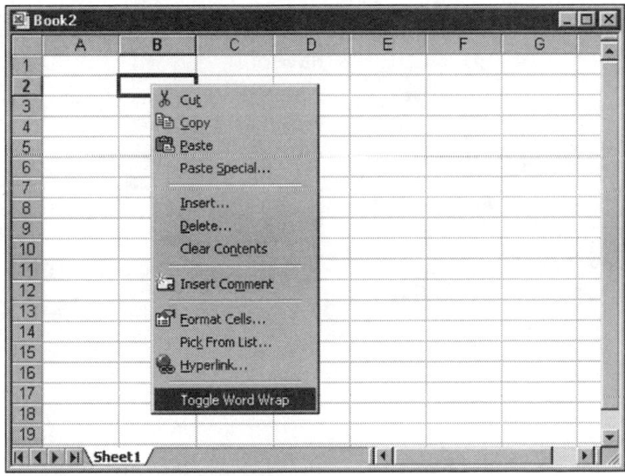

Figure 22-11: This shortcut menu has a new menu item.

Deleting menu items from shortcut menus

The following procedure uses the `Delete` method to remove the menu item added by the procedure in the previous section.

```
Sub RemoveItemFromShortcut()
    On Error Resume Next
    CommandBars("Cell").Controls("Toggle Word Wrap").Delete
End Sub
```

The On Error Resume Next statement avoids the error message that appears if the menu item is not on the shortcut menu.

The following procedure removes the Hide menu item from two shortcut menus: the one that appears when you right-click a row header and the one that appears for a column header.

```
Sub RemoveHideMenuItems()
    CommandBars("Column").Controls("Hide").Delete
    CommandBars("Row").Controls("Hide").Delete
End Sub
```

Disabling shortcut menu items

As an alternative to removing menu items, you may want to disable one or more items on certain shortcut menus while your application is running. When an item is disabled, it appears in a light gray color, and clicking it has no effect. The following procedure disables the Hide menu item from the Row and Column shortcut menus.

```
Sub DisableHideMenuItems()
    CommandBars("Column").Controls("Hide").Enabled = False
    CommandBars("Row").Controls("Hide").Enabled = False
End Sub
```

Disabling shortcut menus

You can also disable entire shortcut menus. For example, you may not want the user to access the commands generally made available by right-clicking a cell. The following DisableCell procedure disables the Cell shortcut menu. After the procedure is executed, right-clicking a cell has no effect.

```
Sub DisableCell()
    CommandBars("Cell").Enabled = False
End Sub
```

If you want to disable *all* shortcut menus, use the following procedure:

```
Sub DisableAllShortcutMenus()
    Dim cb As CommandBar
    For Each cb In CommandBars
        If cb.Type = msoBarTypePopup Then _
          cb.Enabled = False
    Next cb
End Sub
```

Disabling the shortcut menus "sticks" between sessions. Therefore, you'll probably want to restore the shortcut menus before closing Excel. To restore the shortcut menus, modify the preceding procedure to set the `Enabled` property to True.

In the initial release of Excel 97, the Toolbar List shortcut menu cannot be disabled. This is the shortcut menu that appears when you right-click any command bar. In other words, there is no way to prevent the user from displaying this shortcut menu. This problem was corrected in SR-1 and SR-2.

Resetting shortcut menus

The `Reset` method restores a shortcut menu to its original condition. The following procedure resets the Cell shortcut menu to its normal state.

```
Sub ResetCellMenu()
    CommandBars("Cell").Reset
End Sub
```

Creating new shortcut menus

It's possible to create an entirely new shortcut menu. Listing 22-7 creates a shortcut menu named `MyShortcut` and adds six menu items to it. These menu items display one of the tabs in the Format Cells dialog box.

Listing 22-7: Creating an entirely new and separate shortcut menu

```
Sub CreateShortcut()
    Set myBar = CommandBars.Add _
      (Name:="MyShortcut", Position:=msoBarPopup, _
       Temporary:=True)

'   Add a menu item
    Set myItem = myBar.Controls.Add(Type:=msoControlButton)
    With myItem
        .Caption = "&Number Format..."
        .OnAction = "ShowFormatNumber"
        .FaceId = 1554
    End With

'   Add a menu item
    Set myItem = myBar.Controls.Add(Type:=msoControlButton)
    With myItem
```

Continued

Listing 22-7 *(continued)*

```
            .Caption = "&Alignment..."
            .OnAction = "ShowFormatAlignment"
            .FaceId = 217
        End With

'       Add a menu item
        Set myItem = myBar.Controls.Add(Type:=msoControlButton)
        With myItem
            .Caption = "&Font..."
            .OnAction = "ShowFormatFont"
            .FaceId = 291
        End With

'       Add a menu item
        Set myItem = myBar.Controls.Add(Type:=msoControlButton)
        With myItem
            .Caption = "&Borders..."
            .OnAction = "ShowFormatBorder"
            .FaceId = 149
            .BeginGroup = True
        End With

'       Add a menu item
        Set myItem = myBar.Controls.Add(Type:=msoControlButton)
        With myItem
            .Caption = "&Patterns..."
            .OnAction = "ShowFormatPatterns"
            .FaceId = 1550
        End With

'       Add a menu item
        Set myItem = myBar.Controls.Add(Type:=msoControlButton)
        With myItem
            .Caption = "Pr&otection..."
            .OnAction = "ShowFormatProtection"
            .FaceId = 2654
        End With
    End Sub
```

Figure 22-12 shows how this new shortcut menu looks.

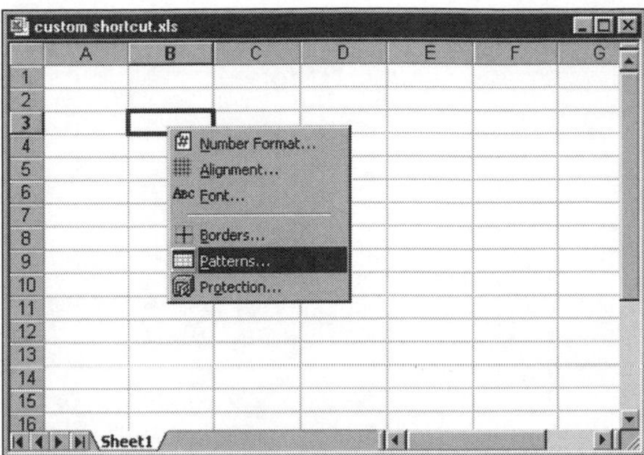

Figure 22-12: This new shortcut menu was created with VBA.

After the shortcut menu is created, you can display it with the `ShowPopup` method. The following procedure, located in the code module for a `Worksheet` object, is executed when the user right-clicks a cell.

```
Private Sub Worksheet_BeforeRightClick _
  (ByVal Target As Excel.Range, Cancel As Boolean)
    If Union(Target.Range("A1"), Range("data")).Address = _
      Range("data").Address Then
        CommandBars("MyShortcut").ShowPopup
        Cancel = True
    End If
End Sub
```

If the cell the user right-clicks is within a range named data, the `MyShortcut` menu appears. Setting the `Cancel` argument to True ensures that the normal shortcut menu is not displayed.

The companion CD-ROM contains an example that creates a new shortcut menu and displays it in place of the normal Cell shortcut menu.

Summary

In this chapter, I covered the topic of custom menus and presented many examples that demonstrate how to modify and create standard menus and shortcut menus.

The next chapter continues the discussion of application development, covering the topic of user help.

✦ ✦ ✦

CHAPTER 23

Providing Help for Your Applications

✦ ✦ ✦ ✦

In This Chapter

Why you might want to provide user help for your applications

How to provide help by using only the components supplied with Excel

How to create Help files with the Windows Help System or the HTML Help System

How to associate a Help file with your applications

How to use the Office Assistant to display help

Other ways to display WinHelp or HTML Help

✦ ✦ ✦ ✦

Computer users have become rather spoiled over the years. Not too many years ago, software rarely provided online help. And the "help" provided often proved less than helpful. Now, just about all commercial software provides online help; and more often than not, online help serves as the primary documentation. Thick software manuals are an endangered species (good riddance!).

In this chapter, I discuss the concept of providing help for your Excel applications. As you'll see, you have lots of options.

Help for Your Excel Applications?

If you develop a nontrivial application in Excel, you may want to consider building in some sort of help for end users. Doing so makes the users feel more comfortable with the application and may eliminate those time-wasting phone calls from users with basic questions. Another advantage is that online help is always available (the instructions can't be misplaced or buried under a pile of books).

You can add user help to your applications in a number of ways, ranging from simple to complex. The method you choose depends on your application's scope and complexity and how much effort you're willing to put into this phase of development. Some applications may require only a brief set of instructions on how to start them. Others may benefit from a full-blown, searchable help system. Most often, applications need something in between.

This chapter classifies online help into two categories:

- ✦ *Unofficial Help System.* This method of displaying help uses standard Excel components (such as a UserForm).
- ✦ *Official Help System.* This help system uses either a compiled HLP file produced by the Windows Help System or a compiled CHM file produced by the HTML Help System.

Creating a compiled Help file is not a trivial task, but it may be worth the effort if your application is complex or if it will be used by a large number of people.

About the Examples in This Chapter

In this chapter, I use a simple workbook application to demonstrate various ways of providing help. The application uses data stored in a worksheet to generate and print form letters.

As you can see in the following figure, cells display the total number of records in the database (C2, calculated by a formula), the current record number (C3), the first record to print (C4), and the last record to print (C5). To display a particular record, the user enters a value into cell C3. To print a series of form letters, the user specifies the first and last record numbers in cells C4 and C5.

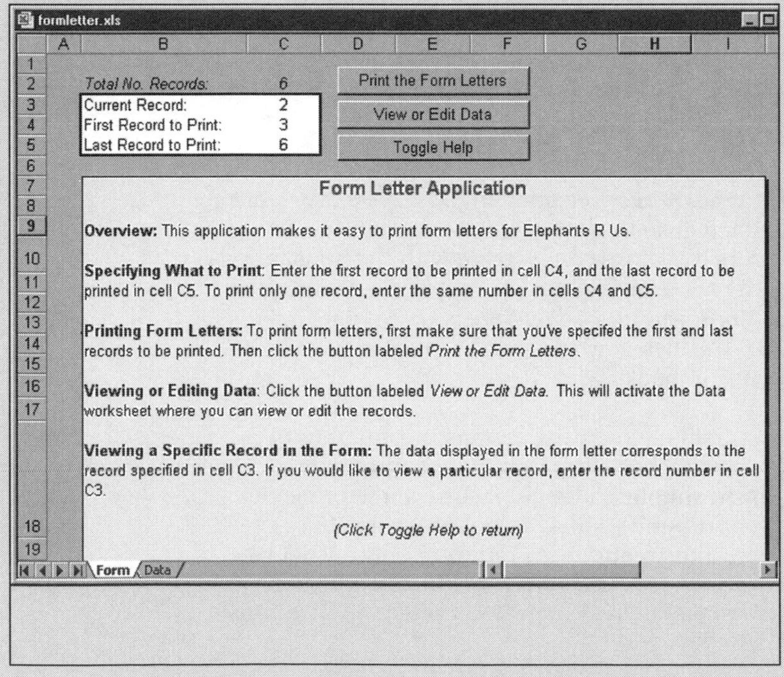

formletter.xls
Total No. Records: 6
Current Record: 2
First Record to Print: 3
Last Record to Print: 6
Print the Form Letters
View or Edit Data
Toggle Help
Form Letter Application
Overview: This application makes it easy to print form letters for Elephants R Us.
Specifying What to Print: Enter the first record to be printed in cell C4, and the last record to be printed in cell C5. To print only one record, enter the same number in cells C4 and C5.
Printing Form Letters: To print form letters, first make sure that you've specifed the first and last records to be printed. Then click the button labeled Print the Form Letters.
Viewing or Editing Data: Click the button labeled View or Edit Data. This will activate the Data worksheet where you can view or edit the records.
Viewing a Specific Record in the Form: The data displayed in the form letter corresponds to the record specified in cell C3. If you would like to view a particular record, enter the record number in cell C3.
(Click Toggle Help to return)
Form
Data

The application is simple, but it does consist of several discrete components in order to demonstrate various ways of displaying context-sensitive help.

The form letter workbook consists of the following components:

`Form`	A worksheet that contains the text of the form letter.
`Data`	A worksheet that contains a seven-field database.
`HelpSheet`	Present only in the examples that store help text on a worksheet.
`PrintMod`	A VBA module that contains macros to print the form letters.
`HelpMod`	A VBA module that contains macros that control the help display. The content of this module varies, depending on the type of help being demonstrated.
`UserForm1`	Present only if the help technique involves a UserForm.

The workbook is available on the companion CD-ROM. You might want to take a few minutes to familiarize yourself with the application.

Help Systems That Use Excel Components

Perhaps the most straightforward method of providing help to your users is to use the features contained in Excel itself. The primary advantage is that you don't need to learn how to create WinHelp or HTML Help files — which can be a major undertaking and may take longer to develop than your application!

In this section, I provide an overview of some help techniques that use the following built-in Excel components:

✦ *Cell comments.* This is about as simple as it comes.

✦ *A Text Box control.* A simple macro is all it takes to toggle the display of a Text Box that shows help information.

✦ *A worksheet.* A simple way to add help is to insert a worksheet, enter your help information, and name its tab "Help." When the user clicks the tab, the worksheet is activated.

✦ *A custom UserForm.* A number of techniques involve displaying help text in a UserForm.

Using cell comments for help

Perhaps the simplest way to provide user help is to use cell comments. This technique is most appropriate for describing the type of input that's expected in a cell. When the user moves the mouse pointer over a cell that contains a comment, that comment appears in a small window. Another advantage is that this technique does not require any macros.

Automatic display of cell notes is an option. The following VBA instruction ensures that cell comment indicators are displayed for cells that contain comments:

```
Application.DisplayCommentIndicator = xlCommentIndicatorOnly
```

A workbook that demonstrates the use of cell comments for help is available on the companion CD-ROM.

Using a Text Box for help

Using a Text Box to display help information is also easy to implement. Simply create a Text Box using the Text Box button on the Drawing toolbar, enter the help text, and format it to your liking. Figure 23-1 shows an example of a Text Box set up to display help information.

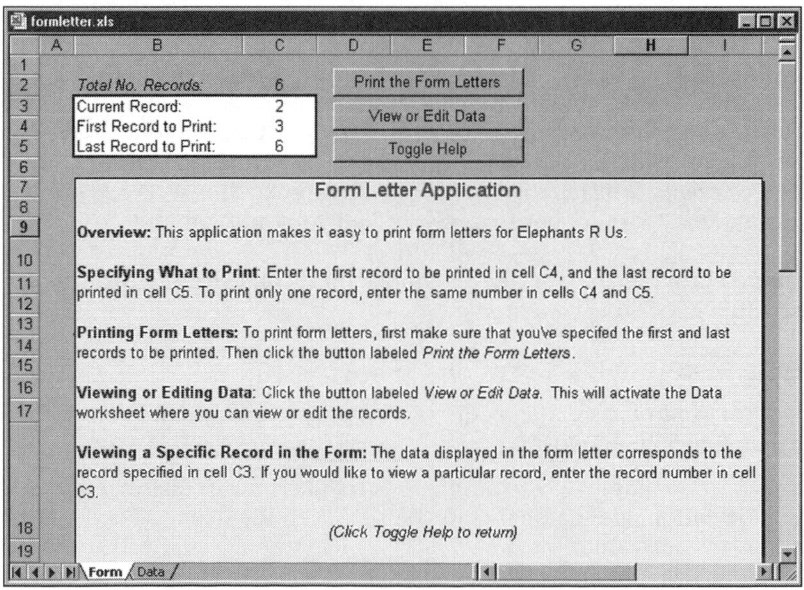

formletter.xls
Total No. Records: 6
Current Record: 2
First Record to Print: 3
Last Record to Print: 6
Print the Form Letters
View or Edit Data
Toggle Help
Form Letter Application
Overview: This application makes it easy to print form letters for Elephants R Us.
Specifying What to Print: Enter the first record to be printed in cell C4, and the last record to be printed in cell C5. To print only one record, enter the same number in cells C4 and C5.
Printing Form Letters: To print form letters, first make sure that you've specifed the first and last records to be printed. Then click the button labeled Print the Form Letters.
Viewing or Editing Data: Click the button labeled View or Edit Data. This will activate the Data worksheet where you can view or edit the records.
Viewing a Specific Record in the Form: The data displayed in the form letter corresponds to the record specified in cell C3. If you would like to view a particular record, enter the record number in cell C3.
(Click Toggle Help to return)
Form
Data

Figure 23-1: Using a Text Box to display help for the user.

Using the Text Box from the Drawing toolbar is preferable to using an ActiveX Text Box from the Control Toolbox toolbar because it allows *rich text* formatting. In other words, the Text Box from the Drawing toolbar enables you to apply formatting to individual characters within the Text Box.

Most of the time, you won't want the Text Box to be visible. Therefore, you might want to add a button to your application to execute a macro that toggles the `Visible` property of the Text Box. An example of such a macro follows. In this case, the Text Box is named HelpText.

```
Sub ToggleHelp()
    ActiveSheet.TextBoxes("HelpText").Visible = _
      Not ActiveSheet.TextBoxes("HelpText").Visible
End Sub
```

Using a worksheet to display help text

Another easy way to add help to your application is to create a macro that activates a separate worksheet that holds the help information. Just attach the macro to a button control, toolbar button, or menu item, and voilà! . . . quick-and-dirty help.

Figure 23-2 shows a sample help worksheet. I designed the range that contains the help text to simulate a page from a yellow notebook pad—a fancy touch that you may or may not like.

To keep the user from scrolling around the HelpSheet worksheet, the macro sets the `ScrollArea` property of the worksheet. Because this property is not stored with the workbook, it's necessary to set it when the worksheet is activated. I also protected the worksheet to prevent the user from changing the text, and I "froze" the first row so that the Return button is always visible, regardless of how far down the sheet the user scrolls.

The main disadvantage of using this technique is that the help text isn't visible along with the main work area. One possible solution is to write a macro that opens a new window to display the sheet.

Displaying help in a UserForm

Another way to provide help to the user is to display the text in a UserForm. In this section, I describe several techniques that involve UserForms.

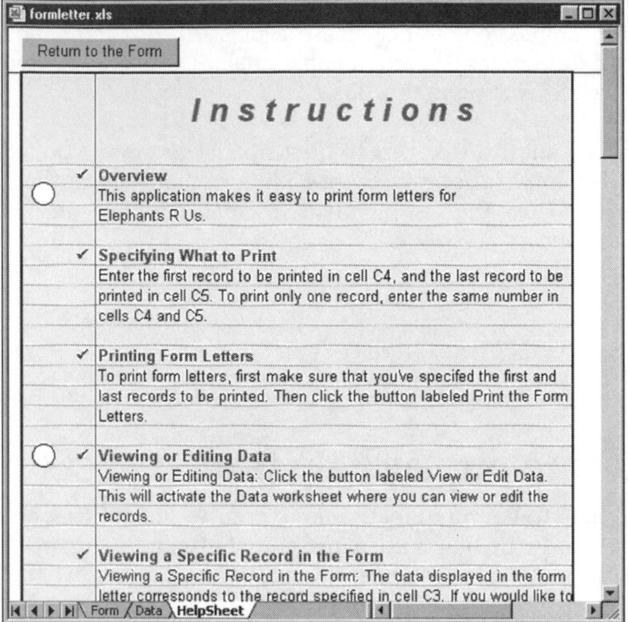

Figure 23-2: Putting user help in a separate worksheet is an easy way to go.

Using Label controls to display help text

Figure 23-3 shows a UserForm that contains two Label controls: one for the title, one for the actual text. A SpinButton control enables the user to navigate among the topics. The text itself is stored in a worksheet, with topics in column A and text in column B.

Figure 23-3: Clicking the SpinButton determines the text displayed in the Labels.

Clicking the SpinButton executes the following procedure. This procedure simply sets the `Caption` property of the two Label controls to the text in the appropriate row of the worksheet (named `HelpSheet`).

```
Private Sub SpinButton1_Change()
    HelpTopic = SpinButton1.Value
    LabelTopic.Caption = Sheets("HelpSheet")._
      Cells(HelpTopic, 1)
    LabelText.Caption = Sheets("HelpSheet").Cells(HelpTopic, 2)
    Me.Caption = APPNAME & ": Topic " & HelpTopic & "/" _
      & SpinButton1.Max
End Sub
```

Here, `APPNAME` is a global constant that contains the application's name.

Using a "scrolling" Label to display help text

This technique displays help text in a single Label control. Because a Label control cannot contain a vertical scrollbar, the Label is placed inside a Frame control, which *can* contain a scrollbar. Figure 23-4 shows an example of a UserForm set up in this manner. The user can scroll through the text by using the Frame's scrollbar.

Elephants R Us Help
To print only one record, enter the same number in cells C4 andC5.
Printing Form Letters
To print form letters, first make sure that you've specified the first and last records to be printed. Then click the button labeled Print
the Form Letters.
Viewing or Editing Data
Click the button labeled View or Edit Data.
Close

Figure 23-4: Inserting a Label control inside a Frame control adds scrolling to the Label.

The text displayed in the Label is read from a worksheet named `HelpSheet` when the UserForm is initialized. Listing 23-1 presents the `UserForm_Initialize` procedure for this worksheet. Notice that the code adjusts the Frame's `ScrollHeight` property to ensure that the scrolling covers the complete height of the Label. Again, `APPNAME` is a global constant that contains the application's name.

Listing 23-1: Making the label control display scrollable text from the worksheet

```
Private Sub UserForm_Initialize()
    Me.Caption = APPNAME & " Help"
    LastRow = Sheets("HelpSheet").Range("A65536") _
     .End(xlUp).Row
    txt = ""
    For r = 1 To LastRow
      txt = txt & Sheets("HelpSheet").Cells(r, 1) _
       .Text & vbCrLf
    Next r
    With Label1
        .Top = 0
        .Caption = txt
        .Width = 160
        .AutoSize = True
    End With
    With Frame1
        .ScrollHeight = Label1.Height
        .ScrollTop = 0
    End With
End Sub
```

Because a Label cannot display formatted text, I used horizontal lines in the `HelpSheet` worksheet to delineate the help topics.

Using a DropDown control to select a help topic

The example in this section improves upon the previous example. Figure 23-5 shows a UserForm that contains a DropDown control and a Label control. The user can select a topic from the DropDown or view the topics sequentially by clicking the Previous or Next button.

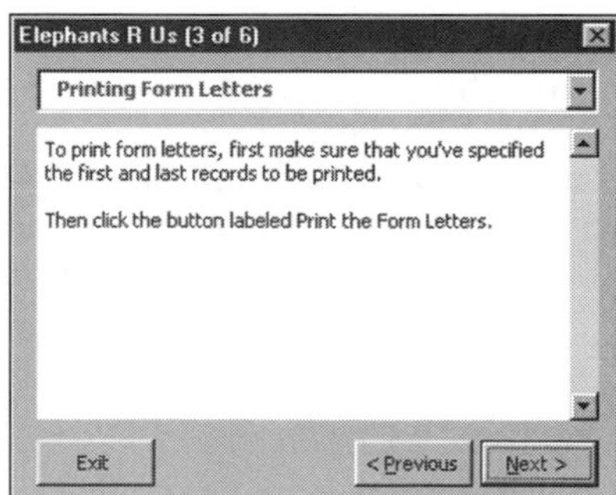
Elephants R Us (3 of 6)
Printing Form Letters
To print form letters, first make sure that you've specified the first and last records to be printed.
Then click the button labeled Print the Form Letters.
Exit
< Previous
Next >

Figure 23-5: Designating the topic of the label's text with a drop-down list control.

This example is a bit more complex than the example in the previous section, but it's also a lot more flexible. It uses the Label-within-a-scrolling-Frame technique (described previously) to support help text of any length.

The help text is stored in a worksheet named `HelpSheet` in two columns (A and B). The first column contains the topic headings and the second column contains the text. The ComboBox items are added in the `UserForm_Initialize` procedure, shown below. The `CurrentTopic` variable is a module-level variable that stores an integer that represents the help topic.

```
Private Sub UserForm_Initialize()
    Set HelpSheet = ThisWorkbook.Sheets(HelpSheetName)
    TopicCount = Application.WorksheetFunction. _
      CountA(HelpSheet.Range("A:A"))
    For Row = 1 To TopicCount
        ComboBoxTopics.AddItem HelpSheet.Cells(Row, 1)
    Next Row
    ComboBoxTopics.ListIndex = 0
    CurrentTopic = 1
    UpdateForm
End Sub
```

The `UpdateForm` procedure is shown in Listing 23-2. This procedure handles the details of setting the Label's caption, adjusting the Frame's scrollbar, and enabling or disabling the Previous and Next buttons.

Listing 23-2: **Making the Label mind the Frame's directive**

```
Private Sub UpdateForm()
    ComboBoxTopics.ListIndex = CurrentTopic - 1
    Me.Caption = HelpFormCaption & _
      " (" & CurrentTopic & " of " & TopicCount & ")"

    With LabelText
        .Caption = HelpSheet.Cells(CurrentTopic, 2)
        .AutoSize = False
        .Width = 212
        .AutoSize = True
    End With
    With Frame1
        .ScrollHeight = LabelText.Height + 5
        .ScrollTop = 1
    End With

    On Error Resume Next
    If CurrentTopic = 1 Then PreviousButton.Enabled = False _
     Else PreviousButton.Enabled = True
    If CurrentTopic = TopicCount Then _
```

Continued

Listing 23-2: *(continued)*

```
        NextButton.Enabled = False _
        Else NextButton.Enabled = True
      If NextButton.Enabled Then NextButton.SetFocus _
        Else PreviousButton.SetFocus
End Sub
```

Using the WinHelp and HTML Help Systems

Currently, the most common help system used in Windows applications is the Windows Help System (WinHelp). This system displays HLP files and supports hypertext *jumps* that let the user display another related topic. However, it seems that Microsoft is attempting to phase out WinHelp in favor of HTML Help. Most of the new applications from Microsoft, including Office 2000, use HTML Help.

Both these help systems enable the developer to associate a context ID with a particular Help topic. This makes it possible to display a particular help topic in a context-sensitive manner.

In this section, I briefly describe these two help-authoring systems. Details on creating such help systems are well beyond the scope of this book.

If you plan to develop a large-scale help system, I strongly recommend that you purchase a help-authoring software product to make your job easier. Help-authoring software makes it much easier to develop Help files because the software takes care of lots of the tedious details for you. Many products are available, including shareware and commercial offerings. Perhaps the most popular help-authoring product is RoboHELP, from Blue Sky Software. RoboHELP creates both WinHelp and HTML help systems. For more information, visit the company's Web site at this address: `http://www.blue-sky.com`.

About WinHelp

Figure 23-6 shows a typical help topic displayed in WinHelp. Some words, called *jump words,* are underlined and displayed in a different color. Clicking a jump word that has a dotted underline makes WinHelp display another window with more explanation — often a definition. Clicking a jump word that has a solid underline makes WinHelp either jump to a new topic or display a secondary help window.

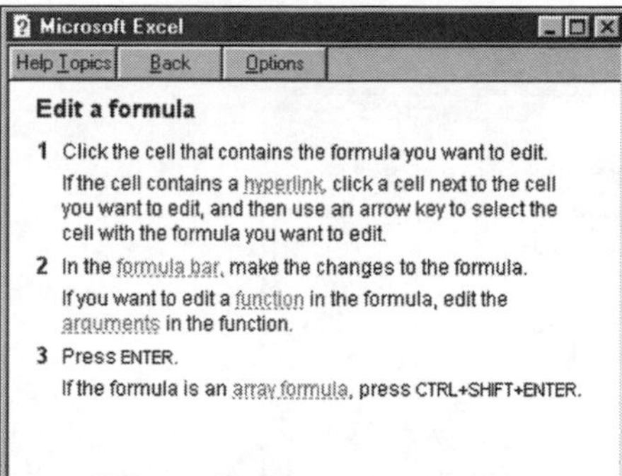

Figure 23-6: An example of WinHelp.

WinHelp's main disadvantage is that creating the HLP files takes a great deal of knowledge and effort. An entire Usenet newsgroup is devoted to this topic (`comp.os.ms-windows.programmer.winhelp`), and I'm constantly amazed at the level of discussions in this group. It's clear that creating a good WinHelp file requires lots of experience and some good programming skills to boot.

To create an HLP file, you need a word processing program that can read and write RTF (Rich Text Format) files. Most major word processors can do this, including Microsoft Word. You also need a copy of the Microsoft Help Workshop, which includes the Help compiler. You can download the Help Workshop from Microsoft's FTP site at this address:

```
ftp://ftp.microsoft.com/softlib/mslfiles/hcwsetup.exe
```

The companion CD-ROM contains a simple compiled HLP file, along with the RTF file and the project file (an HPJ file) that were used to create it.

About HTML Help

As I mentioned, Microsoft is positioning HTML Help as the new Windows standard for online help. This system essentially compiles a series of HTML files into a compact help system. Unlike WinHelp, which uses RTF-formatted documents, HTML Help accepts documents in HTML format. Figure 23-7 shows an example of an HTML Help system.

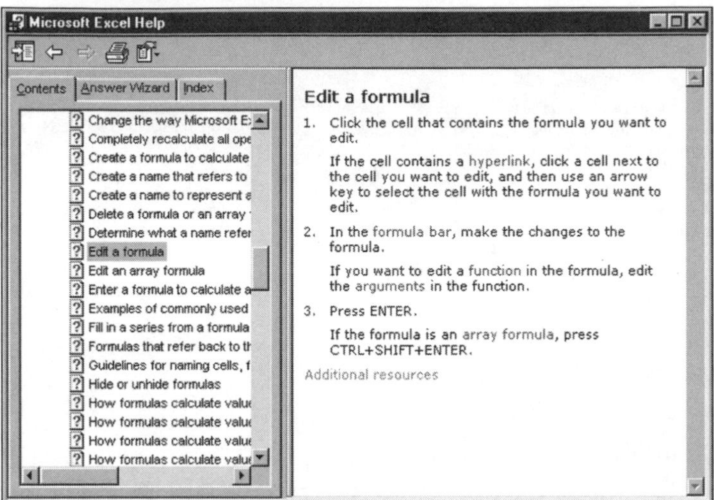

Figure 23-7: An example of HTML Help

HTML Help is displayed in a browser window, and the table of contents, index, and search tools are displayed in a separate pane. In addition, the help text can contain standard hyperlinks that display another topic or even a document on the Internet.

Like WinHelp, you need a special compiler to create an HTML Help system. The HTML Help Workshop is available free from Microsoft's Web site at this address:

```
http://www.microsoft.com/workshop/author/htmlhelp
```

The companion CD-ROM contains an example of a simple HTML Help system, along with the files used to create it.

Associating a Help File with Your Application

If you use one of the "official" Help file systems (that is, WinHelp or HTML Help), you can associate a particular Help file with your application in one of two ways: by using the Project Properties dialog box or by writing VBA code.

In the VB Editor, select Tools→*xxx* Properties (where *xxx* corresponds to your project's name). In the Project Properties dialog box, click the General tab, and specify a Help file for the project — either an HLP file or a CHM file.

It's a good practice to keep your application's Help file in the same directory as the application. The following instruction sets up an association to Myfuncs.hlp, which is assumed to be in the same directory as the workbook.

```
ThisWorkbook.VBProject.HelpFile = _
  ThisWorkbook.Path & "\Myfuncs.hlp"
```

After a Help file is associated with your application, you can call up a particular Help topic in the following situations:

- ✦ When the user presses F1 while a custom worksheet function is selected in the Paste Function dialog box.
- ✦ When the user presses F1 while a UserForm is displayed. The Help topic associated with the control that has the focus is displayed.

Associating a help topic with a VBA function

If you create custom worksheet functions using VBA, you may want to associate a Help file and context ID with each function. Once these items are assigned to a function, the Help topic can be displayed from the Paste Function dialog box by pressing F1.

To specify a context ID for a custom worksheet function, follow these steps:

1. Create the function as usual.
2. Make sure that your project has an associated Help file (refer to the preceding section).
3. In the VB Editor, press F2 to activate the Object Browser.
4. Select your project from the Project/Library drop-down list.
5. In the Classes window, select the module that contains your function.
6. In the Members of window, select the function.
7. Right-click the function, and select Properties from the shortcut menu. This displays the Member Options dialog box, as shown in Figure 23-8.

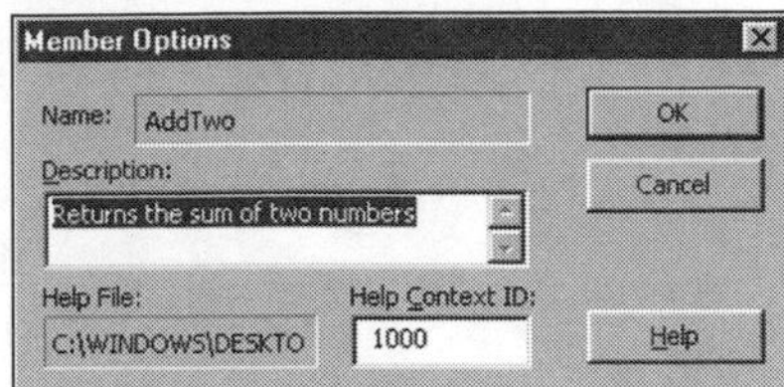

Figure 23-8: Specify a context ID for a custom function in the Member Options dialog box.

8. Enter the context ID of the Help topic for the function. You can also enter a description of the function.

The Member Options dialog box does not let you specify the Help file. It always uses the Help file associated with the project.

You may prefer to write VBA code that sets up the context ID and Help file for your custom functions. You can do this using the `MacroOptions` method. The following procedure uses the `MacroOptions` method to specify a description, Help file, and context ID for two custom functions (`AddTwo` and `Squared`).

```
Sub SetOptions()
'   Set options for the AddTwo function
    Application.MacroOptions Macro:="AddTwo", _
        Description:="Returns the sum of two numbers", _
        HelpFile:=ThisWorkbook.Path & "\Myfuncs.hlp", _
        HelpContextID:=1000

'   Set options for the Squared function
    Application.MacroOptions Macro:="Squared", _
        Description:="Returns the square of an argument", _
        HelpFile:=ThisWorkbook.Path & "\Myfuncs.hlp", _
        HelpContextID:=2000
End Sub
```

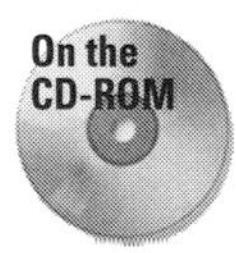

A workbook on the companion CD-ROM demonstrates this technique.

Displaying Help from a custom dialog box

Each control on a UserForm — as well as the UserForm itself — can have a Help topic associated with it. The Help file for the topic is the file associated with the project. The type of help provided is determined by the value of the following two UserForm properties:

✦ `WhatsThisButton`. If True, the UserForm displays a small question mark button in its title bar, like the one in Figure 23-9. The user can click this button and then click a UserForm control to get help regarding the control.

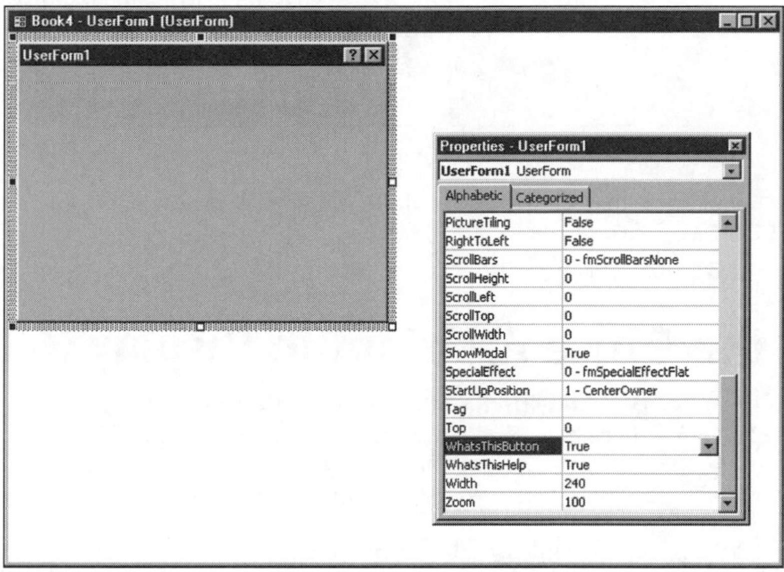

Figure 23-9: A WhatsThisButton setting of True brings up a small question mark button.

✦ `WhatsThisHelp`. If True, the help provided for each control is in the form of a small pop-up window that displays the Help topic's title only.

The `WhatsThisHelp` property must be True for the `WhatsThisButton` property to be True. In other words, only three combinations of values for `WhatsThisHelp` and `WhatsThisButton` are possible. Table 23-1 summarizes the effects of various settings.

Table 23-1
Settings for WhatsThisHelp and WhatsThisButton Properties

WhatsThisHelp	*WhatsThisButton*	*Result*
True	True	Question mark button is displayed; F1 gives pop-up help.
True	False	No question mark button is displayed; F1 gives pop-up help.
False	False	No question mark button is displayed; F1 gives full help.

A workbook that demonstrates these settings is available on the companion CD-ROM.

Using the Office Assistant to Display Help

You're probably familiar with the Office Assistant — the cutesy screen character that's always ready to help out. In my experience, people either love or hate this feature (you can count me among the latter group). The Office Assistant is quite programmable, and you can even use it to display help for the user.

Figure 23-10 shows the Office Assistant displaying some help text.

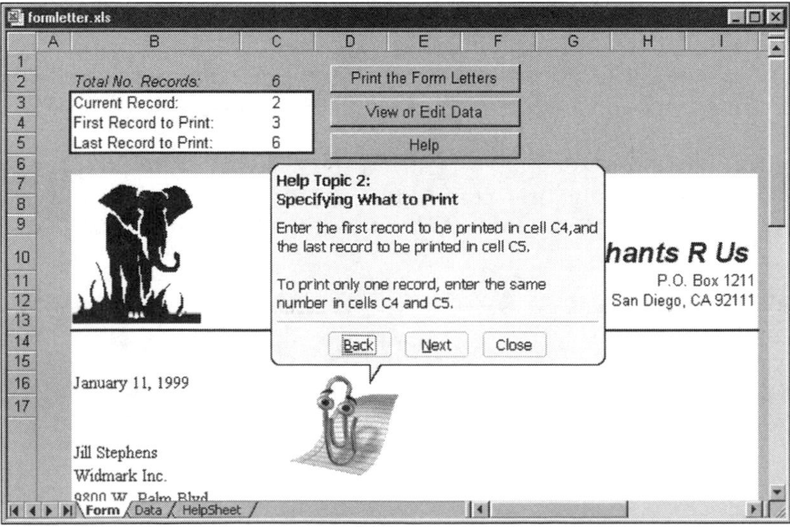

Figure 23-10: Using the Office Assistant to deliver custom help.

The main procedure for using the Office Assistant to display help is shown in Listing 23-3. The help text is stored in two columns on a worksheet named `HelpSheet`. Column A contains the topics, and column B contains the help text.

Listing 23-3: Calling up the Office Assistant to display custom help

```
Public Const APPNAME As String = "Elephants R Us"
Dim Topic As Integer
Dim HelpSheet As Worksheet

Sub ShowHelp()
    Set HelpSheet = ThisWorkbook.Worksheets("HelpSheet")
    Application.Assistant.On = True
    Topic = 1
    With Assistant.NewBalloon
        .Heading = "Help Topic " & Topic & ": " & _
            vbCrLf & HelpSheet.Cells(Topic, 1)
        .Text = HelpSheet.Cells(Topic, 2)
        .Button = msoButtonSetNextClose
        .BalloonType = msoBalloonTypeButtons
        .Mode = msoModeModeless
        .Callback = "ProcessRequest"
        .Show
    End With
End Sub
```

The procedure begins by making sure the Office Assistant is turned on. Then, it creates a new `Balloon` object (you'll recall that the Office Assistant's help text is displayed in a balloon) and uses the first help topic in the `HelpSheet` worksheet to set the `Heading` and `Text` properties. It sets the `Button` property so it displays Next and Close buttons like a wizard. The procedure then sets the `Mode` property to `msoModeModeless` so the user can continue working while the help is displayed. The `Callback` property contains the procedure name that is executed when a button is clicked. Finally, the `Assistant` balloon is displayed using the `Show` method.

The `ProcessRequest` procedure, shown in Listing 23-4, is called when any of the buttons is clicked.

Listing 23-4: Engaging the customized help through the Office Assistant

```
Sub ProcessRequest(bln As Balloon, lbtn As Long, lPriv _
 As Long)
    NumTopics = _
      WorksheetFunction.CountA(HelpSheet.Range("A:A"))
    Assistant.Animation = msoAnimationCharacterSuccessMajor
    Select Case lbtn
        Case msoBalloonButtonBack
            If Topic <> 1 Then Topic = Topic - 1
        Case msoBalloonButtonNext
            If Topic <> NumTopics Then Topic = Topic + 1
        Case msoBalloonButtonClose
            bln.Close
            Exit Sub
    End Select
    With bln
        .Close
        Select Case Topic
            Case 1
                .Button = msoButtonSetNextClose
            Case NumTopics
                .Button = msoButtonSetBackClose
            Case Else
                .Button = msoButtonSetBackNextClose
        End Select
        .Heading = "Help Topic " & Topic & ": " & _
            vbCrLf & HelpSheet.Cells(Topic, 1)
        .Text = HelpSheet.Cells(Topic, 2)
        .Show
    End With
End Sub
```

The `ProcessRequest` procedure displays one of several animations and then uses a `Select Case` construct to take action depending on which button was clicked. The button clicked is passed to this procedure through the `lbtn` variable. The procedure also specifies which buttons to display based on the current topic.

If you have an interest in programming the Assistant, I refer you to the online help for the details.

This example is available on the companion CD-ROM.

Other Ways of Displaying WinHelp or HTML Help

VBA provides several different ways to display specific help topics. I describe these in the following sections.

Using the Help method

Use the `Help` method of the `Application` object to display a Help file — either a WinHelp HLP file or an HTML Help CHM file. This method works even if the Help file doesn't have any context IDs defined.

The syntax for the `Help` method is as follows:

```
Application.Help(helpFile, helpContextID)
```

Both arguments are optional. If the name of the Help file is omitted, Excel's Help file is displayed. If the context ID argument is omitted, the specified Help file is displayed with the default topic.

The following example displays the default topic of Myapp.hlp, which is assumed to be in the same directory as the workbook that it's called from. Note that the second argument is omitted.

```
Sub ShowHelpContents()
    Application.Help ThisWorkbook.Path & "\Myapp.hlp"
End Sub
```

The following instruction displays the help topic with a context ID of 1002 from an HTML Help file named Myapp.chm.

```
Application.Help ThisWorkbook.Path & "\Myapp.chm", 1002
```

Displaying Help from a message box

When you use VBA's `MsgBox` function to display a message box, you include a Help button by providing the `vbMsgBoxHelpButton` constant as the function's second argument. You'll also need to include the Help file name as its fourth argument. The context ID (optional) is its fifth argument. The following code, for example, generates the message box shown in Figure 23-11.

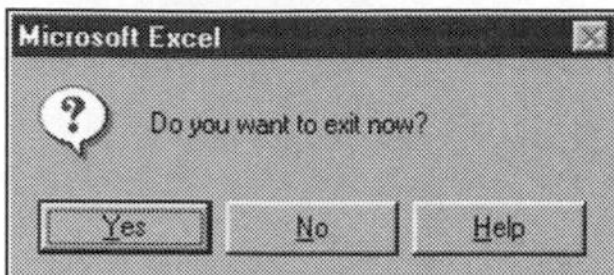

Figure 23-11: A message box with a Help button.

```
Sub MsgBoxHelp()
    Msg = "Do you want to exit now?"
    Buttons = vbQuestion + vbYesNo + vbMsgBoxHelpButton
    He
lpFile = ThisWorkbook.Path & "\AppHelp.hlp"
    ContextID = 1002
    Ans = MsgBox(Msg, Buttons, , HelpFile, ContextID)
    If Ans = vbYes Then Call CloseDown
End Sub
```

Displaying Help from an input box

VBA's `InputBox` function can also display a Help button if its sixth argument contains the Help file name. The following example produces the `InputBox` shown in Figure 23-12.

Figure 23-12: An InputBox with a Help button.

```
Sub ShowInputBox()
    Msg = "Enter a value"
    DefaultVal = 0
    HelpFile = ThisWorkbook.Path & "\AppHelp.hlp"
    ContextID = 1002
    x = InputBox(Msg, , DefaultVal, , , HelpFile, ContextID)
End Sub
```

Summary

In this chapter, I presented several alternative methods of providing online help for end users, including "official" help systems (WinHelp or HTML Help) and "unofficial" help systems that use Excel-specific techniques to display help.

The next chapter wraps up Part VI by providing an example of a user-oriented application.

✦ ✦ ✦

Developing User-Oriented Applications

In This Chapter

A description of a user-oriented application

A close look at the Loan Amortization Wizard, which generates a worksheet with an amortization schedule for a fixed-rate loan

A demonstration of application development concepts and techniques by the Loan Amortization Wizard

An application development checklist

In this chapter, I attempt to pull together some of the information presented in the previous chapters. This discussion centers around a user-oriented application called Loan Amortization Wizard. Useful in its own right, this workbook demonstrates quite a few important application development techniques.

What Is a User-Oriented Application?

I use the term *user-oriented application* for an Excel application that can be used by someone with minimal training. These applications produce useful results even for users who know virtually nothing about Excel.

The Loan Amortization Wizard discussed in this chapter qualifies as a user-oriented application because it's designed in such a way that the end user doesn't need to know the intimate details of Excel to use it. Replying to a few simple prompts produces a useful and flexible worksheet complete with formulas.

The Loan Amortization Wizard

The Loan Amortization Wizard generates a worksheet that contains an amortization schedule for a fixed-rate loan. An amortization schedule projects month-by-month details for a loan. The details include the monthly payment amount, the amount of the payment that goes toward interest, the amount that goes toward reducing the principal, and the new loan balance.

Figure 24-1 shows an amortization schedule generated by the Loan Amortization Wizard.

Book1

	A	B	C	D	E	F	G
1	**Amortization Schedule**						
2	**Prepared by Shirley Miller**						
3	*Generated Wednesday, April 7, 1999*						
4							
5	Purchase Price:		$249,000.00				
6	Down Pmt Pct:		20.00%				
7	Down Pmt:		$49,800.00				
8	Loan Amount:		$199,200.00				
9	Term (Months):		360				
10	Interest Rate:		8.25%				
11	First Payment:		06/01/99				
12							
13	**Pmt No.**	**Year**	**Month**	**Payment**	**Interest**	**Principal**	**Balance**
14	1	1999	6	$1,496.52	$1,369.50	$127.02	$199,072.98
15	2	1999	7	$1,496.52	$1,368.63	$127.90	$198,945.08
16	3	1999	8	$1,496.52	$1,367.75	$128.78	$198,816.30
17	4	1999	9	$1,496.52	$1,366.86	$129.66	$198,686.64
18	5	1999	10	$1,496.52	$1,365.97	$130.55	$198,556.09
19	6	1999	11	$1,496.52	$1,365.07	$131.45	$198,424.64
20	7	1999	12	$1,496.52	$1,364.17	$132.35	$198,292.29
21	***1999 Total***			***$10,475.66***	***$9,567.95***	***$907.71***	***$198,292.29***
22	8	2000	1	$1,496.52	$1,363.26	$133.26	$198,159.02
23	9	2000	2	$1,496.52	$1,362.34	$134.18	$198,024.84
24	10	2000	3	$1,496.52	$1,361.42	$135.10	$197,889.74
25	11	2000	4	$1,496.52	$1,360.49	$136.03	$197,753.71
26	12	2000	5	$1,496.52	$1,359.56	$136.97	$197,616.74
27	13	2000	6	$1,496.52	$1,358.62	$137.91	$197,478.84
28	14	2000	7	$1,496.52	$1,357.67	$138.86	$197,339.98
29	15	2000	8	$1,496.52	$1,356.71	$139.81	$197,200.17
30	16	2000	9	$1,496.52	$1,355.75	$140.77	$197,059.40

Sheet1

Figure 24-1: This amortization schedule shows details for a 30-year mortgage loan.

The Loan Amortization Wizard is available on the CD-ROM that accompanies this book. It's an unprotected add-in.

Using the application

The Loan Amortization Wizard consists of a five-step dialog box sequence that collects information from the user. Typical of a wizard, this enables the user to go forward and backward through the steps. Clicking the Finish button creates the new worksheet.

This application uses a single UserForm with a MultiPage control to display the five steps, shown in Figures 24-2 through 24-6.

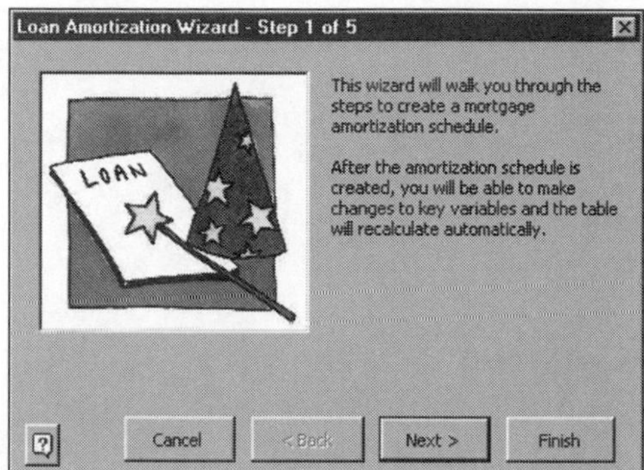

Figure 24-2: Step 1 of the Loan Amortization Wizard.

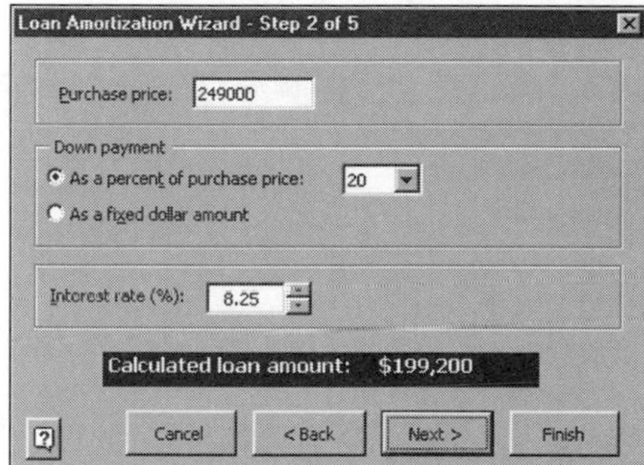

Figure 24-3: Step 2 of the Loan Amortization Wizard.

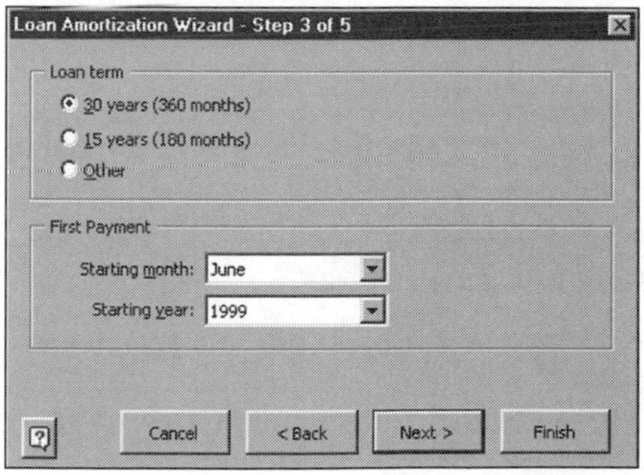

Figure 24-4: Step 3 of the Loan Amortization Wizard.

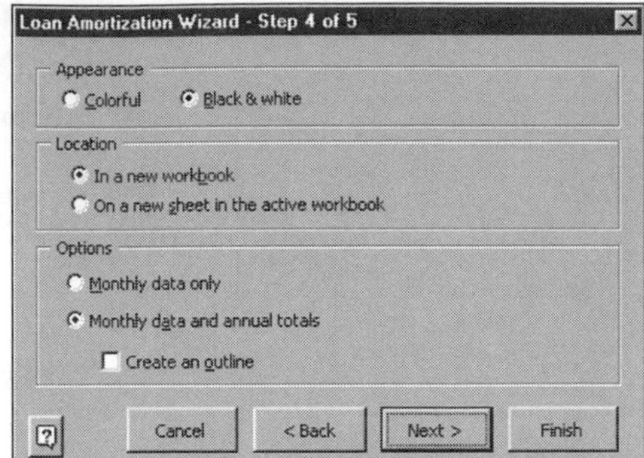

Figure 24-5: Step 4 of the Loan Amortization Wizard.

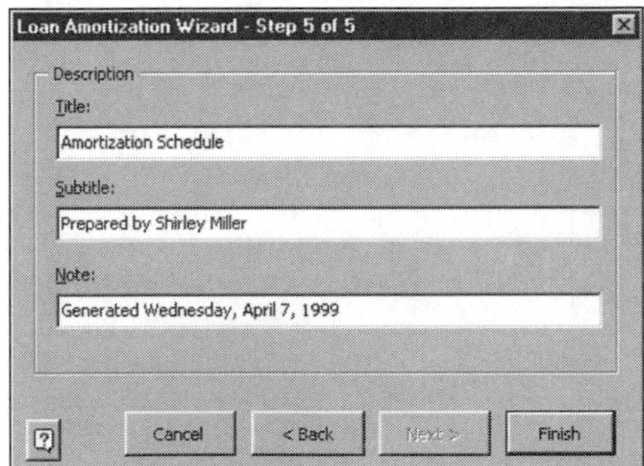

Figure 24-6: Step 5 of the Loan Amortization Wizard.

The workbook structure

The Loan Amortization Wizard consists of the following components:

`FormMain` A UserForm that serves as the primary user interface.

`FormHelp` A UserForm that displays online help.

`HelpSheet` A worksheet that contains the text used in the online help.

`ModMain` A VBA module that contains a procedure that displays the main UserForm.

`ThisWorkbook` The code module for this object contains event-handler procedures `Workbook_Open` and `Workbook_BeforeClose`, which create and delete a menu item, respectively.

Creating the Loan Amortization Wizard

The Loan Amortization Wizard application started out as a simple concept and evolved into a relatively complex project. My primary goal was to demonstrate as many development concepts as possible and still have a useful end product. I would like to say that I clearly envisioned the end result before I began developing the application, but I'd be lying.

My basic idea was much less ambitious. I simply wanted to create an application that gathered user input and created a worksheet. But after I got started, I began thinking of ways to enhance my simple program. I eventually stumbled down several blind alleys. Some folk may consider my wanderings time-wasting, but those false starts became a vital part of the development process.

I completed the entire project in one (long) day, and I spent a few more hours fine-tuning and testing it.

How it works

The Loan Amortization Wizard is an add-in, so it should be installed using the Tools➪Add-Ins command. It works equally well, however, if it's opened with the File➪Open command.

Adding the menu item

When the workbook is opened, the `Workbook_Open` procedure adds a new Loan Amortization Wizard menu item to the Tools menu. Clicking this menu item executes the `StartAmortizationWizard` procedure, which simply displays the `FormMain` UserForm.

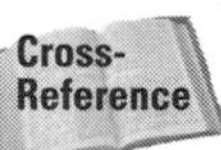

Refer to Chapter 22 for information about creating new menu items.

Initializing FormMain

The `UserForm_Initialize` procedure for `FormMain` does quite a bit of work:

- ✦ It sets the MultiPage control's `Value` property to 0. This ensures that it displays the first page, regardless of its value when the workbook was last saved.
- ✦ It adds items to three ComboBox controls used on the form.
- ✦ It calls the `GetDefaults` procedure, which retrieves the most recently used setting from the Windows Registry (see "Saving and retrieving default settings" later in this section).

✦ It checks to see whether a workbook is active. If not, the code disables the OptionButton that enables the user to create the new worksheet in the active workbook.

✦ If a workbook is active, an additional check determines whether the workbook's structure is protected. If so, the procedure disables the OptionButton that enables the user to create the worksheet in the active workbook.

Processing events while the UserForm is displayed

The code module for the `FormMain` UserForm contains several event-handler procedures that respond to the `Click` and `Change` events for the controls on the UserForm.

Clicking the Back and Next buttons determines which page of the MultiPage control is displayed. The `MultiPage1_Change` procedure adjusts the UserForm's caption and enables and disables the Back and Next buttons as appropriate. See Chapter 14 for more information about programming a wizard.

Displaying help

You have several options when it comes to displaying online help. I chose a simple technique that employs the UserForm shown in Figure 24-7 to display text stored in a worksheet. You'll notice that this help is context sensitive. When the user clicks the Help button, the help topic displayed is relevant to the current page of the MultiPage control.

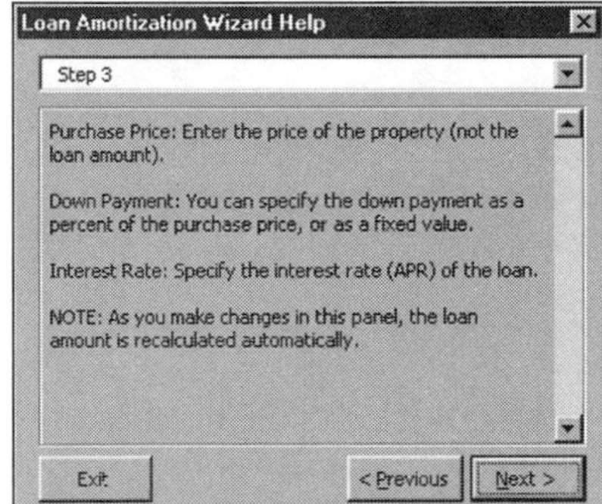

Figure 24-7: User help is presented in a UserForm that copies text stored in a worksheet.

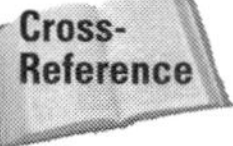

For more information about the technique of lifting worksheet text into a dialog box, consult Chapter 23.

Creating the new worksheet

Clicking the Finish button kicks off all the excitement. The `Click` event-handler procedure for this button performs the following actions:

- ✦ It calls a function named `DataIsValid`, which checks the user's input to ensure that it's valid. If all the entries are valid, the function returns True, and the procedure continues. If an invalid entry is encountered, `DataIsValid` sets the focus to the control that needs to be corrected and returns a descriptive error message (see Figure 24-8).

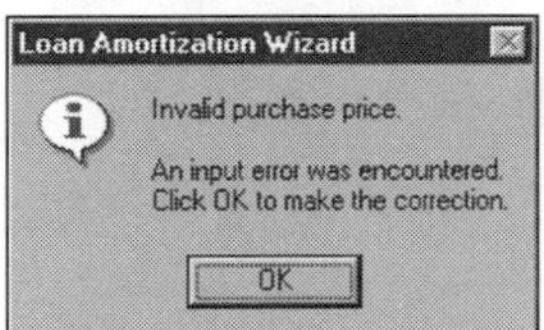

Figure 24-8: If an invalid entry is made, the focus is set back to the control that contains the error.

- ✦ If the user's responses are valid, the procedure creates a new worksheet either in the active workbook or in a new workbook, per the user's request.
- ✦ The loan parameters (purchase price, down payment information, loan amount, term, and interest rate) are written to the worksheet. This requires the use of some `If` statements because the down payment can be expressed as a percentage of the purchase price or as a fixed amount.
- ✦ The column headers are written to the worksheet.
- ✦ The first row of formulas is written below the column headers. The first row is different from the remaining rows because its formulas refer to data in the loan parameters section. The other formulas all refer to the previous row. Notice that I use named ranges in the formulas. In addition, for unnamed references I use R1C1 notation, which is much easier than trying to determine actual cell addresses!
- ✦ The second row of formulas is written to the worksheet and then copied down one row for each month.
- ✦ If the user requested annual totals as opposed to simply monthly data, the procedure uses the `Subtotal` method to create subtotals. This, by the way, is an example of how using a native feature in Excel can save *lots* of coding!
- ✦ Because subtotaling the Balance column isn't appropriate, the procedure replaces formulas in the balance column with a formula that returns the year-end balance.

✦ When Excel adds subtotals, it also creates an outline. If the user didn't request an outline, the procedure uses the `ClearOutline` method to remove it. If an outline was requested, the procedure hides the outline symbols.

✦ If the sheet contains an outline, the procedure adds a CheckBox control captioned "*Hide monthly detail*" and also creates an event-handler procedure that executes when the CheckBox is clicked. This procedure, which is stored in the `Worksheet` object's code module, determines whether the outline is collapsed to hide monthly detail or expanded to show everything. Figure 24-9 shows how the worksheet looks when the outline is collapsed to hide the detail.

Book2

Amortization Schedule

Prepared by Shirley Miller

Generated Wednesday, April 7, 1999

☑ Hide monthly detail

Purchase Price:	$302,000.00
Down Payment:	28500
Loan Amount:	$273,500.00
Term (Months):	360
Interest Rate:	8.10%
First Payment:	07/01/99

Pmt No.	Year	Month	Payment	Interest	Principal	Balance
1999 Total			$12,155.67	$11,058.38	$1,097.29	$272,402.71
2000 Total			$24,311.34	$21,979.30	$2,332.03	$270,070.67
2001 Total			$24,311.34	$21,783.24	$2,528.10	$267,542.57
2002 Total			$24,311.34	$21,570.68	$2,740.65	$264,801.92
2003 Total			$24,311.34	$21,340.26	$2,971.08	$261,830.84
2004 Total			$24,311.34	$21,090.47	$3,220.87	$258,609.96
2005 Total			$24,311.34	$20,819.67	$3,491.67	$255,118.29
2006 Total			$24,311.34	$20,526.10	$3,785.24	$251,333.06
2007 Total			$24,311.34	$20,207.86	$4,103.48	$247,229.57
2008 Total			$24,311.34	$19,862.85	$4,448.49	$242,781.09
2009 Total			$24,311.34	$19,488.84	$4,822.50	$237,958.59
2010 Total			$24,311.34	$19,083.39	$5,227.95	$232,730.64
2011 Total			$24,311.34	$18,643.84	$5,667.50	$227,063.14
2012 Total			$24,311.34	$18,167.34	$6,144.00	$220,919.14
2013 Total			$24,311.34	$17,650.78	$6,660.56	$214,258.59
2014 Total			$24,311.34	$17,090.79	$7,220.55	$207,038.04
2015 Total			$24,311.34	$16,483.72	$7,827.62	$199,210.41

Sheet1

Figure 24-9: The check box denotes whether the sheet contains summary information or detail.

✦ Next, the procedure applies formatting to the cells: number formatting, plus an AutoFormat if the user requested color output.

✦ The procedure then adjusts the column widths, freezes the titles just below the header row, and protects the formulas and a few other key cells that can't be changed. The sheet is protected, but not with a password.

✦ Finally, the SaveDefaults procedure writes the current values of the UserForm's controls to the Registry. These values will be the new default settings the next time the user creates an amortization schedule.

Saving and retrieving default settings

If you run this application, you'll notice that the FormMain UserForm always displays the setting that you most recently used. In other words, it "remembers" your last choices and uses them as the new default values. This is accomplished by storing the values in the Windows Registry and then retrieving them when the UserForm is initialized. When the application is used for the first time, the Registry doesn't have any values, so it uses the default values stored in the UserForm controls.

The following GetDefaults procedure loops through each control on the UserForm. If the control is a TextBox, ComboBox, OptionButton, CheckBox, or SpinButton, it calls VBA's GetSetting function and reads the value to the Registry. Note that the third argument for GetSetting is the value to use if the setting is not found. In this case, it uses the value of the control specified at design time. APPNAME is a global constant that contains the name of the application.

```
Sub GetDefaults()
'   Reads default settings from the registry
    Dim ctl As Control
    Dim CtrlType As String

    For Each ctl In Me.Controls
        CtrlType = TypeName(ctl)
        If CtrlType = "TextBox" Or _
           CtrlType = "ComboBox" Or _
           CtrlType = "OptionButton" Or _
           CtrlType = "CheckBox" Or _
           CtrlType = "SpinButton" Then
           ctl.Value = GetSetting _
             (APPNAME, "Defaults", ctl.Name, ctl.Value)
        End If
    Next ctl
End Sub
```

Figure 24-10 shows how these values appear in the Registry, from the perspective of the Windows Registry Editor program.

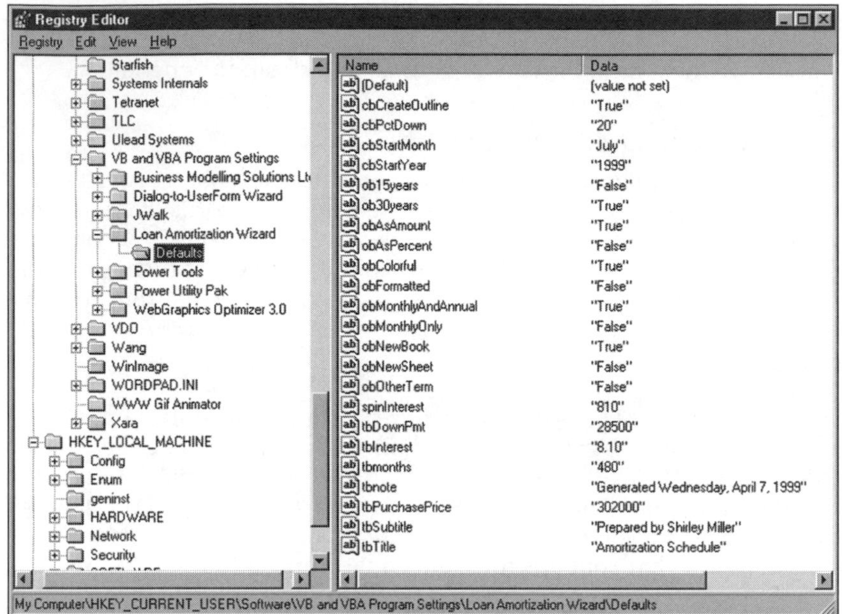

Figure 24-10: The Windows Registry stores the default values for the wizard.

The following `SaveDefaults` procedure is similar. It uses VBA's `SaveSetting` statement to write the current values to the Registry.

```
Sub SaveDefaults()
'   Writes current settings to the registry
    Dim ctl As Control
    Dim CtrlType As String

    For Each ctl In Me.Controls
        CtrlType = TypeName(ctl)
        If CtrlType = "TextBox" Or _
           CtrlType = "ComboBox" Or _
           CtrlType = "OptionButton" Or _
           CtrlType = "CheckBox" Or _
           CtrlType = "SpinButton" Then
           SaveSetting APPNAME, _
              "Defaults", ctl.Name, ctl.Value
        End If
    Next ctl
End Sub
```

The `SaveSetting` statement and the `GetSetting` function always use the following Registry key:

```
HKEY_CURRENT_USER\Software\VB and VBA Program Settings\
```

Potential enhancements

It's been said that you never finish writing an application—you just stop working on it. Without even thinking too much about it, I can come up with several enhancements for the Loan Amortization Wizard:

✦ Add an option to display cumulative totals for interest and principal.

✦ Add an option to work with adjustable rate loans and make projections based on certain interest rate scenarios.

✦ Add more formatting options (for example, no decimal places, no dollar signs, and so on).

✦ Add options to enable the user to specify page headers or footers.

Application Development Concepts

It's often difficult to follow the logic in an application developed by someone other than yourself. To help you understand my work, I included lots of comments in the code and described the general program flow in the preceding sections. But if you really want to understand this application, I suggest that you use the Debugger to step through the code.

At the very least, the Loan Amortization Wizard demonstrates some useful techniques and concepts that are important for Excel developers:

✦ Creating a custom menu item that's displayed only when a particular workbook (or add-in) is open

✦ Using a wizardlike UserForm to gather information

✦ Setting the Enabled property of a control dynamically

✦ Linking a TextBox and a SpinButton control

✦ Displaying online help to a user

✦ Naming cells with VBA

✦ Writing and copying formulas with VBA

✦ Creating an ActiveX control (CheckBox) and an event-handler procedure at run time

✦ Reading from and writing to the Windows Registry

Some Final Words

Developing user-oriented applications in Excel is not easy. You must be keenly aware of how people will use (and abuse) the application in real life. Although I tried to make this application completely bulletproof, I did not do extensive testing, so I wouldn't be surprised if it fails under some conditions.

Application Development Checklist

When developing user-oriented applications, you need to keep in mind many things. Let the following checklist serve as a reminder.

- *Did you clean up after yourself?* Make sure that you restore toolbars and menus to their original state when the application ends.
- *Do the dialog boxes all work from the keyboard?* Don't forget to add hot keys and check the tab order carefully.
- *Did you make any assumptions about directories?* If your application reads or writes files, you can't assume that a particular directory exists or that it's the current directory.
- *Did you make provisions for canceling all dialog boxes?* You can't assume that the user will end a dialog box by clicking the OK button.
- *Did you assume that no other worksheets are open?* If your application is the only workbook open during testing, you may overlook something that happens when other workbooks are open.
- *Did you assume that a workbook was visible?* It's possible, of course, to use Excel with no workbooks visible.
- *Did you attempt to optimize the speed of your application?* For example, you often can speed up your application by declaring variable types and defining object variables.
- *Are your procedures adequately documented?* Will you understand your code if you revisit it in six months?
- *Did you include appropriate end-user documentation?* Doing so often eliminates (or at least reduces) the number of follow-up questions.
- *Did you allow time to revise your application?* Chances are, the application won't be perfect the first time out. Build in some time to fix it.

Summary

In this chapter, I described a relatively complex user-oriented application that creates a worksheet based on user-specified options.

This chapter concludes Part VI. Chapters in the next part cover a variety of topics that you may find helpful, including compatibility issues, manipulating text files with VBA, modifying VBA components, and class modules.

✦ ✦ ✦

PART

VII

Other Topics

The five chapters in this part cover additional topics that you may find helpful. Chapter 25 presents information regarding compatibility. In Chapter 26, I discuss various ways to use VBA to work with files. In Chapter 27, I explain how to use VBA to manipulate Visual Basic components such as UserForms and modules. Chapter 28 covers the topic of class modules. I finish the part with a useful chapter that answers many common questions about Excel programming.

✦ ✦ ✦ ✦

In This Part

✦ ✦ ✦ ✦

CHAPTER 25

Compatibility Issues

In This Chapter

How to make sure your Excel 2000 applications work with previous versions of Excel

Issues to be aware of if you're developing Excel applications for international use

Applications that you develop using Excel 2000 will probably be used only by others who also use Excel 2000. In such a case, you can skip this chapter. But if your application also needs to run on earlier versions of Excel, Excel for Macintosh, or international versions of Excel, you should be aware of some compatibility issues. These issues are the topic of this chapter.

What Is Compatibility?

Compatibility is an often-used term among computer people. In general, it refers to how well software performs under various conditions. These conditions may be defined in terms of hardware, software, or a combination of the two. For example, software that is written specifically for a 32-bit operating system such as Windows 9*x* or Windows NT does not run under the earlier 16-bit versions of Windows 3.*x*. In other words, 32-bit applications are not compatible with Windows 3.*x*. And, as I'm sure you realize, binary applications and executable files written for Windows do not run on other operating systems, such as the Macintosh.

In this chapter, I discuss a more specific compatibility issue involving how your Excel 2000 applications work with earlier versions of Excel for Windows and Excel for Macintosh. The fact that two versions of Excel may use the same file format isn't always enough to ensure complete compatibility between the contents of their files. For example, Excel 97, Excel 2000, and Excel 98 for Macintosh all use the same file format . . . but compatibility issues are rampant. Just because a particular version of Excel can open a worksheet file or an add-in doesn't guarantee that that version of Excel can carry out the VBA macro instructions contained in it.

The compatibility problem is more serious than you may think. You can run into compatibility problems even within the same major version of Excel. For example, Excel 97 exists in at least three different subversions: the original release, SR-1, and SR-2. These later releases fixed some bugs and also introduced a few subtle changes. Therefore, there is no guarantee that an application developed using the original release of Excel 97 performs flawlessly with Excel 97 SR-1 or SR-2.

The point here is that Excel is a moving target and there is really no way that you can guarantee complete compatibility. Unfortunately, cross-version compatibility doesn't happen automatically. In most cases, you need to do quite a bit of additional work to achieve compatibility.

Types of Compatibility Problems

You need to be aware of five categories of potential compatibility problems:

✦ *File format issues.* Workbooks can be saved in several different Excel file formats. Excel may not be able to open workbooks that were saved in a later version file format.

✦ *New feature issues.* It should be obvious that a feature introduced in a particular version of Excel cannot be used in previous versions of Excel.

✦ *32-bit versus 16-bit issues.* If you use Windows API calls, you need to pay attention to this issue if your application must work with a 16-bit version of Excel (such as Excel 5.0).

✦ *Windows versus Macintosh issues.* If your application must work on both platforms, plan to spend lots of time ironing out various compatibility problems.

✦ *International issues.* If your application will be used by those who speak another language, you must address a number of additional issues.

These categories are discussed further in the following sections of this chapter.

After you read this chapter, it should be clear to you that there is only one way to ensure compatibility: You must test your application on every target platform and with every target version of Excel. However, there are measures that you, as a developer, can take to help ensure that your application works with different versions of Excel.

If you're reading this chapter in search of a complete list of specific compatibility issues among the various versions of Excel, you will be disappointed. I frequently see newsgroup postings from people asking where the "master list" of Excel 95/97 differences is stored. As far as I know, no such list exists, and it would be virtually impossible to compile one. Compatibility issues are far too numerous and complex and in many cases, they are extremely subtle.

Excel File Formats Supported

As you probably know, Excel enables you to save a workbook in a format for earlier versions. In addition, you can save a workbook in a *dual version* format that combines two file formats in a single file. These dual version formats result in larger files.

If your application must work with earlier versions of Excel, you need to make sure your file is saved in the appropriate file format. The various Excel file formats that can be saved by Excel 2000 are as follows:

✦ *Microsoft Excel 5.0/95 Workbook* is a dual format that can be opened by Excel 5.0 and later versions.

✦ *Microsoft Excel 97–2000 & 5.0/95 Workbook* is a dual format that can be opened by Excel 5.0 and later versions.

✦ *Microsoft Excel 4.0 Worksheet (*.xls)* can be opened by Excel 4.0 and later versions.

✦ *Microsoft Excel 3.0 Worksheet (*.xls)* can be opened by Excel 3.0 and later versions. This format saves a single sheet only.

✦ *Microsoft Excel 2.1 Worksheet (*.xls)* can be opened by Excel 2.1 and later versions. This format saves a single sheet only.

✦ *Microsoft Excel 4.0 Workbook (*.xlw)* can be opened by Excel 4.0 and later versions. This format saves multisheet workbooks.

You can use VBA to access the `FileFormat` property of the `Workbook` object to determine the file format for a particular workbook. The following instruction, for example, displays a value that represents the file format for the active workbook:

```
MsgBox ActiveWorkbook.FileFormat
```

Predefined constants are available for the `FileFormat` property. For example, the following statement displays True if the active workbook is an Excel 5.0/95 file:

```
MsgBox ActiveWorkbook.FileFormat = xlExcel5
```

Table 25-1 lists the constants and values for various Excel file formats.

Table 25-1
Constants and Values for Various Excel File Formats

Excel Version	*Constant*	*Value*
Excel 2.1	`xlExcel2`	16
Excel 3.0	`xlExcel3`	29
Excel 4.0	`xlExcel4`	33
Excel 5.0	`xlExcel5`	39
Excel 95	`xlExcel7`	43
Excel 97/2000	`xlWorkbookNormal`	–4143

Avoid Using New Features

If your application must work with Excel 2000 and earlier versions, you need to avoid any features that were added after the earliest Excel version that you support. Another alternative is to incorporate the new features selectively. In other words, your code can determine which version of Excel is being used, and either take advantage of the new features or not.

VBA programmers must be careful not to use any objects, properties, or methods that aren't available in earlier versions. In general, the safest approach is to develop your application with the lowest common denominator in mind. For compatibility with Excel 95, Excel 97, and Excel 2000, you should use Excel 95 for development, and then test thoroughly using the other versions.

The online help system describes all new elements in Excel 2000's object model. To locate these help topics, access the Answer Wizard in the VB Editor and search for *new objects, new properties,* or *new methods.* Figure 25-1 shows an example.

If your application must support Excel 95, you can't use any UserForms, which were introduced in Excel 97. Rather, you need to use dialog sheets.

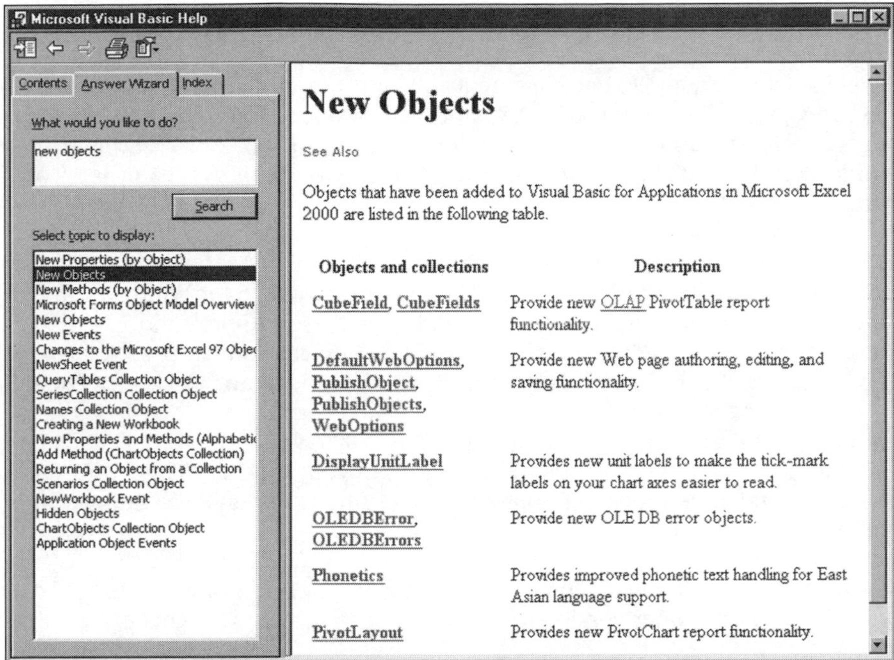

Figure 25-1: Excel 2000's online help lists new objects, properties, and methods.

Determining Excel's Version Number

The `Version` property of the `Application` object returns the version of Excel. The returned value is a string, so you may need to covert it to a value. VBA's `Val` function is perfect for this. The following function, for example, returns True if the user is running Excel 2000 or later (Excel 2000 is version 9).

```
Function XL2KOrLater()
    If Val(Application.Version) >= 9 Then
        XL2KOrLater = True
    Else
        XL2KOrLater = False
    End If
End Function
```

Applications That Use Windows API Calls

Excel 95, Excel 97, and Excel 2000 are all 32-bit programs. Excel 5.0, however, is a 16-bit program. This "bitness" determines which operating system Excel can run under. Excel 5.0 can run on 16-bit Windows 3.*x*, as well as 32-bit Windows 9*x* and Windows NT. The 32-bit versions of Excel run only on Windows 95 or later or Windows NT.

This becomes important when your VBA code uses API function calls, because 32-bit Windows API functions are declared differently than 16-bit Windows API functions. Therefore, an Excel 5.0 application that uses 16-bit Windows API functions does not work with Excel 95 or later. Similarly, an Excel 95 (or later) application that uses 32-bit Windows API functions does not work with Excel 5.0.

For compatibility with Excel 5.0 through Excel 2000, you need to declare both the 16-bit and 32-bit versions of the API functions in your module. Then your code needs to determine which version of Excel is running and call the appropriate function.

Following is an example of a procedure that uses API function calls and works with both Excel 5.0 and later versions. The `Declare` statements for this example are as follows:

```
'   32-bit API declaration
    Declare Function GetSystemMetrics32 Lib "user32" _
     Alias "GetSystemMetrics" (ByVal nIndex As Long) As Long

'   16-bit API declaration
    Declare Function GetSystemMetrics16 Lib "user" _
     Alias "GetSystemMetrics" (ByVal nIndex As Integer) _
     As Integer
```

I declared the 32-bit version and the 16-bit version of the API function. Note the use of the keyword `Alias`. This precedes the actual names of the functions in the Windows API, which are identical here. I declared these functions with different names to distinguish them from one another.

The following `DisplayVideoInfo` procedure displays the video resolution of the user's system:

```
Sub DisplayVideoInfo()
    Const SM_CXSCREEN = 0
    Const SM_CYSCREEN = 1

    If Val(Application.Version) > 5 Then
'       32-bit Excel
        vidWidth = GetSystemMetrics32(SM_CXSCREEN)
```

```
        vidHeight = GetSystemMetrics32(SM_CYSCREEN)
    Else
'       16-bit Excel
        vidWidth = GetSystemMetrics16(SM_CXSCREEN)
        vidHeight = GetSystemMetrics16(SM_CYSCREEN)
    End If

    Msg = "The current video mode is: "
    Msg = Msg & vidWidth & " X " & vidHeight
    MsgBox Msg
End Sub
```

Here, I used the expression `Val(Application.Version) > 5` to determine whether Excel is 16-bit or 32-bit. If the expression returns True, the code calls the 32-bit function; otherwise, it calls the 16-bit function.

But Will It Work on a Mac?

One of the most prevalent problems I hear about concerns Macintosh compatibility. Excel for Macintosh represents a very small proportion of the total Excel market, and many developers choose to simply ignore it. The good news is that Excel file formats are compatible across both versions, and VBA code written on a Windows platform can be loaded into Excel for Macintosh. The bad news is that the features supported by both Excel formats are not identical, and VBA macro compatibility is far from perfect.

You can write VBA code to determine which platform your application is running on. The following function accesses the `OperatingSystem` property of the `Application` object and returns True if the operating system is any version of Windows (that is, if the returned string contains the text "Win"):

```
Function WindowsOS() As Boolean
    If Application.OperatingSystem like "*Win*" Then
        WindowsOS = True
    Else
        WindowsOS = False
    End If
End Function
```

Many subtle (and not so subtle) differences exist between the Windows versions and the Mac versions of Excel. Many of those differences are cosmetic (for example, different default fonts), but others are much more serious. For example, Excel for Macintosh doesn't support maps or ActiveX controls, and it uses "1904" as the default date system, so workbooks that use dates may be off by four years. Excel for Windows, by default, uses the 1900 date system. On the Macintosh, a date serial number of 1 refers to January 1, 1904; in Excel for Windows, that same serial number represents January 1, 1900.

Another limitation concerns Windows API calls: They don't work with Excel for Macintosh. If your application depends on such functions, you need to develop a workaround.

If your code deals with paths and filenames, you need to construct your path with the appropriate path separator (a colon for the Macintosh, a backslash for Windows). A better approach is to avoid hard-coding the path separator character and use VBA to determine it. The following statement assigns the path separator character to a variable named `PathSep`:

```
PathSep = Application.PathSeparator
```

After this statement is executed, your code can use the `PathSep` variable in place of a hard-coded colon or backslash.

Rather than try to make a single file compatible with both platforms, most developers choose to develop on the Excel for Windows platform and then modify the application so that it works on the Mac platform. In other words, you'll probably need to maintain two separate versions of your application.

There is only one way to make sure that your application is compatible with the Macintosh version of Excel: You must test it thoroughly on a Macintosh. And be prepared to develop some workarounds for routines that don't work correctly.

Creating an International Application

The final compatibility issue deals with language issues and international settings. If your application will be used by those who speak another language, you need to ensure that the proper language is used in your dialog boxes. You also need to identify the user's decimal and thousands separator characters. In the United States, these are almost always a period and a comma. But users in other countries may have their systems set up to use other characters. Yet another issue is the date and time format. The United States is one of the few countries that use the month/date/year format.

If you're developing an application that will be used only by people in your company, you probably don't need to be concerned with international compatibility. But if your company has offices throughout the world, or if you plan to distribute your application outside your country, you need to address a number of issues to ensure that your application will work properly. I discuss these issues in this section.

Multilanguage applications

An obvious consideration involves the language that is used in your application. For example, if you use one or more dialog boxes, you may want the text to appear in the language of the user. Fortunately, this is not too difficult (assuming, of course, that you can translate your text or know someone who can).

The companion CD-ROM contains a dialog box wizard that is set up to use any of three languages: English, Spanish, or German. This example is based on a dialog box example presented in Chapter 14.

The first step of the wizard contains three OptionButtons that enable the user to select a language. The text for the three languages is stored in a worksheet. Figure 25-2 shows the UserForm displaying text in all three languages.

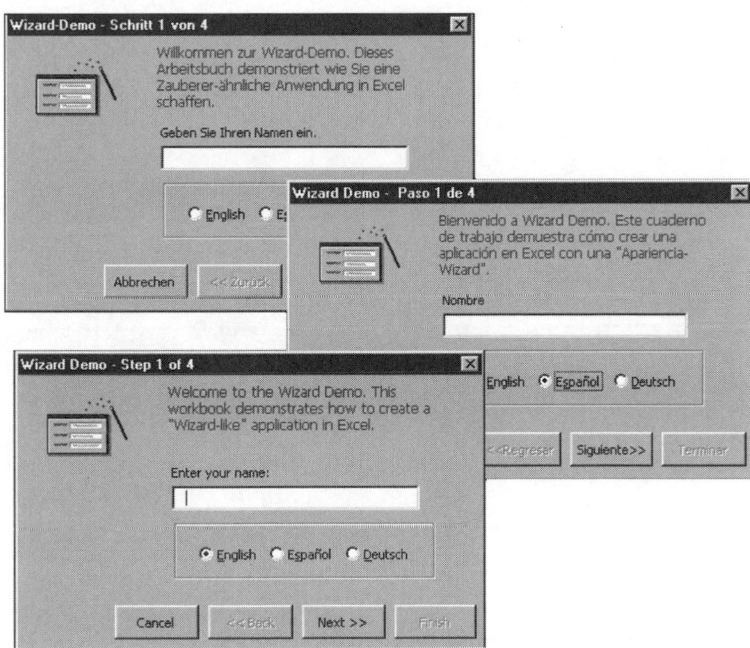

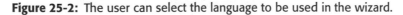

Figure 25-2: The user can select the language to be used in the wizard.

VBA language considerations

In general, you need not be concerned with the language you write your VBA code in. Excel uses two object libraries: the Excel object library and the VBA object library. When you install Excel, it registers the English-language version of these object libraries as the default libraries (this is true regardless of the language version of Excel).

There are other language editions of the object libraries, however. If you install a different language version of the VBA object library (and the corresponding Excel object library), you can write your VBA code in a non-English language. Your code's language can be different from the language of Excel, because the object library translates your code into statements that can run in any language version of Excel.

If your VBA code is not written in English, you need to include the appropriate object libraries for the language your code is written in when you distribute your application, just in case the users don't already have them installed.

Using "local" properties

If your code displays worksheet information such as a range address, you probably want to use the local language. For example, the following statement displays the address of the selected range:

```
MsgBox Selection.Address
```

For international applications, a better approach is to use the `AddressLocal` property rather than the `Address` property:

```
MsgBox Selection.AddressLocal
```

An even better approach is to ensure that the reference style (A1 or R1C1) matches the style that the user has selected. You can accomplish this with the following statement:

```
MsgBox Selection.AddressLocal _
    (ReferenceStyle:=Application.ReferenceStyle)
```

Several other properties also have "local" versions. These are shown in Table 25-2 (refer to the online help for details).

Table 25-2
Properties That Have "Local" Versions

Property	*"Local" Version*	*Return Contents*
`Address`	`AddressLocal`	An address
`Category`	`CategoryLocal`	A function category
`Formula`	`FormulaLocal`	A formula

Property	"Local" Version	Return Contents
`Name`	`NameLocal`	A name
`RefersTo`	`RefersToLocal`	A reference

Identifying system settings

Generally, you cannot assume that the end user's system is set up like the system on which you develop your application. For international applications, you may need to be aware of the following settings:

Decimal separator	The character used to separate the decimal portion of a value
Thousands separator	The character used to delineate every three digits in a value
List separator	The character used to separate items in a list

You can determine the current separator settings by accessing the `International` property of the `Application` object. For example, the following statement displays the decimal separator, which won't always be a period:

```
MsgBox Application.International(xlDecimalSeparator)
```

Table 25-3 lists the 45 international settings that you can access with the `International` property.

Table 25-3
Constants for the International Property

Constant	What It Returns
`xlCountryCode`	Country version of Microsoft Excel.
`xlCountrySetting`	Current country setting in the Windows Control Panel.
`xlDecimalSeparator`	Decimal separator.
`xlThousandsSeparator`	Zero or thousands separator.
`xlListSeparator`	List separator.
`xlUpperCaseRowLetter`	Uppercase row letter (for R1C1-style references).

Continued

Table 25-3 (continued)

Constant	***What It Returns***
`xlUpperCaseColumnLetter`	Uppercase column letter.
`xlLowerCaseRowLetter`	Lowercase row letter.
`xlLowerCaseColumnLetter`	Lowercase column letter.
`xlLeftBracket`	Character used instead of the left bracket ([) in R1C1-style relative references.
`xlRightBracket`	Character used instead of the right bracket (]) in R1C1-style references.
`xlLeftBrace`	Character used instead of the left brace ({) in array literals.
`xlRightBrace`	Character used instead of the right brace (}) in array literals.
`xlColumnSeparator`	Character used to separate columns in array literals.
`xlRowSeparator`	Character used to separate rows in array literals.
`xlAlternateArraySeparator`	Alternate array item separator to be used if the current array separator is the same as the decimal separator.
`xlDateSeparator`	Date separator (/).
`xlTimeSeparator`	Time separator (:).
`xlYearCode`	Year symbol in number formats (y).
`xlMonthCode`	Month symbol (m).
`xlDayCode`	Day symbol (d).
`xlHourCode`	Hour symbol (h).
`xlMinuteCode`	Minute symbol (m).
`xlSecondCode`	Second symbol (s).
`xlCurrencyCode`	Currency symbol.
`xlGeneralFormatName`	Name of the General number format.
`xlCurrencyDigits`	Number of decimal digits to be used in currency formats.
`xlCurrencyNegative`	A value that represents the currency format for negative currency values.
`xlNoncurrencyDigits`	Number of decimal digits to be used in noncurrency formats.

Constant	*What It Returns*
`xlMonthNameChars`	Always returns three characters for backward compatibility. Abbreviated month names are read from Microsoft Windows and can be any length.
`xlWeekdayNameChars`	Always returns three characters for backward compatibility. Abbreviated weekday names are read from Microsoft Windows and can be any length.
`xlDateOrder`	An integer that represents the order of date elements.
`xl24HourClock`	True if the system is using 24-hour time; False if the system is using 12-hour time.
`xlNonEnglishFunctions`	True if the system is not displaying functions in English.
`xlMetric`	True if the system is using the metric system; False if the system is using the English measurement system.
`xlCurrencySpaceBefore`	True if a space is added before the currency symbol.
`xlCurrencyBefore`	True if the currency symbol precedes the currency values; False if it follows them.
`xlCurrencyMinusSign`	True if the system is using a minus sign for negative numbers; False if the system is using parentheses.
`xlCurrencyTrailingZeros`	True if trailing zeros are displayed for zero currency values.
`xlCurrencyLeadingZeros`	True if leading zeros are displayed for zero currency values.
`xlMonthLeadingZero`	True if a leading zero is displayed in months (when months are displayed as numbers).
`xlDayLeadingZero`	True if a leading zero is displayed in days.
`xl4DigitYears`	True if the system is using four-digit years; False if the system is using two-digit years.
`xlMDY`	True if the date order is month-day-year for dates displayed in the long form; False if the date order is day-month-year.
`xlTimeLeadingZero`	True if a leading zero is displayed in times.

Here's an example that writes a value to a cell by combining an integer with a decimal, but first it determines the decimal separator in use on the system. If the decimal separator is a period, this procedure enters 123.45 into cell A1. If the decimal separator is a comma, the procedure enters 123,45 into the cell.

```
Sub WriteValue()
    DecSep = Application.International(xlDecimalSeparator)
    IntegerPart = 123
    Decimalpart = 45
    Range("A1") = IntegerPart & DecSep & Decimalpart
End Sub
```

Date and time settings

If your application writes formatted dates and will be used in other countries, you might want to make sure the date is in a format familiar to the user. The following procedure shows one way to write a formatted date. It uses VBA's `Format` function to write the date in the specified format. For example, it might write "12/01/99" to the cell.

```
Sub WriteDate()
    Today = Now()
    Range("A1") = Format(Today, "mm/dd/yy")
End Sub
```

A non-U.S. user might be confused by this date, interpreting it as January 12 rather than December 1. The best way to avoid such confusion is to use named formats. Here's an example:

```
Sub WriteDate()
    Today = Now()
    Range("A1") = Format(Today, "Short Date")
End Sub
```

Excel provides several other named date and time formats, plus quite a few named number formats. The online help describes all of them (search for *named date/time formats* or *named numeric formats*).

Summary

In this chapter, I discussed some general issues that you should consider if your Excel application must work with earlier versions of Excel, Excel for Macintosh, and foreign language versions of Excel.

The next chapter describes some techniques that enable you to read and write text files with VBA.

✦ ✦ ✦

CHAPTER 26

Reading and Writing Text Files

✦ ✦ ✦ ✦

In This Chapter

A basic overview of VBA's text file manipulation features

Performing common file operations using traditional techniques and the new FileSearch object

Various ways to open a text file

Examples of reading and writing a text file using VBA

✦ ✦ ✦ ✦

Many applications that you develop for Excel require working with multiple external files. For example, you may need to get a listing of files in a directory, delete files, rename files, and so on. Excel, of course, can import and export several types of text files. In many cases, however, Excel's built-in text file handling isn't sufficient. For example, you may need to import a text file that contains more than 256 columns of data. Or the file may use a nonstandard delimiter such as a backslash. In this chapter, I describe how to use VBA to perform common file operations and work directly with text files.

Performing Common File Operations

VBA includes a number of statements and functions that enable you to manipulate files stored on a disk.

New Feature

If you use Excel 2000, you can take advantage of the new FileSearch object, which is easier to use than the VBA statements and functions. The FileSearch object offers some distinct advantages if your application does not need to run under Excel 97.

In the sections that follow, I discuss both the VBA commands and the new FileSearch object, and present examples.

VBA file-related commands

Table 26-1 summarizes the VBA commands you can use to work with files.

Table 26-1
VBA File-Related Commands

Command	*What It Does*
`ChDir`	Changes the current directory
`CurDrive`	Changes the current drive
`Dir`	Returns a filename or directory that matches a specified pattern or file attribute
`FileCopy`	Copies a file
`FileDateTime`	Returns the date and time a file was last modified
`FileLen`	Returns the size of a file, in bytes
`GetAttr`	Returns a value that represents an attribute of a file
`Kill`	Deletes a file
`MkDir`	Creates a new directory
`Name`	Renames a file or directory
`RmDir`	Removes an empty directory
`SetAttr`	Changes an attribute for a file

The remainder of this section consists of examples that demonstrate some of the file manipulation commands.

Displaying a list of files in a directory

Listing 26-1 displays (in the active worksheet) a list of files contained in a particular directory, along with the file size and date.

Listing 26-1: Listing directory contents to a worksheet

```
Sub ListFiles()
    Directory = "c:\windows\desktop\"
    r = 1

'   Insert headers
```

```
    Cells(r, 1) = "FileName"
    Cells(r, 2) = "Size"
    Cells(r, 3) = "Date/Time"
    Range("A1:C1").Font.Bold = True
    r = r + 1

'   Get first file
    f = Dir(Directory, 7)
    Cells(r, 1) = f
    Cells(r, 2) = FileLen(Directory & f)
    Cells(r, 3) = FileDateTime(Directory & f)

'   Get remaining files
    Do While f <> ""
        f = Dir
        If f <> "" Then
            r = r + 1
            Cells(r, 1) = f
            Cells(r, 2) = FileLen(Directory & f)
            Cells(r, 3) = FileDateTime(Directory & f)
        End If
    Loop
End Sub
```

Figure 26-1 shows an example of the `ListFiles` procedure's output.

filelister.xls

	A	B	C
1	**FileName**	**Size**	**Date/Time**
2	DelsL1.isu	41343	08/12/98 13:42
3	PSReadme.wri	43002	05/05/98 19:05
4	AdobeUI.fon	10832	05/06/98 18:29
5	AGM.dll	420352	05/06/98 18:29
6	CoolType.dll	836096	05/06/98 18:29
7	KICCCMSG.SWB	60928	05/06/98 18:18
8	KICCRES.RSL	18432	05/06/98 18:18
9	Photos01.dll	578048	05/06/98 18:29
10	Photos02.dll	2691072	05/06/98 18:30
11	Photoshp.cnt	12940	04/02/98 11:47
12	Photoshp.exe	5687296	08/12/98 13:41
13	Photoshp.GID	112515	11/01/98 15:35
14	PHOTOSHP.HLP	8676723	04/24/98 11:05
15	Photoshp.reg	5501	05/06/98 18:30
16	Plugin.dll	32768	05/06/98 18:30
17	psicon.dll	93184	05/06/98 18:30
18	PSUT9516.DLL	19456	05/06/98 18:19
19	psut9532.dll	18432	05/06/98 18:19
20	TypeLibrary.tlb	123208	05/06/98 18:30
21	Uninst.dll	31232	05/06/98 18:05
22	Photoshp.FTS	425984	08/12/98 15:05
23			

Sheet1

Figure 26-1: Output from the `ListFiles` procedure.

Notice that the procedure uses the Dir function twice. The first time, it retrieves the first filename found. Subsequent calls to the Dir function retrieve additional filenames. When no more files are found, the function returns an empty string.

The companion CD-ROM contains a more sophisticated version of this procedure that enables you to select a directory from a dialog box.

The Dir function also accepts wildcard file specification in its first argument. To get a list of Excel files, for example, you could use a statement such as:

```
f = Dir("c:\files\*.xl?", 7)
```

This statement retrieves the name of the first .xl? file in the c:\files directory. The second argument for the Dir function enables you to specify the attributes of the files. An argument of 7 retrieves filenames that have no attributes, read-only files, hidden files, and system files. Consult the online help for specifics.

If you need to display a list of files and enable a user to select one, this is not the most efficient approach. Rather, you'll want to use the GetOpenFilename method, which is discussed in Chapter 12.

Determining whether a file exists

The following function returns True if a particular file exists and False if not. If the Dir function returns an empty string, the file could not be found, so the FileExists function returns False.

```
Function FileExists(fname) As Boolean
    If Dir(fname) <> "" Then _
      FileExists = True _
      Else FileExists = False
End Function
```

The argument for the FileExists function consists of a full path and filename. The function can be used in a worksheet, or called from a VBA procedure.

Determining whether a path exists

The following function uses the GetAttr function. It returns True if a path exists and False if not:

```
Function PathExists(pname) As Boolean
'   Returns TRUE if the path exists
    Dim x As String
    On Error Resume Next
```

```
    x = GetAttr(pname) And 0
    If Err = 0 Then PathExists = True _
      Else PathExists = False
End Function
```

Using the FileSearch object

The `FileSearch` object essentially gives your VBA code all the functionality of Excel's Open dialog box. For example, you can use this object to locate files that match a file specification (such as *.xls), and even search for files that contain specific text.

The `FileSearch` object is new to Excel 2000. If your application does not need to work with Excel 97, using `FileSearch` is preferable to using the `Dir` function.

Table 26-2 summarizes some of the key methods and properties of the `FileSearch` object.

Table 26-2
Key Properties and Methods of the FileSearch Object

Property or Method	*What It Does*
`FileName`	Specifies the name of the file to be located (wildcard characters are acceptable)
`FoundFile`	Returns an object that contains the names of the files found
`LookIn`	Specifies the directory to be searched
`SearchSubfolders`	Returns True if subdirectories are to be searched
`Execute`	Performs the search
`NewSearch`	Resets the `FileSearch` object

The remainder of this section consists of examples that demonstrate use of the `FileSearch` object.

Displaying a list of files in a directory

Listing 26-2 displays (in the active worksheet) a list of files contained in a particular directory, along with the file size and date.

Listing 26-2: A more complete directory listing to a worksheet

```
Sub ListFiles2()
    Directory = "c:\windows\desktop\"

'   Insert headers
    r = 1
    Cells(r, 1) = "FileName"
    Cells(r, 2) = "Size"
    Cells(r, 3) = "Date/Time"
    Range("A1:C1").Font.Bold = True
    r = r + 1

    With Application.FileSearch
        .NewSearch
        .LookIn = Directory
        .Filename = "*.*"
        .SearchSubFolders = False
        .Execute
        For i = 1 To .FoundFiles.Count
            Cells(r, 1) = .FoundFiles(i)
            Cells(r, 2) = FileLen(.FoundFiles(i))
            Cells(r, 3) = FileDateTime(.FoundFiles(i))
            r = r + 1
        Next i
    End With
End Sub
```

The companion CD-ROM contains a more sophisticated version of this procedure that enables you to select a directory.

Determining whether a file exists

The following function returns True if a particular file exists, and False if not. After the `Execute` method is run, the `Count` property of the `FoundFiles` object is 0 if the file was not found.

```
Function FileExists2(fname) As Boolean
    With Application.FileSearch
        .NewSearch
        .Filename = fname
        .Execute
        If .FoundFiles.Count = 0 Then _
          FileExists = False _
          Else FileExists = True
    End With
End Function
```

It's not possible to use the `FileSearch` object to determine if a path exists. Instead, use the `PathExists` function shown previously in this chapter.

Locating files that contain specific text

The following procedure searches the My Documents directory and its subdirectories for all XLS files that contain the text *budget.* The found filenames are then added to a ListBox on a UserForm.

```
Sub FindFiles()
    With Application.FileSearch
        .NewSearch
        .LookIn = "C:\My Documents"
        .SearchSubFolders = True
        .TextOrProperty = "budget"
        .MatchTextExactly = True
        .Filename = "*.xls"
        .Execute
        For i = 1 To .FoundFiles.Count
            UserForm1.ListBox1.AddItem .FoundFiles(i)
        Next i
    End With
    UserForm1.Show
End Sub
```

Working with Text Files

VBA contains a number of instructions that enable "low level" manipulation of files. These input/output (I/O) instructions give you much more control over files than Excel's normal text file import and export options.

You can access a file in any of three ways:

Sequential access	By far the most common method. This method enables reading and writing individual characters or entire lines of data.
Random access	Used only if you're programming a database application (which you shouldn't be doing in VBA, because better techniques do exist).
Binary access	Reads or writes to any byte position in a file, such as a bitmap image. Rarely (if ever) used in VBA.

Because random and binary access files are rarely used with VBA, this chapter focuses on sequential access files. A sequential access file is accessed in a sequential manner. In other words, your code starts reading from the beginning of the file, and reads each line sequentially. For output, your code writes data to the end of the file.

Opening a text file

VBA's Open statement (not to be confused with the Open method of the Application object) is used to open a text file for reading or writing. Before you can read from or write to a file, you must open it.

The Open statement is quite versatile, and has a rather complex syntax:

```
Open pathname For mode [Access access] [lock] _
  As [#]filenumber [Len=reclength]
```

pathname (Required) The *pathname* argument of the Open statement is quite straightforward. It simply contains the name of the file to be opened, which may include its storage path.

mode (Required) The file mode must be one of the following:

Append — A sequential access mode that enables the file to be read, or data to be appended to the end of the file.

Input — A sequential access mode that enables the file to be read, but not written to.

Output — A sequential access mode that enables the file to be read or written to. In this mode, a new file is always created (an existing file with the same name is deleted).

Binary — A random access mode that enables data to be read or written to on a byte-by-byte basis.

Random — A random access mode that enables data to be read or written in units determined by the *reclength* argument.

access (Optional) Determines what can be done with the file. It can be Read, Write, or Read Write.

lock (Optional) Useful for multiuser situations. The options are Shared, Lock Read, Lock Write, and Lock Read Write.

filenumber (Required) A numeral ranging from 1 to 511. You can use the FreeFile function to get the next available file number.

reclength (Optional) The record length for random access files, or the buffer size for sequential access files.

Reading a text file

The basic process for reading a text file using VBA is as follows:

1. Open the file using the `Open` statement.
2. Specify the position in the file using the `Seek` function (optional).
3. Read data from the file using the `Input`, `Input #`, or `Line Input #` statement.
4. Close the file using the `Close` statement.

Writing a text file

The basic process for writing a text file is as follows:

1. Open or create the file using the `Open` statement.
2. Specify the position in the file using the `Seek` function (optional).
3. Write data to the file using the `Write #` or `Print #` statement.
4. Close the file using the `Close` statement.

Getting a file number

Most VBA programmers simply designate a file number in their `Open` statement. For example:

```
Open "myfile.txt" For Input As #1
```

Then, you can refer to the file in subsequent statements as `#1`.

If a second file is opened while the first is still open, you can designate the second file as `#2`:

```
Open "another.txt" For Input As #2
```

Another approach is to use VBA's `FreeFile` function to get an open file number. Then, you can refer to the file using a variable. Here's an example:

```
FileNumber = FreeFile
Open "myfile.txt" For Input As FileNumber
```

Excel's Text File Import and Export Features

Excel supports three types of text files:

CSV (Comma-Separated Value) — Columns of data are separated by a command, and each row of data ends in a carriage return.

PRN — Columns of data are aligned by character position, and each row of data ends in a carriage return.

TXT (Tab delimited) — Columns of data are separated by tab characters, and each row of data ends in a carriage return.

When you attempt to open a text file with the File➪Open command, the Text Import Wizard may appear to help you delineate the columns. If the text file is tab delimited or comma delimited, Excel usually opens the file without displaying the Text Import Wizard.

Determining or setting the file position

For sequential file access, it's rarely necessary to know the current location (character position) in the file. If for some reason you need to know this, you can use the `Seek` function.

The Text to Columns Wizard (accessed by Data➪Text to Columns) is identical to the Text Import Wizard, but works with data stored in a single column.

Statements for reading and writing

VBA provides several statements to read and write data to a file. Three of these statements are used for reading data from a sequential access file:

`Input`	Reads a single character from a file.
`Input #`	Reads a complete line of data as a series of variables, with each variable separated by a comma.
`Line Input #`	Reads a complete line of data, delineated by a carriage return and/or line feed character.

Two statements are used for writing data to a sequential access file:

`Write #`	Writes a series of values, with each value separated by a comma and enclosed in quotes. If you end the statement with a semicolon, a carriage return/line feed sequence is not inserted after each value. Data written with `Write #` is usually read from a file with an `Input #` statement.

`Print #` Writes a series of values, with each value separated by a tab character. If you end the statement with a semicolon, a carriage return/line feed sequence is not inserted after each value. Data written with `Write #` is usually read from a file with a `Line Input #` or an `Input` statement.

Text File Manipulation Examples

This section contains a number of examples that demonstrate various techniques for manipulating text files.

Importing data in a text file

The following example reads a text file and places each line of data in a single cell, beginning with the active cell:

```
Sub ImportRange1()
    Set ImpRng = ActiveCell
    Open "c:\windows\desktop\textfile.txt" For Input As #1
    r = 0
    Do While Not EOF(1)
        Line Input #1, data
        ActiveCell.Offset(r, 0) = data
        r = r + 1
    Loop
    Close #1
End Sub
```

If the text file contains multiple values in each line, this procedure isn't very useful, because each line of data is simply dumped into a single cell. You can, however, use Excel's Data⇨Text to Columns command after importing the file. This command parses the data into separate columns in the worksheet.

Exporting a range to a text file

Listing 26-3 shows a simple example that writes the data in a worksheet range to a CSV text file. The range is determined by the current region, which is based on the active cell. In this example, the `CurrentRegion` property returns a range around the active cell that is bounded by any combination of blank rows and blank columns.

Listing 26-3: Writing worksheet data to an ordinary text file

```
Sub ExportRange()
    Dim ExpRng As Range
    Set ExpRng = ActiveCell.CurrentRegion
    FirstCol = ExpRng.Columns(1).Column
    LastCol = FirstCol + ExpRng.Columns.Count - 1
    FirstRow = ExpRng.Rows(1).Row
    LastRow = FirstRow + ExpRng.Rows.Count - 1

    Open ThisWorkbook.Path & "\textfile.txt" For Output As #1
        For r = FirstRow To LastRow
            For c = FirstCol To LastCol
                vData = ExpRng.Cells(r, c).Value
                If IsNumeric(vData) Then vData = Val(vData)
                If c <> LastCol Then
                    Write #1, vData;
                Else
                    Write #1, vData
                End If
            Next c
        Next r
    Close #1
End Sub
```

Notice that the procedure uses two `Write #` statements. The first statement ends with a semicolon, so a carriage return/line feed sequence is not written. For the last cell in a row, however, the second `Write #` statement does not use a semicolon, which causes the next output to appear on a new line.

I use a variable named `vData` to store the contents of each cell. If the cell is numeric, the variable is converted to a value. This step ensures that numeric data is not stored with quotation marks.

Figure 26-2 shows the contents of the resulting file.

Importing a text file to a range

Listing 26-4 reads the CSV text file created in Listing 26-3, and stores the values beginning at the active cell. The code parses each character of data in every line, ignoring quote characters and looking for commas to delineate the columns.

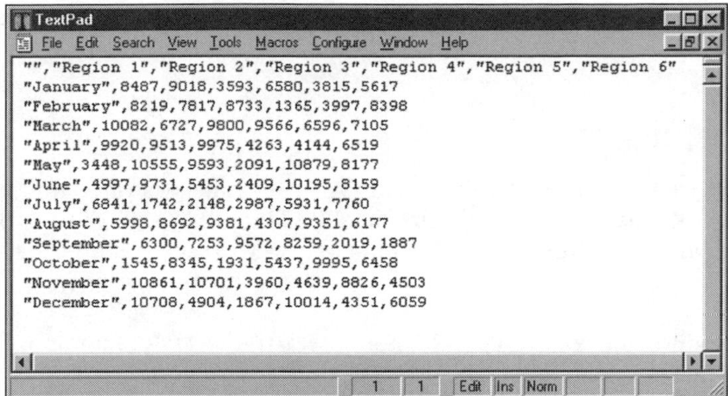

Figure 26-2: VBA generated this text file.

Listing 26-4: Importing data from a text file to a worksheet range

```
Sub ImportRange2()
    Set ImpRng = ActiveCell
    Open ThisWorkbook.Path & "\textfile.txt" _
      For Input As #1
    r = 0
    c = 0
    txt - ""
    Application.ScreenUpdating = False
    Do While Not EOF(1)
        Line Input #1, vData
        For i = 1 To Len(vData)
            char = Mid(vData, i, 1)
            If char = "," Or i = Len(vData) Then
                ActiveCell.Offset(r, c) = txt
                c = c + 1
                txt = ""
            Else
                If char <> Chr(34) Then _
                  txt = txt & Mid(vData, i, 1)
            End If
        Next i
        c = 0
        r = r + 1
    Loop
    Close #1
    Application.ScreenUpdating = True
End Sub
```

Listing 26-4 has a flaw: It doesn't handle data that contains a comma or a quote character.

Logging Excel usage

The example in this section writes data to a text file every time you open and close Excel. For this to work reliably, the procedure must be located in a workbook that is opened every time you start Excel — the Personal Macro Workbook is an excellent choice.

The following procedure, stored in the code module for the `ThisWorkbook` object, is executed when the file is opened:

```
Private Sub Workbook_Open()
    Open Application.Path & "\excelusage.txt" _
      For Append As #1
    Print #1, "Started " & Now
    Close #1
End Sub
```

The procedure appends a new line to a file named excelusage.txt. The new line contains the current date and time, and might look something like this:

```
Started 08/09/99 9:27:43 PM
```

The following procedure is executed when the workbook is closed. It appends a new line that contains the word "Stopped" along with the current date and time.

```
Private Sub Workbook_BeforeClose(Cancel As Boolean)
    Open Application.Path & "\excelusage.txt" _
      For Append As #1
    Print #1, "Stopped " & Now
    Close #1
End Sub
```

Filtering a text file

The example in this section demonstrates how to work with two text files at once. The following `FilterFile` procedure reads a text file (infile.txt) and copies only the rows that contain a specific text string to a second text file (output.txt).

```
Sub FilterFile()
    Open "infile.txt" For Input As #1
    Open "output.txt" For Output As #2
    TextToFind = "January"
    Do While Not EOF(1)
```

```
        Line Input #1, data
        If InStr(1, data, TextToFind) Then
            Print #2, data
        End If
    Loop
    Close
End Sub
```

Importing more than 256 columns of data

It's not uncommon to need to import a text file that exceeds Excel's 256-column capacity. If you attempt to open such a file with the File⇨Open command, Excel simply ignores any data past column 256 (and doesn't even warn you about it!).

Listing 26-5 is a variation of the `ImportRange2` procedure presented earlier in this chapter. It reads a text file and stores the data in Sheet1. If the line contains more than 256 columns of data, the additional data is stored in Sheet2.

Listing 26-5: Importing multicolumn text file contents into two worksheets

```
Sub ImportLongLines()
'   Create new workbook with two sheets
    UserSheets = Application.SheetsInNewWorkbook
    Application.SheetsInNewWorkbook = 2
    Workbooks.Add
    Application.SheetsInNewWorkbook = UserSheets

    Open ThisWorkbook.Path & "\longfile.txt" For Input As #1
    r = 0
    c = 0
    CurrLine = 0
    Set ImpRange = ActiveWorkbook.Sheets(1).Range("A1")
    Application.ScreenUpdating = False

    Do While Not EOF(1)
        CurrLine = CurrLine + 1
        Line Input #1, data
        Application.StatusBar = "Processing line " & CurrLine
        For i = 1 To Len(data)
            char = Mid(data, i, 1)
'           Are we out of columns?
            If c = 256 Then

                c = 0
```

Continued

Listing 26-5 *(continued)*

```
                Set ImpRange = _
                 ActiveWorkbook.Sheets(2).Range("A1")
            End If

'           End of the field
            If char = "," Then
                ImpRange.Offset(r, c) = txt
                c = c + 1
                txt = ""
            Else
'               Skip quote characters
                If char <> Chr(34) Then _
                    txt = txt & Mid(data, i, 1)

'               End of the line?
                If i = Len(data) Then
                    ImpRange.Offset(r, c) = txt
                    c = c + 1
                    txt = ""
                End If
            End If
        Next i
        c = 0
        Set ImpRange = ActiveWorkbook.Sheets(1).Range("A1")
        r = r + 1
    Loop

    Close #1
    Application.ScreenUpdating = True
    Application.StatusBar = False
End Sub
```

This example is available on the companion CD-ROM, along with a text file that contains 100 rows, each with 300 columns of data.

If you import files that contain more than 512 columns of data, you need to modify the procedure in Listing 26-5. You can start with a single worksheet, and then have the procedure determine when to add a new worksheet using the following expression:

```
c Mod 256
```

When this expression returns 0, a new sheet must be added.

Summary

In this chapter, I discussed two ways of working with files on disk: VBA's standard commands and the new `FileSystem` object available in Excel 2000. I also presented several examples of reading and writing text files with VBA.

The next chapter demonstrates how you can make a VBA application generate *another* VBA application on the fly.

✦ ✦ ✦

Manipulating Visual Basic Components

✦ ✦ ✦ ✦

In This Chapter

An overview of the VBA Integrated Development Environment and its object model

How to use VBA to add and remove modules from a project

How to write VBA code that creates VBA code

How to use VBA to help create UserForms

A useful function that creates a UserForm on the fly

✦ ✦ ✦ ✦

This chapter discusses a topic that some readers may find extremely useful: writing VBA code that manipulates components in a VBA project. The VBA Integrated Development Environment (IDE) contains an object model that exposes key elements of your VBA projects, including the Editor itself. You can write VBA code that adds or removes modules, generates other VBA code, or even creates a UserForm on the fly.

Introducing the IDE

The IDE is essentially an OLE Automation interface for the Visual Basic Editor. Once you establish a reference to the Visual Basic Extensibility Library (using the VB Editor's Tools⇨References command), you have access to all the VB Editor's objects, properties, and methods, and you can declare objects as from the IDE's member classes.

In the References dialog box, you may add a reference to **Microsoft Visual Basic for Applications Extensibility.** This gives you access to an object called `VBIDE`. Creating a reference to `VBIDE` gives you access to a number of predefined constants that relate to the IDE. Actually, you can access the objects in the IDE *without* creating a reference, but you won't be able to use the constants in your code nor will you be able to declare specific objects that refer to IDE components.

Refer to Chapter 19 for background information about OLE Automation.

Once you understand how the IDE object model works, you can write code to perform a variety of operations, including the following:

- ✦ Adding and removing VBA modules
- ✦ Inserting VBA code
- ✦ Creating UserForms
- ✦ Adding controls to a UserForm

The IDE Object Model

Programming the IDE requires an understanding of its object model. The top object in the object hierarchy is the VBE (Visual Basic Environment). As with Excel's object model, the VBE contains other objects. A simplified version of the IDE object hierarchy is as follows:

```
VBE
 VBProject
  VBComponent
    CodeModule
    Designer
    Property
  Reference
 Window
 CommandBar
```

This chapter ignores the Extensibility Library's `Windows` collection and `CommandBars` collection, which aren't all that useful for Excel developers. Rather, the chapter focuses on the `VBProject` object, which can be *very* useful for developers.

The VBProjects collection

Every open workbook or add-in is represented by a `VBProject` object. To access the `VBProject` object for a workbook, use the `VBProject` property of the `Workbook` object. The following instructions, for example, create an object variable that represents the `VBProject` object for the active workbook:

```
Dim VBP As VBProject
Set VBP = ActiveWorkbook.VBProject
```

Each VBProject object contains a collection of the VBA component objects in the project (UserForms, modules, class modules, or document modules). Not surprisingly, this collection is called VBComponents. A VBProject object also contains a References collection for the project, representing the libraries being referenced currently by the VBE.

It's not possible to add a new member to the VBProjects collection directly. Rather, you do so indirectly by opening or creating a new workbook in Excel. Doing so automatically adds a new member to the VBProjects collection. Similarly, you can't remove a VBProject object directly; closing a workbook removes the VBProject object from the collection.

The VBComponents collection

To access a member of the VBComponents collection, use the VBComponents property with an index number or name. The following instructions demonstrate the two ways to access a VBA component and create an object variable:

```
Set VBC = ThisWorkbook.VBProject.VBComponents(1)
Set VBC = ThisWorkbook.VBProject.VBComponents("Module1")
```

The References collection

Every VBA project in Excel contains a number of references. You can view, add, or delete the references for a project using the Tools⇨References command (see Figure 27-1). Every project contains some references (such as VBA itself, Excel, OLE Automation, and the Office Object Library), and you can add additional references to a project as needed.

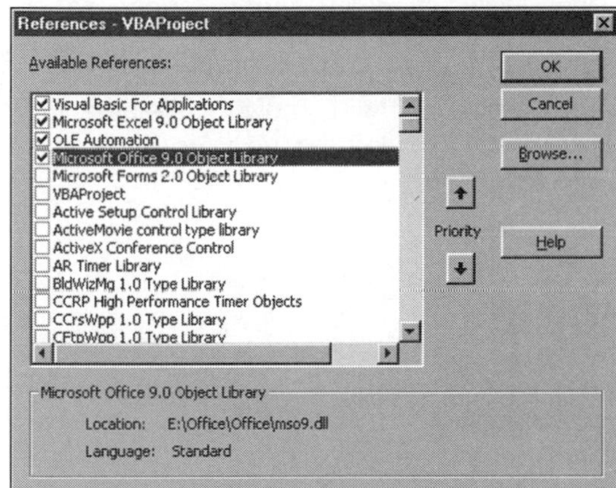

Figure 27-1: The References dialog box shows the references for each project.

You can also manipulate the references for a project using VBA. The References collection contains Reference objects, and the Reference class for these objects has properties and methods. The following procedure, for example, displays a message box that lists the Name property for each Reference object in the active workbook's project:

```
Sub ListReferences()
    Dim Ref As Reference
    Msg = ""
    For Each Ref In ActiveWorkbook.VBProject.References
        Msg = Msg & Ref.Name & vbCrLf
    Next Ref
    MsgBox Msg
End Sub
```

Figure 27-2 shows the result of running this procedure when a workbook that contains six references is active.

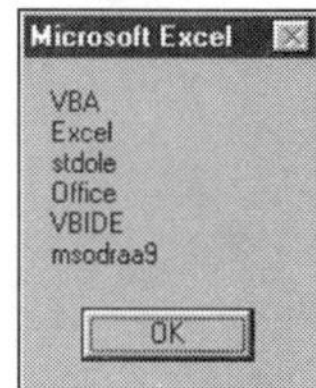

Figure 27-2: This message box displays the names of references for a workbook.

Because it declares an object variable of type Reference, the ListReferences procedure requires a reference to the VBA Extensibility Library. If you declare Ref as a generic Object, the VBA Extensibility Library reference is not needed.

You can also add a reference programmatically using either of two methods of the Reference class. AddFromFile adds a reference if you know its filename and storage path. AddFromGuid adds a reference if you know the reference's *globally unique identifier,* or GUID. Refer to the online help for complete details.

An Introductory Example

The ShowComponents procedure shown in Listing 27-1 loops through each VBA component in the active workbook and writes the following information to a worksheet:

- ✦ The component's name
- ✦ The component's type
- ✦ The number of lines of code in the code module for the component

Listing 27-1: Displaying each active VBA component in a worksheet

```
Sub ShowComponents()
    Dim VBP As VBProject
    Set VBP = ActiveWorkbook.VBProject
    NumComponents = VBP.VBComponents.Count
    Cells.ClearContents
    For i = 1 To NumComponents
'       Name
        Cells(i, 1) = VBP.VBComponents(i).Name

'       Type
        Select Case VBP.VBComponents(i).Type
            Case 1
                Cells(i, 2) = "Module"
            Case 2
                Cells(i, 2) = "Class Module"
            Case 3
                Cells(i, 2) = "UserForm"
            Case 100
                Cells(i, 2) = "Document Module"
        End Select
'   Lines of code
        Cells(i, 3) = _
         VBP.VBComponents(i).CodeModule.CountOfLines
    Next i
End Sub
```

Figure 27-3 shows the result of running the `ShowComponents` procedure. In this case, the VBA project contained five components, and only one of them had a nonempty code module.

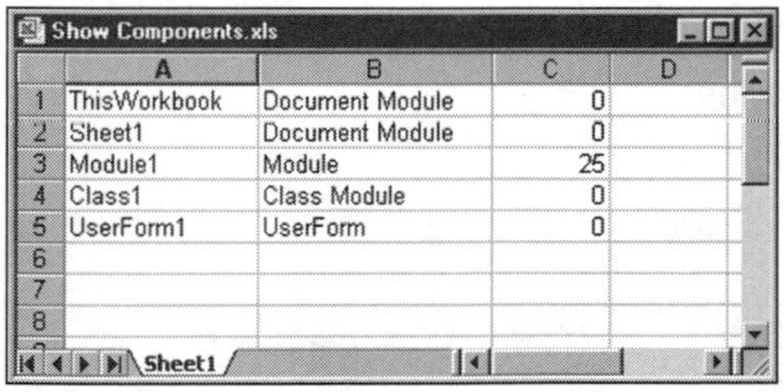

Show Components.xls

	A	B	C	D
1	ThisWorkbook	Document Module	0	
2	Sheet1	Document Module	0	
3	Module1	Module	25	
4	Class1	Class Module	0	
5	UserForm1	UserForm	0	
6				
7				
8				

Sheet1

Figure 27-3: The result of executing the `ShowComponents` procedure.

On the
CD-ROM

This workbook is available on the companion CD-ROM. Notice that it contains a reference to the VBA Extensibility Library.

Replacing a Module with an Updated Version

The example in this section demonstrates how to replace a VBA module with a different VBA module. Besides demonstrating three `VBComponent` methods (`Export`, `Remove`, and `Import`), the procedure also has a practical use. For example, you may distribute a workbook to a group of users, and later discover that a macro contains an error or needs to be updated. Because the users may have added data to the workbook, it would not be practical to replace the entire workbook. The solution, then, is to distribute another workbook that contains a macro that replaces the VBA module with an updated version stored in a file.

This example consists of two workbooks:

UserBook.xls	Contains a module (`Module1`) that needs to be replaced
UpdateUserBook.xls	Contains VBA procedures to replace `Module1` in UserBook.xls with a later version of `Module1` stored in UpdateUserBook.xls

The `BeginUpdate` procedure shown in Listing 27-2 is contained in the `UpdateUserBook` workbook, which would be distributed to users of UserBook.xls. This procedure ensures that UserBook.xls is open. It then informs the user of what is about to happen with the message shown in Figure 27-4.

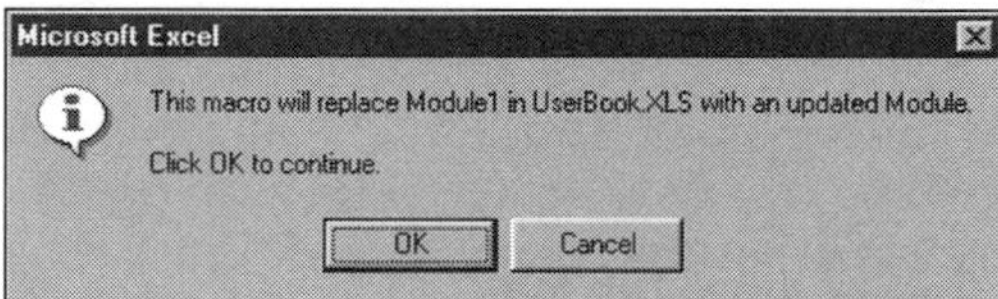
Microsoft Excel
This macro will replace Module1 in UserBook.XLS with an updated Module.
Click OK to continue.
OK
Cancel

Figure 27-4: This message box informs the user that a module will be replaced.

Listing 27-2: Preparing the user for some changes that are afoot

```
Sub BeginUpdate()
    Filename = "UserBook.xls"

'   Activate workbook
```

```
    On Error Resume Next
    Workbooks(Filename).Activate
    If Err <> 0 Then
        MsgBox Filename & " must be open!", vbCritical
        Exit Sub
    End If

    Msg = "This macro will replace Module1 in UserBook.XLS "
    Msg = Msg & "with an updated Module." & vbCrLf & vbCrLf
    Msg = Msg & "Click OK to continue."
    If MsgBox(Msg, vbInformation + vbOKCancel) = vbOK Then
        Call ReplaceModule
    Else
        MsgBox "Module not replaced!", vbCritical
    End If
End Sub
```

When the user clicks OK, the `ReplaceModule` procedure is called. This procedure, shown in Listing 27-3, replaces the existing `Module1` in UserBook.xls with an updated version stored in the `UpdateUserBook` workbook.

Listing 27-3: Updating the existing code module with a revised one

```
Sub ReplaceModule()
'   Export Module1 from this workbook
    Filename = ThisWorkbook.Path & "\tempmodxxx.bas"
    ThisWorkbook.VBProject.VBComponents("Module1") _
      .Export Filename

'   Replace Module1 in UserBook
    Set VBP = ActiveWorkbook.VBProject
    On Error GoTo ErrHandle
    With VBP.VBComponents
        .Remove VBP.VBComponents("Module1")
        .Import Filename
    End With

'   Delete the temporary module file
    Kill Filename
    MsgBox "The module has been replaced.", vbInformation
    Exit Sub

ErrHandle:
'   Did an error occur?
    MsgBox "ERROR. The module may not have been replaced.", _
      vbCritical
End Sub
```

The procedure in Listing 27-3 performs the following steps:

1. It exports `Module1` (the updated module) to a file. The file has an unusual name to reduce the likelihood of overwriting an existing file.
2. It uses the `Remove` method of the `VBComponents` collection to remove `Module1` (the old module) from UserBook.xls.
3. It imports the module (saved in Step 1) to UserBook.xls.
4. It deletes the file saved in Step 1.
5. It reports the action to the user. General error handling is used to inform the user that an error occurred.

This example (which uses two files) is available on the companion CD-ROM.

Using VBA to Write VBA Code

The example in this section demonstrates how you can write VBA code that writes VBA code. The `AddSheetAndButton` procedure does the following:

1. It inserts a new worksheet.
2. It adds a CommandButton to the worksheet.
3. It adjusts the position, size, and caption of the CommandButton.
4. It inserts an event-handler procedure for the CommandButton named `CommandButton1_Click` in the sheet's code module. This procedure simply activates Sheet1.

Listing 27-4 provides the `AddSheetAndButton` procedure.

Listing 27-4: Generating a new worksheet, built-in button, and event handler

```
Sub AddSheetAndButton()
    Dim NewSheet As Worksheet
    Dim NewButton As OLEObject

'   Add the sheet
    Set NewSheet = Sheets.Add

'   Add a CommandButton
    Set NewButton = NewSheet.OLEObjects.Add _
```

```
    ("Forms.CommandButton.1")
  With NewButton
      .Left = 4
      .Top = 4
      .Width = 100
      .Height = 24
      .Object.Caption = "Return to Sheet1"
  End With

'   Add the event handler code
  Code = "Sub CommandButton1_Click()" & vbCrLf
  Code = Code & "    On Error Resume Next" & vbCrLf
  Code = Code & "    Sheets(""Sheet1"").Activate" & vbCrLf
  Code = Code & "    If Err <> 0 Then" & vbCrLf
  Code = Code & "      MsgBox ""Cannot activate Sheet1.""" _
   & vbCrLf
  Code = Code & "    End If" & vbCrLf
  Code = Code & "End Sub"

  With ThisWorkbook.VBProject. _
    VBComponents(NewSheet.Name).CodeModule
      NextLine = .CountOfLines + 1
      .InsertLines NextLine, Code
  End With
```

Figure 27-5 shows a worksheet and CommandButton that were added by the `AddSheetAndButton` procedure.

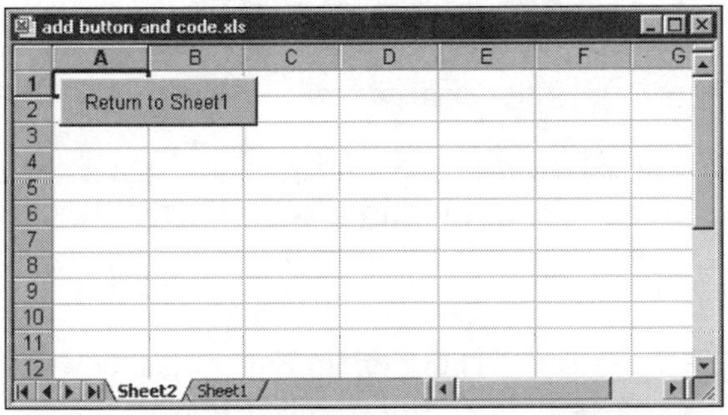

Figure 27-5: This sheet, the CommandButton, and its event handler were added using VBA.

The tricky part of this procedure is inserting the VBA code into the code module for the new worksheet. The code is stored in a variable named `Code`, with each instruction separated by a carriage return and line feed sequence. The InsertLines method adds the code to the code module for the inserted worksheet.

The NextLine variable stores the number of existing lines in the module incremented by one. This ensures that the procedure is added to the end of the module. If you simply insert the code beginning at line 1, it causes an error if the user's system is set up to add an Option Explicit statement to each module automatically.

Figure 27-6 shows the procedure that is created by the AddSheetAndButton procedure in its new home in the code window.

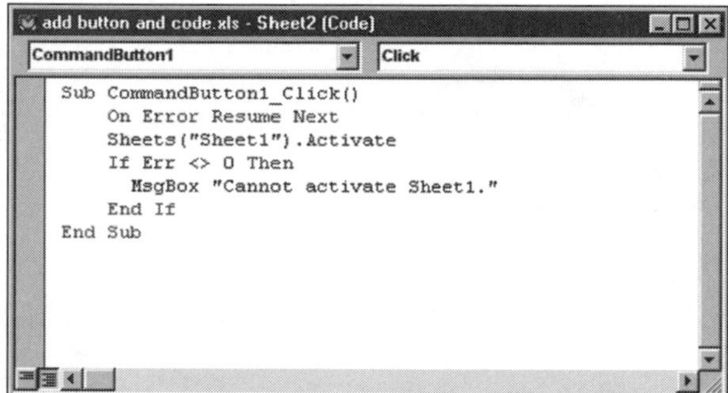

Figure 27-6: VBA generated this event-handler procedure.

Adding Controls to a UserForm at Design Time

If you've spent any time developing UserForms, you probably know that it can be quite tedious to add and adjust the controls so they are sized consistently and aligned. Even if you take full advantage of the VB Editor's formatting commands, it can still take a considerable amount of time to get the controls to look just right.

The UserForm shown in Figure 27-7 contains 100 CommandButtons, all of which are identical in size and positioned precisely on the form. Furthermore, each CommandButton has its own event-handler procedure. Adding these buttons manually and creating their event handlers would take some time . . . lots of time. Adding them automatically at design time using a VBA procedure takes about three seconds.

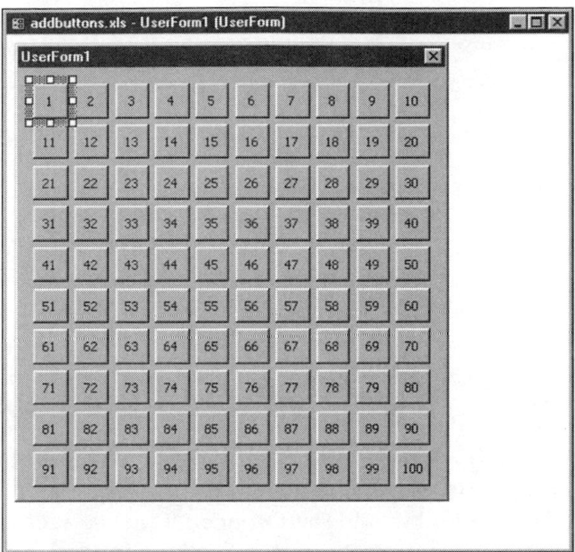

Figure 27-7: A VBA procedure added the CommandButtons on this UserForm.

Design-time versus run-time UserForm manipulations

It's important to understand the distinction between manipulating UserForms or controls at design time and manipulating these objects at run time. Run-time manipulations are apparent when the UserForm is shown, but the changes made are not permanent. For example, you might write code that changes the `Caption` property of the UserForm before the form is displayed. The new caption appears when the UserForm is shown, but when you return to the VB Editor, the UserForm displays its original caption. Part IV of this book contains many examples of code that perform run-time manipulation of UserForms and controls.

Design-time manipulations, on the other hand, are permanent — just as if you made the changes manually using the tools in the VB Editor. Normally, you perform design-time manipulations as a way to automate some of the tedious chores in designing a UserForm. To make design-time manipulations, you access the `Designer` object for the UserForm.

To demonstrate the difference between design-time and run-time manipulations, I developed two simple procedures that add a CommandButton to a UserForm. One procedure adds the button at run time; the other adds it at design time.

The following `RunTimeButton` procedure is very straightforward. Attached to a general (nonform) module, it simply adds a CommandButton, changes a few of its properties, and then displays the UserForm. The CommandButton appears on the form when the form is shown, but when you view the form in the VB Editor, the CommandButton is not there.

```
Sub RunTimeButton()
'   Adds a button at runtime
    Dim Butn As CommandButton
    Set Butn = UserForm1.Controls.Add("Forms.CommandButton.1")
    With Butn
        .Caption = "Added at runtime"
        .Width = 100
        .Top = 10
    End With
    UserForm1.Show
End Sub
```

Following is the `DesignTimeButton` procedure. What's different here is that this procedure uses the `Designer` object, which is contained in the `VBComponent` object. Specifically, it uses the `Add` method to add the CommandButton. Because the `Designer` object was addressed, the CommandButton is added to the UserForm just as if you did it manually in the VB Editor.

```
Sub DesignTimeButton()
'   Adds a button at design time
    Dim Butn As CommandButton
    Set Butn = ThisWorkbook.VBProject. _
      VBComponents("UserForm1") _
      .Designer.Controls.Add("Forms.CommandButton.1")
    With Butn
        .Caption = "Added at design time"
        .Width = 120
        .Top = 40
    End With
End Sub
```

Adding 100 CommandButtons at design time

The example in this section demonstrates how to take advantage of the `Designer` object to help you design a UserForm. In this case, the code adds 100 CommandButtons (perfectly spaced and aligned), sets the `Caption` property for each CommandButton, and also creates 100 event-handler procedures (one for each CommandButton).

Listing 27-5 shows the complete code for the `Add100Buttons` procedure.

Listing 27-5: **Generating an instant 100-button UserForm**

```
Sub Add100Buttons()
  Dim UFvbc As Object 'VBComponent
  Dim CMod As Object 'CodeModule
  Dim ctl As Control
  Dim cb As CommandButton
  Dim n As Integer, c As Integer, r As Integer
  Dim code As String

  Set UFvbc = ThisWorkbook.VBProject.VBComponents("UserForm1")

' Delete all controls, if any
  For Each ctl In UFvbc.Designer.Controls
    UFvbc.Designer.Controls.Remove ctl.Name
  Next ctl

' Delete all VBA code
  UFvbc.CodeModule.DeleteLines 1, UFvbc.CodeModule.CountOfLines

' Add 100 CommandButtons
  n = 1
  For r = 1 To 10
    For c = 1 To 10
      Set cb = _
       UFvbc.Designer.Controls.Add("Forms.CommandButton.1")
      With cb
        .Width = 22
        .Height = 22
        .Left = (c * 26) - 16
        .Top = (r * 26) - 16
        .Caption = n
      End With

'     Add the event handler code
      With UFvbc.CodeModule
        code = ""
        code = code & "Private Sub CommandButton" & n & _
         "_Click" & vbCr
        code = code & "Msgbox ""This is CommandButton" & n & _
          """" & vbCr
        code = code & "End Sub"
        .InsertLines .CountOfLines + 1, code
      End With
      n = n + 1
    Next c
  Next r
End Sub
```

The Add100Buttons procedure requires a UserForm named UserForm1. The procedure starts by deleting all controls on the form using the Remove method of the Controls collection, and then deleting all of the code in the code module using the DeleteLines method of the CodeModule object. Next, the CommandButtons are added and the event-handler procedures are created within two For-Next loops. These event handlers are very simple. Here's an example of such a procedure for CommandButton1:

```
Private Sub CommandButton1_Click()
  MsgBox "This is CommandButton1"
End Sub
```

If you remember to clear the form and its attached code each time before you have the Add100Buttons procedure generate the controls, it'll be easier for you to test various parameters such as button width and spacing. Just change a few values, rerun the procedure, and see how it looks. There's no need to delete the old controls manually before rerunning the procedure.

If you would like to show the form after adding the controls at design time, you need to add the following instruction right before the End Sub statement:

```
VBA.UserForms.Add("UserForm1").Show
```

It took me quite a while to figure out how to actually display the UserForm. When the VBA interpreter generates the 100-button UserForm, it indeed exists in VBA's memory, but it isn't officially part of the project yet. So you need the Add method to formally enroll UserForm1 into the collection of UserForms. The return value of this method (yes, it has one) is a reference to the form itself, which is why the Show method can be appended to the end of the Add method. So as a rule, the UserForm must be added to the UserForms collection before it can be used.

Creating UserForms Programmatically

The final topic in this chapter demonstrates how to use VBA code to create UserForms at run time. I present two examples: one is relatively simple, and the other is quite a bit more complex.

A simple example

The example in this section isn't all that useful — in fact, it's completely useless. But it does demonstrate some useful concepts. The MakeForm procedure performs several tasks:

1. It creates a temporary UserForm in the active workbook using the `Add` method of the `VBComponents` collection.
2. It adds a CommandButton control to the UserForm using the `Designer` object.
3. It adds an event-handler procedure to the UserForm's code module (`CommandButton1_Click`). This procedure, when executed, simply displays a message box and then unloads the form.
4. It displays the UserForm.
5. It deletes the UserForm.

The net result is a UserForm that's created on the fly, put to use, and then deleted. This example and the one in the next section both blur the distinction between modifying forms at design time and modifying forms at run time. The form is created using design-time techniques, but it all happens at run time.

The online documentation for topics dealing with creating UserForms is quite poor. Consequently, I relied heavily on trial and error when I developed this procedure.

Following is the complete listing for the `MakeForm` procedure.

```
Sub MakeForm()
    Dim TempForm As Object
    Dim NewButton As Msforms.CommandButton
    Dim Line As Integer

    Application.VBE.MainWindow.Visible = False

'   Create the UserForm
    Set TempForm = ThisWorkbook.VBProject. _
      VBComponents.Add(3) 'vbext_ct_MSForm
    With TempForm
        .Properties("Caption") = "Temporary Form"
        .Properties("Width") = 200
        .Properties("Height") = 100
    End With

'   Add a CommandButton
    Set NewButton = TempForm.Designer.Controls _
      .Add("forms.CommandButton.1")
    With NewButton
        .Caption = "Click Me"
        .Left = 60
        .Top = 40
    End With
```

```
'   Add an event-hander sub for the CommandButton
    With TempForm.CodeModule
        Line = .CountOfLines
        .InsertLines Line + 1, "Sub CommandButton1_Click()"
        .InsertLines Line + 2, "  MsgBox ""Hello!"""
        .InsertLines Line + 3, "  Unload Me"
        .InsertLines Line + 4, "End Sub"
    End With

'   Show the form
    VBA.UserForms.Add(TempForm.Name).Show
'
'   Delete the form
    ThisWorkbook.VBProject.VBComponents.Remove TempForm
End Sub
```

This procedure creates and shows the simple UserForm shown in Figure 27-8.

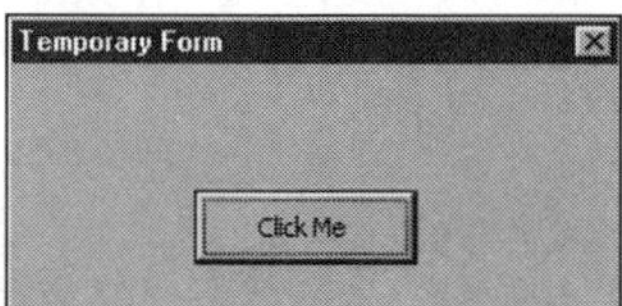

Figure 27-8: This UserForm and its underlying code were generated on the fly.

The workbook that contains the `MakeForm` procedure does not need a reference to the VBA Extensibility Library because it declares `TempForm` as a generic `Object` (not specifically as a `VBComponent` object). Moreover, it doesn't use any built-in constants.

Notice that one of the first instructions hides the VB Editor window by setting its `Visible` property to False. This eliminates the flashing that may occur while the form and code are being generated.

A useful (but not so simple) example

The example in this section is both instructive and useful. It consists of a function named `GetOption` that displays a UserForm. Within this UserForm are a number of OptionButtons, whose captions are specified as arguments to the function. The function returns a value that corresponds to the OptionButton selected by the user. Listing 27-6 shows the complete function.

Listing 27-6: **A dynamically generated option button form**

```
Function GetOption(OpArray, Default, Title)
    Dim TempForm As Object
    Dim NewOptionButton As Msforms.OptionButton
    Dim NewCommandButton1 As Msforms.CommandButton
    Dim NewCommandButton2 As Msforms.CommandButton
    Dim i As Integer, TopPos As Integer
    Dim MaxWidth As Long
    Dim Code As String

'   Hide VBE window to prevent screen flashing
    Application.VBE.MainWindow.Visible = False

'   Create the UserForm
    Set TempForm = _
      ThisWorkbook.VBProject.VBComponents.Add(3)
    TempForm.Properties("Width") = 800

'   Add the OptionButtons
    TopPos = 4
    MaxWidth = 0 'Stores width of widest OptionButton
    For i = LBound(OpArray) To UBound(OpArray)
        Set NewOptionButton = TempForm.Designer.Controls. _
          Add("forms.OptionButton.1")
        With NewOptionButton
            .Width = 800
            .Caption = OpArray(i)
            .Height = 15
            .Left = 8
            .Top = TopPos
            .Tag = i
            .AutoSize = True
            If Default = i Then .Value = True
            If .Width > MaxWidth Then MaxWidth = .Width
        End With
        TopPos = TopPos + 15
    Next i

'   Add the Cancel button
    Set NewCommandButton1 = TempForm.Designer.Controls. _
      Add("forms.CommandButton.1")
    With NewCommandButton1
        .Caption = "Cancel"
        .Height = 18
        .Width = 44
        .Left = MaxWidth + 12
        .Top = 6
    End With
```

Continued

Listing 27-6 *(continued)*

```
'   Add the OK button
    Set NewCommandButton2 = TempForm.Designer.Controls. _
      Add("forms.CommandButton.1")
    With NewCommandButton2
        .Caption = "OK"
        .Height = 18
        .Width = 44
        .Left = MaxWidth + 12
        .Top = 28
    End With

'   Add event-hander subs for the CommandButtons
    Code = ""
    Code = Code & "Sub CommandButton1_Click()" & vbCrLf
    Code = Code & "  GETOPTION_RET_VAL=False" & vbCrLf
    Code = Code & "  Unload Me" & vbCrLf
    Code = Code & "End Sub" & vbCrLf
    Code = Code & "Sub CommandButton2_Click()" & vbCrLf
    Code = Code & "  Dim ctl" & vbCrLf
    Code = Code & "  GETOPTION_RET_VAL = False" & vbCrLf
    Code = Code & "  For Each ctl In Me.Controls" & vbCrLf
    Code = Code & "    If TypeName(ctl) = ""OptionButton"" _
       Then" & vbCrLf
    Code = Code & "      If ctl Then GETOPTION_RET_VAL = _
       ctl.Tag" & vbCrLf
    Code = Code & "    End If" & vbCrLf
    Code = Code & "  Next ctl" & vbCrLf
    Code = Code & "  Unload Me" & vbCrLf
    Code = Code & "End Sub"

    With TempForm.CodeModule
        .InsertLines .CountOfLines + 1, Code
    End With

'   Adjust the form
    With TempForm
        .Properties("Caption") = Title
        .Properties("Width") = NewCommandButton1.Left + _
           NewCommandButton1.Width + 10
        If .Properties("Width") < 160 Then
            .Properties("Width") = 160
            NewCommandButton1.Left = 106
            NewCommandButton2.Left = 106
        End If
        .Properties("Height") = TopPos + 24
    End With

'   Show the form
```

```
    VBA.UserForms.Add(TempForm.Name).Show

'   Delete the form
    ThisWorkbook.VBProject.VBComponents.Remove
VBComponent:=TempForm

'   Pass the selected option back to the calling procedure
    GetOption = GETOPTION_RET_VAL
End Function
```

The `GetOption` function is remarkably fast, considering all that's going on behind the scenes. On my system, the form appears almost instantaneously. The UserForm is deleted after it has served its purpose.

Using the GetOption function

The `GetOption` function takes three arguments:

OpArray	A string array that holds the items to be displayed in the form as OptionButtons.
Default	An integer that specifies the default OptionButton that is selected when the UserForm is displayed. If 0, none of the OptionsButtons is selected.
Title	The text to display in the title bar of the UserForm.

How GetOption works

The `GetOption` function performs the following operations:

1. It hides the VB Editor window to prevent any flashing that may occur when the UserForm is created or the code is added.
2. It creates a UserForm and assigns it to an object variable named `TempForm`.
3. It adds the OptionButton controls, using the array passed to the function via the `OpArray` argument. It uses the `Tag` property of the control to store the index number. The `Tag` setting of the chosen option is the value that's eventually returned by the function.
4. It adds two CommandButtons: the OK button and the Cancel button.
5. It creates an event-handler procedure for each of the CommandButtons.
6. It does some final cleanup work. It adjusts the position of the CommandButtons, as well as the overall size of the UserForm.

7. It displays the UserForm. When the user clicks OK, the `CommandButton1_Click` procedure is executed. This procedure determines which OptionButton is selected, and assigns a number to the `GETOPTION_RET_VAL` variable (a `Public` variable).
8. It deletes the UserForm after it's dismissed.
9. It returns the value of `GETOPTION_RET_VAL` as the function's result.

A significant advantage of creating the UserForm on the fly is that the function is self-contained in a single module, and doesn't even require a reference to the VBA Extensibility Library. Therefore, you can simply export this module (which is named `modOptionsForm`) and then import it into any of your workbooks, giving you access to the `GetOption` function.

The following procedure demonstrates how to use the `GetOption` function. In this case, the UserForm presents five options (contained in the `Ops` array).

```
Sub TestGetOption()
    Dim Ops(1 To 5)
    Dim UserOption
    Ops(1) = "North"
    Ops(2) = "South"
    Ops(3) = "West"
    Ops(4) = "East"
    Ops(5) = "All Regions"
    UserOption = GetOption(Ops, 5, "Select a region")
    Debug.Print UserOption
    MsgBox Ops(UserOption)
End Sub
```

The `UserOption` variable contains the index number of the option selected by the user. If the user clicks Cancel, the `UserOption` variable is set to False.

Figure 27-9 shows the UserForm this function generated.

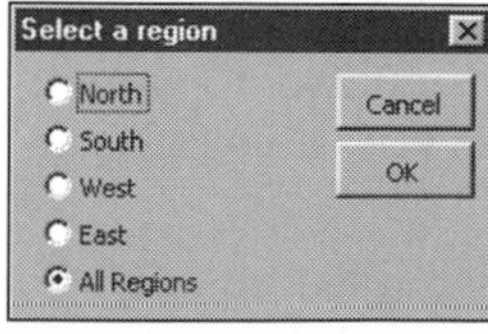

Figure 27-9: The `GetOption` function generated this UserForm.

The UserForm adjusts its size to accommodate the number of elements in the array passed to it. Theoretically, the `UserOption` function can accept an array of any size. Practically speaking, however, you'll want to limit the number of options to keep the UserForm at a reasonable size.

What GetOption makes

Following are the event-handler procedures for the two CommandButtons. This is the code generated within the `GetOption` function and placed in the code module for the temporary UserForm.

```
Sub CommandButton1_Click()
  GETOPTION_RET_VAL = False
  Unload Me
End Sub

Sub CommandButton2_Click()
  Dim ctl
  GETOPTION_RET_VAL = False
  For Each ctl In Me.Controls
    If TypeName(ctl) = "OptionButton" Then
      If ctl Then GETOPTION_RET_VAL = ctl.Tag
    End If
  Next ctl
  Unload Me
End Sub
```

Because the UserForm is deleted after it's used, you can't see what it looks like in the VB Editor. So if you'd like to view the UserForm, convert the following instruction to a comment by typing an apostrophe (') in front of it:

```
ThisWorkbook.VBProject.VBComponents.Remove _
 VBComponent:=TempForm
```

Summary

In this chapter, I provided an introduction to the VBA Integrated Development Environment. I presented examples that demonstrate how to use VBA to add and remove modules, insert VBA code, and create UserForms.

The next chapter introduces another advanced topic: class modules.

✦ ✦ ✦

CHAPTER 28

Understanding Class Modules

In This Chapter

An introduction to class modules

A list of some typical uses for class modules

Examples that demonstrate some key concepts related to class modules

For many VBA programmers, the concept of a class module is a mystery. This feature has been available in Visual Basic for several years and in Excel since Excel 97. This chapter presents an introduction to class modules and includes several examples that may help you better understand this feature and give you ideas for using class modules in your own projects. Class modules can be very complex, and complete coverage is beyond the scope of this book.

What Is a Class Module?

A *class module* is a special type of VBA module that you can insert into a VBA project. Basically, a class module enables the programmer (you) to create new object classes. As you know, programming Excel really boils down to manipulating objects. A class module gives you new objects to manipulate. You can also create properties, methods, and events for your new objects.

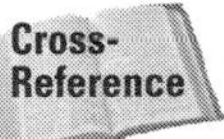

Examples in previous chapters in this book have used class modules. See Chapters 14, 17, 18, and 22.

At this point, you may be asking, "Do I really need to create new objects?" The answer is no. You don't *need* to, but you may want to once you understand some of the benefits of doing so. In many cases, a class module simply serves as a substitute for functions or procedures, but it may be a more convenient and manageable alternative. In other cases, however, you'll find that a class module is the only way to accomplish a particular task.

Following is a list of some typical uses for class modules:

- *To handle events associated with embedded charts.* (See Chapter 17 for an example.)
- *To monitor application-level events,* such as activating any worksheet. (See Chapters 18 and 22 for examples.)
- *To encapsulate a Windows API function to make it easier to use in your code.* For example, you can create a class that makes it easy to detect or set the state of the Num Lock or Caps Lock key. Or you can create a class that simplifies access to the Windows Registry.
- *To enable multiple objects in a UserForm to execute a single procedure.* Normally, each object has its own event handler. The example in Chapter 14 demonstrates how to use a class module so multiple CommandButtons have a single `Click` event-handler procedure.
- *To create reusable components that can be imported into other projects.* Once you create a general-purpose class module, you can import it into other projects to reduce your development time.

Example: Creating a NumLock Class

In this section, I provide step-by-step instructions for creating a useful, albeit simple, class module. This class module creates a NumLock class that has one property: `Value`. Detecting or changing the state of the Num Lock key requires several Windows API functions. The purpose of this class module is to simplify things. All the API declarations and code are contained in a class module (not in your normal VBA modules). The benefits? Your code will be much easier to work with, and you can use this class module in your other projects.

After the class is created, your VBA code can determine the current state of the Num Lock key by using an instruction such as the following, which displays the `Value` property:

```
MsgBox NumLock.Value
```

Or, your code can change the state of the Num Lock key. The following instruction, for example, turns the Num Lock key on.

```
NumLock.Value = True
```

It's important to understand that a class module contains the code that *defines* the object, including its properties and methods. You can then create an instance of this object in your VBA general code modules and manipulate its properties and methods.

To better understand the process of creating a class module, you may want to follow the instructions in the sections that follow. Start with an empty workbook.

Inserting a class module

Activate the VB Editor, and select Insert➪Class Module. This adds an empty class module named `Class1`. If the Properties window isn't displayed, press F4 to display it. Then change the name of the class module to `NumLockClass` (see Figure 28-1).

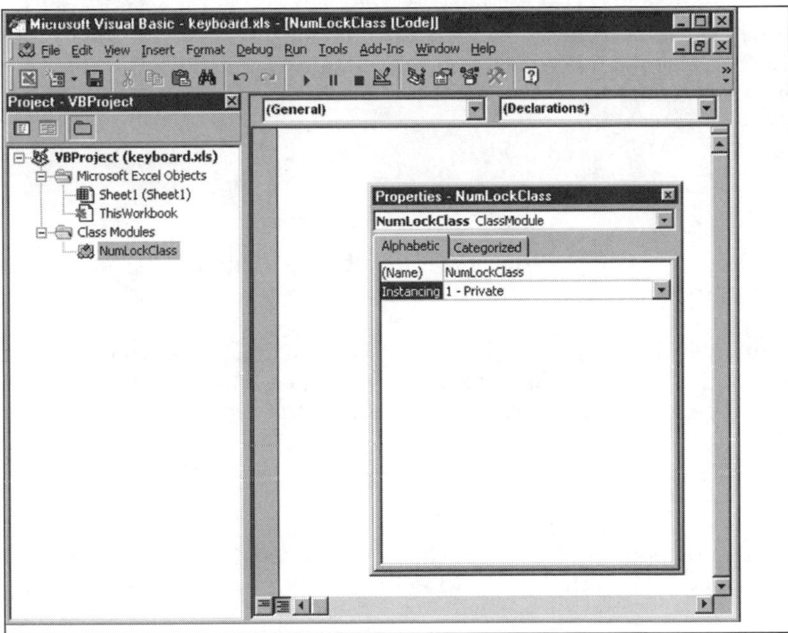

Figure 28-1: An empty class module named NumLockClass.

Adding the VBA code

In this step, you create the code for the `Value` property. To detect or change the state of the Num Lock key, the class module needs the required Windows API declarations that are used to detect and set the Num Lock key. That code is listed below.

```
Private Type KeyboardBytes
     kbByte(0 To 255) As Byte
End Type
```

```
Dim kbArray As KeyboardBytes

Private Declare Function GetKeyState _
  Lib "user32" (ByVal nVirtKey As Long) As Long
Private Declare Function GetKeyboardState _
  Lib "user32" (kbArray As KeyboardBytes) As Long
Private Declare Function SetKeyboardState _
  Lib "user32" (kbArray As KeyboardBytes) As Long

Const VK_NUMLOCK = &H90
```

Next, you need a procedure that retrieves the current state of the Num Lock key. I'll call this the `Value` property of the object. You can use any name for the property; `Value` seems like a good choice. To retrieve the state, insert the following `Property Get` procedure.

```
Property Get Value() As Boolean
    Value = GetKeyState(VK_NUMLOCK) And 1 = 1
End Property
```

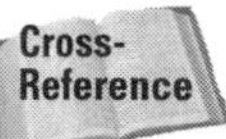

The details of Property procedures are described later in this chapter. See "Programming properties."

This procedure, which uses the `GetKeyState` API function to determine the current state of the Num Lock key, is called whenever VBA code reads the `Value` property of the object. For example, a VBA statement such as this executes the `Property Get` procedure:

```
MsgBox NumLock.Value
```

You now need a procedure that sets the Num Lock key to a particular state: either on or off. You can do this with the following `Property Let` procedure.

```
Property Let Value(boolVal As Boolean)
    GetKeyboardState kbArray
    kbArray.kbByte(VK_NUMLOCK) = Abs(boolVal)
    SetKeyboardState kbArray
End Property
```

The `Property Let` procedure takes one argument, which is either True or False. A VBA statement such as the following executes the `Property Let` procedure.

```
NumLock.Value = True
```

Using the NumLockClass class

Before you can use the NumLockClass class module, you must create an instance of the object. The following statement does just that.

```
Dim NumLock As New NumLockClass
```

Notice that the object type is NumLockClass (that is, the name of the class module). The object itself can have any name, but NumLock certainly seems like a logical name for this.

The following procedure sets the Value property of the NumLock object to True, which results in the Num Lock key's being turned on.

```
Sub NumLockOn()
    Dim NumLock As New NumLockClass
    NumLock.Value = True
End Sub
```

The next procedure displays a message box that indicates the current state of the Num Lock key (True is on; False is off).

```
Sub GetNumLockState()
    Dim NumLock As New NumLockClass
    MsgBox NumLock.Value
End Sub
```

Finally, the following procedure toggles the Num Lock key.

```
Sub ToggleNumLock()
    Dim NumLock As New NumLockClass
    NumLock.Value = Not NumLock.Value
End Sub
```

The completed class module for this example is available on the companion CD-ROM. The workbook also contains a class module to detect and set the state of the Caps Lock key.

More about Class Modules

The example in the preceding section demonstrates how to create a new object class with a single property named Value. An object class can contain any number of properties; it can also contain methods and events.

Naming the object class

The name you use for the class module in which you define the object class is also the name of the object class. By default, class modules are named `Class1`, `Class2`, and so on. Usually, you'll want to provide a more meaningful name for your object class.

Programming properties

Most objects have at least one property, and you can give them as many as you need. After a property is defined, you can use it in your code, using the standard "dot" syntax:

```
object.property
```

The VB Editor's Auto List Members option works with objects defined in a class module. This makes it easier to select properties or methods when writing code.

Properties for the object that you define can be read-only, write-only, or read/write. You define a read-only property with a single procedure, using the `Property Get` keyword. Here's an example of a `Property Get` procedure:

```
Property Get FileNameOnly() As String
    FileNameOnly = ""
    For i = Len(FullName) To 1 Step -1
        Char = Mid(FullName, i, 1)
        If Char = "\" Then
            Exit Function
        Else
            FileNameOnly = Char & FileNameOnly
        End If
    Next i
End Property
```

A `Property Get` procedure works like a Function procedure. The code performs calculations and then returns a property value that corresponds to the procedure's name. In this example, the procedure's name is `FileNameOnly`. The property value returned is the filename part of a path string (contained in a `Public` variable named `FullName`). For example, if `FullName` is `c:\windows\myfile.txt`, the procedure returns a property value of `myfile.txt`. The `FileNameOnly` procedure is called when VBA code references the object and property.

For read/write properties, you create two procedures: a `Property Get` procedure, which reads a property value, and a `Property Let` procedure, which writes a property value. The value being assigned to the property is treated as the final argument (or the only argument) of a `Property Get` procedure.

Two example procedures follow:

```
Property Get SaveAsExcelFile as Boolean
    SaveAsExcelFile = XLFile
End Property

Property Let SaveAsExcelFile(boolVal) as Boolean
   XLFile = boolVal
End Property
```

Note: Use `Property Set` in place of `Property Let` when the property is an object data type.

In the unlikely event that you need to create a write-only property, you create a single `Property Let` procedure with no corresponding `Property Get` procedure.

The preceding examples assume a Boolean module–level variable named `XLFile`. The `Property Get` procedure simply returns the value of this variable as the property value. If the object were named `FileSys`, for example, the following statement would display the current value of the `SaveAsExcelFile` property.

```
MsgBox FileSys.SaveAsExcelFile
```

The `Property Let` statement, on the other hand, accepts an argument and uses the argument to change the value of a property. For example, you could write a statement such as the following to set the `SaveAsExcelFile` property to True:

```
FileSys.SaveAsExcelFile = True
```

In this case, the value True is passed to the `Property Let` statement, changing the property's value.

The preceding examples use a module-level variable named `XLFile` that actually stores the property value. You'll need to create a variable that represents the value for each property that you define within your class module.

Note: Normal procedure-naming rules apply to Property procedures, and you'll find that VBA won't let you use some names if they are reserved words. So if you get a syntax error when creating a Property procedure, try changing the name of the procedure.

Programming methods

A method for an object class is programmed using a standard Sub or Function procedure placed in the class module. An object may or may not use methods. Your code executes a method using standard notation:

```
object.method
```

Like any other VBA method, a method that you write for an object class will perform some type of action. The following procedure is an example of a method that saves a workbook in one of two file formats, depending on the value of the XLFile variable. As you can see, there is nothing special about this procedure.

```
Sub SaveFile()
    If XLFile Then
        ActiveWorkbook.SaveAs FileName:=FName, _
          FileFormat:=xlWorkbookNormal
    Else
        ActiveWorkbook.SaveAs FileName:=FName, _
          FileFormat:=xlCSV
    End If
End Sub
```

The example in the next section should clarify the concepts of properties and methods for object classes defined in a class module.

Class module events

Every class module has two events: Initialize and Terminate. The Initialize event is triggered when a new instance of the object is created; the Terminate event is triggered when the object is destroyed. You might want to use the Initialize event to set default property values.

The frameworks for these event-handler procedures are as follows:

```
Private Sub Class_Initialize()
'    Initialization code goes here
End Sub

Private Sub Class_Terminate()
'    Termination code goes here
End Sub
```

An object is *destroyed* (and its memory is freed) when the procedure or module in which it is declared finishes executing. You can destroy an object at any time by setting it to Nothing. The following statement, for example, destroys the object named MyObject.

```
Set MyObject = Nothing
```

Example: A CSV File Class

The example presented in this section defines an object class called CSVFileClass. This class has two properties and two methods:

Properties

`ExportRange`	(Read/write) A worksheet range to be exported as a CSV file
`ImportRange`	(Read/write) The range into which a CSV file will be imported

Methods

`Import`	Imports the CSV file represented by the `CSVFileName` argument into the range represented by the `ImportRange` property
`Export`	Exports the range represented by the `ExportRange` property to a CSV file represented by the `CSVFileName` argument

Class module–level variables

A class module must maintain its own private variables that mirror the property settings for the class. The `CSVFileClass` class module uses two variables to keep track of the two property settings. These variables are declared at the top of the class module:

```
Private RangeToExport As Range
Private ImportToCell As Range
```

`RangeToExport` is a `Range` object that represents the range to be exported. `ImportToCell` is a `Range` object that represents the upper-left cell of the range into which the file will be imported. These variables are assigned values by the `Property Get` and `Property Let` procedures listed in the next section.

Property procedures

The Property procedures for the `CSVFileClass` class module are shown in Listing 28-1. The `Property Get` procedures return the value of a variable, and the `Property Let` procedures set the value of a variable.

Listing 28-1: Property procedures for the CSVFileClass module

```
Property Get ExportRange() As Range
    Set ExportRange = RangeToExport
End Property

Property Let ExportRange(rng As Range)
    Set RangeToExport = rng
```

Continued

Listing 28-1 *(continued)*

```
End Property

Property Get ImportRange() As Range
    Set ImportRange = ImportToCell
End Property

Property Let ImportRange(rng As Range)
    Set ImportToCell = rng
End Property
```

Method procedures

The CSVFileClass class module contains two procedures that represent the two methods. These are listed and discussed in the sections that follow.

The Export procedure

The Export procedure in Listing 28-2 is called when the Export method is executed. It takes one argument: the full name of the file receiving the exported range. The procedure provides some basic error handling. For example, it ensures that the ExportRange property has been set by checking the RangeToExport variable. The procedure sets up an error handler to trap other errors.

Listing 28-2: Exporting a worksheet range with a class module method

```
Sub Export(CSVFileName)
'   Exports a range to CSV file
    If RangeToExport Is Nothing Then
        MsgBox "ExportRange not specified"
        Exit Sub
    End If

    On Error GoTo ErrHandle
    Set ExpBook = Workbooks.Add
    RangeToExport.Copy
    Application.DisplayAlerts = False
    Application.ScreenUpdating = False
    With ExpBook
        .Sheets(1).Paste
        .SaveAs FileName:=CSVFileName, FileFormat:=xlCSV
        .Close SaveChanges:=False
```

```
        End With
        Application.CutCopyMode = False
        Application.ScreenUpdating = True
        Exit Sub
    ErrHandle:
        ExpBook.Close SaveChanges:=False
        Application.CutCopyMode = xlCopy
        Application.ScreenUpdating = True
        MsgBox "Error " & Err & vbCrLf & vbCrLf & Error(Err), _
          vbCritical, "Export Method Error"
    End Sub
```

The `Export` procedure works by copying the range specified by the `RangeToExport` variable to a new temporary workbook, saving the workbook as a CSV text file, and closing the file. Because screen updating is turned off, the user does not see this happening. If an error occurs — for example, an invalid filename is specified — the procedure jumps to the `ErrHandle` section and displays a message box that contains the error number and description.

The Import procedure

The `Import` procedure in Listing 28-3 imports a CSV file specified by the `CSVFileName` argument and copies its contents to a range specified by the `ImportToCell` variable, which maintains the `ImportRange` property. The file is then closed. Again, screen updating is turned off, so the user does not see the file being opened. Like the `Export` procedure, the `Import` procedure incorporates some basic error handling.

Listing 28-3: Importing text file contents into a range with a class module method

```
Sub Import(CSVFileName)
'   Imports a CSV file to a range
    If ImportToCell Is Nothing Then
        MsgBox "ImportRange not specified"
        Exit Sub
    End If

    If CSVFileName = "" Then
        MsgBox "Import FileName not specified"
        Exit Sub
    End If
```

Continued

Listing 28-3 *(continued)*

```
    On Error GoTo ErrHandle
    Application.ScreenUpdating = False
    Application.DisplayAlerts = False
    Workbooks.Open CSVFileName
    Set CSVFile = ActiveWorkbook
    ActiveSheet.UsedRange.Copy
    ImportToCell.Parent.Parent.Activate
    ImportToCell.Range("A1").Select
    ActiveSheet.Paste
    CSVFile.Close SaveChanges:=False
    Application.ScreenUpdating = True
    Exit Sub
ErrHandle:
    CSVFile.Close SaveChanges:=False
    Application.ScreenUpdating = True
    MsgBox "Error " & Err & vbCrLf & vbCrLf & Error(Err), _
      vbCritical, "Import Method Error"
End Sub
```

Using the CSVFileClass object

To create an instance of a CSVFileClass object in your code, start by declaring a variable as type CSVFileClass. Here's an example:

```
Dim CSVFile As New CSVFileClass
```

You may prefer to declare the object variable first and then create the object when needed. This requires a Dim statement and a Set statement:

```
Dim CSVFile As CSVFileClass
' other code may go here
Set CSVFile = New CSVFile
```

The advantage of using the two-statement method is that the object isn't actually created until the Set statement is executed. You may want to use this technique to save memory by not creating an object if it's not needed. For example, your code might contain logic that determines whether the object is actually created. In addition, using the Set command enables you to create multiple instances of an object.

After creating an instance of the object, you can write other instructions to access the properties and methods defined in the class module.

As you can see in Figure 28-2, the VB Editor's Auto List Members feature works just like any other object. After you type the variable name, followed by a dot, you'll see a list of properties and methods for the object.

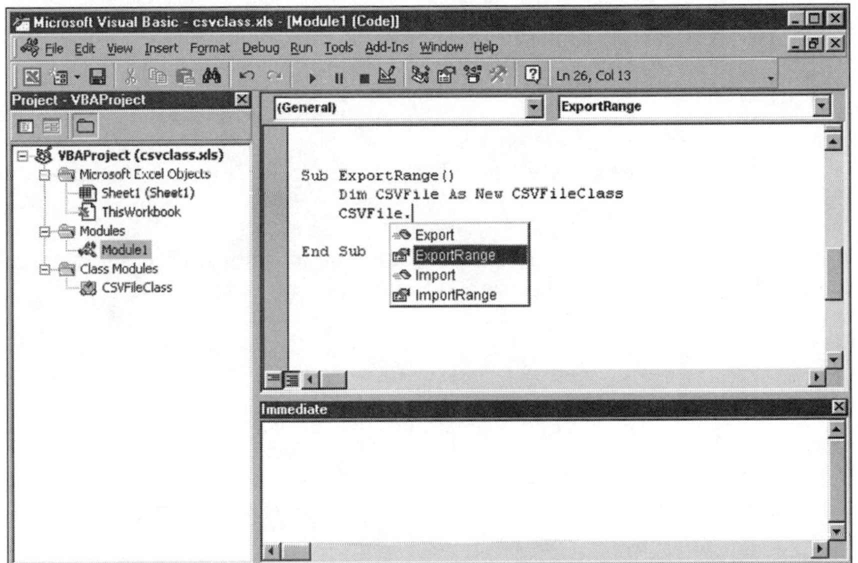

Figure 28-2: The Auto List Members feature displays the available properties and methods.

The following procedure demonstrates how to save the current range selection to a CSV file named temp.csv, which is stored in the same directory as the current workbook.

```
Sub ExportARange()
    Dim CSVFile As New CSVFileClass
    With CSVFile
        .ExportRange = ActiveWindow.RangeSelection
        .Export CSVFileName:=ThisWorkbook.Path & "\temp.csv"
    End With
End Sub
```

Using the `With-End With` structure isn't mandatory. For example, the procedure could be written as follows:

```
Sub ExportARange()
    Dim CSVFile As New CSVFileClass
    CSVFile.ExportRange = ActiveWindow.RangeSelection
    CSVFile.Export CSVFileName:=ThisWorkbook.Path & "\temp.csv"
End Sub
```

The following procedure demonstrates how to import a CSV file, beginning at the active cell.

```
Sub ImportAFile()
    Dim CSVFile As New CSVFileClass
    With CSVFile
    On Error Resume Next
        .ImportRange = ActiveCell
        .Import CSVFileName:=ThisWorkbook.Path & "\temp.csv"
    End With
    If Err <> 0 Then _
      MsgBox "Cannot import " & ThisWorkbook.Path & "\temp.csv"
End Sub
```

Your code can work with more than one instance of an object. The following code, for example, creates an array of three `CSVFileClass` objects.

```
Sub Export3Files()
    Dim CSVFile(1 To 3) As New CSVFileClass
    CSVFile(1).ExportRange = Range("A1:A20")
    CSVFile(2).ExportRange = Range("B1:B20")
    CSVFile(3).ExportRange = Range("C1:C20")

    For i = 1 To 3
        CSVFile(i).Export CSVFileName:="File" & i & ".csv"
    Next i
End Sub
```

Summary

In this chapter, I presented an introduction to class modules and included examples that demonstrate how to create new object classes containing properties and methods. Previous chapters in this book contain other examples of class modules.

The next chapter wraps up Part VII with a handy list of frequently asked questions.

✦ ✦ ✦

CHAPTER 29

Frequently Asked Questions about Excel Programming

✦ ✦ ✦ ✦

In This Chapter

Lists of frequently asked questions about Excel programming

Where to go if your question isn't answered here

✦ ✦ ✦ ✦

If you like to cruise the Internet, you're undoubtedly familiar with *FAQs* — lists of *frequently asked questions* (and their answers) about a particular topic. FAQs are prevalent in the Usenet discussion groups and are posted in an attempt to reduce the number of messages that ask the same questions over and over again. But they rarely serve their intended purpose because the same questions keep appearing despite the FAQs.

I've found that people tend to ask the same questions about Excel programming, so I put together a list of FAQs that cover programming topics for Excel 97 and Excel 2000. Although this FAQ list certainly won't answer *all* of your questions, it covers many common questions and may set you straight about a thing or two. The questions (and many of the answers) came from the following sources:

- `microsoft.public.excel.*` newsgroups
- The `comp.apps.spreadsheets` newsgroup
- Microsoft's Knowledge Base
- *PC World* readers, who wanted them answered in my monthly column
- E-MAIL sent to me in an attempt to get some free consulting

What If My Question Isn't Answered Here?

If this chapter doesn't provide you an answer to your question, start by checking the index of this book. This book includes lots of information that doesn't qualify as a frequently asked question. If you come up empty-handed, check out the resources listed in Appendix A.

I organized this list of questions by assigning each question to one of eight categories:

- General Excel
- The Visual Basic Editor
- Sub procedures and Function procedures
- Objects, properties, methods, and events
- VBA instructions
- UserForms
- Add-ins
- CommandBars

In some cases, my classifications are rather arbitrary; a question could justifiably be assigned to other categories. Moreover, questions within each category are listed in no particular order.

By the way, most of the information in this chapter is discussed in greater detail in other chapters in this book.

General Excel Questions

Why does Excel have two macro languages?

Early versions of Excel used a macro language called XLM. The VBA language was introduced in Excel 5 and is vastly superior in every way. XLM has been phased out, so you should use VBA for new macro development.

I need to distribute a workbook to someone who still uses Excel 4. Is there a way to have Excel 97 or Excel 2000 record my actions to an XLM macro?

No, the macro recorder in these versions can generate only VBA macro code.

Do XLM macros written for previous versions of Excel work in Excel 97 and Excel 2000?

In most cases, they will work perfectly.

I'm looking for a third-party utility that will convert my Excel 4 macros to VBA. Am I out of luck?

Yes, you are. No such utility exists, and it is unlikely that one will be written. Such conversions must be done manually. Because all versions of Excel can execute XLM macros, however, there is really no reason to convert these macros . . . unless, of course, you'd like to update the macro to include new features.

Is it possible to call a VBA procedure from an Excel 4.0 XLM macro?

Yes, you can do so by using XLM's `RUN` function. For example, the following macro runs the `Test` procedure contained in `Module1` in workbook Book1.xls:

```
=RUN(Book1.xls!Module1.Test)
```

Is there a way to automatically convert 1-2-3 or Quattro Pro macros to VBA macros?

No. You must rewrite the macros for Excel.

Where can I find examples of VBA code?

The Internet has hundreds of examples. A good starting point is my Web site:

```
http://www.j-walk.com/ss/
```

Is there a utility that will convert my Excel application into a stand-alone EXE file?

No.

How can I add a drop-down list to a cell so the user can choose a value from the list?

Type the list of valid entries in a single column. You can hide this column from the user if you wish. Select the cell or cells that will display the list of entries, choose Data➪Validation, and select the Settings tab. From the Allow drop-down list, select List. In the Source box, enter a range address or a reference to the items in your sheet. Make sure the In-cell dropdown check box is selected. This technique does not require any macros.

How can I increase the number of columns in a worksheet?

You can't. This number is fixed and cannot be changed.

How can I increase the number of rows in a worksheet?

See the answer to the previous question.

Is it possible to change the color and font of the sheet tabs?

You can't change the color. You can, however, change the font size. In the Windows Control Panel, select Display. In the Display Properties dialog box, click the Appearance tab. In the Item list, select Scrollbar. Use the spinner to increase or decrease the size. This setting will affect other programs.

How can I print the workbook's full path and filename in a page header?

Amazingly, Microsoft continues to ignore what must amount to thousands of requests per year for this feature. The only way to print a workbook's path in a header or footer is to use VBA. The best approach is to take advantage of the `WorkbookBeforePrint` event. For example, place the following procedure in the code module for the `ThisWorkbook` object to print the workbook's full path and filename in the left header of each sheet.

```
Private Sub Workbook_BeforePrint(Cancel As Boolean)
    For Each sht In ThisWorkbook.Sheets
        sht.PageSetup.LeftHeader = ThisWorkbook.FullName
    Next sht
End Sub
```

I've heard that some programs have "secret" commands that display a list of the program's developers. Is there such a command in Excel?

These hidden messages are sometimes known as *Easter Eggs*. Each version of Excel has its own Easter Egg. To view Excel 97's Easter Egg, follow these steps:

1. Open a new workbook.
2. Press F5.
3. Enter **X97:L97**, and press Enter.
4. Press Tab.
5. Press Ctrl+Shift, and click the Chart Wizard button on the toolbar.

You'll be greeted with a full-screen animated image. Use the mouse to "fly" over the landscape (the mouse changes direction: left button moves the image forward and right button moves it backward). Fly around a bit, and you'll see a grey stone pyramid. Fly to the black side of the pyramid, and you'll see the credits scroll by. If this doesn't work, select the Tools➪Options command and then click the Transition tab. Remove the check mark from Transition navigation keys, and click OK. Then try it again.

What about the Easter Egg for Excel 2000?

As this book was going to press, the Excel 2000 Easter Egg had not yet been discovered. Check my Web site (`http://www.j-walk.com/ss/excel/eastereg.htm`) for the latest Excel Easter Egg news.

The Visual Basic Editor

In Excel 95, my VBA modules were located in my workbook. I can't see them when I open the file using Excel 97 or Excel 2000.

The modules are still there, but you view and edit them in the Visual Basic Editor. Press Alt+F11 to toggle between the VB Editor and Excel.

Can I use the VBA macro recorder to record all of my macros?

No. Recording is useful for very simple macros only. Macros that use variable, looping, or any other type of program flow changes cannot be recorded. You can, however, often take advantage of the macro recorder to write some parts of your code or to discover the relevant properties or methods.

Excel 95 had a "record at mark" feature that enabled you to record a macro beginning at a particular location within an existing macro. Is that feature still available?

No, it was removed beginning with Excel 97. To add new recorded code to an existing macro, you need to record it and then cut and paste the code to your existing macro.

I have some macros that are general in nature. I would like to have these available all the time. What's the best way to do this?

Consider storing those general-purpose macros in your Personal Macro Workbook. This is a (normally) hidden workbook that is loaded automatically by Excel. When you record a macro, you have the option of recording it to your Personal Macro Workbook. The file, Personal.xls, is stored in your \XLStart directory.

I can't find my Personal Macro Workbook. Where is it?

The Personal.xls file doesn't exist until you record a macro to it.

Every time my macro copies a worksheet, the new sheet name appears in the Project window of the VB Editor as something like Sheet11111111111(Sheet 1(9)). What's the deal with this?

These strange names are the "code names" for `Worksheet` objects, and they can get very unwieldy if you do a lot of sheet copying. You can change the code name by using the Properties window in the VB Editor.

I locked my project with a password, and I forget what it was. Is there any way to unlock it?

Although Excel 97 and Excel 2000 workbooks are more secure than previous versions, several third-party password-cracking products exist. Use a Web search engine, and search for *Excel password*.

How can I write a macro to change the password of my project?

You can't. The protection elements of a VBA project are not exposed in the object model. Most likely, this was done to make it more difficult for password-cracking software.

When I insert a new module, it always starts with an Option Explicit line. What does this mean?

If `Option Explicit` is included at the top of a module, it means that you must declare every variable before you use it (which is a good idea). If you don't want this line to appear in new modules, activate the VB Editor and select the Tools➪Options command, click the Editor tab, and uncheck the Require Variable Declaration check box. Then you can either declare your variables or let VBA handle the data typing automatically.

Why does my VBA code appear in different colors? Can I change these colors?

VBA uses color to differentiate various types of text: comments, keywords, identifiers, statements with a syntax error, and so on. You can adjust these colors and the font used by selecting the Tools➪Options command (Editor Format tab) in the VB Editor.

I want to delete a VBA module by using VBA code. Can I do this?

Yes. The following code deletes `Module1` from the active workbook.

```
With ActiveWorkbook.VBProject
    .VBComponents.Remove .VBComponents("Module1")
End With
```

I'm having trouble with the concatenation operator (&) in VBA. When I try to concatenate two strings, I get an error message.

VBA is probably interpreting the ampersand as a type-declaration character. Make sure that you insert a space before and after the concatenation operator.

I can't seem to get the VBA line continuation character (underscore) to work.

The line continuation sequence is actually two characters: a space followed by an underscore.

In Excel 95, I set my VBA module to be "very hidden" to prevent users from seeing it. When the workbook is opened in Excel 97, the module can be viewed in the VB Editor. Is this right?

I don't know if it's right, but that's the way it is. Excel 97 and later does not support the `xlVeryHidden` property setting for modules.

After deleting a major amount of VBA code, I've noticed that the XLS file size is not reduced accordingly. Why is this?

Excel doesn't always do a good job of cleaning up after itself. This sometimes causes some subtle problems with variables that you no longer use. One way to fix it is to export your module to a file, delete the module, and then import it again.

My workbook contains a VBA procedure named Test. I tried to use Excel's Name box to create a range named Test, and Excel dumped me to the VB Editor, with the cursor on my Test procedure. What's this all about?

I can only guess that it's a bug of some sort. Apparently, Excel thinks the name is already defined, possibly as an XLM macro. If you use the Insert⇨Name⇨Define command to define your range name, the problem won't occur.

I distributed an XLS application to many users. On some machines, my VBA error-handling procedures don't work. Why not?

The error-handling procedures won't work if the user has the Break on All Errors option set. This option is available in the Options dialog box (General tab) in the VB Editor. Unfortunately, you can't change this setting with VBA. To avoid this problem, you can distribute your application as an XLA add-in.

Procedures

What's the difference between a VBA procedure and a macro?

Nothing, really. The term *macro* is a carry-over from the old days of spreadsheets. These terms are now used interchangeably.

What's a procedure?

A procedure is a grouping of VBA instructions that can be called by name. If these instructions are to give an explicit result, such as a value, back to the instruction that called them, they most likely belong to a Function procedure. Otherwise, they probably belong to a Sub procedure.

What is a variant data type?

Variables that aren't specifically declared are assigned the variant type by default, and VBA automatically converts the data to the proper type when it's used. This is particularly useful for retrieving values from a worksheet cell when you don't know in advance what the cell contains. Generally, it's a good idea to specifically declare your variables with the `Dim`, `Public`, or `Private` statement because using variants is quite a bit slower and is not the most efficient use of memory.

What's the difference between a variant array and an array of variants?

A variant is a unit of memory with a special data type that can contain any kind of data: a single value or an array of values (that is, a *variant array*). The following code creates a variant that contains an array.

```
Dim X As Variant
X = Array(30, 40, 50)
```

A normal array can contain items of a specified data type, including nontyped variants. The following statement creates an array that consists of twelve variants.

```
Dim X (0 To 2) As Variant
```

Although a variant containing an array is conceptually different from an array whose elements are of type variant, the array elements are accessed in the same way.

What's a type-definition character?

VBA lets you append a character to a variable's name to indicate the data type. For example, you can declare the `MyVar` variable as an integer by tacking `%` onto the name, as follows:

```
Dim MyVar%
```

Here's a list of the type-declaration characters supported by VBA:

```
Integer    %
Long       &
Single     !
Double     #
Currency   @
String     $
```

Can a custom worksheet function written in VBA perform the same types of actions as a procedure?

No. Functions called from a worksheet formula have some limitations. In general, they must be strictly "passive"—they can't change the active cell, apply formatting, open workbooks, or change the active sheet.

Functions can only perform calculations and return a value. An exception to this rule is the VBA `MsgBox` function. A custom function can display a message box whenever it is recalculated. This is very handy for debugging a custom function.

I would like to create a procedure that automatically changes the formatting of a cell based on the data I enter. For example, if I enter a value greater than 0, the cell's background color should be red. Is this possible?

It's certainly possible, and you don't need any programming. Use Excel's Conditional Formatting feature, accessed with the Format⇨Conditional Formatting command.

The Conditional Formatting feature is useful, but I'd like to perform other types of operations when data is entered into a cell.

In that case, you can take advantage of the `Change` event for a worksheet object. Whenever a cell is changed, the `Change` event is triggered. If the code module for the `Sheet` object contains a procedure named `Worksheet_Change`, this procedure will be executed automatically.

What other types of events can be monitored?

Lots! Search the online help for *events* to get a complete listing.

I tried entering an event procedure (Sub Workbook_Open), but the procedure isn't executed when the workbook is opened. What's wrong?

You probably put the procedure in the wrong place. Workbook event procedures must be in the code module for the `ThisWorkbook` object. Worksheet event procedures must be in the code module for the appropriate `Sheet` object, as shown in the VB Editor's Project window.

I can write an event procedure for a particular workbook. Is it possible to write an event procedure that will work for any workbook that's open?

Yes, but you need to use a class module. Details are in Chapter 18.

I'm very familiar with creating formulas in Excel. Does VBA use the same mathematical and logical operators?

Yes. And it includes some additional operators that aren't valid in worksheet formulas. These additional VBA operators are listed in the following table:

Operator	*Function*
`\`	Division with an integer result
`Eqv`	Returns True if both expressions are True or both are False
`Imp`	Logical implication on two expressions
`Is`	Compares two object variables
`Like`	Compares two strings, using wildcard characters
`Xor`	Returns True if only one expression is True

How can I execute a procedure that's in a different workbook?

Use the `Run` method of the `Application` object. The following instruction executes a procedure named `Macro1` located in the Personal.xls workbook.

```
Run "Personal.xls!Macro1"
```

I've used VBA to create several custom functions. I like to use these functions in my worksheet formulas, but I find it inconvenient to precede the function name with the workbook name. Is there any way around this?

Yes. Convert the workbook that holds the function definitions to an XLA add-in. When the add-in is open, you can use the functions in any other worksheet without referencing the function's filename.

In addition, if you set up a reference to the workbook that contains the custom functions, you can use the function without preceding it with the workbook name. To create a reference, use the Tools⇨References command in the VB Editor.

I would like a particular workbook to be loaded every time I start Excel. I would also like a macro in this workbook to execute automatically. Am I asking too much?

Not at all. To open the workbook automatically, just store it in your \XLStart directory. To have the macro execute automatically, create a `Workbook_Open` macro in the code module for the workbook's `ThisWorkbook` object.

I have a workbook that uses a Workbook_Open procedure. Is there a way to prevent this from executing when I open the workbook?

Yes. Hold down Shift when you issue the File⇨Open command. This technique also works with the `Workbook_BeforeClose` procedure. However, it does not work if the workbook you're opening is an add-in.

Can a VBA procedure access a cell's value in a workbook that is not open?

No. A formula in a worksheet can do this, but VBA cannot.

How can I prevent the "save file" prompt from being displayed when I close a workbook from VBA?

Insert the following instruction to eliminate this and other prompts:

```
Application.DisplayAlerts = False
```

How can I set things up so my macro runs once every hour?

You need to use the `OnTime` method of the `Application` object. This enables you to specify a procedure to execute at a particular time of day. When the procedure ends, use the `OnTime` method again to schedule another event in one hour.

How do I prevent a macro from showing in the macro list?

Declare the procedure using the `Private` keyword:

```
Private Sub MyMacro()
```

Or you can add a dummy optional argument:

```
Sub MyMacro (Optional FakeArg)
```

I wrote a macro that creates lots of charts. After some of the charts are created, I get a "not enough memory" error. My system has lots of memory, so what's the problem?

Most likely, your system is running low on system resources. In some versions of Excel, creating charts uses system resources that are not returned to the system. The only way to regain the system resources is to restart Windows. The problem was supposedly fixed in Excel 2000. If you're using Excel 97, try upgrading to SR-2.

Is it possible to save a chart as a GIF file?

Yes. The following code saves the first embedded chart on Sheet1 as a GIF file named Mychart.gif.

```
Set CurrentChart = Sheets("Sheet1").ChartObjects(1).Chart
Fname = ThisWorkbook.Path & "\Mychart.gif"
CurrentChart.Export Filename:=Fname, FilterName:="GIF"
```

Are variables in a VBA procedure available to other VBA procedures? What if the procedure is in a different module? Or in a different workbook?

You're talking about a variable's *scope*. There are three levels of scope: local, module, and public. Local variables have the narrowest scope and are declared within a procedure. A local variable is visible only to the procedure in which it was declared. Module-level variables are declared at the top of a module, prior to the first procedure. Module-level variables are visible to all procedures in the module. Public variables have the broadest scope, and they are declared using the `Public` keyword.

Functions

I created a custom worksheet function. When I access this function with the Insert Function dialog, it says, "Choose the Help button for help on this function and its arguments." How can I get the Insert Function dialog box to display a description of my function?

As you discovered, the message displayed in the Insert Function dialog box is erroneous and misleading. To add a description for your custom function, select Tool⇨Macro⇨Macros to display the Macro dialog box. Your function won't be listed, so you must type it into the Macro name box. After typing the function's name, click Options to display the Macro Options dialog box. Enter the descriptive text in the Description box.

Can I also display help for the arguments for my custom function in the Paste Function dialog box?

Unfortunately, no.

My custom worksheet function appears in the User Defined category in the Insert Function dialog box. How can I make my function appear in a different function category?

You need to use VBA to do this. The following instruction assigns the function named `MyFunc` to Category 1 (Financial):

```
Application.MacroOptions Macro:="MyFunc", Category:=1
```

The following table lists the valid function category numbers:

Number	*Category*
0	No category (appears only in All)
1	Financial
2	Date & Time
3	Math & Trig
4	Statistical
5	Lookup & Reference
6	Database
7	Text
8	Logical
9	Information
10	Commands (this category is normally hidden)
11	Customizing (this category is normally hidden)
12	Macro Control (this category is normally hidden)
13	DDE/External (this category is normally hidden)
14	User Defined (default)
15	Engineering (this category is valid only if the Analysis Toolpak add-in is installed)

How can I create a new function category?

You can't.

I have a custom function that will be used in a worksheet formula. If the user enters arguments that are not appropriate, how can I make the function return a true error value (#VALUE)?

If your function is named MyFunction, you can use the following instruction to return an error value to the cell that contains the function:

```
MyFunction =  CVErr(xlErrValue)
```

In this example, xlErrValue is a predefined constant. Constants for the other error values are listed in the online help.

Can I use Excel's built-in worksheet functions in my VBA code?

In most cases, yes. Excel's worksheet functions are accessed via the WorksheetFunction method of the Application object. For example, you could access the POWER worksheet functions with a statement such as the following:

```
Ans = Application.WorksheetFunction.Power(5, 3)
```

This example raises 5 to the third power.

Generally, if VBA includes an equivalent function, you cannot use Excel's worksheet version. For example, because VBA has a function to compute square roots (Sqr), you cannot use the SQRT worksheet function in your VBA code.

Excel 95 doesn't support the WorksheetFunction method. Does that mean I can't make my Excel 2000 application compatible with Excel 95?

No. Actually, using the WorksheetFunction method is superfluous. The following statements have exactly the same result:

```
Ans = Application.WorksheetFunction.Power(5, 3)
Ans = Application.Power(5, 3)
```

Is there any way to force a line break in the text of a message box?

Use a carriage return or a line feed character to force a new line. The following statement displays the message box text on two lines. vbCr is a built-in constant that represents a carriage return.

```
MsgBox "Hello" & vbCr & Application.UserName
```

Objects, Properties, Methods, and Events

I don't understand the concept of objects. Is there a listing of the Excel objects I can use?

Yes. The online help includes the information in a graphical format.

I'm overwhelmed with all the properties and methods available. How can I find out which methods and properties are available for a particular object?

There are several ways. You can use the Object Browser available in the VB Editor. Press F2 to access the Object Browser and then choose Excel from the Libraries/Workbooks drop-down list. The list on the left shows all the Excel objects. When you select an object, its corresponding properties and methods appear in the list on the right.

The online help system for VBA is very extensive; it lists the properties and methods available for most objects of importance. The easiest way to access these lists is to type the object name into the Immediate window at the bottom of the VB Editor and move the cursor anywhere within the object name. Press F1, and you'll get the help topic appropriate for the object.

What's the story with collections? Is a collection an object? What are collections?

A *collection* is an object that contains a group of related objects. A collection is designated by a plural noun. For example, the `Worksheets` collection is an object that contains all the `Worksheet` objects in a workbook. You can think of this as an array: `Worksheets(1)` refers to the first `Worksheet` object in the `Workbook`. Rather than use index numbers, you can also use the actual worksheet name, such as `Worksheets("Sheet1")`. The concept of a collection makes it easy to work with all related objects at once and to loop through all objects in a collection by using the `For Each-Next` construct.

When I refer to a worksheet in my VBA code, I get a "subscript out of range" error. I'm not using any subscripts. What gives?

This error occurs when you attempt to access an element in a collection that doesn't exist. For example, the following instruction generates the error if the active workbook does not contain a worksheet named `MySheet`.

```
Set X = ActiveWorkbook.Worksheets("MySheet")
```

How can I prevent the user from scrolling around the worksheet?

You can either hide the unused rows and columns or use a VBA instruction to set the scroll area for the worksheet. The following instruction, for example, sets the scroll area on `Sheet1` so the user cannot activate any cells outside of B2:D50.

```
Worksheets("Sheet1").ScrollArea = "B2:D50"
```

To set scrolling back to normal, use a statement like this:

```
Worksheets("Sheet1").ScrollArea = ""
```

Be aware that the `ScrollArea` setting is not saved with the workbook. Therefore, you'll need to execute the `ScrollArea` assignment instruction whenever the workbook is opened. This instruction can go in the `Workbook_Open` event-handler procedure.

What's the difference between using Select and Application.Goto?

The `Select` method of the `Range` object selects a range on the *active* worksheet only. Use `Application.Goto` to select a range on any worksheet in a workbook. `Application.Goto` may or may not make another sheet the active sheet. The `Goto` method also lets you scroll the sheet so that the range is in the upper-left corner.

What's the difference between activating a range and selecting a range?

In some cases, the `Activate` method and the `Select` method have exactly the same effect. But in other cases, they produce quite different results. Assume that range A1:C3 is selected. The following statement activates cell C3. The original range remains selected, but C3 becomes the active cell — that is, the cell that contains the cell pointer.

```
Range("C3").Activate
```

Again, assuming that range A1:C3 is selected, the following statement selects a single cell, which also becomes the active cell.

```
Range("C3").Select
```

I know how to write a VBA instruction to select a range by using a cell address, but how can I write one to select a range if I know only its row and column number?

Use the `Cells` method. The following instruction, for example, selects the cell in the 5th row and the 12th column:

```
Cells(5, 12).Select
```

Is there a VBA command to quit Excel? When I try to record the File⇨Exit command, Excel closes down before I can see what code it generates!

Use the following instruction to end Excel:

```
Application.Quit
```

How can I turn off the screen updating while a macro is running?

The following instruction turns off screen updating and speeds up macros that modify the display:

```
Application.ScreenUpdating = False
```

Is it possible to display messages in the status bar while a macro is running? I have a lengthy macro, and it would be nice to display its progress in the status bar.

Yes. Assign the text to the `StatusBar` property of the `Application` object. Here's an example:

```
Application.StatusBar = "Now processing File " & FileNum
```

When your routine finishes, return the status bar back to normal with the following instruction:

```
Application.StatusBar = False
```

I recorded a VBA macro that copies a range and pastes it to another area. The macro uses the Select method. Is there a more efficient way to copy and paste?

Yes. Although the macro recorder generally selects cells before doing anything with them, selecting is not necessary and may actually slow down your macro. Recording a very simple copy-and-paste operation generates four lines of VBA code, two of which use the `Select` method. Here's an example:

```
Range("A1").Select
Selection.Copy
Range("B1").Select
ActiveSheet.Paste
```

These four lines can be replaced with a single instruction, such as the following:

```
Range("A1").Copy Range("B1")
```

Notice that this instruction does not use the `Select` method.

I have not been able to find a method to sort a VBA array. Does this mean that I have to copy the values to a worksheet and then use the Range.Sort method?

There is no built-in way to sort an array in VBA. Copying the array to a worksheet is one method, but you'll probably be better off if you write your own sorting procedure. Many sorting algorithms are available, and some are quite easy to code in VBA. This book contains VBA code for several sorting techniques.

My macro works with the selected cells, but it fails if something else (like a chart) is selected. How can I make sure that a range is selected?

You can use VBA's `TypeName` function to check the `Selection` object. Here's an example:

```
If TypeName(Selection) <> "Range" Then
    MsgBox "Select a range!"
    Exit Sub
End If
```

Another approach is to use the `RangeSelection` property, which returns a `Range` object that represents the selected cells on the worksheet in the specified window, even if a graphic object is active or selected. This property applies to a `Window` object, not a `Workbook` object. The following instruction, for example, displays the address of the selected range:

```
MsgBox ActiveWindow.RangeSelection.Address
```

My VBA macro needs to count the number of rows selected by the user. Using Selection.Rows.Count doesn't work when nonadjacent rows are selected. Is this a bug?

Actually, this is the way it's supposed to work. The `Count` method returns the number of elements in only the *first* area of the selection (a noncontiguous selection has multiple areas). To get an accurate row count, your VBA code must first determine the number of areas in the selection and then count the number of rows in each area. Use `Selection.Areas.Count` to count the number of areas. Here's an example that stores the total number of selected rows in the `NumRows` variable:

```
NumRows = 0
For Each areaCounter In Selection.Areas
    NumRows = NumRows + areaCounter.Rows.Count
Next areaCounter
```

By the way, this process is also relevant to counting columns and cells.

Is there a workbook property that forces an Excel workbook always to remain visible so it won't be hidden by another application's window?

No.

Is there a way to stop Excel from displaying messages while my macro is running? For example, I'd like to eliminate the message that appears when my macro deletes a worksheet.

The following statement turns off most of Excel's warning messages:

```
Application.DisplayAlerts = False
```

Is there a VBA instruction to select the last entry in a column or row? Normally, I can use Ctrl+Shift+down arrow or Ctrl+Shift+right arrow to do this, but how can I do it with a macro?

The VBA equivalent for Ctrl+Shift+down arrow is the following:

```
Selection.End(XLDown).Select
```

The constants used for the other directions are `XLToLeft`, `XLToRight`, and `XLUp`.

How can I determine the last nonempty cell in a particular column?

The following instruction displays the address of the last nonempty cell in column A:

```
MsgBox ActiveSheet.Range("A65536").End(xlUp).Address
```

But that instruction won't work if cell A65536 is not empty!

To handle that unlikely occurrence, use this code:

```
With ActiveSheet.Range("A65536")
    If .Value <> "" Then
        MsgBox .Address
    Else
        MsgBox .End(xlUp).Address
    End If
End With
```

VBA references can become very lengthy, especially when you need to fully qualify an object by referencing its sheet and workbook. Is there a way to reduce the length of these references?

Yes. Use the Set statement to create an object variable. Here's an example:

```
Dim MyRange as Range
Set MyRange = _
  ThisWorkbook.Worksheets("Sheet1").Range("A1")
```

After the Set statement is executed, you can refer to this single-cell Range object simply as MyRange. For example, you can assign a value to the cell with the following:

```
MyRange.Value = 10
```

Besides making it easier to refer to objects, using object variables can also help your code execute more quickly.

Is there a way to declare an array if you don't know how many elements it will have?

Yes. You may declare a dynamic array with the Dim statement, using empty parentheses, and then allocate storage for that array later with the ReDim statement when you know how many elements the array should have. Use ReDim Preserve if you don't want to lose the current array contents when reallocating it.

How can I write a macro to select some, but not all, of the sheets in a workbook?

Use False as the argument for the Select method. For example, the following procedure selects all chart sheets in the active workbook:

```
Sub SelectSheets()
    For Each sht In Sheets
        If TypeName(sht) = "Chart" Then _
          sht.Select False
    Next sht
End Sub
```

Can I let the user undo my macro?

Yes, but it's not something that can be done automatically. To enable the user to undo the effects of your macro, your VBA code module must keep track of what was changed by the macro and then be capable of restoring the original state if the user selects Edit⇨Undo.

To enable the Edit➪Undo command, use the OnUndo method as the last action in your macro. This method enables you to specify text that will appear on the Undo menu item and also to specify a procedure to run if the user selects Edit➪Undo. Here's an example:

```
Application.OnUndo "The Last Macro", "MyUndoMacro"
```

I have a 1-2-3 macro that pauses so the user can enter data into a certain cell. How can I get the same effect in a VBA macro?

Excel can't duplicate that type of behavior, but you can use Excel's InputBox statement to get a value from a user and place it in a particular cell. The first instruction below, for example, displays an input box. When the user enters a value, that value is placed in cell A1.

```
UserVal = Application.InputBox("Value?", , , , , , 1)
If UserVal <> False Then Range("A1") = UserVal
```

VBA has an InputBox function, but there's also an InputBox method for the Application object. Are these the same?

No. Excel's InputBox method is more versatile because it allows validation of the user's entry. The preceding example uses 1 (which represents a numeric value) for the last argument of the InputBox method. This ensures that the user enters a value into the input box.

When I use the RGB function to assign a color, the color sometimes isn't correct. What am I doing wrong?

Probably nothing. An Excel workbook can use only 56 different colors (the color palette). If a specified RGB color isn't in the palette, Excel uses the closest match it can find.

I'm trying to write a VBA instruction that creates a formula. To do so, I need to insert a quote character (") within quoted text. How can I do that?

Assume you want to enter the following formula into cell B1 with VBA:

```
=IF(A1="Yes",TRUE,FALSE)
```

The following instruction generates a syntax error:

```
Range("B1").Formula = "=IF(A1="Yes",TRUE,FALSE)"   'erroneous
```

The solution is to use two double quotes side by side. The following instruction produces the desired result:

```
Range("B1").Formula = "=IF(A1=""Yes"",TRUE,FALSE)"
```

Another approach is to use VBA's `Chr` function with an argument of `34`, which returns a quotation mark. The following example demonstrates:

```
Range("B1").Formula = _
  "=IF(A1=" & Chr(34) & "Yes" & Chr(34) & ",TRUE,FALSE)"
```

I created an array, but the first element in that array is being treated as the second element. What's wrong?

Unless you tell it otherwise, VBA uses 0 as the first index number for an array. If you want all your arrays to always start with 1, insert the following statement at the top of your VBA module:

```
Option Base 1
```

Or you can specify the upper and lower bounds of an array when you declare it. Here's an example:

```
Dim Months(1 To 12) As String
```

I would like my VBA code to run as quickly as possible. Any suggestions?

Here are a few general tips: Make sure that you declare all your variables. Use `Option Explicit` at the top of your modules to force yourself to do this. If you reference an Excel object more than once, create an object variable for it. Use the `With-End With` construct whenever possible. Finally, if your macro writes information to a worksheet, turn off screen updating by using `Application.ScreenUpdating = False`.

UserForms

I need to get just a few pieces of information, and a UserForm seems like overkill. Are there any alternatives?

Yes, check out VBA's `MsgBox` function and its `InputBox` function. Alternatively, you might want to use Excel's `InputBox` method.

I have 12 CommandButtons on a UserForm. How can I assign a single macro to be executed when any of the buttons is clicked?

There is no easy way to do this because each CommandButton has its own `Click` event procedure. One solution is to call another procedure from each of the `CommandButton_Click` procedures. Another solution is to use a class module to create a new class. This procedure is described in Chapter 14.

Is there any way to display a chart in a UserForm?

There is no direct way to do this. One solution is to save the chart to a GIF file and then load the GIF file into an `Image` control.

How can I remove the "X" from the title bar of my UserForm? I don't want the user to click that button to close the form.

You can't remove the Close button on a UserForm's title bar. However, you can intercept all attempts to close the UserForm by using a `UserForm_QueryClose` event procedure in the code module for the UserForm. The following example does not allow the user to close the form by clicking the Close button:

```
Private Sub UserForm_QueryClose _
  (Cancel As Integer, CloseMode As Integer)
    If CloseMode = vbFormControlMenu Then
        MsgBox "You can't close the form like that."
        Cancel = True
    End If
End Sub
```

I've created a UserForm whose controls are linked to cells on the worksheet with the ControlSource property. Is this the best way to do this?

In general, you should avoid using links to worksheet cells unless you absolutely must. Doing so can slow your application down because the worksheet is recalculated every time a control changes the cell.

Is there any way to create a control array for a UserForm? It's possible with Visual Basic 6.0, but I can't figure out how to do it with Excel VBA.

You can't create a control array, but you can create an array of `Control` objects. The following code creates an array consisting of all CommandButton controls:

```
Private Sub UserForm_Initialize()
    Dim Buttons() As CommandButton
    Cnt = 0
    For Each Ctl In UserForm1.Controls
```

```
            If TypeName(Ctl) = "CommandButton" Then
                Cnt = Cnt + 1
                ReDim Preserve Buttons(1 To Cnt)
                Set Buttons(Cnt) = Ctl
            End If
        Next Ctl
    End Sub
```

Is there any difference between hiding a UserForm and unloading a UserForm?

Yes, the `Hide` method keeps the UserForm in memory but makes it invisible. The `Unload` statement unloads the UserForm, beginning the "termination" process (invoking the `Terminate` event for the UserForm) and removing the UserForm from memory.

How can I make my UserForm stay open while I do other things?

By default, each UserForm is *modal*, which means that it must be dismissed before you can do anything else. In Excel 2000, however, you can make a UserForm modeless by writing `vbModeless` as the argument for the `Show` method. Here's an example:

```
UserForm1.Show vbModeless
```

Excel 97 gives me a compile error when I write UserForm1.Show vbModeless. How can I make the form modeless in Excel 2000, while allowing it to remain modal in Excel 97?

Test for the version of Excel that the user is running and then execute a separate procedure if the version is Excel 2000 or later. The following code demonstrates how:

```
Sub ShowUserForm()
    If Val(Application.Version) > 8 Then
      ShowModelessForm
    Else
      UserForm1.Show
    End If
End Sub

Sub ShowModelessForm()
    UserForm1.Show vbModeless
End Sub
```

Because the `ShowModelessForm` procedure is not executed in Excel 97, it will not cause a compile error.

I need to display a progress indicator like those you see when you're installing software while a lengthy process is being executed. How can I do this?

You can do this with a UserForm. Chapter 14 describes several different techniques, including one where I gradually stretch a shape inside a frame while the lengthy process is running.

How can I generate a list of files and directories into my UserForm so the user can select a file from the list?

There's no need to do that. Use VBA's `GetOpenFilename` method. This displays a "file open" dialog box in which the user can select a drive, directory, and file.

I have several 1-2-3 for Windows files and Quattro Pro for Windows files that contain custom dialog boxes. Is there a utility to convert these to Excel dialog boxes?

No.

I need to concatenate strings and display them in a ListBox control. But when I do so, they aren't aligned properly. How can I get them to display equal spacing between strings?

You can use a monospaced font such as Courier New for the ListBox. A better approach, however, is to set up your ListBox to use two columns (see Chapter 13 for details).

Is it possible to display a built-in Excel dialog box from VBA?

Most, but not all, of Excel's dialog boxes can be displayed by using the `Application.Dialogs` method. For example, the following instruction displays the dialog box that enables you to format numbers in cells:

```
Application.Dialogs(xlDialogFormatNumber).Show
```

Use the Object Browser to display a list of the constants for the built-in dialog boxes. Press F2 from the VB Editor, select the `Excel` library, and then select the `Constants` object. The Method/Properties list displays the constants for the built-in dialog boxes (they all begin with `xlDialog`).

I tried the technique in the preceding question and received an error message. Why is that?

The Dialogs method will fail if the context isn't appropriate. For example, if you attempt to display the Chart Type dialog box (xlDialogChartType) when a chart is not activated, you'll get an error message.

Every time I create a UserForm, I go through the steps of adding an OK button and a Cancel button. Is there a way to get these controls to appear automatically?

Yes. Set up a UserForm with the controls you use most often. Then select File⇨Export File to save the UserForm. When you want to add a new form to another project, select File⇨Import File.

Is it possible to create a UserForm without a title bar?

No. The closest you can get is to make the dialog box's caption blank by setting the Caption property to an empty string.

I recorded a VBA macro that prints to a file. However, there seems to be no way to supply the filename in my code. No matter what I try, I keep getting the prompt to supply a filename.

This common problem was corrected in Excel 2000. In Excel 2000, you can provide a PrToFileName argument for the PrintOut method. Here's an example:

```
ActiveSheet.PrintOut PrintToFile:=True, _
  PrToFileName:="test.prn"
```

When I click a button on my UserForm, nothing happens. What am I doing wrong?

Controls added to a UserForm do nothing unless you write event-handler procedures for them.

I wrote a procedure named Workbook_Open, but it doesn't get executed when the workbook is opened.

The most likely cause is that your procedure is located in a general VBA module. Workbook event procedures must be located in the code module for the ThisWorkbook object.

Can I create a custom dialog box whose size is always the same, regardless of the video display resolution?

You can, but it's probably not worth the effort. You can write code to determine the video resolution and then make use of the Zoom property of a UserForm to change its size. The normal way to deal with this matter is simply to design your UserForm for a 640 × 480 display.

Is it possible to create a UserForm box that lets the user select a range in a worksheet by pointing?

Yes. Use the RefEdit control for this. See Chapter 13 for an example.

Is there a way to change the startup position of a UserForm?

Yes, you can set the UserForm's `Left` and `Top` properties. But for these to be effective, you need to set the UserForm's `StartUpPosition` property to `0`.

Can I add an Excel 5/95 dialog sheet to my workbook?

Yes. Right-click any sheet tab in a workbook, and select Insert from the shortcut menu. In the Insert dialog box, select MS Excel 5.0 Dialog.

Add-ins

Where can I get Excel add-ins?

You can get Excel add-ins from a number of places:

- ✦ Excel includes several add-ins you can use whenever you need them.
- ✦ Third-party developers distribute and sell add-ins for special purposes.
- ✦ Many developers create free add-ins and distribute them via their Internet sites.
- ✦ You can create your own add-ins.

How do I install an add-in?

You can load an add-in by selecting either the Tools➪Add-Ins command or the File➪Open command. Using Tools➪Add-Ins is the preferred method. An add-in opened with File➪Open cannot be closed without using VBA.

When I install my add-in using Excel's Add-Ins dialog box, it shows up without a name or description. How can I give my add-in a description?

Before creating the add-in, use the File➪Properties command to bring up the Properties dialog box. Click the Summary tab. In the Title box, enter the text that you want to appear in the Add-Ins dialog box. In the Comments field, enter the description for the add-in. Then create the add-in as usual.

I have several add-ins that I no longer use, yet I can't figure out how to remove them from the Add-Ins Available list in the Add-Ins dialog box. What's the story?

Oddly, there is no direct way to remove unwanted add-ins from the list directly from Excel. You must edit the Windows Registry and remove the references to the add-in files you don't want listed. Another way to do this is to move or delete the add-in files. Then, when you attempt to open the add-in from the Add-Ins dialog box, Excel will ask if you want to remove the add-in from the list.

How do I create an add-in?

Activate any sheet, and select File⇨Save As. Then select Microsoft Excel Add-in (*.xla) from the Save as type drop-down list.

I try to create an add-in, but the Save as type drop-down box doesn't provide Add-in as an option.

The most likely reason is that your workbook doesn't contain at least one worksheet.

Should I convert all my essential workbooks to add-ins?

No! Although you can create an add-in from any workbook, not all workbooks are suitable. When a workbook is converted to an add-in, it is essentially invisible. For most workbooks, being invisible isn't a good thing.

Is it necessary to keep two copies of my workbook, the XLS version and the XLA version?

With versions prior to Excel 97, maintaining an XLS and an XLA version was necessary. Beginning with Excel 97, however, this is no longer necessary. An add-in can be converted back to a normal workbook.

How do I modify an add-in after it's been created?

Activate the VB Editor (Alt+F11), and set the `IsAddIn` property of the `ThisWorkbook` object to False. Make your changes, set the `IsAddIn` property to True, and resave the file.

What's the difference between an XLS file and an XLA file created from an XLS file? Is the XLA version compiled? Does it run faster?

There isn't a great deal of difference between the files, and you generally won't notice any speed differences. VBA code is always "compiled" before it is executed. This is true whether it's in an XLS file or an XLA file. However, XLA files contain the actual VBA code, not compiled code.

How do I protect the code in my add-in from being viewed by others?

Activate the VB Editor and select Tools➪*xxxx* Properties (where *xxxx* is the name of your project). Click the Protection tab, select Lock project for viewing, and enter a password.

Are my XLA add-ins safe? In other words, if I distribute an XLA file, can I be assured that no one else will be able to view my code?

Protect your add-in by locking it with a password. This prevents most users from being able to access your code. The password can be broken, however, by using any of a number of utilities. Bottom line? Don't think of an XLA as being a secure file.

CommandBars

I have a macro attached to a toolbar button. Is it possible to have the macro perform a different action if the user presses Shift while the button is clicked?

Yes, but you have to use a Windows API call to do it. Refer to Chapter 11 for details.

Excel 95 had a handy menu editor, but it's missing in Excel 97 and Excel 2000. What gives?

Beginning with Excel 97, the toolbars and menus in Excel are entirely different. Both are called CommandBars. The menu editor is gone, but users can edit CommandBars by using the Customize dialog box (select Tools➪Customize).

When I change a menu with the Customize dialog box, the menu is changed permanently. How can I make the menu change apply to only one workbook?

You'll need to perform your menu changes with VBA code when the workbook is opened, and restore the menu to normal when the workbook is closed.

I know you can use the FaceId property to add an image to a toolbar control. But how do I figure out which FaceId value goes with a particular image?

Microsoft didn't provide any way to do this, but several utilities exist that make it easy to identify the `FaceId` values. The companion CD-ROM for this book includes such a utility.

I attached a new version of my toolbar to a workbook, but Excel continues to use the older version. How do I get it to use the new version of my toolbar?

When Excel opens a workbook that has an attached toolbar, it displays the toolbar only if one with the same name does not already exist on the user's system. The best solution is to write VBA code to create the toolbar on the fly when the workbook is opened and to delete it when the workbook is closed.

I've made lots of changes to Excel's toolbars. How can I restore all of these toolbars to their original state?

You can use the Customize dialog box and reset each one manually. Or run the following procedure.

```
Sub ResetAllToolbars()
    For Each tb In CommandBars
        If tb.Type = msoBarTypeNormal Then
            If tb.BuiltIn Then tb.Reset
        End If
    Next tb
End Sub
```

How can I set things up so my custom menu is displayed only when a particular workbook is active?

You need to make use of the `WorkbookActivate` and `WorkbookDeactivate` events. In other words, write procedures in the code module for the `ThisWorkbook` object that hide the custom menu when the workbook is deactivated and unhide the custom menu when the workbook is activated.

How can I add a "spacer" between two buttons on a toolbar?

Set the `BeginGroup` property of the control after the spacer to True.

How do you display a check mark next to a menu item?

A check mark on a menu item is controlled by the menu item's `State` property. The following instruction, for example, displays a check mark next to the menu item called `My Item`.

```
CommandBars(1).Commands("MyMenu"). _
  Commands("My Item").State = msoButtonDown
```

To uncheck the menu item, set the `State` property to `msoButtonUp`.

I accidentally deleted some items from the Worksheet menu and can't get them back. Restarting Excel doesn't fix it.

Select Tools⇨Customize, and select the Toolbars tab in the Customize dialog box. Select the Worksheet Menu Bar item, and click the Reset button.

How can I disable all the right-click shortcut menus?

The following procedure will do the job.

```
Sub DisableAllShortcutMenus()
    Dim cb As CommandBar
    For Each cb In CommandBars
        If cb.Type = msoBarTypePopup Then _
          cb.Enabled = False
    Next cb
End Sub
```

Is there a way to disable the shortcut menus that appear when the user clicks the right mouse button?

Yes, the following instruction will do the job:

```
CommandBars("Toolbar List").Enabled = False
```

I just entered CommandBars("Toolbar List").Enabled = False, and it doesn't work on my system!

The original version of Excel 97 had a problem with this instruction. It was corrected in the SR-1 service release for Excel 97.

✦ ✦ ✦

APPENDIX A

Excel Resources Online

If I've done my job, the information provided in this book will be useful to you. It is, however, by no means comprehensive. In addition, new issues tend to crop up, so you'll want to make sure that you're up-to-date. Therefore, I've compiled a list of additional resources that may help you become more proficient in Excel application development. I've classified these resources into three categories:

- Microsoft technical support
- Internet newsgroups
- Internet Web sites

Microsoft Technical Support

Technical support is the common term for assistance provided by a software vendor. In this case, I'm talking about assistance that comes directly from Microsoft. Microsoft's technical support is available in several different forms.

Support options

To find out your support options, choose the Help ➪ About Microsoft Excel command. Then click the Tech Support button.

This opens a help file that lists all the support options offered by Microsoft, including both free and fee-based support.

My experience is that you should use vendor *standard telephone* support only as a last resort. Chances are, you'll run up a big phone bill (assuming you can even get through) and spend lots of time on hold, but you may or may not find an answer to your question.

The truth is, the people who answer the phone are equipped to answer only the most basic questions. And the answers to these basic questions are usually readily available elsewhere.

Microsoft Knowledge Base

Your best bet for solving a problem may be the Microsoft Knowledge Base. This is the primary Microsoft product information source — an extensive, searchable database that consists of tens of thousands of detailed articles containing technical information, bug lists, fix lists, and more.

You have free and unlimited access to the Knowledge Base via the Internet. The URL is: `http://support.microsoft.com`

Microsoft Excel home page

The official home page of Excel is at:

```
http://www.microsoft.com/excel
```

Microsoft Office update

For information about Office 2000 (including Excel), try this site:

```
http://officeupdate.microsoft.com
```

About the URLs Listed Here

As you know, the Internet is a dynamic entity that tends to change rapidly. Web sites are often reorganized, so a particular URL listed in this appendix may not be available when you try to access it. Each URL was accurate at the time of this writing, but it's possible that a URL may have changed by the time you read this.

Internet Newsgroups

Usenet is an Internet service that provides access to several thousand special interest groups that enable you to communicate with people who share common interests. There are thousands of newsgroups covering virtually every topic you can think of (and many that you haven't). Typically, questions posed on a newsgroup are answered within 24 hours — assuming, of course, that the questions are asked in a manner that makes others want to reply.

Besides an Internet connection, you need special newsreader software to access newsgroups. Microsoft Outlook Express (free) is a good choice. This product is available on your Office 2000 CD-ROM.

Spreadsheet newsgroups

The primary Usenet newsgroup for general spreadsheet users is

```
comp.apps.spreadsheets
```

This newsgroup is intended for users of any brand of spreadsheet, but about 90 percent of the postings deal with Excel.

Microsoft newsgroups

Microsoft has an extensive list of newsgroups, including quite a few devoted to Excel. If your Internet service provider doesn't carry the Microsoft newsgroups, you can access them directly from Microsoft's news server. You'll need to configure your newsreader software or Web browser to access Microsoft's news server, which is at this address:

```
msnews.microsoft.com
```

Table A-1 lists the key newsgroups you'll find on Microsoft's news server.

Table A-1
Microsoft.com's Excel-Related Newsgroups

Newsgroup	*Topic*
`microsoft.public.excel.programming`	Programming Excel with VBA or XLM macros
`microsoft.public.excel.123quattro`	Converting 1-2-3 or Quattro Pro sheets into Excel sheets

Continued

Table A-1 (continued)

Newsgroup	*Topic*
microsoft.public.excel .worksheet.functions	Worksheet functions
microsoft.public.excel .charting	Building charts with Excel
microsoft.public.excel .printing	Printing with Excel
microsoft.public.excel .queryDAO	Using Microsoft Query and Data Access Objects (DAO) in Excel
microsoft.public.excel .datamap	Using the Data Map feature in Excel
microsoft.public.excel .crashesGPFs	Help with General Protection Faults or system failures
microsoft.public.excel .misc	General topics that do not fit one of the other categories
microsoft.public.excel .links	Using links in Excel
microsoft.public.excel .macintosh	Excel issues on the Macintosh operating system
microsoft.public.excel .interopoledde	OLE, DDE, and other cross-application issues
microsoft.public.excel .setup	Setting up and installing Excel
microsoft.public.excel .templates	Spreadsheet Solutions templates and other XLT files
microsoft.public.excel .sdk	Excel Software Development issues

Searching newsgroups

Many people don't realize that you can perform a keyword search on past newsgroup postings. Often, this is an excellent alternative to posting a question to the newsgroup because you can get the answer immediately. The best source for searching newsgroup postings is DejaNews, at the following Web address:

```
http://www.dejanews.com
```

Tips for Posting to a Newsgroup

1. Make sure that your question has not already been answered. Check the FAQ (if one exists) and also perform a DejaNews search (see "Searching newsgroups" in this appendix).
2. Make the subject line descriptive. Postings with a subject line such as "Help me!" and "Excel Question" are less likely to be answered than postings with a subject such as "VBA Code to Resize a Chart in Excel 2000."
3. Specify the spreadsheet product and version that you are using. In many cases, the answer to your question depends on your version of Excel.
4. Make your question as specific as possible.
5. Keep your question brief and to the point, but provide enough information so it can be adequately answered.
6. Indicate what you've done to try to answer your own question.
7. Post in the appropriate newsgroup, and don't cross-post to other groups unless the question applies to multiple groups.
8. Don't type in all uppercase or all lowercase, and check your grammar and spelling.
9. Don't include a file attachment.
10. Avoid posting in HTML format.
11. If you would like an e-mail reply, don't use an "anti-spam" e-mail address that requires the responder to modify your address. Why cause extra work for someone who's doing *you* a favor?

For example, assume you're having a problem with the ListBox control on a User-Form. You can perform a search using the following keywords: **Excel, ListBox,** and **UserForm.** The DejaNews search engine will probably find dozens of newsgroup postings that deal with these topics. It may take a while to sift through the messages, but there's an excellent chance that you'll find an answer to your question.

Internet Web Sites

If you have access to the World Wide Web (WWW), you'll find some very useful Web sites. I list a few of my favorites here.

The Spreadsheet Page

This is my own Web site. All humility aside, this is the best site on the Web for developer information. It contains files to download, developer tips, instructions for accessing Excel Easter Eggs, spreadsheet jokes, and links to other spreadsheet sites. The URL is

```
http://www.j-walk.com/ss
```

This site also contains updates on the topics covered in my books, including the book you're reading now.

Chip Pearson's Excel Pages

This site contains dozens of useful examples of VBA and clever formula techniques. The URL is

```
http://home.gvi.net/~cpearson/excel.htm
```

Stephen Bullen's Excel Page

Stephen is an Excel developer based in the United Kingdom. His Web site contains some fascinating examples of Excel code, including a section titled "They Said it Couldn't be Done." The URL is

```
http://www.bmsltd.co.uk/excel
```

Spreadsheet FAQ

Many newsgroups have *FAQ*—a list of frequently asked questions. The purpose of FAQs is to prevent the same questions from being asked over and over. The FAQ for the `comp.apps.spreadsheets` newsgroup is available at

```
http://www.faqs.org/faqs/spreadsheets/faq
```

APPENDIX B

VBA Statements and Functions Reference

This appendix contains a complete listing of all VBA statements and built-in functions. For details, consult Excel's online help.

Table B-1
Summary of VBA Statements

Statement	*Action*
`AppActivate`	Activates an application window
`Beep`	Sounds a tone using the computer's speaker
`Call`	Transfers control to another procedure
`ChDir`	Changes the current directory
`ChDrive`	Changes the current drive
`Close`	Closes a text file
`Const`	Declares a constant value
`Date`	Sets the current system date
`Declare`	Declares a reference to an external procedure in a DLL
`DefBool`	Sets the default data type to Boolean for variables that begin with a specified letter
`DefByte`	Sets the default data type to byte for variables that begin with a specified letter
`DefDate`	Sets the default data type to date for variables that begin with a specified letter

Continued

Table B-1 *(continued)*

Statement	***Action***
`DefDec`	Sets the default data type to decimal for variables that begin with a specified letter
`DefDouble`	Sets the default data type to double for variables that begin with a specified letter
`DefInt`	Sets the default data type to integer for variables that begin with a specified letter
`DefLng`	Sets the default data type to long for variables that begin with a specified letter
`DefObj`	Sets the default data type to object for variables that begin with a specified letter
`DefSng`	Sets the default data type to single for variables that begin with a specified letter
`DefStr`	Sets the default data type to string for variables that begin with a specified letter
`DeleteSetting`	Deletes a section or key setting from an application's entry in the Windows Registry
`Dim`	Declares an array locally
`Do-Loop`	Loops
`End`	Exits the program
`Enum`*	Declares a type for enumeration
`Erase`	Reinitializes an array
`Error`	Simulates a specific error condition
`Event`*	Declares a user-defined event
`Exit Do`	Exits a block of Do-Loop code
`Exit For`	Exits a block of Do-For code
`Exit Function`	Exits a Function procedure
`Exit Property`	Exits a Property procedure
`Exit Sub`	Exits a subroutine procedure
`FileCopy`	Copies a file
`For Each-Next`	Loops
`For-Next`	Loops

Statement	*Action*
Function	Declares the name and arguments for a Function procedure
Get	Reads data from a text file
GoSub-Return	Branches
GoTo	Branches
If-Then-Else	Processes statements conditionally
Implements*	Specifies an interface or class that will be implemented in a class module
Input #	Reads data from a sequential text file
Kill	Deletes a file from a disk
Let	Assigns the value of an expression to a variable or property
Line Input #	Reads a line of data from a sequential text file
Load	Loads an object but doesn't show it
Lock-Unlock	Controls access to a text file
LSet	Left-aligns a string within a string variable
Mid	Replaces characters in a string with other characters
MkDir	Creates a new directory
Name	Renames a file or directory
On Error	Branches on an error
On-GoSub	Branches on a condition
On-GoTo	Branches on a condition
Open	Opens a text file
Option Base	Changes default lower limit
Option Compare	Declares the default comparison mode when comparing strings
Option Explicit	Forces declaration of all variables in a module
Option Private	Indicates that an entire module is Private
Print #	Writes data to a sequential file
Private	Declares a local array
Property Get	Declares the name and arguments of a Property Get procedure
Property Let	Declares the name and arguments of a Property Let procedure
Property Set	Declares the name and arguments of a Property Set procedure

Continued

Table B-1 *(continued)*

Statement	***Action***
`Public`	Declares a public array
`Put`	Writes a variable to a text file
`RaiseEvent`	Fires a user-defined event
`Randomize`	Initializes the random number generator
`ReDim`	Changes the dimensions of an array
`Rem`	Specifies a line of comments (same as an apostrophe ['])
`Reset`	Closes all open text files
`Resume`	Resumes execution when an error-handling routine finishes
`RmDir`	Removes an empty directory
`RSet`	Right-aligns a string within a string variable
`SaveSetting`	Saves or creates an application entry in the Windows registry
`Seek`	Sets the position for the next access in a text file
`Select Case`	Processes statements conditionally
`SendKeys`	Sends keystrokes to the active window
`Set`	Assigns an object reference to a variable or property
`SetAttr`	Changes attribute information for a file
`Static`	Changes the dimensions of an array, keeping the data intact
`Stop`	Pauses the program
`Sub`	Declares the name and arguments of a Sub procedure
`Time`	Sets the system time
`Type`	Defines a custom data type
`Unload`	Removes an object from memory
`While-Wend`	Loops
`Width #`	Sets the output line width of a text file
`With`	Sets a series of properties for an object
`Write #`	Writes data to a sequential text file

* Not available in Excel 97 and earlier editions

Invoking Excel Functions in VBA Instructions

If a VBA function that's equivalent to one you use in Excel is not available, you can use Excel's worksheet functions directly in your VBA code. Just precede the function with a reference to the `WorksheetFunction` object. For example, VBA does not have a function to convert radians to degrees. Because Excel has a worksheet function for this procedure, you can use a VBA instruction such as the following:

```
Deg = Application.WorksheetFunction.Degrees(3.14)
```

The `WorksheetFunction` object was introduced in Excel 97. For compatibility with earlier versions of Excel, you can omit the reference to the `WorksheetFunction` object and write an instruction such as the following:

```
Deg = Application.Degrees(3.14)
```

Table B-2
Summary of VBA Functions

Function	*Action*
Abs	Returns the absolute value of a number
Array	Returns a variant containing an array
Asc	Converts the first character of string to its ASCII value
Atn	Returns the arctangent of a number
CallByName*	Executes a method, or sets or returns a property of an object
CBool	Converts an expression to a Boolean data type
CByte	Converts an express to a byte data type
CCur	Converts an expression to a currency data type
CDate	Converts an expression to a date data type
CDbl	Converts an expression to a double data type
CDec	Converts an expression to a decimal data type
Choose	Selects and returns a value from a list of arguments
Chr	Converts a character code to a string
CInt	Converts an expression to an integer data type
CLng	Converts an expression to a long data type
Cos	Returns the cosine of a number
CreateObject	Creates an OLE Automation object

Continued

Table B-2 (continued)

Function	*Action*
CSng	Converts an expression to a single data type
CStr	Converts an expression to a string data type
CurDir	Returns the current path
CVar	Converts an expression to a variant data type
CVDate	Converts an expression to a data data type
CVErr	Returns a user-defined error number
Date	Returns the current system date
DateAdd	Adds a time interval to a date
DateDiff	Returns the time interval between two dates
DatePart	Returns a specified part of a date
DateSerial	Converts a date to a serial number
DateValue	Converts a string to a date
Day	Returns the day of the month of a date
DDB	Returns the depreciation of an asset
Dir	Returns the name of a file or directory that matches a pattern
DoEvents	Yields execution so the operating system can process other events
Environ	Returns an operating environment string
EOF	Returns True if the end of a text file has been reached
Error	Returns the error message that corresponds to an error number
Exp	Returns the base of the natural logarithms (*e*) raised to a power
FileAttr	Returns the file mode for a text file
FileDateTime	Returns the date and time when a file was last modified
FileLen	Returns the number of bytes in a file
Fix	Returns the integer portion of a number
Format	Displays an expression in a particular format
FormatCurrency*	Returns an expression formatted with the system currency symbol
FormatDateTime*	Returns an expression formatted as a date or time
FormatNumber*	Returns an expression formatted as a number
FormatPercent*	Returns an expression formatted as a percentage

Function	*Action*
FreeFile	Returns the next available file number when working with text files
FV	Returns the future value of an annuity
GetAllSettings	Returns a list of settings and values from the Windows Registry
GetAttr	Returns a code representing a file attribute
GetObject	Retrieves an OLE Automation object from a file
GetSetting	Returns a specific setting from the application's entry in the Windows Registry
Hex	Converts from decimal to hexadecimal
Hour	Returns the hour of a time
Iif	Evaluates an expression and returns one of two parts
Input	Returns characters from a sequential text file
InputBox	Displays a box to prompt a user for input
InStr	Returns the position of a string within another string
InStrRev*	Returns the position of a string within another string, from the end of the string
Int	Returns the integer portion of a number
IPmt	Returns the interest payment for a given period of an annuity
IRR	Returns the internal rate of return for a series of cash flows
IsArray	Returns True if a variable is an array
IsDate	Returns True if a variable is a date
IsEmpty	Returns True if a variable has been initialized
IsError	Returns True if an expression is an error value
IsMissing	Returns True if an optional argument was not passed to a procedure
IsNull	Returns True if an expression contains no valid data
IsNumeric	Returns True if an expression can be evaluated as a number
IsObject	Returns True if an expression references an OLE Automation object
Join*	Combines strings contained in an array
LBound	Returns the smallest subscript for a dimension of an array
LCase	Returns a string converted to lowercase
Left	Returns a specified number of characters from the left of a string

Continued

Table B-2 *(continued)*	
Function	***Action***
`Len`	Returns the number of characters in a string
`Loc`	Returns the current read or write position of a text file
`LOF`	Returns the number of bytes in an open text file
`Log`	Returns the natural logarithm of a number
`LTrim`	Returns a copy of a string with no leading spaces
`Mid`	Returns a specified number of characters from a string
`Minute`	Returns the minute of a time
`MIRR`	Returns the modified internal rate of return for a series of periodic cash flows
`Month`	Returns the month of a date
`MsgBox`	Displays a modal message box
`Now`	Returns the current system date and time
`NPer`	Returns the number of periods for an annuity
`NPV`	Returns the net present value of an investment
`Oct`	Converts from decimal to octal
`Partition`	Returns a string representing a range in which a value falls
`Pmt`	Returns a payment amount for an annuity
`Ppmt`	Returns the principal payment amount for an annuity
`PV`	Returns the present value of an annuity
`QBColor`	Returns an RGB color code
`Rate`	Returns the interest rate per period for an annuity
`Replace*`	Returns a string in which a substring is replaced with another string
`RGB`	Returns a number representing an RGB color value
`Right`	Returns a specified number of characters from the right of a string
`Rnd`	Returns a random number between 0 and 1
`Round`	Returns a rounded number
`RTrim`	Returns a copy of a string with no trailing spaces
`Second`	Returns the seconds portion of a specified time
`Seek`	Returns the current position in a text file
`Sgn`	Returns an integer that indicates the sign of a number
`Shell`	Runs an executable program

Function	*Action*
Sin	Returns the sine of a number
SLN	Returns the straight-line depreciation for an asset for a period
Space	Returns a string with a specified number of spaces
Spc	Positions output when printing to a file
Split*	Returns a one-dimensional array containing a number of substrings
Sqr	Returns the square root of a number
Str	Returns a string representation of a number
StrComp	Returns a value indicating the result of a string comparison
StrConv	Returns a converted string
String	Returns a repeating character or string
StrReverse*	Returns a string, reversed
Switch	Evaluates a list of Boolean expressions and returns a value associated with the first True expression
SYD	Returns the sum-of-years' digits depreciation of an asset for a period
Tab	Positions output when printing to a file
Tan	Returns the tangent of a number
Time	Returns the current system time
Timer	Returns the number of seconds since midnight
TimeSerial	Returns the time for a specified hour, minute, and second
TimeValue	Converts a string to a time serial number
Trim	Returns a string without leading spaces and/or trailing spaces
TypeName	Returns a string that describes the data type of a variable
UBound	Returns the largest available subscript for a dimension of an array
UCase	Converts a string to uppercase
Val	Returns the numbers contained in a string
VarType	Returns a value indicating the subtype of a variable
WeekdateName*	Returns a string indicating a day of the week
Weekday	Returns a number representing a day of the week
Year	Returns the year of a date

* Not available in Excel 97 and earlier editions

APPENDIX C

VBA Error Codes

This appendix contains a complete listing of the error codes for all trappable errors. This information is useful for error trapping. For complete details, consult Excel's online help.

Error Code	*Message*
3	Return without GoSub
5	Invalid procedure call
6	Overflow
7	Out of memory
9	Subscript out of range
10	This array is fixed or temporarily locked
11	Division by zero
13	Type mismatch
14	Out of string space
16	Expression too complex
17	Can't perform requested operation
18	User interrupt occurred
20	Resume without error
28	Out of stack space
35	Sub, Function, or Property not defined
47	Too many code resources or DLL application clients
48	Error in loading code resource or DLL
49	Bad code resource or DLL calling convention
51	Internal error
52	Bad filename or number

Continued

Error Code	*Message*
53	File not found
54	Bad file mode
55	File already open
57	Device I/O error
58	File already exists
59	Bad record length
61	Disk full
62	Input past end of file
63	Bad record number
67	Too many files
68	Device unavailable
70	Permission denied
71	Disk not ready
74	Can't rename with different drive
75	Path/File access error
76	Path not found
91	Object variable or With block variable not set
92	For loop not initialized
93	Invalid pattern string
94	Invalid use of Null
97	Can't call Friend procedure on an object that is not an instance of the defining class
98*	A property or method call cannot include a reference to a private object, either as an argument or as a return value
298	System DLL could not be loaded
320	Can't use character device names in specified filenames
321	Invalid file format
322	Can't create necessary temporary file
325	Invalid format in resource file
327	Data value named not found
328	Illegal parameter; can't write arrays
335	Could not access system registry
336	Component not correctly registered

Error Code	Message
337	Component not found
338	Component did not run correctly
360	Object already loaded
361	Can't load or unload this object
363	Control specified not found
364	Object was unloaded
365	Unable to unload within this context
368	The specified file is out of date. This program requires a later version
371	The specified object can't be used as an owner form for Show
380	Invalid property value
381	Invalid property-array index
382	Property Set can't be executed at run time
383	Property Set can't be used with a read-only property
385	Need property array index
387	Property Set not permitted
393	Property Get can't be executed at run time
394	Property Get can't be executed on write-only property
400	Form already displayed; can't show modally
402	Code must close topmost modal form first
419	Permission to use object denied
422	Property not found
423	Property or method not found
424	Object required
425	Invalid object use
429	Component can't create object or return reference to this object
430	Class doesn't support Automation
432	Filename or class name not found during Automation operation
438	Object doesn't support this property or method
440	Automation error
442	Connection to type library or object library for remote process has been lost

Continued

Error Code	*Message*
443	Automation object doesn't have a default value
445	Object doesn't support this action
446	Object doesn't support named arguments
447	Object doesn't support current locale setting
448	Named argument not found
449	Argument not optional or invalid property assignment
450	Wrong number of arguments or invalid property assignment
451	Object not a collection
452	Invalid ordinal
453	Specified code resource not found
454	Code resource not found
455	Code resource lock error
457	This key is already associated with an element of this collection
458	Variable uses a type not supported in VBA
459	This component doesn't support the set of events
460	Invalid Clipboard format
461	Method or data member not found
462*	The remote server machine does not exist or is unavailable
463*	Class not registered on local machine
480	Can't create AutoRedraw image
481	Invalid picture
482	Printer error
483	Printer driver does not support specified property
484	Problem getting printer information from the system. Make sure the printer is set up correctly
485	Invalid picture type
486	Can't print form image to this type of printer
520	Can't empty Clipboard
521	Can't open Clipboard
735	Can't save file to TEMP directory
744	Search text not found

Error Code	*Message*
746	Replacements too long
31001	Out of memory
31004	No object
31018	Class is not set
31027	Unable to activate object
31032	Unable to create embedded object
31036	Error saving to file
31037	Error loading from file

* Not supported by Excel 97 or earlier editions

ANSI Code Reference

✦ ✦ ✦ ✦

This appendix contains the ANSI codes, the character (if any) they produce, their hex value, binary value, and the keystroke (if any) that generates the code.

ANSI Code	*Character*	*Hex Code*	*Binary Code*	*Keystroke**
1	<None>	&H01	0000 0001	<None>
2	<None>	&H02	0000 0010	<None>
3	<None>	&H03	0000 0011	<None>
4	<None>	&H04	0000 0100	<None>
5	<None>	&H05	0000 0101	<None>
6	<None>	&H06	0000 0110	<None>
7	<None>	&H07	0000 0111	<None>
8	<Backspace>	&H08	0000 1000	Backspace
9	<Tab>	&H09	0000 1001	Tab
10	<Line feed>	&H0A	0000 1010	<None>
11	<None>	&H0B	0000 1011	<None>
12	<None>	&H0C	0000 1100	<None>
13	<Carriage return>	&H0D	0000 1101	Return
14	<None>	&H0E	0000 1110	<None>
15	<None>	&H0F	0000 1111	<None>
16	<None>	&H10	0001 0000	<None>
17	<None>	&H11	0001 0001	<None>
18	<None>	&H12	0001 0010	<None>
19	<None>	&H13	0001 0011	<None>
20	<None>	&H14	0001 0100	<None>
21	<None>	&H15	0001 0101	<None>
22	<None>	&H16	0001 0110	<None>
23	<None>	&H17	0001 0111	<None>
24	<None>	&H18	0001 1000	<None>
25	<None>	&H19	0001 1001	<None>
26	<None>	&H1A	0001 1010	<None>
27	<None>	&H1B	0001 1011	<None>
28	<None>	&H1C	0001 1100	<None>
29	<None>	&H1D	0001 1101	<None>
30	<None>	&H1E	0001 1110	<None>
31	<None>	&H1F	0001 1111	<None>
32	<Space>	&H20	0010 0000	Space

ANSI Code	*Character*	*Hex Code*	*Binary Code*	*Keystroke**
33	!	&H21	0010 0001	!
34	"	&H22	0010 0010	"
35	#	&H23	0010 0011	#
36	$	&H24	0010 0100	$
37	%	&H25	0010 0101	%
38	&	&H26	0010 0110	&
39	'	&H27	0010 0111	'
40	(	&H28	0010 1000	(
41	)	&H29	0010 1001	)
42	*	&H2A	0010 1010	*
43	+	&H2B	0010 1011	+
44	,	&H2C	0010 1100	,
45	-	&H2D	0010 1101	-
46	.	&H2E	0010 1110	.
47	/	&H2F	0010 1111	/
48	0	&H30	0011 0000	0
49	1	&H31	0011 0001	1
50	2	&H32	0011 0010	2
51	3	&H33	0011 0011	3
52	4	&H34	0011 0100	4
53	5	&H35	0011 0101	5
54	6	&H36	0011 0110	6
55	7	&H37	0011 0111	7
56	8	&H38	0011 1000	8
57	9	&H39	0011 1001	9
58	:	&H3A	0011 1010	:
59	;	&H3B	0011 1011	;
60	<	&H3C	0011 1100	<
61	=	&H3D	0011 1101	=
62	>	&H3E	0011 1110	>
63	?	&H3F	0011 1111	?

Continued

ANSI Code	*Character*	*Hex Code*	*Binary Code*	*Keystroke**
64	@	&H40	0100 0000	@
65	A	&H41	0100 0001	A
66	B	&H42	0100 0010	B
67	C	&H43	0100 0011	C
68	D	&H44	0100 0100	D
69	E	&H45	0100 0101	E
70	F	&H46	0100 0110	F
71	G	&H47	0100 0111	G
72	H	&H48	0100 1000	H
73	I	&H49	0100 1001	I
74	J	&H4A	0100 1010	J
75	K	&H4B	0100 1011	K
76	L	&H4C	0100 1100	L
77	M	&H4D	0100 1101	M
78	N	&H4E	0100 1110	N
79	O	&H4F	0100 1111	O
80	P	&H50	0101 0000	P
81	Q	&H51	0101 0001	Q
82	R	&H52	0101 0010	R
83	S	&H53	0101 0011	S
84	T	&H54	0101 0100	T
85	U	&H55	0101 0101	U
86	V	&H56	0101 0110	V
87	W	&H57	0101 0111	W
88	X	&H58	0101 1000	X
89	Y	&H59	0101 1001	Y
90	Z	&H5A	0101 1010	Z
91	[	&H5B	0101 1011	[
92	\	&H5C	0101 1100	\
93	]	&H5D	0101 1101	]
94	^	&H5E	0101 1110	^
95	_	&H5F	0101 1111	_

ANSI Code	*Character*	*Hex Code*	*Binary Code*	*Keystroke**
96	'	&H60	0110 0000	'
97	a	&H61	0110 0001	a
98	b	&H62	0110 0010	b
99	c	&H63	0110 0011	c
100	d	&H64	0110 0100	d
101	e	&H65	0110 0101	e
102	f	&H66	0110 0110	f
103	g	&H67	0110 0111	g
104	h	&H68	0110 1000	h
105	i	&H69	0110 1001	i
106	j	&H6A	0110 1010	j
107	k	&H6B	0110 1011	k
108	l	&H6C	0110 1100	l
109	m	&H6D	0110 1101	m
110	n	&H6E	0110 1110	n
111	o	&H6F	0110 1111	o
112	p	&H70	0111 0000	p
113	q	&H71	0111 0001	q
114	r	&H72	0111 0010	r
115	s	&H73	0111 0011	s
116	t	&H74	0111 0100	t
117	u	&H75	0111 0101	u
118	v	&H76	0111 0110	v
119	w	&H77	0111 0111	w
120	x	&H78	0111 1000	x
121	y	&H79	0111 1001	y
122	z	&H7A	0111 1010	z
123	{	&H7B	0111 1011	{
124	|	&H7C	0111 1100	|
125	}	&H7D	0111 1101	}
126	~	&H7E	0111 1110	~

Continued

ANSI Code	*Character*	*Hex Code*	*Binary Code*	*Keystroke**
127	▯	&H7F	0111 1111	Del
128	▯	&H80	1000 0000	Alt+0128
129	▯	&H81	1000 0001	Alt+0129
130	‚	&H82	1000 0010	Alt+0130
131	ƒ	&H83	1000 0011	Alt+0131
132	„	&H84	1000 0100	Alt+0132
133	…	&H85	1000 0101	Alt+0133
134	†	&H86	1000 0110	Alt+0134
135	‡	&H87	1000 0111	Alt+0135
136	ˆ	&H88	1000 1000	Alt+0136
137	‰	&H89	1000 1001	Alt+0137
138	Š	&H8A	1000 1010	Alt+0138
139	‹	&H8B	1000 1011	Alt+0139
140	Œ	&H8C	1000 1100	Alt+0140
141	▯	&H8D	1000 1101	Alt+0141
142	▯	&H8E	1000 1110	Alt+0142
143	▯	&H8F	1000 1111	Alt+0143
144	▯	&H90	1001 0000	Alt+0144
145	‘	&H91	1001 0001	Alt+0145
146	’	&H92	1001 0010	Alt+0146
147	“	&H93	1001 0011	Alt+0147
148	”	&H94	1001 0100	Alt+0148
149	•	&H95	1001 0101	Alt+0149
150	–	&H96	1001 0110	Alt+0150
151	—	&H97	1001 0111	Alt+0151
152	˜	&H98	1001 1000	Alt+0152
153	™	&H99	1001 1001	Alt+0153
154	?	&H9A	1001 1010	Alt+0154
155	›	&H9B	1001 1011	Alt+0155
156	œ	&H9C	1001 1100	Alt+0156
157	▯	&H9D	1001 1101	Alt+0157
158	▯	&H9E	1001 1110	Alt+0158

ANSI Code	*Character*	*Hex Code*	*Binary Code*	*Keystroke**
159	Ÿ	&H9F	1001 1111	Alt+0159
160	<None>	&HA0	1010 0000	Alt+0160
161	¡	&HA1	1010 0001	Alt+0161
162	¢	&HA2	1010 0010	Alt+0162
163	£	&HA3	1010 0011	Alt+0163
164	¤	&HA4	1010 0100	Alt+0164
165	¥	&HA5	1010 0101	Alt+0165
166	|	&HA6	1010 0110	Alt+0166
167	§	&HA7	1010 0111	Alt+0167
168	¨	&HA8	1010 1000	Alt+0168
169	©	&HA9	1010 1001	Alt+0169
170	ª	&HAA	1010 1010	Alt+0170
171	«	&HAB	1010 1011	Alt+0171
172	¬	&HAC	1010 1100	Alt+0172
173	–	&HAD	1010 1101	Alt+0173
174	®	&HAE	1010 1110	Alt+0174
175	¯	&HAF	1010 1111	Alt+0175
176	°	&HB0	1011 0000	Alt+0176
177	±	&HB1	1011 0001	Alt+0177
178	2	&HB2	1011 0010	Alt+0178
179	3	&HB3	1011 0011	Alt+0179
180	´	&HB4	1011 0100	Alt+0180
181	µ	&HB5	1011 0101	Alt+0181
182	¶	&HB6	1011 0110	Alt+0182
183	·	&HB7	1011 0111	Alt+0183
184	,	&HB8	1011 1000	Alt+0184
185	1	&HB9	1011 1001	Alt+0185
186	º	&HBA	1011 1010	Alt+0186
187	»	&HBB	1011 1011	Alt+0187
188	_	&HBC	1011 1100	Alt+0188
189	_	&HBD	1011 1101	Alt+0189

Continued

ANSI Code	*Character*	*Hex Code*	*Binary Code*	*Keystroke**
190	_	&HBE	1011 1110	Alt+0190
191	¿	&HBF	1011 1111	Alt+0191
192	À	&HC0	1100 0000	Alt+0192
193	Á	&HC1	1100 0001	Alt+0193
194	Â	&HC2	1100 0010	Alt+0194
195	Ã	&HC3	1100 0011	Alt+0195
196	Ä	&HC4	1100 0100	Alt+0196
197	Å	&HC5	1100 0101	Alt+0197
198	Æ	&HC6	1100 0110	Alt+0198
199	Ç	&HC7	1100 0111	Alt+0199
200	È	&HC8	1100 1000	Alt+0200
201	É	&HC9	1100 1001	Alt+0201
202	Ê	&HCA	1100 1010	Alt+0202
203	Ë	&HCB	1100 1011	Alt+0203
204	Ì	&HCC	1100 1100	Alt+0204
205	Í	&HCD	1100 1101	Alt+0205
206	Î	&HCE	1100 1110	Alt+0206
207	Ï	&HCF	1100 1111	Alt+0207
208	_	&HD0	1101 0000	Alt+0208
209	Ñ	&HD1	1101 0001	Alt+0209
210	Ò	&HD2	1101 0010	Alt+0210
211	Ó	&HD3	1101 0011	Alt+0211
212	Ô	&HD4	1101 0100	Alt+0212
213	Õ	&HD5	1101 0101	Alt+0213
214	Ö	&HD6	1101 0110	Alt+0214
215	x	&HD7	1101 0111	Alt+0215
216	Ø	&HD8	1101 1000	Alt+0216
217	Ù	&HD9	1101 1001	Alt+0217
218	Ú	&HDA	1101 1010	Alt+0218
219	Û	&HDB	1101 1011	Alt+0219
220	Ü	&HDC	1101 1100	Alt+0220
221	Y	&HDD	1101 1101	Alt+0221

ANSI Code	*Character*	*Hex Code*	*Binary Code*	*Keystroke**
222	_	&HDE	1101 1110	Alt+0222
223	ß	&HDF	1101 1111	Alt+0223
224	à	&HE0	1110 0000	Alt+0224
225	á	&HE1	1110 0001	Alt+0225
226	â	&HE2	1110 0010	Alt+0226
227	ã	&HE3	1110 0011	Alt+0227
228	ä	&HE4	1110 0100	Alt+0228
229	å	&HE5	1110 0101	Alt+0229
230	æ	&HE6	1110 0110	Alt+0230
231	ç	&HE7	1110 0111	Alt+0231
232	è	&HE8	1110 1000	Alt+0232
233	é	&HE9	1110 1001	Alt+0233
234	ê	&HEA	1110 1010	Alt+0234
235	ë	&HEB	1110 1011	Alt+0235
236	ì	&HEC	1110 1100	Alt+0236
237	í	&HED	1110 1101	Alt+0237
238	î	&HEE	1110 1110	Alt+0238
239	ï	&HEF	1110 1111	Alt+0239
240	∂	&HF0	1111 0000	Alt+0240
241	ñ	&HF1	1111 0001	Alt+0241
242	ò	&HF2	1111 0010	Alt+0242
243	ó	&HF3	1111 0011	Alt+0243
244	ô	&HF4	1111 0100	Alt+0244
245	õ	&HF5	1111 0101	Alt+0245
246	ö	&HF6	1111 0110	Alt+0246
247	÷	&HF7	1111 0111	Alt+0247
248	ø	&HF8	1111 1000	Alt+0248
249	ù	&HF9	1111 1001	Alt+0249
250	ú	&HFA	1111 1010	Alt+0250
251	û	&HFB	1111 1011	Alt+0251
252	ü	&HFC	1111 1100	Alt+0252

Continued

ANSI Code	*Character*	*Hex Code*	*Binary Code*	*Keystroke**
253	y	&HFD	1111 1101	Alt+0253
254	_	&HFE	1111 1110	Alt+0254
255	ÿ	&HFF	1111 1111	Alt+0255

* For keystrokes that use the Alt key, use the numeric keypad with Num Lock on.

What's on the CD-ROM

This appendix describes the contents of the companion CD-ROM.

CD-ROM Overview

The CD-ROM consists of four components:

- *Chapter Examples.* Excel workbooks that I discussed in this book.
- *Bonus Files.* Excel workbooks that I did not discuss in this book but that I developed and added to the CD-ROM because I thought you'd find them useful or instructive.
- *Power Utility Pak.* The shareware version of my popular Excel add-in. Use the coupon in this book to order the full version *free!* The complete VBA source code is also available for a small fee.
- *Sound-Proof.* The demo version of my audio proofreader add-in.

Chapter Examples

Each chapter of this book that contains example workbooks has its own subdirectory on the CD-ROM. For example, the example files for Chapter 3 are found in the following directory:

```
chapters\chap03\
```

Following is a list of the chapter examples, with a brief description of each.

Chapter 3

`array examples.xls`	Examples of array formulas.
`named formula.xls`	Examples of using named formulas.
`megaformula-1.xls`	The "remove middle name" formula example that uses intermediate formulas.
`megaformula-2.xls`	The "remove middle name" formula example that uses a megaformula.
`megaformula-3.xls`	The "remove middle name" formula example that uses a custom VBA function.

Chapter 7

`comment objects .xls`	Examples of VBA code that manipulates `Comment` objects.

Chapter 9

`sheet sorter.xls`	The sheet-sorting application.
`better sheet sorter .xls`	The sheet-sorting application, improved so that it better handles sheet names that end in numbers.

Chapter 10

`uppercase.xls`	Contains the `UpCase` function that emulates Excel's `UPPER` function.
`commission.xls`	Contains various versions of the `Commission` function used to calculate a sales commission.
`draw.xls`	Contains the `Draw` function, which randomly chooses one cell from a range.
`monthnames.xls`	Demonstrates the `MonthNames` function, which returns an array.
`reverse.xls`	Demonstrates the `Reverse` function, which returns an error value if its argument is not a string.
`mysum.xls`	Demonstrates the `MySum` function, which emulates Excel's `SUM` function.
`windows directory .xls`	Demonstrates the `ShowWindowsDir` function, which uses an API function to display the Windows directory name.

`key press.xls`	Demonstrates how to use an API function to determine whether the Shift, Ctrl, or Alt key is pressed.
`winapi.txt`	Contains Windows API declarations and constants.

Chapter 11

`range selections .xls`	Demonstrates several common types of range selections relative to the active cell. After opening this file, use the Selection Demo menu.
`input.xls`	Contains examples of using the `InputBox` function to prompt for a value.
`next empty row.xls`	Demonstrates how to insert data into the next empty row of a worksheet.
`auto average.xls`	Demonstrates how to insert an `AVERAGE` function in a manner similar to Excel's AutoSum feature. When this workbook is open, you have access to a new menu command: Tools ⇨ Enter Average Formula.
`about selection.xls`	Contains a procedure that describes the current range selection.
`selective color.xls`	Contains a procedure that colors cells based on their contents.
`delete empty rows .xls`	Contains a procedure that deletes all empty rows in a worksheet.
`in range.xls`	Contains a function that returns True if a range is contained inside of another range.
`data type.xls`	Uses the `CellType` function to determine the type of data in a cell.
`write and read range .xls`	Contains procedures that write data to a range and read data from a range.
`fill range.xls`	Contains two procedures that demonstrate how to fill a range with data from an array.
`select max.xls`	Contains a procedure that selects the cell that contains the maximum value.
`toggles.xls`	Contains procedures that toggle various settings.
`page count.xls`	Contains a procedure that Counts the number of pages to be printed.
`date and time.xls`	Contains a procedure that displays the current date and time.
`sorting demo.xls`	Demonstrates three VBA array-sorting procedures.

batch processing .xls	Demonstrates how to process a series of files. The example uses three additional files: text01.txt, text02.txt, and text03.txt.
utility functions .xls	Contains the following functions: `FileExists`, `FileNameOnly`, `PathExists`, `RangeNameExists`, `SheetExists`, and `WorkbookIsOpen`.
worksheet functions .xls	Contains the following worksheet functions: `SheetName`, `WorkbookName`, `AppName`, `CountBetween`, `LastInColumn`, `LastInRow`, and `IsLike`.
extract element.xls	Demonstrates the `ExtractElement` function.
stat functions.xls	Demonstrates the `StatFunction` function.
sheet offset.xls	Demonstrates two versions of the `SheetOffset` function.
disk info.xls	Demonstrates various API functions that return information about disk drives.
file association .xls	Demonstrates an API function that returns the full path to the application associated with a particular file.
printer info.xls	Demonstrates an API function that returns information about the default printer.
video mode.xls	Demonstrates an API function that returns the current video resolution.
registry.xls	Demonstrates API functions that enable you to read from and write to the Windows Registry.
sound.xls	Demonstrates API functions that play sound files.

Chapter 12

get a filename.xls	Demonstrates how to use the `GetOpenFilename` method.
get directory.xls	Demonstrates API functions that display a dialog box that enables the user to select a directory.
excel dialogs.xls	Contains a procedure that displays all of Excel's built-in dialog boxes.
dlgwiz.xla	Converts Excel 5/95 dialog sheets to UserForms. See dlgwiz.doc for additional information about this add-in.

`worksheet controls .xls`	Demonstrates the use of dialog box controls placed on a worksheet.
`all controls.xls`	Demonstrates all UserForm controls.
`get name and sex.xls`	Is the end result of the hands-on example described in Chapter 12.
`userform events.xls`	Demonstrates the sequence of events pertaining to UserForms.
`spinbutton events.xls`	Demonstrates the sequence of events pertaining to SpinButton controls.
`spinbutton textbox .xls`	Demonstrates how to pair a SpinButton control with a TextBox control.
`newcontrols.pag`	Contains customized controls for your Toolbox. To import this file as a new page, right-click a Toolbox tab, and select Import Page.

Chapter 13

`dialog box menus.xls`	Demonstrates two simple menu systems using CommandButton controls and a ListBox control.
`refedit.xls`	Demonstrates the RefEdit control.
`splash.xls`	Demonstrates a splash screen that is displayed when the workbook is opened.
`queryclose.xls`	Demonstrates a technique that ensures that the user can't close a UserForm by clicking its Close button.
`change size.xls`	Demonstrates a dialog box that changes sizes.
`zoom.xls`	Demonstrates the use of the `Zoom` property to zoom a dialog box.
`zoom and scroll sheets .xls`	Demonstrates how to use dialog box controls to zoom and scroll a worksheet.
`fill listbox.xls`	Demonstrates two ways to add items to a ListBox control.
`unique.xls`	Demonstrates how to fill a ListBox control with unique items.
`selected items.xls`	Demonstrates how to identify selected items in a ListBox control.
`multiple lists.xls`	Demonstrates how to display multiple lists in a single ListBox control.
`item transfer.xls`	Demonstrates how to let the user transfer items between two ListBox controls.

`move items.xls`	Demonstrates how to enable the user to move items within a ListBox control.
`select rows.xls`	Demonstrates how to use a multicolumn ListBox control to enable the user to select rows in a worksheet.
`activate sheet.xls`	Demonstrates how to display a list of sheet names in a ListBox control.

Chapter 14

`progress-1.xls`	Demonstrates how to display a progress indicator while a macro is running. (The progress indicator is not initiated by a dialog box.)
`progress-2.xls`	Demonstrates another way to display a progress indicator while a macro is running. (The progress indicator is initiated by a dialog box.)
`scrolling text.xls`	Demonstrates how to use a third-party timer control (ccrpTmr.dll) to display moving text on a UserForm.
`flashing text.xls`	Demonstrates how to use a third-party timer control (ccrpTmr.dll) to display flashing text on a UserForm.
`chart in userform.xls`	Demonstrates how to display a chart on a UserForm.
`wizard.xls`	Demonstrates how to create a multistep "wizard."
`my msgbox.xls`	Contains the `MyMsg` box function, which emulates VBA's `MsgBox` function.
`modeless.xls`	Demonstrates a modeless dialog box.
`multiple buttons.xls`	Demonstrates how to use a single event-handler procedure for multiple controls.
`color picker.xls`	Demonstrates a function that enables the user to select a color from a dialog box.
`dataform.xla`	Is an add-in that serves as a replacement for Excel's Data Form. This add-in is protected, but the VBA code is available for a nominal fee.

Chapter 15

`text tools.xls`	Is the text manipulation utility described in Chapter 15 (workbook version).
`undo.xls`	Demonstrates one way to undo the effects of a VBA procedure.

Chapter 16

`budget.xls`	Demonstrates how to create a pivot table from a worksheet database with VBA.
`external db.xls`	Demonstrates how to create a pivot table from an external database table with VBA. This workbook uses the budget.mdb database file.
`survey data.xls`	Demonstrates how to create multiple pivot tables to analyze survey data.
`modify pivot.xls`	Demonstrates how to write VBA code to modify a pivot table.

Chapter 17

`create chart.xls`	Contains a recorded macro to create a chart, plus a "cleaned up" version of the macro.
`chart active cell .xls`	Demonstrates how to change a chart's data series based on the active cell.
`combo box chart.xls`	Demonstrates how to use a ComboBox control to change a chart's data series.
`get chart range.xls`	Contains a custom function that returns a `Range` object that represents the data used in a chart.
`data labels.xls`	Demonstrates how to use a range for data labels in a chart.
`chart in userform .xls`	Demonstrates how to create a chart on the fly and display it in a UserForm.
`chart events.xls`	Demonstrates chart events.
`chart image map.xls`	Demonstrates how to create a chart that serves as a type of image map.
`hiding data.xls`	Demonstrates how to use a filtered list to prevent data from being displayed in a chart.
`animated chart.xls`	Is an example of an animated chart.
`trig chart.xls`	Is a chart that displays interesting patterns by using trigonometric functions.
`clock chart.xls`	Is a chart that looks like an analog clock.
`xy sketch.xls`	Is a chart that doubles as a primitive sketching tool.

Chapter 18

`track changes.xls`	Demonstrates a procedure that uses comments to track changes made to cells.
`validate entry1.xls`	Demonstrates how to validate data entered into a cell; uses the `EnableEvents` property.
`validate entry2.xls`	Demonstrates how to validate data entered into a cell; does not use the `EnableEvents` property.
`log file.xls`	Demonstrates how to keep track of every workbook that is opened by storing information in a text file.
`application events 2k .xls`	Demonstrates how to monitor Application-level events (Excel 2000 version, which uses a modeless UserForm).
`application events 97`	Demonstrates how to monitor Application-level events (Excel 97 version).
`onkey demo.xls`	Demonstrates the use of the `OnKey` method to remap keyboard keys.

Chapter 19

`start charmap.xls`	Demonstrates two ways to execute the Windows Character Map program.
`start calculator.xls`	Demonstrates how to execute (or activate) the Windows Calculator program.
`system dialogs.xls`	Demonstrates how to display any of 50 system dialog boxes.
`make memos.xls`	Demonstrates Automation by using Microsoft Word to generate memos using data stored in a worksheet.
`projections.doc`	Is a Word 2000 file that demonstrates Automation. It creates a new document and uses Excel to calculate data and create a chart.
`phone dialer.xls`	Demonstrates how to use `SendKeys` to control the Windows Phone Dialer application.

Chapter 20

`text tools.xls`	Is the text manipulation utility described in Chapter 15 (add-in version).
`addin installed.xls`	Contains code that determines whether an add-in is properly installed.

Chapter 21

`list commandbars.xls`	Contains a procedure that lists each CommandBar's name, index number, and type.
`autosense.xls`	Contains a procedure that creates an "autosense" toolbar that is displayed only when the active cell is in a particular range.
`hide and restore.xls`	Contains procedures that hide and then later restore toolbars.
`list all controls.xls`	Contains a procedure that displays the `Caption` property for each control on every toolbar.
`faceids.xla`	Is an add-in that makes it very easy to determine the `FACEId` property setting for a particular image. This add-in uses additional files and is contained in a separate `\faceids` subdirectory.
`toggle toolbars.xls`	Contains a procedure that toggles the `Visible` property of each CommandBar.
`dynamic caption.xls`	Creates a toolbar button that displays the number format string for the active cell.
`month list.xls`	Demonstrates the use of a drop-down list control on a CommandBar.

Chapter 22

`list menu info.xls`	Contains a procedure that displays the caption for each item (menu, menu item, and submenu item) on the Worksheet Menu Bar.
`add new menu.xls`	Contains a procedure that adds a new menu with menu items.
`add tools item.xls`	Contains a procedure that adds a new menu item to the Tools menu on the Worksheet Menu Bar.
`shortcut key.xls`	Contains a procedure that adds new menu items with a shortcut key.
`hide menu.xls`	Demonstrates how to display a menu only when a particular workbook is active.
`toggle gridlines.xls`	Demonstrates how to display a "toggle" menu with a check mark.
`menu maker.xls`	Demonstrates an easy way to create a menu with information contained in a worksheet.
`new menubar.xls`	Demonstrates how to replace Excel's menu bar with one of your own.

`menu shenanigans.xls`	Contains a procedure that reverses the text in all menus and menu items.
`list shortcut menus.xls`	Contains a procedure that lists all shortcut menus.
`new shortcut menu.xls`	Contains a procedure that creates a new shortcut menu.

Some of the examples in Chapter 23 use multiple files, and many use the same filename. Therefore, each example is contained in a separate subdirectory.

Chapter 23

`\comments\formletter.xls`	Demonstrates how to display help by using cell comments.
`\textbox\formletter.xls`	Demonstrates how to display help by using a TextBox control on a worksheet.
`\worksheet\formletter.xls`	Demonstrates how to display help by activating a worksheet.
`\userform1\formletter.xls`	Demonstrates how to display help by using Label controls in a UserForm.
`\userform2\formletter.xls`	Demonstrates how to display help by using a "scrolling" Label control in a UserForm.
`\userform3\formletter.xls`	Demonstrates how to display help by using a DropDown control and a Label control in a UserForm.
`\winhelp\formletter.xls`	Demonstrates a simple WinHelp Help system (includes the source files).
`\htmlhelp\formletter.xls`	Demonstrates a simple HTML Help system (includes the source files).
`\function\myfuncs.xls`	Demonstrates how to display help for custom functions.
`\assistant\formletter.xls`	Demonstrates how to display help by using the Office Assistant.
`\other\myapp.xls`	Demonstrates other ways to display help: with the Help method, from a message box, and from an input box.

Chapter 24

`loan amortization wizard.xla`	Is an add-in "wizard" that creates an amortization schedule for a fixed-rate loan. This add-in is not protected.

Chapter 25

`video mode.xls`	Demonstrates how to use an API function that works with both 16-bit and 32-bit versions of Excel.
`multilingual wizard .xls`	Is a simple wizard that lets the user choose from three languages.

Chapter 26

`list files.xls`	Contains a procedure that displays a list of files contained in a particular directory, along with the file size and date.
`list files2.xls`	Contains a procedure that displays a list of files contained in a particular directory, along with the file size and date; uses the `FileSearch` object (requires Excel 2000).
`export import.xls`	Contains procedures to export a range to a CSV file and to import a CSV file at the active cell position.
`filter text file.xls`	Contains a procedure that reads a text file (infile.txt) and copies only the rows that contain a specific text string to a second text file (output.txt).
`import 256.xls`	Contains a procedure that reads a text file and stores the data in Sheet1. If the line contains more than 256 columns of data, the additional data is stored in Sheet2.

Chapter 27

`show components.xls`	Contains a procedure that displays information about each VB component in the active workbook.
`replace module.xls`	Contains a procedure that replaces a module with another module. This example uses the UserBook.xls file.
`add button and code .xls`	Contains a procedure that adds a CommandButton and a VBA procedure.
`add controls.xls`	Demonstrates how to add controls to a UserForm at design time and at run time.
`add 100 buttons.xls`	Contains a procedure that adds 100 CommandButtons and that creates an event-handler procedure for each.
`add userform.xls`	Contains a procedure that creates a UserForm on the fly.

`options form.xls`	Contains a function that creates a UserForm (with OptionButtons) on the fly and that returns an integer corresponding to the user's choice.

Chapter 28

`keyboard.xls`	Contains a class module that defines a NumLock and a CapsLock class.
`csvclass.xls`	Contains a class module that makes it easy to import and export a CSV file.

Bonus Files

I don't discuss the files contained in the Bonus directory in the book, but you may find these files useful or instructive. Following is a list of these workbooks, with a brief description of each.

Bonus directory

`number formats.xls`	A workbook that contains a variety of custom number formats.
`mileage.xls`	A workbook that demonstrates how to use the `INDEX` and `MATCH` functions to display the mileage between various cities.
`timesheet.xls`	A workbook that contains an easy-to-use time sheet for tracking hours worked daily.
`appointment pages .xls`	A workbook that enables you to generate and print daily appointment calendar pages.
`permutations.xls`	A macro that generates all possible permutations of a sting. The macro uses a recursive VBA procedure.
`tic tac toe.xls`	An Excel version of tic-tac-toe.
`moving tiles.xls`	An Excel version of the common moving tile puzzle.
`keno.xls`	An Excel version of keno.
`keno odds.xls`	A workbook that calculates the odds of winning in keno.
`animated shapes .xls`	A workbook that that contains some animated `Shape` objects.
`guitar.xls`	A workbook that displays a guitar fret board and the notes in various scales and keys.

Power Utility Pak

Power Utility Pak is a collection of Excel add-ins that I developed. The companion CD-ROM contains a copy of the shareware version of this product. The shareware version contains a subset of the features of the commercial version.

The CD-ROM contains PUP97, which works with both Excel 97 and Excel 2000. A significantly enhanced version, PUP 2000, was being finalized as this book went to press. If you would like to try the shareware version of PUP 2000, download a copy from `http://www.j walk.com/ss/pup`.

Registering Power Utility Pak

The normal registration fee for Power Utility Pak is $39.95. You can use the coupon in this book, however, to get a free copy of PUP 2000 (you pay shipping and handling only). In addition, you can purchase the complete VBA source code for only $20.00.

Installing the shareware version

To install the shareware version of Power Utility Pak, follow these steps:

1. Make sure Excel is not running.
2. Locate the PUP97R3.EXE file on the CD-ROM. This file is located in the PUP\ directory.
3. Double-click PUP97R3.EXE. This expands the files to a directory you specify on your hard drive.
4. Start Excel.
5. Select Tools ➪ Add-Ins, and click the Browse button. Locate the POWER97.XLA file in the directory you specified in Step 3.
6. Make sure Power Utility Pak 97 is checked in the add-ins list.
7. Click OK to close the Add-Ins dialog box.

After you install Power Utility Pak, it will be available whenever you start Excel, and Excel will have a new menu: Utilities. Access the Power Utility Pak features from the Utilities menu.

Power Utility Pak includes extensive online help. Select Utilities ➪ Help to view the Help file.

Uninstalling Power Utility Pak

If you decide that you don't want Power Utility Pak, follow these instructions to remove it from Excel's list of add-ins:

1. In Excel, select Tools ➪ Add-Ins.
2. In the Add-Ins dialog box, remove the check mark from Power Utility Pak 97.
3. Click OK to close the Add-Ins dialog box.

After performing these steps, you can reinstall Power Utility Pak at any time by placing a check mark next to the Power Utility Pak 97 item in the Add-Ins dialog box.

To remove Power Utility Pak from your system after you've followed the preceding steps to uninstall it from Excel, delete the directory into which you originally installed it.

Sound-Proof

Sound-Proof is an Excel add-in that I developed. It uses a synthesized voice to read the contents of selected cells. It's the perfect proofreading tool for anyone who does data entry in Excel.

Cells are read back using natural language format. For example, 154.78 is read as "one hundred fifty-four point seven eight." Date values are read as actual dates (for example, "June fourteen, nineteen ninety-eight") and time values are read as actual times (for example, "six forty-five a.m.").

The companion CD-ROM contains a demo version of Sound-Proof. The full version is available for $19.95. Ordering instructions are provided in the online Help file.

The demo version's only limitation is that it reads no more than 12 cells at a time.

Installing the demo version

To install the demo version of Sound-Proof, follow these steps:

1. Make sure Excel is not running.
2. Locate the SP.EXE file on the CD-ROM. This file is located in the SP\ directory.
3. Double-click SP.EXE. This expands the files to a directory you specify on your hard drive.
4. Start Excel.
5. Select Tools ➪ Add-Ins, and click the Browse button. Locate the SOUNDPRF.XLA file in the directory you specified in Step 3.
6. Make sure Sound-Proof is checked in the add-ins list.
7. Click OK to close the Add-Ins dialog box.

After you install Sound-Proof, it will be available whenever you start Excel, and Excel will have a new menu command: Tools ➪ Sound-Proof. This command displays the Sound-Proof toolbar.

Uninstalling Sound-Proof

If you decide that you don't want Sound-Proof, follow these instructions to remove it from Excel's list of add-ins:

1. In Excel, select Tools ➪ Add-Ins.
2. In the Add-Ins dialog box, remove the check mark from Sound-Proof.
3. Click OK to close the Add-Ins dialog box.

After performing these steps, you can reinstall Sound-Proof at any time by placing a check mark next to the Sound-Proof item in the Add-Ins dialog box.

To remove Sound-Proof from your system after you have performed the preceding steps to uninstall the add-in from Excel, delete the directory into which you originally installed it.

Index

A

(continued)

D

F

(continued)

M

N

V

X

Z

IDG BOOKS WORLDWIDE, INC. END-USER LICENSE AGREEMENT

READ THIS. You should carefully read these terms and conditions before opening the software packet(s) included with this book ("Book"). This is a license agreement ("Agreement") between you and IDG Books Worldwide, Inc. ("IDGB"). By opening the accompanying software packet(s), you acknowledge that you have read and accept the following terms and conditions. If you do not agree and do not want to be bound by such terms and conditions, promptly return the Book and the unopened software packet(s) to the place you obtained them for a full refund.

1. **License Grant.** IDGB grants to you (either an individual or entity) a nonexclusive license to use one copy of the enclosed software program(s) (collectively, the "Software") solely for your own personal or business purposes on a single computer (whether a standard computer or a workstation component of a multiuser network). The Software is in use on a computer when it is loaded into temporary memory (RAM) or installed into permanent memory (hard disk, CD-ROM, or other storage device). IDGB reserves all rights not expressly granted herein.
2. **Ownership.** IDGB is the owner of all right, title, and interest, including copyright, in and to the compilation of the Software recorded on the disk(s) or CD-ROM ("Software Media"). Copyright to the individual programs recorded on the Software Media is owned by the author or other authorized copyright owner of each program. Ownership of the Software and all proprietary rights relating thereto remain with IDGB and its licensers.
3. **Restrictions on Use and Transfer.**
   - **(a)** You may only (i) make one copy of the Software for backup or archival purposes, or (ii) transfer the Software to a single hard disk, provided that you keep the original for backup or archival purposes. You may not (i) rent or lease the Software, (ii) copy or reproduce the Software through a LAN or other network system or through any computer subscriber system or bulletin-board system, or (iii) modify, adapt, or create derivative works based on the Software.
   - **(b)** You may not reverse engineer, decompile, or disassemble the Software. You may transfer the Software and user documentation on a permanent basis, provided that the transferee agrees to accept the terms and conditions of this Agreement and you retain no copies. If the Software is an update or has been updated, any transfer must include the most recent update and all prior versions.
4. **Restrictions on Use of Individual Programs.** You must follow the individual requirements and restrictions detailed for each individual program in Appendix E of this Book. These limitations are also contained in the individual license agreements recorded on the Software Media. These limitations may

include a requirement that after using the program for a specified period of time, the user must pay a registration fee or discontinue use. By opening the Software packet(s), you will be agreeing to abide by the licenses and restrictions for these individual programs that are detailed in Appendix E and on the Software Media. None of the material on this Software Media or listed in this Book may ever be redistributed, in original or modified form, for commercial purposes.

5. Limited Warranty.

(a) IDGB warrants that the Software and Software Media are free from defects in materials and workmanship under normal use for a period of sixty (60) days from the date of purchase of this Book. If IDGB receives notification within the warranty period of defects in materials or workmanship, IDGB will replace the defective Software Media.

(b) **IDGB AND THE AUTHOR OF THE BOOK DISCLAIM ALL OTHER WARRANTIES, EXPRESS OR IMPLIED, INCLUDING WITHOUT LIMITATION IMPLIED WARRANTIES OF MERCHANTABILITY AND FITNESS FOR A PARTICULAR PURPOSE, WITH RESPECT TO THE SOFTWARE, THE PROGRAMS, THE SOURCE CODE CONTAINED THEREIN, AND/OR THE TECHNIQUES DESCRIBED IN THIS BOOK. IDGB DOES NOT WARRANT THAT THE FUNCTIONS CONTAINED IN THE SOFTWARE WILL MEET YOUR REQUIREMENTS OR THAT THE OPERATION OF THE SOFTWARE WILL BE ERROR FREE.**

(c) This limited warranty gives you specific legal rights, and you may have other rights that vary from jurisdiction to jurisdiction.

6. Remedies.

(a) IDGB's entire liability and your exclusive remedy for defects in materials and workmanship shall be limited to replacement of the Software Media, which may be returned to IDGB with a copy of your receipt at the following address: Software Media Fulfillment Department, Attn.: *Microsoft Excel 2000 Power Programming with VBA*, IDG Books Worldwide, Inc., 7260 Shadeland Station, Ste. 100, Indianapolis, IN 46256, or call 1-800-762-2974. Please allow three to four weeks for delivery. This Limited Warranty is void if failure of the Software Media has resulted from accident, abuse, or misapplication. Any replacement Software Media will be warranted for the remainder of the original warranty period or thirty (30) days, whichever is longer.

(b) In no event shall IDGB or the author be liable for any damages whatsoever (including without limitation damages for loss of business profits, business interruption, loss of business information, or any other pecuniary loss) arising from the use of or inability to use the Book or the Software, even if IDGB has been advised of the possibility of such damages.

(c) Because some jurisdictions do not allow the exclusion or limitation of liability for consequential or incidental damages, the above limitation or exclusion may not apply to you.

7. **U.S. Government Restricted Rights.** Use, duplication, or disclosure of the Software by the U.S. Government is subject to restrictions stated in paragraph (c)(1)(ii) of the Rights in Technical Data and Computer Software clause of DFARS 252.227-7013, and in subparagraphs (a) through (d) of the Commercial Computer — Restricted Rights clause at FAR 52.227-19, and in similar clauses in the NASA FAR supplement, when applicable.

8. **General.** This Agreement constitutes the entire understanding of the parties and revokes and supersedes all prior agreements, oral or written, between them and may not be modified or amended except in a writing signed by both parties hereto that specifically refers to this Agreement. This Agreement shall take precedence over any other documents that may be in conflict herewith. If any one or more provisions contained in this Agreement are held by any court or tribunal to be invalid, illegal, or otherwise unenforceable, each and every other provision shall remain in full force and effect.

CD-ROM Installation Instructions

The CD-ROM that accompanies this book contains author John Walkenbach's award-winning Power Utility Pak, his Sound-Proof add-in, a complete set of workbook files for the macros discussed in the book, and bonus files for additional macros that you'll find useful. Appendix E contains detailed descriptions of these items, along with installation guidelines. When you copy the workbook files from the CD-ROM to your own disk, you should remove the read-only attribute by right-clicking the file and selecting Properties; then, uncheck the Read-only check box.